transformative
LEADERSHIP

Studies in the
Postmodern Theory of Education

Shirley R. Steinberg
General Editor

Vol. 409

The Counterpoints series is part of the Peter Lang Education list.
Every volume is peer reviewed and meets
the highest quality standards for content and production.

PETER LANG
New York • Washington, D.C./Baltimore • Bern
Frankfurt • Berlin • Brussels • Vienna • Oxford

transformative
LEADERSHIP

A READER

Edited by Carolyn M. Shields

PETER LANG
New York • Washington, D.C./Baltimore • Bern
Frankfurt • Berlin • Brussels • Vienna • Oxford

Library of Congress Cataloging-in-Publication Data

Transformative leadership: a reader / edited by Carolyn M. Shields.
p. cm. — (Counterpoints; v. 409)
Includes bibliographical references.
1. Educational leadership. 2. Leadership. I. Shields, Carolyn M.
LB2806.T688   371.2'011—dc23   2011028982
ISBN 978-1-4331-1310-9 (hardcover)
ISBN 978-1-4331-1309-3 (paperback)
ISBN 978-1-4539-0150-2 (e-book)
ISSN 1058-1634

Bibliographic information published by **Die Deutsche Nationalbibliothek**.
Die Deutsche Nationalbibliothek lists this publication in the "Deutsche
Nationalbibliografie"; detailed bibliographic data is available
on the Internet at http://dnb.d-nb.de/.

The paper in this book meets the guidelines for permanence and durability
of the Committee on Production Guidelines for Book Longevity
of the Council of Library Resources.

© 2011 Peter Lang Publishing, Inc., New York
29 Broadway, 18th floor, New York, NY 10006
www.peterlang.com

Printed in the United States of America

Contents

Transformative Leadership

An Introduction

Carolyn M. Shields

What's in a name? that which we call a rose
By any other name would smell as sweet
— William Shakespeare, *Romeo and Juliet (II, ii, 1–2)*

Would that which we call *transformative leadership* by any other name have the same import? Indeed, it is tempting to become cynical about the proliferation of leadership theories and to argue, as Shakespeare apparently did, that names and labels are but artificial and meaningless conventions. At the same time, as Juliet protested so powerfully, it is the inherent characteristics—the qualities of the person so labeled—that are important. Indeed, Juliet's appeal is to find agreement over the characteristics and not to battle over the label and, of course, given the extent to which so many leadership theories overlap, it is the qualities of the leader and his or her beliefs, values, and practices that are of paramount importance. The roles and responsibilities of leaders are increasingly complex, the contexts within which leadership is exercised are ever more diverse, the pressures for performance accountability are progressively greater, and the challenges presented by declining resources are severe. Strewn throughout this landscape are traditional and emerging theories of leadership, each purporting to help educational leaders to operate effective and efficient schools, to respond to parental and community wants and needs, and, invariably, to meet the needs of all students. Because the metaphoric landscape of educational leadership in the 21st century is as convoluted and diverse as natural geography itself, it is important to carefully consider which elements, commitments, skills, beliefs, knowledge, and so forth are inherent in different leadership theories—each represented, of course, by a particular name.

Despite the myriad of leadership theories and reform strategies, the critiques and complaints about the current state of education continue unabated. In developed countries, educators repeatedly protest high-stakes testing, lack of funding and resources, and pressures for performativity

(Foucault, 1995; Perryman, 2009). There is still an "achievement gap" between dominant-culture students and their peers from other ethnic, linguistic, religious, or cultural backgrounds. There are still too few students from minoritized groups accessing advanced or international baccalaureate—or gifted—classes, too few successfully attending or completing college or university, and too many of these same students dropping out (or being pushed out) of high school before completion. Worldwide, 75 million children never have the opportunity to attend school at all. Many who do attend school encounter poorly trained teachers, few resources, and low expectations; moreover, high numbers of students in developing countries fail to even complete elementary school. It is little wonder that, in recent decades, forms of leadership related to advancing social justice (Bogotch, 2002; Brown, 2004; Larson & Murtadha, 2002; Theoharis, 2007), democracy (Ryan, 2009; Woods, 2004), equity reform (Oakes & Rogers, 2006), or transformation (Foster, 1986; Shields, 2003, 2009) have arisen.

Psychologists and scholars tell us that names are important. Volumes are published explaining the histories and qualities associated with names. Parents spend hours deliberating over choices for unborn children, and in many cultures a naming ceremony celebrates not only the birth of a child but the inherent hopes and dreams of the parents for the child's future. The powerful naming ceremony of Haley's Kunta Kinte in *Roots* (1974) is a case in point, as the name itself, according to the traditions of the tribe, helps a person to know who he or she is. Studies also indicate that a child's body build, ethnicity, gender, and name all affect how a teacher may respond to the child and, in turn, how that child will be expected to perform (Vail, 2005).

This suggests that there may be some import to choosing a name (or a theory), especially, perhaps, one that might guide and ground one's leadership practice. Here, we offer for consideration the concept of *transformative* leadership—a theory of leadership that is increasingly delineated and conceptualized as distinct from its etymological sibling *transformational* leadership. Situated squarely within a number of new approaches, transformative leadership emphasizes the need for education to focus both on academic excellence and on social transformation.

Although, as indicated earlier, we can quibble over an appropriate name or label for the kind of leadership we believe to be desirable, we must ultimately find a way to describe and embody it. This is the goal of the *Transformative Leadership Reader*. In the 24 chapters of this volume, you will find theoretical work that explains and conceptualizes transformative leadership in various contexts, and you will read empirical studies that demonstrate its practical utility on several continents and, thus, in contexts that vary considerably. First, I provide an overview of transformative leadership itself, its historical development, its underlying principles, and its distinguishing features, and attempt to provide an argument for adopting a form of transformative leadership to further the transformative goals of education in this century.

Transformative Leadership: An Overview

Elsewhere, I have provided an overview of some of the salient aspects of transformative leadership. These include starting with a global perspective that attends to the material realities and daily experiences of the community from which members of an organization come; deconstructing and reconstructing knowledge frameworks that perpetuate inequities in the status quo; offering a balance of critique and promise related to existing beliefs, structures, policies, and practices; acknowledging the pervasiveness and hegemony of power and privilege; and focusing on liberation, emancipation, deep democracy, equity, and justice as prerequisites to achieving the more specific goals of an organization. Hence, for educational institutions such as schools, colleges, and universities, as well as less formal educative sites, creating learning contexts of liberation, democracy, equity, and justice is necessary for fostering the high achievement of all students as well as for the fulfillment of requisite accountability measures.

Although the goals of liberation, deep democracy, equity, and justice are generally supported by most citizens, their conceptualization is deeply embedded in ideological perspectives. Hence, the goals will play out very differently from site to site in the details of their implementation. At the same time, there are some general, underlying principles that, together, inform the theory and practice of transformative leadership—principles I will expand upon in a later section. At this point, it is sufficient to assert that transformative leadership requires the leader to have a clear sense of the values and beliefs that undergird his or her own identity, be willing to take stands that may require moral courage, to live with tension, and, to some degree, to engage in activism and advocacy. Although these characteristics are rarely placed in the forefront of leadership practices, none is new as we shall see in a brief examination of the historical development of transformative leadership.

Historical Development[1]

The emergence of formal scholarly leadership studies in the United States is sometimes attributed to what has become known as the Chicago School—a group of more than 50 scholars from 20 leading universities who travelled by car, train, and plane to Chicago, Illinois on November 10, 1957, to attend a seminar entitled "Administrative Theory in Education" (Culbertson, 1995, p. 34). What has become known as the "theory movement" emerged from this seminar. This movement, as Halpin explained, centered in large part on the belief that "theory must be concerned with how the superintendent *does* behave, not with someone's opinion of how he *ought* to behave" (in Culbertson, 1995, p. 41). This approach, as has often been discussed and critiqued, undergirded the strong positivist approach to administration and leadership studies of the last half of the 20th century, an approach in which scholars and practitioners generally believed that "ought" questions—for example, questions about ethics and moral purpose or right and wrong—have no place in science, and thus lie outside of the study and practice of educational administration. Unfortunately, the influence of this approach is pervasive, and too many elements of it still dominate thinking about leadership in the 21st century.

More recently, of course, the concept of moral leadership (Evans, 2000; Starratt, 2007), with its emphasis on ethics and justice, has re-emerged as central to many leadership theories. At the same time, it is important to acknowledge that these concepts were never totally repressed, with a minority group of scholars and practitioners continuing to recognize the importance of beliefs and values in educational leadership. Culbertson (1988) reports, for example, that in 1875 William Harold Payne, Superintendent of Schools in Adrian, Michigan—who wrote the first book on school administration, *Chapters on School Supervision*—said:

> that educational organizations are not "objective" phenomena regulated by general laws; rather they are mental constructs that reflect the perceptions and interpretations of their members. Students of organizations should turn their backs, then, upon logical positivistic science and adopt interpretive modes of inquiry. (p. 3)

A century later, Greenfield (1975) picked up on this argument and restored it to prominence in educational administration. He emphasized the importance of understanding organizations as "invented social reality," saying that when one does so, "the notion of discovering the ultimate laws which govern social reality becomes an ever receding fantasy" (p. 79). Transformative leadership takes the notion of invented social reality further and draws on critical theories, theories of cultural and social reproduction, and concepts of leadership for social justice to help leaders understand how to create educational organizations that combine excellence with equity, inclusion, and justice.

Recent origins of transformative leadership are sometimes traced to Burns's (1978) seminal book, simply called *Leadership*. His discussion ranged widely, covering topics such as moral leadership, social sources of leadership, political leadership, reform leadership, and even revolutionary leadership. To introduce his discussion, Burns stated that he would identify "two basic types of leadership: the *transactional* and the *transforming*" (p. 4). In differentiating between them, he explained that "the result of transforming leadership is a relationship of mutual stimulation and elevation that converts followers into leaders and may convert leaders into moral agents" (p. 5). He then added that it was "this last concept, *moral leadership*," that concerned him most. He described moral leadership as "the kind of leadership that can produce social change" (p. 4) and suggested it is one of the most important and salient characteristics of transforming leadership.

One additional important element of transforming leadership, according to Burns, was "the concept of intellectual *leadership* [that] brings in the role of *conscious purpose* drawn from values" (p. 142). The intellectual leader stands inside society and fully embraces the conflicts and tensions of social and "political combat." As he described the intellectual leader, Burns emphasized that, like the French *philosophes* of the 18th century, these leaders need to be "hommes engagés" (p. 145)—communicating, exchanging, and vigorously debating their ideas. Indeed, the intellectual leader, according to Burns, is embattled but not lonely. The contrast between this embattled leader, standing for a conscious and controversial purpose, and the administrator described by Halpin, for whom ethics and moral purpose play no role in his daily activities, is striking.

For Burns, the absence or presence of the foregoing characteristics—moral and conscious purpose, social change, and engagement—formed the basis for his now well-known distinction between transactional and transforming leadership. It is interesting to note that, despite frequent acknowledgement of Burns as the originator of transformative leadership, he never used that term. He did, however, write about transformational leadership in a way that is evocative of the current use of transformative leadership. For Burns, transactions that include an exchange of valued goods (economic, political, or psychological) are an acceptable and normal part of organizational processes, but they do not bind "leader and follower together in a mutual and continuing pursuit of higher purpose" (p. 20). Through *transforming* leadership, on the other hand, purposes "become fused" (p. 20):

> Transforming leadership is dynamic leadership in the sense that the leaders throw themselves into a relationship with followers who will feel "elevated" by it and often become more active themselves, thereby creating new cadres of leaders. Transformative leadership is leadership *engagé*. (p. 20)

Thus, as Starratt asserts (this volume), the current iteration of transformational leadership has moved away from these radical and revolutionary roots to emphasize organizational effectiveness and internal operations, while transformative leadership remains closely tied to Burns's original concept of leadership. Thus, transformational leadership remains clearly focused on the need to "improve employee performance" (Leithwood, Harris, & Hopkins, 2008, p. 30), and on the tasks of building vision and setting directions, understanding and developing people, redesigning the organization, and managing the teaching and learning program (p. 30)—all broad practices that uphold the effective and efficient operation of any organization and are necessary, but likely are not sufficient, for achieving the transformation implied by the theories discussed here. Transformative leadership, on the other hand, could be said to pass Burns's test of conscious moral purposing and intellectual leadership:

The test of transforming power is "the capacity to conceive values or purpose in such a way that ends and means are linked analytically and creatively and that the implications of certain values for political action and governmental organization are clarified" (p. 163)

To be truly transformative, the processes of leadership must be linked to the ends of equity, inclusion, and social justice. Extending the conception of educational purpose in such as way as to engage political action and governmental organization is fundamental to the recognition of social injustice and to the organization's ability to address (and attempt to redress) inequities that emerge from the uneven playing field experienced by students in their daily lives. To that end, Burns later explains that "transformational leadership is more concerned with *end-values,* such as liberty, justice, equality. Transforming leaders 'raise' their followers up through levels of morality, though insufficient attention to means can corrupt the ends" (p. 426).

Here we can clearly see how and why the two concepts of transformational and transformative leadership have become confounded, and can understand the necessity for the clarification offered by this present volume. What Burns called transforming leadership as exemplified in his mind by the term *transformational leadership* has become, in the 21st century, closely associated with the theory of transformative leadership. Indeed, this is the concept picked up by Foster (1986) when he calls for leadership that is "critically educative," that not only looks "at the conditions in which we live, but it must also decide how to change them" (p. 185). To confuse matters even more, one finds in most dictionaries reference to the two terms as synonyms. Nevertheless, despite the common, vernacular confusion and confounding of the two concepts, in terms of scholarship and educational leadership theory, it is important to clarify the basic tenets of transformative leadership and to clearly elucidate how it can form the basis for leadership that is truly transforming—both for individuals and for society as whole.

Transformative Leadership: Underlying Principles and Distinguishing Features

Transformative leadership is grounded in a number of principles that distinguish it from other leadership theories, although it does not eschew the practices of other theories as strategies for accomplishing its goals. Negotiating acceptable transactions, distributing leadership responsibilities, and even demonstrating servant leadership may well serve to advance its desired goals. However, the following tenets, to be discussed in turn, are basic to transformative leadership. It focuses on:

- acknowledging power and privilege

- articulating both individual and collective purposes (public and private good)

- deconstructing social-cultural knowledge frameworks that generate inequity and reconstructing them

- balancing critique and promise

- effecting deep and equitable change

- working towards transformation: liberation, emancipation, democracy, equity, and excellence

- demonstrating moral courage and activism.

Acknowledging Power and Privilege

Burns (1978), writing of transforming leadership, emphasized the need to "analyze power in the context of human motives and physical constraints." He argued that "if we can come to grips with these aspects of power, we can hope to comprehend the nature of leadership" (p. 11). This is critically important, in that understanding the nature of power and the accompanying privilege it typically accords to those who wield it is rarely expressed as a starting point of leadership. Yet it is essential to recognize how thinking of power as a finite good or as a zero-sum game perpetuates practices that preserve the privilege of those who have traditionally held positions of influence and who have had the ability to make decisions and create policies for both society and its organizations. Starting by taking into account the material realities and disparities of the wider society, and considering how they impinge on the ability of organizations to successfully meet their goals or the ability of individuals within organizations to be deemed successful, promotes change. This approach recognizes and addresses the reality that some groups and individuals within a given organization are advantaged and included in the daily operations and decisions of the institution and that other people are generally excluded, disadvantaged, and often marginalized.

For that reason, Burns's (1978) concept of power as a relationship must be taken seriously. He writes:

> power is first of all a relationship and not merely an entity to be passed around like a baton or a hand grenade; that it involves the intention or purpose of both power holder and power recipient; and hence that it is collective, not merely the behavior of one person. (p. 13)

In this concept, power is an organizational quality, a relationship among all participants that must be nurtured, developed, and understood as a way of moving towards a collective purpose. Thus, a policy related to discipline or bullying that targets students whose behavior does not meet acceptable standards may well eliminate the "problem" if students fearing suspension choose to limit their aggressive behavior while at school. On the other hand, the myriad "microaggressions" (Ladson-Billings, 2006) these students encounter on a daily basis—the teasing about their dress, home life, or accent—and the marginalization they experience when they do not see themselves reflected in school curricula or in classroom discussions are therefore never addressed. The hand grenade remains explosive. No relationship is formed with the students or their families, no understanding of their situation or feelings of inferiority or exclusion is developed, and no meaningful change occurs. Power has been used inappropriately, resentment likely builds, and transformation remains elusive. Moreover, the possibility of achieving a collective goal of a safer, more inclusive school community remains unrealized.

Articulating Purpose

Undoubtedly, it has become clear at this point that transformative leadership is to some extent normative. It emphasizes the need for educational organizations to articulate and attain purposes related to equity and excellence, public and private good, and individual and collective advancement. Moreover, it is necessary to articulate such purposes in terms of mutual benefit and societal change. Astin and Astin (2000), for example, assert that:

> the value ends of leadership should be to enhance equity, social justice, and the quality of life; to expand access and opportunity; to encourage respect for difference and diversity; to strengthen democracy, civic life, and civic responsibility; and to promote cultural enrichment, creative ex-

pression, intellectual honesty, the advancement of knowledge, and personal freedom coupled with responsibility. (p. 11)

To accomplish these ends requires that leaders not only have a clear conception of the purposes of their endeavor, but also that they engage with others to ensure that the sense of purpose is shared.

At the beginning of the 2010 fall term, I asked members of my introductory master's-level class in educational leadership (all practicing teachers and educators) what they believed to be the goals and purposes of education. They stared blankly, obviously dumbfounded, until one student ventured a response, "To help all students pass the tests." Others nodded their agreement. As we discussed what comprises a "good school," we touched on issues of deep democracy (Green, 1999), racism (Ladson-Billings, 1996; Tatum, 2007), social class (hooks, 2000), and deficit thinking (Shields, 2009; Valencia, 1997) and began to explore how these and other issues create an institutional environment that privileges some and tends to disadvantage other students. Later in the evening, one student posed a question that reflected the group consensus: "We have never discussed these topics—not at our schools, nor in our teacher training programs—so how are we supposed to know how to address them when we become principals and leaders?"

It was my turn to be dumbfounded. I inquired, "You mean, you have did not have discussions like this at the beginning of the year at your opening faculty meeting? You have never had conversations about privilege, racism, sexism, and so forth, and how different practices and beliefs affect the ability of students to achieve? You have never thought about the collective purposes of schooling, but instead, have only discussed strategies to ensure all students pass the requisite state tests?" I was dismayed. I thought of Burns's (1978) assertion that "ideological leaders dedicate themselves to explicit goals that require substantial social change and to organizing and leading political movements that pursue these goals" (p. 248).

Here, it seems to me, is one of the critical differences between transformative leadership and other current theories that call for distribution of leadership or shared and collaborative processes. As desirable as these strategies are for attaining an organizational goal, it is essential that the goals and purposes of the educational endeavor be made explicit. Coming from a critical and transformative point of view, I would argue that it is equally, if not more, important for the goal to be one of transformation, equity, and substantial social change. It is certainly important to arouse in every child a sense of curiosity and a passion for intellectual excellence; although, obviously this is not adequately assessed by a once-a-year standardized test. Moreover, it is equally important to create an understanding of what it means to be a global citizen—for students to learn to take their places as caring, fulfilled, and contributing members of society. And although "contributing" often implies economic contribution and self-sufficiency, I posit that it must always be accompanied by a clear understanding of social, cultural, and political participation in a civil society.

New Knowledge Frameworks

It seems obvious that in order to change the ways in which we think about schooling, it is important to engage in conversations about difficult, emotional, and important topics such as race, social class, sexual orientation, or religious perspective. Further, we must not remain silent when we hear expressed an opinion that "blames the victim" or that assumes that because Michael Jordan, Oprah Winfrey, President Barack Obama, or (insert a name) have been able to overcome difficult circumstances, anyone can if they only struggle hard enough and work to "pull themselves up by their bootstraps." In a previous article (Shields, 2004), I wrote about what I then called *pathologies of silence*—avoiding difficult situations because they are so sensitive. At that time, I suggested that adopting what has come to be known as a "color-blind" position, or remaining silent about class differences, is a stance of the privileged, who can afford to affirm that people are all the same by virtue of their humanity and that differences are immaterial and superficial. In fact, this hegemonic stance ignores the fact that for those who are not part of the dominant culture, many differences matter on a daily basis as they are refused housing or jobs, taxis are locked to them, doors are slammed in their faces, or prejudicial statements are made with no consideration given to their impact.

During the introductory session of my master's class described earlier, a student mentioned that on the following night his school would hold parent-teacher conferences and that, as usual, only the parents one did not really need to see would attend. He noticed my grimace and in the ensuing discussion admitted he had never considered the unequal ability of some parents to attend school events, take time off work, hire baby sitters for younger siblings, or have accessible transportation. Moreover, he quickly understood that the physical presence (or lack thereof) of parents could not be equated with interest in or support for their children's education. This insight, attained during the first class session, was soon known as "Chet's comment" and became a sort of class code for inappropriate assumptions about families whose lived experiences were in some way different from those of most of the teachers in my students' schools.

Deconstructing inappropriate attitudes and assumptions, including common wisdom that has been passed on for years, is one of the primary tasks of the transformative leader. But it must not stop there; for to begin the process of deep and equitable reform and social transformation requires reconstructing our images of students and families as knowledgeable, caring, and being capable of high achievement and of full participation in every decision and activity of the organization.

Balancing Critique and Promise

One of the first steps in deconstructing existing inappropriate knowledge frameworks is, of course, critique. It is important to recognize, for example, how standards movements can—and often do—perpetuate a hierarchy of knowledge such that current norms and beliefs remain unchallenged (Columbus did "discover" America, after all). It is essential to understand how accountability can become associated with performativity (Foucault, 1995; Perryman, 2009), which results in elaborate plans and programs purported to bring about the desired reform but that, in practice, serve to include some and marginalize others. It is easy to critique current remedial programs for the "bubble kids"—those on the cusp of achieving the specified score—decrying the ways in which we narrow the curriculum, forcing these students to enroll in additional language arts or math classes at the expense of electives, or to spend their noon hours, Saturdays, or afterschool time in remedial academic-support activities. It is much more difficult to offer promise—to find ways, in the current climate of high-stakes testing and accountability, to enrich the learning experiences of all students. It is much more difficult for the school leader to focus on strategies for including all students. To reject the prescriptive programs that de-skill teachers and "widgitize" kids, and to accept the possible consequences of their school not achieving adequate yearly progress (AYP in the United States) in a given year, requires moral courage.

Maxine Greene (1988) asserts that the promise of education is to prepare students to be "citizens of the free world—having the capacity to choose, the power to act to attain one's purposes, and the ability to help transform a world lived in common with others" (p. 32). This is indeed the goal of a transformative educational leader. This goal does not preclude ensuring that all students have learned to read, write, and compute; it does not preclude ensuring that the school functions efficiently and effectively; but it goes well beyond. This goal not only asks leaders to help students understand and develop their own potential, but includes the need to recognize and address the inequities in their school, community, and around the world and to learn to live and act in such a way as to make a difference. Indeed, this is the basis for achieving the next tenet—deep and equitable change.

Effecting Deep and Equitable Change

For years, scholars have written about the failure of educational reform. Twenty years ago, Sarason (1990) even entitled his book *The Predictable Failure of Educational Reform*, asking in his subtitle, "Can we change course before it's too late?" In the same year, Cuban (1990) discussed reform in terms of a pendulum, entitling a well-known and oft-cited article "Reforming Again, Again, and Again." More recently, Oakes and Rogers (2006) discussed the failure of education in America to be the "great equalizer," to narrow the gaps between the "haves" and "have-nots," and to fulfill Horace Mann's vision of schools as places "where students of all backgrounds come together to share fair and equal opportunities for success in the educational system and, as a consequence, fair and equal life chances" (p. 7). They argue that, in part, the failure is due to a lack of purposeful reform strategies and assert that "merely documenting inequality will not, in and of itself, lead to adequate and equitable schooling" (p. 13). If we want reform to fulfill Mann's vision, they maintain, we must stop tinkering around the edges of needed change. We must instead be explicit about the kind of reform needed, about the material disparities I mentioned earlier; we must acknowledge the inadequacy of technical change; and we must "treat equity reforms as distinctly different from other school improvement initiatives" (p. 30). This is the basis for the kind of deep and equitable reform that will preoccupy a transformative leader.

Instead of quickly adopting the most recent prescription for improvement (Response to Intervention, Reading First, or Positive Behavioral Interventions and Supports, to name a few), transformative leaders will first consider their goals: They will examine the nature of the inequity they wish to address and, instead of de-skilling teachers or narrowing student opportunities, they will find ways to introduce deep and meaningful reform. Again, this is not to suggest that the earlier-mentioned programs in themselves are inappropriate or ineffective. It is meant to suggest that a state-wide mandate for all schools to adopt a given program denies educators the agency to identify the specific changes needed in their own context in order to achieve the goals of equity, excellence, and social justice. Spending time reorganizing teachers' planning time to allow for meetings of existing teams (now to be called "professional learning communities") may satisfy an accountability mandate, but it does not guarantee that the discussions will focus on the broader citizenship goals of education or will consider the relationship of deficit thinking, racism, or classism to the failure of students to make academic progress.

Thus, as previously stated, transformative leaders are explicit about both the goals to be achieved and the processes required to attain them. These include the transformative goals of liberation, emancipation, democracy, equity, and excellence.

Transforming Schools

Although the goals of liberation, emancipation, democracy, equity, and excellence are not intended to be exhaustive, they do indicate a different direction from many of the goals specified in typical school improvement plans. For example, most plans required at present in the United States under a provision of the No Child Left Behind Act require a focus on meeting the standards of AYP. In Illinois, a school improvement plan is required to "identify the current achievement level, be measurable outcomes in terms of the AYP achieved for each year of the plan, focus on fundamental teaching and learning issues, and ensure that each subgroup meets the State's target" (Illinois State Board of Education, 2010). There is no discussion or critique of what current achievement level is under consideration; hence, rather than considering a broad range of individual and collective achievement categories, the standard is presumably limited to that which is tested on the requisite standardized tests. In fact, the requirement that the measurable outcomes be stated in terms of the AYP level achieved makes testing the almost-singular focus of discussion and planning. Further, in Illinois, as in many other states, unless a school is in "academic watch" status (i.e., not currently meeting AYP), school improvement plans are optional. Perhaps this helps to explain the perplexed look on my students' faces when asked about the goals and purposes of education. It certainly helps to explain Thompson's (2007) analysis of the history of school improvement plans; she wrote, "Simply stated, the purpose of planning is to define the process whereby the school will achieve its stated improvement goals and meet state and federal mandates" (p. 2). Ravitch (2010) echoed this sentiment when she wrote, "The standards movement was replaced by the accountability movement. What once was an effort to improve the quality of education turned into an accounting strategy. Measure, then punish or reward" (Kindle location 342). The improvement plan is neither reflective of a wider conversation about the goals and purposes of education nor, in most cases, does it serve as a catalyst for such a conversation.

In 1998, Freire contended "that education is not the ultimate lever for social transformation, but without it transformation cannot occur" (p. 37). Somehow, it is difficult to determine how transformation can occur without a focus on liberation, emancipation, democracy, equity, or excellence—concepts that seem far removed from high-stakes testing, cut scores, test prep classes, data-driven decisions, or measurable objectives. Indeed, Ravitch (2010), once a strong proponent of these latter reforms, recently asserted:

> If we want to improve education, we must first of all have a vision of what good education is. We should have goals that are worth striving for. Everyone involved in educating children should ask themselves why we educate. What is a well-educated person? What knowledge is of most worth? What do we hope for when we send our children to school? (Kindle location 5778)

These questions are at the heart of transformative leadership: How can educators create learning environments that empower all students? How do race, class, ability, or disability affect a child's motivation to learn? Who is marginalized, excluded, or disadvantaged by a given decision and who is privileged and included? To answer such questions, one must take seriously Freire's (1970) call for personal, dialogic relationships to undergird education. He wrote, "Each time the 'thou' is changed into an object, an 'it,' dialogue is subverted and education is changed to deformation" (1970, p. 89). Without dialogic relationships, as argued later by Burns (1978), education acts to deform rather than to transform. Weiner (2003) summarized it well: "Transformative leadership is an exercise of power and authority that begins with questions of justice, democracy, and the dialectic between individual accountability and social responsibility" (p. 89). Transformative leaders base their decisions and actions on this moral dialectic and not on technical strategies and solutions.

Demonstrating Moral Courage and Activism

From the previous discussion, it becomes apparent that the leader who strives to acknowledge the relationships of power and privilege, to articulate both the public and private goods of education, to deconstruct existing knowledge frameworks and replace them with new, more inclusive norms, and who works to ensure that critique leads to promise and that change focuses on liberation, equity, and social justice, as well as excellence and individual growth, is not only rare but also likely experiences a considerable sense of isolation and even rejection. Weiner, recognizing this, calls for leaders to "confront more than just what is, and work toward creating an alternative political and social imagination that does not rest solely on the rule of capital or the hollow moralism of neoconservatives, but is rooted in radical democratic struggle" (2003, p. 97). At the same time, he recognizes the dilemma in which many educational leaders find themselves—caught with "one foot in the dominant structures of power and authority" (p. 102) while at the same time, needing to:

> take risks, form strategic alliances, to learn and unlearn their power, and reach beyond a "fear of authority" toward a concrete vision of the work in which oppression, violence, and brutality are transformed by a commitment to equality, liberty, and democratic struggle. (p. 102)

This is not only the quandary of the transformative leader but the mandate as well. This mandate requires a clear sense of self and knowledge of what guides and grounds one. It also requires a clear vision of the task ahead, for without such a vision, as we have seen, we will lead an endeavor that deforms rather than transforms education.

Why Adopt Transformative Leadership?

When the transformative task is so difficult, so broad, so fraught with resistance and tradition that it acts as an impediment to significant and equitable reform, how and why would a school leader want to put on its mantle?

Educational leaders know how to effect short-term change. Although they recognize that tests are not precise measures, that they are often ambiguous, flawed, or simply wrong, leaders have often been captivated by an emphasis on data, or have succumbed to the pressures of district and state, parents and the general public, to ensure their school meets the annual standard. They recognize how to raise test scores by providing extensive test preparation to certain students, by restricting the enrolment of (or even suspending) students unlikely to succeed, by reducing the number of students eligible to take the test on a given day (manipulating the enrolment and grade level of certain students, assigning them to different classes, having them change schools after a certain date, and so forth), or even by "cleaning up" the test data. There is virtually no administrator who is not fully familiar with ways to make his or her school appear to be performing better than it actually is.

But the real question is: What is accomplished by these strategies? Burns (1978) wrote that "it is purpose that puts man into history" (p. 442) and indeed, for good or ill, we can recognize the truth of these words. One might assert that Sun Wu's purpose was to humanize warfare; for Hitler, that purpose was ethnic dominance; for Machiavelli, it was to remain in power (being hated rather than loved, if that was necessary); and for Gandhi, to demonstrate the possibility of nonviolent solutions to political oppression.

But what of the educational leader? Horace Mann (1948) believed that education "beyond all other devices of human origin, is the great equalizer of the conditions of men, the balance-wheel of the social machinery" (cited in Oakes & Rogers, 2006, p. 7). About the same time, century, Dewey (2001) elaborated a vision for public schools, arguing that each school should be "an embryonic community life." He expanded this statement, explaining:

> When the school introduces and trains each child of society into membership within such a little community, saturating him with the spirit of service, and providing him with the instruments of

effective self-direction, we shall have the deepest and best guarantor of a larger society which is worthy, lovely, and harmonious" (p. 177)

More recently, political theorist Barber (1991/2001) held that "the fundamental task of education in a democracy is the apprenticeship of liberty—learning to be free" (p. 12). For Palmer (2007), it is to "protect and support the inner journey that is at the heart of authentic teaching, learning, and living" (p. ix).

The myriad of quotations over centuries that emphasize the potential of education to transform society, to teach individuals to know themselves and to serve others, and, through these lessons, to become "free," stands in direct opposition to today's emphasis on high-stakes testing, narrow forms of accountability, and performativity. Yet they provide strong support for adopting the tenets of transformative leadership—for understanding the critically important role of education in preparing students to become caring, engaged global citizens. In a society in which the gap between rich and poor is widening, in which the goal of economic development and dominance is prime, in which over two million children a year die because of lack of access to clean water, and in which 295 million people are chronically hungry (World Hunger and Poverty Facts and Statistics, 2010), the current excessive preoccupation with league tables, test scores, and rankings is unconscionable.

That is the message of this volume: We educational leaders, at every level of educational organization—from pre-school to graduate school—must join forces to renew commitment to transforming education as a fundamental means of transforming our world.

Overview of the Chapters

This volume is divided into four sections. In the first section, Conceptualizing Transformative Leadership, several authors wrestle with, and attempt to clarify, the meanings associated with transformative leadership, and several actually develop additional models to emphasize their specific concept of interest. Here, the authors draw on theories related, and relevant, to transformative leadership in order to clarify and extend our understanding. Jill Blackmore introduces this section with a thoughtful elaboration of the historical development of popular, competing theories of leadership and, like many of the authors, emphasizes the critical roots of transformative leadership. By drawing on data from four Australian case studies, she demonstrates the significant impact of various policy contexts and decisions on school leaders and the need for a transformative response. Paul Carr draws on a framework of critical pedagogy to position an argument in favour of a more engaged, politically meaningful, and counter-hegemonic form of transformative leadership, and focuses on the place of democratic schooling "in which myriad dialogs, debates and decisions are hashed out" (p. TK, this volume). Erica Mohan argues that if transformative leadership is to be able to successfully foster engaged citizenry, then in the United States courageous dialogue about race and ethnicity must be central components. David Requa uses "border theory" to discuss how a robust concept of identity can lead to the engagement of a transformative leader and to being a "radical" in the Freirean sense. This is followed by a powerful narrative chapter in which Anish Sayani also examines identity, demonstrating the interconnections between theories of identity and transformative leadership, thus enhancing our understanding of both. Lyse Langlois extends the discussion of transformative leadership by showing how a deep understanding of ethics, especially the ethic of critique, enhances transformative leadership. Steve Rayner further develops the concept of transformative leadership by introducing what he describes as an "integrative model for the management of educational diversity." The section concludes with a literature review by Deneca Avant that includes a brief historical overview of other, more traditional approaches to leadership, and again argues the need for transformative leadership, as well as the need for transformative action.

In the second section, Curriculum Through the Lens of Transformative Leadership, including the curriculum required to prepare transformative leaders, the authors take insightful and original approaches to the relationship between transformative leadership and curriculum. Jerry Starratt's short piece introduces this section with some reflections on what transformative leadership is (and is not) and how leaders might be prepared to work with teachers on transforming the curriculum so as to ground the learning of social justice and citizenship in its connections with human flourishing. In a comprehensive and thoughtful essay, Daniel Reyes-Guerra and Ira Bogotch discuss the need for transformative leaders and propose, as a way of preparing them, to re-center curriculum theory and inquiry as a "complicated conversation" inside educational leadership (this volume). In other words, they argue that re-centering curriculum inquiry is essential to the field of educational leadership. Michael Dantley cogently articulates the place of spirituality, aligned with a critical theoretical frame, in forging a new conception of transformative instructional leadership. Anne Marie Tryjankowski introduces the need to prepare leaders to understand the bureaucratic contexts within which they work in order for them to be able to have a transformative influence. This section concludes with an innovative and creative piece by Eric Weiner in which he takes seriously the relationship between leadership and curriculum. Weiner presents a fictitious Transformative Institute and provides comment by its founder (also fictional, of course) to show how "we can begin to see the truth in possibility and then more accurately locate the projects of equity, justice, and freedom shimmering just above the horizon of hope and probability" (p. TK, this volume). His lengthy prologue is followed by some specific pedagogical activities that may help to shape transformative leaders.

Part 3, Transformative Leadership in Practice, focuses on reflections informed by the authors' fields of practice, in which they either demonstrate the potential of transformative leadership or long wistfully for its appearance in their setting. Andy Barrett is an elementary school principal in a predominantly white, wealthy, upper-middle-class suburb of a large American city. His chapter ponders both the need for transformative leadership and the attendant challenges related to introducing a form of leadership that advocates both private and public good in a setting such as his. Paula Bieneman, also an elementary school principal but in a setting that is much more diverse in terms of both ethnicity and socioeconomic status, reflects on her 10 years of school leadership and the potential and encouragement she has found in concepts associated with transformative leadership. Iris Jun, in contrast, is a department head in a large and diverse high school where, although she tries to exercise transformative leadership, the concepts are neither widely understood nor practiced by others. She presents some compelling vignettes (Metal Detectors at the Cinco de Mayo Celebration, the "Brown Line," and Committing to the Mustangs) and argues that they beg for leaders who are transformative to address them through dialogue and the promotion of critical reflection. Claire Lapointe's study of principals who work in linguistic minority schools in Northern Canada again shows clearly, through their own words, how tenets of transformative leadership can help leaders understand how to promote equity and social justice in various settings. The section concludes with a chapter by Shirley Steinberg in which she argues that in order to work transformatively *with* youth, we need to transform the ways in which we think about, and represent, youth as leaders. Hence, with the other authors in this section, she argues the need to stop marginalizing and pathologizing youth and to reconceptualize them as capable of talented and creative leadership.

Table I.1. Core Components of Transformative Leadership in Comparison with Other Forms of Leadership

	Transactional Leadership	Transformational Leadership	Transformative Leadership
Starting Point	A desired agreement or item	Need for the organization to run smoothly and efficiently	Material realities and disparities outside the organization that impinge on the success of individuals, groups, and organization as a whole.
Foundation	An exchange	Meet the needs of complex and diverse systems	Critique and promise
Emphasis	Means	Organization	Deep and equitable change in social conditions
Processes	Immediate cooperation through mutual agreement and benefit	Understanding of organizational culture, setting directions, developing people, redesigning the organization, and managing the instructional program	Deconstruction and reconstruction of social-cultural knowledge frameworks that generate inequity, acknowledgement of power and privilege, dialectic between individual and communal
Key Values	Honesty, responsibility, fairness, and honoring commitments	Liberty, justice, equality	Liberation, emancipation, democracy, equity, justice
Goal	Agreement; mutual goal advancement	Organizational change; effectiveness	Individual and organizational learning; inclusive pedagogy; societal transformation; global citizenship
Power	Mostly ignored	Inspirational	Positional, hegemonic, tool for oppression as well as for action; moral and ethical use
Leader	Ensures smooth and efficient organizational operation through transactions	Looks for motive, develops common purpose, focuses on organizational goals	Lives with tension and challenge; requires moral courage, inclusive organizations, participation, advocacy, activism
Related Theories	Bureaucratic leadership; scientific management	School effectiveness; school reform; school improvement; instructional leadership;	Critical theories (race, gender); cultural and social reproduction; leadership for social justice, democratic leadership

Source: Adapted from Shields (2010).

In the fourth and final section, Studying Transformative Leadership, we provide both original research using the lens of transformative leadership and reanalyses of existing studies through this new lens. Here the authors unite to show the relevance of a transformative lens for empirical work. Jorunn Møller studied the practices of two principals in Norway five years after their participation in an International Successful School Principals Project (ISSPP). Their practices, as reported by the principals and the teachers, have been analyzed through the framework of transformative leadership, which offers a lens to understanding leadership for democratic education. Similarly, Jean Archambault and Rosaline Garon developed a transformative leadership framework to analyze how school principals worked successfully in some of Montreal's most disadvantaged schools. George Theoharis and Marcia Ranieri provide a secondary analysis of four different studies to demonstrate "the ways transformative school administrators lead in contrast to other leaders tackling similar issues" (p. TK, this volume). In particular, they pick up on Avant's appeal for action and emphasize the need for advocacy to be part of transformative leadership. Lauren Stephenson and Barbara Harold are colleagues at Zayed University in Dubai. Lauren describes a project developed by Zayed University called Conversations on Leadership, and uses the data from this project to inquire about the extent to which perceptions of leadership in that part of the world are, or perhaps could be, transformative. Barbara's chapter analyzes the conceptions of leadership of some their graduate students and practicing school administrators. Both chapters demonstrate the emerging utility of the theory of transformative leadership for non-Western contexts, including Arabic countries in the Middle East. Finally, Christa Boske's chapter focuses on the impact of a leadership preparation program in terms of how an emphasis on transformative leadership helps participants to understand their relation to self and others in addressing issues of social justice in U.S. public schools. I conclude this Introduction with a table modified from a recently published article (Shields, 2010 EAQ).

Clearly, each of these authors, coming from different continents, cultural contexts, and positions, has a uniquely individual perspective on transformative leadership. In the Afterword, I try to pull together some of the key themes and ideas that reflect the richness and diversity of these chapters. It is our hope that you will take time to reflect on how the ideas explicated here may help educational leaders to address the myriad tasks that confront them. In some ways, the challenges are daunting, and the call to engaged, transformative action does not represent a safe or easy approach. Nevertheless, we anticipate you will be inspired and encouraged by the words you find here. Before we proceed, let me provide a figure that attempts to capture some of the key differences I perceive between transformative leadership and common iterations of transactional or transformational leadership (see Table I.1).

Note

1. For a more complete discussion of this history see Shields and Edwards (2005), on which this section is loosely based. Moreover, during this discussion, and reflective of the writers, speakers, and dominant stances of the times, I continue to use the male pronouns to describe leaders, cognizant, as Shakeshaft argued in 1989, that women are systematically neglected and excluded from these discussions.

References

Astin, A. W., & Astin, H. S. (2000). *Leadership reconsidered: Engaging higher education in social change.* Battle Creek, MI: Kellogg Foundation. Available at: http://www.wkkf.org/knowledge-center/resources/2007/01/Leadership-Reconsidered-Engaging-Higher-Education-In-Social-Change.aspx (accessed Dec. 2006).

Barber, B. R. (1991/2001). An aristocracy of everyone. In S. J. Goodlad (Ed.), *The last best hope: A democracy reader* (pp.11–22). N. San Francisco, CA: Jossey-Bass.

Bogotch, I. E. (2002). Educational leadership and social justice: Practice into theory. *Journal of School Leadership, 12*(2), 138–156.

Brown, K. M. (2004), Leadership for social justice and equity: Weaving a transformative framework and pedagogy. *Educational Administration Quarterly, 40*(1), 77–108.

Burns, J. M. (1978). *Leadership*. New York: Harper & Row.

Cuban, L. (1990). Reforming again, again, and again. *Educational Researcher, 19*(1), 3–13.

Culbertson, J. A. (1988). A century's quest for a knowledge base. In N. J. Boyan (Ed.), *Handbook of research on educational administration* (pp. 3–26). New York: Longman.

Culbertson, J. A. (1995). *Building bridges: UCEA's first two decades.* University Park, PA: UCEA.

Dewey, J. (2001). John Dewey 1859–1952. In J. A. Palmer, (Ed.), *Fifty major thinkers on education* (pp. 177-182). New York: Routledge.

Evans, R. (2000). The authentic leader. In M. Fullan (Ed.), *The Jossey-Bass reader on educational leadership* (pp. 287–308). San Francisco, CA: Jossey-Bass.

Foster, W. (1986). *Paradigms and promises.* Buffalo, NY: Prometheus.

Foucault, M. (1995). *Discipline and punish.* New York: Vintage.

Freire, P. (1970). *Pedagogy of the oppressed.* New York: Herder & Herder.

Freire, P. (1998). *Pedagogy of freedom: Ethics, democracy, and civic courage.* Lanham, MD: Rowman & Little-field.

Green, J. M. (1999). *Deep democracy: Diversity, community, and transformation.* Lanham, MD: Rowman & Littlefield.

Greene, M. (1988). *The dialectic of freedom.* New York: Teachers College Press.

Greenfield, T. B. (1975). Theory about organization: A new perspective and its implications for schools. In T. Greenfield & P. Ribbons (Eds.) *Greenfield on educational administration: Towards a humane craft* (pp. 1–25). London: Routledge.

Haley, A. (1974). *Roots.* New York: Vanguard.

hooks, b. (2000). *Where we stand: Class matters.* New York: Routledge.

Illinois State Board of Education. (2010). *Developing school improvement plans* [Power Point]. Available at: http://www.isbe.net/sos/htmls/district.htm (accessed Dec. 26, 2010).

Ladson-Billings, G. (1996). "Your blues ain't like mine": Keeping issues of race and racism on the multicultural agenda. *Theory into Practice, 35*(4), 248–255.

Ladson-Billings, G. (2006). Once upon a time when patriotism was what you did. *Phi Delta Kappan, 87*(8), 585–588.

Larson, C. L., & Murtadha, K. (2002). Leadership for Social Justice. *Yearbook of the National Society for the Study of Education, 101*(1), 132–161.

Leithwood, K., Harris, A., & Hopkins, D. (2008). Seven strong claims about successful school leadership. *School Leadership and Management, 28*(1), 27–42.

Oakes, J., & Rogers, J. (2006). *Learning power.* New York: Teachers College Press.

Palmer, P. J. (2007). *The courage to teach.* San Francisco, CA: Jossey-Bass/Wiley.

Perryman, J. (2009). Inspection and the fabrication of professional and performative processes. *Journal of Education Policy, 24*(5), 611–631.

Ravitch, D. (2010). *The death and life of the great American school system.* New York: Basic Books. (Kindle version)

Ryan, J. (2009). Struggling for democracy. *Educational Management Administration Leadership, 37*(4), 473–496.

Sarason, S. (1990). *The predictable failure of educational reform.* San Francisco, CA: Jossey-Bass.

Shakeshaft, C. (1989). *Women in educational administration.* Newbury Park, CA: Corwin.

Shields, C. M. (2003). *Good intentions are not enough: Transformative leadership for communities of difference.* Lanham, MD: Scarecrow.

Shields, C. M. (2004). Dialogic leadership for social justice: Overcoming pathologies of silence. *Educational Administrative Quarterly, XI*(1), 111–134.

Shields, C. M. (2009). *Courageous leadership for transforming schools: Democratizing practice.* Norwood, MA: Christopher-Gordon.

Shields, C. M., & Edwards, M. M. (2005). *Dialogue is not just talk: A new ground for educational leadership.* New York: Peter Lang.

Starratt, R. J. (2007). Leading a community of learners. *Educational Management Administration & Leadership, 35*(2), 165–183.

Tatum, B. D. (2007). *Can we talk about race? And other conversations in an era of school resegregation.* Boston, MA: Beacon.

Tauber, R. T. (2007). *Classroom management: Sound theory and effective practice.* Westport, CT: Praeger.

Theoharis, G. 2007. Social justice educational leaders and resistance: Toward a theory of social justice. *Educational Administration Quarterly, 43*(2), 221–258

Thompson, J. (2007). *A history and analysis of school improvement planning.* Unpublished document, Michigan State University. Available at: https://www.msu.edu/user/thomp603/improvement.pdf (accessed Dec. 26, 2010).

Vail, K. (2005). What's in a name? Maybe a student's grade. *American School Board Journal, 192,* 6–8. Available   at: http://web.ebscohost.com/ehost/pdfviewer/pdfviewer?hid=108&sid=c9792b9f-3ac3–415f-acc4–d40a8b2b8c23%40sessionmgr113&vid=11 (accessed Dec. 28, 2010).

Valencia, R. R. (Ed.). (1997). *The evolution of deficit thinking.* London: Falmer.

Weiner, E. J. (2003). Secretary Paulo Freire and the democratization of power: Toward a theory of transformative leadership. *Educational Philosophy and Theory, 35*(1), 89–106.

Woods, P. A. (2004). Democratic leadership: Drawing distinctions with distributive leadership. *International Journal of Leadership in Education, 7*(Part 1), 3–26.

World Hunger and Poverty Facts and Statistics. (2010). *2011 World Hunger and Poverty Facts and Statistics.* Available at: http://www.worldhunger.org/articles/Learn/world%20hunger%20facts%202002.htm (accessed Dec. 28, 2010).

Conceptualizing
Transformative Leadership

I

Leadership in Pursuit of Purpose

Social, Economic and Political Transformation

Jill Blackmore

Transformation is the word on every leadership scholar and practitioner leader's lips, hailed as the next solution after 'best practice' in school reform (Hallinger, 2003). Transformation is the lexicon of new leadership in the 21st century (Gronn, 1999; Gunter, 2001). According to its advocates, *transformational leadership* addresses key issues in education and redresses past neglect—for example, about teacher emotions, inequality of student learning outcomes, cultural diversity, and pedagogy (Leithwood & Jantzi, 2005). In this chapter I argue that, while seductive, this transformational leadership discourse appropriates critical perspectives while depoliticising their social-justice intent, as the notion of transformational leadership has been framed narrowly within the school effectiveness improvement paradigms (see Gunter & Butt, 2007; Thrupp & Willmott, 2003). In contrast, *transformative leadership* discourses derive from a critical tradition, promoting emancipatory pedagogies that arise from political and social movements, feminist perspectives, and critical pedagogy (Darder, Baltodano, & Torres, 2009). These have historically focused not only on what *can* be done—confined by a 'what works' frame—but also on what *should* be done for a better and more just society. Transformative approaches raise key questions about the purposes of education and leadership and about issues of social justice addressing social and economic inequality more broadly within democratic societies (Marshall & Olivia, 2006).

This chapter draws on four three-year empirical studies in schools[1] undergoing restructuring and redesign in Victoria, Australia, in the context of neo-liberal reforms and economic globalisation. The findings identified how, in each instance, it was the overarching desire of leaders and teachers to provide a 'just' education—including for those most disadvantaged, such as refugees and children living in poverty—that was the underlying purpose for serial redesign, as each school's circumstances changed over time. At the same time, schools had to address the performative context and demands of marketised systems where schools, their students, teachers, and principals lived under constant scrutiny and threat of closure if seen to be failing against pre-determined and externally defined criteria of success. The socio-cultural, spatial, and material positioning of these schools indicated that schools cannot sustain equity work on their own and that more democratic and community practices, aligned with redistributive notions of justice, are required and need to be supported by political will.

Transformative Leadership: Why Now?

In 1978, out of the context of the political unrest and activism of the civil rights movement of the previous decades, James McGregor Burns argued that there were serious failures in leadership studies because of the 'bifurcation between the literature on leadership and the literature on followership' (p. 3): between heroic or demonic leaders, as represented through anecdote or biography, and their 'audiences', depicted as 'drab and powerless masses' (p. 2).

> I describe leadership here as no mere game among elitists and no mere populist response but as a structure of action that engages persons, to varying degrees, throughout the levels and among the intersices of society. . . (Burns, 1978, p. 3)

Burns not only coined the notion of transforming leadership, but his quote also signals that, in his view, the field of educational leadership continues to suffer from the same malaise. Burns also argues that because leadership is about relationships, it is about the complex dynamic between power and values as well. His theory of power is premised on the view that

> not all human influences are necessarily coercive and exploitative, that not all transactions among persons are mechanical, impersonal, ephemeral. It lies in seeing that the most powerful influences consist of deeply human relationships in which two or more persons *engage* with one another. It lies in a more realistic, and more sophisticated understanding of power, and the often far more consequential exercise of mutual persuasion, exchange, elevation and transformation—in short leadership. . . .We must see power—and leadership—as not things but as *relationships*. We must analyse power in a context of human motives and physical constraints. (Burns, 1978, p. 11)

Here Burns identifies issues of mutuality, engagement, relationships, and material constraints for action. He then goes on to focus on moral purpose and values, even in the practical relations of leaders (Burns, 1978, p. 32). That is, the purpose of leadership is to assist in making the everyday decisions be, not about self-interest, but about mutual needs, aspirations, and values. Followers, he suggests, should have opportunities to choose between leadership alternatives, and leaders should take responsibility for their commitments to their followers.

Thus Burns seeks to obliterate the historical divide in the literature on political leadership between structural (class, institutional, etc.) and cultural (individual, psychological) understandings of leadership. The conditions and context of leadership are also significant. His prepostmodernist notion of historical causation is informed by a sense of contingency and of how multiple economic, social, and political factors inform leadership. While his search for a cross-cultural 'general theory of leadership' (p. 26) is worrisome for some postmodernists, his assertion that any theory of leadership requires the perspective of various disciplines—psychology, sociology, politics, and history (Burns, 1978, p. 27)—is not. The role of leaders is to purposefully 'make conscious what lies unconscious in followers'—for instance, aspects of their identity (sexual, communal, ethnic, class, national, ideological). But the issue is, for what purpose (Burns, 1978, p. 41)?

Burns's notions of transforming and transactional leadership were popularised during the early 1990s and again in the 2000s in management and educational leadership literature. *Transactional* leadership is about the everyday exchanges negotiated between leaders and followers, where there may be little coincidence between their interests or aims for transacting this exchange. *Transforming* leadership is when the leader recognises and 'exploits' the potential needs of the followers, but where there is a collective agreement as to a purpose or higher goal. And 'in satisfying their needs... the leader elevates and converts the followers into leaders' and moral agents, because leadership is about teaching (pp. 4, 425). Leadership is therefore an educative process for both leaders and followers that occurs through dialogue about purpose, minimising any leader-follower hierarchy. The transforming leader undertakes work of a higher moral order than that of transactional leaders who focus on management functions.

At the same time, Burns was also a man of his time. While recognising that leadership is relational and about power, his leaders are disembodied, although, through implication from his examples of Roosevelt, Kennedy, and Martin Luther King Jr., they are male. His work arises out of the civil rights and student movements, but he neglects to mention the emerging women's movement that was yet to display its political, social, and epistemological force. And finally, in discussing moral leadership, he draws on the work of Lawrence Kohlberg in claiming that transformational leaders have greater moral virtue and that they can convert others to moral agency. One reading of this is that followers do not have the same levels of moral virtue, and, as feminist critics of Kohlberg, such as Gilligan (1982), have argued, such levels of moral distinction tend to position women as followers and of lesser moral capacity. His use of the term *convert* implies that leaders impart power or moral virtue onto others, a questionable supposition. Feminist scholars have argued (Luke & Gore, 1992) that power is not something to be given by the 'powerful' within the context of unequal relations, and that 'higher order' morality is also situated in the everyday dilemmas of living together. What leaders (or the powerful) *can* do is transform unequal conditions of power and resources and in so doing create conditions that may enable others to mobilise their own sense of agency. Alternatively, Burns can be seen to view leadership as mutually uplifting, centered around a shared commitment to moral endeavours in which the leader is also a learner (Collard, 1998).

Popularised in the management field by Avolio and Bass (1994), *transformational* leaders 'convert followers to disciples', 'develop followers into leaders', and 'provide followers with a cause around which they can rally'. Bass (1990) was quick to eliminate the distinction between leadership and management, or transforming and transactional leadership, arguing that different forms of leadership were undertaken by the same people, some more disposed towards one form than another. Managers are potential leaders and leadership is critical to good management. Transactional leadership thus became defined as an exchange relationship between subordinate and superior, premised upon rewards and punishments, which is a reductionist reading of Burns's sophisticated notion of interests. Transformational leaders, according to Bass:

> attempt and succeed in raising colleagues, subordinates, followers, clients, or constituencies to a greater awareness about the issues of consequence. This heightening of awareness requires a leader with vision, self-confidence, and inner strength to argue successfully for what he [sic] sees is right or good, not for what is popular or is acceptable according to the established wisdom of the time. (1990, pp. 17–18)

Bass reduces a political process of negotiation, dialogue, and contestation to that of one leader at the top motivating workers to meet specified organisational aims, a view readily collapsed into the bundle of soft and visionary new leadership studies of the early 21st century (Gronn, 1995).

Transformational leadership is a seductive notion because it 'overcomes virtually every shortcoming that brought erstwhile great-man theory of history and leadership into disrepute:

its paternalism and gender exclusiveness, its aristocratic pretensions and social-class bias, and its exaggerated, eccentric conception of human agency and causality' and reasserts the 'power of one' implicit in charismatic leadership (Gronn, 1995, p. 15). But leadership is not a product of circumstance: leaders create circumstances. Transformational leadership reasserts:

> a deeply ingrained cultural pre-disposition to accept the efficacy of individual leaders and members of elites as in control of, responsible for and able to make a difference to, levels of organisational performance and effectiveness. . .and the mindset chiefly responsible for the learned helplessness experienced by followers. (Gronn, 1995, p. 16)

According to Bass (1999), transformational leadership cascades down through the organisation as leaders modelled behaviours on the one hand and empowered followers on the other. If transformational behaviour is found lower down in the organisation, it is seen to be evidence of a trickle-down effect of the organisational leader rather than leadership being practised by many within an organisation (Gronn, 1995, p. 18).

Ironically, although the embodiment of leadership was masculine in most studies, the single empirical study addressing gender concluded that women were seen to be more transformational than male leaders (Bass & Aviolo, 1994; Druskat, 1994), an irony requiring more sophisticated theories of how inequality works. While Bass recognised leadership as multilevel and multifaceted, there was no wider sense of the public good. Thus, the educational discourse of the 1990s inherited the business assumption that transformational leadership was equated to a formal position within a hierarchical organisation (Collard, 1998; Gronn, 1995; Leithwood, 1992; Silins, 1994).

Why Is Transformational Leadership Such an Enduring Concept?

In Western nation-states, fundamental shifts in the role of education—from a public good to a positional good—have arisen as a consequence of a regressive mix of unstable socioeconomic contexts, fast capitalism, and neo-liberal policies of managerialism and marketisation redefining equity as choice (Blackmore & Sachs, 2007). At the same time, a progressive educational discourse promotes reinventing schools so that they better meet the needs of 21st-century self-reflexive and flexible citizen workers, as evident in pedagogical discourses about the personalization of learning to address student diversity. Within systems of devolved schooling, governments rely heavily on leaders of 'self-managing' schools to implement their policies. Professional development has therefore focused on leadership capacity building—for example, the National College of School Leadership in England and the standards movement in leadership. Within the dominant school-effectiveness and school-improvement paradigms that accept these parameters, Bass's conceptualisation of transformational leadership—strong leaders who are prepared to make radical changes—is therefore a good fit. Governments can deflect responsibility and blame onto individual leaders, as policies of parental choice produce successful or failing schools (and leaders).

The failure of the notion of transformational leadership to address the complexity of educational work (Wrigley, 2004; Hartley, 2007)—particularly in schools in challenging circumstances—led to a new focus on distributed leadership in the 2000s (Harris & Chapman, 2006). This discourse aligned well with discourses about how the knowledge economy requires innovation, emotional work, problem solving, evidence-based practice, and organisational learning (Brown & Moshavi, 2005; Leithwood & Jantzi, 2005; Mulford & Silins, 2003; Silins, Zarins & Mulford, 2002). This discourse recognized that teachers undertook leadership work. Quantitative methodological advances in the school-effects paradigm have also caught up with qualitative research's conclusion that student-teacher interaction is critical to improving student outcomes; teacher efficacy is central to innovative pedagogies; and executive leadership provides the conditions that enable productive relationships and is thus indirectly connected to outcomes (Barker, 2007; Ross & Gray, 2006; Hattie, 2003).

But as with transformational leadership, distributed leadership is more about delegating responsibility without redistributing authority or resources. The rhetoric is normative, as it is aligned with the social and communal concerns of employees derived from the human relations movement, participative decision making, and organisational cultures (Hartley, 2007; Hatcher, 2005). Yet it is the rational 'logic' that drives policy: that of standardisation and formalisation, as derived from the tradition of scientific management and reengineering (Hartley, 2007, p. 204). While reengineering does not pretend to be democratic, both transformational and distributed leadership are often couched in democratic terms, such as the ownership of change and knowledge production, shared leadership, and being consensus driven. But from within the school-effectiveness and management paradigm, this softer turn is less the dissolution of the emotionality-rationality divide and is more attributable to liquid modernity producing another 'contemporary cultural shift. . .towards a general weakening of classifications', with the shift from a 'social structure to network culture' (Hartley, 2007, pp. 208–209). Transformational leadership in its latest reincarnation continues to focus on:

- individual schools and not education for the public good;

- teacher efficacy driven by standards rather than a wider sense of education professionalism and advocacy;

- knowledge production to improve effectiveness rather than coproduction of knowledge for more inclusive schools;

- evidence-based practice rather than research informed inquiry;

- heroic individualism rather than collective activism;

- emotional intelligence as an acquired skill to better manage others, rather than emotionality as a way of being and thinking about the self and with regard to others; and

- viewing diversity at a second-order level, as elaborated in pedagogical notions of personalisation, while ignoring how first-order difference is constituted through unequal structural, social, and economic relations of gender, race, and class.

In the end, the leader continues to be positioned as the one with agency and as the source of innovation, vision, and, indeed, moral virtue. Issues of power relations, structures, processes of inequality, and unequal economic resources, or how perceptions of leadership are gendered and racialised, are still pushed into the background. The leader is still expected to operate within and be judged by the paradigm of school effectiveness which is 'associated with a narrow understanding of what education is for' (Gorard, 2010, p. 759; Potter et al., 2002). What many of the (flawed) measures of success used by school-effectiveness research and replicated in public websites and rankings, such as MySchool in Australia do is to make invisible the very things that make the difference in outcomes: differences between rich and poor, between ethnic and language groups, and the significance of prior educational attainment and background (Gorard, 2010) and social mix (Thrupp & Lupton, 2006).

Transformative Leadership

There is a second body of literature that informs discourses around transforming education: that of critical pedagogy arising from the work of libertarian educators, such as Freire and feminist educators (e.g., Luke & Gore, 1992). Transformative leadership emerges out of the politics of difference—how schools are racialised and gendered in terms of their curriculum, organisation, and pedagogies—and favours some students more than others (Ladson-Billings, 1998; Shields, 2003). Transformative leadership considers how the work conditions of teachers are also the work conditions of students. It also values diversity and seeks to provide inclusive learning environments based on relationships of respect and trust. While aspirational in intent, transformative leadership is also analytical. Schools are seen as integral to unequal economic, social, and political structures, relationships, and processes (Lupton, 2005; Lipman, 2009). Thus, context matters in terms of what leaders can—and should—do (Thrupp & Lupton, 2006). Leadership requires a clear ethical (in the professional sense) and moral (doing the right thing) imperative linked to a strong sense of purpose in order to reduce inequality and promote social justice for all.

A transformative perspective views leadership as a social practice aligned with democratic practices more broadly (Shields, 2003). Education is a means by which to achieve social and economic change and individual opportunity and is an institution serving the wider public good. Transformative leadership is a collective and educative process—as typified by Burns—aiming for more inclusive, democratic, and equitable education. Whereas transformational leadership accepts the context and parameters within which a school works and predetermined organisational objectives as a given, transformative leadership seeks also to change the context to better suit the needs of the students and community and thus takes school contexts seriously (Thrupp & Lupton, 2006). As Burns related, transformative leadership calls upon a range of disciplinary fields—such as sociology, history, cultural studies, and psychology—and multiple perspectives within each field—feminist, critical, indigenous, and post-colonial. It also means working across professional boundaries when problem-setting and researching, and going outside one's comfort zone and field, in order to achieve a just society (Marshall & Olivia, 2006). A just society is one which provides conditions of possibility for all its citizens to achieve, through the recognition of difference and establishing redistributive policies within a democratic framework.

Leadership with Purpose: Some Australian Case Studies

Data from four qualitative three-year research projects undertaken by the author and others over the past 15 years facilitate tracking the impact of various policy shifts on the work of principals and teachers in government schools in the state of Victoria. One study is from the period of neoliberal educational restructuring of women leaders during the 1990s (Blackmore & Sachs, 2007). A second looks at a Local Learning and Employment Network (LLEN) as a policy response to students at risk in the early 2000s (Blackmore & Sachs, 2007). A third study focused on why there were fewer applicants for the school leadership positions. The fourth study—Redesigning Schools and Leadership—captured responses as schools underwent fundamental redesign—of organisation, space, time, and pedagogy—in response to discourses about changing needs to accommodate 21st-century students and locational disadvantage.

Australia, while ranking high in the international league tables of PISA, is characterised as high quality but low equity, the latter signalled by a long tail in underachievement that has increased over the past decade. Socioeconomic background (often the proxy for rurality, indigeneity, or ethnicity) is *the* greatest indicator after family background of educational achievement, more so in Australia than any other Organisation for Economic Co-operation and Development (OECD) country. Recent Australian studies point to the concentration of educational underachievement, poor community health and well-being, as well as inadequate government and nongovernment infrastructure, most often in rural or isolated, largely indigenous, communities, or rapidly expanding outer-suburban areas experiencing deindustrialisation (Teese, Lamb, & Duru-Bellat, 2007). Similar patterns have occurred in other Anglophone nation-states, such as the United Kingdom and United States, with some correlation between the degree of devolution to self-managing schools and increased competition between schools arising from neo-liberal policies (Teese et al., 2007).

Victoria has a particular policy history that has shaped leadership practices. During the 1990s, the neo-liberal Kennett government radically restructured the government school sector, moving to create internal labour markets within the public system, as schools competed for enrolments, per capita funding was reduced, student-to-staff ratios were increased, support services were outsourced, and performance management was imposed. As a consequence of this devolved system resulting from deregulation and downsizing, two reviews by a Labour government found many students at risk 'slipped through the cracks', because there was little sense of systemic responsibility (Connors, 2000; Kirby, 2000). A number of initiatives sought to address the negative effects of competition and the growing disparity between rich and poor students, schools, and regions. In order to recreate a sense of system-wide responsibility, schools were encouraged to work in clusters around shared issues and projects; LLENs were established to better coordinate services for young people at risk. A state-wide reform agenda—The Blueprint for Victorian Government Schools—focused on teacher professional development, leadership capacity building, student learning outcomes, evidence-based practice, a leading-schools fund to encourage innovation, and development of a 'performance culture'. Phase Two of the Blueprint (2008 to present) recognised the need for additional resources and support for schools in more 'challenging circumstances'. A Building Futures program (2004 to 2010) sought to revive the depleted and neglected infrastructure of public schools. Victoria also focused on transitions through early years intervention; a middle years strategy; and On Track data seeking to support students in their first year after leaving school. Victoria has led with the introduction of the Victorian Certificate of Applied Learning alongside its more academic Victorian Certificate of Education and Vocational Education and Training (VET) programs in schools. Federal policies also encouraged VET, Mapping Individual Pathways, as well as School-Based Apprenticeships in schools.

At the same time, state governments and schools are framed by federal policies. While public schools are a state government responsibility, and federal governments fund nongovernment schools (now 34% of Australian students), federal policies have shifted since 1996 from need to choice, based on postcode and not on the social mix of student population. This has encouraged nongovernment schools to expand into new areas, offering transport and scholarships to more families (Morgan & Blackmore, 2012). The greatest expansion has been of small, fundamentalist, religious schools of all persuasions, and poaching of high-achieving students from low-socioeconomic status (SES) postcodes, a practice benefitting already advantaged schools. Meanwhile, state-run government schools have been restructured due to demographic shifts, with many being closed, only to be replaced by smaller nongovernment schools that are federally funded.

Furthermore, since 1996 there has been a centralising trend, with greater policy coherence emerging between the states and territories through the federal Ministerial Council of Youth Employment and Education and Youth Affairs, the Adelaide (1999) and Melbourne Declarations (2009), the push towards a national curriculum (2012), national teacher and leadership professional standards, standardised testing through the National Assessment Program—Literacy and Numeracy (NAPLAN)—and most recently via MySchool, which provides performance data on every Australian school on an open-access website. Federal-state funding agreements are based on performance outcomes and retention rates to Year 12, foci evident in Victoria's push for increased literacy and numeracy outcomes in schools below state or national average on NAPLAN. Thus, there is intensified scrutiny of under-achieving schools by governments, parents, and the media; stronger external accountability demands based on narrower measures of success; and a trend to standardisation. At the same time, there is a discourse about the need to personalise learning, utilise evidence-based practice, improve teacher leadership, and use innovative pedagogies in new learning spaces in order to improve student learning (McNeil, 2009). This is the policy mix that teachers and leaders contend with in their daily practice.

Leadership and Educational Restructuring: 1990s

During the 1990s, women entered into leadership roles in Victorian schools, spurred by 1980s gender-equity policies to aspire and apply. Many feminists had the desire to make a difference in creating a more equitable education system. But women's entrée into this masculine domain coincided with the radical restructuring of school education by the neo-liberal Kennett government, which punished resistance through withdrawal of funds and threats against teachers who spoke out, closed 300 out of over 1800 schools, and resulted in a reduction of 20% of the teacher workforce. Principals were not informed or consulted, with new initiatives often published in the press the day directives were faxed down from the department (Blackmore, Bigum, Hodgens, & Laskey, 1996). Parents were positioned as consumers and individuals and no longer as policymakers and partners. Parent organisations opposing these reforms were marginalised and lost funding. Thus, these women leaders found themselves undertaking the emotional management work of a system in crisis and teachers under great stress while managing moves to dismantle the public education system (Blackmore, 1999).

The women principals' responses were various, agreeing not to set up schools to be in competition for students, and buffering staff and students from the deluge of reforms that reshaped principals' and teachers' work and conditions (Blackmore et al., 1996). Some fought publically alongside teacher unions to oppose standardised testing, for which they were officially reprimanded. Others encouraged parents to collectively protest against the reforms. Many principals joined with a coalition of student, teacher, parent, public-sector and not-for-profit, and philanthropic organisations in the Purple Sage movement to work against the decimation of public health, welfare, and education sectors. Most principals made the hard decisions but did so in the most transparent and democratic manner. This was possible if they had built their leadership on mutual respect and were trusted to do the right and fair thing within the above constraints (Bishop, 1999). Most principals experienced personal distress, and many expressed extreme anger—often physically manifested—as they perceived a radical values-drift in viewing education as an individual positional good and not as a public good and away from equity towards efficiency (Blackmore, 1999, 2004).

In this context, the discourse was about entrepreneurial, visionary, and transformational leadership as schools were likened to small businesses. Professional development focused only on principals, with a focus on promoting one's school. But the clear message from this study was that the external accountabilities and market orientation led to a focus on the performative work and not the real work of teaching and learning in schools. The tension they managed was between 'being good' in pragmatic terms of complying with system-wide demands, and 'doing good' in normative terms of seeking to meet the particular needs of their students, their families, and communities (Blackmore & Sachs, 2007).

LLENs: A Policy Response to Risk in the 2000s

In the 1999 election, the surprise loss of the neo-liberal Kennett government after seven years in power led to a reassessment of public education. While self-management and devolution were retained, as the principles of new public management had become deeply embedded in the public sector, there were concerns about the decline and residualisation of the public education system. Students had been encouraged to move to the private sector by a neo-conservative federal policy change in the funding rules. In response to low retention rates and an increase in the students 'at risk' of dropping out, the Kirby report on training (2000) and Connors report on public education (2000) both recommended greater cooperation between public schools and better coordination of services through 'joined-up' government, returning to the notion of a public education *system*. While many clusters between schools had emerged organically in response to local need—setting up welfare units, working on transitions, agreeing to codes of practice on marketing, and developing professional networks in subject areas—now clusters and networks were policy solutions in response to public school-system fragmentation. With a focus on at-risk youth—those most likely to drop out of school before completing Year 12—LLENs were established to coordinate all local services available to young people and facilitate their transitioning into work or further education and training. The LLENs' role was to mobilise and fund new initiatives through interagency activities and improve communication and collaboration between government agencies, NGOs, schools, and the individual student.

In a large provincial city, young people, as individuals, had to navigate 38 organisations that catered to young people out of school and work (Kamp, 2006). This LLEN built on existing networks of organisations and teachers. Many teachers and school leaders had already developed multiple strategies and specific programs for students at risk, working with local employers and training providers as well as with community agencies. One principal of a senior secondary college had, without departmental support, mobilised the school's limited funds to develop in-school childcare for young mothers in order to encourage them to finish their schooling. Another principal had, through the restructuring of three schools in one region, developed a one-stop shop for students where welfare, health, career, and advisory services were located, in an effort to encourage all students to use these services. These programs were coordinated and enhanced by the LLEN, which sought to encourage seamlessness between educational providers to facilitate student pathways, offering welfare, employment, and training support where possible. The LLEN partnered with the local university to develop a program to train and recruit new teachers—people out of the trades and professions to teach the new Certificate of Applied Learning, as an alternative pathway.

While schools were judged on retention rates, principals and teachers defined success as when a student found work or training out of school, often with their help. Getting a job was preferable to constant failure at school. For many students, the first step to academic success is just turning up at school each day; for others any sense of success lies outside school in work or sport, achievements that do not boost retention statistics. This requires a comprehensive curriculum rather than the current trend towards a narrower curriculum, specialisation, and niche markets—particularly for students seen to be at risk, who benefit from a diverse range of learning experiences. As Lipman argues, regimes of accountability in education 'concretely and symbolically produce a highly segmented and economically polarised labour force' (2009, p. 365).

While most public schools offered a breadth of programs to meet the multiple needs of their diverse student groups, advantaged elite schools offered a more traditional academic-liberal curriculum. These were usually enhanced by extracurricular activities that are unaffordable in disadvantaged schools but that provide alternative avenues of achievement (Muschamp, Bullock, Edge, & Wideley, 2009). Measuring success through standardised outcomes, rather than a range of social and emotional as well as academic outcomes, also reduces innovation: compliance regimes reduce teachers' professional capacity to think analytically, be creative, and they even desensitise them to thinking critically (Lipman, 2009; McNeil, 2009). While policies encouraged families and communities to work in partnership with schools, performance indicators did not recognise different forms of learning in different contexts. As in the English context:

> an effectiveness framework that assigns disproportionate value to examination results seems to have created a leadership paradox, where heads reported to be transformational produce only limited gains in performance. The study concludes that the government's determination to assume a strongly positive relationship between leaders and outcomes has compromised the principle of evidence-informed policy-making and that we need a different approach based on a broadly defined, qualitative conception of student success. (Barker, 2007, p. 21)

Leadership in the Australian context was undertaken by teachers, as well as principals, working in fluid and short-term networks across industry, health, welfare, and retail professions based on single-issue concerns (Blackmore, 2006). Working with students at risk was the common purpose and how to mobilise a range of resources—people, knowledge, and funds—to that end was the underpinning rationale for the network to survive. Leadership was premised upon expertise and relationships of trust, as well as a capacity to get things done, and not official position (Kamp, 2006). Respect was earned through recognition of, learning about, and sharing other forms of expertise. Network sociality was more fluid, tenuous, and open to new ideas, while at the same time more focused (Wittel, 2000). But serial networks based on relationships meant that success, in terms of measurable outcomes, was difficult to track and measure, and thus it was difficult to be accountable in the managerial sense.

Disengagement with Leadership

Cross-nationally, the early 2000s also saw a crisis in leadership, with declining applications for school principalship from amongst potential aspirants. This was in part due to demographics of an ageing workforce but also because the job was perceived as threatening to one's health due to a work-life imbalance. Principals were seen to take the brunt of blame and shame if their schools were labelled as 'underachieving', while implementing heavy-handed policies that were viewed as often being counterproductive to student learning. Increasingly the focus of leadership was less on pedagogy and more about administration, accountability, risk management, and marketing and the daily routine of imposed administration. Hence, there was a dissonance between the rhetorical employment of the discourse of transformational and distributed leadership and the reality of leaders' work in schools. Finally, many minority aspirants felt excluded due to the lack of diversity in leadership, as selection panels were seen to make 'safe' choices—for instance, Anglos and males. But the dominant theme was value-driven: most simply did not 'want to be like that' (Barty, Thomson, Blackmore, & Sachs, 2005).

Redesigning Schools and Leadership

By the mid-2000s, it was evident that locational disadvantage was entrenched, with numerous schools in deindustrialised areas facing declining enrolments and increasingly diverse student needs (Teese et al., 2007). In a project focusing on the redesign of schools and leadership, we sought to identify the rationale, processes, and outcomes of schools that 'voluntarily' underwent a collective decision to implement fundamental changes in practice in order to better meet the needs of their students. In one outer-suburban region, Highgrove, unemployment was three times the national average due to the closure of manufacturing industries, which were decamping overseas to seek cheaper labour. Three secondary schools had experienced declining enrolments as students bypassed them to attend other government and nongovernment schools. Realising they were no longer serving the community or students with their low retention rates and high levels of underachievement, the school principals resolved to restructure local provision in association with a government neighbourhood regeneration project. Consequently, over two years health and welfare infrastructure was built in close proximity to three new, well-designed school campuses—two P–9 schools and one senior college (Years 10–12)— to create new learning environments and social centres.

A new executive principal, brought from a high-achieving, middle-class school, developed a distributed leadership structure, imparting some responsibility to most staff. Prior to moving in to the new flexible spaces, teachers and leaders explored how to capture the possibilities of personalised learning, before default pedagogies could be institutionalised. Whole school approaches to learning were developed around common vocabularies and rubrics. The students were recruited to the mantra of achieving "Two years in one'. Within a year, there was a sign of improved student learning outcomes and morale. The new buildings renewed community interest and enabled innovative pedagogical practices. Government investment provided additional personnel, infrastructure, and professional development (Blackmore, 2009). But this improvement is fragile, as external factors can lead to unexpected and unexplained 'dips' as new waves of refugees arrive or students drop out due to sudden rises in unemployment. Whereas it is easy to argue that community deprivation or individual issues are not excuses for any school's incapacity to improve learning outcomes, raising unreasonable expectations and experiencing continual failure has a deflating effect.

But with all schools under the same pressure, Highgrove's ranking, relative to similar schools on the MySchool website and within NAPLAN data, may not alter, even though student performance had markedly improved in one year. Continual improvement of everyone produces a no-win solution, as standards rise. The reality not recognised in school effects research and policy is that an individual school may add value to the student intake through innovative pedagogies, but learning outcomes are determined mostly by a school's capacity to be selective of its students (Gorard, 2010). If schools are segregated socially—due to specialisation, selectiveness, location, or fees—then this will impact the equity of the system overall (Alegre & Ferrer, 2010). Individual schools cannot be expected to remedy or ameliorate what system-wide policies have produced. As Thrupp and Lupton (2006, p. 311) argue, a less 'neutral discourse on schooling' is required as it would give a 'fairer evaluation of school performance, a fairer distribution of resources, and the provision of more appropriate advice and support to schools in less favourable contexts'.

Leadership Lessons

A number of themes emerge from these studies. First, context does matter. Context is informed by social and demographic—as well as economic—factors, geography, temporality, and policy. When leadership is decontextualised and all leadership is invested in the exemplary practice of a 'good leader', then leaders are set up for failure. As one principal joked, one year he had been a mentor principal of colleagues in 'failing' schools and the next was being mentored as a failure when he moved to a school in a disadvantaged area. An assistant principal reflected on how, in a middle-class school, it was possible to undertake certain types of innovation with a computer-intensive Year 6 claymation project because the students were already performing above the state average on literacy and numeracy tests, but that instigating a similar project in his former disadvantaged school would lead to the centre and parents questioning why they were 'wasting time' and 'not concentrating on the basics'. Strong external accountabilities are often prioritised more in disadvantaged schools whereas high-achieving schools are left free to innovate; and yet improvement is most likely when there is strong internal accountability based on peer review (McNeil, 2009; Elmore, 1997). School context, as well as social mix, also matters in terms of the resources that can be brought to bear and the time required in getting students to attend school and address their welfare needs (Thrupp & Lupton, 2006; Gorard, 2010).

Second, each case study indicated that a key element was an enabling policy framework that provided legitimation for action as well as resources. This also required a level of system reflexivity. In the mid-2000s, education bureaucrats recognized after evaluations that some children cost more to educate, and that education reform was best achieved by resourcing bottom-up initiatives, distributing resources more equitably, as well as 'working alongside teachers to actually address the problems that they're confronting with that particular cohort and within that particular community' (personal interview, senior bureaucrat, 2008). Leadership, together with central and regional support, was critical in providing teachers with professional development and in encouraging risk-taking and exploration of innovative pedagogies, teamwork, and collaborative learning in the new learning spaces. Excess staff due to amalgamations and special consideration meant learning coaches could be mobilized to work with teachers on literacy and numeracy. Targeted funding from the Leading Schools Fund (a state fund) and National Partnerships provided additional resources that could not be raised by parents or the community. Students were involved in planning and responded favourably to government investment in buildings. Likewise, investment in community infrastructure and governmental agencies—so they could support student transitions and well-being—facilitated both teachers' and the LLEN's functions to better coordinate support for young people at risk and to promote new initiatives. Schools were also networked with other government and nongovernment agencies as part of community capacity building. Policymakers had to move beyond the individual school, as reducing educational inequality is contingent on wider structural, cultural, social, and economic factors within both a global and a local frame.

Third, leadership was in each study characterised by complexity, contradiction, and ethical dilemmas, as well as questions about what constitutes a 'just' education. Certainly these studies indicate that the practices of leadership fit with the concept of transformational leadership, as espoused by School Effectiveness and School Improvement research: whole-of-school approach, collaboration, collegiality, strong internal accountability, shared goals, and distributed leadership (Harris & Chapman, 2006, Leithwood & Jantzi, 2005). But as Lavié (2006) argues, such notions have different discursive frames and meanings. Within the SE and SI framing of transformational leadership, collaboration is part of cultural management by the principal, whereas collaboration is, within a critical transformative frame, underpinned by democratic and inclusive practices. Teacher collaboration, from within a restructuring discourse of the new professionalism, is about organisational learning and knowledge transfer; from a cultural perspective it is about blending the personal and the political. Leaders are confronted with all these understandings of collaboration and can only work for social justice by seeking to negotiate and navigate what these understandings mean in a specific context (Gewirtz & Cribb, 2003).

Fourth, these studies fail to recognise the difference between being professional (e.g., meeting standards) and being in a profession. Teachers were also leaders in these networks and partnerships. Teachers saw the purpose of educational reform as going beyond their particular school. Their professionalism entailed a wider obligation to the community, and indeed the public good, as well as to their students. Teachers were motivated to radically change their practices in many instances because they wished all students to experience success. In these studies, most of the principals and teachers in the schools lived and worked in these working-class regions, which had become culturally diverse with the ebb and flow of migration and refugees. Many had never left the region after training or returned after teaching elsewhere. The new executive principal of Highgrove College was motivated by the memory of having to change which local secondary school he attended in order to get into university. He wanted Highgrove to be the best local school that offered all students the full range of opportunities. Many teachers and potential leaders were discouraged by how professional ethics were being devalued and replaced by the values of the market, as a new vocabulary of leadership was required. Thus 'the pedagogy of the market "teaches" and disseminates "a new morality"' (Ball, 2003, p. 31). This was evident in the struggle these leaders endured between focusing on the real (educational) work and the performative (market and accountability) work of leadership; between doing good and being good. This struggle was about the role of education—its purpose, possibilities, and the wider public good—in the production of an active citizenry that was not just a malleable and flexible workforce.

Fifth, principals constantly faced circumstances beyond their control. While principals can do much to change structures and processes and develop productive relationships within the school environment, other background variables seem to explain the apparent improvement in student outcomes: new buildings improving morale or collective teacher investment in changing their practices. Policy and access to resources shaped the possibilities of leadership practice—some policies and contexts were more enabling and others more disabling. Those leaders who could be depicted as transformational also had to negotiate the complexities around the dilemma of undertaking leadership for social justice—whether a focus on class or culture was to the detriment of addressing gender differences or whether a focus on personalised learning meant missing patterns of group disadvantage (Gewirtz & Cribb, 2003). Parents and communities did not necessarily support innovative pedagogies. Principals continue to be caught between political and performative education systems demanding unrealistic ongoing improvement.

Finally, systemic support was in each instance critical, in the form of targeted systemic assistance to address specific school-based needs, hiring additional teachers, or developing networks and clusters. Transforming schools so they would reduce educational inequality requires not only transformative leadership from below—principals and teachers—but also from above. These studies indicate the significance of political will and investment in creating systems of education that serve the wider public by improving student learning and educational outcomes, and not just creating individual schools that pander to an aggregate of individual parents' choices. It also requires policymakers to see education as more than merely producing human capital to service fast capitalism: education is about the creation of global citizens for inclusive, democratic societies in which work is a productive activity and not the sole definer of self and society, and where success is more broadly defined. This is part of the exchange relationship within a democracy. The research also indicates that schools and leaders cannot do it alone and that educational justice requires transforming wider social and economic structures and practices. This is because schools in high-poverty areas do not fail, but rather, political, economic, and social systems fail to deliver on their promises. Transformative, as distinct from transformational, leadership is political in both its intent and practice.

Note

1   These four studies were funded by the Australian Research Council: *Women, Leadership and Educational Restructuring; How Learning Networks Support Young People at Risk; Investigating the Declining Supply of Leadership Applicants;* and *Redesigning Schools and Leadership.*

References

Alegre, A., & Ferrer, G. (2010). School regimes and education equity: Some insights based on PISA 2006. *British Educational Research Journal, 36*(3), 433–461.

Barker, B. (2007). The leadership paradox: Can school leaders transform student outcomes? *School Effectiveness and School Improvement, 18*(1), 21–43.

Ball, S. (2003). The teacher's soul and the terrors of performativity. *Journal of Education Policy,* 18 (2), 215–228.

Barnett, K., & McCormick, J. (2001). Transformational Leadership in Schools—Panacea, Placebo, or Problem? *Journal of Educational Administration, 39*(1), 24–46.

Barty, K., Thomson, P., Blackmore, J., & Sachs, J. (2005). Unpacking the issues: Researching the shortage of school principals in two states in Australia. *Australian Educational Researcher, 32*(3), 1–25.

Bass, B. M. (1990). From transactional to transformational leadership: Learning to share the vision. *Organizational Dynamics, 18*(3), 19–31.

Bass, B. M. (1999). Two decades of research and development in transformational leadership. *European Journal of Work and Organizational Psychology, 8*(1), 9–32.

Bass, B. M., & Avolio, B. (1994). Shatter the glass ceiling: Women may make better managers. *Human Resource Management, 33*(4), 549–560.

Bass, B.M. & Avolio, B.J. (Eds.). 1994. *Improving organizational effectiveness through transformational leadership.* Thousand Oaks, CA: Sage Publications.

Bishop, P. (1999). School-based trust in Victoria: Some telling lessons. *Australian Journal of Education, 43*(3), 273–284.

Bishop, P., & Mulford, B. (1999). When will they ever learn? Another failure of centrally-imposed change. *School Leadership & Management, 19*(2), 179–187.

Blackmore, J. (1999). *Troubling women: Feminism, leadership, and educational change.* Buckingham, U.K.: Open University Press.

Blackmore, J. (2004). Leading as emotional management work in high risk times: The counterintuitive impulses of performativity and passion. Invited article in special issue, *School Leadership and Management, 24*(4), 439–460.

Blackmore, J. (2006, November). *Networking leadership and educational governance: New flows of power?* Paper presented at the AARE Annual Conference, Adelaide, Australia.

Blackmore, J. (2009, December). Schools cannot do it alone: Radical redesign from the ground up. In J. Blackmore (Chair), *Symposium on the complexity of school redesign.* Symposium conducted at the AARE Conference, Canberra, Australia.

Blackmore, J., Bigum, C., Hodgens, J., & Laskey, L. (1996). Managed change and self-management in Victorian schools of the future. *Leading and Managing, 2*(3), 195–226.

Blackmore, J., & Sachs, J. (2007). *Performing and reforming leaders: Gender, educational restructuring and organizational change.* New York, NY: SUNY.

Brown, F. W., & Moshavi, D. (2005). Transformational leadership and emotional intelligence: A potential pathway for an increased understanding of interpersonal influence. *Journal of Organizational Behaviour, 26*(7), 867–871.

Burns, J. M. (1978). *Leadership.* New York, NY: Harper and Row.

Collard, J. (1998). The debate on transformational leadership: Semantic shifts and conceptual drifts. *Leading and Managing, 3*(2), 75–80.

Connors, L. (2000). *Public education. The next generation.* Melbourne: Victorian Government Printer.

Darder, A., Baltodano, M., & Torres, R. (Eds.). (2009). *Critical pedagogy reader.* New York, NY: Routledge.

Druskat, V. (1994). Gender and leadership style: Transformational and transactional leadership in the Roman Catholic church. *Leadership Quarterly, 5*(2), 99–119.

Elmore, R. (1997). *School reform from the inside-out. Policy, practice and performance.* Cambridge: Harvard Education Press.

Gewirtz, S., & Cribb, A. (2003). Plural conceptions of social justice: Implications for policy sociology. *Journal of Education Policy, 17*(5), 499–509.

Gilligan, C. (1982). *In a different voice.* Boston, MA: Harvard University Press.

Gorard, S. (2010). Serious doubts about school effectiveness. *British Educational Research Journal, 36*(5), 745–766.

Gronn, P. (1995). Greatness revisited: The current obsession with transformational leadership. *Leading and Managing, 1*(1), 14–27.

Gronn, P. (1999). *The new work of educational leaders.* Thousand Oaks, CA: Sage Publications.

Gunter, H. (2001). Critical approaches to leadership in education. *Journal of Educational Inquiry, 2*(2), 94–108s.

Gunter, H. M., & Butt, G. (2007). *Modernizing schools: People, learning, and organizations.* London: Continuum.

Hallinger, P. (2003). Leading educational change: Reflections on the practice of instructional and transformational leadership. *Cambridge Journal of Education, 33*(3), 329–352.

Harris, A., & Chapman, C. (2006). Improving schools in challenging contexts: Exploring the possible. *School Effectiveness and School Improvement, 17*(4), 409–424.

Hartley, D. (2007). The emergence of distributed leadership. Why now? *British Journal of Educational Studies, 55*(2), 202–214.

Hatcher, R. (2005). The distribution of leadership and power in schools. *British Journal of Sociology of Education, 26*(2), 253–267.

Hattie, J. (2003). *Visible learning.* London: Routledge.

Kamp, A. (2006). *A Study of the Geelong Local Learning and Employment Network.* Unpublished Doctoral Thesis, Deakin University.

Kirby, P. (2000). *Review of the postcompulsory sector.* Office of Postcompulsory Tertiary Education, Melbourne, Australia.

Ladson-Billings G.(1998). Just what is critical race theory and what's it doing in a nice field like education? *International Journal of Qualitative Studies in Education,* 11(1),7–24.

Lavié, J. M. (2006). Academic discourses on school-based teacher collaboration: Revisiting the arguments. *Educational Administration Quarterly, 42*(5), 773–805.

Leithwood, K. A. (1992). The move toward transformational leadership. *Educational Leadership, 49*(5), 8–12.

Leithwood, K. A., & Jantzi, D. (2005). A review of transformational school leadership research, 1996–2005. *Leadership and Policy in Schools, 4*(3), 177–199.

Lipman, P. (2009). Beyond accountability: Towards schools that create new people for a new way of life. In A. Darder, M. Baltodano, & R. Torres (Eds.), *Critical Pedagogy Reader* (pp. 364–383). New York, NY: Routledge.

Luke, C., & Gore, J. (Eds.). (1992). *Feminisms and critical pedagogy.* London: Routledge.

Lupton, R, (2005) Social justice and school improvement: improving the quality of schooling in the poorest neighbourhoods. *British Educational Research Journal 31*(5) pp. 589–604

McNeil, L. (2009). Standardisation, defensive teaching, and the problem of control. In A. Darder, M. Baltodano, & R. Torres (Eds.), *Critical Pedagogy Reader* (pp. 384–396). New York, NY: Routledge.

Marks, H. M., & Printy, S. M. (2003). Principal leadership and school performance: An integration of transformational and instructional leadership. *Educational Administration Quarterly, 39*(3), 370–397.

Marshall, C., & Olivia, M. (2006). *Leaders for social justice: Making revolutions in education.* Boston, MA: Allyn & Bacon.

Morgan, R., & Blackmore, J. (2012). How rural education markets shape parental choice of schooling: An Australian case study. *Journal of Educational Administration and History.*

Mulford, B., & Silins, H. (2003). Leadership for organisational learning and improved student outcomes. *Cambridge Journal of Education, 33*(2), 175–195.

Muschamp, Y., Bullock, K., Edge, T., & Wideley, F. (2009). 'Nothing to do': The impact of poverty on pupils' learning identities within out-of-school activities. *British Educational Research Journal, 35*(2), 305–321.

Potter, D., Reynolds, D., & Chapman, C. (2002). School improvement for schools facing challenging circumstances: A review of research and practice. *School Leadership & Management, 22*(3), 243–256.

Ross, J. A., & Gray, P. (2006). Transformational leadership and teacher commitment to organizational values: The mediating effects of collective teacher efficacy. *School Effectiveness and School Improvement, 17*(2), 179–199.

Shields, C. M. (2003). *Good intentions are not enough: Transformative leadership for communities of difference.* Lanham, MA: Scarecrow Press.

Silins, H. (1994). The relationship between transformational and transactional leadership. *School Effectiveness and School Improvement, 5*(3), 272–298.

Silins, H., Zarins, S., & Mulford, B. (2002). What characteristics and processes define a school as a learning organisation? Is this a useful concept to apply to schools? *International Education Journal, 3*(1), 24–32.

Teese, R., Lamb, S., & Duru-Bellat, M. (Eds.). (2007). *International studies in educational inequality, theory and policy* (Vol. 3, *Inequality: Educational theory and public policy*). Dordrecht, the Netherlands: Springer.

Thrupp, M., & Lupton, R. (2006). Taking school contexts more seriously: The social justice challenge. *British Journal of Educational Studies, 54*, 308–328.

Thrupp, M., & Willmott, R. (2003). *Education management in managerialist times: Beyond the textual apologists.* Buckingham, U.K.: Open University Press.

Wittel, A. (2000). Ethnography on the move: From field to net to Internet. *Forum: Qualitative Social Research, 1*(1). Available at: http://www.qualitative-research.net/fqs-texte/1–00/1–00wittel-e.htm (accessed 23 March 2009).

Wrigley, T. (2004). 'School effectiveness': The problem of reductionism. *British Educational Research Journal, 30*(2), 227–44.

2

Transforming Educational Leadership Without Social Justice?

Looking at Critical Pedagogy as More Than a Critique, and a Way Toward "Democracy"[1]

Paul R. Carr

One thing we know for sure, as common wisdom has it, is that you can always count on change. *Change is everywhere*, we are told constantly. *We are about change*, political parties extoll. *If you don't change, you'll be left behind*, is what we are taught. While advertisers, business gurus, pundits, and highly remunerated futurists all agree that change is in the air, that progress is the way to go, and that evolution means embracing change, I'm left wondering: what type of change, defined by whom, for whom, contextualized, understood, and embraced in what manner, by whom, and why? If change is a certainty, as we are led to believe, then why is there still poverty? One would think that social inequities— including racism, sexism, income gaps, homelessness, religious intolerance, discrimination of all forms, and so on —would be history; that, with all of the change going on, there would be no room for such anti-change variables. While, undoubtedly, much *has* changed—and there is evidence of this—social inequities, in many regards, are widening, not dissipating. This, I would argue, relates to power and how it is exercised, challenged, and considered. This chapter on transformative leadership, building on the work of Carolyn Shields (2004, 2010), takes the posture that power is directly related to the educational project and, moreover, that it can only take place within a broad framework that acknowledges social inequities (Kincheloe, 2007, 2008a, 2008b; Macrine, 2009). Critical pedagogy provides such a framework, and I will use that framework here to position an argument in favour of a more engaged, politically meaningful, and counter-hegemonic transformative leadership, one that deemphasizes neo-liberalism, the reproduction of social relations, and the solidification of a rigid educational system that too willingly weeds out those with lower cultural capital, incongruent lived experiences, and divergent identities (see the work of Paulo Freire, 1973, 1985, 1998, 2004, 1973/2005).

In discussing the transformative leadership project, I will focus on democracy as a means of reframing a way of understanding change in education within a critical pedagogy–pedagogical perspective (Carr, 2007, 2008a, 2008b, 2008c, 2010; Lund & Carr, 2008). Democracy is key to this debate because if democracy is not an objective of education, then what is its purpose (Westheimer, 2008; Westheimer & Kahne, 2003, 2004)?[2] Principals and vice-principals, along with superintendents and other senior education officials, form a group that I, and others, call administrators, and they are the focus of the first line of implementation in the quest for transformative leadership. Added to this group, we must also consider policymakers, decisionmakers, and other leaders, who have a direct stake in what happens in schools. Interest groups, think-tanks, teachers' federations, parents' groups, and others are also enmeshed in how we define, orchestrate, evaluate, and produce education. Transformative leadership, therefore, involves many sectors, interests, concepts, and realities (Shields & Edwards, 2005). Significantly, it is something that is a product of society; is socially, economically, and politically constructed, and is an appendage of the power structures in which it exists. For this chapter, I will argue that democracy is a useful concept to guide our thinking here because it forces us to acknowledge the broader macro-portrait of society, something that inevitably impinges on the individual actions of administrators and, moreover, is shaped by the concerns and priorities of various groups in society. Thus, the critical pedagogy of democracy in relation to transformative leadership is the focus of this chapter and will guide the analysis and discussion throughout. The chapter presents thoughts, concepts, and research related to democracy, critical pedagogy, and the critical pedagogy of democracy, and concludes with some proposals for more engaged, critical, and meaningful transformative change in education, with particular attention being paid to the leadership role.

Democracy and Transformative Leadership

What can be done to contribute to democracy in and through education, and how does leadership fit into the equation? Clearly, there is no one answer, especially not an easy or simplistic one. A fundamental, and perhaps obvious, argument is that democracy and education must be inextricably linked. One might ask: What kind of education? Part of the formulation of a response comes in the form of how we choose to elucidate what we mean by *democracy*. My interpretation surpasses the electoral politics (representative) model, embracing a *thicker* version of inclusion, participation, dialog, interrogation, and critical engagement, which is underpinned by a vigorously and humbly formulated critical pedagogy (Carr, 2008c). This form of democratic education seeks to embrace the experiences and perspectives of diverse peoples, including those traditionally marginalized from the national narratives that have enshrined a partisan allegiance to patriotism; these narratives were not often included and accepted military conquest as a normative value, and, conversely, often excluded and rejected those groups and actions that ran counter to hegemonic reasoning (Carr, 2010). It is problematic, therefore, to consider democracy in exclusion of a meaningful analysis of inequitable power relations, and this links directly with the notion of transformative leadership as opposed to traditional forms of leadership that privilege maintaining the status quo (Kincheloe & Steinberg, 2006; Macrine, 2009; McLaren & Kincheloe, 2007).

I caution that there is no one thing, menu, or recipe that can be produced to inculcate a democratic state, government, citizen, or education system (Carr, 2008a). Indeed, even addressing an amalgam of concerns is no guarantee of reinforcing democracy. However, the desire for a more meaningful, just, and decent form of democracy is something that requires—borrowing from the contemporary vernacular within mainstream politics—a certain measure of *hope*. One must remain confident and strident in order to improve the current situation, because to simply endorse it uncritically is to further entrench vast swaths of the landscape, figuratively and literally, to a permanently deceptive existence in which the quest for human rights becomes a mere fictional legal manoeuvre reserved largely for those with their hands firmly on the economic levers of power.

Ultimately, seeking a more democratic society in and through education is tantamount to seeking the truth. Never comfortable, nor easily achieved, such a proposition requires a multitude of measures as well as the belief that people can, ultimately, function together without self-destruction. War is not the answer, nor is violence. Corruption and greed are also areas that can be addressed, provided that the will of the people is respected. Racism, sexism, and poverty are not virtues—they are man- and woman-made, and can be addressed. Cycles of disenfranchisement do not mesh well with the oft-repeated mantra of American "greatness" and the superiority of a highly-developed, advanced nation, one often invoked as being blessed by God. Rather than reducing inequities, society is actually (according to all of the standard measures used to demonstrate development and superiority) becoming less united, less equal, less resolutely inclusive, and ultimately, I would argue, less democratic. The space provided for elections has usurped the place of education in many regards (Carr, 2010; Denzin, 2009).

Critical Pedagogy and Democratic (Sur)Realities

Can we have democracy without democratic literacy? Without democratic engagement? Is critical pedagogy an appropriate means for achieving democratic literacy and democratic engagement? Relying, in large part, on the critical pedagogical foundation of Paulo Freire, it is helpful here to highlight the epistemological salience of Freire's work, which Au (2007) argues is steeped in the Marxist tradition. Epistemological interrogation is a necessary function in the quest for transformative change in education. Although the terminology may change from context to context, Freire's "conscientization" has meaning across diverse milieus and environments. Achieving meaningful experiences in and through education, cognizant of differential power relations, is the core of a critical pedagogical, democratic education. Whether or not a critical Marxist perspective is germane in nurturing democratic education should not obfuscate the reality that critical pedagogy can lead to the process of personal and collective transformation.

Brosio (2003), in citing leading radical political philosopher Michael Parenti, highlights that normative neo-liberal, capitalistic structures have, and continue to have, a significant effect on people and societal development:

> What we need is a 180-degree shift away from unilateral global domination and toward equitable and sustainable development among the peoples of the world. This means U.S. leaders would have to stop acting like self-willed unaccountable rulers of the planet. They must stop supporting despots, and stop opposing those democratic movements and governments that challenge the status quo. The struggle is between those who believe that the land, labor, capital, technology, markets, and natural resources of society should be used as expendable resources for transnational profit accumulation, and those who believe that such things should be used for the mutual benefit of the populace. What we need is to move away from liberal complaints about how bad things are and toward a radical analysis that explains why they are so, away from treating every situation as a perfectly new and befuddling happening unrelated to broader politico-economic interests and class power structures. What we need is a global anti-imperialist movement that can challenge the dominant paradigm with an alternative one that circumvents the monopoly ideological control of officialdom and corporate America. (Brosio, 2003)

Bellamy Foster, Holleman, and McChesney (2008) support this perspective, arguing for a more comprehensive, critical, and global analysis of the American empire, suggesting that the degree to which U.S. society is controlled by militarization is poorly understood by the population, which then leads to the military having far-reaching potential to dominate, marginalize, and diminish the vibrancy of vast swaths of society. Willinsky (1998) further addresses the need to critique empire as a necessary step in bringing forth the prospect for change, which relates to Freire's (1973/2005) oppressor-oppressed dichotomy. Anticolonial education should, therefore, not be uniquely a discussion reserved for the archives, as the historical is intertwined with the present, and appreciating how current problems and issues are connected with previous actions is pivotal to avoiding simplistic, essentialized education responses.

Taking account of the dialectical relationship between hegemony and ideology (Fischman & McLaren, 2005) is a fundamental part of the critical pedagogical equation. As highlighted in the first section of their book, critical epistemological interrogation is fundamental to the dissection and unravelling of how power is infused in and through (supposed) democratic processes. The relevance for education, therefore, is clear:

> Critical pedagogy problematizes the relationship between education and politics, between socio-political relations and pedagogical practices, between the reproduction of dependent hierarchies of power and privilege in the domain of everyday social life and that of the classroom and institutions. In doing so, it advances an agenda for educational transformation by encouraging educators to understand the socio-political contexts of educative acts and the importance of radically democratizing both educational and larger social formations. In such processes, educators take on intellectual roles by adapting to, resisting, and challenging curriculum, school policy, educational philosophies, and pedagogical traditions. (Fischman & McLaren, 2005, p. 425)

A critical pedagogy of democracy can cultivate a vigorous and meaningful interrogation of the various strands underpinning power structures, including the functioning of the military, the limited but populism-laden visions of politics, and the infusion of right-wing Christian fundamentalism into decision-making (Giroux, 2005; Steinberg & Kincheloe, 2009). Giroux and Giroux (2006) provide a thoughtful synthesis of critical democratic pedagogy:

> The democratic character of critical pedagogy is defined largely through a set of basic assumptions, which holds that power, values, and institutions must be made available to critical scrutiny, be understood as a product of human labor (as opposed to God-given), and evaluated in terms of how they might open up or close down democratic practices and experiences. Yet, critical pedagogy is about more than simply holding authority accountable through the close reading of texts, the creation of radical classroom practices, or the promotion of critical literacy. It is also about linking learning to social change, education to democracy, and knowledge to acts of intervention in public life. Critical pedagogy encourages students to learn to register dissent as well as to take risks in creating the conditions for forms of individual and social agency that are conducive to a substantive democracy. (p. 28)

Challenging neo-liberalism is a central feature to this project, shining a light on nefarious practices, marginalization, and conservative interpretations of success that serve to blame the victim rather than critique the trappings and inner-working of power (Giroux & Giroux, 2006). Decoding signals, omissions, directives, and the meaning of rhetoric is a key component of the critical pedagogy of democracy (Engels, 2007; Kellner & Share, 2007; Macedo & Steinberg, 2007). State authority is not obliged to be oppressive, and ingratiating students with a critical pedagogy of democracy can lead to thicker experiences and interpretations of democracy.

A radical democratic pedagogy, as outlined by Denzin (2009), speaks to hope: "Hope is ethical. Hope is moral. Hope is peaceful and nonviolent. Hope seeks truth of life's sufferings. Hope gives meaning to the struggles to change the world. Hope is grounded in concrete performative practices, in struggles and interventions that espouse sacred values of love, care, community, trust, and well-being" (p. 385).

Compelling arguments can be made for a more deliberately conscious, engaged, and loving connection to others (Darder & Miron, 2006). Freire spoke of radical love and the inescapable prospect of indignation, which need not be considered weakness, cynicism, or hopelessness (Freire, 2004). The capacity, and necessity, to love is entrenched in the very essence of the human condition. Accepting human and humane interactions and relations, without exploitation and discrimination, is a fundamental consideration for a critical pedagogy of democracy. Darder and Miron (2006) emphasize that our experiences are not disconnected from the broader politico-economic context but, as Brosio (2003) maintains, are interwoven into a socially constructed narrative:

> Capitalism disembodies and alienates our daily existence. As our consciousness becomes more and more abstracted, we become more and more detached from our bodies. For this reason, it is absolutely imperative that critical educators and scholars acknowledge that the origin of emancipator possibility and human solidarity resides in our body. (p. 16)

As Darder and Miron (2006) argue, everyone is capable of contesting, resisting, and challenging nefarious neo-liberal policies and manifestations:

> If we, as citizens of the Empire, do not use every opportunity to voice our dissent, we shamefully leave the great task of dissent to our brothers and sisters around the world who daily suffer greater conditions of social, political, and economic impoverishment and uncertainty than we will ever know. For how long will our teaching and politics fail to address the relevant and concrete issues that affect people's daily lives? (p. 18)

Not every action or gesture need be representative of a grandiose, sweepingly transformative manifestation. For transformative leadership to be meaningful, individuals can, and must, make their voices heard: They can resist imperialism, hegemony, and patriotic oppression, and, importantly, they can choose love over hate, peace over war, and humanity over inhumanity. This may seem abstract and outside of the boundaries of the proverbial three Rs, student-based learning, high academic standards, No Child Left Behind–like system reforms, and the like, but, as argued throughout this chapter, there is a direct, visceral relation between power and change, and transformative leadership is hinged, according to this thinking, on a broad platform of macro-level thinking combined with micro-level transformative leadership within school and educational sites.

Fifty Proposals That Could Contribute to Democracy Through Education

Building on the backdrop outlined above—at the risk of being criticized for including some ideas that may not mesh with a democratic education focus, or others that seem to be superfluous to the debate or that may not seem too original or innovative—what follows is a list of 50 proposals that could contribute to a thicker democratic education. Importantly, these proposals should be considered as an ensemble, not as disparate, individual efforts at reform. Within the spirit of this chapter and book, all of these proposals would require a vigorous, engaged, and critical transformative leadership. Based on a critical pedagogical conceptualization of education, change, and democracy, these proposals are offered as an alternative to the neo-liberal, hegemonic reform models currently in place, which have largely overlooked and underplayed social justice.

1. Make education a *societal* responsibility, removing the false narrative of it somehow being only a *local* responsibility. The nation-state should undertake a public education campaign

to acknowledge and promote public education as the engine behind societal growth, development, harmony, and ingenuity.

2. Democratic conscientization should be integrated into educational planning, and political, critical, and media-centric forms of literacy should become mandatory aspects of teaching and learning.

3. Eradicate the mainstream representation of education as being neutral and devoid of politics. Emphasize that education can lead to change and that regressive forms of education can lead to docile, compliant citizens, the antithesis of thick democracy.

4. Redefine the notion of accountability in education to more centrally focus on ethics, bone fide diversity, social justice, and thick democracy. Just because No Child Left Behind (NCLB) declares that there is greater accountability does not necessarily mean that this is true.

5. The state should only fund public education, and charters, vouchers, private schools, and other offshoots should be discouraged and not be eligible for public support. Public education is a public good, benefitting all of society, and it should be viewed as a collective, global responsibility.

6. End the ranking of schools and school boards. Such efforts are divisive, punish the marginalized, are not appropriately contextualized, and serve to disintegrate rather than integrate, thus diminishing the possibility of enhancing the public good and the notion of education being a fundamental pillar to solidifying the thicker and more humane elements of a democracy.

7. Do not let high cultural capital areas—those with high property values and other advantages—graduate their high schools without having them work closely with schools in their areas that are facing serious challenges. The notion here is that all schools will see that they are part of a common struggle, existence, and society, and are not simply, as within the neo-liberal mindset, individuals demonstrating how hard they work as opposed to others who are supposedly not committed.

8. All subject areas of the curriculum should explicitly diagnose how power works as well as the meaning of social justice. This should include a critical pedagogical analysis of whiteness; racial, gender, and class inequities; and other forms of marginalization, discrimination, and disenfranchisement. It may be considered impolite to discuss such matters, but to avoid them is only to further entrench and ingratiate harm, damage, and the antithesis of democracy.

9. Education-systems and educators should embrace the following saying: *"The more I know, the less I know."* If education is to sincerely be about life-long learning, then it should involve an endless process of critical interrogation, lived experiences, and dialectical questioning and dialog, which far overshadows the notion of standards, high-stakes testing, and a prescriptive curriculum.

10. Men and women of all origins, races, ethnicities, and backgrounds should be involved in teaching and education. Some elementary schools lack male teachers, and some schools have no racial minorities or no females in leadership positions, which can further lead to false stereotypes about leadership, role models, and learning.

11. Educational policymaking and curriculum development should involve more consultation and collaboration with diverse groups and interests, and the decision-making process should necessarily become more transparent. Educators, parents, students, and the broader community should be able to understand how decisions are made and why, and they should be involved in these processes that will, ultimately, have an effect on all of society.

12. All schools should be twinned within local areas (for example, an urban school could be twinned with a suburban school, and a suburban school twinned with a rural school, or schools from different demographic areas could be twinned in the same area). This twinning would involve bone fide academic and curriculum work in addition to cultural exchange. No student should be allowed to say that they do not know, understand, or experience diversity because "everyone in their school is white," which does not sufficiently encapsulate a thicker version of critical thinking and engagement with pluralism.

13. School boards should use technology to twin classrooms in the United States with those around the world so that educators can exchange language and culture with colleagues in other countries. The government should provide seed funding to schools that require it in order to undertake this program.

14. If there must be standards in education, there should be standards for democratic education, citizenship education, peace education, media literacy, and social justice. Standards should be focused on building a more decent society, not on testing basic skills that are predefined largely because of cultural capital.

15. Teachers should not be remunerated on how well their students do. Teachers' salaries should be increased and other measures of acknowledgement for their contributions should be pursued. The objective should not be to diminish those working in more challenging situations or those whose students have lower levels of cultural capital. The role of the teacher has to be understood in a broader societal context, not simply related to mercantilist outcomes.

16. The curriculum should be significantly revamped. Freire's generative themes and Dewey's constructivism should be incorporated into classrooms at all levels, instilling values of respect, critical interrogation, engagement, and appreciation of how power works.

17. All schools should emphasize deliberative democracy and young people should learn how to listen, articulate, debate, and diagnose difference. Significantly, students should learn how to respectfully seek to construct further knowledge in a peaceful way. Condemning those with critical opinions needs to be stopped as group-think can lead to societal paralysis and a nefarious form of patriotism.

18. Rather than protecting students from controversial subject matter, they should be encouraged to critically understand not only the *what* but also the *how* and *why* behind significant events, issues, and concerns. The mythology that politics is about Democrats and Republicans needs to be rectified, and students need to learn that critical reflection can lead to more appropriate and effective resolutions of systemic problems and conflicts than the use of force, whether it be wars, racial profiling, or the neglect of impoverished groups.

19. Peace and peace education should become centerpieces of the educational project. If peace is not a fundamental part of education, what then is its purpose?

20. A thicker interpretation of the environment and environmental education should be taught throughout the educational program. The effects of war and military conflict on the environment, for example, should be explored.

21. Poorer areas should not be punished because of wealth concentration, and everyone should be able to enjoy the outdoors without cost.

22. Accessible, fair-play, sportsmanlike values should be reasserted in place of a win-at-all-costs mission and the drive for notoriety and the supremacy of money.

23. All students should be introduced to critical service learning. The experiences should be accompanied by courses and debriefings on why societal problems exist. To do a service-learning placement without some sociopolitical contextualization may only reinforce the opposite of what is sought through the actual experience.

24. Contracts for superintendents of education and principals should contain a clause that they will be evaluated on how well they inculcate democratic education, political literacy, and social justice. Their renewal should hinge, in part, on how well they address these matters within their educational institutions.

25. There should be no place in schools for military recruitment, especially not in schools in poorer areas. All students should be afforded the possibility of higher education, not just those with higher levels of cultural capital, and the message should not be transmitted, either explicitly or implicitly, that poor people have no other option than to join the army.

26. All American students should learn at least one foreign language starting in first grade and then be introduced to a second language in high school. The notion that English will get Americans everywhere they wish to go at all times and will lead to inter-cultural development, not to mention the visible concern of achieving peace and good relations with the world, must be recast in a more holistic and democratic form of education.

27. The enticement to enter into contracts with for-profit enterprises as a way of funding schools should be eliminated. Communities should be made aware of economic situations that pressure and coerce some localities more than others, and should also be invited to critique the role of marketing, advertising, and the drive to capture market-share within schools. Educational policymaking should also address this area. Programs such as Channel One should be prohibited from schools. They are not benevolent services; moreover, they come with strings attached, and are not problematized.

28. The differentiated experiences of schools that have a larger wealth-base, as compared to poorer districts, should be addressed. The research on this reality, including the social context, should be concisely and critically presented to parents, students, educators, and the broader community. The approach should not be to illustrate blame, pity, guilt, or incompetence but, rather, to seek to underscore systemic problems, resource allocation, and ineffectual curriculum and policy development.

29. The limited accessibility to field trips to museums, cultural events, and even foreign countries only serves to further increase the educational, cultural, and political gap between Americans. Governments should provide an appropriate level of funding so that all schools can benefit from such indispensable activities.

30. Parents should be required, except in extraordinary circumstances, to provide one-half day of service per month to their children's schools. The objective is to make all parents

knowledgeable of what happens at school, to create support for progressive activities, and to provide a vehicle to discuss education and democracy. Legislation should be passed to ensure that no parent would be penalized for participating in such a program (and these days would not count as formal vacation-days). School principals should be supported in finding the appropriate ways to liaise with parents.

31. Teacher-education programs should focus on qualitative teaching and learning experiences and develop assessment schemes that monitor and support innovation, engagement, collaboration, and critical pedagogical work that emphasizes learning and the *construction* of knowledge over the *acquisition* of knowledge. Similarly, these programs should forge meaningful relationships with local school boards. All education faculty should have some type of formal relationship with their schools.

32. All schools should implement a guest program, whereby a range of professionals, academics, and people with diverse experiences could liaise with students. The access to a diversity of guests should be distributed equally throughout all schools, and no schools should be without some form of a regular, regimented, and engaging program in place. Special attention should be paid to diversity and the public good (i.e., high cultural-capital schools should not be the only ones exposed to leading business and political figures; conversely, critical alternative movements and grass-roots figures should not be invited only to working-class schools).

33. Public officials, including politicians, diplomats, and mainstream media, should be invited into schools to dialog with students, all the while being open to critical questions about social justice, bias, patriotism, propaganda, and why systemic issues exist, in addition to the traditional reasons that such figures visit schools (e.g., to extol the virtues of democracy, to sell support for a particular platform, to discuss career choices, how to a good citizen, etc.).

34. All schools should embark on a range of community projects that could count for credit toward graduation. These projects could involve service-learning, undertaking research, writing narratives and ethnographies, and making presentations on how social problems might be addressed.

35. State departments of education, overseen by a board of professionals and activists, should gather data on inputs and outputs of the education system, and report on how diversity, social justice, media literacy, democracy, and other program areas are relevant. These reports should be available online, free of cost, through the state's Department of Education website.

36. The study of democracy and elections should not be concentrated within a single course (often labelled as a Civics or Government course). Democracy must be demonstrated, acted upon, and lived, not relegated to a course that focuses on encouraging voting.

37. Require school boards and schools to implement participatory budgeting in an inclusive and meaningful fashion, involving diverse interests in determining the allocation of funds for education.

38. Prohibit fundraising within schools, and have educators focus exclusively on critical teaching, learning, and engagement. If schools are not concerned with raising funds they will then be able to freely target the best interests of the students and also to not be beholden to any outside interests.

39. Schools should focus on the prevention of bullying and violence, and work with communities, families, and students at various levels to establish a conducive environment for learning, and, at the same time, seek to avoid the nefarious zero-tolerance, criminalization route.

40. Schools should undertake community violence and criminality projects, examining the form, substance, and degree of violence and criminality in their localities. The data-collection and analysis should include white-collar crime, corruption, racial profiling, and un- and under-documented crimes, including abuse against women, gang activities, and police misconduct. The results, which would form part of a process of critical interrogation, could be publicly presented on an ongoing basis in order to lead to a more rigorous understanding of how and why criminal activities and violence take place, and, moreover, what is done about it.

41. Similar to point 40, schools should undertake community health projects to determine the types of diseases, infections, and illnesses that exist in local communities, with a view to undertaking critical comparative analyses. Are poorer people more at risk, do they live shorter lives, do they have access to adequate health care, do they contribute equally to the formulation of health policy, and so on? The ongoing results of the research should be exposed, and acted upon.

42. Students should be invited, as per Lawrence Kohlberg's moral-development model, to determine some of the rules, guidelines, and conditions of their school experience. Students should not be uniquely the recipients of the formal education experience but should also be full participants in shaping their knowledge and reality.

43. No child should be placed in special education without a full determination of the socio-economic context, thus diminishing the possibility of marginalized and racialized communities being disproportionately streamed into these programs. Despite formal procedures outlined in present processes, there is still wide-spread concern about the types of children directed to special education.

44. Make humility a virtue for teaching and learning, and downgrade the emphasis placed on economic gain accrued by business leaders, actors and professional athletes.

45. All schools should have a garden that produces fruits and vegetables. While working one to two hours a week on the garden, students will also learn, and will have opportunities to make concrete curricular connections to the environment, agriculture, nutrition, the economics of food, and globalization. The fruits and vegetables produced could also be consumed by the students.

46. All schools should have music, arts, and physical education programs. Funding and wealth should not be an impediment to children having access to a broad liberal arts education.

47. A war tax of 20% should be applied to all spending on the military and militarization, and the resultant funding should be applied to education. In present times, with approximately $1 trillion being spent annually on the military in the United States, the government would be obligated to allocate an additional $200 billion to the education section. Education should not be used to subsidize war, nor should poorer people be forced into fighting other people's battles.

48. The federal government should organize an annual education summit, in which diverse civil society, educational, and *alter-mondialiste/counter-globalization* organizations could contribute to a debate on the formal measures, data, policies, resources, and goals of public education. This education summit could be considered as an accountability forum for governments and education authorities. The summit would generate a detailed annual report and plan, which would be reviewed the following year.

49. Humility should be emphasized over nationalism and patriotism.

50. Radical love should be the starting point for the conceptualization of education.

Whether or not the above proposals appear to be realistic is not the fundamental question. The reality that there are diverse proposals, movements, interests, and people seeking a different kind of democracy should be kept in mind. Transformative leadership, being ideologically positioned to engage and act upon inequitable power relations, is afforded unique and meaningful access to formal educational structures in which myriad dialogs, debates, and decisions are hashed out. The above set of proposals could be considered and massaged by transformative leaders, who might be able to shift some portions of the bedrock underpinning the neo-liberal monopoly within mainstream education circles that prevents many progressive and social-justice–based reforms from making it to the table.

A Democratic Education Planning Model

This democratic education planning model (Figure 2.1) can assist in mapping what individuals, schools, and communities are thinking and experiencing in relation to democracy and democratic engagement. Schools could document the context, content, experiences, and outcomes of what takes place within the realm of education. There are many ways of promoting constructive collaboration, and I would encourage critical, dialectical, and harmonious efforts aimed at understanding and constructing more meaningful experiences, rather than imposing haphazard, incongruent, and inauthentic ones. For this model, schools could work with diverse interests— or stakeholders, in public-policy jargon—who are not, to use the neoliberal terminology, clients. Involving teachers, parents, students, members of the community, and others, and being cognizant of differential power relations, may facilitate some important synergetic planning as well as the formulation of proposals. This approach is inspired by the participatory budget planning process (Gandin & Apple, 2005), established in Porto Alegre, Brazil, in which the community comes together to consider how portions of the budget will be spent. Using a critical pedagogical analysis, participants in the democratic education planning model should be highly sensitized to systemic and institutional barriers to change and should also consider the *lived* experiences of individuals and groups, being vigilant to grasp the nuanced existence of marginalized interests.

Figure 2.1 Democratic Education Planning Model

	Context	Content	Experiences	Outcomes
Individual				
School				
Community				

This model does not seek the typical (supposed) accountability report that is skewed toward illustrating the virtue of the funder or the institutional interest. Rather, the focus should be on bone fide, tangible critical engagement, questioning why policies and programs have been developed, in whose interest, and to what end. For example, how do individuals, the school, and the community contribute to the democratic foundation, growth, and tension of what takes place locally within an educational site?

One way to use this model would be to chart out the context for democratic education: to define it, to highlight the historic and contemporary achievement, issues, and challenges, and to address fundamental concerns, such as those related to patriotism, socioeconomic development, and political participation, in an inclusive and thick way. The notion is not to draft volumes here but, rather, to attempt to link to our actions the epistemological and philosophical foundation of what we know, and how we know and believe it (Kincheloe, 2008b). Often, education policies seem to drop from the sky, disconnected from the lived realities of students, and are inconsistent with scientific research—although NCLB specifically prescribes that reforms be based on scientific research, can educational leaders enumerate the literature that has informed their philosophies? (Gordon, Smyth, & Diehl, 2008).

Concluding Thoughts

In focusing on democracy, it is clear that a thicker, more critical version of democracy—outside of representative, electoral politics—necessarily involves an inter-disciplinary approach (touching on sociology, history, philosophy, political science, economics, education, cultural studies, and the social sciences in general), and close consideration should be given to a number of directly related subjects and issues (peace studies, media literacy, environmental education, intercultural relations, etc.). There is no set answer, list, or menu to the question of how to *do* democracy, or how to create a *thicker* democracy. Rather, as suggested in the earlier list of what might be done, an amalgam of thinking, interrogation, critical analysis, experience, and humility may lead to a more meaningful and sustainable democracy, one that seeks to inspire and cultivate critical engagement of all people and interests. A more radical determination toward a more radical democracy requires thinking well outside of constricted, hegemonic boundaries, and must address how power works (Hill & Boxley, 2007).

How does transformative leadership fit into this discussion? One might argue that the discussion would remain theoretical, conceptual, and academic without considering the real-world problems and challenges that encapsulate the educational arena, experience, and institution. How do we actually promote change—not just the discourse of change, which is surely important—but the actual process of change? For it to be transformative, it would be important to consider diverse epistemologies, values, strategies, and variables, and, especially, to understand how power works (Shields, 2010). Power is not neutral, nor is democracy, and change of a transformative type can only happen when there is serious, critical engagement. Thus, for the purposes of this chapter, the administrative class must be attuned to the power dynamic. Administrators are not employed simply to carry our orders: They are not soldiers on the battle-field. They provide, one would hope, insight, knowledge, intelligence, and compassion as to how to consider change.

If administrators, individually and as a group, are dissuaded from considering alternative perspectives, as was once the case when women were not taken seriously within the leadership realm, then meaningful transformative change in and though education would be almost impossible. Transformative leaders must be courageous to point out institutional deficiencies that harm groups and populations, and they must be open to that which they do not know. How they are taught, trained, cultivated, and promoted are important pieces of the equation. I have argued that critical pedagogy may be one area in which administrators could benefit a great deal, even if they, at first, react negatively. In a nutshell, administrators are a necessary piece of the puzzle of promoting change in formal education. The issue of whether change is transformative or not depends on how we evaluate power, from what angle, and who is doing the evaluating.

Regarding the 50 proposals enunciated earlier, it is clear that administrators would have an important role to play in endorsing, debating, accepting, shaping, implementing, and evaluating the implications, ramifications, and measures related to them. Such change requires vision and transformative leadership, not merely leaders who oversee incremental change. Are the proposals too radical or not radical enough; too precipitous, too poorly conceived, too costly, too jarring, and so on? I can only answer that they form part of what I call the critical pedagogy of democracy, and they could lead to transformative change. Are they the only proposals to transform education? Most certainly not, but, given the history, political economy, traditions, and context of education, I believe that they are certainly worth considering.

Neither Paulo Freire, nor Joe Kincheloe, nor other well-known critical pedagogues, I believe, would want students, educators, and others to simply replicate what they've done or to simply believe that what they've experienced and developed in theory and in praxis is the ultimate answer. The quest for critical humility and radical love encourages all of us to seek new, innovative, and reflective thoughts and actions in the quest for a more decent society. What Freire, Kincheloe, and others offer us, however, is an enormous wealth and insightful archive of *constructed* knowledge, something that is, I would argue, of tremendous value to those wishing to have a more conscious connection to what society was, is, and is evolving into. The critical pedagogy of democracy is not about counting votes, but relates more fundamentally to an unending critical interrogation of the human experience, focused on humane encounters, social justice, peace, a more equitable and respectful distribution of resources, a more dignified and just recognition of indigenous cultures, and an acknowledgement that hegemonic forces exist that marginalize peoples at home and abroad.

Does your vote count? (Or we might ask, *Are our schools democratic?*) It might (or they might be), but there are a multitude of other factors that are most likely more germane—not to mention that voting, in and of itself, does not make a democracy. As argued throughout my book, any definition of democracy that omits a central place for a meaningful, engaged, and critical education is problematic. *People* construct a democracy, not political parties and institutions (albeit they are relevant), and, therefore, *people* must construct their political, economic, social, cultural, and philosophic destinies. The people are the ones who define their circumstances, values, affiliations, interpersonal relations, and essence to live. Yet, as per the central hypothesis of this book, the people must also be vigilant and suspicious of how power affects their daily lives, their abilities, their relations, and their connection to the world. Education is the key intersecting vehicle that can reinforce or, conversely, interrupt patriotic bondage, racialized marginalization, essentialized visions of poverty and impoverishment, and an uncritical assessment of how power works. Freire and Kincheloe offer much inspiration for this journey, and their willingness to question and accept questions provides for a vibrant, dynamic, and engaged democracy within the spirit of critical pedagogy. Alongside the mantra of the *alter-mondialiste* movement that *another world is possible*, I would like to conclude by suggesting that *another democracy is possible.*

Postscript: Good People in Difficult Jobs

For five years, from 2005 to 2010, I had the pleasure to teach in an educational leadership doctoral program at Youngstown State University. I taught three of the mandatory courses—Qualitative

Methods, Theories of Inquiry, and Diversity and Leadership—providing me with significant exposure to the students, in addition to sitting on dissertation committees. The students, who were largely white, with a majority being male, and were, for the most part, principals and superintendents, came from rural, suburban, and urban schools boards within a roughly two-hour radius. My learning experience in working with the students was not only important but also transformative. I learned that my views, concerns, opinions, beliefs, values, ideology, proclivities, idiosyncrasies, and way of being may not be common, shared, accepted, and embraced by others.

I learned that sustained and meaningful critical analysis, discussion, and engagement can help transform thinking. I refer to myself because I learned a great deal from the students, from their questions, critiques, presentations, papers, justifications, and positioning as students, people, and colleagues. Much of the material I presented was not necessarily what might come quickly to mind when thinking of educational leadership; for instance, we focused on epistemology and what we do not know, which is not easy for educational leaders, when thinking about theory. We started with what we did and did not know about Cuba, and why, and what the signification was for us in deconstructing political reality and intercultural relations; and when we started to study diversity, I had them focus on white power and privilege rather than the much-vaunted benefits of a heterogeneous society. In both cases, the initial reaction was: *Why this?* and *What does this have to do with what we're all about?*

I recall a professor of political science from my undergraduate studies warning that we should not focus too narrowly on the target, lest we miss the framework. Thus for me, during this period, the objective was to engage and accept, with humility, that we were limited in our knowledge, and, moreover, that knowledge is socially constructed. We also sought to ingratiate ourselves in the comfort that we could change, perhaps not as radically and quickly as we would like, but for the better, in seeking to refocus our comprehension of our limitations. Ultimately, the process of dialectical engagement in this way aimed to liberate us from the strictures and structures that are ensconced in hegemonic relations, which limit how we consider and address social justice.

Did the students benefit? I can only speak for myself, but the experience was one that instilled in me the notion that transformative leadership requires a process, humility, and a rejection of rubrics, matrices, tools, instruments, and measures that provide one answer only (or, rather, one hegemonic viewpoint only). Administrators are surely a fundamental part of the change equation, and engaging them in ways that encourage transverse thinking can help facilitate change. As important as this is, the next and even more transformative step involves confronting power, not sustaining it, and transformative leadership will reach its full potential when this becomes a central feature of the educational debate, not a peripheral one.

Notes

1. Parts of this chapter borrow from a book I recently completed: Carr, P. (2010). *Does Your Vote Count? Democracy and Critical Pedagogy.* New York: Peter Lang.

2. As elaborated in Carr (2010), formal, normative, hegemonic interpretations of democracy based on electoral processes to the behest of critical, meaningful engagement through education can be understood through a thin to thick spectrum of democracy, with the former (electoral processes) being more at the thin end, and the latter (critical engagement) being more at the thick end.

References

Au, W. (2007). Epistemology of the oppressed: The dialectics of Paulo Freire's *Theory of knowledge*. *Journal for Critical Education Policy Studies*, 5(2). Retrieved from http://www.jceps.com/index.php?pageID= article&articleID=100

Bellamy Foster, J., Holleman, H., & McChesney, R. (2008). The U.S. imperial triangle and military spending. *Monthly Review*, 60(5), 1–19.

Brosio, R. (2003). High-stakes tests: Reasons to strive for better Marx. *Journal for Critical Education Policy Studies*, 1(2). Retrieved from http://www.jceps.com/index.php?pageID= home&issueID=17

Carr, P. R. (2007). Experiencing democracy through neo-liberalism: The role of social justice in education. *Journal of Critical Education Policy Studies*, 5(2). Retrieved from http://www.jceps.com/index. php?pageID= article&articleID=104

Carr, P. R. (2008a). "But what can I do?": Fifteen things education students can do to transform themselves in/through/with education. *International Journal of Critical Pedagogy*, 1(2), 81–97. Retrieved from http://freire.mcgill.ca/ojs/index.php/home/article/view/56/31

Carr, P. R. (2008b). Educating for democracy: With or without social justice? *Teacher Education Quarterly*, fall, 117–136.

Carr, P. R. (2008c). Educators and education for democracy: Moving beyond "thin" democracy. *Inter-American Journal of Education and Democracy*, 1(2), 147–165. Retrieved from http://www.riedijed.org/english/ articulo.php?idRevista=4&idArticulo=16

Carr, P. R. (2010). *Does your vote count? Democracy and critical pedagogy*. New York: Peter Lang.

Darder, A., & Miron, L. F. (2006). Critical pedagogy in a time of uncertainty: A call to action. *Cultural Studies—Critical Methodologies*, 6(1), 5–20.

Denzin, N. K. (2009). Critical pedagogy and democratic life or a radical democratic pedagogy. *Cultural Studies—Critical Methodologies*, 9(3), 379–397.

Engels, J. (2007). Floating bombs encircling our shores: Post 9/11 rhetorics of piracy and terrorism. *Cultural Studies—Critical Methodologies*, 7(3), 326–349.

Fischman, G. E., & McLaren, P. (2005). Rethinking critical pedagogy and the Gramscian and Freirean legacies: From organic to committed intellectuals or critical pedagogy, commitment, and praxis. *Cultural Studies—Critical Methodologies*, 5(4), 425–447.

Freire, P. (1973). *Education for critical consciousness*. New York: The Continuum Publishing Company.

Freire, P. (1985). *The Politics of education*. South Hadley, MA: Bergin & Garvey Publishers.

Freire, P. (1998). *Pedagogy of freedom: Ethics, democracy, and civic courage*. Lanham, MD: Rowman & Littlefield.

Freire, P. (2004). *Pedagogy of indignation*. Boulder, CO: Paradigm Publishers.

Freire, P. (1973/2005). *Pedagogy of the oppressed*. New York: Continuum.

Gandin, L. A., & Apple, M. (2005). Thin versus thick democracy in education. Porto Alegre and the creation of alternatives to neo-liberalism. *International Studies in Sociology of Education*, 12(2), 99–116.

Giroux, H. (2005). The passion of the right: Religious fundamentalism and the crisis of democracy. *Cultural Studies—Critical Methodologies*, 5(3), 309–317.

Giroux, H., & Giroux, S. S. (2006). Challenging neo-liberalism's new world order: The promise of critical pedagogy. *Cultural Studies—Critical Methodologies*, 6(1), 21–32.

Gordon, S. P., Smyth, J., & Diehl, J. (2008). The Iraq war, "sound science," and "evidence-based" educational reform: How the Bush administration uses deception, manipulation, and subterfuge to advance its chosen ideology. *Journal for Critical Education Policy Studies*, 6(2), 173–204. Retrieved from http://www.jceps.com/PDFs/6-2–10.pdf

Hill, D., & Boxley, S. (2007). Critical teacher education for economic, environmental and social justice: An ecosocialist manifesto. *Journal for Critical Education Policy Studies*, 5(2). Retrieved from http://www. jceps.com/index.php?pageID=article&articleID=96

Kellner, D., & Share, J. (2007). Critical media literacy, democracy, and the reconstruction of education. In Macedo, D., and Steinberg, S. (Eds.), *Media literacy: A reader* (pp. 3–23). New York: Peter Lang.

Kincheloe, J. L. (2007). Critical pedagogy in the twenty-first century. In McLaren, P., & Kincheloe J. (Eds.), *Critical pedagogy: Where are we now?* (pp. 9–42). New York: Peter Lang.

Kincheloe, J. L. (2008a). *Critical pedagogy: Primer*. New York: Peter Lang.

Kincheloe, J. L. (2008b). *Knowledge and critical pedagogy: An introduction*. London: Springer.

Kincheloe, J. L., & Steinberg, S. R. (2006). An ideology of miseducation: Countering the pedagogy of empire. *Cultural Studies—Critical Methodologies, 6*(1), 33–51.

Lund, D. E., & Carr, P. R. (Eds.). (2008). *"Doing" democracy: Striving for political literacy and social justice.* New York: Peter Lang.

Macedo, D., & Steinberg, S. (2007). *Media literacy: A reader.* New York: Peter Lang.

Macrine, S. (Ed.). (2009). *Critical pedagogy in uncertain times: Hopes and possibilities.* New York: Palgrave Macmillan.

McLaren, P., & Kincheloe, J. L. (Eds.). (2007). *Critical pedagogy: Where are we now?* New York: Peter Lang.

Shields, C. M. (2004). Dialogic leadership for social justice: Overcoming pathologies of silence. *Educational Administration Quarterly, 40*(1), 109–113.

Shields, C. M. (2010). Transformative leadership: Working for equity in diverse contexts. *Educational Administration Quarterly, 46*(4), 558–589

Shields, C. M., & Edwards, M. M. (2005). *Dialogue is not just talk: A new ground for educational leadership.* New York: Peter Lang.

Steinberg, S., & Kincheloe, J. (Eds.). (2009). *Christotainment: Selling Jesus through popular culture.* Boulder, CO: Westview Press

Westheimer, J. (2008). *No child left thinking: Democracy at-risk in American schools* (Democratic Dialog series, no. 17). Ottawa, Canada: Democratic Dialog, University of Ottawa.

Westheimer, J., & Kahne, J. (2003). Reconnecting education to democracy: Democratic dialogs. *Phi Delta Kappan, 85*(1), 9–14.

Westheimer, J., & Kahne, J. (2004). What kind of citizen? The politics of educating for democracy. *American Educational Research Journal, 41*(2), 237–269.

Willinsky, J. (1998). *Learning to divide the world: Education at empire's end.* Minneapolis: University of Minnesota Press.

3

From Cowardice to Courage

Breaking the Silence Surrounding Race in Schools

Erica Mohan

Even silence speaks. —Hausa proverb

According to Shields (2010), "transformative concepts and social justice are closely connected through the shared goal of identifying and restructuring frameworks that generate inequity and disadvantage" (p. 28). They also share the related goal of raising the critical consciousness of students so as to prepare them for participation as critical and engaged citizens (see McKenzie et al., 2008; Shields, 2004, 2010). We immediately perceive the influence of Freire's concepts of dialogue, critical consciousness, transformation, and praxis on current theories of education for social justice and transformative leadership (Freire, 1970, 1998) We also hear the call for school leaders to ensure that students have opportunities for meaningful engagement with topics such as race, class, gender, and sexual orientation so that they may understand, challenge, and replace oppressive belief structures.

Although each of the aforementioned topics, among others, requires our attention, my focus here is on the dialogue and deep engagement with the topics of race and ethnicity required if we are to challenge oppressive frameworks, raise the critical consciousness of students, and prepare them for engaged citizenship. More precisely, my primary concern here is the *lack* of dialogue regarding these topics in schools. Drawing on both literature and empirical data, I discuss the perennial silence regarding race and ethnicity in schools and students' perceptions regarding this silence.

As the epigraph starting the chapter indicates, silence is not neutral. Indeed, Shields, in the Introduction to this reader, reminds us of the insidiousness of what she terms "pathologies of silence" and a colorblind approach that refuses to acknowledge "that for those who are not part of the dominant culture, differences matter on a daily basis as they are refused housing or jobs, taxis are locked, and doors slammed in their faces, or prejudicial statements are made thoughtlessly with no consideration of their impact" (this volume, p. 8; see also Schofield, 2009; Sleeter, 1993). I contend that it is the responsibility of transformative school leaders to reject such cowardly pathologies of silence and colorblind approaches that claim neutrality while reproducing injustice and inequities. The persistent silence surrounding race cannot be ignored, tolerated, or perpetuated by transformative leaders; they must play an active role in shattering it.

A Nation of Cowards

As was widely publicized at the time, in early 2009 the United States Attorney General Eric Holder called the American people "essentially a nation of cowards" for failing to openly discuss race and race-related issues. He said, "Though this nation has proudly thought of itself as an ethnic melting pot, in things racial we have always been and continue to be, in too many ways, essentially a nation of cowards" (para. 2). Holder claimed that Americans avoid discussions about race because they are uncomfortable and asserted that "certain subjects are off limits and that to explore them risks, at best embarrassment, and, at worst, the questioning of one's character" (para. 4). He stated, during a news conference following his speech, "It's a question of being honest with ourselves and racial issues that divide us. . .It's not easy to talk about it. We have to have the guts to be honest with each other, accept criticism, [and] accept new proposals" (CNN, 2009).

In his speech, Attorney General Holder specifically pointed to affirmative action as an issue around which there can and should be "nuanced, principled and spirited" debate. He noted, however, that such debates seldom take place and that conversations about affirmative action often become "simplistic" and are used to advance individuals' self-interests. In his words:

> There can, for instance, be very legitimate debate about the question of affirmative action. This debate can, and should, be nuanced, principled and spirited. But the conversation that we now engage in as a nation on this and other racial subjects is too often simplistic and left to those on the extremes who are not hesitant to use these issues to advance nothing more than their own, narrow self interest. (para. 5)

Clearly, Holder recognizes the occurrence of *some* conversations and debates about affirmative action and other emotionally charged topics related to race, but his concern stems from the simplistic, polarizing, and unproductive nature of many such conversations and debates.

Take, for example, the so-called "affirmative-action bake sales" that have taken place on several U.S. university campuses over the past decade. During these bake sales, baked goods are sold to members of the student body, with prices linked to the buyer's (perceived) racial background. Several students at Wesleyan University who are members of the group Cardinal Conservatives, for example, recently hosted one such bake sale offering items according to the following price scale: white/Caucasian $2.00, Asian/Asian American $1.50, Latino/Hispanic $1.00, black/African American $0.75, and Native American $0.00 (Wood, 2010). In his discussion of the purpose of the Wesleyan bake sale, Peter Wood explains that:

> Affirmative-action bake sales are meant to bring home to students that a sliding scale giving favorable treatment to some students, based on their race or ethnicity, is disturbing and indeed offensive. Generally it was up to the spectators to take the analogical jump: If racial hierarchy is bad when it comes to selling cookies, might it also be bad when it comes to granting college admissions, financial aid, and other amenities that colleges have at their disposal? (para. 4)

When I first heard about affirmative-action bake sales nearly a decade ago, and again this year, several questions immediately came to mind: What is the agenda of the students holding such bake sales? Are they intended as merely a statement of the host students' positions and perspectives, or are the bake sales genuine attempts to inspire dialogue and debate? How did other students respond? How did faculty members and the administration respond? I hoped that affirmative-action bake sales, however crude and absurd, would prompt the lively, "nuanced, principled and spirited" debates called for by Holder. In actuality, however, they have, it seems, resulted in silencing, accusations, and (likely as a consequence of their over-simplification of complex issues) understandable anger. As Wood explains:

> We know that at the dozens of colleges and universities where conservative student groups have staged these events, the result is seldom a sudden flood of illumination on the part of students that institutional racial preferences are a form of racial discrimination. Rather, the result every single time is that some students become offended (and say so) and some faculty and administrators cry racism. In a good many cases, administrators have also shut down the sales and tried to punish the would-be vendors. (2010, para. 6)

Indeed, to the extent that affirmative-action bake sales fail to stimulate meaningful dialogue about affirmative action, race, and ethnicity, they are, in the most gentle of terms, merely another polarizing force with the potential to do great harm.

It is a safe assumption that, based on their respective affiliations and positions, Attorney General Holder and Peter Wood do not agree on a host of policies and issues, yet they both feel strongly about the need for frank and rigorous conversations about racial issues, and that these conversations need to be inclusive. Of course, neither Holder nor Wood is specifically addressing my concern here, which is the need for dialogue and debate in K-12 schools about issues related to race and ethnicity, but I cannot imagine that either would accept that K-12 schools are somehow exempt from their mutual call for increased discussion of these issues. Indeed, if Holder and Wood are to have their wish, it is essential that individuals participate in earnest dialogue about race and ethnicity early and often. Silence in schools on issues of race and ethnicity sets the tone for society. Conversely, and more positively, schools can play an important role in preparing students for dialogue about race and ethnicity and, thus, for engaged citizenship in our rapidly diversifying country.

The Need for Courage

If the American people are truly "essentially a nation of cowards" in failing to openly discuss race and race-related issues, then, given that the most common definition of cowardice is the lack of courage, it should not be surprising that in recent years we have seen the proliferation of calls for more courage—for example, courageous conversations about uncomfortable topics, moral courage in the classroom, and courageous leadership—especially as courage pertains to race-related issues (see, e.g., Ayers & Ayers, 2011; Singleton & Linton, 2006; Shields, 2009a, 2009b, 2010). In fact, the word *courage* pervades educational literature, and Shields identifies "demonstrating moral courage" as one of the distinguishing features of transformative leadership (see Shields, 2010, this volume). But what do we mean by courage? What does it look like? How does a transformative leader exercise courage? Surely, what courage "looks like" or how it is manifested is dependent on the individual, the context, and the possible consequences of one's actions, but there must also be some general principles that can guide transformative leaders. In trying to understand the unique types of courage demanded of educators in general, and specifically of transformative leaders, it is useful to consider Edward Said's discussion of the public intellectual (1994).

Said's discussion of the roles and responsibilities of public intellectuals captures many of the key attributes and, more particularly, the courage required of transformative educational leaders. Indeed, Said argues that the role of a public intellectual entails a specific set of responsibilities, which overlaps closely with the responsibilities of a transformative leader as conceptualized by Shields (2009a, 2009b, 2010, this volume). Said asserts that the role of the intellectual

> has an edge to it, and cannot be played without a sense of being someone whose place it is publically to raise embarrassing questions, to confront orthodoxy and dogma (rather than to produce them), to be someone who cannot easily be co-opted by governments or corporations, and whose raison d'être is to represent all those people and issues that are routinely forgotten or swept under the rug. The intellectual does so on the basis of universal principles: that all human beings are entitled to expect decent standards of behavior concerning freedom and justice from worldly powers or nations, and that deliberate or inadvertent violations of these standards need to be testified and fought against courageously. (1994, p. 9)

Borrowing Said's language, and reflecting previously outlined descriptions of transformative leadership (Shields, 2009 a, 2009b, 2010, this volume; Weiner, 2003), I call on transformative leaders (and all educators) to raise embarrassing questions about race, to confront the racial orthodoxy that has been used to defend and justify centuries of racial inequality, to resist being co-opted by those with the loudest voices or the most power, to pull out from "under the rug" racial issues and the perspectives of those whose voices are often silenced, and to defend every individual's right to freedom and justice.

Certainly I am not alone in calling on educators to summon the courage to perform these tasks. Beverly Tatum (2007), for example, in her book *Can We Talk about Race? And Other Conversations in an Era of School Resegregation*, calls on educators to find the courage to have honest and open conversations about race, no matter how uncomfortable these conversations might be. She asks, "Can we get beyond our fear, our sweaty palms, our anxiety about saying the wrong thing, or using the wrong words, and have an honest conversation about racial issues?" (p. xiii). Tatum specifically calls on those in leadership positions in education, whom she identifies as faculty, administrators, and men and women of influence, to promote dialogue about racial issues, to serve as role models for younger generations, and to "cross racial and ethnic boundaries and connect with others different from ourselves" (p. xiii).

There are, then, many individuals, from different contexts and representing distinct perspectives, who recognize the importance of open, meaningful, and spirited conversations about race and related topics. While most recognize that such conversations might be difficult and require courage, the perceived benefits of such conversations are widely understood as significantly outweighing the potential risks. We might reasonably assume, then, with so many unambiguous calls for dialogue coming from so many different perspectives, and especially from those in education, that the conversations envisioned by Holder and Wood are already taking place in our schools, and increasingly so. Surprisingly, and unfortunately, research that I recently conducted suggests otherwise.

Silence and Surveillance in Schools

In 2007, I embarked on my dissertation study, the central purpose of which was to gain a deep understanding of the K-12 schooling experiences of multiethnic students and the perceived influence of these experiences on their racial and ethnic identity development (Mohan, 2010). The central research question for this study was: In what ways does K-12 schooling influence the racial and ethnic identity construction of multiethnic students? Related questions included: In what ways do school initiatives such as multicultural and antiracism education influence their identity development? What other aspects of K-12 schooling (for example, the curriculum, the racial and ethnic makeup of the school, and extracurricular activities) influence the racial and ethnic identity construction of multiethnic students? And, how might K-12 schools become more inclusive of their multiethnic students? For the study, I interviewed 23 self-identified multiethnic high school students drawn from eight schools in Northern California. All of the students participated in a semi-structured interview, nine participated in one of two optional focus groups, and five completed an optional writing activity.

Given the purpose of the study and the research questions, it is not surprising that much of the interview and focus-group discussions focused on how and what students learn about race and ethnicity in schools. Quite unexpectedly, during our conversations, many of the students echoed Tatum's request for more engagement with race-related topics. Given that the data for this study were collected in a particularly racially and ethnically diverse part of the country (Lopez, 2003), and given the prevalence of calls for engagement with the topics of race and ethnicity in schools, I was surprised to find so few students reporting such engagement. Moreover, nearly all of them expressed a sincere desire that their teachers would have more authentic and detailed conversations with them about race and ethnicity. Indeed, recurring themes in the data include the observation that race and ethnicity are seldom addressed in school and, when they are, it is often in simplistic and superficial ways; and the students' desire for more frequent and more meaningful engagement with the topics of race and ethnicity. Of particular interest here, however, are participants' explanations for why such engagement with these topics does not take place in their schools.

One participant, Renee,[1] sensed fear on the part of her teachers, which prevents them from talking about race, culture, or anything not in the textbook. She said:

> I think teachers are too afraid to talk, to be the first person to talk with their students about race and culture. And unless it is in your textbook, you don't learn about it, because teachers are still afraid to step outside of the box in that category because they're too afraid to step on anyone's toes, get in trouble, offend anyone.

Another student, Jill, discussed the discomfort people feel when talking about race and ethnicity and the lack of a safe space to discuss these topics in her school. Although she acknowledged that some people might try to broach the topics, such attempts are rarely successful. In her words:

> I think it's just uncomfortable because people just don't like to talk about race and ethnicity, because there's so much hush on it in our culture. It's like, "Don't talk about that." . . .So that when you're in an environment where people say "Let's talk about race,". . .the people who want to open up shut down because there's not a safe space for them to talk about it.

Yet another student, Barry, discussed the silence in his school regarding race and ethnicity and the fear surrounding these topics. Barry was quite explicit about the risks associated with talking about race and ethnicity, but he also recognized that the silence surrounding these topics reinforces their taboo status:

> [I think teachers don't talk about race and ethnicity] because they might get it wrong and a person might be offended and they tell the principal and then punishment comes down to that. I think teachers should [talk about race and ethnicity], but I think also they need to be careful, because a

lot of people might take offense to certain things. But I think the fact that we don't talk about it, makes it more kind of a taboo thing. . .. But talking about it, I think that's how you fix anything.

Again, my primary interest here is the participants' explanations for why there is so little meaningful engagement with race and ethnicity in their schools. According to Renee, teachers are "too afraid to talk. . .too afraid to step on anyone's toes, get in trouble, offend anyone." According to Jill, her schools have not provided a safe space to talk about race and ethnicity. And according to Barry, if they talk about race and ethnicity in class, teachers might offend someone and, as a result, get punished. These observations are consistent with the explanations offered by the majority of study participants.

When reading these and related data, what immediately strikes me is the implied role of the school leader. Indeed, on closer examination, these data smack of a hierarchical structure in schools, topped with school leaders, and a culture of surveillance in which teachers might be punished or "get in trouble." Regardless of whether teachers in participants' schools actually get in trouble for talking about race and ethnicity with students, something must have informed the students' perceptions. Again and again, words such as *fear, trouble, offend, careful, taboo*, and *silence* appear in the data. Somewhere along the way, it seems, participants in my study—attending different schools in very different contexts—have picked up the idea that someone with authority over their teachers is responsible for the culture of silence in their schools. They sense that there is an administration that creates an environment, not of safety, but of surveillance, and, thus, teachers are in a vulnerable position that requires them to eschew discussion of potentially controversial or "taboo" topics. Nevertheless, and regardless of the risks associated with conversations about race and related topics, my data show that students want to have them. This, in my opinion, holds important implications for school leaders and provides a clear mandate for those who believe in the transformative potential of their role.

Courageous Transformative Leadership

To review, many of the participants in my dissertation research cited perceived surveillance and the threat to teachers of "getting in trouble" from school leaders as reasons for the lack of meaningful discussion about race, ethnicity, and related issues in their respective schools. This finding clearly points to the need for school leaders to explicitly communicate with teachers and students that conversations involving race and related topics, to the extent that they are respectful, are not only welcomed but *expected* in their schools. This does not mean merely stating that one's school is a "safe space" for conversations about race (and other "taboo" topics) but actually demonstrating that it is. This may require, for example, holding round-table discussions with groups of students about such topics, having students listen to their peers (or teachers, or administrators) debate racial issues in a respectful manner, or visiting classrooms and facilitating honest and open conversations about affirmative action, residential segregation, and other contentious topics. Setting aside the substantive aspects of such conversations, it also requires school leaders to establish and broadcast guidelines for respectful dialogue. Making one's school a safe space for conversations about race, while critically important, does not, alone, make one a transformative leader, and superficial conversations about race will not have a transformative effect.

According to Shields, moral courage, which she describes as "the willingness to take risks, and to become actively engaged in the struggle and challenge of creating schools that are more equitable, inclusive, excellent, and socially just," is a key aspect of transformative leadership (2009b, p. 13). Clearly, the notions of risk and active engagement are at the heart of transformative leadership, the immediate goal of which is to create excellent and equitable schools for all children, and the ultimate goal of which is to redress persistent social inequities. As Shields explains, transformative leadership:

> recognizes the need to begin with critical reflection and analysis and to move through enlightened understanding to action—action to redress wrongs and to ensure that all members of the organization are provided with as level a playing field as possible—not only with respect to access, but also with regard to academic, social, and civic outcomes. (2010, p. 31)

What I take all of this to mean, in relation to engaging with race and related topics in schools, is that the goal and, indeed, responsibility, of the transformative leader is to, despite the risks, raise the critical consciousness of students and foster enlightened understanding that may lead to critical action.

How, then, does one foster enlightened understanding about race-related issues? Again, during my dissertation research, most students discussed the notable silence in their schools regarding race and ethnicity. When students did discuss engagement with these topics in their classrooms, they most often described it as "superficial," "basic," or "meaningless," and they discussed an over-emphasis on the food, clothing, heroes, and holidays associated with different racial and ethnic groups. While students probably enjoy enchilada day, Chinese New Year's celebrations, and learning about Native American heroes, they are unlikely to glean from such activities enlightened understanding about the historical exploitation of immigrant and slave labor in the United States or the destruction of Native American communities and how these atrocities continue to shape modern day life in the United States.

I am, therefore, not merely calling for more frequent engagement with the topics of race and ethnicity in schools, but for a certain type of engagement—one that might lead to enlightened understanding and critical action, one that deconstructs oppressive belief structures, and one that will make it difficult for students, as they become contributing members of society, to sit back and allow the inequities of yesteryear to continue in the future. I am, in short, calling on transformative school leaders to encourage and facilitate the type of dialogue about race and ethnicity envisioned by Holder (2009), Singleton and Linton (2006), Tatum (2007), and Wood (2010), among others. Here, again, I find Edward Said's words useful (1994). The transformative leader will see his or her role as having an edge to it, as requiring him or her to confront the orthodoxy and dogma that justifies entrenched inequities, to raise embarrassing questions such as those which concern the appalling treatment faced by various groups of people, and to defend the right of all individuals to freedom, justice, and decent treatment. Can frequent, open, honest, and principled dialogue about race and related issues in K-12 schools, alone, redress the enduring racial inequities and resolve the persistent racial tensions found in North America? I suspect not, but can I see no better starting point if our attempts to do so are to be successful.

A Personal Confession

It is very easy, especially for those of us who are not on the front lines of education, working in K-12 schools, to create a laundry list of "shoulds" for teachers and school leaders (do this, don't do that, read this book, try this strategy, and so on). When talking or working with K-12 educators, however, I often hear phrases like "easier said than done" or "wouldn't it be nice if I had the time to do that." I have also heard quiet confessions about missed opportunities to raise uncomfortable topics with staff and students, to adopt an unpopular position despite one's belief in the value of doing so, or to try out innovative strategies. Just recently, I, too, missed one such opportunity.

At a workshop whose participants included ten adults representing a variety of racial heritages who would be working with those who are commonly considered "at-risk" youth, the issue of racial identity came up. Almost immediately, the tone of the conversation and the feeling in the room changed. Whereas earlier in the workshop we all seemed to identify with each other in relation to a common goal, upon the emergence of the topic of racial identity, words like *you, us, them, we,* and *they* quickly emerged. Some participants fell silent, others seemed agitated and irritated by others' comments, and almost everyone seemed defensive. The facilitator appeared threatened, and several people used the word *vulnerable* to describe their feelings. So uncomfortable did the conversation become, that we failed to return to the topic of race at any other point in the remaining eight hours of the workshop. In other words, this conversation foreclosed any other substantive engagement with the topic of race during the workshop.

Looking back, I, of course, wish that our conversation about racial identity had not become so uncomfortable and heated. I wish that comments had not taken a defensive tone and that those who fell silent had felt more comfortable or able to participate in the conversation. I also wish that I had felt more comfortable stepping in and trying to diffuse the situation, but as a participant in the workshop, I did not want to infringe on the facilitator's role. Rather, my response in this situation was to participate in the conversation about racial identity in what I thought to be a productive manner, but truth be told, I just wanted the conversation to end. I have spent nearly a decade studying racial and ethnic identity formation and strategies for addressing race, ethnicity, and related topics in the classroom, and I am truly astounded (and a bit ashamed) by how uncomfortable I felt during the conversation at our workshop and how relieved I was when the conversation ended. To borrow Attorney General Holder's term, I felt like a coward.

I share this story here for several reasons. Firstly, it is, I believe, a sad story that is indicative of the magnitude of the task before us. If adults who have self-selected into a workshop regarding "at-risk" youth experience difficulty in having an open and productive conversation about race, surely educators trying to encourage such conversations in their schools will face significant challenges. As discussed previously, Tatum (2007) calls on educators to set an example for younger generations and to model how to "cross racial and ethnic boundaries and connect with others different from ourselves" (p. xiii). I am glad that there were not young students attending the workshop as we would have set a poor example for them. Secondly, this story illustrates the danger of continuing to treat race and related topics as taboo and dangerous. The change in tone of our conversation occurred almost immediately after the introduction of the topic of race and before any substantive comments were made. What this indicates to me is that the mere topics of race and ethnicity, and not necessarily particular comments or ideas, can rile and cause discomfort. Here we see the insidiousness of the silence surrounding these topics: Silence begets silence. Accordingly, this story demonstrates the need to encourage children to engage with race and related topics at an early age, before the silence surrounding, and fear of, these topics get entrenched for another generation. As my participant Barry so aptly said, "But I think the fact that we don't talk about it makes it more kind of a taboo thing. . . .. But talking about it, I think that's how you fix anything."

Final Thoughts

If we use as our starting point the notion that transformative school leaders have the responsibility to help foster engaged citizenship in a pluralistic democracy; to raise issues that students will confront in their lives; to address social inequities that too often determine the educational opportunities and outcomes for certain students; and to engage in courageous conversation about topics that are too often, in Said's words, "forgotten or swept under the rug" (1994, p. 9), then the silence regarding race and ethnicity reported by students can only be taken as an indication that we, as educators and leaders, have yet to fulfill our responsibilities.

Students fully recognize the risks inherent in conversations about race and ethnicity for both teachers and students, yet they nonetheless desire those conversations. They recognize that no one wants to be the first to broach such topics in the classroom, yet they wish someone would. And they recognize the need for an environment in which discussions of race and ethnicity can take place safely without fear of being attacked or silenced. Our students, then, do not want to be another generation of cowards, and they are eager to play their part in meaningful discussions that address pressing social issues such as race. Transformative school leaders should embrace the opportunity their students' eagerness presents and bring such pressing and heretofore "taboo" issues into the classroom in authentic, thoughtful, and sincere ways.

Note

1.   All names used here are pseudonyms.

References

Ayers, R., & Ayers, W. (2011). *Teaching the taboo: Courage and imagination in the classroom.* New York: Teachers College Press.

CNN (Cable News Network). (February 18, 2009). Holder: U.S. a 'nation of cowards' on race discussions [Electronic Version]. Retrieved December 14, 2010 from http://articles.cnn.com/2009-02-18/politics/holder.race.relations_1_holder-affirmative-action-black-history-month?_s=PM:POLITICS

Freire, P. (1970). *Pedagogy of the oppressed.* New York: Herder and Herder.

Freire, P. (1998). *Pedagogy of freedom. Ethics, democracy, and civic courage* (P. Clarke, Trans.). Lanham, MD: Rowman & Littlefield Publishers.

Holder, E. (2009). *Attorney General Eric Holder at the Department of Justice African American History Month Program* [Remarks as prepared for delivery]. Retrieved March 2009, from http://www.justice.gov/ag/speeches/2009/ag-speech-090218.html

Lopez, A. M. (2003). Mixed-race school-age children: A summary of census 2000 data. *Educational Researcher, 32*(6), 25–37.

McKenzie, K. B., Christman, D., Hernandez, F., Fierra, E. Capper, C., Dantley, M., Cambron-McCabe, N. & Scheurich, J. J.(2008). From the field: A proposal for educating leaders for social justice. *Educational Administration Quarterly, 44*(1), 111–138.

Mohan, E. (2010). *The influence of K–12 schooling on the identity development of multiethnic students.* (Unpublished doctoral dissertation). University of British Columbia, Vancouver.

Said, E. W. (1994). Representations of the intellectual. In E. W. Said (Ed.), *Representations of the intellectual: The 1993 Reith lectures* (pp. 3–17). London: Random House.

Schofield, J. W. (2009). The colorblind perspective in school: Causes and consequences. In J.A. Banks & C.A. McGee Banks (Eds.), *Multicultural education: Issues and perspectives* (7th ed., pp. 271–295). New York: John Wiley & Sons.

Shields, C. M. (2004). Dialogic leadership for social justice: Overcoming pathologies of silence. *Educational Administration Quarterly, 40*(1), 111–134.

Shields, C. M. (2009a). *Courageous leadership for transforming schools: Democratizing practice.* Norwood, MA: Christopher-Gordon.

Shields, C. M. (2009b, May). *Transformative leadership: Working for equity in diverse contexts.* Paper presented at the annual meeting of the Canadian Association for Studies in Educational Administration, Ottawa.

Shields, C. M. (2010). Leadership: Transformative. In P. Peterson, E. Baker, & B. McGraw (Eds.), *International Encyclopedia of Education* (Vol. 5, pp. 26–33). Oxford: Elsevier.

Singleton, G. E., & Linton, C. (Eds.). (2006). *Courageous conversations about race: A field guide for achieving equity in schools*. Thousand Oaks, CA: Corwin Press.

Sleeter, C. E. (1993). How white teachers construct race. In C. McCarthy & W. Crichlow (Eds.), *Race, identity and representation in education* (pp. 157–171). New York: Routledge.

Tatum, B. D. (2007). *Can we talk about race? and other conversations in an era of school resegregation*. Boston: Beacon Press.

Weiner, E. J. (2003). Secretary Paulo Freire and the democratization of power: Toward a theory of transformative leadership. *Educational Philosophy and Theory, 35*(1), 89–106.

Wood, P. (2010, December 7). Racism at Wesleyan? [Electronic Version]. *The Chronicle of Higher Education*. Retrieved December 8, 2010 from http://chronicle.com/blogs/innovations/racism-at-wesleyan/28029?sid=at&utm_source=at&utm_medium=en

4

Radical Leadership on the Borders of Difference

David Requa

The radical, committed to human liberation, does not become the prisoner of a 'circle of certainty' within which reality is also imprisoned. On the contrary, the more radical the person is, the more fully he or she enters into reality so that, knowing it better, he or she can better transform it. This individual is not afraid to confront, to listen, to see the world unveiled. This person is not afraid to meet the people or to enter into dialogue with them. This person does not consider himself or herself the proprietor of history or of all people, or the liberator of the oppressed; but he or she does commit himself or herself, within history, to fight at their side.
—P. Freire, *Pedagogy of the Oppressed*, p. 39

Inequity arises in the social context from the presence of difference—a constant in human society that is increasing with the shrinking global community, which brings new cultures, beliefs, languages, and images into communities across the globe. Increasing differences too often mean that some coalesce into an "us" while labeling those unlike themselves as "other," to be kept out of power and seen as the intruders. That separation and labeling build an inequity and a valuing and devaluing that fly in the face of freedom, democracy, and the opportunity for each person to fulfill their potential as productive and participative citizens of the community, whether that community is local or global. A transformative leader must then address the inequities in communities of increasing diversity by first understanding the "conflicts and contradictions" (Quantz, Rogers, & Dantley, 1991) that are inherent in that social context.

In this chapter, I use Freire's image of the transformative leader as a radical, and lay out one way to get to know difference and diversity better, in order to engage in the dialectic relationship with those who differ from the dominant and whose difference is devalued in the larger social context. Freire's image of the radical reveals an approach to others that avoids the pitfall of viewing the transformative leader as a missionary out to liberate others from their oppressed condition. The radical, like the transformative educational leader, has the purpose of changing what it is that should not be and addressing ongoing inequities in the greater social context (Shields, 2010). The transformative leader must unveil and understand, confront and engage the social structures that tend to value some and devalue others and thus provide inequitable opportunities for growth and fulfillment. It is not only individual growth and fulfillment that is the concern of the transformative educational leader, for merely providing individual economic opportunity for more students will not prepare them to actively enter into a democratic society and engage in the ongoing dialogue that prevents the reproduction of the past to occur. To fully enter into reality as a radical, a transformative leader must establish a framework for understanding and must find a way to share that framework within and beyond the school walls, in order to transform the society that reproduces the inequities.

By looking through the eyes of Latino migrant students, we see one view of difference and the result of the inequities that exist for one group of students. I propose that a framework for understanding these students and other communities of difference can be found in border theory, first by applying it to the literal border and then moving into the metaphorical and personal borders that divide people into "us" and "them" categories of all types. Using this framework, educational leaders can gain a more nuanced understanding of difference and the effects of ignoring the social structures that disadvantage difference. By taking a radical stand, the transformative leader can more fully enter into the reality of the social context and find ways to fight at the side of—rather than swoop in as the liberator of—those who are devalued by a social order in need of change.

The Radical as Transformative Leader

The Freirean radical must first fully enter into reality to engage in the required dialectical relationship with the other. That reality is easily ignored or misunderstood by leaders who are often from a dominant class and may never have experienced the position of one who is not valued. Quantz et al. (1991, p. 99) hold that inequities need not be intentional, and often are not. They cite Bourdieu, stating that inequities often result from a process that treats all students as equal, ignores reality, and perpetuates a status quo that disadvantages some. It is this simple act of not paying attention to reality that allows the inequities to continue and flourish. The radical, in the role of transformative educational leader, is bound to the concept of critique (Shields, 2010) that requires an active drive to see reality as it exists and to continue to "more fully enter into" (Freire, 2007, p. 39) what is actually happening in order to avoid perpetuating it.

Too often, academic failure of students outside the dominant group is blamed on forces other than the school itself, without taking a critical look at the reality of the situation. Parents are accused of not being involved in their child's education, and conditions of poverty, substandard housing, and lack of proper nourishment are blamed, all without performing a critical examination of how those conditions are the result of socially constructed orders that disadvantage some to the advantage of others. By being imprisoned in Freire's so-called circle of certainty, which does not examine the reality of those different from the privileged group, a leader fails to meet the requirement of radical inquiry that transformative leadership calls for. Without that level of critical inquiry and a vision beyond apparent certainties, a leader cannot transform the social structures that prevent equitable outcomes for all students.

Ogbu's work addresses the issues of African American students trying to adapt to the social order by "acting white," confusing and devaluing the rich cultural reality of those students (Ogbu & Spring, 2008). Other studies have shown similar attempts to assimilate or accommodate by students outside of the dominant group (Lee, 2005; Maira, 2009; Thompson, 2004). By adapting to the existing structure of white dominance, those students experienced alienation, a lowered self-esteem, and a dissonance of identity that built a wall of difference around them, while dominant groups moved on, imprisoned in their wall of certainty that the social order was what it should be. Only through examination of the reality of the situation could someone inside that wall break out and begin to understand what the reality was. They could then see how to engage with those experiencing the dissonance in order to transform the social order. That is the work of the radical as a transformative leader.

The Borders of Difference

The study of difference can take many perspectives. The researcher can observe as a detached gatherer of data and, having collected the targeted information, leave to write what has been observed and move on to the next project. That is the one common way to study and teach the issues that surrounded the Mexican-United States borders. Writers too often observe what happened along the border, and for the people that inhabit that area, and report differences or distinctions, often from a north-of-the-border perspective. Michaelsen and Johnson (1997) describe this form of study as exclusionary—creating borders around the Mexican population and those living near the border with Mexican roots, inevitably infusing inferior and superior viewpoints into the description.

Another perspective—and the one modern border theorists take—is to understand the borders as a fluid locus, not necessarily placed at the geopolitical lines of demarcation but within each person as a line of difference, even distinction, that is a part of the cultural and personal identity of that person. It is what Bhabha (1994) refers to as a problematic and ambivalent ground of study that cannot sum its observations into identity but must allow identity to be a goal unreached and always subject to redefinition. It is in naming and defining the other that we exercise dominance and abandon the possibility of what Freire set out as our goal—to fight side by side with the other. Bhabha (1994) is careful to avoid seeing one or the other as resisting but sees the struggle from each side of difference as ongoing and not the sole effort of one labeled as other.

What this means for the transformative leader as we study difference—and in particular the Latino migrant students—is that we must not observe them as prescribed difference exercising resistance to a dominant culture. We cannot afford to draw a border around them and fix their identity based on our observations; we must recognize that their struggle is also ours as we seek to move toward our own identity and to join them side-by-side in the struggles that are a part of each of us. To get to know difference is to begin to understand the struggles within us, finding our own borders and the boundaries of our own culture. This is the border theory that will assist the radical in moving toward the reality that will allow the dialogue to proceed.

I cannot continue without acknowledging that this study of difference is, in fact, an ideal and is not attainable in full. We must all be aware in our desire to enter into reality, as Freire calls us to do, that we carry baggage that cannot be left behind. Our own cultural and individual biases cling to us and we can only see through or around them as best we can. The best-intentioned transformative leader-as-radical still has those biases, which cannot be ignored or denied. We can, by examining them closely, minimize their effect on our own understanding to some extent, but they will always taint our vision and understanding in some ways.

To understand the framework of modern border theory requires an examination of the construct of culture. Culture can be said to guide much of what we do and how we behave toward each other; yet, it has been described as invisible to our own observations of ourselves—as if we have no culture and it exists only in others (Rosaldo, 1993). Notions of "high" culture— perhaps to describe the opera or art museums—as opposed to "low" culture—to describe what is less formal, such as local food or music offerings—compound this view. We are drawn to ranking cultural levels as we study others and their perceived culture, which too often means the ways in which they differ from our own norms.

Rosaldo (1993) describes the "invisibility" of our own culture and the culture of those whom we perceive to be like us. He calls it the "invisibility within which the North American upper middle class hides itself from itself" (p. 203). Describing the study of borderlands and culture, he exposes how attempts to describe the so-called blending of two or more cultures at a border makes "the fiction of the uniformly shared culture increasingly. . .more tenuous than useful" (p. 207). He describes how we are constantly crossing borders "around such lines as sexual orientation, gender, class, race, ethnicity, nationality, age, politics, dress, food or taste" (p. 208). He rejects the whole notion of fixed cultures and concludes "the notion of an authentic culture as an autonomous internally coherent universe no longer seems tenable" (p. 217).

As radicals we do not move toward reality by creating a construct of culture, but rather, we must look at a much more nuanced self that is more individualized and unique. We cannot enter into a dialogue with those whom we do not know. Buber's (1970) *I and Thou* cannot be "I and whomever-you-are"; it requires a knowing and understanding to enter into the dialectic relationship (Shields & Edwards, 2005). To be a radical transformative leader, we must know the other without drawing boundaries around those who are not like ourselves. We must truly know them to engage in the dialogue that allows us to fight side-by-side with them.

Unveil the World and Meet the People

Freire calls on us to be unafraid to unveil the world and meet the people, in order to enter into dialogue with them. I use a group of Latino migrant high school students to provide an example of what we can learn as radical transformative leaders when we work to more fully enter into reality. By examining deeply what is revealed in the words and observations of these youth, we see reflected our own world of actions unveiled, and perhaps better understand the differences among us. It is not my goal to depict these students as victims or lacking agency. In fact, they have, in many cases, surpassed significant barriers erected by schools and communities to reach their goals. My purpose is to show how we are able to see our own possible openings for dialogue and to unveil the realities of what we are doing as educational leaders.

The Latino migrant students in my study were all of high-school age, and most had worked for a few years themselves in Midwestern cornfields during the month of July, removing the flowers, or tassels, from the tops of corn stalks destined to be harvested later as seed corn. All had traveled from a border state, as they had traveled in years previous, with their parents or other family members, so that the adults could work in the fields. Later, in the early fall, they would work in seed-corn plants, assisting in the preparation of the seed corn for the coming year. The companies that hired them would enter into agreements with a few crew chiefs, who then arranged for housing and transportation to and from the fields for the workers each morning. The day started at around 4:30 a.m. with a bus ride, and ended around 5:30 p.m. with another bus ride back to the apartments where many families stayed. Often, the housing arrangements were substandard; some stayed in an abandoned government building three stories tall that had kitchen facilities on only a single floor. It was the norm to grill outside and keep chilled food in ice chests.

The local school district operated a summer school program under the sponsorship of the state, with federal funds. That program provided an evening session for high school students that allowed them to receive extra instruction in areas they might need for state assessments in their home state or might be useful for college preparation. The program in the area where these students lived was the largest in the state, which offered more than a dozen such programs, but none of the students

I spoke with attended the program regularly. In order to attend, the students would have to clean up quickly from the work in the fields and get on a bus to be taken into the school for a three-hour session before returning home on a bus in time to sleep and repeat the process the next day. A few of the students I spoke to attended occasionally because of the food offered at the beginning of the nightly sessions.

Jorge[1] aspired to go to college along with his cousins of his age, and the three of them would be the first in his family to attend. As a sophomore, he had experienced some trouble in schools because, as he described it, he had fallen in with some people who were supposed to be his friends, but who he later found out may not have had his best interests in mind. He had often been in fights in previous years and had been suspended from school. In the current year he had changed his ways and was working at doing well in school and pursuing his goal of attending college, with the encouragement of a girlfriend who kept him focused. He had decided not to return to his home near the Mexican border but to finish school where he was working summers because he felt he had made a fresh start there and could succeed without the distractions of home. He stayed with relatives, but not with his two brothers, one of whom he supported in private school in his home state because of his perceived aptitude for school.

Camila was also a sophomore and wanted to become a member of the Border Patrol when she graduated from high school so she could "send people back to Mexico if they should not be in the United States." She had attended three different high schools, including two in the Midwest and one in her home state. She did not work in the fields in the summer but babysat for other families who were working. She found changing schools difficult and felt that she could keep up if she had extra help at her home school, where many teachers and students spoke Spanish. There, she also participated in extracurricular activities, but she did not at her Midwestern school. Her parents felt that school was important, in hopes that she could have a better life than they had. She had failed to pass one grade in elementary school but had since passed all of her classes.

Clara wanted to be a lawyer after high school. As a sophomore, she was earning Bs and Cs and had attended schools in two states. She found it difficult to catch up when she returned to her home school almost halfway through the first semester each fall. She was required to catch up with study packets, mostly on her own time, with one study hall that was designated for migrant students to work on their homework. Her courses didn't always match up when she returned home, because the two schools had different schedules and she took a different number of classes at each school. In that way, some of what she did in the Midwest did not transfer to her home school. She maintained her credits by taking an exam in Spanish to earn one class worth of credit. She did work in the fields during the summer and her parents worked in the seed-corn plants in the fall, until their mid-October return home.

Isabel was a sophomore who worked in the fields in the summer, traveling with relatives to the Midwest because it was the best way for her to earn money in the summer, which she had done for the past four years. She wanted to be a pediatrician but anticipated that it would take an additional four or five years past high school to reach that goal. She earned As and Bs in school, but found it took hard work to catch up with her classes when she returned to Texas. She didn't think working as a migrant worker made it much harder than any other student to succeed in school but said others would probably not answer that the same way.

The students differed in how they saw their parents' connection to school, and that changed in nature in their home state, where the staff mostly spoke Spanish. Some felt that their parents were at school and in touch with staff often. Others did not believe their parents made it to school at all. Their paths, their approaches to school, and their manners of dealing with the transience all differed.

These students could be analyzed as a group in order to define a culture if we draw a cultural border around them. Who they are was undoubtedly shaped, in part, by their close proximity to the border and to their shared Mexican heritage and Spanish first-language skills. To classify and characterize them as a singularity would, however, be erroneous as revealed by their stories, even in brief summary.

What does appear is the occasional exposure of the reality that these students were often handled with "equality" by schools. They did not receive any treatment other than that any other student would have, not even if their circumstances were quite different. They were not given a coordinated program of study to connect their two schools so that they could make a smooth transition from one to the other, nor were they offered opportunities to earn credits outside of the normal plan for all students. It appeared that in each school, assimilation was expected, and little more than a special study hall was provided to acknowledge their individual needs. Some succeeded under those circumstances— others did not.

In large numbers, Latino students—and migrant students in particular—fail in school for a variety of reasons. Mehta and colleagues (2000) report that 85% of migrant workers have less than a high school education, with the average being about six years of schooling; many are functionally illiterate. More than one third of the children of migrant workers fall behind academically or drop out of school (Huang, 2002, p. 6). Yet, the schools seem to stand apart and offer the regular program, rather than to stand alongside those who appear in need within the community, and to engage in dialogue with those in need to address the best ways to offer them a pathway to success. Is it because we lack the radical's lack of fear to "meet the people or to enter into dialogue with them," or is it that we do not see them or the world we build around them as they really are? Freire calls on us to radicalize our views and actions to the point that we no longer fear the confrontation of what is real and we see the world unveiled. He calls on us to meet the people and enter into dialogue with them, not to swoop in to save them but to commit ourselves to fight at their side.

The Transformative Leader as Radical

Transformative leadership calls for more than just an observation of the world around us and a critical analysis of the interrelationships and interactions we see. It calls, as Shields (2010) says, for critique, or as Freire calls it, the unveiling of the world as we move toward reality. Certainly we must engage in that critical analysis and dig into those relationships that provide one group an advantage over another. But more than just being called to critique, we are also called to what Shields calls possibility—that is, the call to action to enter into dialogue and to fight at the side of the other, as a joint effort to change what *is* into what *could be*. Transformative leadership is not clean and aloof from the fray but requires us to enter into the possibilities and join in the effort *with* the other and at their side.

We cannot claim radical transformative leadership unless we fully embrace Freire's warning not to be the proprietor of history ("We've always done it this way") or the liberator of the oppressed ("I'm here to right the wrongs of the past"). Truly radical transformative leadership calls us to embrace the other with the dignity of Buber's (1970) "Thou," and to stand with others in dialogue and understanding in order to enter more fully into reality. Included in that concept is the fact that we can only move more fully into reality and cannot find it intact as a whole. We must always seek to critically understand and engage in building the possibilities that will serve all students and communities, and build a world of interrelatedness that does not create walls around borders.

As transformative leaders in the image of Freire's radical, we are obligated to address those issues of inequity that occur as difference increases in our communities. We cannot allow those inequities to deny the future of so many young people simply because we fear the changes. We cannot shrink from the larger task of building a whole society of dialogue and acceptance, as Freire calls us to do. In meeting the other and entering into reality we open a world to all students of all backgrounds, and we build that community of difference that will benefit not just the privileged few, but all students. It is in moving toward that new reality that we can claim to be transformative leaders and true radicals for positive change.

Note

1.   All names are pseudonyms.

References

Bhabha, H. K. (1994). *The location of culture*. New York, NY: Routledge.

Buber, M. (1970). *I and thou* (W. Kaufmann, Trans.). New York, NY: Simon & Schuster.

Freire, P. (2007). *Pedagogy of the oppressed* (M. B. Ramos, Trans. 30th anniversary ed.). New York, NY: The Continuum International Publishing Group, Ltd.

Huang, G. G. (2002). *What federal statistics reveal about migrant farmworkers: A summary for education*. (Education Resources Information Center [ERIC] Digest no. ED471487.) Retrieved from http://www.eric.ed.gov/PDFS/ED471487.pdf

Lee, S. J. (2005). *Up against whiteness: Race, school, and immigrant youth*. New York, NY: Teachers College Press.

Maira, S. M. (2009). *Youth, citizenship, and empire after 9/11*. Durham, NC: Duke University Press.

Mehta, K., Gabbard, S. M., Barrat, V., Lewis, M., Carroll, D., & Mines, R. (2000). *Findings from the national agricultural workers survey (NAWS), 1997–1998: A demographic and employment profile of United States farmworkers*. (ERIC Document Reproduction Service no. ED446887.) Washington, DC: U.S. Department of Labor. Retrieved from http://www.eric.ed.gov/PDFS/ED446887.pdf

Michaelsen, S., & Johnson, D. (Eds.). (1997). *Border theory: The limits of cultural politics*. Minneapolis, MN: University of Minnesota Press.

Ogbu, J. U., & Spring, J. (2008). *Minority status, oppositional culture, and schooling*. (Sociocultural, Political, and Historical Studies in Education series). New York: Routledge.

Quantz, R., Rogers, J., & Dantley, M. (1991). Rethinking transformative leadership: Toward democratic reform of schools. *Journal of Education, 173*(3), 96–118.

Rosaldo, R. (1993). *Culture and truth: The remaking of social analysis*. Boston, MA: Beacon Press.

Shields, C. M. (2010). Leadership: Transformative. In P. Peterson, E. Baker, & B. McGraw (Eds.), *International Encyclopedia of Education* (Vol. 5, pp. 26–33). Oxford: Elsevier.

Shields, C. M., & Edwards, M. (2005). *Dialogue is not just talk: A new ground for educational leadership* (Vol. 289). New York, NY: Peter Lang.

Thompson, G. L. (2004). *Through ebony eyes: What teachers need to know but are afraid to ask about African American students*. San Francisco, CA: Jossey-Bass.

5

Transformative Leadership and Identity

Anish Sayani

Diversity Blooms in Many Ways

Our university president was making her rounds and was scheduled to visit our education department for a check-in and update. To brandish the diversity and many exciting innovations and directions of our department, our educational department leaders reserved a few minutes from an already burgeoning agenda for new faculty and seconded instructors, of which I was one, to introduce themselves. Certainly, this was a laudable and respectful gesture on their part. The day before the meeting, one of the department leaders contacted me and, in passing, hinted that since diversity was the theme our department was featuring, I should mention my own diversity in my introduction.

Since diversity blooms in many ways, I consciously decided to instead position my identity as a student and teacher. As planned, during the meeting I was given the stage for a couple of minutes, whereby I introduced myself as a seconded teacher instructing five pre-service teacher-education courses. I also referenced that I was an experienced high school English and humanities teacher of 14 years, in both the Canadian and American school systems. As a doctoral student, I was examining issues in areas of leadership, identity, and critical narrative inquiry. Before I could sit down, I was requested by one of the department's educational leaders to share with the president and other faculty members who did not know me, "where I was from and the circumstances by which I arrived in Canada."

Raised to always respect authority and, specifically, to pay deference to one's teachers, I began, obsequiously, to stammer out a few incoherent words about 1972, Uganda, refugees, and coup d'état.

My chest hardened. My throat began to swell and choke my words. With a grimace, I sat down.

Later, I was told that the silence that followed my grimace was deafening. In the coming days, several colleagues and peers acknowledged and condemned how I was positioned that afternoon. Perhaps no one captured my feelings better than a decorated senior professor; she shook with anger as she declared with *disgust, "When will we not be required to wear our wounds in public? Shame on [the leader] for subject-ing you to that type of indignity."*

Are We Really Muslims?

I was asked to lead a discussion on "the perception of Islam in the West" for a high school class attending a weekly religious education (RE) class for Shia Ismaili Muslim[1] students. My fifteen-year-old nephew, Alykhan,[2] who attends St. Alexander High School, a prestigious all-boys' prep school with a prodigious reputation for academic excellence, was one of the 28 students present for the interactive session. Many students shared their personal experiences of how Islam is so easily essentialized and, consequently, mis-represented, not only in the media, but very frequently in their schools. Alykhan's story was one of many that day that left me confounded and disturbed. Alykhan began describing wistfully how he felt while his social studies teacher explained the principles of Islam to her class[3]:

> *She explained Islam using the five pillars approach: A good practicing Muslim must fast during Rama-dan; fulfill the Hajj; pay Zakat; et cetera. I was waiting for her to explain that although these were some of the key principles, there was much more to Islam than these five pillars. I was waiting for her to explain that Islam is not only a religion but constitutes civilizations, cultures, and ways of life. I wanted her to ask me or Armaan (another Ismaili Muslim student in the class) to share our understanding of Islam. I was waiting for her to explain how some people in power have made Islam a dangerous political term. Those explanations, however, never came. She talked about Islam in a way that made me wonder if both Armaan and myself were indeed Muslims.*
>
> *After class, I told her how I was feeling. She was very nice about it; she even told me that she, too, had a lot to learn about Islam. I mentioned to her that my mom could guest lecture about Islam. She nodded but never followed up.*
>
> *The shocker came after I wrote the unit test on Islam. She gave me a 65%! I talked to her after school and tried to explain my answers on the test. For one of the questions, I had written that religious authority did not only reside with Prophet Muhammad but, for Shia Ismaili Muslims, it also resides with the Imam[4] of the time. I tried to explain to her that pilgrimage was not only to the Kaaba in Mecca, but could also be seen as a daily pilgrimage to Jamat Khana[5] to recite daily prayers. I explained some other things I had written. She told me that all this may be so, but for the purposes of the test, I had to answer the questions according to the information found in the textbook.*

Although I was incredulous at what I had heard, for the rest of the students in that RE class, the story was prosaic and common knowledge. Sadly, most of them recognized in that story a parallel in their own lives.

Leadership and Identity

These two narratives capture a fundamental challenge in education today: How do educational leaders "negotiate" the critical issues of identity that form an integral aspect of the teaching and learning acts, without falling prey to an all-too-familiar tendency of essentialization? In the first narrative, although Anish was cognizant of the diversity theme underlying the university presi-dent's visit and consciously chose to represent himself using the elastic and indeterminate scripts of *student* and *teacher,* one of the educational leaders chairing the meeting, for a variety of different reasons—which we will speculate on at the end of this chapter—chose to see diversity through the scripts of *culture, homeland,* and *immigration,* which Anish purposely avoided. In the second narrative, Alykhan, and many of his Muslim peers, experienced an identity crisis. Alykhan's reli-gious identity—a central and defining feature of how he sees himself—was ironically erased in a curricular conversation that was ostensibly conceived not only to legitimate the extensive diversity of world faiths but, more importantly, to *normalize* the fact that people from all over the world have different ways of knowing. Instead of the curricular conversation in Alykhan's humanities class opening up to the fact that having people with diverse epistemologies in our great Nation is an absolute and unconditional virtue, the conversation insidiously shut down and unwittingly reinscribed a hegemonic essentialist construct of identity. For minoritized[6] students and teachers, this crisis of representation has profound negative consequences that range from alarming student failure rates (Dei, 2003; Dei, Mazzuca, McIsaac, & Zine, 1997; Gibson & Bhachu, 1991; Klassen & Georgiou, 2008) and pathologizing experiences (Bishop & Glynn, 1999; Delpit, 1993; Sayani, 2010; Scheurich & Skryla, 2003; Shields, Bishop, & Mazawi, 2005; Valencia & Solorzano, 1997) to marginalization, silence, shame, and overall anomie of both students and teachers (Dei, 2003; Delpit, 1993; Valencia & Solorzano, 1997).

In this chapter, I address the following question: How can transformative educational leaders help create spaces where identities can be explored and negotiated rather than essentialized? In a personal but critical attempt to address this question, I organize the chapter as follows. First, I highlight some key features of transformative leadership. Second, I critique the essentialist construct of identity ubiquitous in education today and propose an alternate, more robust construct of identity that transformative educational leaders can reason from when they make curricular, programmatic, policy, and fiduciary decisions for their schools. Third, I use dialogue—situated in a relational epistemology—to examine how transformative educational leaders can effectively lead in a context of diversity. Last, I use the opening two narratives, which I interleave at strategic moments, in order to wed theory with practice; to develop an intricate, nuanced, and relational perspective of transformative educational leadership and identity politics and to humanize the arguably disembodied nature of these theoretical discourses.

Transformative Educational Leadership

At the heart of school change and reform is effective educational leadership. Reforming the *habitus* (Bourdieu, 1990) of schools is unlikely without enlightened educational leadership (Robinson, Lloyd, & Rowe, 2008). During the last half of the 20th century, many innovative and promising educational theories have emerged (Shields, 2003) as alternatives to the traditional leadership paradigm, with its roots in scientific management and modernist thinking (Dantley, 2005; Foster, 1986; Hodgkinson, 1991; Sackney & Mitchell, 2002). These emerging educational leadership theories that are fashioning a new leadership paradigm are based on the fundamental assumption that "leadership highlights the capacity of individuals to shape the world and to have a say in determining their own destiny" (Ogawa, 2005, p. 91). Unlike the modernist leadership paradigm, which privileges reason at its center and emphasizes the discourse of "order, accountability, structure, systemization, rationalization, expertise, specialization, linear development, and control" (Cherryholmes, 1988, p. 4), the new leadership paradigm negates the very concept of center and emphasizes the discourse of uncertainty, ambiguity, difference, diversity, incommensurability, and pluralism. This epistemological turn has enabled scholars and researchers of educational administration and leadership to critically engage with axiological issues of diversity, difference, and pluralism that have for too long been silenced or pathologized by the hegemonic discourses of the positivist paradigm. In short, "traditional [educational] research," as Heck and Hallinger (2005) state, "has too narrowly focused on administrative processes and improvement while accepting the premises of an unjust educational system" (p. 234). *Au courant* educational leadership research, however, has become a moral enterprise (English, 2008; Furman, 2002) with an imperative to challenge primary inequities in our system (Anderson, 2004; Dantley, 2005; Heck & Hallinger, 2005; McKenzie et al., 2008; Sackney & Mitchell, 2002; Shields, 2003; Shields et al., 2005). By asking a rhetorical question, English (2005) emphasizes this point well:

> The problem of educational leadership is that it has been thoroughly saturated with the kind of thinking that has ignored social justice. . ..If the schools keep reinforcing the existing social order, with its inequities and injustices perpetuated, what service has education rendered to such an unjust society? (p. xi)

Many leadership theories from this new educational leadership paradigm that organizes for education and justice abound; among them are transformative, transformational, feminist, multi-cultural, democratic, critical, emancipatory (Shields, 2003), and moral or purpose-driven leadership (Dantley, 2005).[7] Of these, I believe that transformative educational leadership—a theory of leadership that Shields (2008, 2009) has further developed by drawing from multiple theories and disparate concepts—holds the most promise because, among other reasons which I elaborate on later in this chapter, it is perhaps the only leadership theory in education that underscores the centrality of dialogue and, as a corollary, the identity-shaping possibilities and responsibilities that ensue when leadership intersects with education.

Crediting the seminal work of Freire for inspiring the ideals of transformative leadership, Shields (2009) argues that at the heart of this leadership theory are "the twin concepts of critique and possibility" (p. 5). The concept of critique —leaders confronting moral issues of schools that disproportionately benefit some students and fail others—must be balanced with the concept of possibility—leaders ensuring that hope, an "ontological need" (Freire, 2004, p. 2), lights the path of all their aims, intents, and actions—for transformative leaders to escape being "trapped in a malaise of powerlessness" (Quantz, Rogers, & Dantley, 1991, p. 107) and to believe, ardently, that change is always possible.

Elements that undergird the theory of transformative leadership include "the need for social betterment, for enhancing equity, and for a thorough reshaping of knowledge and belief structures" (Shields, 2009, p. 3). She continues:

> [transformative leadership] recognizes the need to begin with critical reflection and analysis and to move through enlightened understanding to action—action to redress wrongs and to ensure that all members of the organization are provided with as level a playing field as possible —not only with respect to access, but also with regard to academic, social, and civic outcomes. (p. 6)

It is not enough for educational leaders to help improve the academic achievement of minoritized students; they must also ensure that all their students are critically conscious of inequities that persist in our society and that they have the necessary knowledge, abilities, and opportunities to redress these inequities. Without increasing the political, social, and cultural capital of *all* students, the hegemonic practices that have invaded and pathologized the social spaces of the disenfranchised will continue to prevail.

Two hallmarks of transformative leadership are that it is an "engaged" (Shields, 2009, p. 2) and a dialogical form of leadership, which I will elaborate on extensively later in the chapter. Unlike transformational leadership (Leithwood & Jantzi, 1990), which it is often confused with, transformative leadership champions an activist agenda. Transformative leaders understand that education is a "terrain where power and politics are given fundamental expression" (Giroux, 1985, p. viii) and that it is precisely in this terrain—deeply engaged in the field with all the stakeholders—that leaders must advocate for those who are denied their rights of thought, belief, opinion, participation, and expression. In an era of high-stakes accountability and public transparency, transformative leaders are not fearful of speaking out. They realize that they are part of the culture of power (Delpit, 1993): They were educated in it and currently work within its authority and influence. Hence, it is their responsibility to use the power apparatuses they are privileged with to fight against the persistent inequities that beleaguer both schools and society.

Dialogical, as opposed to hierarchical, in their approach, transformative leaders orient their voices among other voices (Bakhtin, 1984) because they understand that their voices participate with other voices to represent the world. They attempt to listen and understand others, even if what they hear is contrary to their own ideas, values, and beliefs. Even in the tension of disagreement or conflict, transformative leaders are fully present to the "other," aspiring to understand and learn his or her worldview and context. Shields and Edwards (2005) elaborate:

> As educational leaders, we must first and foremost focus on knowing ourselves. Then, conscious of our own voice—sometimes muting it temporarily in order to hear others, sometimes silencing it altogether to set aside our positional authority and formal knowledge, we come more fully into dialogical relationship with those who live and work in our organizations. But sometimes, too, we must speak loudly and eloquently and share our insights, our understanding, and our wisdom for the good of community. Being a dialogic leader does not require losing oneself, but finding oneself in the richness of the polyphonic community. (p. 170)

Transformative leaders know when to speak and when not to speak. They understand that, sometimes, because of their position of authority, silence may be the best option to encourage others to speak. They also understand that, at other times, they have a responsibility to speak, forcefully, in a way that champions the rights, security, and dignity of the disenfranchised others. In essence, transformative leaders believe that no individual is bequeathed with the truth. Always mindful that meanings are created in dialogue, they maintain that no individual can ever see the entire picture or understand the totality of any situation. It is only when individuals share their perspectives; engage deeply, respectfully, and resolutely to understand each other; and invite the other to enter into their worldviews, which shape their perspectives, that meanings become relevant, inclusive, and wholly understood.

Identity

In this section, I examine and critique the prevailing theory of identity representation and construction—the essentialist construct—that undergirds current educational practice, and then propose an alternate, more robust, theory of identity—the postpositivist realist construct—that transformative educational leaders can reason from when they engage with the identities of others. A compass that I use to help navigate this discussion is Hall's (1997b) outwardly simple, but inwardly complex, definition of identity: "Identities are the names we give to the different ways we are positioned by, and position ourselves. . ." (p. 52). He continues, "we should think of identity as a 'production', which is never complete, always in process, and always constituted within not outside of representation" (p. 51).

Essentialist Construct of Identity

The essentialist construct of identity is most commonly based on the Enlightenment subject—which is seen as stable, unified, determinate, and complete (Hall, 1997a). Within this modernist paradigm, groups are identified by characteristics that are assumed and accepted as inherent and intrinsic (Dolby, 2000; Gosine, 2002). That is, groups are viewed as having an essence or "core" identity that unites the individuals that comprise the group. This group or cultural identity is based on a "collective of one true self, hiding inside the many other, more superficial or artificially imposed 'selves', which people with a shared history and ancestry hold in common" (Hall, 1997b, p. 51). These common historical experiences and joint cultural customs produce an identity of "one people," which anchors and defines the group. Simply put, "essentialism expresses itself through the tendency to see one social category (class, gender, race, sexuality, etc. . .) as determinate in the last instance for the cultural identity of the individual or group in question" (Moya, 2000, p. 80). Often, essentialism can be read as biological or natural (Woodward, 1997).

The politics of essentialization is complex and multidirectional. Who essentializes and who is essentialized are two questions that uncover the centrality of power that undergirds the discourses of representation and difference. Difference, in the modernist paradigm, has predominately been understood in the either-or realm of binary logic. Anything that is outside the habitus (Bourdieu, 1990) of the dominant group is considered different and referred to disparagingly as "other." Hall (1997b) claims that difference is negatively interpreted as the marginalization and exclusion of those who are seen as "other." Referencing Derrida, Laclau, and Butler, Hall (2000) states that,

> it is only through the relation to the Other, the relation to what it is not, to precisely what it lacks, to what has been called its constitutive outside that the 'positive' meaning of any term—and thus its 'identity'—can be constructed. (p. 17)

Alluding to the powerful and deeply entrenched concept of binaries, which is common to the modernist's system of thought, Hall argues that clear oppositions such as white-black, spiritual-material, and East-West are differentially weighted so that one constituent of the dichotomy is more authoritative or prized than the other (Woodward, 1997). One of the two terms in the dualism is situated as the "norm" while the other, contrasting term, is positioned as "abnormal." Similarly, the secondary term of the modernist's identity binary, self other, is positioned as "aberrant," "deviant," or "alien." Contrastingly, the first term in that binary, *"self,"* reflects the dominant point of view and is read as "legitimate," "natural", or "normal." The power differential inherent between the two terms results in the privileging of one term and the marginalizing of the other term. Hall (2000) quotes Laclau, who argues compellingly that the act of identity construction is an act of power:

> If. . .an objectivity manages to partially affirm itself it is only by repressing that which threatens it. Derrida has shown how an identity's constitution is always based on excluding something and establishing a violent hierarchy between the two resultant poles—man/woman, etc. . . . What is peculiar to the second term is thus reduced to the function of an accident as opposed to the essentiality of the first. It is the same with the black-white [sic] relationship, in which white [sic], of course, is equivalent to 'human being'. 'Woman' and 'black' are thus 'marks' (i.e., marked terms) in contrast to the unmarked terms of 'man' and 'white.' (p. 18)

Imposed and Self-Ascribed Essentialization

The most common form of essentialization, which I call *imposed* essentialization, arises when a dominant group ascribes characteristics of identity onto a minoritized group, claiming that these attributes best represent and describe all the people in that minoritized group. It can be even more severe than this: Groups can be seen to have an immutable and definite "essence" that characterizes their innate nature. Through the processes of signification and power, markers—which are usually derogatory—are affixed to a group of people that eventually become the defining features of that group.

The other form of essentialism, which I call *self-ascribed* essentialism, arises when minoritized groups resist their marginalization by reclaiming and unequivocally reaffirming their ethnic and national identities. Under the policies of multiculturalism (Fleras, 2009), colonized people, who have lost or concealed their identities for the purposes of survival, are now resurrecting these identities to counter their experiences of marginalization. May (1999) is precise:

> Such a conception may well be motivated by a principal concern to acknowledge positively cultural difference, to address historical and current patterns of disadvantage, racism and marginalization, and, from that, to effect the greater pluralization of the nation-state, particularly in its public sphere. (p. 21)

Similarly, to cope with the perceived fragmentation and dissolution of their societies as a result of "multiculturalism gone awry," dominant groups are also "soul-searching" for their old ethnic certainties. "We must return to our good old family values" and "Here, we speak English; if 'they' do not want to speak English, let them go back to where they came from" are examples of nostalgia for a culturally homogenous lost past or "golden age." The heritage "industry" (Woodward, 1997), which includes books, film, and media, not only packages an identity that most reflects the values of the dominant group but implicitly implies that this version of identity is the best and only acceptable version possible. In both cases, nevertheless, old ethnic certainties are reclaimed and naturalized in order for the minority or dominant groups to mobilize their social and political projects.

For a theory of identity that escapes the assaults of essentialism and begins to theorize the connections among social locations, representation, experience, cultural identity, materiality, and knowledge, I draw on the work of Mohanty's (1995, 2000) construction of postpositivist realist theory.

Postpositivist Realist Theory of Identity

The major claim of a postpositivist reality theory of identity states that "personal experience is socially and theoretically constructed, and it is precisely in this mediated way that it yields knowledge" (Mohanty, 2000, p. 31). Using examples from Scheman's illuminating essay, "Anger and the Politics of Naming" (1980), Mohanty argues that human experiences have a cognitive and theoretical component that must be recognized. Mohanty (2000) questions the validity of a fundamental assumption that is deeply embedded in many of the educational and counselling theories practiced in the field: Emotions are a private and an inner possession of a subject; these emotions have an inherent private logic that must be represented or released from the inner sanctum of that subject. Both Mohanty (2000) and Scheman (1980) argue that this assumption is flawed and must be reexamined. They posit that emotions become meaningful through the mediation of theoretical, political, and social frameworks that the subject employs for herself. That is, emotions and personal feelings do not have intrinsic or transparent meanings; they are, among other things, theoretical matters that rely on epistemologies to make sense. Mohanty (2000) explains:

> This new emotion, say, anger, and the ways it is experienced are not purely personal or individual. A necessary part of its form and shape is determined by the non-individual social meanings that the theories and accounts supply. It would be false to say that this emotion is the individual's own "inner" possession and that she alone has "privileged access" to its meaning or significance. Rather, our emotions provide evidence of the extent to which even our deepest personal experiences are socially

constructed, mediated by visions and values that are "political" in nature, that refer outward to the world beyond the individual. (p. 34)

This epistemic status of experience, then, eloquently attends to the essentialist predicament of cultural identity that postmodernism fails to address. That is, in this theoretically mediated form, it is not assured or guaranteed that my experiences will be similar to or the same as others from my social or cultural group. This argument forms the second important claim of a postpositivist realist theory of identity: A subject's experiences will shape, but not completely determine, the creation of his or her identity (Moya, 2000). Even though I may share core values and a similar lifestyle with others in my social group, my experiences are different because my meaning-making systems that allow me to interpret these experiences are particular to my individual history, context, and abilities. Moya (2000) is precise:

> Because the theories through which humans interpret their experiences vary from individual to individual, from time to time, and from situation to situation, it follows that different people's interpretations of the same kind of event will differ. (p. 82)

Hence, in the narrative *Are We Really Muslims?*, even though my nephew Alykhan was challenging his teacher's monolithic interpretation and understanding of Islam, his interpretation of Islam—the Shia Ismaili Muslim perspective—must not become essentialized, monolithic, or the privileged interpretation of Islam either. Although Alykhan's interpretation and perspective of Islam will converge in understanding with other Ismaili Muslims—particularly those of his age and developmental level—his interpretation is only one of many and cannot represent all Ismaili Muslims. Within any group of people that share a common bond, there will always be a plurality in interpretation of that bond. My personal meaning-making systems, which are shaped by so many factors, such as social location (as we will see below), will make sense of my group's common experiences differently than someone else who belongs to that group. Alykhan's interpretation of being an Ismaili Muslim, therefore, may differ in discernable ways from another fifteen-year-old Ismaili Muslim boy, who as a refugee, has moved to Vancouver from a war-torn Afghanistan. Both will affirm they are Ismaili Muslims, but how they express their personal faith may differ dramatically.

I must note that, like the Nobel Prize winner Ilya Prigogine's dissipative structures,[8] our meaning-making systems are not static and thus do not interpret experiences the same way every time. Although our meaning systems shape our understanding of the world, they, too, are shaped by that understanding and those experiences; this iterative process allows our meaning systems to continually evolve and adapt to new circumstances. To recap, postpositivist thought claims that experiences in their theoretically mediated form contain a "cognitive component through which we can gain access to knowledge of the world" (Moya, 2000, p. 81). It is these experiences that will influence the formation of a subject's identity.

The third important claim of a postpositivist realist theory of identity is that a person's experience will, for the most part, be determined by his or her social location in a given society (Moya, 2000). So, different social categories, such as race, gender, sexuality, and class, which together determine a person's social location, will influence her life experiences. Hence, an individual who is socially coded "Brown, Muslim, male, and heterosexual" will experience different situations, experiences, and realities than another individual who is socially coded "White, Christian, female, and heterosexual." Similarly, however, a Brown, heterosexual, Muslim male with abundant financial resources will have decidedly different experiences than a Brown, male, heterosexual Muslim with minimal or scarce financial resources. Obviously, these examples can multiply indefinitely;

however, of salience here is that social locations and their varying combinations will extensively influence the experiences of any individual.

It is crucial to clarify here that there does not exist an a priori relationship between experience and social location (Moya, 2000); not every individual in a particular social location will accrue the same or similar experiences. Social location does not beget specific knowledge that everyone in that social location shares. Rather, social locations may structure or organize certain circumstances, but inevitably, as mentioned earlier, it is how the individual theoretically interprets these circumstances that make it an "experience."

Let me employ Bourdieu's ingenious and discerning concept of habitus to clarify this point further. Bourdieu (1990) defines habitus as "a system of dispositions common to all products of the same conditionings" (p. 59). That is, habitus is a repository term for all the possible experiences—social, cultural, economic, religious, and so on—that help shape or forge an individual's identity. Using this concept, Bourdieu theorizes how individuals from a social group "acquire, as a result of their socialization, a set of *embodied* dispositions—or ways of viewing, and living in the world" (May, 1999, p. 28). Similarly then, social locations, like habitus, are "both shaped by, and also *shape,* objective social and cultural conditions which surround it" (May, 1999, p. 28). Nash (1999) deftly advances this point, which we can apply to our understanding of social locations:

> The habitus is thus a system of durable dispositions inculcated by objective structural conditions, but since it is embodied, the habitus develops a history and generates its practices, for some period of time, even after the original material conditions which gave rise to it have disappeared. (p. 184)

However, like habitus, social location is not structurally deterministic. Social locations do not singularly determine experiences and behaviours of individuals; instead, they orient rather than precisely shape the individual's actions (May, 1999). Thus, again like habitus, at the core of social locations is a varying degree of choice. Some choices may be restrained and others spurned by the different mixture of social locations and, subsequently, their ways of structuring and organizing the world. An individual's experience depends both on the nature of the social locations and the theoretically mediated interpretations of his or her position in those social locations. Bourdieu closes this point:

> Habitus, like every art of inventing. . .makes it possible to produce an infinite number of practices that are relatively unpredictable (like the corresponding situations) but [which are] also limited in their diversity. (quoted in May, 1999, p. 28)

The fourth major claim of a postpositivist realist theory is a logical inference from the first two claims: Since there is a cognitive element to experiences and experiences influence the formation of identities, then one can conclude that there is a cognitive element to identity. This is a critical point because, like postmodern thought that claims identities are fluid, mutable, and contradictory, postpositivist thought claims that a subject's identity can undergo many revisions and reinterpretations as his or her interpretations of experiences change over time. In other words, as subjects redescribe or reinterpret their experiences with their perpetually reconstituted and reflexive epistemological frameworks, they may change, in varying degrees, their views of themselves, others, or their circumstances.

To sum up, a postpositivist realist theory of identity—with its focus on the epistemic status of experience—provides transformative educational leaders with critical lenses to better apprehend the complexities of identity construction and representation without sliding into the allure and deception of essentialism. I now examine another conceptual framework that undergirds transformative educational leadership: polyphonic dialogue. I contend that transformative educational leaders help create spaces where identities can be explored and negotiated rather than essentialized when they engage in polyphonic dialogue.

Polyphonic Dialogue

To understand Bakhtin's notion of polyphony, I must first clarify, briefly, the larger concept of *dialogue* that contextualizes it. Bakhtin (1984)—a philosopher of language, a literary theorist, and a neologist—advances arguably the most formative work on dialogue. The following quote provides a quick précis of how Bakhtin (1984) views dialogic relations:

> I am conscious of myself and become myself only while revealing myself for another, through another, and with the help of another. The most important acts constituting self-consciousness are determined by a relationship toward another consciousness (toward a thou). . . . The very being of man (both external and internal) is the deepest communion. To be means to communicate. . . . To be means to be for another, and through the other, for oneself. A person has no internal sovereign territory, he is wholly and always on the boundary: looking inside himself, he looks into the eyes of another or with the eyes of another. . . . I cannot manage without another, I cannot become myself without another; I must find myself in another by finding another in myself (in mutual reflection and mutual acceptance). (p. 287)

For Bakhtin, dialogue is not only an instrument of communication, a conversation, or a medium to achieve a goal. It is, like relationships (Bakhtin, 1984; Buber, 1970; Sidorkin, 1999, 2002; Taylor, 1994; Thayer-Bacon, 2003; Wheatley, 1992; Wheatley & Kellner-Rogers, 1996), the very essence of being. It is a person's raison d'être. It is an orientation and desire to understand and be understood through the presence of and participation with the other. Bakhtin argues that, to fully exist, one must live in the dialogical.

Dialogue is not an instrumental approach or strategy for communication, but communication itself (Shields & Edwards, 2005). Unlike Saussure and other structuralists, Bakhtin posits that dialogue is more than a static triad of sender, message, and receiver. The message, for Bakhtin, is fluid and evolving, formulated and formulating as a result of what the speaker has already uttered, what he or she will utter, and the anticipation of what the speaker will or will not utter. Each message is uttered in a context, which has in its memory the dialogue partners themselves, the formulations and intentions of previous utterances, and possible future utterances which will contribute to the dialogue. There are multiple messages or viewpoints vying for understanding in a dialogue. This leads to Bakhtin's concept of *polyphony*.

Bakhtin, in explicating the literary work of Dostoevsky, describes polyphony (a concept appropriated from music) as a dialogic exchange of multiple voices that replaces the singularity of monologism by allowing disparate and conflicting voices to compete with one another. In Dostoevsky's polyphonic novels, all characters have an equal say; the author, who moderates between the voices of these characters and usually has the final word in more common homophonic novels, does not wield this power in a polyphonic novel. All the voices, including that of the author, are engaged in a dialogue; no one voice is privileged. The author does not take an omniscient point of view and does not preside as a higher authority. In fact, the author stands alongside the other characters, abdicating her "surplus of vision" (Danow, 1991). That is, the author surrenders her prescient knowledge of the novel's characters and their life trajectories, and instead participates in an ongoing dialogue as an equal. In Bakhtin's (1984) own words:

In his work a hero appears whose voice is constructed exactly like the voice of the author himself in a novel of the usual type. A character's word about himself and his world is just as fully weighted as the author's word usually is; it is not subordinated to the character's objectified image as merely one of his characteristics, nor does it serve as a mouthpiece for the author's voice. It possesses extraordinary independence in the structure of the work; it sounds, as it were, alongside the author's word and in a special way combines both with it and with the full and equally valid voices of other characters. (p.7)

This authorial position is "a fully realizable and thoroughly consistent dialogic position" (Bakhtin, 1984, p. 63), one in which the author has a dialogue *with*, not about, a character. The characters, in turn, engage in this to and fro, not as objects of the author's consciousness, but as *"free* people, capable of standing *alongside* their creator, capable of not agreeing with him and even of rebelling against him" [italics in original] (Bakhtin, 1984, p. 6). Clearly, the character, with respect to the author, in Buberian terminology, is not an *it* but a full and voluble *Thou* (Buber, 1970). So for Bakhtin, when one is engaged in a Thou dialogue, fully available to the speaker, to what he or she has uttered, and to what he or she will utter, one becomes part of "a genuine polyphony of fully valid voices" (Bakhtin, 1984, p. 6).

Bakhtin's concept of polyphony deepens not only our understanding of dialogue, in general, but also how dialogical relations should occur in schools. It not only buttresses our understanding that meanings in dialogue are coauthored but, more importantly, it also makes apparent that meanings occur at "an intersection of two consciousnesses" (p. 289). That is, meanings are created in dialogue on the edges and borders where two or more consciousnesses meet. Danow (1991) advances this thought:

Meanings as Truth may thus be said to belong to neither the self nor the other but inheres within an ideal third category, in which the word and intention of each are intermeshed but transcended. 'From the point of view of truth, there are no individual consciousnesses,' writes Bakhtin, suggesting that someone's earlier fragmented 'truth'—as well as the disintegrative self—are potentially made whole, if only fleetingly, by the interaction of several viewpoints. (p. 65)

In other words, meaning—or interpretative "truth"—does not belong to anyone; rather, it is a social construction born of dialogue and context with explicit material consequences. No one person is bequeathed with the truth; no one person can ever see the entire picture or understand the totality of any situation. No single voice has the scope or sweep to beget the truth (Bakhtin, 1984). It is only when individuals share their perspectives; engage deeply, respectfully, and resolutely to understand each other; and invite the other to enter into their worldviews that shape their perspectives, that meanings become relevant, inclusive, and wholly understood. It is, therefore, precisely in difference that a polyphonic dialogue can bring about a commonality of understanding. In that understanding, however, there must exist the potential for misunderstanding. In that understanding, there must exist the potential for controversy and dissonance. In that understanding, there must exist the potential for difference. Understanding, therefore, does not mean a single way of seeing or a unified viewpoint. It does not mean that everyone agrees and shares a similar perspective. Understanding harbours, in its composition, the possibility of incongruity. In fact, according to Bakhtin, "to understand something means to embrace two or more incongruous views on the subject" (quoted in Sidorkin, 2002, p. 168). Therefore, as we have seen, genuine understanding, which is robust enough to contain a surfeit of meanings and perspectives, is constructed at the intersections where many voices are engaged in a polyphonic dialogue.

In the process of polyphony, misunderstandings, misinterpretations, and miscommunication may occur; however, these setbacks must not hinder the "bigger" purposes of dialogue and understanding. What must occur is the inclusion of all possible voices. Different interpretations and perspectives drive the dialogue. As Sidorkin (2002) declares, "No existing statement is refused to enter the big dialogue or the polyphonic truth. . .any concept of truth implies both existence and exclusion of false statements" (p. 169). Hence, even if some voices are interpreted as disturbing, ignorant, or hopeless, they must have the space to be heard. Only in this deep diversity—where difference speaks in all her voices—can we begin to expand understanding. Bakhtin (1984) expands upon this:

> The essence of polyphony lies precisely in the fact that the voices remain independent and, as such, are combined in a unity of a higher order than in homophony. If one is to talk about individual will, then it is precisely in polyphony that a combination of several individual wills takes place that the boundaries of the individual will can be in principle exceeded. One could put it this way: the artistic will of polyphony is a will to combine many wills, a will to the event. (p. 21)

Of salience then is that in polyphony, when all voices have the freedom to engage in dialogue in all their candour, a "deep" understanding emerges that far exceeds any form of individual understanding. That is, when a group of voices interact in an intense dialogue of *I* and *Thou*, the resulting understanding of each voice eclipses any form of understanding arrived at individually. The understanding that issues from polyphony is rich in perspectives. It is an estuary thick with diverse viewpoints and context. Sidorkin (2002) is explicit in his explanation:

> If one wants to know the truth about something, one should attempt to solicit everything everyone has to say about it, make all these voices talk to each other, and include one's own voice as one among equals. One should listen to this big dialogue, not to get the main idea but only to get all the voices to address each other. . .Everyone can probably remember such a high-intensity conversation when all the opposing positions present themselves as distinct and yet really address each other. At a certain point, one notices that in order to really talk, the voices should implicitly include each other, echo each other, so that the difference 'travels down into depths,' ultimately splitting every individual voice. And just before it falls apart again, the truth emerges as in musical polyphony, where the multitude of voices forms a higher of harmony. (p. 170)

In no way, however, is this "deeper" and more robust understanding complete. Instead, the new understanding becomes a new starting point for further polyphonic dialogue. As mentioned earlier, polyphonic dialogue is a result of what the speaker has already uttered, what he or she will utter, and the *anticipation* of what the speaker will or will not utter.

Implications for Leaders

To this point, I have explicated some key features of transformative leadership. I have claimed that transformative leaders must use a more nuanced construct of identity to ensure they avoid essentializing the identities of their minoritized constituencies. I have also elucidated that dialogic interaction is the foundation of a transformative leader's ability to effectively lead in our rapidly shifting educational contexts. By using these two lenses—postpositivist realist theory of identity and polyphonic dialogue—to analyze the two narratives that prefaced this chapter, I conclude by illustrating how transformative educational leaders can, indeed, create spaces where identities are explored and negotiated rather than essentialized.

In *Diversity Blooms in Many Ways,* Anish wanted to represent himself using the identity scripts of *teacher* and *student*. To extricate himself from the discourses of affirmative action and minority hiring practices that have recently created dissention between departments and fault lines among many of the faculty members, he did not want to trade in the social locaters of culture, race, ethnicity, and religion. Anish was judicious in how he wanted to position himself in front of the university president and the department's faculty. Like the "White" students and faculty, who were present but did not acknowledge or feature their cultural background, Anish, too, in this circumstance, wanted to remain racially, ethnically, or culturally invisible. If everyone, including the "White" students and faculty, were asked to share their cultural background, perhaps Anish too would have participated. However, in this situation and given the optics of various faculty members, Anish wanted to represent his diverse identity as innocuously as possible. He did not want to be seen as an unofficial affirmative-action prop.

From postpositivist reality theory, we understand that among other factors, the experiences of an individual will help forge that person's identity. Importantly, the individual's identity is not fixed or ossified but indeterminate and fluid because the cognitive element of his or her identity affords that person to revisit and reinterpret past experiences, often leading to new ways of seeing him- or herself. As a minoritized instructor and student, Anish's collective experiences of indigent refugee life, racism, and covert marginalization in schools, his identity as a practicing Muslim living in a terrorist-obsessed continent, and a plethora of other negative experiences have helped forge his identity. The way he makes sense of his world—his epistemological framework—is very much shaped by these and other experiences. Some experiences, more than others, embed themselves in the memory of his mind, body, and spirit. For him, however, to choose only from a cultural frame—which from a mainstream perspective has predominately cast him as Other—to represent his diversity is limiting and unfair. If Anish wanted to represent himself from a cultural framework, he could have done so easily. However, to expect him to speak from this location in the name of diversity not only reinforces the essentialist binaries of Self and Other but reinscribes the hegemonic propensity of the "culture of power" (Delpit, 1993) that determines how he and "others" are positioned and represented. Given the circumstances that I have already shared, Anish deliberately chose to speak about his diversity from the locations of *teacher* and *student*. Because he knew his cultural and immigrant identity was an issue and that it needed to be made transparent by some educational leaders, he chose very much to make it a nonissue. He chose consciously not to play that game. He chose to use an unearned privilege from an invisible knapsack of privileges that "White people count on every day (MacIntosh, 1988). That, of course, did not work.

Ironically, even though he located himself in a noncultural way, he did so by consciously negating his cultural frame. He was profoundly aware of this fact. As he momentarily "erased" his cultural identity from a presentation that the department's educational leader expected him to manifest, Anish still spoke from the cultural frame. Behind each word that he spoke about his research and the courses he taught, he consciously and deliberately did not speak about his cultural and immigrant identity, which very much shaped his student and teacher identities. His cultural identity, however, was hiding behind every verbal intonation, pitch, and modulation. It became the secret code which his entire presentation could have been "re-read" (Hall, 1997a) Nonetheless, one of the department's educational leaders publicly positioned Anish to speak from his cultural frame, which he began to do but aborted once the violation of it paralyzed his speech.

The principles behind this incident can be very instructive to transformative educational leaders. Clearly, we, as educational leaders, must create spaces in schools where students can choose to speak from respectful locations of their choice. That is, we must provide opportunities for all students, but specifically minoritized students, to speak from positions they choose. Too often, we predetermine where students will speak from, how they will speak, and what they will say. When they do in fact speak, even if they say something different, we filter their meanings through our own deeply entrenched frameworks. We must be very careful, even vigilant, of how we construct this dialogue.

Let me say it another way: All students will speak from identities that have been shaped by myriad forces. For minoritized students, in particular, their identities are, too often, essentialized. That is, there is a tendency, as we have seen, for educational leaders from a dominant group to ascribe characteristics of identity onto a minoritized group, claiming that these attributes best represent all the people in that minoritized group. Through the processes of signification and power—apparent in the authority of the curriculum, common pedagogical practices, and various multicultural school programs and policies—markers are fixed to groups of students that become the defining features of that group. As a result, the individual lives and experiences of the students trapped under the heavy weight of these essentializing markers are predominately denied, rejected, or pathologized (Sayani, 2010; Shields et al., 2005).

We must see student identities differently. As I have already explained, students' personal experiences are socially and theoretically constructed. These experiences are theoretically mediated in many different ways so that a student, even though she belongs to a similar cultural or faith-based group, or may share a similar social location, does not necessarily share similar or the same experiences as others from her group or social location. For example, in the narrative *Are We Really Muslims?*, even though Alykhan may share core Ismaili Muslim values and a similar lifestyle with other Ismaili Muslims, such as Armaan, Alykhan's experiences are different because his meaning-making system—which allows him to interpret these experiences—is particular to his history, context, and ability. We must give our students a choice to speak from identities—epistemological frameworks—of their choice. As educational leaders, we should not always equate diversity with culture or expect our students to speak from a cultural framework. Depending on the circumstances, as we saw in Anish's case, to expect students to speak from this location every time diversity is the focus could have the opposite effect— reinforcing the essentializing binaries of self and other. Not giving minoritized students a choice of where they want to speak from and what terms of reference they want to use to express their own diversity is reinforcing the hegemonic project of determining how Others are presented. Minoritized students, whose epistemological frameworks continue to be shaped by their previous experiences and social locations, will speak from these diverse locations anyway; ensuring they have a choice of how best to represent themselves, how they choose to interpret events, and how they best learn are the more faithful markers of a committed, pluralist society. Educational leaders equipped with this interpretation of identity would not only eschew the perils of essentialism but, more importantly, would begin to create safe spaces where all students and teachers could profitably explore and negotiate their identities.

In *Diversity Blooms in Many Ways*, it is very easy to accuse the department's educational leader of essentializing identities, exploiting or exotizing difference, or even reinscribing the hegemonic tendency to determine how others are represented. However, to come to any of these conclusions without engaging him in the type of dialogue that Buber, Bakhtin, Sidorkin, and others advocate would be unprincipled, unjust, and unfair. Clearly, the very act of truly listening to him and encountering him as a Thou (Buber, 1970) would provide us with an opportunity to understand his intentions and motivations. If he, too, reciprocates with a commitment to a polyphonic dialogue, then the potential exists for new meanings and new understandings, which occur at "an intersection of two consciousnesses" (Bakhtin, 1984, p. 289). Genuine understanding that is robust enough to contain a surfeit of meanings and perspectives about this issue can only be constructed at the intersection where his voice, my voice, and others who care to join engage in this polyphonic dialogue. Undoubtedly, the possibility for disagreement is sizable, but this should not impede the process of dialogue and understanding; as Bakhtin states, "to understand something means to embrace two or more incongruous views of the subject" (quoted in Sidorkin, 2002, p. 168). Of salience here is that each perspective, each voice, is genuinely listened to and considered judiciously in hopes of precipitating a "deep" understanding that far exceeds any form of individual understanding. If mutual agreement or consensus results, wonderful; if it does not, our different points of view will have *changed* us by the very presence of another point of view. We may still disagree with each other, but we will have explored each other's reasons and rationales for thinking that way. The memory of this dialogue, the insights gleaned from both the dialogue and the incident, and the symbolic and material consequences resulting from the incident itself will not only determine the future actions of both me and the department's educational leader, but they will further shape and deepen our identities and epistemological frameworks so that we can negotiate effectively—or ineffectively—other circumstances of this ilk.

In our world of rapid change, people with differing identities mix and mingle, shoulder to shoulder, in ways that were once inconceivable. In these inevitable encounters, how we honour, encourage, and strengthen difference will determine the health of our society and the promise of democracy. As educational leaders, we have been entrusted with this imperative. It is then incumbent on us, as transformative educational leaders, to create programmatic, policy, curricular, and pedagogical spaces where all whom we lead can speak from identities of their choice with integrity and responsibility. I submit we can begin to achieve some measure of success by using the two lenses of postpositivist realist theory of identity and polyphonic dialogue that I have examined in this chapter to enrich our understanding and practice of transformative leadership.

Notes

1. "The Shia Imami Ismaili Muslims, generally known as the Ismailis, belong to the Shia branch of Islam. The Shia form one of the two major branches of Islam, the Sunni being the other. The Ismailis live in over 25 different countries, mainly in Central and South Asia, Africa and the Middle East, as well as in Europe, North America and Australia" (Institute of Ismaili Studies, 2011, p.1). For more information, please see: http://www.iis.ac.uk/WebAssets/Small/The%20Ismaili%20Community/ismaili_community.pdf

2. All the names of people and institutions in these narratives are pseudonyms.

3. Quotes reconstructed from memory.

4. Spiritual leader.

5. Persian word for "House of prayer."

6. I employ in this chapter the term "*minoritized*" in the same way Shields et al. (2005) define it: "the term . . . minoritized stress[es] the importance of institutional and societal power structures that have marginalized a group that by virtue of sheer numbers alone (some could argue) should have the dominant, legitimate, decision-making voice" (p. 59).

7. See Shields (2003) for a concise description and comparison of each leadership theory.

8. Wheatley (1992) describes dissipative structures as living systems that regenerate themselves to higher levels of self-organization in response to environmental demands. She states, "He [Prigogine] called these systems dissipative structures because they dissipate their energy in order to recreate themselves into new forms of organization. Faced with amplifying levels of disturbance, these systems possess innate properties to reconfigure themselves so that they can deal with the new information. For this reason, they are frequently called self-organizing or self-renewing systems" (p. 89).

References

Anderson, G. L. (2004). William Foster's legacy: Learning from the past and reconstructing the future. *Educational Administration Quarterly, 40*(2), 240–258.

Bakhtin, M. (1984). *Problems of Dostoevsky's poetics.* Minneapolis: University of Minnesota Press. H. Tiffin (Eds.), *The post-colonial studies reader* (pp. 206–209). New York: Routledge.

Bishop, R., & Glynn, T. (1999). *Culture counts: Changing power relations in education.* Palmerston North, NZ: Dunmore.

Bourdieu, P. (1990). *The Logic of practice.* Cambridge: Polity Press.

Buber, M. (1970). *I and Thou.* New York: Charles Scribner.

Cherryholmes, C. (1988). *Power and criticism.* New York: Teachers College Press.

Danow, D. K. (1991). *The thought of Mikhail Bakhtin: From word to culture.* New York: St. Martin's Press.

Dantley, M. (2005). Moral leadership: Shifting the management paradigm. In F. W. English (Ed.), *The Sage handbook of educational leadership advances in theory, research, and practice.* Thousand Oaks, CA: Sage Publications.

Dei, G. J. S. (2003). Schooling and the dilemma of youth disengagement. *McGill Journal of Education, 38*(2), 241–256.

Dei, G. J. S., Mazzuca, J., McIsaac, E., & Zine, J. (1997). *Reconstructing "dropout": A critical ethnography of the dynamics of black students' disengagement from school.* Toronto: University of Toronto Press.

Delpit, L. (1993). *Other people's children: Cultural conflict in the classroom.* New York: The New Press.

Derrida, J. (2000). *Différance.* In P. Du Gay, J. Evans, & P. Redman (Eds.), *Identity: A reader* (pp. 87–93). London: Sage Publications and the Open University.

Dolby, N. (2000). Changing selves: Multicultural education and the challenge of new identities. *Teacher College Record, 102*(5), 898–912.

English, F. (2008). *The art of educational leadership: Balancing performance and accountability.* Thousand Oaks, CA: Sage Publications.

Fleras, A. (2009). *The politics of multiculturalism.* New York: Palgrave Macmillan.

Foster, W. (1986). *Paradigms and promises.* Buffalo, NY: Prometheus.

Freire, P. (2004). *Pedagogy of hope: Reliving pedagogy of the oppressed.* London and New York: Continuum.

Furman, G. (2002). The 2002 UCEA presidential address. *UCEA Review, 45*(1), 1–6.

Gibson, M. A., & Bhachu, P. K. (1991). The dynamics of decision making: A comparative study of Sikhs in Britain and the United States. In M. A. Gibson & J. U. Ogbu (Eds.), *Minority status and schooling: A comparative study of immigrant and involuntary minorities* (pp. 63–95). New York: Garland.

Giroux, H. (1985). Introduction. In P. Freire, *The politics of education.* (pp. viii–xxvi). Westport, CT: Bergin & Garvey.

Gosine, K. (2002). Essentialism versus complexity: Conceptions of racial identity construction in educational scholarship. *Canadian Journal of Education, 27*(1), 81–99.

Hall, S. (1997a). *Representation: Cultural representations and signifying practices.* London: Sage.

Hall, S. (1997b). Cultural identity and diaspora. In K. Woodward (Ed.), *Identity and difference* (pp. 51–58). London: Sage Publications.

Hall, S. (2000). Who needs identity? In P. Du Gay, J. Evans, & P. Redman (Eds.), *Identity: A reader* (pp. 15–30). London: Sage Publications and the Open University.

Heck, R., & Hallinger, P. (2005). The study of educational leadership and management: Where does the field stand today? *Educational Management Administration and Leadership, 33*(2), 229–244.

Hodgkinson, C. (1991). *Educational leadership: The moral art.* Albany: State University of New York Press.

Institute of Ismaili Studies. (2011). *The Ismaili Community.* Retrieved from http://www.iis.ac.uk/WebAssets/Small/The%20Ismaili%20Community/ismaili_community.pdf

Klassen, R. M., & Georgiou, G. K. (2008). Spelling and writing self-efficacy of Indo-Canadian and Anglo-Canadian early adolescents. *Journal of International Migration & Integration, 9*(3), 311–326. Retrieved from DOI 10.1007/s12134–008-0068-6

Leithwood, K., & Jantzi, D. (1990). Transformational leadership: How principals can help to reform school cultures. *School effectiveness and school improvement. 1*(4), 249-280.

MacIntosh, P. (1988). *White privilege and male privilege: A personal account of coming to see correspondences through work in women's studies.* (Working paper no. 189). Wellesley College Center for Research on Women, Wellesley, MA.

May, S. (1999). Critical multiculturalism and cultural difference: Avoiding essentialism. In S. May (Ed.), *Critical multiculturalism: Rethinking multicultural and antiracist education* (pp. 11–41). London : Falmer Press.

McKenzie, K. B., Christman, D., Hernandez, F., Fierro, E., Capper, C., Dantley, M., Gonazlez, M., Cambron-McCabe, N., & Scheurich, J. (2008). From the field: A proposal for educating leaders for social justice. *Educational Administration Quarterly, 44*(1), 111–138.

Mohanty, S. P. (1995). Epilogue. Colonial legacies, multicultural futures: Relativism, objectivity, and the challenge of otherness. *PMLA 110*(1), 108–118.

Mohanty, S. P. (2000). The epistemic status of cultural identity: On *Beloved* and the postcolonial condition. In P. M. L., Moya, & M. R. Hames-Garcia (Eds.), *Reclaiming identity: Realist theory and the predicament of postmodernism* (pp. 67–101). Berkeley, CA: University of California.

Moya, P. M. L. (2000). Postmodernism, "Realism," and the Politics of Identity: Cherrie Moraga and Chicana Feminism, In P. M. L. Moya, & M. R. Hames-Garcia (Eds.), *Reclaiming identity: Realist theory and the predicament of postmodernism* (pp. 67–101). Berkeley, CA: University of California.

Nash, R. (1999). Bourdieu, 'habitus', and educational research: Is it all worth the candle? *British Journal of Sociological Education, 20*(2), 175–187. Retrieved from DOI: 10.1080/01425699995399

Ogawa, R. T. (2005). Leadership as social construct: The expression of human agency within organizational constraint. In F. W. English (Ed.), *The Sage Handbook of Educational Leadership Advances in Theory, Research, and Practice* (pp. 89–108). Thousand Oaks, CA: Sage Publications.

Quantz, R. A., Rogers, J., & Dantley, M. (1991). Rethinking transformative leadership: Toward democratic reform of schools. *Journal of Education, 173*(3), 96–118.

Robinson, V. M. J., Lloyd, C. A., & Rowe, K. (2008). The impact of leadership on student outcomes: An analysis of differential effects of leadership types. *Educational Administration Quarterly, 44*(5), 635–674. Retrieved from DOI: 10.1177/0013161X08321509

Sackney, L., & Mitchell, C. (2002). Postmodern expressions of educational leadership. In K. Leithwood & P. Hallinger (Eds.), *The second international handbook of educational leadership and administration* (pp. 881–913). Dordrecht, NL: Kluwer.

Sayani, A. (2010). *Pathologies and complicities: High school and the identities of disaffected South Asian "brown boys"* (Unpublished doctoral thesis). University of British Columbia, Vancouver.

Scheman, N. (1980). Anger and the politics of naming. *Women and Language in Literature and Society.* Ed. Sally McConnell-Ginet, Ruth Borker, and Nelly Furman. New York: Praeger.

Scheurich, J. J., & Skryla, L. (2003). *Leadership for equity and excellence.* Thousand Oaks, CA: Corwin Press.

Shields, C. M. (2003). *Good intentions are not enough: Transformative leadership for communities of difference.* Lanham, MD: Scarecrow/Technomics.

Shields, C. M. (2008). *Courageous leadership for transforming schools: Democratizing practice.* Norwood, MA: Christopher-Gordon.

Shields, C. M. (2009). Leadership: Transformative. In E. Baker, B. McGaw, & P. Peterson (Eds.), *International encyclopedia of education* (3rd ed.) Oxford: Elsevier.

Shields, C. M., Bishop, R., & Mazawi, A. E. (2005). *Pathologizing practices: The impact of deficit thinking on education.* New York: Peter Lang.

Shields, C. M., & Edwards, M. M. (2005). *Dialogue is not just talk: A new ground for educational leadership.* New York: Peter Lang.

Sidorkin, A. M. (1999). *Beyond discourse: Education, the self, and dialogue.* Albany, NY: SUNY Press.

Sidorkin, A. M. (2002). *Learning relations.* New York: Peter Lang.

Taylor, C. (1994). *Multiculturalism and the politics of recognition.* Princeton: Princeton University Press.

Thayer-Bacon, B. J. (2003). *Relational "(e)pistemologies.* New York: Peter Lang.

Valencia, R. R., & Solorzano, D. G. (1997). Contemporary deficit thinking. In R.R. Valencia (Ed.), *The evolution of deficit thinking* (pp 124–133). Washington, DC: Falmer Press.

Wheatley, M. (1992). *Leadership and the new science.* San Francisco, CA: Berrett-Koehler Publishers.

Wheatley, M., & Kellner-Rogers, M. (1996). *A simpler way.* San Francisco, CA: Berrett-Koehler Publishers

Woodward, K. (Ed.). (1997), *Identity and difference.* London: Sage Publications.

6

Looking at Transformative Leadership Through the Concept of Ethics

Lyse Langlois

When our intentions are egotistical, the fact that our actions might seem good does not guarantee that they are positive or ethical.
—*Dalai Lama*

In the last forty years, leadership models have abounded. In a thematic *American Psychologist* issue dealing with the topic, Bennis (2007) states that, in spite of the insight gained into the concept, researchers have yet to identify a highly accurate vision of leadership or to agree on what constitutes a leader today. For Burns, the problem of properly identifying leadership is rooted primarily in the crisis resulting from the mediocrity and irresponsibility of those in power (1978, 3).

In recent years, headlines have reported several scandals related to financial embezzlement, corruption, conflict of interest, and collusion in the political, administrative, and financial arenas. These scandals simply confirm Burns's words. There have been a number of repercussions, but they have resulted primarily in weakening the very concept of leadership, to the extent that many citizens have begun to lose faith in our establishments. The school system has not been spared from this. Many questions about resource allocation and school dropout rates increasing alarmingly in several countries are but telltale signs of the importance of changing the way we manage organizations and human resources.

For Montréal management guru Henri Mintzberg,[1] the main causes of the recession that recently shook the world do not reside in economic factors, but in organizational management. Organizations are social institutions, or communities, for Mintzberg; they are at their best when human beings are committed to working together in a spirit of cooperation, respect, and trust. For Mintzberg, the entire institution collapses when these conditions are no longer met.

These findings are part of an increasingly complex context faced by today's leaders. Some want to make sustainable changes, but they must consider new factors[2] that have had very little impact on their management practices to date. Maintaining a practice of "in silo" leadership dissociated from current challenges is a major risk for organizations and their development.

Changes currently observed are part and parcel of a reportedly knowledge-based society where the emphasis on knowledge and skills is an important strategic and economic issue. Therefore, the development of a knowledge-based economy is a determining factor that is forcing organizations and managers not only to introduce new work and management practices but also to review the way they administer their organizations. Such innovation is, for the most part, strongly questioned when it does not appear sustainable to organizations. Individual commitment, often instrumental in achieving these changes, implies the mobilization of workers who might become involved but not at any price or in any way. As a result, developing organizations depend progressively more on ever-increasing human capital, in the sense that the people with this capital are more and more educated, specialized, and experienced. The move from an industrial society to a knowledge-based society emphasizes the contrast between two visions of work: individuals carrying out well-defined tasks versus individuals accomplishing intellectual work that is focused on solving complex problems requiring autonomy and freedom of action.

Indeed, not only will leaders in a knowledge-based society have to exhibit management skills, but they will also require special skills to support and stimulate new professionals in their intellectual work in a sustainable manner. We believe that the concept of ethical leadership is an important part of transformative leadership and represents an avenue filled with opportunities to follow this trajectory towards the knowledge-based society currently establishing itself.

The purpose of this chapter is to explore the concept of ethics as an essential condition to exercising transformative leadership. First, this concept is defined and, secondly, the social regulation that it mirrors is highlighted. Once these concepts are detailed, the potential links between ethics and the concept of transformative leadership are demonstrated, supported by the research work that we have been conducting in the field of applied ethics and school management for several years.

The Rise of Ethics: The Codes

In recent years, the inclusion of ethics has been observed in most industrialized countries through the development of codes of conduct. In 2001, the Organisation for Economic Co-operation and Development (OECD)[3] identified no less than 256 codes in both individual businesses and sector organizations. These codes constitute but a fraction of all the codes promoted and implemented in organizations. Ballet and De Bry (2001, 372) estimated that 80% to 93% of large businesses in the United States have a code or an ethics charter. This percentage is 77% for Japan and 62% for France (Gendron, 2005). However, ethics cannot be reduced to a code; ethics are a process in which it is important to clarify related terms to establish a common language.

The Concept of Ethics: Specifications and Confusion

There is agreement in philosophy to identify ethics as the science and study of morality. In this context, ethics are viewed as an intellectual discipline offering tools for reflection. Ethics can also be approached in terms of specific language, such as vocabulary, concepts, or reasoning modes, in order for those who use ethics to identify and gain knowledge of certain fundamental aspects of the human experience.

In the concept of applied ethics, ethics become a process allowing the analysis of underlying principles, such as a decision that leads to specific action. As such, ethical analysis applies to norms (interdictions, possibilities) that guide human action, such as the practical values and rules making one choose one particular path over another, and the moral principles that individuals attempt to respect in their relations with themselves and others (Langlois, 2004, 2008).

However, the concept of ethics can be destabilized depending on the approach some may have, such as the ethics of virtue (Aristotle, McIntyre), consequentialism, teleology, or simply for the principle of precaution (Jonas). There are multiple ethical movements and sometimes it is difficult to find one's way around them, especially when individuals in a position of authority wish to impose their ethical practices. How does one judge whether an action is really appropriate or not? What is good for one person is not necessarily good for someone else. In the light of the aforementioned approaches and the wide range of interpretations likely to be made regarding ethics and morality, we suggest relying on the precision given by French philosopher Monique Canto-Sperber, who affirmed that ethics and morality are synonymous because they both refer to reflecting on action and whether it is good or just. Their essential proximity lies in the fact that they are back-to-back with a process of reflection, critique, and justification (Canto-Sperber, 2001).

Within this perspective, ethics aim at better understanding reality, driving deliberation, and allowing one to justify one's decisions, namely to be responsible for one's actions. This perspective involves placing one's moral conscience and imagination at the forefront of action as justified by reason. Ethics mean questioning, which involves reference points for reflection on leads to responses that are clarified during one's reflection process.

Ethical Distinction, Law, and Professional Ethics: Which Regulations?

Ethics move from bottom to top: The bottom represents civil society and the top, the state, which translates into a self-regulatory force. This requires self-control and discipline, in terms of taking action. This process is different than the law, which refers to a collection of norms affecting people and groups from a hetero-regulatory perspective. The law moves from top to bottom, which can be translated into a hetero-regulatory force. Conduct irrespective of established norms is liable to sanctions. To live together in harmony and take into account the different interests of individuals making up a given society, a regulatory framework is needed to administer our conduct with one another. Naturally, this framework provides an indication of things to do and not do, while ethics provide a meaning—the why and how, or the substance that underlies our relationships with others. As concerns professional ethics, this relates to responsibilities imposed on professionals through the exercise of their function (G. Giroux, 1997). When professional ethics are imposed on professionals, they are integrated into the scope of a hetero-regulatory vision. Furthermore, professional ethics can be part of a self-regulatory purpose when values are defined by members in a voluntary support process. The state develops by way of a code of hetero-regulatory practices, while civil society self-regulates through ethical practices. This paradigm of hetero-regulation (code of ethics or committee) or auto-regulation (autonomy and responsibility) allows the verification of what ethics are actually all about (G. Giroux, 1997, 46–47).

Ethical Derivatives and the Law

There is often confusion between ethics and the law, or worse, the taking over of ethics by the law, which in fact is a significantly perverse effect. The issue lies in wanting to codify ethics, which may result in the loss of their primary substance or original purpose as they are submerged in the mechanics and aim of the law. It is not unusual to see organizations wishing to pursue an ethical trajectory begin by establishing a code of conduct or issuing several standards to emphasize conduct that is considered acceptable. Such codification never reaches consensus, but it is imposed from top to bottom. In this case, the top represents the managers of an organization, and the bottom, employees. Once the code is established, updating it is futile, difficult, and worse yet, assimilated into forgotten procedures.

Institutionalizing ethics in structures and administrative practices is a major challenge. At first glance, it can be seen as an interesting way to empower individuals to respect their decisions or their conduct at work. The problem arises when one appoints a group of individuals or one individual in particular as responsible for establishing ethics at work. Deterioration observed in this type of situation refers to the weakening of individual responsibility and reliance on the group or person in charge of ethics. Thus, people without this responsibility are led to suspend their own moral judgment and delegate it to those responsible for ethics within the organization. We consider the establishment of so-called ethical codes as a kind of "ethical *technicization.*" This concept seems more similar to a deontological view— a list of rules to be followed—than to an ethical view, because these codes are contained in an immediate prolongation of legal texts. But, as Dufresne (2009) indicates:

> [. . .] to ensure the common good, all we have are ethics and the law. Even if some worshipers of the charters of law still exist, increasingly more people understand the limitations of the law. What is a right without a corresponding responsibility? What is left is ethics, but cut off from the transcendent, and reduced to its codes, and not condemned to increasingly resemble the law? [Translation] (para. X)

In human resources management, normative deontological and legal regulation is obviously widespread, as it helps decision making. It must be pointed out that the end purpose of this type of regulation is equality. In addition, apparent progress in equity has been observed. To illustrate such progress, what follows is an example demonstrating that the concept of equity originates from ethical concerns. For more than 15 years, several groups of women have claimed the right to pay equity. As a result of promoting this concept, some organizations have included the concept of equity in their regulations and applied it to particular working conditions, such as wages and tasks. Other civil society groups are also claiming major adjustments to specific values. These requests may change things and lead to legal acknowledgment (for instance, the abolition of racism, equality between women and men, and women's right to vote). Such claims are often rooted in a critical reflection process or major ethical concerns. More likely than not, these claims are shaped by an in-depth analysis that reveals the presence of injustice and disavowal of particular values.

But Where Are Ethics?

During a particular decision-making process, we noticed that a school administrator's first action was to check to see if there was a rule, a regulation, a directive, or a law that could be applied in the situation at hand. If administrators have such legal justification in hand, their decision will be in conformity with the regulatory framework in place and will constitute a fair decision. They will even claim that their decision is ethical. Thus, this regulatory framework will serve to dictate their conduct, while at times minimizing their reasoning, because the rule indicates what they should do to be within the law and to make their decision ethical. As explained above, ethics are not law.

In an opposite situation, when an issue or problem is in a grey area given the absence of normative perspective, is when we believe administrators are subject to an ethical test. In other words, they will have to reason on other bases to find what is just and acceptable to do in terms of the situation at hand. Therefore, they enter the ethical dimension quite similar to the claims and ethical concerns previously raised. What must be done in this situation when the norm provides no guidance? How will administrators proceed to deliberate and find the necessary perspective to justify their decision? Does what has been done still suit the situation? Is it still acceptable to behave this way in spite of the fact that the rule no longer seems to suit the current situation?

Here, ethics will play a paramount role in allowing leaders to turn towards organizational or professional values in order to justify their decisions. In a context where an organization has no clearly established value statements, inspiration and justification can become more difficult and generate some degree of arbitrary decision-making. If professional values are clearly enacted, they will provide food for reflection vis-a-vis other personal and social values. Thus, ethics will provide a broader view of the facts available by questioning what is best done under given circumstances and by looking at what is best understood as fair and acceptable. Thus, in a nebulous situation, ethics will serve to evaluate the potential stakes and consequences, therefore avoiding problems and or conflicts and making the best choice possible. This is where ethics find its true position, by being perceived as reflexive capacity. It sometimes takes a certain amount of courage to make a decision that does not benefit from a regulatory framework. Courage will be measured against elements that were considered and justifications offered for the validation of the decision. In this way, administrators assume responsibility in terms of their role and ethical responsibility, in each specific situation.

The words of Epictetus can help us better identify certain situations that make the work of educational administrators more complex: "*Some things* are up to us and *some* are not up to us." Wisdom lies in recognizing these situations, in having the ability of discernment to distinguish them and attempt to keep at least the ones within the administrator's power on an ethical trajectory.

Defining Reflective Ethics from a Critical Perspective

Following clarification of these concepts that are often juxtaposed, a definition of *reflective ethics* is proposed, based on a critical approach. Important links can even be made in the field of education by proposing critical ethics through references to the work of Paulo Freire, who became the most influential educator of the 20th century for his most-recognized work, *Pedagogy of the Oppressed* (1970). Several of the following premises of Freire's concept can apply to our concept of critical reflective ethics:

- The development and exercise of critical consciousness is the product of "critical educational work."

- The task of education as an instrument in the process of development of consciousness depends on two basic attitudes and activities: criticism and dialogue.

- A critical consciousness is typical of societies with a truly democratic structure.

These premises are in line with our definition of ethics as being a critical reflective ability involving various elements likely to guide an individual's thinking process and conduct. These elements may be personal, professional, or organizational values, rules, standards, or procedures.

In regards to the first premise, ethics are also self-regulatory. In other words, they call upon an individual's autonomy, moral responsibility, and exercise of personal and professional judgment. This critical thinking and discernment process raises the following questions:

- How should I behave in such a situation?

- What value should I choose?

- Is this the best decision to make?

- How will my decision affect me and others?

Ethical reflection is an attempt to promote some values, considered as significant by an individual, who will make a judgment following careful self-evaluation. Ethics are also flexible in character because they are rooted in reality and adapted to given circumstances, contrary to rights and professional ethics, which are more static. Therefore, several authors consider ethics to be a mode of interrogation and questioning aimed at finding moral certainties that remain uncertain nonetheless (Bourgeault, 2004; Legault, 2004). The challenge during such internal deliberation is to find the meaning or credible and reasonable arguments likely to provide public justification without presenting the decision as absolute truth.

Regarding Freire's second premise, authors such as Patenaude and Legault suggest initiating collective questioning based on dialogue and deliberation. This process aims at finding collectively what makes sense and what would constitute the best decision to make in a given situation (Legault, 2004). Exchanging ideas with others is important in ethics because, as philosopher Bégin suggests, ethics are a mode of relation with others that develops with day-to-day situations and challenges (Bégin, 2004).

Freire's last premise can be linked to ethics of critique, as proposed by Starratt (1991). The ethics of critique is founded in the "critique theory." This way of thinking is drawn from the Frankfurt school of philosophy and researchers such as Theodor Adorno (1973), Jürgen Habermas (1987), Max Horkheimer (1974), Henry Giroux (2003) and Iris M. Young (1990), who were interested in perspectives offered by the theory. The tenets of this approach look to uncover injustice occasionally found in social relations or created by laws, the structure of an organization, or language used to obscure the real problem or serving to dominate a relationship. In short, people reflecting on ethics were looking to discover all situations that could benefit one person or a group to the detriment of another person or another group. For Starratt, the ethics of critique serves to discover if one group is dominating another group and to show how this state of affairs comes about, in order to correct injustice (1991).

Four questions aimed at understanding the relation of power are connected to ethics of critique: Who benefits from this situation? Is there a dominant group? Who defines the way in which things should be structured? Who defines what should be valued or undervalued? When injustice is uncovered, those who adopt this ethical perspective tend to sensitize others in order to obtain a better balance in the distribution of social benefits. Starratt states that "their basic stance is ethical for they are dealing with questions of social justice and human dignity, although not with individual choices" (Starratt, 1991, 189). The intention of those acting according to the ethics of critique is to ensure that organizational and social arrangements are more in line with the rights of all humans. Their goal is also to allow people concerned by these arrangements or privileges to express their opinion regarding already-made decisions that affect one group in particular. One way of describing this is through the concept of *transformative leadership*.

Transformative Leadership

Several authors draw the concept of transformative leadership from the work of Burns (1978), Bass (1985), and Conger and Kanungo (1987). For some, transformative leadership is a mere derivative of transformational leadership. However, Burns generally uses the terms *transforming* and *transformational* instead of *transformative*. Carolyn Shields (2003, 2008, 2009, 2010) considers *transformative leadership* as distinct from transactional and transformational leadership. Foster (1987); Quantz, Rogers, and Dantley (1991); and Weiner (2003) consider transformative leadership in the same way. Transformative leadership is distinguished from other forms of leadership in that it takes as its starting point recognition and acknowledgement of the material disparities and inequities in the wider society and how they impinge on the ability of schools to adequately and equitably educate all students. Transformative leadership therefore recognizes the need for leaders to deconstruct and reconstruct knowledge frameworks that generate inequity; to understand and challenge the ways in which power and privilege create and sustain inequity; to focus on liberation, emancipation, democracy, and justice; to emphasize both the private and the public good; and to demonstrate moral courage and activism (Shields, 2010).

During the Global Development of Feminist Leadership conference held in South Africa in 1997, the concept of transformative leadership was highlighted as part of the efforts of several women working within communities to abolish prejudice and eliminate social inequalities. They take positive action, leading to the transformation of the present inequalities between women and men in all forms and at all the levels of society. Their actions are closely related to the definition proposed by Shields (2010) regarding transformative leadership, and to the ideas of Quantz et al. (1991), who invite leaders in agreement with this perspective to reduce the "undemocratic power relationship and use their power to transform present social relations" (1992, 102–103). Transformative leadership is defined by Shields (2010) as follows:

> Transformative leadership, therefore, recognizes the need to begin with critical reflection and analysis and to move through enlightened understanding to action—action to redress wrongs and to ensure that all members of the organization are provided with as level a playing field as possible—not only with respect to access but also with regard to academic, social, and civic outcomes. (p. 573)

The Ethics of Critique and Transformative Leadership

After clarifying the concept of ethics and providing an operational definition of transformative leadership that is rooted in Shields's work, we would like to highlight a few research results related to Shields's concept of transformative leadership. In a recent article, the author confirms the existence of a corpus of knowledge regarding this concept, which is, however, creating confusion because of its wide range of orientations. She points out that there is very little empirical data to make this concept operational: "Few studies have operationalized transformative leadership and examined its effect in real-life settings" (2010, 573). Hence, we attempted to add more insight by operationalizing the element of ethics, in the hope that it will serve to clarify some aspects of transformative leadership.

Ethics of Critique: Potentially Complementary

Over several years, we conducted research on organizational ethics with educational leaders. This research was carried out with several groups of school administrators. Four major research stages were developed based on a systematic program. Here is a summary of the main stages of this program, which was started in 1995.

The first stage consisted of determining the presence of ethical dimensions in decision-making practices arising from ethical dilemmas. An interview guide was validated based on ethical dilemmas (Langlois, 1997). A qualitative method was used to collect all data. At that stage, a typology was constructed summing up the moral actions— associated to two ethical dimensions recognized in moral theories: justice and care (Kohlberg, 1981; Gilligan, 1982)—completed by critique. It should be pointed out that it was Starratt in 1991 who proposed integrating the two ethical dimensions of justice and care by completing his theoretical proposition with critique.

In keeping with the same qualitative method, the second stage of this scientific program served to conduct several interviews with peer-acknowledged school leaders to highlight their leadership profiles. This stage helped to define the concept of ethical leadership and an ethical decision-making model. During the third stage, a questionnaire was developed, using the qualitative data collected to assess the presence of ethical leadership based on three ethical dimensions: care, justice, and critique. During that stage, data were collected from school administrators across Canada and the United States. We also conducted more specific studies in minority French-language settings (Langlois & Lapointe, 2007, 2010). The fourth stage served to validate this questionnaire and our ethics training program. Based on results obtained at that stage, interesting correlations were established between transformative leadership and a particular ethical dimension: the ethics of critique (Langlois & Lapointe, 2010). It is primarily based on these results that we made observations on the possible links between the ethics of critique and transformative leadership. To fully understand this study, following is a brief summary of the methodology used.

The methodology for this study (Langlois & Lapointe, 2010) combines both quantitative and qualitative approaches. Prior to the first session and during the last meeting, participants answered a questionnaire designed to assess the presence of ethical leadership (ELQ, Langlois, 2005). The questionnaire data were analysed using Statistical Package for the Social Sciences (SPSS) software. Descriptive statistics, such as frequency, and mean scores for ethical dimensions and standard deviations were calculated both for pre- and post-testing. Considering our specific goal—to provide participants with individual feedback—and the general purposes of the study, statistical diagrams of individual scores were produced. The following demographic variables were considered in the general analysis of results: gender, age, years of teaching experience, years of educational administration experience, language, and membership of a professional association. As a complement to the questionnaire, we used Langlois' guide (1997) on the decision-making process in a moral-dilemma situation to conduct interviews with the participants. To document participant learning and the transformation in their administrative practice, qualitative data were collected throughout the training period using group interviews and subgroup interviews. Data from the interviews were analyzed using thematic analysis.

It should be noted that three groups of educational administrators were invited to participate in this three-year research project. One group consisted of educational leaders working in the same school district in the province of Québec, Canada (Group 1). Two other groups were composed of educational leaders who belonged to the same professional association in the province of Ontario, Canada (Groups 2 and 3).

We looked into several theoretical frameworks to identify ethical dimensions in management practices in both the field of applied ethics and administration. Starratt's framework (1991) seemed the most appropriate; it proposes three ethical dimensions, including care, justice, and critique. Two of these dimensions—justice and care—obtained some unanimity among the research community involved in management, administration, medicine, moral theory, and psychology.

Links Between the Results and Transformative Leadership

Figure 6.1 following provides characteristics associated with the ethical dimension of critique. They help to better understand the thought process of individuals concerned with a moral conflict and how they react in relation to the dimension of critique.

Figure 6.1 Ethics of Critique

	Moral Action Associated with Ethics of Critique
	Bringing power struggles and conflicts of interest to light;
	Reveal Injustice and racial, sexual and discriminatory biases;
	Highlighting disproportionate benefits;
	Uncovering groups benefiting from advantages over others;
	Raising consciousness among stakeholders on arrangements, power, privileges and power struggles;
	Seeking consensus through deliberation to ensure that what unites triumphs over what divides;
	Demystifying technical language used for the purpose of making an enlightened decision.
Values of Ethics of Critique	Transparency, Emancipation, Empowerment

Source: ©Langlois, L. (2000)

During the two last stages of our research program, Stages 3 and 4, very interesting links were established with transformative leadership as identified by Shields. By analyzing the ethical leadership profiles of educational leaders, and more particularly, minority French-language school leaders, and their efforts to follow an ethical trajectory (Langlois & Lapointe, 2010), we found that those who considered the dimension of ethics of critique in their work exhibited leadership quite similar to transformative leadership as proposed by Shields (2010). These individuals showed strong ethics of critique (Langlois & Lapointe, 2007) when reasoning and analyzing ethical issues they faced. In these schools, the leaders had to struggle to maintain the French language, preserve their schools, and protect the stakeholders—or those entitled to receive an education in French. By analyzing their ethical dilemma and decision-making process, these leaders exhibited the following characteristics:

They undertook or had

- actions aimed at transforming and improving;

- a reasoning process based on a critical and social analysis of reality;

- struggles to reduce injustice and abolish privileges;

- motivation based on values of equity and transparency;

- an ability to raise others' consciousness and help them liberate themselves;

- the courage to act in spite of obstacles and hardships; and

- the will to protect minorities or vulnerable individuals.

Results obtained from school administrators working in minority settings are particularly useful in gaining an understanding of the exercise of ethics of critique apparently based on transformative leadership. These results have revealed the presence of the ethics of critique more convincingly, as opposed to other school leaders working in non-minority settings. Given that the prime directive is to preserve and protect the French language, the former have to deal with several constraints exceeding their managerial tasks, including historical, political, legal, and cultural constraints. The historical background of these schools reveals the number of struggles waged to preserve the French-language identity. French-language schools in Canada have struggled for recognition since the onset of confederation. School administrators working in these institutions are continually aware of this historical burden. In spite of the adoption of the Canadian Charter of Rights and Freedoms in 1982, it took more than 20 years for French-language schools to define a school system of their own, which, nonetheless, remains incomplete even today for French-language minorities. Recognition has certainly been acquired, but it remains fragile with regard to the survival of these rights and this identity. School leaders work with this ever-precarious legacy and seek to preserve this identity by offering an educational system conducive to the academic achievement of students. However, this service is subjected to unrelenting struggles to secure qualified staff and adequate financial resources, which are not necessarily easy to obtain.

By analyzing the ethical dilemmas of the school administrators, we highlighted the characteristics associated more particularly with the ethics of critique, based on the typology discussed earlier. Through such analysis, we found that the leaders seemed to demonstrate transformative leadership in their management practices. For Shields (2010):

> Transformative leadership, therefore, recognizes the need to begin with critical reflection and analysis and to move through enlightened understanding to action—action to redress wrongs and to ensure that all members of the organization are provided with as level a playing field as possible—not only with respect to access but also with regard to academic, social, and civic outcomes. (p. 572)

We believe that exhibiting ethics of critique can play an important role in the development of transformative leadership. Identifying this ethical dimension in an educational leader's reasoning process and practice highlights a form of complementarity between ethical sensitivity and action needed to enact transformative leadership.

Two types of individuals emerged from this analysis: the "transformative agent" and the "critical ethics agent." Transformative agents do not consider themselves as pawns of the organizational scene or society but rather as agents of change determined to reestablish greater social justice. This position is marked by the critical analysis of social inequalities and leaders' individual commitment to action fostering change (Freire, 1987; Bourdieu, 2001). As for critical ethics agents, individual bases underpin their every action. They determine which action to take through an analysis of their relationships with themselves, others, and their organization by highlighting the values of equity, transparency, and empowerment.

According to Quantz et al. (1991) and quoted in Shields (2010), "transformative educational leaders must learn to diminish "undemocratic power relationships" (p. 102) and use their "power to transform present social relations" (p. 103). Transformative leadership, they asserted, "requires a language of critique and possibility" (p. 105); a "transformative leader must introduce the mechanisms necessary for various groups to begin conversations around issues of emancipation and domination" (2010, p. 569).

For complementarity to exist and to power critical analysis and social action, as set forth by Quantz and contributors, it appeared important that leaders be in a position to develop such a perspective, a concern for injustice or a form of sensitivity regarding issues at stake in the public arena that might go unnoticed if society as a whole does not perceive them. Hence, sensitivity or consciousness becomes a necessary lever of transformative leadership. But how can this concept be defined?

Sensitivity and ethical consciousness are synonymous. According to Chalmers (1996), consciousness is hard to define. He basically refers to the concept as the subjective quality of a given experience, as perceived by the cognitive agent. Ethical sensitivity calls on an individual's ability for introspection. Church (2003) adds that it is a reflection process rooted in the assessment of potential actions and their likely effects on others. Consciousness building and reflection are the two poles of sensitivity. Sensitivity is an ability that can be developed; it involves the analysis of factors in conflict, understanding the intricacies of advantages and the deterioration of elements. Sensitivity is activated through this reflection process. It is meant as an exercise of comprehension, analysis, comparison, and evaluation, differentiated from reality.

Transformative leadership and ethics of critique cannot be interconnected without such sensitivity. Once activated, it leads to a reflection process that is constructed, deconstructed, and reconstructed in light of the social context. In our opinion, some sort of close interaction among action, reflection, and capacity is vital to properly exercise transformative leadership. Freire proposes a praxis of education where action is based on critical reflection, which is in turn based on practice.

The following diagram (Figure 6.2) illustrates the components essential to the exercise of transformative leadership positioned along an ethical trajectory.

Figure 6.2 Transformative Leadership Positioned Along an Ethical Trajectory

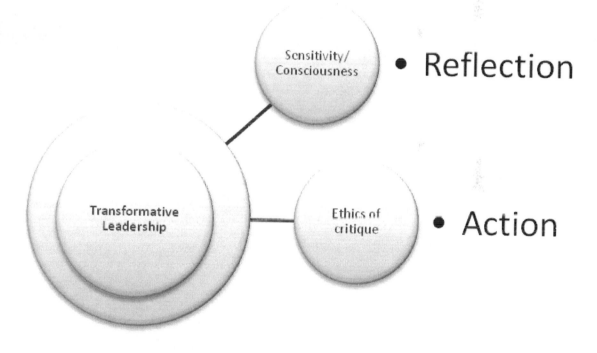

Conclusion

We started this chapter by highlighting the fact that, even today, it is hard to define the concept of leadership, in spite of all the research work conducted on the topic. However, most researchers agree that leadership is the ability to foster the voluntary participation of people and the community regarding objectives to be achieved. In other words, it is an art to try and be a leader, in contexts ranging from extreme organizational control to deregulation in utter freedom. A Canadian fellow researcher had already stated that addressing the topic of leadership was like using alternative medicine to address the exercise of power. It would be interesting to consider transformative leadership as traditional medicine, in the light of the recovery it fosters regarding injustice within organizations. Given the definitions provided on the concept of transformative leadership, it can be affirmed that leadership refers to the preventive as much as to the curative. Shields (2009) stated that transformative leadership "starts with justice and democracy issues; it provides a critical perspective on unfair practices and fosters not only greater individual success among youth, but also a better life in community with others" [translation] (p. 2). By questioning justice and democracy, transformative leadership initiates the critical analysis of the structural and cultural constraints limiting equity in education. Once analysis is done, protective action can be implemented to prevent any deterioration that may jeopardize values of social justice. Sensitivity to injustice translates into commitment to action intended for groups of people clearly disadvantaged by the school system and society. This secures an important ethical position for transformative leadership, because ethics are also rooted in reality and question social arrangements, as highlighted in this chapter.

To conclude, developing transformative leadership is part of a process likely to help renew educational institutions and visibly transform them in a fair and, hopefully, sustainable manner. We believe that in these times of gloom and disenchantment, the interest in transformative leadership is promising.

Notes

1   Interview granted to the newspaper *Le Devoir*, published in the December 4–5, 2010 weekend edition under the title: *Rencontre avec Henry Mintzberg, gourou du management—La productivité à l'américaine tue les entreprises*

2   Generally speaking, reference is made here to the following factors: demographic growth, the deterioration of the atmosphere, deforestation, land desertification, the preservation of oceans and drinking water resources, waste processing and disposal, literacy, the social role of women, urban planning, the preservation of biological, and cultural diversity, and so on.

3   The OECD is celebrating its 50th anniversary, but its roots go back to the rubble of Europe after World War II. Determined to avoid the mistakes of their predecessors in the wake of World War I, European leaders realised that the best way to ensure lasting peace was to encourage co-operation and reconstruction rather than punish the defeated. Now OECD uses its wealth of information on a broad range of topics to help governments foster prosperity and fight poverty through economic growth and financial stability. We help ensure the environmental implications of economic and social development are taken into account. (http://www.oecd.org)

References

Adorno, T. W. (1973). *Negative dialectics*. New York: The Seabury Press.

Ballet, J., & Bry, F. de. (2001). *L'entreprise et l'éthique*. Paris: Seuil.

Bass, B. M. (1985). *Leadership and performance beyond expectation*. New York: Free Press.

Bégin, L. (2004). L'autorégulation. In M. Jutras & A. Marchildon (Eds.), *Deux perspectives régulatoires de l'éthique* (pp. 9–15).ENAP, Laboratoire d'éthique publique, ENAP, éditions Liber.

Bennis,W. (2007). Introduction to the Special Issue. *American Psychologist, Special Issue: Leadership*, 62(1), 2–5.

Burns, J. M. (1978). *Leadership*. New York: HarperCollins.

Bourdieu, P. (2001). *Langage et pouvoir symbolique*. France: Livre de Poche.

Bourgeault, G. (2004). *Éthiques, Dit et non-dit, contredit, interdit*.Québec: Presses Université du Québec.

Canto-Sperber, M. (2001). *L'inquiétude morale et la vie humaine*. Paris: Presses Universitaires de France.

Chalmers, D. (1996). *The conscious mind: In search of a fundamental theory*. New York: Oxford University Press.

Church, J (2003) Depression, depth and the imagination, In J. Phillips & J. Morley (Eds.), *Imagination and its pathologies*, Cambridge, MA: MIT Press, p. 175-209.

Conger, J. A., & Kanungo, R. N. (1987). Towards a behavioral theory of charismatic leadership in organizational settings. *Academy of Management Review, 12*(4), 637–647.

Dufresne, J. (2009). *Encyclopédie de l'Agora*. Retrieved from http://agora.qc.ca/reftext.nsf/Documents/Ethique/ethique__un_systeme_complexe_par_Jacques_Dufresne

Foster, W. (1987) *Paradigms and Promises: New Approaches to Educational Administration*, Buffalo, NY: Prometheus Books, October 1987, 71: 149-150.

Freire, P. (1970). *Pedagogy of the oppressed.* New York: Herder & Herder.

Freire, P. (1987). *A pedagogy of liberation, dialogue of transforming education.* New York: Bergin and Garvey.

Gendron, C. (2005). Les codes d'éthiques: de la déontologie à la responsabilité sociale, In L. Langlois, Jean Sexton, Sylvie Montreuil, Rodrigue Blouin. (Eds.), *Éthique et dilemme dans les organisations*. Québec: Presses Université Laval.

Gilligan, C. (1982) In a different voice. *Psychological Theory and Women's Development*, Cambridge, Harvard University Press.

Giroux, G. (1997). La demande sociale de l'éthique, autorégulation ou hétérorégulation? In Bellarmin (Ed), pp.27-47, *Dans la pratique sociale de l'éthique*, Montréal, Québec: Bellarmin, 286p.

Giroux, H.A. (2003). Critical theory and educational practice. *In* A. Darder, M. Baltodano, & R.D. Torres (Eds.), *The critical pedagogy reader* (pp. 27–56). New York, NY: RoutledgeFalmer.

Habermas, J. (1987). *The philosophical discourse of modernity.* Cambridge: Polity Press.

Horkheimer, M. (1974). *Eclipse of reason.* New York: Continuum.

Honas, H. (1990). Le principe responsabilité. *Une éthique pour la civilisation technologique*, Paris, Éditions du Cerf, Passages.

Kolhberg, L. (1981) *The philosophy of moral development*, San Francisco, Harper and Row.

Langlois, L. (1997). Relever les défis de la gestion scolaire d'après un modèle de leadership éthique : une étude de cas. Thèse de doctorat, Université Laval.

Langlois, L. (2004). "Responding ethically: Complex decision-making by school district superintendents". *International Studies in Educational Administration and Management, 32*(2), 78–93.

Langlois, L. (2008). *Anatomie d'un leadership éthique.* Québec, Canada: Presses Université Laval.

Langlois, L. (2005) Ethical leadership questionnaire, Measuring instrument, unpublished document

Langlois, L. & Lapointe, C. (2010). Can we learn ethics? Results from a three-year action-research project. *Journal of Educational Administration, 48*(2), 147–163

Langlois, L., & Lapointe, C. (2007). Ethical leadership in Canadian school organizations: Tensions and possibilities. *Educational Management, Administration and Leadership, 1*(2), 247–260

Legault, G. (2004). "L'autorégulatoire." In M Jutras et A Marchildon (Ed.), *Deux perspectives régulatoires* (pp.54–59). ENAP: Laboratoire d'éthique publique, éditions Liber.

Quantz, R. A., Rogers, J., & Dantley, M. (1991). Rethinking transformative leadership: Toward democratic reform of schools. *Journal of Education, 173*(3), 96–118.

Shields, C. M. (2003). Dialogic leadership for social justice: Overcoming pathologies of silence. *Educational Administrative Quarterly, XI*(1), 111—134.

Shields, C. M. (2008). *Democratizing practice: Courageous leadership for transforming schools.* Norwood, MA: Christopher-Gordon Publishers.

Shields, C. M. (2009, September). *Le leadership transformatif.* Paper presented at the cadre d'un séminaire de 2e cycle, Quebec, QC: Université Laval.

Shields, C.M. (2010). Transformative leadership: Working for equity in diverse contexts. *Educational Administration Quarterly, 46*(4), 558–591.

Starratt, J. (1991). Building an ethical school: A theory for practice in educational leadership. *Educational Administration Quarterly, 27*(2), 185–202.

Weiner, E. J. (2003). Secretary Paulo Freire and the democratization of power: Toward a theory of transformative leadership. *Educational Philosophy and Theory, 35*(1), 89–106.

Young, I. M. (1990). *Throwing like a girl and other essays in feminist philosophy and social theory.* Bloomington: Indiana University Press.

7

Managing Educational Diversity

Developing Transformative Leadership and Professional Praxis in the 21st-Century Learning Community

Steve Rayner

The complexities created by multicultural and interfaith societies forming and reforming across the globe inevitably raise difficult questions surrounding issues of diversity, inclusive education, and the nature of school community. There is an increasingly urgent need to share in the challenge of reconstructing and managing fit-for-purpose systems, agency, and provision in this changing educational setting (Caldwell, 2004; Grossman, 2004; Moses & Chang, 2008; Rayner, 2007). It is in part as a response to these challenges that the idea of *learning leadership,* embracing aspects of instructional and inclusive leadership, is presented (see Rayner, 2009a).

This model is intended as a part of a fit-for-purpose approach to managing issues of equity and efficacy in the educational system. It is also perhaps self-evident that this or, indeed, any successful approach must contain and inform many of the complexities now faced in the contemporary classroom, which is increasingly imagined as space rather than place, involving digital divides that span global or virtual worlds, and as technology-led spatial pedagogies servicing diverse and sometime remote communities of practice. Such an approach will need to be concerned with professional praxis and, therefore, be primarily focused upon the 'who', 'how', and 'why' of learning and pedagogy.

The idea of a bespoke form of educational management is an approach that is strengthened considerably when linked to a reconceptualization of learning and knowing, which in the final analysis of leading invokes notions of enabling growth, transformation, and adaptation. The role of transformative leadership is examined in a developing model of integrative management, as a particular and constructive basis for better developing provision for educational diversity. Integrative management is, in conclusion, identified as an approach to knowledge and professional practice that is deliberately oriented toward learning in a transformative paradigm.

Envisioning Education 2020: New Ways of Learning

In this 'brave new world' of education futures, practitioners are, for example, wrestling with a need to refocus upon learning and the learner as digital natives, especially in the design of e-pedagogy and adaptive learning systems that center upon the learner, firstly as an individual (Shi, Revithis, & Chen, 2002); secondly when learning in a social context (Naismith, 2005); and thirdly as a learning tool to be used by the practitioner in leading pedagogic change (Laurillard, 2007; Rayner, 2009b; Sheth, Ramakrishnan, & Thomas, 2005). What is clearly and equally crucial for continuing efficacy in education is the role of the educator in valuing and exercising forms of leadership that are holistically grounded upon the work of successful learning. It is these concerns, chiefly, that make apparent the need for a facilitating model of integrative management in the educative process. This model of management is educational. It is purposeful in this sense and is also task-specific. This model is grounded in an approach to management and leadership that is about building the capability to deal with an increasing number of issues and decisions related to uncertain, complex, and sometimes irresolvable dilemmas that are faced in day-to-day practice. It is, however, ultimately a model of management that is concerned with the production of new knowledge, learning, growth, and development.

An early and powerful example of this mutating educational scenario experienced by school leaders was captured in a study of secondary school headteachers coping with educational reform at the beginning of the decade in England (see Day, Harris, Hadfield, Tolley, & Beresford, 2000; Day, Harris, & Hadfield, 2001). The translation of policy imperatives in these headteachers' management of externally driven reform was consistently found to reflect deeper concerns for an educative function and for developing new forms of leadership that were firmly grounded in pedagogic and professional conceptions of learning and teaching (instruction). This process of a rapid and generally turbulent continuing institutional change in education has gathered pace since the turn of the century (Fullan, 2001; Leithwood, Begley, & Cousins, 1994); the tasks and roles asked of any individual member of the school workforce are, moreover, and irrespective of status or function, demanding the take-up of new and shared role responsibilities. The result has been a dismantling of traditional professional boundaries and an increasing adoption of distinctive, distributing forms of leadership, which are embedded in notions of a less fixed and more uncertain context, characterized by increasing forms of social diversity in the learning community (see Carroll, Levy, & Richmond, 2008; Lance, Rayner, & Szwed 2007; Rayner & Gunter, 2007; Turner, 2007).

The conceptual back-cloth for much of this change is reflected in the recent decade of school reform in England (and mirrored across much of the Western world). It has helped to reinforce notions of transformational leadership and modernisation in the form of a government-inspired remodelling of school and workforce (Gunter et al., 2007; Gunter & Rayner, 2007; PricewaterhouseCoopers, 2007; Rayner, 2008; Rayner & Gunter, 2005). *Managerialism* is defined as performativity-based regimes and associated types of administration, dominated by an accountability-led surveillance method or technology (see Ball, 2003; Lyotard, 1984). This approach is typically characterised by the managerial use of a top-down, standards-driven, performance-data-driven metric, and is very often fused with transformational claims for the place of visionary innovation, driven by new technology producing politically driven warrants of quality and service, as for example reflected in league tables of high performing schools, colleges and universities (Gunter & Rayner, 2007; Rayner & Gunter, 2005).

Indeed, the widening popularity for so-called evidence-led, research-based management— dealing in constantly expanding sets of school-generated information (tagged as evidence-based data), evaluation protocols, and accountability procedure—is linked to the same approach. Data management and tracking and analysing performance are forming an ever-bigger part of school administration. It is set to be reinforced in the United Kingdom with a fresh wave of new legislation and national policy that will enact massive contraction of resources and the funding of a review programme. This educational policy is bound together with the rationale of neo-liberal economic theory and the idea of education as a utilitarian and/or entrepreneurial enterprise (Lauder, Brown, Dillabough, & Halsey, 2006). The result is the continuing story of the dismantling of the public-service sector and further engineering of a quasi-education marketplace for the English educational system, bringing new meaning to Wilde's quip that we now know the cost of everything but the value of little, if anything.

Much of this is captured in the predicted trends for the development of school managers identified by Hallinger and Snidvongs (2005, p. 2), and echoed in the PricewaterhouseCoopers report (2007) commissioned by the English government. The model of good educational leadership in this report is one comprising a mix of qualities associated with entrepreneurial, transformational, and managerialist practice. It is also set against a predicted need for the reconstruction of an educational system located in an age of constant change and with multiple functions and sites but with a school leadership securely framed within a set of measurable standards.

Valuing Meaning and Worth in Education

The alternative to this direction of utilitarian policy and related practice, which uncannily resembles a conversion of the educational system into a retail mall, is to pause and consider the idea of education and leadership as being grounded in dealing with knowledge, diversity, complexity, inclusion, and equity, and which reflects an imperative for facilitating access, engagement, and a widening participation of a full and active membership of individuals within a defined community. The learning community stands or falls on its contribution to the integrated management of this same community, rather than relying on a list of data-smart performance indicators and standards frameworks used to securely frame or, perhaps more accurately, constrain the school system (Rayner, 2007).

Such a shift in focus, because it is concerned with means and ends, as well as process and equity, requires the work and character of educational leadership and management to remain an integral part of the civic—as well as academic—function of education. It also arguably offers a more meaningful way to effectively deal with the inequities and uncertainty found in the contemporary school setting. Much of this discussion, it seems, is reflected in Shields's description of transformative leadership—that is, of a model of leadership valuing

> questions of justice and democracy; it critiques inequitable practices and offers the promise not only of greater individual achievement but of a better life lived in common with others. Transformative leadership, therefore, inextricably links education and educational leadership with the wider social context within which it is embedded. (Shields, 2010, p. 26)

This particular recipe for education and educational leadership encourages or demands thinking more seriously about the implications associated with notions of organizational learning, practitioner learning, pedagogic leadership, and the theory-practice relationship. This in turn raises questions about the place, value, and continuing development of teacher education and knowledge production (Boyer, 1990; Shulman, 1986; Walker, 2010). It also infers a rich potential and relevance for revisiting traditional ideas of knowledge, virtue, and ethics, as presented in Aristotelian philosophy (Grundy, 1987; Rayner, 2007, 2009a).

The idea of virtue, for example, in Aristotle's *Nicomachean Ethics*, refers to a practical philosophy in which the idea of perfect form or goal serving as a guiding intention (*eidos*) shapes the learner's action (*phronesis*) to attain the purpose or stated end of realising happiness (*eudemonia*) and by so doing achieving practical wisdom (*telos*). The use of praxis, as presented here, is an active acquisition and exercise of knowledge, which in itself reinforces the processes of praxis and phronesis. The notion of educating the good citizen in this way ideally permeates actions of learning, teaching, and education (see Carr, 2004; Carr & Skinner, 2008; Eikeland, 2010; Kristjánsson, 2005, 2006; Lundie, 2007; Squires, 2003). Such a model of person-centred education is related to the renewed notion of an ethical foundation underpinning complementary interpretation of teacher engagement in knowledge production (learning and teaching). The key points of this approach lie with reemphasizing the core function of the educational project as being a process involved in the realization of the 'good', and a concomitant concept, that of learning leadership (see Rayner, 2009).

An approach to knowledge management that is deliberately oriented toward learning in a transformative paradigm is therefore presented as an alternative to the prevailing neo-liberal paradigm, in which education is conceived as a utilitarian venture, knowledge as an asset or commodity, and learning as a form of capital to be gathered and spent by the learner as a consumer (Lauder et al., 2006). In contrast, a transformative paradigm is interpreted as a moral rather than economic emphasis upon education: It is predicated upon the notion of learning as personal growth, as well as being a key to fulfilment and happiness. It emphasises the centrality of well-being with integrity, values, and virtue, and focuses upon the facilitating of the good citizen based upon an understanding of fulfilment that is civic as well as personal. This rationale for education is, in part, resting upon a particular model of change leadership and a pragmatic process for professional learning. It also infers a deeply embedded respect for the individual and social diversity as part of an indigenous learning community. Moreover, this idea of education implies, in turn, recognition of the school curriculum as a vehicle for social justice (Freire, 1972; Lee, 2008; Mertens, 2007). The interactive model of education management adopts a tradition of positioning the idea of the good citizen, reflected in Classical philosophy, and an ethical understanding of knowledge (Aristotle, 1985). It is then, in turn, useful to locate this approach within the wider framework of a transformative paradigm, thereby tapping the rich potential for further developing a knowledge-oriented approach to deepening a more inclusive approach to education.

When approached in this way, a *transformative* paradigm most certainly does not easily fit with the managerialist rendition of a *transformational* model of leadership (see Bass & Reggio, 2006; Rayner, 2007, pp. 4–6). The label *transformation*, however, given the danger of confusion in terminology, needs careful explanation. It is perhaps more helpful to think of transformative leadership as a process of bottom-up growth rather than top-down, imposed alchemy or instant transformation. Shields (2010) and Poutiatine (2009) provide a more detailed examination of this distinction, while making a sensible linkage between 'transformational [transformative] learning' and the 'perspective-shifting' associated with learning found in Mezirow's work (Mezirow, 1997; Mezirow, Taylor, & Associates, 2009). Taking this idea forward, the following discussion in this chapter proposes adopting a conceptual framework for developing an inclusive or transforming model of educational leadership comprising three key constructs:

1. INTEGRATIVE MANAGEMENT: describing a pragmatic but functional model made up of five levels and forming a rational representation of normative structures, principles, and agency that are at play in the process and practice of the management task. As a framework, it can both prompt and act as a template for framing an integrative approach to managing inclusive education (see Rayner, 2007, chapter 3).

2. INCLUSIVE LEADERSHIP: representing a professional form of learning leadership concerned with educational theory, professional knowledge, and the growth of praxis. It is, therefore, leadership that is about establishing dynamic sets comprising people, systems, and context. The key to this approach to learning leadership is the concept of a professional ethic grounded in the notion of a learning community (see Rayner, 2009a).

3. PROFESSIONAL WISDOM AS PRAXIS: As Bernstein argued, in praxis there can be no prior knowledge of the right means by which we realize the end in a particular situation, as this is only finally specified in deliberating about the means appropriate to a particular situation (Bernstein, 1983, p. 147). The practicum envisaged in this use of wisdom is predicated upon Aristotelian ethics but closely reflects that which is described by Walker (2010): in adopting this approach to a practicum of professional knowledge, there is a need to be very deliberate about what we intend as an outcome of our learning, teaching, and exercising learning-instructional and/or school leadership (reflecting an important set of distinctions around the concepts of wisdom, understanding, knowledge, and information).

The intention here is to present a conceptual framework that can be used in dealing with the issues and challenges raised in this introduction. Education as an idea is fixed at the heart of this model, and so is its *conditio sine qua non* or absolute requirement or condition. It is a model of leadership and management that inhabits and is infused with notions of growth, adaptability, involvement, enfranchisement, and progression, through a cycle of change that mirrors passage of time and seasons of the year (see Rayner, 2007). It is, when applied to the actual work of a learning community, a pragmatic approach; it is facilitating, inclusive, and integrating of people, agency, and knowledge. This, in turn, is understood to have relevance for developing a form of transformative leadership (Rayner, 2007), thereby contributing to the professional practicum, practitioner knowledge as professional wisdom, and learning leadership, implicating all those involved in the management of educational policy, provision, and practice—echoing similar arguments presented by Shulman (2005), Shields (2010), and Walker (2010).

Establishing Integrative Management

Integrative management as presented in this chapter embodies a knowledge-led process reflecting a pragmatic philosophy. The true measure of worth in this approach is its effect and how it determines an educational endeavour in the generation and governance of experience and outcome. In respect to learning and the individual, much of the thinking behind the construction of this model is captured in Lundie's account of the application of Aristotelian ethics to the educative process (Lundie, 2007). A theory of motivation and ontological enhancement provides evidence of how framing the process of knowledge synthesis is an enabling tool, which can be used in the management of educational diversity. Taking higher education as an example, Lundie asserts that he "*would like to posit a Janus-faced approach* to the operation of ontological enhancement on disability policy in an institution—one part shaping the individual, the other part shaping the institution" (2007, p. 11). This account of developing a pedagogic-learning relationship aimed at providing better support for students experiencing difficulties with study lends weight to the wider argument claiming that Aristotelian philosophy represents a useful basis for developing a better understanding of educational practice and offers the potential of being a transformative tool for working with individual differences and educational diversity in the learning community.

It is this aspect of praxis that is most easily recognised as a political process associated with education and emancipatory knowledge and as empowerment (Freire, 1972). A separate, but perhaps more recently formed, notion of praxis has been adopted by academics and researchers interested in Marxist-inspired feminist epistemology and critical theory (Lather, 1984, 1986). In respect to conceptualizing methods of educational management, and taking this idea to its next level, Carroll et al. (2008) argue that the ontology, epistemology, and methodologies reflected in the theory of social practice (Chia & MacKay, 2007), tied to a resulting conception of praxis, offer both a challenge and also considerable potential for transformation, in a model of leadership bounded and constrained by current organizational and managerial conventions.

The idea of developing a model of integrative management is, therefore, presented as a twin-track approach to leadership and the management of educational diversity. It is rehearsed in Rayner (2007). The idea, however, starts from a point of departure that dismisses a widely held view that leadership and management are a dichotomy, and so should result in practice that reflects separate and divorced action. This view (see West-Burnham, 1997) is often summed up as leadership being about doing the right things (strategic-policy), while management is described as doing things right (technical-operational). In the contemporary mode typically favoured by policymakers and administrators involved in reform, the transformational notion of leadership takes on the mystical mantle of a kind of manna to be found and consumed as an activity in the strategic domain, while being separately supported by an accountability-driven, managerialist model in an operational domain. Simplistically, and perhaps literally, management follows and is sustained by leadership (Rayner, 2007). It produces a non-educative pattern of action and a kind of consumption that, quite crucially, is not about growth and does not concern itself with grounded development or sustainability. It is, in its logical conclusion, simply an approach about valuing and driving production and success as measured by consumption.

Knowing and Not Knowing: Uncertainty, Learning, and Transformation

Quite clearly, attempting this person-centred, growth-oriented approach in schooling and education—with its leading concern for diversity, equity, knowledge, and learning—cannot hope to be successful if it is only predicated upon a consumerist valuing of utility and production. At a second level, dealing with diversity engenders a range of issues that require thinking through how organizational systems and individual agency interact, particularly as, in an educational setting, many of these systems are complex and are characterised by a pluralistic combination of unexpected and hard to predict patterns of agency. Complexity theorists (Stacey, 1992) emphasize openness to accident, coincidence, and serendipity. Strategy is the emerging resultant.

Rather than trying to consolidate stability, advocates of chaos theory argue that the organization is better advised to position itself in a region of bounded instability or, in other words, to seek 'the edge of chaos'. In a way, this logic is reminiscent of the argument that learning requires conflict and perspective-shift (Mezirow, 1991). What remains important in navigating this change, however, is to retain a need for rational knowledge and a synthesis based upon reason (thinking) and emotion (affect), as chaos will not spontaneously produce sense and meaning. Stacey (1993), applying this theory to management, argues that effective organizations will

- both adapt to and help create their situated environments;

- ensure that organisational success flows from contradiction as well as consistency in the work-place;

- ensure opportunities for success in a self-reinforcing cycle of learning, rather than from explicit vision; and

- realize that transforming, as well as incremental, changes may lie on the route to organisational success.

Diversity, as a description of social and individual differences, may perhaps be usefully understood as a working example of the dynamic systems described in a theory of complexity. Framing and harnessing the many different aspects of these social and personal worlds, which combine to make up the learning community that is school, college, or university, is the 'right stuff' of educational leadership and management. It is in adopting this approach to learning and education that integrative management is presented as an essential and useful tool with which to enable transformative learning and ensure widening participation in the learning community (Rayner, 2007).

Integrative Management

Arguably, any form of leadership will involve strategic problem-posing, direction-finding, and sense-making, and is in this way very much about knowledge management (Rayner, 2007). Such action encompasses utilizing the past, in terms of both local and global history. It draws upon formal and tacit knowledge and, in so doing, is about synthesizing and resynthesizing knowledge as a decision-making process that determines future purposes and action. For policymakers, as well as practitioners, deliberately engaging in praxis to assist the management of diversity should always be located in a wider framework of functional and integrative management (see Rayner, 2007, 2008). Such an approach reasserts the need for a pragmatic base in any theorizing of diversity, difference, and difficulty. To this end, it is useful to think of an integrative and interrelational dynamic as representing social and personal forms of diversity or differences in the school community.

The idea of integrative management at its most elemental is represented as a structure in Figure 7.1. It comprises three integrative principles, which are construed as a framework for containing what is described by Goldkuhl as an epistemology of action knowledge made up of the theories, strategies, and methods governing peoples' actions in social practice (1999, pp. 1–2).

Figure 7.1 The Structure of Integrative Management

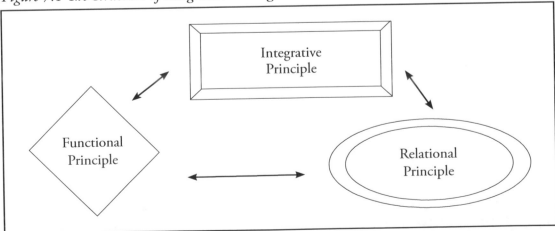

The first element in this model is the *integrative principle* of facilitating knowledge management. This is a strategic process tied to managing actions and practice. It includes, moreover, the continuing and adaptive reconstruction of institutional identity and organizational culture, ideally reflecting an emphasis on learning, with a readiness to continuously invest resources in a cycle of personal and communal problem posing, decision making, problem solving, and decision-taking as an outcome to decision-making and a particular activity. It is a cognitive and intellectual activity aimed at a synthesis and reintegration of knowledge. It is, in essence, a learning-centred approach to enabling the production and transfer of new knowledge.

The second element is the *relational principle* of leadership and action knowledge working as a dynamic system, comprising an unfolding series of structures and agency. It produces activity focusing upon both ways and means and is always situated in social contexts defined by purpose, people, and an evolving praxis. It shapes culture, ethos, and milieu. It is an extremely powerful factor in determining transformative learning and a successful school community. It is, at its most straightforward, evidenced in collaborative process and the work of an effective team or group at work.

The third element is the *functional principle* of leadership. As a process, leadership requires continuous learning and management of knowledge as part of its operation. A pragmatic application of knowledge—in any form—is a key component for any example of leading and leadership at any level or place of the organizational setting. In the deployment of integrative management, activity will generally utilize reflective enquiry, sense-making, and a research-led approach to decision making and taking. It reflects the need for a manager to understand, facilitate, and actively monitor the structures, agency, and preferred outcomes articulated in their institutional policy.

These principles are interactive but interdependent aspects of work that form the exercise of integrative management. As a theory of social practice (see Reckwitz, 2002), and sharing many of the same characteristics described in an integrative model of management (see Rayner, 2007), the idea of praxis (as defined in this context by Carroll et al., 2008) as being the interconnection and embeddedness of action, actor, and institution, is by far the most important. The notion of 'action knowledge' production and management of learning, which should arguably represent the ultimate purpose and core work of the educative project, is a continuing dynamic process that is simultaneously relational (collaborative exchange), an integration of extant knowledge (eclectic synthesis), and by definition and purpose must always be functional (pragmatic application). A practitioner exercising this kind of management is likely to be a member of a team or group and hopes to serve a specific purpose but equally might be a lone practitioner organizing a programme of study. The task might be almost anything; for example, an intervention at the casework level with an individual student, institutional-change management and work with issues in the school community, or policy development in a regional or even national forum. Professionalism and its related knowledge base as teacher education or pedagogy (practical wisdom and tradecraft) lie at the heart of this concept of integrative management. It requires continuing opportunities for personal and professional learning. Such learning is not simply a set of skills, qualities, or even a collection of best-practice scenarios but rather, the management and application of several forms of action knowledge combining to produce praxis (see Goldkuhl, 1999).

Transformative Learning, Leadership, Knowledge, and Practising Praxis

Transformative learning is generally understood to involve a holistic engagement of thought, feelings, and actions in generating new perceptions and understandings of the world (O'Sullivan, 2003). Experience, awareness, emotions, and sense-making are critical aspects of transformative learning. At the core of transformative learning is the process of perspective transformation, which has three dimensions: psychological (changes in understanding of the self), convictional (revision of belief systems), and behavioural (changes in lifestyle). Indeed, Cranton asserts that transformative learning occurs when emancipatory knowledge is gained (2006). This connection is identified in Mezirow's definition of transformative learning (2000), that is, when transformative learning is conceived as:

> ... a process by which previously uncritically assimilated assumptions beliefs, values, and perspectives are questioned and thereby become more open, permeable, and better validated. (Cranton, 2006, p. 2)

This idea of transformation as a process or an event (epiphany) is largely informed by the description of conflict fuelling perspective-shift and ego-based growth within the individual. It is more generally described as a key concept in Mezirow's theory of learning (1991). Change-as-growth is an important aspect of this model of learning, but this does not equate with a constant and evenly spread rate of progression. Levy and Mary (1986) describe how transformational change in organizational settings is, by its nature, discontinuous and having stops and starts and running in cycles; then there are typically lengths of time in what is still marked down as a period of continuing change where there isn't any transformational change actually taking place. Individual development and learning cycles are seen to be closely linked and operate in a similar manner.

Shields (2010) refers to critical theory and social justice as key elements in an emerging model of transformative leadership. While these social dimensions to transformation, usually linked to notions of equity and social justice, remain a key part of the wider notion of transformative leadership, there is, however, a need to align the social with the 'personal growth' when describing the relevance of a transformative model. Elias et al., (1997) for example, argue that transformative leadership is one in which change is characterized by a willingness to realign structures and relationships in the school curriculum to achieve genuine and sustainable change.

Leadership Knowledge: Establishing a Practicum

There is a great deal of scope here for further developments linked to a model of inclusive leadership (see Rayner, 2007, 2009a, b) and, more generally, emerging models of instructional leadership in the United States (Blase & Blase, 1998) or learning leadership in Australia, New Zealand, and the United Kingdom (MacBeath, Pedder, & Swalfield, 2007; O'Donoghue & Clarke, 2010). Rayner (2009a, b) makes the case for a proposition that inclusive leadership should be regarded as an exercise in teacher education and developing practice, involving the blending of theory (knowledge) with provision (practice), and producing what is essentially an applied or pragmatic theory (praxis). In doing this work, the individual or group is engaged in a learning process that can be construed as producing new knowledge, as well as contributing to a personal phronesis forming part of an individual member's educational professionality. It is literally and entirely a learning process. It is also an individual and a social activity, reflecting and often involving interplay between agency and structures found in the educational setting. Put simply, the case here is for the organizational and transformative potential of a combination of social structures and individual agency in reconceptualizing educational leadership as generically being about learning leadership and specifically being about leadership of learning as practice.

Harris, Lowery-Moore, and Farrow (2008) also describe how transformative leadership involves the practitioner moving beyond the point of knowledge acquisition to focus more specifically on connecting theory to practice. In following this pathway, future educational leaders develop as reflective practitioners, or as Rayner (2009a, b) argues, they go on to become thinking practitioners, constructing and reconstructing new ways of knowing, which lead to an enhanced personal capability in the learning context and a deepening engagement with social justice. This aligns closely with the model of Aristotelian philosophy examined in an earlier part of this discussion, with the concept of action knowledge (Goldkuhl, 1999), and also with Habermas's (1974) taxonomy of technical, communicative, and emancipatory knowledge on which Mezirow (1991) based his transformative learning theory. For the present, however, it is the wider movement of a phronesis-praxis perspective associated with critical theory, emancipatory research, action research, and teacher empowerment that merits yet further consideration as a source for ideas about knowledge and its relevance for the management of education (Lather, 1986; Carr, 2004; Kristjánsson, 2005).

Moreover, the adoption of virtue ethics as a pragmatic methodology will, according to Carr (2004), enable the individual to take advantage of a practical philosophy that offers a mode of reflective inquiry that will:

> . . . enable them to expose and examine the taken-for-granted presuppositions implicit in their practice in order that they may reflectively reconstruct their understanding of their practice and of how its internal good may, in their own practical situation, be more appropriately pursued. (2004, p. 62)

The work of practicing praxis and/or developing phronesis as a leader and manager in the learning community—that is, drawing upon theory in practice to develop practical wisdom—involves divers forms of knowledge management as identified by Rayner (2007) and Wain (2006), and located in organizational learning by Thomas and Allen (2006).

Rediscovering Practitioner Wisdom

In a more closely elaborated consideration of praxis, Eikeland (2008, p. 53) tells us that, for Aristotle, a virtue is what makes something work at its best. The ability to exercise virtue only comes about through a *hexis* or *habitus*, in that it is an acquired ability, rather than being an inherent capability, such as seeing, which a person can do well without any practice. Furthermore, and in what offers yet another indication of the relevance of Aristotelian philosophy in reconceptualizing models of educational leadership, Eikeland explains that what does seem important is that 'how we know anything' is a very complex interpenetration of both logic and experience, and that, according to Aristotle, we can only really know anything in relation to its context. This tells us that praxis is entwined with phronesis—that is, prudence or practical wisdom—and it is produced by using the ability to reflect on practice (thus its relevance to experiential theory and action orientated research). But, and this is the important point, phronesis is so much more than the ability to reflect on and learn from practice. It involves thinking, knowledge synthesis, and perspective formation; that is, it is about integrating theory and practice, and, furthermore, recognizing that these actions and forms of knowledge are not helpfully construed as separate or distinctive, as they have become for us. Aristotle, Eikeland claims, would have seen them as much more intertwined and interactive—each penetrating the other in ways that it is hard for contemporary minds to comprehend (2008). If this view is accurate, then there is an exciting prospect of yet greater benefits in realigning knowledge and learning as the basis for combining modern practices in transformative and inclusive models of educational leadership, as part of an integrative management of education.

Conclusion

The exercise of integrative management requires a commitment to the idea of the action of learning as a first principle in an educational organization. Continuing professional development and organizational learning represent key factors in this concept of an effective educational community of practice. Such an approach enshrines the idea that each individual member of the community represents both a contributor and a source of learning and knowledge creation. The three key values, which surely must lie at the heart of a community culture of this kind, are integrity, respect, and responsibility. How each of these are surfaced and resurfaced in a community will offer vital evidence as to the levels of inclusive practice and form an important and alternative counterweight in stories of school effectiveness and quality that only employ managerialist data comprising measures of efficiency rather than equity and effectiveness (see Mertens & McLaughlin [2004] for some interesting case examples and a discussion of research design for evaluating special school populations in this way). A further compelling case example of practitioner research revealing the key role for inclusive forms of learning leadership is presented by Riehl (2000).

As previously argued, transformational leadership is not be confused with the model identified in this discussion as transformative leadership. The former is vulnerable to the excesses of a 'charismatic tyranny' very often associated with an approach that deliberately injects intense self-serving uncertainty and/or anxiety in any kind of management. It is often characterized by a deliberate shaking-down of structures and a visionary-led demand for high-impact and instantaneous change in and of cultures and practice. The method adopted is essentially controlling, and the by-product of such management is often a high dependency of so-called subordinate followers or workforce. Transformational leadership of this sort does not lead to sustainability or growth in the medium term but can produce a quick win and surface make-over that looks good for the short term. All in all, it is difficult to envisage how approaches of this kind, grounded in turnover and profit, are anything but anathema to an educationist genuinely interested in people, learning, and knowledge.

The model of integrative management described in this chapter is therefore presented as a pragmatic tool for use in both expanding and exploiting professional knowledge and in developing the notion of praxis as a continuing opportunity to reimagine the promise and potential of educational research, knowledge growth, and teacher education (see Carr & Skinner, 2008; Golde & Walker, 2006; Grundy, 1987). This process, in turn, is closely related to the notion of transformative leadership (see Poutiatine, 2009; Shields, 2010) when it is defined as a critical and normative concept located in both a sociological and psychological paradigm. It is a situated concept that is uniquely and arguably a highly relevant paradigm within which to locate a prime site for educational management. The educational endeavour and educative process are both valued as key aspects of this site, comprising systems and structures as well as evolving social agency. Each is interrelated and remains generally coherent in relation to core concepts, such as change and mutability, but at the same time each is often found to comprise loosely coupled adaptive systems that are plastic, nonlinear, and complex. In this respect, an emphasis upon transformative leadership and education is one that should not separate the social from the personal, or individual from the communal, and recognizes the need to combine an approach that directly but concurrently deals with equity, differences, and diversity in the learning community.

References

Aristotle. (1985). *Nicomachean Ethics* (W. Kaufman edition). Mineola, NY: Dover Thrift, Inc.

Ball, S. J. (2003). The teacher's soul and the terrors of performativity. *Journal of Education Policy, 18*(2), 215–228.

Bass, B., & Reggio, R. (2006). *Transformational leadership.* Mahwah, NJ: Lawrence Erlbaum.

Bernstein, R. J. (1983). *Beyond objectivism and relativism.* Oxford: Blackwell.

Blase, J., & Blase, J. (1998). *Handbook of instructional leadership: How really good principals promote teaching and learning.* Thousand Oaks, CA: Corwin Press.

Boyer, E. L. (1990). *Scholarship reconsidered: Priorities of the professoriate.* Princeton, NJ: The Carnegie Foundation for the Advancement of Teaching.

Caldwell, B. J. (2004). A strategic view of efforts to lead the transformation of schools. *School Leadership and Management, 24*(1), 81–99.

Carr, W. (2004). Philosophy and education. *Journal of Philosophy of Education, 38*(1), 55–73.

Carr, D., & Skinner, D. (2008). The cultural roots of professional wisdom: Towards a broader view of teacher expertise. *Educational Philosophy and Theory, 41*(2), 141–154.

Carroll, B., Levy, L., & Richmond, D. (2008). Leadership as practice: Challenging the competency paradigm. *Leadership, 4*(4), 363–379.

Chia, R., & MacKay, B. (2007). Post-processual challenges for the emerging strategy-as-practice perspective: Discovering strategy in the logic of practice. *Human Relations, 60*(1), 217–242.

Cranton, P. (2006). *Understanding and promoting transformative learning* (2d ed.). San Francisco, CA: Jossey-Bass.

Day, C., Harris, A., & Hadfield, M. (2001). Grounding knowledge of schools in stakeholder realities: A multi-perspective study of effective school leaders. *School Leadership and Management, 21*(1), 9–42.

Day, C., Harris, A., Hadfield, M., Tolley, H., & Beresford, J. (2000). *Leading schools in times of change.* Milton Keynes, U.K.: Open University Press.

Eikeland, O. (2008). *The ways of Aristotle: Aristotelian phronesis, Aristotelian philosophy of dialogue, and action research* (Vocational and Continuing Education, Vol. 5). Berlin: Peter Lang.

Elias, M. J., Zins, J. E., Weissberg, R. P., Frey, K. S., Greenberg, M. T., & Haynes, N. M. (1997). *Promoting social and emotional learning: Guidelines for educators.* Alexandria, VA: Association for Supervision and Curriculum Development.

Freire, P. (1972). *Pedagogy of the oppressed.* London: Penguin.

Fullan, M. (2001). *Leading in a culture of change.* San Francisco, CA: Jossey-Bass.

Golde, C. M., & Walker, G. E. (Eds.) (2006). *Envisioning the future of doctoral education: Preparing stewards of the discipline.* Stanford, CA: The Carnegie Foundation for the Advancement of Teaching.

Goldkuhl, G. (1999). *The grounding of usable knowledge: An inquiry in the epistemology of action knowledge.* Paper accepted to *Högskolor och Samhälle i Samverkan.* Falun, Sweden.

Grossman, H. (2004). *Classroom behaviour management for diverse and inclusive schools.* Oxford: Rowman and Littlefield.

Grundy, S. (1987). *Curriculum: Product or praxis?* London: RoutledgeFalmer.

Gunter, H., & Rayner, S. (2007). Modernising the school workforce in England: Challenging transformation and leadership? *Leadership, 3*(1), 47–64.

Gunter, H., Rayner, S., Butt, G., Fielding, A., Lance, A., & Thomas, H. (2007). Transforming the school workforce: Perspectives on school reform in England. *Journal of Educational Change, 8*(1), 825–839.

Habermas, J. (1974). *Theory and practice* (trans. J. Viertel). London: Heinemann.

Hallinger, P., & Snidvongs, K. (2005). *Adding value to school leadership and management. A review of trends in the development of managers in the education and business sectors.* Paper commissioned by the National College of School Leadership. Nottingham: National College of School Leadership.

Harris, S., Lowery-Moore, H., & Farrow, V. (2008). Extending Transfer of Learning Theory to Transformative Learning Theory: A Model for Promoting Teacher Leadership. *Theory into Practice, 47*, 318–326.

Kristjánsson, K. (2005). Smoothing it: Some Aristotelian misgivings about the *phronesis-praxis* perspective on education. *Educational Philosophy and Theory, 37*(4), 455–473.

Kristjánsson, K. (2006). Habituated reason: Aristotle and the 'paradox of moral education'. *Theory and Research in Education, 4*(1), 101–122.

Lance, A., Rayner, S., & Szwed, C. (2007). Challenging and changing role boundaries. In G., Butt & H. Gunter (Eds.), *Modernising schools: People, learning and organisations* (pp. 47–60). London: Continuum.

Lather, P. (1984). Critical theory, curricular transformation, and feminist mainstreaming. *Journal of Education, 166*(1), 49–62.

Lather, P. (1986). Research as Praxis. *Harvard Educational Review, 56*(3), 257–277.

Lauder, H., Brown, P., Dillabough, J., & Halsey, A. H. (2006). Introduction: The prospects for education: Individualization, globalization, and social change.. In, H. Lauder, P. Brown, J. Dillabough, & A. H. Halsey (Eds.), *Education, globalization and social change* (pp. 1–70). Oxford: Oxford University Press.

Laurillard, D. (2007). Technology, pedagogy and education: Concluding comments. *Technology, Pedagogy and Education, 16*(3), 357–360.

Lee, C. D. (2008). How an ecological framework in education research facilitates civic responsibility. *Educational Researcher, 37*(5), 267–279.

Leithwood, K., Begley, P. T., & Cousins, J. B. (1994). *Developing expert leadership for future schools*. London: The Falmer Press.

Levy, A., & Mary, U. (1986). *Organizational transformation*. New York, NY: Praeger.

Lundie, D. (2007). A theory of motivation and ontological enhancement: The role of disability policy in student empowerment and institutional change. *Educational Philosophy and Theory, 41*(5), 1–14.

Lyotard, J. F. (1984). *The postmodern condition: A report on knowledge* (trans. by Bennington, G., & Massumi, B.). Minneapolis: University of Minnesota Press.

MacBeath, J., Pedder, D., & Swalfield, S. (2007). Unlocking transforming practice within and beyond the classroom: Messages for practice and policy. In M. James, R. McCormick, M. J. Drummond, A. Fox, J. MacBeath, B. Marshall, D. Pedder, R. Proctor, S. Swalfield, J. Swann, & D. Wiliam (Eds.), *Improving learning how to learn. Classrooms, schools and networks* (pp. 64–88). London: Routledge.

Mertens, D. M. (2007). Transformative paradigm: Mixed methods and social justice. *Journal of Mixed Methods Research, 1*(3), 212–225.

Mertens, D. M., & McLaughlin, J. A. (2004). *Research and evaluation methods in special education*. Thousand Oaks, CA: Corwin.

Mezirow, J. (1991). *Transformative dimensions of adult learning*. San Francisco, CA: Jossey-Bass.

Mezirow, J. (1997). Transformative learning: Theory to practice. *New Directions for Adult and Continuing Education, 74*, 5–12.

Mezirow, J. (2000). Learning to think like an adult: Core concepts of transformation theory. In J. Mezirow, & Associates (Eds.), *Learning as transformation: Critical perspectives on a theory in progress* (pp. 3–33). San Francisco, CA: Jossey-Bass.

Mezirow, J., Taylor, E., & Associates. (Eds.). (2009). *Transforming learning into practice*. San Francisco, CA: Jossey-Bass.

Moses, M. S., & Chang, M. J. (2008). Toward a deeper understanding of the diversity rationale. *Educational Researcher, 35*(1), 6–11.

Naismith, E. (2005). Enabling personalization through context awareness. In S. De Freitas & C. Yapp (Eds.), *Personalizing learning in the 21st century* (pp. 103–108). Stafford, U.K.: Network Educational Press.

O'Donoghue, T., & Clarke, S. (2010). *Leading learning: Process, themes and issues in international contexts*. Abingdon, U.K.: Routledge.

O'Sullivan, E. (2003). Bringing a perspective of transformative learning to globalized consumption. *International Journal of Consumer Studies, 27*(4), 326–330.

Poutiatine, M. I. (2009). What is transformation? Nine principles toward an understanding of transformational process for transformational leadership. *Journal of Transformative Education, 7*(3), 189–208.

PricewaterhouseCoopers. (2007). *Independent study into school leadership: The main report*. Nottingham, U.K.: Department for Education and Skills.

Rayner, S. (2007). *Managing special and inclusive education*. London: Sage.

Rayner, S. (2008). Complexity, diversity and management: Some reflections on folklore and learning leadership in education. *Management in Education, 22*(2), 40–46.

Rayner, S. (2009a). Educational diversity and learning leadership: A proposition, some principles and a model of inclusive leadership? *Educational Review, 61*(4), 433–447.

Rayner, S. (2009b). Personalizing style in learning: Activating a differential pedagogy. In C. Mourlas, N. Tsianos, & P. Germanakos (Eds.), *Cognitive and emotional processes in web-based education: Integrating human factors and personalization* (pp. 25–45). Hershey, PA: IGI Global.

Rayner, S., & Gunter, H. (2005). Rethinking leadership: Perspectives on remodelling practice. The challenges of modernisation in education. *Educational Review, 57*(2), 151–162.

Rayner, S., & Gunter, H. (2007). Remodelling leadership: Moving beyond modernising reform. In G. Butt & H. Gunter. (Eds.), *Modernising schools: People, learning and organisation* (pp. 75–90). London: Continuum.

Reckwitz, A. (2002). Toward a theory of social practices: A development in cultural theorizing. *European Journal of Social Theory, 5*(2), 243–263.

Riehl, C. J. (2000). The principal's role in creating inclusive schools for diverse students: A review of normative, empirical, and critical literature on the practice of educational administration. *Review of Educational Research, 70*(1), 55–81.

Sheth, A., Ramakrishnan, C., & Thomas, C. (2005). Semantics for the semantic web: The implicit, the formal and the powerful. *International Journal of Semantic Web and Information Systems, 1*(1), 1–18.

Shi, H., Revithis, S., & Chen, S. (2002). An agent enabling personalized learning in e-learning environments. In M. Gini & T. Ishida (conf. chairs), *International conference on autonomous agents: Proceedings of the First International Joint Conference on Autonomous Agents and Multi-agent Systems, Part 2* (pp. 847–848). New York: ACM.

Shields, C. M. (2010). Leadership: Transformative. In P. Peterson, E. Baker, & B. McGaw (Eds.), *International Encyclopedia of Education* (Vol. 5, pp. 26–33). Oxford: Elsevier.

Shulman, L. S. (1986). Those who understand: Knowledge growth in teaching. *Educational Researcher, 15*(2), 4–14.

Shulman, L. S. (2005). Signature pedagogies in the professions. *Daedalus, 134*(3), 52–59.

Squires, G. (2003). OP-ED. Praxis: A dissenting note. *Journal of Curriculum Studies, 35*(1), 1–7.

Stacey, R. D. (1992). *Managing the unknowable: Strategic boundaries between order and chaos in organizations.* San Francisco. CA: Jossey-Bass.

Stacey, R. D. (1993). *Strategic management and organizational dynamics.* Pitman: London.

Thomas, K., & Allen, S. (2006). The learning organization: A meta-analysis of themes in literature. *The Learning Organization, 13*(2), 123–139.

Turner, C. (2007). Leading from the middle: Dealing with diversity and complexity. *School Leadership & Management, 27*(5), 401–403.

Wain, K. (2006). This thing called 'the philosophy of education'. *Journal of Philosophy of Education, 40*(3), 391–403.

Walker, K. (2010). Wisdom for developing professionals. In E. G. Ralph, K. D. Walker, & R. Wimmer (Eds.), *The Practicum in Professional Education: Canadian Perspectives* (pp. 180–210). Calgary, Alberta: Detselig Enterprises.

West-Burnham, J. (1997). *Managing quality in schools* (2d ed.). London: Financial Times.

8

Unwrapping Tradition

Shifting from Traditional Leadership to Transformative Action

Deneca Winfrey Avant

Leadership is one of the most observed yet least understood phenomena on earth (Burns, 1978); thus, scholars find that people respond differently to various leadership styles. Upon review of the literature, it is particularly important to understand traditional leadership in order to appreciate transformative action. Research suggests that traditional leadership focuses one on organizational culture and leadership style. This notion is essentially true in acknowledging where leadership began to move forward and in comprehending how action is a necessity within society.

Because practice standards have evolved throughout history, it is especially important to comprehend the road to great leadership in order to further the enhancement of any organization. For example, the cliché "you won't know where you're going if you don't know where you've been" holds value in leadership. Accordingly, leadership has transformed in response to historical conditions and theoretical developments, which provide a framework for leading, understanding, and controlling behaviors. The most appropriate and effective forms of leadership are subjects of constant debate. One example is provided by Blake and Mouton's (1985) managerial grid, which distinguished a leader's concern for people from a concern for task. Later, Kouzes and Posner (1997) provided the concept of encouraging the heart of others by recognizing individual contributions, and developing the capacities of their employees through opportunities for continuous learning. Another leadership model is illustrated by Schein's (1996) participatory management, in which feelings of staff are taken into consideration and followers can say "we did it" after implementing change efforts. For instance, this leadership practice understands that when change seems imposed on staff and is totally against the norm, red flags go up because of the lack of ownership. However, if staff are allowed the opportunity to express their thoughts about particular concerns and suggest ways to address them, they will be more apt to accept the finished product of change and take actions as outlined by the leader's vision. Ultimately, Schein encouraged innovative leadership approaches and follow-through of action.

Another approach to leadership stems from McGregor's research in 1960. McGregor applied organizational management by arguing that self-fulfilling prophecies are generated through assumptions that managers have about their employees. He believed that leadership practices should be based on an accurate understanding of human nature. McGregor used the example of Theory X and Theory Y to illustrate that what leaders believe about their workers influences their actions. In the Theory X model, leaders felt that their workers were lazy and demonstrated autocratic leadership style by announcing their decisions and inviting questions regarding expectations. In contrast, in the Theory Y model leaders trusted their workers and expressed more positive actions based on democratic leadership, in which the leaders delegated authority and responsibility (Cunningham & Cordeiro, 2000). In 1981, Ouchi formed a more practical leadership approach, Theory Z, suggesting that it leads to improvements in organizational performance. Theory Z prescribes that organizations can enjoy many of the advantages of both Theory X and Theory Y systems while motivating employees for increased productivity. By enhancing professional standards, Theory Z promotes a holistic concern for the employee and their family, including collective decision making, individual responsibility, and moderately specialized career paths. This theory characterizes long-term employment with slow evaluation and promotion, noting implicit, informal control with explicit, formalized measures. Theory Z is clearly linked to the work of McGregor (1960), with the addition of more humanistic and effective management styles.

Burns's (1978) transactional and transformational leadership models are among the most recognized styles of traditional leadership paving the way to a transformative shift. Transactional leadership focuses on organizational transactions and is based on exchanging one thing for another. In this kind of leadership, people enter into agreements through a process of "bargaining between the individual interests of persons or groups in return for their cooperation in the leader's agenda" (p. 109). Burns contends that with transactional leadership, the goal of both leader and follower is to fulfill self-interest. Thus, transactional leadership refers to a non-creative but stable environment in which the leader responds to problematic situations or to otherwise enforce the rules.

Transformational leadership is the other of Burns's two prominent types of leadership (1978). This kind of leadership concentrates on what Burns calls "end-values," such as liberty, equality, freedom, justice, equity, care, peace, and security. These internal values and standards create important fundamental changes in society and are considered the highest and most comprehensive of human ambitions. Transformational leadership requires people to bond over organizational goals. This refers to leaders and followers inspiring each other to achieve higher levels of morality and motivation, thus creating a collaborative change process and contributing to the performance of the whole organization. Transformational leadership is a broad step on the path from traditional leadership to transformative action. Additionally, it is clear that while we have ample knowledge of traditional leadership, our knowledge of transformative action is still developing. It is imperative to further cultivate our understanding of transformative action, in order to better address issues of inequality and seek social change. I turn now to the fundamentals of transformative leaders.

Transformative Leaders

In recent years, a considerable number of questions have been raised about the transformative leader concept in relation to earlier, traditional leadership models. Because traditional models did not always recognize all stakeholders, traditional leaders had a limited capacity to realign the relationships and organizations necessary to attain transformation. In contrast, the transformative leader concept undertakes many tasks beyond any single individual to sustain copious and equitable results within community organizations and society.

Transformative leaders play an integral role within society and have high expectations to accompany their responsibilities. Society looks to transformative leaders to act in important roles, including as strategists, motivators, developers, sustainers, innovators, and catalysts for change, to name a few. Transformative leaders are aware of issues simmering below the surface, are able to decipher complex cultural codes, and they understand what is needed for social change (Henze, Katz, Norte, Sather, & Walker, 2001). These leaders are conscious of operating in a world dominated by national interests and therefore must act as visionaries to facilitate a global community. As such, transformative leaders have the vision to recognize perspectives of social justice and understand the consequences of ignoring those perspectives. According to Green (1998), understanding equality means recognizing another individual's circumstances. Leaders also must recognize racial and ethnic barriers and develop strategies to lessen and overcome these obstacles.

By acknowledging and addressing personal challenges, transformative leaders can act with the necessary consideration to avoid the stressors of communal conditions. Due to the many individuals affected by societal disparities, there are differences in how categories of people are treated. Understanding that moral exclusion is conceivably a dangerous form of oppression, transformative leaders work to enhance the moral development of both the dominant oppressing group and individuals subjected to inhumane or discriminatory treatment (Shields, 2004). Transformative leaders find ways to help individuals envision new possibilities that challenge institutionalized knowledge on improving society and transforming themselves (Lindsey, Terrell, & Robins, 2003). This enables transformative leaders to identify and collaborate with individuals who are influential in their communities to address fundamental inequalities. One way for transformative leaders to demonstrate this deep responsibility for others is by making a commitment to utilize their influence as an instrument to question the existing norms of exclusion and to create spaces that ensure equal opportunities for marginalized groups. In short, transformative leaders must critique inequitable practices in an effort to meet the needs of diverse and intricate systems and to achieve harmony within all organizations.

Leaders serve the interests of the people as citizens and public servants. In other words, they should seek the common good of their constituents prior to their own benefit. Transformative leaders exemplify these characteristics of ethical responsibility by forgiving, being compassionate, and working with everyone in their communities. Starratt (2004) noted that leaders should have a basic level of respect and dignity for human beings, thus ensuring that all voices are heard. An example comes from Furman and Shields's (2005) recognition of interdependence and the significance of communal efforts to provide balance of equity and also to create a safe space for dialogue, professional development, and for people to voice opinions and concerns.

Transformative leaders have many characteristics that set them apart from traditional leaders. These include, but are not limited to, democratic participation, commitment to deep and equitable social change, an understanding of institutionalized power, and cultural competence. I will discuss each of these elements in detail and give a practical example to provide a deeper understanding of transformative leadership.

Democratic Participation

Transformative leaders work toward democratic participation that involves the notion of inclusiveness by understanding how disparities may affect individuals. In its very nature, democracy suggests that all individuals have the same divine potential, but not everyone is at the same level of manifesting that potential. The principles of democracy are inherently inclusive in that they bestow equal opportunity, political rights, and decision-making power upon all individuals, and encourage the development of their full potential (McLaughlin & Davidson, 1996). Green (1999) argues that democracy "expresses the experience-based possibility of more equal, respectful, and mutually beneficial ways of community life" (p. vi). Because of this, democratic participation should focus on respect, participation, communication, and cross-cultural cooperation. As such, egalitarian solidarity is the belief that all people are equal and should enjoy the harmony of social, political, and economic rights and opportunities, with mutual support and collective action for achievement (Green, 1998).

Thoughtful concentration on the essence of democracy and cohesion are necessary to provide a level playing field for individuals to think critically and gain a sense of agency. According to Winfrey (2009), leaders should understand that cultural, ethnic, racial, and ideological differences may enhance or detract from dialogue, trust, and solidarity. Comprehending these differences assists transformative leaders in taking the proper steps to best engage with the public. Simons (2010) describes democratic participation as being elemental in sustainable community and social development. Democratic participation also has become the central route to self-development, as it enhances personal growth and provides community association regardless of culture differences. In that sense, politics of difference should use multiple notions of differentiation where gender, ethnicity, race, and class mediate each other. An example of this comes from Foster (1989), who emphasized the moral and ethical quality of human beings and sought to empower diverse followers through engaging in a mutual vision of freedom and equality. As such, democratic participation implies movement toward a partnership in which personal empowerment is essential for success (Eisler & Carter, 2010).

Empowerment is based on the principle of using an individual's strengths and structure to enable his or her ability to function as a self-advocate. Transformative leaders engage in internal critique and emancipation to cultivate self-knowledge while empowering others. Foster believes that leadership "must be critically educative; it cannot only look at the conditions in which we live, but it must also decide how to change them" (1989, p. 185). This form of leadership begins by acknowledging the link between community issues and individual reactions. For example, should a neighborhood attempt to discriminate against certain types of families (i.e., same-sex couples, people of color), a transformative leader would invoke compassionate understanding by establishing open dialogue, with the goal of educating and empowering all parties in order to achieve a consensus. This leadership role encompasses addressing all concerns when dealing with the degree of personal biases and internal changes needed. Change is difficult due to several assumptions that people place between themselves and change efforts. People tend to have traditions and become comfortable with the way they do things. Transformative leaders recognize that the change process is delicate and requires time and careful navigation. According to Schein (2004), transformation change implies that the person or group that is the target of change must unlearn something, as well as learn something new. Change causes transition, which requires people to adjust their behavior, attitudes, and thoughts. Bridges and Mitchell (2002) say that, while change is external (i.e., policies, practices, or structures), transition is internal (a psychological reorientation that people have to go through before the change will work). Transformative leaders understand that transition is not automatic and it will not occur just because the change is happening. This notion leads to encouraging a deeper commitment of both societal and internal social change.

Commitment to Deep and Equitable Social Change

The primary responsibility of transformative leaders consists of pursuing sustainable and equitable social change, particularly with and on behalf of vulnerable and oppressed groups. According to Burns (1978), social change leaders respond to pluralistic value sets by building advocacy and conflict into the planning process. Social change efforts focus primarily on issues of poverty, unemployment, discrimination, and other forms of social injustice. These efforts seek a creative transformation, not only of the external world, but also of internal processes, in order to promote sensitivity to and knowledge about oppression and cultural and ethnic diversity. As vehicles for change, transformative leaders seek to strengthen relationships between people in a purposeful effort to promote, restore, maintain, and enhance the well-being of individuals, families, social groups, organizations, and communities. These areas reiterate the importance of connecting social change to democratic participation.

In 1986, Foster promoted a higher level of democratic participation for transformative leadership as an exploration of individual constructions, interpretations of reality, and critical inquiry as a reflective process. Hence, transformative leadership encourages critical self-examination. Self-reflection or heightened self-awareness, knowledge, and practice skills are essential to understanding how our actions affect others. Additionally, transformative leadership involves engaging in self-reflection to comprehend how personal beliefs and attitudes may affect individuals, as well as society. According to Furman and Shields (2005), careful examination of one's own beliefs and practices and those of the institution in which one works is vital for social change, as injustice exists both in individual relationships and systemically.

Assessing Institutionalized Power

Transformative leadership demands a critical assessment of asymmetrical power relationships in organizational contexts, and that those relationships meet the needs of complex, diverse, and stressed systems. Transformative leaders work to identify all factors related to power: the leader, the intention, and the organization. Bennis (1986) defines transformative leadership power as "the ability of the leader to reach the souls of others in a fashion which raises human consciousness, builds meanings, and inspires human intent that is the source of power" (p. 70). These characteristics embody the level of engagement needed to make a change from traditional leadership to transformative action.

There is a critical need to examine systematic inequalities of power within our society, in order to better understand how this imbalance perpetuates hegemonic and dominating behaviors, cultures, and structures. Misrepresented power not only encourages societal dominance but also overlooks the crucial ingredient of power symmetry within the politics of ethnic identification. Failure to acknowledge and appreciate differences challenges inequalities due to inappropriate use of power. In 1992, Quantz, Rogers, and Dantley considered transformative leadership as a forum to raise the promise of moral purpose. They questioned assumptions upon which a vision is based, asked on whose behalf power is used, and uncovered distortions that may exist in our language and our view of the world. Furthermore, they found that leaders must exert their own positions of power to transform or balance inequitable power relationships (Quantz, Rogers, & Dantley, 1992). In other words, transformative leaders seek to uncover the ways in which dominant groups use power and strategies to promote their interests. In this way, transformative leadership is an "exercise of power and authority that begins with questions of justice, democracy, and the dialectic between individual accountability and social responsibility" (Weiner, 2003, p. 89). Additionally, Shields (2009) notes that the inequities and struggles caused by unbalanced power could have a negative effect on the leader's ability to effectively execute responsibilities. Ultimately, transformative leadership behaviors that acknowledge the injustices related to power and privilege are moving in the right direction to address societal disparities.

Demonstrating Cultural Competence

Increasing diversity in the United States requires that leaders amplify their awareness and appreciation of cultural differences. To meet this cultural-competence responsibility, leaders must continually strive to enhance their professional knowledge and skills so that they may apply them in practice. Cultural competence encompasses distinct behaviors, attitudes, and policies within a system that are necessary for effective interactions and communication in cross-cultural situations (Cross, Bazron, Dennis, & Isaacs, 1989). Transformative leaders integrate knowledge about individuals and groups of people into their practices and policies to supplement the qualities of their services and their capacity to function within the cultural context. This cultural awareness is defined as the knowledge of one's own culture as well as competencies to effectively interact across different cultures. Cultural competence implies understanding differences that individuals may identify within the categories of race, gender, sex, national origin, sexual orientation, ability, and religion. Transformative leaders value cultural differences and see them as potential strengths rather than shortcomings (Creighton, 1998; Winfrey, 2009). This perspective encourages optimism and lets a transformative leader celebrate the differences in others while including people who were previously excluded. The mission is initiated by advocating for the changes in thought and behavior necessary to cease the perpetuation of stereotypes. Moreover, transformative leaders embed professional development in collaborative structures, a context involving seeing the world through a lens of equity in order to make gains toward fair treatment for all.

Culture is not solely a race or a category, but rather, it is an experience. It is the way people understand their lives and how they feel, talk, and think about other groups of people (Lynn, 2006). Cultural assumptions profoundly weigh on societal mentalities, such as how they influence philosophy, determine policy, and incite action. In addition to understanding that an individual's culture informs his or her actions and beliefs, it is just as important to note that cultural groups have different perspectives based on their group's societal status. For instance, a certain cultural group may have varied perceptions associated with opportunities afforded to that group. Therefore, transformative leaders must take into account how a particular group experiences privilege or oppression and consider the societal inequalities that generate distinctive accounts of natural and social relationships.

Another decisive concept to examine within cultural competence is the perception or consciousness of stereotypes. Stereotypes are defined as a conceptualization of another person based on a group she or he belongs to that we use to guide our interactions in the absence of other information (Lee, Jussim, & McCauley, 1995). All individuals have an internal list of stereotypes they have yet to understand, let alone appreciate. Additionally, all individuals have biases, even prejudices, toward specific groups of people. In our personal circles, individuals may even discuss our hopes and fears when relating to or hurting others unintentionally. These hopes may include the possibility of dialogue, of learning something new, establishing rapports, developing friendships, and comprehending different points of view. At any moment that we are dealing with people different from ourselves, it is likely that they also carry similar hopes and fears. That being said, people must understand how stereotypes are both good and bad. Stereotypes are good when they encourage people to seek a deeper understanding of a person or group and when they assist people in making decisions in the absence of other information. However, stereotypes are also viewed as negative because they are factually incorrect and are usually generalizations, especially if they are simply applied and one assumes that all people one meets will follow their stereotyped roles when one treats them as such. According to Lee et al. (1995), the following are additional reasons why stereotypes should be avoided:

- Stereotypes lead to biased perceptions of individuals and ignoring individual differences.

- Stereotypes create self-fulfilling prophecies.

- Stereotypes are illogical in origin.

- Stereotypes are based in prejudice and are ethnocentric.

- Stereotypes are exaggerations of real group difference and imply genetic origins, such as "They all look alike to me."

- Stereotypes are irrationally resistant to new information.

I hope that this overview will help readers to challenge cultural stereotypes in order to contribute to societal changes. Acknowledging the various levels of progress toward cultural competence, transformative leaders seek to provide solutions for the challenges of cross-cultural interactions. These strategies go beyond promoting multiculturalism by encouraging individuals to critically examine their practices for possible bias. I now shift to a discussion of transformative actions that are essential for positive change.

Transformative Action

"Hope for a new beginning" is frequently uttered across society, as scholars recognize the dire need to take action and create transformative change. Talk is cheap unless followed by action. It is easy to talk about the numerous disparities manifested in our society, but to actually incorporate strategies that address these behaviors is difficult. To better understand the contributing components of transformative leaders, it is vital to discuss the implication of the term *transformative action*. Temes (1996) defines *leadership* as an action of ideas to make change. Action is what separates transformative leadership from traditional perspectives. Transformative action is a new entrepreneurial social-change model that focuses on the betterment of society. As stated previously, transformative leaders focus on concepts such as oppression, prejudice, and powerlessness to revolutionize attitudes, policies, and practices. The purpose of discussing transformative action is to provide a better understanding of how democracy, social justice, and inclusivity can improve societal change. Transformative leaders recognize that actions must be taken beyond simply complaining about unjust practices or policies, and work must be done to incorporate strategies for change. Leadership must be translated into action for a transformation to occur. Action involves leaders successfully manipulating events and people so their vision becomes reality. In other words, transformative leaders are able to touch on the passion of their followers by tapping into their core beliefs in order to inspire action. For example, reaching into the spiritual realms of followers lets transformative leaders seek the nature of good within themselves. As a result, transformative leaders can demonstrate how that good nature can positively affect the entire community by taking action against injustices. Such action against injustice is crucial to transformative leaders; as King (1963) noted, injustice anywhere is a threat to justice everywhere. In essence, by deeply reflecting on and integrating the message noted in the aforementioned quotation, transformative leaders arouse the inner qualities of their followers, which will serve the common good. In this section of the chapter, I will focus on characteristics of transformative action to further explain its role of transformative leadership.

Being a Change Catalyst

As change agents, transformative leaders seek to break the silence, build allies, and empower others. In other words, their actions consist of working toward democratic participation and building consensus, while helping individuals find their voices via dialogue (Eisler & Carter, 2010; Shields, 2004; Starratt, 2004). In many cases, individuals are written off or dismissed, especially people of color, simply due to lack of knowledge or intentional discrimination. In recent years, we have become increasingly aware of how these actions lead to various notions of injustice and the need for societal change (Bass & Steidlmeier, 1999). As major icons for building strong foundations for tomorrow's society, transformative leaders work to create spaces for individuals to express their innermost thoughts and understand their followers without assumptions. More specifically, we should not interpret silence from people of color as ignorance, but instead recognize it as a difference that results from many circumstances that we may not fully understand. Because of this, the goal of transformative leaders is to help break the silence and implement effective conflict-resolution strategies in order to institutionalize change. A transformative leader works to heighten societal consciousness so that society can accept differences and similarities within a larger milieu (Petranker, 2010). This is usually demonstrated via community forums, educational workshops, and within class or seminar discussions. These assemblies provide people with opportunities to debate and deliberate in an effort to achieve a compromise that results in building an alliance.

Transforming enemies into allies, repugnance into compassion, and conflict into collaboration is the ultimate accomplishment for transformative leaders. They achieve these actions by devoting their energy to creating solutions and better alternatives for all constituents. Once they understand the purpose and effect of problematic behaviors, transformative leaders are able to disseminate information for developing interventions that avoid adversarial approaches. They seek to resolve conflicts between individual and societal interests in a socially responsible manner that is consistent with the values, principles, and ethical standards of the profession. For example, this act involves treating each person in a caring and respectful fashion and being mindful of individual differences and of cultural or ethnic diversity. Ultimately, transformative action utilizes personal life-changing strategies to unite unseen threads, which may have initially been a source of negativity or oppression. This process is a necessity in assisting individuals to find their voices and empower change.

Change arises when a "win-win" solution changes a negative situation into a positive opportunity. To accomplish this level of transformation and to combat the lasting effects of societal disparities, individual and societal empowerment is crucial. That being said, transformative leaders also work with individuals to support their needs through socially responsible self-determination. According to Petranker (2010), the temporal dynamic of transformative action involves keeping the interests of others in mind through the realms of past, present, and future. Additionally, by empowering others to enhance their internal and external capacities and to address their own needs, transformative leaders help people realize their dual responsibilities—to each other and to the broader society. Transformative leaders understand that empowerment involves an adaptation to different cultural mores, and that this requires flexibility and a respect for other viewpoints. Therefore, transformative actions ensure that everyone has access to needed information, services, and resources; that they have equality of opportunity; and that they have meaningful participation in decision making.

Employing Democratic Power

Leaders must highlight democracy to address fundamental inequalities within their communities. Transformative leadership not only calls for a change in the vision and commitment of leaders but also emphasizes the need for leaders to follow a different set of institutional processes and behaviors (Bennis, 1986). For example, people in leadership roles should be committed to using power, not as an instrument of domination and exclusion but as an apparatus of liberation, inclusion, and equality. Furthermore, they should display a strong commitment to the principle of social justice, with concrete policies and actions in place that enable marginalized groups to have equal access to new knowledge and opportunities (Eisler & Carter, 2010). For instance, power controls our level of understanding of societal hierarchy and barriers, such as lack of understanding languages, jargon, and norms. As transformative leaders, we can utilize our position to provide others with information and power.

Transformative leaders mobilize people by focusing on common ideas, as opposed to the personality of a particular person. Transformative leaders understand what is important and necessary for a good society prior to taking action. In addition, these leaders have a clear sense of their own values, which they need to function ethically. Understanding pressure points or triggers and when to compromise personal values is of vital essence, and it requires integrity to do what is right for the common good. This phrase reminds me of a childhood lesson from my mother. She told me "right is right even if no one is doing it and wrong is wrong if everyone is doing it." To that end, leaders are sometimes placed in the position where they must make difficult decisions. Transformative leaders are careful of how they use their power, which says a great deal about their ethics. Ethics apply to our actions and moral values. We all want to be loved, have a need for respect, and desire honesty. Unfortunately, there will be times when these values conflict and leaders will face an ethical dilemma. It is during these moments that transformative leaders recall their personal and educational foundation. Hence, transformative leaders use their awareness of what grounds them to draw the correct conclusion.

Enacting Cultural Competence

Addressing cultural competence is imperative in combating the growing diversity and the persistent disparities within our society. Transformative leaders have an ethical responsibility to be culturally competent. Unfortunately, this concept is usually accompanied with varied perceptions that do not always serve the best interest of those in need. The notion of difference begins with individuals understanding their own lens, and that understanding stems from evaluating the personal biases that may unintentionally influence their actions (Sisneros, Stakeman, Joyner, & Schmitz, 2008). This reflection establishes a framework for exploration that goes beyond what is traditionally taught to reform oppressive ideas. Some individuals are uncomfortable with contentious issues of difference—perhaps due to fear of potential conflict, insufficient knowledge, or lack of experience or preparation (Sisneros et al., 2008; Winfrey, 2009). Nevertheless, transformative leaders understand this apprehension and can motivate others to take into account the divergence of perspectives and differences related to race, class, gender, sexual orientations, age, ability, and religion.

Truthful acknowledgement of injustices related to privilege and oppression is necessary in order to accept diversity and delivery of cultural-competent practice. Transformative leaders display cultural competence by valuing and celebrating differences. Moreover, competence implies that they understand the divergence that exists within a single culture. They also understand how cultural barriers or a language breakdown could falsely identify nondominate individuals as non-compliant or as people with problem behaviors if they fail to coincide with societal expectations. These leaders display compassion in knowing that, in certain cultures, people are taught to give up their cultural norms so they can adequately assimilate into the melting pot (Sisneros et al., 2008).

Leaders can be very effective if they know their audience. Transformative leaders present the opportunity for people to learn about and meet individuals from various cultures; for example, knowing one's audience and utilizing terminology that all individuals are able to comprehend. Transformative leaders teach lessons with built-in choices by asking questions that avoid sending negative messages. As a lack of understanding could be detrimental and lead to inaccurate reactions, transformative leaders should always use tact when acknowledging racial or cultural differences (Eisler & Carter, 2010; Sisneros et al., 2008). They might take an initial action step by research-ing cultural characteristics and examples of verbal and nonverbal communication, so as to avoid unknowingly offending others with the wrong words, tone, or body language (Taylor, 1987). As I discuss cultural examples, it is particularly appropriate to address stereotypes when noting actions for transformative leaders. Stereotypes are pervasive, automatic, and easily accessible. Everyone has stereotypes. They are hard to ignore and they influence our behavior. Although sometimes we know when we are implementing stereotypes, there are other times when we are unaware. Awareness of stereotypes is important in determining whether or not to apply them and what to do about it. Therefore, it requires extra vigilance to monitor our biased reactions to different groups of people. It is important to process our personal views and connect them with how powerful stereotypes can be. This self-examination process is essential to integrating transformative actions within our community and provides a foundation for exploring cultural differences. Please note that examin-ing cultural characteristics should not be confused with endorsing stereotypes but instead as a way to enhance personal growth. As transformative leaders, we should take action to become familiar with the known cultural differences. While acknowledging that cultural awareness varies among individuals, feelings of apprehension are common when experiencing another culture. This is par-tially due to the fact that people tend to stress cultural differences and overlook the similarities that are essential for societal evolution. More specifically, instead of seeing said differences as deficits, one should look at them as areas of value and uniqueness; for instance, individuals should exert an effort to accept traditions or characteristics that may seem illogical or unimportant due to lack of knowledge regarding different cultures.

Taylor (1987) describes various examples of racial and cultural differences, such as while some African Americans consider it offensive when someone touches their hair, some Anglo-Americans see hair-touching as a sign of affection. Also, in certain cultures listeners are expected to avert their eyes to indicate respect and attention, whereas other cultures expect individuals to look at a speaker directly. As another example, while some cultural groups do not mind when outsiders borrow ele-ments of their language, many African Americans are insulted when people outside of their race talk "black" without authorization. Ultimately, the concept of cultural competence has different meaning to various people, beyond the boundary of skin color to identity, institutions, policies, and practices. As a final call for activism, we must all do our part—through actions, sensitivity, and understanding difference—to demonstrate a commitment to seeking the necessary changes in thought and behavior for culturally competent and responsive practice.

Implications

Growing complexities in relation to diverse forms of ethnicity, culture and economic challenges, privilege and oppression, and institutional power and practices remain at the forefront of societal issues. To achieve success, it is imperative to have leaders who are sensitive to all needs and are able to address social injustices. Transformative leaders accept this mission of change. These leaders are committed to employing their influence and promoting the enhancement of consciousness to empower change that delves beneath the surface level. This action requires knowledge, personal development, leadership strategies, and the implementation of social justice in daily practices. What follows is a look at implications of this review of literature, as far as taking traditional leadership to another level of transformative action is concerned.

Strive to Be a Culturally Competent Practitioner

Acknowledging cultural competence is imperative in order to address growing diversity and persistent disparities. Cultural competence emphasizes the importance of being sensitive and understanding that relationships are important. Cross et al. (1989) note five essential elements that contribute to an institution or agency's ability to become more culturally competent. These include valuing diversity, having the capacity for cultural self-assessment, being conscious of the dynamics inherent when cultures interact, having institutionalized cultural knowledge, and having developed adaptations of service-delivery reflecting an understanding of cultural diversity. The task of enhancing cultural competence begins with transforming the commonsense understanding of race. Areas of difference to consider include: taking turns versus interrupting during conversations, using silence as a communicative device, interjecting humor at appropriate times, knowing appropriate topics of conversation, successfully interpreting nonverbal behavior, and accepting discipline techniques or expressions of love.

Using Power to Promote Ethical Practices

Transformative leaders should promote ethical practices on the part of the organizations with which they are affiliated (Bass, 1998). It is essential to understand how leaders make societal climates welcoming and inclusive for all, especially those from non-dominant backgrounds. Moreover, leaders must demonstrate trust, open communication, mutual respect, collaboration, and effective coordination to facilitate societal change. Transformative leaders are responsive and accountable to the general members of the organization and understand that it is vital to use power positively so the organization can survive and prosper (Benfari, Wilkinson, & Orth, 1986). They work toward building consensus through consultation, and their participation through these processes is time-consuming and challenging. Consensus is very powerful for an organization because it means that every voice is being heard. Decision-making processes should be open and transparent, as opposed to a system of bureaucratic, top-down institutional judgments. Instead of manipulating and controlling people, transformative leaders attempt to empower them. For example, they provide training programs and initiate activities to overcome barriers and discrimination, and thus they address deficiencies in resources.

Advocate for and Support the Needs of Disadvantaged Individuals

Understanding inequality requires the recognition of an individual's circumstances and to then try to change those circumstances within the democratic system. Recognizing the complexities of historical and current perspectives related to privilege and oppression is crucial to enhancing work toward the transformation of society that brings about social justice. It is crucial for transformative leaders to confront systematic inequities and to not be afraid to disrupt the dominant way of life. This begins by questioning the existing norms of inequality and exclusion and creating spaces for the participation and empowerment of marginalized and excluded groups. Ultimately, leaders need to take heed from Giroux (1995) and focus on democracy and solidarity in order to inspire critical thinking and belonging and to provide a level playing ground.

Implementing these suggestions will be the catalyst for changes that will create a winning situation for all parties involved. Thus, they will aid in the aspiration for socially just environments and promote social responsibility, which is the epitome of transformative leadership. Values of equity and social justice that ultimately support diversity are essential in unwrapping traditional leadership and shifting to a more action-oriented approach of change. Once transformative action receives a greater sense of acceptance and understanding, a new kind of leadership will be produced.

Summary

The purpose of this chapter was to discuss the kind of leadership needed to address disparities manifested within our society. To achieve the model of transformative leadership, this chapter provided a review of literature and emphasized the need for shifting away from traditional leadership and towards transformative action. The chapter elaborated on how developing an understanding of transformative leadership brings about and sustains social conscience. To understand traditional leadership and appreciate transformative action, this chapter began by acknowledging Burns's (1978) analysis of transactional and transformational leadership. The fundamentals of transformative leaders were provided, as these leaders demonstrate a strong commitment in the principles of equality, equity, and empowerment. In addition to the eminence of action, this chapter then moved on to strategies for building sustainable, nurturing change. A prominent aspect of this chapter was transformative leadership's role in breaking the vicious cycle of stereotypes that govern our society and its dynamic structures. Illustrating systemic inequalities and the abuse of power as a threshold to injustices clearly advocates how effective transformative leadership can be in creating a just and proactive society.

Transformative leaders have many characteristics that set them apart from traditional leaders. These include democratic participation, commitment to social change, an understanding of institutionalized power, and cultural competence. Each aforementioned fundamental of transformative leadership was discussed in an effort to unwrap the traditional shift of leadership. Democratic participation involves the notion of inclusiveness by understanding how disparities may affect individuals. Democracy is therefore essential so that all individuals receiving equitable opportunities achieve their full potential. By understanding this, transformative leaders work to empower individuals toward a partnership that values freedom and equality. In 1992, Quantz, Rogers, and Dantley argued that traditional leadership theories were inadequate for democratic empowerment and that "only the concept of transformative leadership appears to provide an appropriate direction" (p. 96). To that end, transformative leadership involves motivating individuals to reflect on how their personal beliefs and attitudes may unintentionally or unconsciously affect others as well as society (Winfrey, 2009). These solidarity strategies clearly denote a critical need to examine the inequitable distribution of power within our society. Also, transformative leaders need to provide a better understanding of how the power imbalance perpetuates hegemonic and dominating behaviors, cultures, and structures. One way to address these disparities is to integrate a level of cultural competence sufficient for effective transformative leadership. Cultural competence refers to how a transformative leader demonstrates acceptance and consideration for an individual's challenges or experiences. Additionally, cultural competence involves learning new patterns of behavior and effectively applying them in the appropriate settings.

Overall, transformative leaders recognize that actions must be taken beyond simply complaining about unjust practices or polices and that they must work to incorporate strategies for change.

Action was noted as a keystone in fostering the transformative leadership vision. Implementing and advocating for change in both thought and behavior were noted to provide a deeper understanding of the meaning and suitability of transformative action. This process includes encouraging equality in an effort to build empathy and sensitivity toward the oppressed. Moreover, there was discussion of developing an egalitarian outlook within a societal structure that is a by-product of norms and human behaviors representing the non-dominant culture.

Although we have come very far in dealing with social injustices as a people, we still have many rivers to cross and miles to go before we sleep, if you'll allow me the clichés. If we can create a just social order through acceptance and equality rather than through inequity and conflict, then we will be empowered in seeing our ability to bring about a transformation; a fundamental change from past discriminatory practices. This shift from traditional to transformative leadership forces us to think critically about injustices, encourage a heightened consciousness regarding differences, maintain our commitment to confront existing norms of exclusion, and take on a deeper responsibility of advocating for consistent social change.

References

Bass, B. M. (1998). The ethics of transformative leadership. In J. Ciulia (Ed.), *Ethics, the heart of leadership* (pp. 169–192). Westport, CT: Praeger.

Bass, B. M., & Steidlmeier, P. (1999). Ethics, character and authentic transformational leadership behavior. *The Leadership Quarterly, 10*, 181–218.

Benfari, R., Wilkinson, H., & Orth, C. (1986). The effective use of power. *Business Horizon, 29*(3), 12–16.

Bennis, W. (1986). Transformative power and leadership. In T. J. Sergiovanni & J. E. Corbally (Eds.), *Leadership and organizational culture* (pp. 64–71). Urbana, IL: University of Illinois Press.

Blake, R., & Mouton, J. S. (1985). *The managerial grid III: The key to leadership excellence.* Houston: Gulf Publishing Co.

Bridges, W., & Mitchell, S. (2002). Leading transition: A new model for change. *Leader to Leader, 16*, 30–36. Retrieved July 19, 2005, from http://www.pfdf.org/leaderbooks/121/spring2000/bridges.html

Burns, J. M. (1978). *Leadership.* New York: Harper & Row.

Creighton, T. (1998). Rethinking school leadership: Is the principal really needed? In R. Muth (Ed.), *Toward the year 2000: Leadership for quality schools* (Sixth Yearbook of the National Council of Professor of Educational Administration, pp. 14–19). Lancaster, PA: Technomic Press.

Cross T., Bazron, B., Dennis, K., & Isaacs, M. (1989). *Towards a culturally competent system of care* (Vol. I). Washington, DC: Georgetown University Child Development Center, CASSP Technical Assistance Center.

Cunningham, W. G., & Cordeiro, P. A. (2000). *Educational administration: A problem-based approach.* Needham Heights, MA: Allyn & Bacon.

Eisler, R., & Carter, S. (2010). Transformative leadership: From domination to partnership. *ReVision, 30*(3–4), 98–106.

Foster, W. (1986). *Paradigms and promises: New approaches to educational administration.* Buffalo, NY: Prometheus.

Foster, W. (1989). The administrator as a transformative intellectual. *Peabody Journal of Education, 66*(3), 5–18.

Furman, G. C., & Shields, C. M. (2005). How can educational leaders promote and support social justice and democratic community in school? In W. A. Firestone Riehl (Ed.), *A new agenda for research in educational leadership* (pp. 119–137). New York: Teachers College Press, Columbia University.

Giroux, H. A. (1995). Educational visions: What are schools for and what should we be doing in the name of education? In J. L. Kincheloe & S. R. Steinberg (Eds.), *Thirteen questions* (pp. 295–302). New York: Peter Lang.

Green, P. (1998). Egalitarian solidarity. In S. J. Goodlad (Ed.), *The last best hope* (pp. 176–193). San Francisco, CA: Jossey-Bass.

Green, J. M. (1999). *Deep democracy: Community, diversity, and transformation*. Lanham, MD: Rowman & Littlefield.

Henze, R., Katz, A., Norte, E., Sather, S., & Walker, E. (2001). *Leading for diversity: How school leaders promote positive interethnic relations* (Educational practice report no. 7). Santa Cruz, CA, & Washington, DC: Center for Research on Education, Diversity & Excellence.

King, M. L. (1963). Letter from a Birmingham jail. Retrieved October 5, 2010, from http://www.mlkonline.net/jail.html

Kouzes, J. M., & Posner, B. Z. (1997). *The leadership challenge*. San Francisco, CA: Jossey-Bass.

Lee, Y. T., Jussim, L., & McCauley, C. R. (Eds.). (1995). *Stereotype accuracy: Toward appreciating group differences*. Washington, DC: American Psychological Association.

Lindsey, R. B., Terrell, R. D., & Robins, K. N. (2003). *Cultural proficiency: A manual for schoolleaders* (2d ed.). Thousand Oaks, CA: Sage Publications.

Lynn, M. (2006). Race, culture, and the education of African Americans. *Educational Theory, 56*, 107–119.

McGregor, D. (1960). *The human side of enterprise*. New York: McGraw-Hill.

McLaughlin, C., & Davidson, G. (1996). *The new leadership: A synthesis of hierarchy and democracy* [book excerpt]. Retrieved October 20, 2008 from http://www.visionarylead.org/sp_hier.htm

Ouchi, W. (1981). *Theory Z: How American business can meet the Japanese challenge*. Reading, MA: Addison-Wesley.

Petranker, J. (2010). Leading from within the whole time. *ReVision, 30*(3), 57–62.

Quantz, R. A., Rogers, J., & Dantley, M. (1992). Rethinking transformative leadership: Toward democratic reform of schools. *Journal of Education, 173*(3), 96–118.

Schein, E. H. (1996). *Organizational culture and leadership* (2d ed.). San Francisco, CA: Jossey-Bass.

Schein, E. H. (2004). *Organizational culture and leadership* (3d ed.). San Francisco, CA: Jossey-Bass.

Shields, C. M. (2004). Dialogic leadership for social justice: Overcoming the pathologies of silence. *Educational Administration Quarterly, 40*(1), 109–132.

Shields, C. M. (2009). *Courageous leadership for transforming schools: Democratizing practice*. Norwood, MA: Christopher-Gordon.

Simons, S. (2010). The heart of hearing: A story of transformative leadership and sustainable development. *ReVision, 30*(3), 63–68.

Sisneros, J., Stakeman, C., Joyner, M., & Schmitz, C. (2008). *Critical multicultural social work*. Chicago: Lyceum Books.

Starratt, R. J. (2004). The dialogue of scholarship. *Educational Administration Quarterly, 40*(2), 259–267.

Taylor, O. L. (1987). *Cross-cultural communication: An essential dimension of effective education*. Washington, DC: Mid-Atlantic Equity Center.

Temes, P. (1996). *Teaching leadership*. New York: Peter Lang.

Weiner, E. J. (2003). Secretary Paulo Freire and the democratization of power: Toward a theory of transformative leadership. *Educational Philosophy and theory, 35*(1), 89–106.

Winfrey, D. (2009). *How teachers perceive their job satisfaction is influenced by their principals' behaviors and attitudes related to race and gender* (Doctoral dissertation, University of Illinois at Urbana-Champaign). Retrieved March 5, 2010 from ProQuest Dissertation and Theses database at http://gradworks.umi.com/33/63/3363112.html (UMI no. 3363112).

II

Curriculum Through the Lens of Transformative Leadership

9

Preparing Transformative Educators for the Work of Leading Schools in a Multicultural, Diverse, and Democratic Society

Jerry Starratt

The distinction between transformational leadership and transformative leadership is an important one, not only for the field of education, but also for leadership theory and research in other fields, including public administration, business administration, and leadership in the professions. The earlier distinction between transactional and transformational leadership, proposed by James MacGregor Burns (1978), illuminated the difference between transactional leaders who got things done—who achieved strategic objectives for their organization or institution through bargaining, negotiation, or exchange of benefits that satisfied pragmatic self-interests of the parties involved (political opponents, labor-management divisions, executives, and managers)—and transformational leaders, who mobilized the energies and commitments of others in the organization or institution around a common cause or ideal *beyond* self-interest. That common cause pointed toward a deeper or richer human value for the larger community. Burns did not disparage transactional leadership, which is the glue that motivates many arrangements in organizational life. Rather, he pointed toward a form of leadership that was called for during times of upheaval, of social fragmentation and institutional stagnation, and of political division and competing camps being mobilized around institutional survival. Self-interest in these circumstances only feeds the problem. Transformational leaders promote a vision of large and fulfilling possibilities that lift people's horizon beyond self-interest, toward higher, common ideals.

Burns, a historian, was primarily interested in understanding how the great political leaders were able to appeal to their followers and peers to have them put aside immediate self-interest and join together, in a more or less common effort, to overcome the challenges they faced. He documented how those leaders transformed the way their peers and followers thought about themselves as a society, how they defined the human ideals they were striving for, and whether they thought that ideal was democracy, equality, free enterprise, or the Kingdom of God on Earth.

Burns's categories of *transformational* and *transactional* began to be adopted by scholars studying organizational leadership across a variety of fields (Avolio & Bass, 2002; Bass, 1998; Bass & Avolio, 1994). Earlier critiques of charismatic leadership, which led to political, religious, and ideological excesses, had already resulted in a toning down of the notion of transformational leadership into a more modest concept: transforming organizations from current dysfunctions toward greater efficiency and effectiveness; to a more rationalized, rather than a political, internal structure; to greater productivity and, therefore, a more competitive edge in a marketized environment; or, more recently, to a more environmentally sensitive—though nonetheless still profitable—enterprise.

In the field of education, the research of Kenneth Leithwood (1992) has attempted to identify transformational leadership within these more modest notions of transformation. To his credit, he admits that the research findings, when measured by student achievement on state or national tests, point to rather small differences between what he calls transformational leadership and other forms of leadership. Perhaps those modest findings are related more to the attachment of transformational leadership to increases in student test scores rather than to a more generous understanding of transformational leadership as defined by Burns. Using Burns's definition, transformational leadership would be understood to be a far less frequent phenomenon than is assumed by the research on principals and other school leaders, found through the sampling process of educational researchers, who are attempting to identify the organizational strategies of "successful" educational leaders.

Thus, transformative leadership is appropriately distinguished from both Burns's and Leithwood's definitions of transformational leadership. Though it may well be tied to a vision of education that elevates the horizons of all stakeholders beyond self-interest toward a more transformative communal experience of learning and teaching, rather than to a simple and exclusive metric of higher test scores, transformative leadership starts out with a focus on the most obviously disadvantaged students who arrive at the schoolhouse door on the first day of school. Then, having identified who these students are and what the disadvantages are that hinder their learning, and having begun to marshal supports for them, some of Leithwood's findings on the reculturing and restructuring of the school might enter into the work of the transformative leader. Nevertheless, while that reculturing and restructuring might have one eye on improving all students' test scores, the other eye is on the education of the whole child, engaging the whole humanity of the child in an educating process that brings the interests, talents, and cultural background of the child, and youth in general, into dialogue with the learning agenda of the school.

What Might Transformative Educational Leadership Look Like?

Consistent with the theme of this book, I would describe transformative educational leadership as follows. Transformative educational leaders:

1. Identify and create supports for both individuals and groups of students who come to school unprepared for the schooling agenda, due to a variety of conditions, such as the following: difficult or dysfunctional home situations; health issues; socioemotional issues; a history of underperformance in earlier years of school; and underdeveloped language skills. Transformative educational leaders would be involved with creating connections with multiple service agencies, both voluntary and local governmentally supported agencies, that serve families and children in need. Those connections would include: health-related agencies that can help identify health risks like asthma and diabetes, which disproportionately affect children in poverty and negatively impact their academic performance; referrals to health and family services; counseling or intensive intervention for children

with physical or emotional trauma; and an office of home-family communication staffed by a social worker who can provide referrals for housing and clothing, transportation to services, language assistance for recent immigrants, and a general ballast for families in transition. Since academics is at the heart of the school's agenda, transformative leaders would set up an assessment process at the intake of new students to evaluate their developmental needs and connect students with tutoring and mentoring support or enrichment services in the community, such as opportunities in music, art, sports, boys and girls clubs, and so forth. These kinds of full-service school sites can be found in many cities, such as Boston, New York, and Detroit. Affiliations with nearby universities can open up links to both undergraduate and graduate student volunteer groups, as well as academic internships for those in professional schools, such as nursing, social work, law, business, and education. In many communities, groups of retired senior volunteers are also eager to serve in a variety of capacities.

2. Identify and adjust structures in the schooling process that advantage some and disadvantage others; deculturalize some and reinforce the cultural hegemony of others; denormalize some and demand conformity of all to one standard or type; or reward the privileged and penalize, patronize, or neglect the needs of children of poverty. Transformative leaders would establish a committee of teachers and parents to review the school's responsiveness to diversity in the student body and attend to a more generous opportunity to learn for all students.

3. Nurture a sense of democratic community and a school culture where all voices, languages, and interests are respected, and where all students can participate and contribute according to their abilities and interests. Transformative leaders promote the ideal of a self-governing community, with representatives from the student body, the parents, and the teachers involved in discussions and decisions that promote the primary agenda of the school—the agenda of teaching and learning. Within that primary agenda, the learning process will continually probe aspects of the curriculum that concern the needs of a democratic community and polity.

4. Promote a rich understanding, appreciation, and application of the lessons of the academic curriculum, wherein learners can connect the subject matter to their experience, to the life of the community, to the trajectory of their lives, to a sense of membership in the world at large, and to a sense of responsibility to participate within the world at large. This aspect of transformative educational leadership will, of course, require a deep commitment to work with the faculty over many years, in order to replace the current exclusive understanding of curriculum as prefixed, stable content that must be replicated on tests that measure "mastery" of such content, with a dialogical understanding of curriculum and learning that is related to human flourishing within a democratic polity.

What Might the Education of Transformative Educational Leaders Look Like?

Logically, that education would attempt to develop the understandings, dispositions, and skills that would enable these educators to do what the above four leadership capacities describe. Normally, the development of these understandings, dispositions, and skills would be embedded in specific courses within a master's degree program—a program, moreover, that met the requirements for licensure by the state department of education. Courses where one would expect to find attention given to these specific understandings, dispositions, and skills would be, for example, school law, ethics in education, school-community relations, curriculum leadership, leadership for social justice, instructional supervision, the principalship, the field practicum in educational administration, leading change in schools, leading school renewal, and data-influenced decision making at the district, school, and classroom levels. The specifics and quality of attention to the consistent development of the above four leadership capacities throughout these courses would depend, however, on the scholarly perspectives and capacities of the professors teaching the courses; the leadership of the department chair in promoting attention toward this kind of transformative leadership; the orientation of the school of education toward serving urban, suburban, and rural schools; the core values and commitments of the school of education toward equity and social justice in the practice of education, as well as the program evaluation criteria used by the department and by the school of education.

The faculty in master's programs in educational leadership need to assess how well and often individual courses are involved with understandings and dispositions, as well as with actual skills of engagement that will be used to change existing conditions in schools they are likely to work in. Professors tend to focus on identifying unjust and dysfunctional aspects in the operation of schools, and on constructing possible ways to respond to them but often leave it to field-based internships to provide students with opportunities to develop skills to engage with issues of disadvantage and bias. Whenever possible, opportunities to apply their learning to specific, school-based, skill-developing situations should be offered in each course in the program.

One needed addition to the course offerings and experiences in preparation programs would be a course that introduced prospective principals to the many local agencies and services available to families and students. Such a course would expose participants to model collaborations between schools and such agencies, and allow them to have conversations with leaders of these agencies. School districts sometimes provide exceptional leadership in introducing new school principals to this aspect of their leadership role—that of interacting with community agencies. In some instances, local universities provide additional help to local schools through student volunteer groups and professional internships in schools. Educators preparing for principal leadership positions should be prepared to step into these roles with a ready knowledge of what is available, as well as what is possible to nurture, as they link the school with its community.

Transformative Leaders Also Need a Vision of Academic Learning

An important theme that preparation programs should stress is the leader's articulation and cultivation of a vision of learning that honors the three purposes behind the mission of public education: development of skills, understandings, and dispositions for (1) participation as a citizen in a democratic society, (2) productive employment or successful further education, and (3) personal human flourishing. In addition to all of the lessons schools teach in their cocurricular, counseling, and student-life programs, the teaching—and learning—of the academic curriculum should be seen as a primary contributor to those three purposes of learning.

In their work with teachers, students, and parents, educational leaders need to highlight that learning an academic discipline involves these three important goals just outlined. First, students learn the major conceptual perspectives and the skills necessary to employ the research methodologies of the scholar-researcher. For example, in the study of biology, students learn the scientific methodology of doing research in the biology laboratory and can reproduce the knowledge that biology researchers produce. In this way, they can appreciate how biologists think about the living universe and how they practice their science. In the nation's effort to produce more scientists and thus to further the nation's production of new knowledge—which will benefit the health and welfare of its citizens and advance the nation's prosperity in a competitive market for biological research—this approach to learning biology motivates some students to pursue careers in scientific research, thus aligning with the second purpose of education outlined earlier.

However, there are other values to the learning of biology that should be *equally* emphasized in the school's curriculum and pedagogy, such as preparing knowledgeable citizens who can debate public policies that deal with environmental sustainability and public health, which aligns with our first purpose of education, as outlined earlier. This kind of learning entails understanding what biological science teaches about healthy living; about medical options in treating illnesses; about biological effects of toxic chemicals in food, cosmetics, and pesticides; and about the need for governments to cooperate on global environmental sustainability. These issues have enormous implications for the personal and political choices of citizens to support (or not) policies concerning public health and environmental sustainability. While schools might encourage students to contemplate careers in biological research, most students will not become biologists. They will all, however, become citizens, and as such, they should know enough basic biology to understand debates over government policies that affect the public weal. Since nations invest huge sums of money to educate not only future scholars but, equally important, an educated citizenry that is capable of intelligent participation in governing the public welfare, this kind of learning should be especially promoted, even while students are developing skills and understandings derived from a challenging involvement with the science of biology.

The third value educational leaders should promote in the study of biology is the students' gradual appreciation of the intelligence and intelligibility of all life forms in nature—including human nature, which includes the learners' own biological functioning (Starratt, 1998, 2010). This type of learning legitimately connects to the students' understandings of their own identity as biological organisms and leads to human flourishing, our final purpose of education outlined at the start of this section. It would seem as important to have this knowledge about one's physical person—about one's very self—as it would be about one's emotional makeup or about one's spiritual longings and aspirations. The study of biology can help one to appreciate oneself as a biological person, connected to humans everywhere who share the same complex and marvelous history of biological evolution (Csikszentmihalyi, 1994).

Similarly, the study of psychology, while it might be useful to some students' search for a fulfilling career as a research professor of psychology or a clinical professional, can serve these other two larger purposes: the relevance of a broad understanding of human psychology firstly to their involvement as citizens in public policies involving mental health, and secondly to managing their own emotions and motivations in dealing with others on the job. Indeed, human flourishing requires the self-knowledge derived from this knowledge of one's defenses, one's fears, one's biases, and one's need to be loved and to love, so as to develop a more intentional human agency in their human relationships and their work.

Indeed, all of the academic disciplines could take on a richness and a depth if the pedagogy and the curriculum were to deal with the potential embedded in all three dimensions of learning the academic curriculum. The arts and humanities have much to teach the young about the cultural worlds they inhabit and about the variety of expressions of taste, of virtue and vice, of courage and folly, that exist. Questions can be raised about their own preferred cultural expressions of themselves; again, to connect with their journey of constructing an identity, of learning how to be a *someone*—to belong, to do some good (Starratt, 1998, 2010). While teachers might love to see their students choose to become poets or journalists, the humanities also have value for students who will not become professional poets, composers, playwrights, or journalists, but whose lives as citizens and parents are enriched by public involvement in the arts, and whose lives as individual human beings flourish in the self-knowledge and pleasures the arts and humanities convey.

Finally, transformative educational leaders need to consider that the pedagogical approach to these three areas of learning might, in most instances, begin with the significance of particular curriculum units to learners' personal flourishing, for that is the most important and immediate concern for students—though not for testing companies. To be sure, the expression of human flourishing may very well involve critique of and resistance to the picture of the world presented in the curriculum unit, perhaps seen by the students as distorted, biased, unintelligible, or oppressive. Human flourishing requires resistance to a perspective that demeans or excludes the learners' humanity. Teachers should help learners uncover the reasons for and reasonableness of that resistance. In any event, emphasizing the connection between the curriculum unit and the learners' struggle to create their identities and to understand how their world works might considerably energize the other two important learning concerns.

As they address their role as leaders of learning in their training programs, prospective leaders need to be challenged to explore in greater depth the ways in which the learning process can—within the current, exclusive policy emphasis on scholarly academic learning—give greater attention to citizenship and personal flourishing concerns. This focus on the transformative potential of the academic curriculum should be one of the defining characteristics of a preparatory process that seeks to prime educators for the challenging work of transformative leadership.

References

Avolio, B., & Bass, B. (Eds.). (2002). *Developing potential across a full range of leadership: Cases on transformational leadership.* Mahwah, NJ: Lawrence Erlbaum.

Bass, B. (1998). *Transformational leadership: Industrial, military, and educational impact.* Mahwah, NJ: Lawrence Erlbaum.

Bass, B., & Avolio, B. (Eds.). (1994). *Improving organizational effectiveness through transformational leadership.* Thousand Oaks, CA: Corwin Press.

Burns, J. M. (1978). *Leadership.* New York: Harper & Row.

Csikscentmihalyi, M. (1993). *The evolving self.* New York: Harper Collins.

Leithwood, K. A. (1992). The move toward transformational leadership. *Educational Leadership, 49*(5), 8–12.

Starratt, R. J. (1998). Grounding moral educational leadership in the morality of teaching and learning. *Leading and Managing, 4*(4), 243–255.

Starratt, R. J. (2010). The moral character of academic learning: Challenging the exclusivity of the reigning paradigm of school learning. In A. Hargreaves, A. Lieberman, M. Fullan, & D. Hopkins (Eds.), *Second International Handbook of Educational Change* (pp. 631–645). London: Springer International Handbooks of Education.

10

Curriculum-Inquiry as a Transformative Educational Leadership Skill

Daniel Reyes-Guerra and Ira E. Bogotch

We will begin and end this chapter with a single, albeit complicated, message: We believe that the field of educational leadership needs to profoundly embrace the teachings of curriculum theorists. For, without curriculum theory and inquiry as a transformative leadership skill, public education and school leadership will remain captive to externally developed theories, externally mandated policies, managerial practices, and loud, miseducative voices that are all destructive to the historic purposes of public schooling in the United States—and to our profession

Beginning with Purposes

Most readers are familiar with the "recorded history" (Bogotch, in press, 2005/2011) of educational administration from the late 19th century onward, as depicted by textbooks, national reports, seminal authors, timelines, and sweeping metaphors of the different eras. Those who have studied history, however, know that recorded history glosses over the cacophony of diverse voices and eyewitness details that make up the narratives of history. In this chapter, we pick up the historical narrative with Rosemary Papa (2009):

> Perhaps and for the purpose of constructive debate, we can best describe the last 114 year history as a field that 'regresses to the mean' when change comes upon us. The early 20th century was focused on the science of school management. The mid 20th century was characterized by administration as a science. The business model of management gave way to the medical model of theory building. The later part of the 20th century embraces cultural pluralism while moving to narrow the education administration curriculum to a very prescribed path. (p. 14)

While educational administration debates centered on the relationships of theory and practice, objective-versus-subjective research methods, organizational theory, schools and communities, and leadership theories, this "history" was not connected to the purposes and processes of curriculum theory and inquiry. The field of curriculum theory and inquiry has been grounded in educational concepts, such as development, growth, discovery, progressivism, democracy, morality, and reconstruction. In the spirit of writing a "what if" scenario, we ask you, our readers, to consider how we might rewrite the field and profession of educational leadership as if curriculum theory and inquiry were a transformative leadership skill.

Using curricular purposes and processes, we would be able to see our field's grounding as a profession related, not to organizational theory, business, or medical models but rather to other quasi-professional fields, such as nursing and social work, which in their public service roles have displayed a professional courage of conviction not yet found in educational leadership. These other fields have made caring and social justice, respectively, the central purposes of their professions. Educational leadership, however, has never been able to achieve this kind of purpose and has been split by the philosophical differences that emerge when debating the role of education (Donmoyer, Imber, & Scheurich, 1995; Greenfield & Ribbins, 1993). Without professional conviction, then, the profession follows the lead of others, measuring itself on borrowed yardsticks, shifting from workforce productivity to student achievement; from comprehensive school reform back to basics in literacy and numeracy; from top-down or bottom-up reforms to shared decision making and distributive leadership; from single-school culture to culturally relevant pedagogies. It is not that educational leadership does not promote educative values but rather that it dances to many different tunes depending on which tune (policy) the DJ (powerholder) du jour is spinning. In this environment, it is impossible for the public to know—and therefore to support—what the field of educational leadership stands for. Should the purposes of public schools, and therefore our educational leadership programs, be to promote democracy? humanism? workforce readiness? the aesthetic, creative, and spiritual growth and development of citizens? Or what?

In addition to deciding how to answer the above question about purpose, we must also ask the process question: Who should legitimately participate in deciding purposes? To what extent should our business and government leaders—noneducators who wield power throughout society—decide on the purposes of public education? Should public school purposes come from university professors, practicing school administrators, teachers, parents, or school communities? Should the answers come from foundation think-tank scholars or wealthy philanthropists (e.g., Bill Gates)? These are complicated questions for sure. But what we assert here is that the lessons of curriculum theory and inquiry will help us all to reestablish both purposes and processes for educational leadership.

We further believe that both the purpose and process questions depend on the values and goals of democracy. Yet, how often do we hear and stand silent when a school administrator at the national, state, district, or school level, while acknowledging the primary purpose of U.S. education is to promote good citizenry and human potential, states, "But I don't run this [insert an organizational level] as a democracy." Knowing that the "but" negates all that comes before it, we tacitly nod, not challenging such a miseducative and un-American assertion. As well-intentioned human beings, we would never do this when hearing a racist, bigoted, or sexist comment, would we? But, as Carolyn Shields reminded us when she introduced transformative leadership to our profession, "good intentions are not enough" (2003). We agree and, therefore, will argue that if curriculum theory and inquiry does not become central to leadership program development and redevelopment, there can be no transformative leadership in public education.

In this chapter, we will document the relevant teachings of curriculum theory and inquiry, while pointing out that such teachings have never been central to the field of educational leadership. Instead, program "refinement and revisiting"—to meet the needs of "stakeholders"—has been the driving force in today's leadership standards and accountability movement. We in educational leadership have tended to begin with authorities—for example, national standards, state departments of education, superintendent fiats—and not with the educative and moral needs of our adult students and the needs of their diverse young students in schools. We are the first to teach our students about complexity and chaos, yet we allow our professional practice to adopt these binary systems, linear thinking, and universal responses in a profession that should be "responding with its own awareness, and response, a syncopation of diversity, conflict, and complexity" (McClellan & Dominguez, 2006, p. 236).

Our argument is unequivocal: Unless and until we can refocus on the learners' needs in context, we will remain captive inside the political apparatus of external state and institutional authorities, and education will not become the professionals many of us had hoped for as professors of educational leadership. Using curriculum theory and inquiry teachings to develop educational leadership programs, we can educate school leaders in ways that are grounded in transformative leadership theory and practice and affirm the democratic values and processes of the American educational leadership profession.

Why This Conversation Is Complicated

As you continue reading, you will see the importance of collaborative, cooperative, and collegial (3C programs) faculty relationships. Curriculum inquiry and transformative leadership are built upon democratic values, dialogue, and shared decision making, which are not only difficult to conceptualize but also difficult to operationalize. Our situation is problematic. University faculty profiles are characterized by autonomous work ethics, migration, individual expertise, private practice values, and rewards and incentives tied to tenure and promotion decisions (Bogotch & Maslin-Ostrowski, 2010), all of which make building 3C programs difficult.

Each year, educational leadership faculty members migrate for a host of reasons: some seeking colleagues more aligned with their professional values, others just trying to escape toxic departmental climates. Oftentimes, state university faculty migrate based on state levels of higher education funding, the so-called "brain-drain." But whatever the reasons given to explain why faculty come and go, at some point, program design and implementation—that is, curriculum development—become agenda items for both a program and for individual educational leadership faculty members. And, when it does, the critical questions of collegiality, social relationships, professional responsibility, departmental citizenship, leadership, and expertise come to the program faculty table.

Experiences Matter to Learning

In preparation for reading the rest of this curriculum chapter, we want you to recall your own experiences with colleagues when program reform has come to the departmental table. How did you respond, if and when you heard the following comments: "just tell me what you want or need me to do?" "Here's my two cents' worth, if anyone cares." "I don't see why what I teach [in law, policy, management, etc.] has to change." "I don't think we need to include [fill this space with words like *adjuncts, school-district personnel, alumni, current students, community representatives, business leaders,* etc.] in these discussions. It will only prolong this discussion. And, in any case, they won't add anything important." "Let's just do what NCATE wants to see." "Where is [insert the name of a faculty member]? She has missed the last two meetings and we need her input." "Can we move on? We're wasting time." "We haven't heard from [again insert the name of a faculty member] this meeting. What do you think?"

A program faculty is more than the sum of individual faculty members, for it requires a willingness to discuss and debate purposes, processes, values, priorities, commitments, content, sequencing, staging, spiraling, and integrating—all curricular terms that will be highlighted here as necessary for curriculum inquiry as a transformative leadership skill. It was encouraging when, five years ago, the Stanford Educational Leadership Institute School Leadership Study report (Davis, Darling-Hammond, LaPointe, & Meyerson, 2005) recommended that "the learning activities provide a scaffold on which new self-directed knowledge is constructed, foster deep self-reflection, link past experiences with newly acquired knowledge, are problem—rather than subject—centered, and offer multiple venues for applying new knowledge in practice" (pp. 8–9). The language used by these authors is explicitly taken from curriculum theory. Yet, five years later, how many of us are engaged in the constant dialogue needed, using this vocabulary, and can say we have experienced the 3Cs? Likewise, it is discouraging to see that the latest Wallace Foundation report (Orr, King, & LaPointe, 2010) has lost this terminology, and perhaps reflects an omission that we need to reconsider.

Our own experiences have not always been what we would recommend. And yet, we can state honestly that, even through difficult curriculum conversations, we have asked members of our faculties to recommit themselves to our shared purposes, as well as to our adult learners' needs (Bogotch, 2010; Reyes-Guerra & Mountford, 2009). We know the difference between student-feedback data regarding an individual professor or course and student feedback regarding the program as a whole. The former pertain to learning specific course content, course objectives and evaluation, grades, and personal satisfaction with the course; the latter can be truly transformative, not only professionally, but also personally. The following students' comments from unpublished qualitative and quantitative studies, conducted from 1993 to 2000 at the University of New Orleans, speak to the connectedness of courses—the curriculum—when perceived as a leadership program:

> In retrospect, the [courses] did not turn out to be activities in isolation. Rather, ideas became interconnected and interdependent upon each other. I could not contemplate one exercise from one professor and not be able to connect it to another. . . . [This] educational leadership program has taught me to be proficient in what was once foreign. Now it is becoming fluent. Upon reflection, many of the concepts and activities undertaken as a result of this program are more related than different. They are interconnected like threads on a garment. (UNO student communication, June 1999)

> [The course titled] School Community Relations was the first time I began to see the whole program flowing together and merging into one huge learning experience. I guess by that time I had taken enough classes that they were beginning to gel in my mind. I also found myself taking more leadership roles in class during Clinical Supervision and School Community Relations than ever before. I guess that was a personal indication of evolving leadership. (UNO student communication, 1995)

> To be honest, my understanding of school leadership has not just evolved during this program, it has made me into a different person. I entered this program as a second-year, inexperienced teacher. I am learning as a potential school leader for the future. I will take with me more "gems" than I can count. I just hope I can transform them into an educational treasure. (UNO student communication, 1995)

It is the explicit understanding of the program as a whole (i.e., purpose and processes) that influences the kind of leadership we have in university departments and in our K-12 schools.

Why (We Need) Transformative Leadership

Shields (2010) has asserted that transformative leadership moves beyond transactional and transformational leadership to a higher scaffold of change that encompasses individual, organizational, and societal transformation. Other theorists, too, have argued that educational leadership requires taking the high road through educative values, morals, and community building. Yet, a study by Murphy, Moorman, and McCarthy (2008) found that "leadership preparation programs frequently have no explicit mission, perspective, philosophy, or point of view that provides the seedbed upon which all elements of the program build" (p. 8). This curricular gap between "what is" and "what should be" turns on the concepts that transformative leadership shares with curriculum inquiry—democratic principles, processes, and ends. Not even the latest iterations of other modernist leadership theories, such as distributive leadership, can move the conversation beyond the job tasks or work activities. That is, until we specify and debate the moral values and purposes of public education for a community, society, and the world, we remain mired in transactional practices and strategic leadership, perforated with inspirational slogans taken from transformational leadership authors. We hope to demonstrate here that curriculum theory and inquiry is central to our rebuilding programs that will educate transformative school leaders.

Why (We Need) Curriculum Theory

To echo William Pinar (2004, p. 185), curriculum theory and development is a "complicated conversation." How can it be otherwise? Curriculum is both a matter of content, a reorganizing of knowledge and relationships as well as a process or journey for growth. Curriculum has a long and rich theory-base that raises intellectually challenging questions—what Murphy et al. (2008) found missing from their document analyses—and calls for critical analysis of the purposes of schooling. In so doing, participants reaffirm their professional roles, taking control of content, sequence, integration, and purpose. While the formal definition of *curriculum* found inside catalogues, brochures, and Web pages describe it as what is taught and learned in single classrooms, curriculum, as we learned in our undergraduate teacher-education years, is the totality of experiences—with multiple dimensions, including cognitive, social, political, economic, moral, aesthetic, cultural, and spiritual aspects of life—not just for living today, but also to be transmitted generatively from generation to generation. As such, curriculum inquiry demands that participants have the freedom to be creative and innovative. We deliberately intend the word *participant* to be inclusive of teachers, administrators, staff, parents, and community members. Thus, as you read the following curriculum-inquiry quote, please substitute progressively all of the participants for the word *teacher*.

A teacher who does not understand the obvious fact that education is a moral affair, and that a skill has to be learned in a way that makes it likely a person will use it for moral ends in a good and democratic society, is not discharging his responsibility (Foshay, 1975, p. 72). In fact, it is originally from curriculum theorists that we in educational leadership have come to better understand the sociocultural and ideological power that schools hold over a society. Whether the theories are based on the writings of Bowles and Gintis, Pierre Bourdieu, Paulo Freire, Michael Apple, Henry Giroux, Peter McLaren, William Pinar, Elliot Eisner, Gloria Ladson-Billings, Christine Sleeter, Sonia Nieto, Jeannie Oakes, Kenneth Zeichner, William Ayers, or others, "the realization that powerful social and structural relationships in the larger society are embedded in school curricula is largely due to the work of the reconceptualists, who have elevated the discussion of curricular leadership from the purely technical to the larger socio-political domain" (English & Steffy, 2005, p. 423). This is not to say that educational leadership theorists—from Ernest Melby, Donald Willower, William Foster, and Thomas Greenfield, Spencer Maxcy, Fenwick English, Carolyn Shields, and others—have not added to our legitimate knowledge base. All we are saying is that we, the field of educational leadership, are indebted to curriculum theorists who pioneered sociocultural theories of practice.

Thus, we want to reintroduce you to a few of these influential curricular theorists in this chapter. Most of their names and some of their writings should be familiar to professors of educational leadership, as well as to aspiring and veteran school administrators. Among the thought-leaders in curricular inquiry we have read and cited here are John Dewey, Ralph Tyler, Arthur Foshay, Alice Miel, Jerome Bruner, and William Pinar. Our objective is to integrate their curricular teachings into the new reform work of educational leadership.

The Primacy of Curriculum Inquiry over Educational Leadership

We begin by asserting that curriculum inquiry precedes leadership, in the same way that practice precedes theory. We base this analogy on the historical fact that the field of educational leadership was not always subsumed within its current paradigm of management and workforce productivity being transmitted through externally mandated curricula and accountability measures (see Bogotch, 2005/2011). Of the eight historical dimensions of public school leadership, Bogotch identified two rooted in the dynamic relationship between curriculum and educational leadership: (1) "in-depth knowledge of curriculum and instruction" and (2) "school leadership that is democratic with a small 'd'" (p. 27). The first held that when, out of necessity, it became essential to institute managerial processes within schools and school systems, it had to be done in the service of teaching and learning; the second dimension equated democratic practices, whether with respect to classroom teaching or school administration, with a love for children and community (Koopman, Miel, & Miser, 1943; Mann, 1846).

Curriculum organizes and prioritizes the knowledge that educators decide needs to be transmitted from generation to generation. It starts with already-existing knowledge but, because knowledge is not inert (Whitehead, 1929), there have to be constructivist processes through which teachers and students make meanings from the past, in the present, and into the future. Dewey called this laboratory learning and reconstructivist philosophy. As such, curriculum becomes more than the formal content of classroom, or course-by-course, instruction. Rather, curriculum is dynamic, promoting growth and development. According to Grumet (1995), "curriculum is never the text, or the topic, never the method or syllabus; [it is] the conversation that makes sense of things. . . . It is the process of making sense with a group of people of the systems that shape and organize the world we can think about together" (p. 19).

Dewey argued throughout his long career that practice—specifically the consequences of human behaviors and thoughts—a priori precedes theory. Therefore, not only must we conclude that leadership-in-action is prior to articulating a theory of leadership, so must we acknowledge that curriculum development—for example, the organization and purpose of knowledge—is prior to leadership, both as practice and as theory. Having reviewed the literature of curriculum inquiry for this chapter, we have come to the following four conclusions:

- First, that curriculum inquiry begins and continues the processes of growth and development by asking questions, not by prescribing solutions or giving "one best" or "best practice" answers.

- Second, there are stages of development in curricular understanding, rather than fixed, definitive, or one-time measures of achievement.

- Third, the categories of schools of thought (namely, perennialists, essentialists, progressives, and reconstructivists) are not fixed, but rather they overlap each other.

- Fourth, the field of curriculum invests in specifying and clarifying values as it progressively seeks to connect and reconnect to the needs of students, communities and societies.

These four conclusions define the distinguishing features of curriculum inquiry and differentiate it from how educational leadership approaches its own curricular development.

Distinguishing Between Curriculum Inquiry and Educational Leadership

It is important that readers see how differently curricular theorists conceptualize their field from how we in educational leadership write about our roles and our preparation programs. It is also important to understand how curriculum makes leadership stronger and how educational leadership can potentially make curriculum theory stronger. Our argument hinges on this codependency. Thus, we are looking toward the redevelopment of an integrated education profession connecting curriculum theory with educational leadership.

While we emphasize the primacy of curriculum inquiry, we remain staunch proponents of educational leadership, holding firm to the beliefs that it is through leadership practice and research that we best understand how to confront dilemmas, paradoxes, and structural barriers in schools (Starratt, 2011). It is only with a firm knowledge of leadership, and especially transformative leadership, that we can even envision making structural, organizational, and societal changes. The study and practice of leadership come from the professional responsibility to act on the larger stages that exist beyond the classroom. Further, we see this leadership responsibility as more than an accommodation, a seeking out of a strategic advantage, more than the cliché of "it is better to ask for forgiveness than get permission," more than "working under the radar," and more than "creative insubordination." Such strategic survival phrases limit our ability as leaders to think creatively at advanced theoretical levels. They hold us back professionally. They remove us from the primacy of developing our own field, to simply the implementation of dictates and external direction. We are seeking here more than accommodation, compliance, or even transformational changes that are more rhetorical and inspirational rather than substantive; our profession, we hold, should be about the struggles for and deepening of democracy and social justice (Bogotch, 2002a; Jenlink, 2009; Shields, 2004).

But before we in educational leadership can fully realize the scope of our leadership responsibilities, it is important to clarify the distinguishing features (Smith, 1971) between curriculum inquiry and educational leadership. In setting forth the three essential differences—conceptual and process gaps that need to be closed—we build on the conclusions mentioned in the previous section.

1. Whereas curricular theorists speak to the needs of children and to the purposes of education, school leadership programs emphasize the technical skills of monitoring, mapping, prioritizing, and assessing curriculum. If we use the Interstate School Leaders Licensure standards as our curriculum content, we see how the processes of curriculum inquiry are usually absent and even the use of the word "curriculum" is ignored.

2. Whereas curricular theorists define *structure* as a fundamental idea, that is, how a subject is meaningfully related to other ideas (Bruner, 1960/1963), educational leadership uses this word to mean the actual rules, roles, policies, and norms of an organization (Bolman & Deal, 2003). Structures are blatantly removed from the teaching and learning process (Shields, 2003). In contrast, Bruner's structure is a conceptual framework from which new ideas and relationships are developed by students themselves.

3. Whereas curricular theorists begin and end with process-oriented questions (see Tyler, 1949), educational leadership continually looks to experts with already-formulated answers, and many of these experts come from professions other than our own.

The challenge we all face, regardless of the differences in roles and responsibilities between teachers, staff, and administrators, is that we all have to use our professional talents and skills to "develop intelligent human beings who know how the world works and are prepared to participate in the world as healers of the ills and stakeholders in its development" (Starratt, 2011, p. vii). It takes no more than a cursory look at educational history, from Raymond Callahan to David Tyack, to see why and how our leadership profession has allowed these theories and technologies to drive a wedge between the purposes of education and the managerial roles and responsibilities of educational leadership. What has happened is a tragedy, really, for the world needs the best of educational leadership far more than education needs leadership theories built upon business models or organizational dynamics. To again quote Robert Starratt (2011):

> This does not deny that both teacher leaders and administrative leaders come into schools as already established organizations and therefore initially have to accommodate to existing organizational structures, procedures, and arrangement. However, their primary allegiance is not to the organization of the school (or district or state department of education), but rather, to the core work of the school which is down by the learners, and to the human development of those workers. (p. viii)

Starratt understands deeply how educational leadership has made structures into fixed organizational and institutionalized constructs. He, like Jerome Bruner in the 1960s, argues that structures serve as conceptual frameworks from which we can open up possibilities beyond existing systems. But in order for educational leadership to free itself from structuralism, it must acknowledge the historical truth that there was leadership-in-practice before the academic fields of leadership and organization theory emerged in the mid-20th century. Not only was leadership in practice prior to theory development, but so also were the political and economic ideas of democracy and social justice. Why then, do we teach aspiring administrators leadership beginning with the development of leadership as theory? Should we not teach leadership historically, as it emerged inside schools as they existed and evolved? But even if we were to make this curricular change, as advocated by Fenwick English in his many administrative theory texts, we would still not have integrated educational leadership with curriculum inquiry. More conceptual work is needed for this integration to emerge.

All of the special fields of education need to come together programmatically in undergraduate and graduate education if we are to return our chosen field—educational leadership—to "the work of educating" (Starratt, 2011). What Starratt's words mean to us is that teacher leaders and administrative leaders need to engage in curriculum inquiry in terms of program development, program design, program implementation, and program evaluation. If today's critical leadership "success" factors, as determined by the Southern Regional Educational Board (Bottoms & O'Neill, 2001), focus exclusively on the monitoring and assessing of curriculum, then today's leaders will come to know only how to deliver, monitor, and assess already existing curriculum and knowledge, rather than know how to design, develop, and build curriculum based on the needs of learners, local communities, and society at large. This implies that schools and school systems would have to abandon the current practices of "canned" curricula delivered to students based on published textbooks— purchased with taxpayers' monies—a single "best practice" theory of instruction (e.g., direct instruction or scripted instruction), normative practices (i.e., externally mandated), and standardized tests. As Patrick Slattery (2006) reminds us, ". . . any author, professor, or program that offers students an uncritical master plan for curriculum development is only offering a recipe for disaster" (p. 31). And yet, that is exactly the recipe that many prominent experts, school reformers, professional developers, and the top-down political and business-minded individuals promote from their positions of dominance into our public schools. Their messages at times have been coercive, patronizing, and made with no apologies or excuses. Student outcomes and achievement take precedence over educator and student well-being. Is that who we are as professional educators?

Our role within universities is not to reinforce what we already know does or does not work but rather to conduct research studies that ask difficult, critical, and uncomfortable questions. Should we be using our extensive talents and research skills to figure out how best to deliver a ready-made curriculum, or should we engage and promote democratic practices that are grounded in curriculum development through cooperation and mentoring? We stand with those who believe we need an educational leadership curriculum that, first and foremost, teaches the joy of learning (Bogotch, 2002b) and humanitarian values that lie at the center of science, politics, literacy, and numeracy. Why should this message be an exercise in going against the grain? At stake are the reclaiming and rebuilding of the field of educational leadership into a professional voice heard in all aspects of society—politically, economically, socially, and intellectually.

A Primer on Curriculum Theory

Let's look first at the four questions raised by Ralph Tyler at the beginning of his classic 1949 text, *Basic Principles of Curriculum and Instruction*. Note that the questions revolve around purposes, experiences, organization, and judgments—the same format we are using to write this chapter. Here, Tyler is consistent with Dewey. Tyler's questions were:

1. What educational purposes should the school seek to attain?

2. What educational experiences can be provided that are likely to attain these purposes?

3. How can these educational experiences be effectively organized?

4. How can we determine whether these purposes are being attained? (1949, p. x)

Immediately following these questions, Tyler told his readers that this book was not written to answer these four questions. He argued that answers were a responsibility belonging to the participants within schools, primarily their faculties. What he shared with his readers, however, were the ways of learning in terms of knowing *how* to answer these questions. To paraphrase Tyler, the focus is on the learners, the locales, and the materials at hand, for it is from purposes that we determine our teaching materials, and instructional moves, not vice versa (1949). Here, he is being quintessentially Dewey-like and, as such, he is presenting curricular principles quite different from those which have guided the development of educational administration.

We as a field are known for our many cacophonous and contradictory answers to questions which are presented again and again as disconnected "to-do lists." It was our own Roland Barth (1990) who described this phenomenon as "list logic" when he wrote *Improving Schools from Within*. And yet, his call to end this practice has not been heard, as study after study concludes with a list of 3, 4, 10, 15—pick your number—"to-do" items, regardless of context, research method, or sample size. That is not how the processes of curriculum theory should proceed.

In contrast, Dewey and others in curriculum theory would like educators to embrace experimentation—that is, formulating tentative hypotheses and informally, in practice, test them—while learning from experiences (Bogotch & Taylor, 1993). Dewey (1927) asserted that "thinking and beliefs should be experimental, not absolutistic" (p. 202). In order to do that, he prescribes a "logic of method" (p. 202) that has the following two rules:

1. All concepts, principles, and theories applied to systematic knowledge should be formed and tested as tools for inquiry.

2. Policies and proposals for social action are working hypotheses, not static programs that must be dogmatically followed. (p. 202)

His is not a list of answers, solutions, or conclusions. It is a logic of method, which recognizes that there will be differences of opinion in terms of what is the best course to follow, but, as such, allows for understanding other points of view. "[N]o longer will views generated in view of special situations be frozen into absolute standards and masquerade as eternal truths" (p. 203). Dewey maintained that a person who holds an absolutist doctrine, especially when it concerns social matters, winds up using it in place of a "discussion of concepts and their logical relations to one another for inquiry" (p. 201). This is a failure to question the phenomenon observed or considered, which is supported by the scientific approach of using "laws which phenomena 'obey'" (p. 201). According to Dewey, "the appeal to causal forces at large not only misleads inquiry into social facts, but it affects equally seriously the formation of purposes and policies" (p. 202). The absolutist no longer needs to find "out the particular thing that needs to be done and the best way, under the circumstances, of doing it" (p. x).It is an affair of applying a hard and fast doctrine, which follows logically from his preconceptions of the nature of ultimate causes. He is exempt from the responsibility of discovering the concrete correlation of changes, from the need of tracing particular sequences or histories of events through their complicated careers. He knows in advance the sort of thing which must be done, just as in ancient physical philosophy the thinker knew in advance what must happen, so that all he had to do was to supply an answer.

In *The Process of Education* (1960/1963), Jerome Bruner, like Dewey and Tyler, focused on methods, rather than on predigested answers delivered to willing, obedient, and compliant students. Bruner's seminal question is: "What shall we teach and to what end?" (p. 1). It is, to use Pinar's phrase, a "complicated conversation," because it continuously questions the elements of foundational (already known) understanding. It requires reconceptualizations—new learning leading to new knowledge. What makes it so very complicated is that curriculum itself covers multiple human dimensions—moral, political, cognitive, and so on—as well as holding out the possible rejection of dominant ways of knowing and dominant ideas promoted by those in power (Foucault, 1980; Lyotard, 1984). Curriculum strives to understand the past, present, and future as "contextual, multidimensional, ironic, proleptic, contingent, evolving, and autobiographical" (Slattery, 2006, p. 41). These literatures, among others, have been outside the boundaries of educational leadership program-development discourse. What they ask, what we would ask, of leadership curriculum developers is to think, reflect, make value and professional judgments, and not just focus on how to accomplish a specific task. In so doing, the work moves from technical proficiency to enhancing the quality of life for adults in leadership programs, for teachers working in schools, and for the children learning in them. That is the humanistic power of curriculum inquiry.

Generating a Leadership Curriculum

From our tentative conclusions, distinguishing features, and primer on curriculum theory, we begin formulating hypotheses for integrating the language and ideals of curriculum theory into school leadership preparation development—both programmatically and systemically. That means, first and foremost, not focusing on specific course titles and the technical work lives of school administrators. In the development of leadership preparation programs:

- the language of curricular principles and processes should precede discussions of specific course content and administrative tasks and roles;

- the purposes of education and educational leadership should precede discussions of mandated policies and the efficient transmission of content knowledge;

- questions pertaining to the needs of learners should precede answering technical questions and expertise;

- the inclusive experiences of faculty, practitioners, students, and other members of the educational leadership community should precede drafting course titles, selecting texts, and writing syllabi; and

- informal educators and sociocultural dynamics should be used to review the previous stages of development.

These hypotheses prioritize curriculum principles and processes as dynamic sociocultural dimensions (a complicated conversation) rather than provide answers to technical and content knowledge (a simple conversation). Our desire is to see the field of educational leadership in the United States figure out how to integrate concepts of discovery, inquiry, democracy, creativity, and aesthetics alongside standards, structures, top-down delivery systems, unfunded mandates, accreditation and fidelity criteria, and measures of assessment. Instead of leadership faculty divvying up tasks by courses and NCATE–demanded critical assignments and decision points, instead of conversations focusing on the prescriptions of fidelity, delivery, accreditation, and compliance, we ought to hold difficult and complicated conversations based on the teachings of curriculum theory that rely on specifying values and purposes of public education, and then on how to sequence and spiral important concepts and integrate course content across subject areas. We must move from the individual to the social; from private practices to public responsibilities.

Guiding Curricular Principles Towards Transformative Leadership

The task now is to integrate the social aspects of schooling with leadership responsibilities, cooperative relationships, and adaptive contexts. Reclaiming our profession will take civic courage (Etzioni, 2010; Giroux, 1998; Quantz, Rogers, & Dantley, 1991), but if tenure has any practical meaning, then civic courage has to be made explicit in the conversation. What follows now are the curricular principles, a how-to for developing curriculum. As Tyler and others advised, the participants themselves engage in discovery processes that result in naming the specific courses. Our role here is to establish the democratic conditions—both purposes and processes—for curriculum development in educational leadership. In so doing, we will put forth brief justifications for prioritizing the social over the individual and for reinterpreting the meaning of educational responsibility as a sociocultural construct. Again, our explicit understanding is that curriculum theory and inquiry are codepend with educational leadership, and that civic courage is already present because of tenure, seniority, and membership in the profession. Throughout his career, William Foster (1986) raised critical questions regarding the legitimacy of school leadership. His critical questions are more relevant than ever in today's era of standards and accountability: How can school leadership foster and support a democratic polity? What does it mean to be an ethical leader? How do we combine the means of administering schools with an awareness of the larger ends of education? What does it mean for a leader to be transformative? (Angus, 2006, p. 374). While responses to these questions deserve a fuller scholarly treatment, we can provide two justifications for the legitimacy of school leadership, connecting curricular theory and inquiry with leadership principles: namely, a justification for the priority of the social and a justification for expanding educational responsibility:

- A social basis for curriculum and transformative leadership. This entails a philosophical construction of curriculum on the social aspects and not the individual, and its implications for the approach concerning the concepts of freedom, rights, and responsibilities within democratic organizations.

- The responsibility for education. This builds on the idea that curriculum is not social engineering (Pinar, 2006) and that we need to be careful not to make the mistake of conjoining curriculum and teaching—thereby allowing the teacher and schools, ergo school leaders, to be completely responsible for student learning (Pinar, p. 110).

Justification 1: A Social Basis for Curriculum and Transformative Leadership

The ancient Greeks' conception of individual humanity was quite different from our modern Western perspective. For the ancient Greek, an individual human life was part of a whole, a life shaped by membership in a family, community, and state. The polis defined that central identity. In this collectivist context, it makes sense that Socrates chose state-assisted suicide by voluntarily drinking hemlock, as opposed to seeking exile as a possibility. Socrates was following his conception of the purpose of living in and being an active member (as a teacher) in a state or community. At the same time, the individual Greek lives of Socrates, Plato, and Aristotle were extraordinary because of their intellectual prowess, work ethic, and creative talents. There is no contradiction between individual accomplishments and service and membership to a larger enterprise or purpose, if and only if the notions of the social incorporate cooperation, purpose, participation, and membership, over competition. One of the architects of U.S. community education, Ernest Melby, wrote:

> One of the major functions of educational administration is the release of creative talent on the part of individuals connected with the enterprise. Thus freed to be unique, to create, to think along new and original lines is an absolute requisite for a dynamic school. (cited in Koopman et al., 1943, p. 71)

In his essay, titled "Educational leadership and social justice (2002a), Bogotch proposed two pathways to social justice—one through community efforts, the other through individual efforts. What connected the two, however, was that even the individual actions were part of larger sociocultural movements, beyond the specific subject being taught; for example, connecting science, math, or English to the global environment or peace movement helped to make classroom lessons meaningful for both teachers and students.

To practice democratic values is to believe that the *what* and *how* we teach can make the world better. Here we are following Dewey (1927), who argued that a human being cannot be treated as an isolated individual, but rather is "moved and regulated by his associations with others; what he does and what the consequences of his behavior are, what his experience consists of, cannot even be described, much less accounted for, in isolation" (p. 188). The idea that we all belong to a collective first, that humans belong to different and multiple groups at all times and that the word *individual*—which carries with it an understood separateness from everything—should probably be substituted, as Dewey would, by the word *member*. The implications that we are members (of multiple social groups) afford us opportunities to look at the freedoms and responsibilities that come with participation in a democratic society. In and out of schools, these opportunities are operationalized through cooperation, coordination, participation, group work, relations, and self-discovery and identity—all elements of democratic practices. With respect to justice, it is the addition of the term *social* that brings ideas of equity and fairness to our everyday interactions, so that we come to live our ideals in actions, not just through words.

Justification 2: The Responsibility for Education

Drawing upon the writings of Pinar, curriculum is not social engineering and, therefore, we need to be careful to address the mistake of totalizing responsibility for educating society. Schools play a shared responsibility role in society; yet, our profession—teacher and administrator leaders—has been maneuvered into a present-day corner of total responsibility. We are not completely responsible for student learning (Biesta, 2007; Pinar, 2006, p. 110). "Schools are important but only to the extent that they are part of a larger, thoughtful pattern" (Sizer, 2004, quoted in Pinar, 2006, p. 123).

By constantly and continually forcing the business-imported language of *stakeholders* and *clients* into our lexicon, we have let others in society shirk, ignore, or discount their responsibilities in Sizer's "larger, thoughtful pattern." In opposition, we have to define the brackets of responsibility and invite and educate others to their responsibilities in transforming society through education. The professoriate can play a key role in leading this bordercrossing, or partnership collaboration. We can also include participants who have historically been excluded—students, parents, extended families, social organizations, small businesses, large corporations, religious organizations, and the media—in educational discussions so that they work with us and do not stand on the sidelines blaming educators for societal problems, such as poverty.

We need critical friends who accept responsibility for educating all members of society. If, as a society, we have determined that our children's education is inadequate or failing to meet our goals, then each partner needs to discover where and how their piece of education's puzzle needs reform. Using this collective perspective, it follows that in recreating an educational leadership curriculum, we should bring in more participants, not circle the wagons in a siege mentality. The field of knowledge management (KM) speaks specifically to the role that each societal member and group or organization plays when discussing the need for societal knowledge management (SKM). "Acceptable quality of life is achieved when the society is capable, balanced, and just and when appropriate intellectual capital is possessed by citizens, public servants, and organizations and incorporated in their practices, systems, and procedures" (Wiig, 2007, p. 141). For the media, policymakers, industry, and others—including even the well-meaning foundations that fund educational reform—to concentrate their attention on the curriculum and teaching of formal education, while ignoring the demands (or lack thereof) and influences of informal education, is to fail to address the most influential educative processes taking place in the formation of our citizenry.

Over the last few decades, informal educators, supported by politicians and policymakers, have consciously or unconsciously looked to formal educators to assume the responsibility for education that traditionally pertains to their own sphere of influence. By creating an atmosphere of crisis (Berliner & Biddle, 1995), those seeking change target blame on formal educators. Businesses, casting themselves only as the consumers of public education, continually push for vocational-specific programs and demand that students come "job-ready" into the marketplace, as opposed to taking on the responsibility for educating the citizen who comes to the workplace from school with common knowledge, skills, and dispositions. Parents and faith-based organizations push for further values and religious education that goes beyond or ignores the scope of the teaching and learning of democratic or social-justice values. The media in all forms highlight the "educational crisis" without addressing their responsibility in everything from the failure to provide an unbiased reporting of educational success and failure to conducting thorough investigations of public claims about education. The curriculum process of "totality of experiences" makes visible the shared responsibilities for education throughout society.

Ogawa and Kim (2005) described how businesses influence society by (a) consuming the products of education, (b) supplying the inputs to education, (c) competing against education, (d) shaping public policy for education, and (e) indirectly affecting education simply by doing business with education. That they also are in the business of curriculum development (2005, p. 76) indicates how business understands the power of education without their having to take public responsibilities for the success of education. An example of taking the spoils but not the responsibility was illustrated in research by Iske, Klein, Kutscher, and Otto (2008) in a study of Internet use by the current, "Internet-savvy" generation. They found significant and long-lasting inequalities of educational outcomes based on the informal education these young people receive through their out-of-school, independent use of the Internet. These findings have important implications for school-leadership development in terms of collaborations with Internet-dominant sources like Wikipedia, Google, and Facebook, all of which have an impact on the education of future generations. The study further demonstrates the significant and growing influence and responsibility that these media and information sources now have in terms of informal education. However, instead of addressing those issues, these Internet organizations look to school curricula and teaching to educate the student in their use. School-leadership curricular development needs to consider who is responsible for providing the skills and dispositions necessary for a discriminating selection and analytical processing of the information being presented.

Conclusion

Curriculum theory and inquiry is, in its essence, a study of a nation's culture through the needs of its learners. It begins and continues as the practice of democratic values. As such, the legitimacy of educational leadership as a profession is not in raising test scores but rather in ministering to meet the needs of its citizenry. That said, it is curriculum theory and inquiry that alerts educators to their role as "political subjects capable of exhibiting critical sensibilities, civic courage, and forms of solidarity rooted in a strong commitment to freedom and democracy" (Giroux, 1992, p. 201). This is the civic courage from which educational leadership as a profession has shied away.

In the foreword to *Democracy in School Administration* (Koopman et al., 1943), Courtis wrote that "an educator's work is no less important for defense than that of soldiers in the front-line trenches" (p. xi). That is why it has to be disconcerting and disappointing to report that the field of educational leadership has never been an effective ethical and political voice of democracy, especially when it has been threatened in the 20th and 21st centuries. It is not as if democracy was not threatened externally by Nazi Germany or Imperial Japan (two nations which would have ranked near the very top on international literacy and numeracy scales). It is not as if democracy was not threatened internally by Joseph McCarthy and Jim Crow. It is not as if American democracy is still not threatened by authoritarian regimes and non–state sponsored terrorism, Al Qaeda, our own "military-industrial complex," an economic system beholden to banks and corporations deemed "too big to fail," and an electoral system dominated by campaign funding abuses.

We have entered and sustained wars based on misinformation deliberately fabricated and sold to a very literate American public (the Spanish-American War, the Vietnam War, and the War in Iraq are infamous examples). We are living today amid genocidal policies in sub-Saharan Africa, human-rights abuses abroad and at home through state-sponsored torture (i.e., waterboarding), and public displays of intolerance of Islam and its followers. How can we justify not teaching educative and democratic responses to these local, national, and international happenings in our leadership preparation programs and professional consultancies? Where is the response to Foster's critical questions of legitimacy related to the priority of the social and educational responsibilities? While the rhetorical phrase "front-line trenches" seems to have survived as a description of the work of school teachers and administrators, the context of threats to democracy has been ignored and deleted from our preparation programs. Like Koopman et al. (1943), it is not as if there are not educators in both curriculum and school leadership who are not writing to awaken us—there are. But their ideas stand apart from the standards and accountability movements of today. Student achievement and test preparation have become the dominant discourses in both government and privately sponsored reforms, even at this juncture where democracy is being tested by the current economic crisis and long-term threats, such as North Korea, terrorist groups, and nuclear proliferation. When will we frame the educative responses for democracy as part of our profession?

At the very moment of writing this curriculum chapter, the nations with the highest Program for International Student Assessment (PISA) test scores were printed in the *New York Times*. The headline read: "Top Test Scores from Shanghai Stun Educators." Yes, the country with the most people, one of the largest land masses, and the second-largest and one of the fastest-growing economies in the world, using its students from the city of Shanghai, has placed first to in reading, math, and science. The American Secretary of Education's response: "We have to see this as a wake-up call. . . . We can quibble, or we can face the brutal truth that we're being out-educated." Is that what our nation's highest-ranking educator sees as our patriotic duty? From the literature on social justice, the two most repressive organizational environments are totalitarian regimes and closed bureaucracies. Here is what Dewey (1939/1991) saw in Nazi Germany: "Its schools were so efficient that the country had the lowest rate of illiteracy in the world, the scholarship and scientific researches of its universities were known through the civilized globe . . ." (p. 42); and who today would say we were "being out-educated" by Nazi Germany? The times have changed: The nations ranked high in PISA are not threats to the world today, but the educative principles based on democratic values are still the same. What is the purpose of public education in a democracy and how should educational leaders respond?

As described by Shields (2003, 2004, 2010), transformative leadership is centered on a critical, normative concept that "focuses on both democratic process and content and on critical approaches to the practice of leadership" (p. 1). Transformative leadership centers leadership on moral and technical capacities, addressing "beliefs, assumptions, practices, and policies (whether long-standing or newly emerging, ideological, discursive, or material) that oppress and exclude some groups" (p. 1). Ultimately, transformative leaders, followers, and organizations have a moral responsibility to be "agents of change and transformation who are committed to action that will redress inequities in the wider global society" (p. 1). Shields (2004) holds that transformative educational leaders should work to create school communities where educators understand their responsibility for advancing the value-ends defined by Astin and Astin (2000) as equity, social justice, and the quality of life.

The curricular processes that we have considered in this chapter lead to the understanding that learning and instruction must be a process of ongoing, critical questioning. As Pinar (2006) stated, "contemporary curriculum research is nothing less than the intellectual formation of a public sphere in education, a resuscitation of the progressive project in contemporary subjective and social terms, in which we come to understand that self-realization and democratization are inextricably intertwined" (p. 2). What becomes clear is that both transformative leadership and curriculum inquiry are dependent upon one another, because both make democracy and social justice explicit goals, as both ends and means. Using curriculum theory and processes, we can rebuild our educational leadership curricula to create transformative leaders and, they, in turn, will bring these same teachings to the schools and systems they lead to develop democratic and relevant teaching, curricula, and citizens.

References

Angus, L. (2006). Educational leadership and the imperative of including student voice, student interests, and student lives in the mainstream. *International Journal of Leadership in Education, 9*(4), 369–379.

Astin, A. W., & Astin, H. S. (2000). *Leadership reconsidered: Engaging higher education in social change.* [Online publication]. Retrieved March 23, 2011 from http://www.wkkf.org/knowledge-center/resources/2007/01/Leadership-Reconsidered-Engaging-Higher-Education-In-Social-Change.aspx

Barth, R. (1990). *Improving schools from within: Teachers, parents, and principals can make the difference.* San Francisco, CA: Jossey-Bass.

Berliner, D. C, & Biddle, B. J. (1995). *The manufactured crisis: Myths, fraud, and the attack on America's public schools.* Reading, MA: Addison-Wesley.

Biesta, G. (2007). Why "what works" won't work: Evidence-based practice and the democratic deficit in educational research. *Educational Theory, 57*(1), 1–22.

Bogotch, I. (2002a). Educational leadership and social justice: Practice into theory. *Journal of School Leadership, 12*(2), 138–156.

Bogotch, I. (2002b). "Enmeshed in the work": The educative power of developing standards. *Journal of School leadership, 12*(5), 503–525.

Bogotch, I. (2010, April). *State rule for approval of school leadership programs: The matrix* [Audio podcast Vol. 5, no. 1]. *Journal on Research in Leadership Education* [producer] . Retrieved March 23, 2011, from http://www.ucea.org/jrle/2010/4/26/state-rule-for-approval-of-school-leadership-programs-the-ma.html

Bogotch, I. (2011). A history of public school leadership: The first century, 1835–1942. In F. English (Ed.), *The Sage handbook of educational leadership* (pp. 7–33). Thousand Oaks, CA: Sage Publications. (Originally published in 2005.)

Bogotch, I. (In press). U.S. perspectives in leadership and training: Above and beyond recorded history. *School Leadership and Management.*

Bogotch, I., & Maslin-Ostrowski, P. (2010). Internationalizing educational leadership: How a university department jumps the curve from local to international. *Educational Administration Quarterly, 46*(2), 210–240.

Bogotch, I., & Taylor, D. (1993). Discretionary assessment practices: Professional judgments and principal's actions. *The Urban Review, 25*(4), 289–306.

Bolman, L. G., & Deal, T. E. (2003). *Reframing organizations: Artistry, choice, and leadership*. San Francisco, CA: Jossey-Bass.

Bottoms, G., & O'Neill, K. (2001). *Preparing a new breed of school principals: It's time for action*. Atlanta, GA: Southern Regional Education Board. Retrieved March 23. 2011: http://www.sreb.org/main/Leadership/pubs/LeadershipMatters.pdf

Bruner, J. (1963). *The process of education*. New York: Vintage Books. (Originally published in 1960.)

Davis, S., Darling-Hammond, L., LaPointe, M., & Meyerson, D. (2005). *School leadership study: Developing successful principals*. Stanford, CA: Stanford University, Stanford Educational Leadership Institute.

Dewey, J. (1927). *The public and its problems*. New York: H. Holt.

Dewey, J. (1991). Creative democracy: The task before us. In J. Boydston (Ed.), *John Dewey: The later works, 1925–1953* (Vol. 14, pp. 224–230). Carbondale, IL: Southern Illinois University Press. (Originally published in 1939.)

Donmoyer, R., Imber, M., & Scheurich, J. J. (1995). *The knowledge base in educational administration: Multiple perspectives*. Albany, NY: State University of New York Press.

English, F., & Steffy, B. (2005). Curriculum leadership: The administrative survival skill in a test-driven culture and a competitive educational marketplace. In F. English (Ed.), *The Sage handbook of educational leadership* (pp. 407–429). Thousand Oaks, CA: Sage Publications.

Etzioni, A. (2010, November 5). Symposium: Reflections of a sometime-public intellectual [Web log post]. Retrieved March 23, 2011, from http://blog.amitaietzioni.org/2010/11/symposium-reflections-of-a-sometime-public-intellectual.html

Foshay, A. (1975). A modest proposal. In A. W. Foshay (Ed.), *Essays on curriculum: Selected papers by Arthur W. Foshay* (pp. 70–81). New York: The A.W. Foshay Fund, Teachers College Press, Columbia University.

Foster, W. (1986). *Paradigms and promises: New approaches to educational administration*. Buffalo, NY: Prometheus Books.

Foucault, M. (1980). *Power/knowledge: Selected interviews and other writings 1972–1977*. (C. Gordon, Ed.). New York: Pantheon.

Freire, P. (1998). *Pedagogy of freedom: Ethics, democracy, and civic courage*. Lanham, MD: Rowman & Littlefield.

Giroux, H. (1992). *Border crossings*. London, U.K.: Routledge.

Giroux, H. (1998). Education in unsettling times: Public intellectuals and the promise of cultural studies. In D. Carlson & M. W. Apple (Eds.), *Power/knowledge/pedagogy: The meaning of democratic education in unsettling times* (pp. 41–60). Boulder, CO: Westview Press.

Greenfield, T., & Ribbins, P. (Eds.). (1993). *Greenfield on educational administration: Towards a humane science*. New York: Routledge

Grumet, M. (1995). The curriculum: What are the basics and are we teaching them? In J. L. Kincheloe & S. R. Steinberg (Eds.), *Thirteen questions: Reframing education's conversation* (2d ed., pp. 15–21). New York: Peter Lang. [Cited in Shields, C. M. (2004). Dialogic leadership for social justice: Overcoming pathologies of silence. *Educational Administration Quarterly, 40*(1),109–132.]

Iske, S., Klein, A., Kutscher, N., & Otto, H. (2008). Young people's Internet use and its significance for informal education and social participation. *Technology, Pedagogy and Education, 17*(2), 131–141.

Jenlink, P. (2009). *Dewey's democracy and education revisited*. Lanham, MA: Rowman & Littlefield.

Koopman, R., Miel, A., & Miser, R. (1943). *Democracy in school administration*. New York: D. Appleton-Century Company.

Lyotard, J. F. (1984). *The postmodern condition: A report on knowledge*. Minneapolis: University of Minnesota Press.

Mann, H. (1846). *Tenth annual report to the secretary of the Massachusetts State Board of Education retrieved March 13, 2011, from http://www.akidmore.edu/~tkuroda/hi323/mann.htm*

McClellan, R., & Dominguez, R. (2006). The uneven march toward social justice: Diversity, conflict, and complexity in educational administration programs. *Journal of Educational Administration, 44* (3), 225–238.

Murphy, J., Moorman, H., & McCarthy, M. (2008). The changing face of educational leadership preparation: Insights from whole state reform efforts. *Teachers College Record, 110*(10), 2172–2203.

Ogawa, R. T., & Kim, R. H. (2005). The business-education relationship: Using organization theory to conceptualize a research agenda. *Journal of Educational Administration, 43*(1), 72–85.

Orr, M. T., King, C., & LaPointe, M. (2010). *Districts developing leaders: Lessons on consumer actions and program approaches from eight urban districts* [Report commissioned by The Wallace Foundation]. Boston: Education Development Center. Retrieved March 23, 2011 from http://www.wallacefoundation. org/KnowledgeCenter/KnowledgeTopics/CurrentAreasofFocus/EducationLeadership/Pages/districts-developing-leaders.aspx

Papa, R. (2009, November 3) The discipline of educational administration: Crediting the past. In T. Creighton, S. Harris, & J. C. Coleman (Eds.), *Crediting the past, challenging the present, creating the future.* Ypsilanti, MI: National Council for Professors of Educational Administration. Retrieved March 23, 2011, from http://cnx.org/content/m12868/latest/4papasmall.pdf

Pinar, W. F. (2004). *What is curriculum theory?* New York: Routledge.

Pinar, W. F. (2006). *The synoptic text today and other essays: Curriculum development after the reconceptualization.* New York: Peter Lang.

Quantz, R., Rogers, J., Dantley, M., (1991). Rethinking transformative leadership toward democratic reform of schools. *Journal of Education, 173*(3), 96–118.

Reyes-Guerra, D., & Mountford, M. (2009). *Partnerships and internships: How partnerships between districts and universities during internship development and implementation increase learning gains of developing leaders.* Paper presented at the 22nd Annual UCEA Convention, Anaheim, CA.

Shields, C. M. (2003). *Good intentions are not enough: Transformative leadership for communities of difference.* Boston, MA: Scarecrow.

Shields, C. M. (2004). Dialogic leadership for social justice: Overcoming pathologies of silence. *Educational Administration Quarterly, 40*(1),109–132.

Shields, C. M. (2010). Transformative leadership: Working for equity in diverse contexts. *Educational Administration Quarterly, 46*(4), 558–589.

Sizer, T. (2004). *The red pencil: Convictions from experience in education.* New Haven, CT: Yale University Press.

Slattery, P. (2006). *Curriculum development in the postmodern era.* New York: Routledge/Taylor and Francis.

Smith, F. (1971). *Understanding reading: A psycholinguistic analysis of reading and learning.* New York: Holt, Rinehart, & Winston.

Starratt, R. (2011). *Refocusing school leadership.* New York: Routledge/Taylor and Francis.

Tyler, R. W. (1949). *Basic principles of curriculum and instruction.* Chicago: University of Chicago Press.

Whitehead, A. N. (1929). *The aims of education and other essays.* New York: Macmillan.

Wiig, K. M. (2007). Effective societal knowledge management. *Journal of Knowledge Management, 11*(5), 141–156.

11

Transformative Instructional Leadership

A Critical and Spiritual Engagement

Michael Dantley

Educational leadership has undergone a type of metamorphosis, where the traditional tenets of the field have been deconstructed through a critical theoretical lens (Foster, 1986; Maxcy, 1995, 2002).

> Critical theory unravels the hegemony, that is the accepted way of thinking or the dominant ideologies that form the traditions and rituals practiced and celebrated in our society. The whole point of critical theoretical thought is not only to unmask those systemic ways in which institutions such as schools marginalize and disenfranchise those deemed to be outside of the accepted traditions and classifications, but also to propose an oppositional rearrangement of these institutions. (Dantley, 2009, p. 45).

The poignant question of whose interests are being served through administrative practices, as well as the issue of how policies and procedures perpetuate asymmetrical relations of power, have been, for progressive scholars in the field, the fodder for close scrutiny of school leaders' work. This query is of significant importance to a critical theorist.

Within most contexts of leadership, the issue of power takes on an unproblematized nature. That is, one simply speaks about the categories of power and the nuances of power from a perspective that sees this dynamic in all organizations as inherent, unquestioned, and not troubled. Scholars have attempted to couch power in a positive light, delineating the varieties of its manifestation—for example, expert, referent, legitimate, reward, and coercive (French & Raven, 1962)—as if power has no political genesis or negative, oppressive consequences that accompany its ubiquitous presence. The critical theorist, however, sees power as alienating and dismissive. They see power, in its hegemonic manifestations, as an efficacious tool to continue and extend the atrocities of racism, classism, sexism, homophobia, ableism, and other markers of identity that dare to offer a counter-voice to the celebrated ways of perceiving and behaving in organizations, such as schools.

In fact, the critical theorist posits a project of resistance that not only denudes and demystifies marginalizing practices but also, more importantly, lodges a campaign to cause the people in schools to reflect on their conceptual framework and professional behaviors that minimize equity and scoff at democracy.

While notions of leadership and social justice (Dantley, Beachum, & McCray, 2008; Marshall & Oliva, 2001, 2006; Theoharis, 2009) do not always emanate from a critical paradigm, the focus on race, class, gender, ability, age, sexual orientation, and other identity markers and how these are used to marginalize and perpetuate inequitable leadership practices in schools has caused scholars and practitioners alike to examine carefully the plethora of ways schools and their leaders extend the boundaries of unequal and discriminatory practices in educational sites. What transformative leadership highlights is power—its use, abuse, and possessors; its impact and systemic strategies of sustenance; and its debilitating effects on those oppressed by it.

Concomitantly, a substantive deconstructing element in the scholarship on educational leadership has been spirituality (Dantley, 2005, 2007, 2009; Hafner & Capper, 2005; Shields, 2005). Scholars who have positioned spirituality as a lens by which to critique educational leadership practices have argued that the issues of ontology, teleology, and human connectedness, all integral pieces of one's spiritual self, compel educational leaders to interrogate their practices in light of the troubling traditional notions of schooling and its sustaining work as part of a capitalist hegemony.

This chapter articulates the place of spirituality aligned within a critical theoretical frame to forge a new conception of transformative instructional leadership. Such a construction problematizes instruction and pedagogy as being vehicles that sustain the fiats of assessment and accountability and purports an educational leadership that promotes interrogation of disenfranchising curricula, marginalizing pedagogy, and silencing procedures and practices. Further, this chapter aligns instructional leadership with the creation of critical democratic citizens and a civil-rights, hegemony-dismantling agenda in schools, and thus aligns it with the critical concept of transformative leadership as well.

It is no longer sufficient for scholars to offer critique, even critique with hope. There is, even in such a progressive mindset, a sense of acquiescence and even of docility, which mutes the essential revolutionary voice that ought to rise after the deconstruction and demystification of discriminating practices. Our schools are in a state now where the luxury of critique without concomitant action cannot be afforded. To merely recite the voluminous ways in which our schools are failing children of color and poverty, or to rehearse the multiple ways in which educational institutions propagate manifold forms of discrimination, is a horrendous waste of valuable time. To do that placates a theorist's penchant for pontification and not action, theorizing without strategy, and conceptually framing without offering pragmatic action steps.

It is imperative however, to provide a broader context for these action steps. A critical perspective that impacts educational leadership practice does not relax in making schools better at what hegemony purports they are to do. It is not sufficient for the critical theorist to argue that new, democratically grounded curricula must be enacted or to espouse that more equity-based pedagogical practices are to be implemented in schools in order to make them better. While such expectations are admirable, they fall short in helping to make schools more efficacious to society writ large. As at other institutions, schools, from a critical perspective, must engage in social change (Marcuse, 2001). This means that within the purpose and agenda of schools is the mandate to serve as one societal institution that meets the challenge of bringing about positive, qualitative change in our society. Clearly, this means that the educational institution must take the time to reflect on its purposes and to grapple with the idea that, far beyond preparing workers to propagate a capitalist economy, schools exist to help other institutions "establish essentially different forms of human existence, with a new social division of labor, new modes of control over the productive process, a new morality" (Marcuse, 2001, p. 37).

How formidable is the challenge to establish a new morality? A new morality eschews the notions of what has been esteemed to be rational, because it is within these modernistic ideas of rationality that we have created multiple hierarchical social structures that celebrate one group and denigrate the other. It is through rational explications of social phenomena that a hermeneutic of expediency and implications of social and national superiority stem. That which delivers the goods, meets the goal, or triumphs over the challenge is celebrated and creates the parameters for what is reasonable, rational, and what should be expected for all. The critical theorist, however, questions the validity of such claims of rationality by deconstructing the very makeup of notions of expediency, the goal, and the challenge themselves. The critical theorist challenges the primacy of the contest and even the struggle that establishes the expectations. Such a theorist interrogates these notions from the premise that within the establishing of expectations and the rituals and challenges to set these expectations there are relations of power that are inherently asymmetrical and that abrogate the very tensions and contention surrounding the establishment of one group as being crowned superior over another.

Foster (1986) wrote the seminal text on educational leadership and critical theory and introduced the concept of transformative leadership to the field. He dared to deconstruct the hegemonic, asymmetrical relations of power that are inherent in traditional prescriptions of educational leadership and offered a subversive tact to school leadership. Such an approach not merely questioned the status quo of educational administration but also prophesied how schools would be radically reconstructed when a critical theoretical frame was used to ground leadership practice. At the conclusion of this hallmark text, Foster offered ways how this radical approach to educational leadership could be used to impact the enterprise of working with teachers, students, the community, and organizations. According to Foster, all of these spaces, when the labor of leadership is couched in a critical motif, are radically different, effuse a more democratic and equitable context, and portend a learning environment that is not only sensitive to racism, classism, sexism, homophobia, and other markers of identity, but that also builds a project to eradicate these ills from the school setting, as well as from the external community. Leaders of this ilk become the organic catalysts or civil rights activists who facilitate a progressive, egalitarian agenda in purposeful and intentional ways. The intentionality of such leadership tactics can also emanate from a critically spiritual (Dantley, 2005) grounding, a foundation that comes from the aligning of critical theory and African American spirituality. The succeeding portion of this chapter explores the concept of critical spirituality. At its conclusion, the chapter extends Foster's notions of critical theory and how it would impact teachers, students, and community using a critically spiritual lens.

Critical Spirituality: Its Tenets and Place in Educational Leadership

One of the ways school leaders may work from a transformative agenda is through the conceptual frame of critical spirituality. Inherent in this theoretical grounding is the radical work of reflection, resistance, and reconstruction. This way of perceiving the work of educational leaders blends the tenets of critical theory with the notions of African American spirituality. Critical theory proposes that we interrogate the uses—as well as the abuses—of power but falls short in taking its adherents to the next step, that of actually enacting a radical or subversive agenda to create a new, more democratic reality. Critical spirituality embraces the action orientation of African American spirituality and moves the essential critical self-reflection to the actions of resistance deemed to create fodder for reconstruction. In critical spirituality, there are the notions of calling, hope, and reimagination. Essentially, this conceptual frame celebrates the idea that there is labor that we absolutely cannot help but to embrace, because we acknowledge a "calling" or a commissioning to do the work, a calling that is actually outside of ourselves. We also acknowledge that such work enhances our lives ontologically and teleologically; there is added meaning to our lives because of our labor. Also inherent in the work is the hope that our endeavors will result in a reimagined reality that celebrates equity, democracy, and inclusion.

Critical spirituality includes four components: critical self-reflection, deconstructive interpretation, performative creativity, and transformative action. The goal of this compilation of transactions is ". . . to cause school leaders to become grassroots activists or organic intellectuals for the progressive reconstruction of schools" (Dantley, 2007, p. 160). Critical self-reflection is engaged, as persons within educational institutions are assigned to come to grips with the multiple ways schools marginalize and silence those they have "othered." That is, the school community is asked to engage the notion that, because schools have historically helped to propagate a capitalist hegemony, inherent in such a political, social, and ideological paradigm is the disenfranchisement of those who, by nature of the economic fundamentals, will find themselves at the bottom of the social-cultural food chain. Such a revelation must be followed by educators inquiring as to the democracy or equity manifested by such silencing in our schools. Educators may be asked to consider the multiple ways students of color and poverty are dealt short shrift by the ways education is organized and delivered throughout the United States. Closer to the individual, critical self-reflection requires the educator to consider how his or her professional and personal practices militate against the equitable delivery of the educational experience to the children and youth with whom they interface. They are compelled to grapple with the facts that the majority of students receiving discipline through suspension and expulsion are black males; that the preponderance of students in special education classes are black males; and that the majority of students in advanced placement and international baccalaureate programs are white children from affluent backgrounds.

In keeping with this reflective work, educators are asked, through the frame of critical spirituality, to embrace a deconstructive hermeneutic or to deal forthrightly with how their own dispositions have been crafted through their personal socialization. Indeed, they are required to determine the genesis of their attitudes and the conclusions they have drawn about people and circumstances diametrically opposed to their own. Further, through deconstructive interpretation, educators are asked to articulate how their dispositions and resolutions concerning the other have played out in their interactions with those with whom they have come in contact throughout the educational process.

The third component, performative creativity, takes the reflective process to the next stage and empowers educators to envision schools or educational sites where democracy is the undergirding value. Creativity is a spiritual endeavor in which the educator is able to believe that a radical reconstruction of schools is eminent and to then devise strategies to bring such reconstruction to pass. Dantley (2007) writes:

> Creativity and authorship are both exceptionally spiritual activities, and the school leader who is serious about imagining a new way to educate children must have the courage as well as the hope to visualize the process and the results of the process leading to schools that are equitable and democratic for the entire learning community. (p. 161)

The final step is putting this reimagination into practice. This is called transformative action. The goal of critical spirituality is the creation of radically reconstructed schools, where academic achievement is not limited to what happens in the classroom or performance on standardized tests, but rather, where students become activists themselves, whose goal is the radical transformation of the community, as well as the society.

The blend of critical theory and critical spirituality in the work of an educational leader certainly has a profound impact on the lives and the work of teachers. It is vitally important to see the substantive changes that are called for in the role of teachers when a titular school leader subscribes to the tenets of critical and critical-spirituality theories.

Critical Theory, Spirituality, and Teachers

The current accountability movement in education has robbed creativity from the art of teaching, reducing teachers to clerks, test proctors, and purveyors of a celebrated curriculum. All in the name of leaving no child behind, the artistry and science of teaching have been replaced by scripts, reportedly fool-proof best practices, and a perspective that, left to their own devices, teachers will overwhelmingly fail to appropriately educate our school-age population. Foster wrote about this deteriorating condition of the teaching profession:

> This deskilling of the profession occurs through the development of standardized curricula with little or no relevance for the tapestry of local conditions; through mandated competencies that disregard the professional knowledge of the teacher. (p. 191)

In this season of obsessive assessment, it is very easy for teachers to find themselves in conditions of strict prescription and little-to-no professional autonomy. This epistemological position is one that celebrates answers and not questions, and definition rather than inquiry and discovery. Indeed, it has taken the spirit out of the teaching-learning dynamic. Giroux (1997) argued that in this market-based epistemological context, ". . . teachers are being shorn of their skills and increasingly treated more and more as impersonal instruments in a bureaucratic process than as thoughtful and creative intellectuals whose personal vision of education really matters" (p. 92). So what can be done? What, beyond decrying this situation, can take place to reconstruct what happens in U.S. classrooms writ large?

One of the elements of critical spirituality is performative creativity. Inherent in this practice is the notion that seeing beyond the current and envisioning a radically different future is a spiritual endeavor. It requires the interrogation of current practices and paradigms under a lens that asks how these hegemonic ways of conceptualizing education can often marginalize creative thinking as well as deaden intellectual curiosity. Performative creativity would ask teachers to reimagine their performances and rituals were they empowered to facilitate spaces of exploration. How would classrooms look if teachers meshed the demands of assessment with intellectual inquiry? How might teachers use inquiry and exploration, critical thinking and academic rigor, as subversive weapons to ameliorate the onslaught of assessment creep?

Reimagination demands the actions of releasing and replacing. Both of these are spiritually reflective endeavors that get to the core of one's personal and professional self. It is also an encounter with teleology. That is, in order to release and replace, one has to embrace one overarching mission for education while relinquishing an older one. A more critically grounded educational mission would focus on those ways schools must desist in their penchant to perpetuate the status quo. More specifically, how can the work of educational institutions be reimagined to minimize racism, sexism, classism, ableism, and homophobia?

School leaders, particularly school principals, may facilitate a reflective and resistant space in schools, a space where teachers are asked to couch their practices in a broader frame, to consider pedagogy as an act of resistance, and to create experiences with students that relegate standardized testing and unnecessary assessment to a secondary position, while giving inquiry and intellectual curiosity the top place in instruction. This type of ambience will free teachers to return the artistry as well as the science to pedagogical practices, and will concomitantly cause them to see teaching as a political project replete with societal ramifications that can literally assist in releasing more genuinely democratic practices in society. Teachers may find themselves laboring within notions of purpose and could, hopefully, come to see their work as providing greater meaning to their lives. As teachers are encouraged by school principals to align their work in the classroom with a larger social-justice agenda, their work becomes more purposeful and prophetic. That is, the work in the classroom has much greater intentionality than simply passing tests to demonstrate students' grasp of minimum competencies. What happens in classrooms would be designed to set a different societal course, one that celebrates democracy, equity, and the self, as well as communal efficacy of all people no matter their individual markers of identity. In sum, principals and teachers create a space where teachers are given the room to connect instruction to a much broader context, so that their work becomes replete with meaning and purpose. As Foster wrote, "administrators face a dominant problem in the constant struggle to create an organization where personnel are bureaucratically aligned; the leadership of an organization, however, transforms this problem by transforming personnel attitudes through creating a meaning-full system" (p. 193).

To implement a new ontological position for teachers means that a good deal of risk taking must take place on their part. The risk is manifested in their first locating their work in a broader public space, embracing the fact that the educational process is deeper than the casting and catching of incongruous, inane bits of information. Second, the risk involves teachers seeing themselves from a different teleological stance, one that views their work as that of a transformative or organic intellectual. What this means is that teachers couch their work in the creation of more democratic spaces throughout the community and society. This requires challenging the parochial notions of schools and the myopic visions of academic achievement. All of this is risky because it is built upon a subversive and empowering platform that questions the efficacy of almost every traditional notion of the teaching-learning process. Teaching for societal transformation frees the sphere of the school to serve as a space of questioning and struggle. Teachers become reflective, intentional, and strategic about inculcating a progressive, democracy-based agenda in the classroom. As Giroux suggests, the transformative intellectual helps students to gain the critical knowledge about those structures, institutions, rituals, and practices that exist all around them—for example, the economy, the government, the world of work, and popular culture—in order to explore the ways they all serve to propagate an undemocratic motif and reify racism, sexism, homophobia, classism, and the like. Just as profoundly impactful for teachers is the way students are perceived through a critical and critically spiritual frame.

Critical Theory, Spirituality, and Students

When a school leader practices from a critical perspective, and particularly a critically spiritual perspective, then opportunities for students to become self-reflective and deconstructive are inherent in classroom practices. Essentially, as with teachers, the students are encouraged to view their classroom labors through a broader lens that is attached to an agenda of social change. So indeed, academic achievement is not simply measured by standardized test performance but, more importantly, learning is accomplished within a context of societal change, the infusion of greater democratic practices, and the projection of ways of seeing equity and antidiscriminatory behaviors injected into the very fiber of our society. This means that the community, in its broadest sense, becomes the classroom, and its issues become the curriculum. Foster argued that schooling has traditionally served not only to transmit knowledge but also to create what he called structures of personal and social meaning. He maintained that schooling opened up avenues of liberation and protest. In this way, schools are able to promote a certain type of agency where the students' voices—as well as their sense of efficacy—are tied to their efforts or projects to transform community. The very difficult dynamic here, however, is that challenging students to bring about transformation could be seen as taking a patriarchal stance, rather than being a counter-hegemonic purpose of education. In other words, building a school around these critical, progressive notions, while emanating from a genuinely liberating grounding, may come off as paternalistic, authoritarian, and manipulative. This can particularly be the case with students.

One who adopts a critical theoretical grounding for educational leadership practices assuages the very idea that such a position resembles the setting in place of the dominant, patriarchal paradigm by disrupting the hegemonic notions of authority. Giroux (1997) posits the concept of the emancipatory model of authority to assist in reframing or reconstituting the oppressive notions of that phenomenon. The idea of emancipatory authority embraces the essential struggle against traditional concepts of power and authority. Essentially, Giroux argues:

> . . . authority exists as a terrain of struggle and as such reveals the dialectical nature of its interests and possibilities: moreover, it provides the basis for viewing schools as democratic public spheres within an ongoing wider movement and struggle for democracy. (p. 102)

It is the struggle, as well as the highlighting of the dialectical nature of authority, that radical educators keep prominently in mind when facilitating a public sphere like schools; their efforts are taken in order to ground its work in a progressive, critical epistemology.

Our fear of behaving in a contradictory fashion where this whole notion of authority is concerned, however, is ameliorated through the use of a Freirean model (Freire, 1970). As we transform the pedagogical practices from banking to problem posing, leaders also are transforming their positions with students. They are creating spaces where students are actually helping to determine the curriculum. Through their opportunities to explore, critique, create, inquire, self-reflect, and deconstruct, students operate in an anti-oppressive space and come to know that their partnership and contributions to the learning process are welcomed and celebrated. In order for this to come to fruition, teachers and principals are compelled to reject a position regarding students that has been traditionally pervasive throughout educational institutions. As Freire commented:

> Implicit in the banking concept is the assumption of a dichotomy between human beings and the world: a person is merely in the world, not with the world or with others; the individual is spectator, not re-creator. In this view, the person is not a conscious being (corpo consciente); he or she is rather the possessor of a consciousness: an empty 'mind' passively open to the reception of deposits of reality from the world outside. (p. 56)

So, to offer a counter-hegemonic pedagogy, one has to understand that students too, like the adults who facilitate the education process, are agents and cocreators of their own subjectivities. They too possess intentionality and are purpose- or meaning-driven, and education must tap that deep reservoir within them to inspire their participation in the teaching-learning dynamic. Such pedagogical practices imply that students are free enough in their interactions with teachers and principals to participate in a self-reflective project, while concomitantly exploring how the social realities of their lives have been crafted and what their role has been in shaping their own subjectivities. Essentially, it is important for students to be able to inquire about their racial, gender, ability, and sexual-orientation positions and to see them in a larger context of contestation, fluidity, and competition for primacy.

In order for a critical ideology to become a guiding principle for schools, students can no longer be viewed as ". . . a unitary body removed from the ideological and material forces that construct their subjectivities, interests, and concerns in diverse and multiple ways" (Giroux, 1997, p. 122). What a total shift in epistemological formulations! To assume the consciousness of students, their ability to reflect, deconstruct, create, and then to take action means that teachers and principals celebrate and encourage student voice. The use of dialogic pedagogy, creating classroom spaces where critical inquiry, problem-based learning, and exploration are manifested demonstrates that students are being held mutually responsible for their learning and, indeed, are accountable, along with their teachers and principals, for their academic achievement.

There is also the role the community plays and the nuances of community that must be embraced through a critical and critically spiritual way of perceiving educational leadership.

Critical Theory, Spirituality, and Community

We are remiss in our thinking when we look at community as a monolithic phenomenon. Such a myopic perspective negates the multiple communities that are both internal as well as external to the proverbial schoolhouse. When a leader practices her or his craft, grounded in a critical or critically spiritual conceptual frame, there is an accurate exposition of the ways in which particular communities struggle for prominence and dominance. This struggle may be between the communities of the students and teachers, the communities of the teachers and the staff, or the communities of the males and the females that work in the school. Each, with its multiple subcommunities, is vying for the status that supposedly accompanies the possession of power. Beyond this, leaders whose administrative practices emanate from a more critical perspective also negotiate with the multiple communities that are external to schools. These include grassroots or community-based organizations, special-interest groups, political-action coteries, members of the clergy, business leaders, and so on. Each of these groups of people vies for the power to intimately impact what takes place in the school.

As a part of critical transformative leadership, those who construct curriculum clearly understand that the struggles inherent in any collection of human beings become the fodder for study. What is most intriguing is that schools can become those sites where the tensions and the ubiquitous conflicts that inevitably arise actually become those test spaces where democratic practices can be exercised. It is the navigating of these conflicts and the negotiating between the multiple interests where the tenets of democracy and equity are most greatly tested. It is the element of deconstructive interpretation, accompanied by critical self-reflection, where all those engaged in the education project are invited to explore how and from where their dispositions and positions regarding the contending or oppositional interests emanate. It is through this process of critical self-reflection that one interrogates the foundations for the prejudices, stereotypes, and misperceptions one has utilized in building dispositions, as well as behaviors, regarding whatever community, interest, or predisposition that has been deemed antithetical to one's own.

Reenvisioning Educational Leadership Practices

What a formidable task it is to believe that one person, the titular leader, can actually manage all of these social and political dynamics. However, two suggestions seem to be plausible solutions to this mammoth problem. First, it is incumbent upon leadership preparation programs to deal squarely with the competing interests that run rampantly in any school. To leave educational leadership students miseducated through the dismissal of the exploration of these tensions and struggles through omission is almost unpardonable. What is essential is for prospective school leaders to grapple with the messiness of leadership, the irrational aspects of leadership, and the more often than not labyrinthine nature of the relationships within and without the schools, with which leaders must contend.

Second, school leadership must be perceived through a jazz metaphor. That is, the ensemble has a named leader; however, throughout the playing of the piece, members, by turns, take the lead, often in presenting variations on the theme of the piece. While each member of the ensemble "gets 'em some," the other members accompany and begin to catch the creative thinking and nuances that each leader brings to the work. The differences in playing the theme are manifold. What is so intriguing, however, is the constancy of the theme. No matter the creative interpretation and even what at first-listen may seem to be a departure from the undergirding theme, eventually, through a course to resolution, the ensemble gets back to the clear articulation of the piece's theme, its main emphasis or message. Such must be the case of leadership within the multiple communities in the school. The overarching theme must be established: the goal of transforming the school, its environs, and, ultimately, the society into more genuinely democratic spaces has to become the substantive goal for what happens in schools. The multiple layers and leadership players, stepping forward at various junctures in the educative process, allows for an essential distribution of leadership that empowers a host of players other than the principal, in order to impact the practices, policies, and performances in schools.

Conclusion

Through the lens of critical theory and critical spirituality, academic achievement—as well as the work done in educational spaces by the staff, teachers, principals, parents, and community—takes on a much more political and galvanizing tenor. The work in schools loses its mundane character. Indeed, what happens in the schoolhouse is aligned with a much more impacting agenda. The world becomes what is read and deciphered. The textbooks become the situations that are important to both the internal and external communities. There is a sense that the radical reconstruction of schools portends the creation of a new society.

Undoubtedly, this kind of work demands faith and bravery. It demands that antiquated paradigms be replaced with more progressive ones. Progressive paradigms need not simply call for revisions to make the schools work better. Rather, progressive notions of schools must interrogate the very purpose of educational sites and their role in perpetuating societal views and values. What do we want to be transmitted to students that will upset the status quo? In what projects must students be involved in order to bring about societal transformation? Finally, how do we prepare leaders to acknowledge the intangibles of calling, faith, hope, and creativity, and to promote equity, inclusion, and democracy? All of these dynamics must be engaged as the work to reimagine the places called schools continues.

References

Dantley, M. E. (2005). African American spirituality and Cornel West's notions of prophetic pragmatism: Restructuring educational leadership in American urban schools. *Educational Administration Quarterly, 41*(4), 651–674.

Dantley, M. E. (2007). Re-radicalizing the consciousness in educational leadership: The critically spiritual imperative toward keeping the promise. In D. Carlson & C. P. Gause (Eds.), *Keeping the promise* (pp. 159–176). New York: Peter Lang.

Dantley, M. E. (2009). African American educational leadership: Critical, purposive, and spiritual. In L. Foster & L. C. Tillman (Eds.), *African American perspectives on leadership in schools: Building a culture of empowerment* (pp. 39–56). Lanham, MD: Rowman & Littlefield.

Dantley, M. E., Beachum, F. D., & McCray, C. R. (2008). Exploring the intersectionality of multiple centers within notions of social justice. *Journal of School Leadership, 18*(2), 124–133.

Foster, W. (1986). *Paradigms and promises: New approaches to educational administration.* Buffalo: Prometheus Books.

Freire, P. (1970). *Pedagogy of the oppressed.* New York: Continuum Publishing Company.

French, J., & Raven, B. (1962). The bases of power. In D. Cartwright (Ed.), *Group dynamics: Research and theory* (pp. 259–269). Evanston, IL: Row Publishing.

Giroux, H. A. (1997). *Pedagogy and the politics of hope: Theory, culture and schooling.* Boulder: Westview Press.

Giroux, H. A. (2000)

Hafner, M. M., & Capper, C. A. (2005). Defining spirituality: Critical implications for the practice and research of educational leadership. *Journal of School Leadership, 15*(6), 624–637.

Marcuse, H. (2001). *Towards a critical theory of society.* New York: Routledge.

Marshall, C., & Oliva, M. (2001), *Leadership for social justice: Making revolutions in education,* Columbus, OH: Allyn & Bacon.

Marshall, C., & Oliva, M. (Eds.). (2006). *Leadership for social justice: Making revolutions in education.* New York: Allyn & Bacon.

Maxcy, S. J. (1995). *Democracy, chaos and the new school order.* Thousand Oaks, CA: Corwin Press.

Maxcy, S. J. (2002). *Ethical school leadership.* Lanham, MD: Scarecrow Press.

Shields, C. M. (2005). Liberating discourses: Spirituality and educational leadership. *Journal of School Leadership, 15*(6), 608–623.

Theoharis, G. (2009). *The school leaders our children deserve: Seven keys to equity, social justice, and school reform.* New York: Teachers College Press.

12

Transformative Leaders in Bureaucratic Environments

A Juxtaposition of Assessment Leadership

Anne Marie Tryjankowski

Strong leaders are imperative for success in any venue. Some leaders are essential for maintaining organizational structures that are performing optimally, while other leaders are brought into organizations to bring about change in those organizations. Leadership comes in different forms.

Many would argue that educational systems today are transactional in nature. Transactional leadership is a behavioral theory. Transactions in systems are based on reward and punishment. The leader is powerful and allocates tasks to a subordinate employee. A clear chain of command is in place. If the employee successfully completes the task, a reward exists. The reward in most transactional systems is pay and benefits. The tacitly understood punishment is loss of employment. Bureaucracies are transactional systems. Educational systems tend to be highly bureaucratic.

The value that the educational system places on high-stakes assessments is clearly transactional. National legislation dictates that states must develop standards and assessments to measure student progress toward meeting those standards. When states comply, they are rewarded with funding to support these initiatives. At the local level, school districts comply with state mandates for high-stakes testing and measures of adequate yearly progress, in order to receive some funds from the state. When schools and districts fail to make progress toward meeting the standards, they are sanctioned for their inadequate performance. The most severe of these sanctions is school takeover or closure. Rewards, punishments, bureaucracies—all are indicators of a transactional system.

Another transactional practice in school assessment protocol is the rewarding of teachers with merit bonuses for high performance by their students on standardized tests. In an attempt to achieve their adequate yearly progress goals, some districts and schools have implemented merit systems to motivate teachers to increase student performance on these standardized assessments. Goals for class or school performance are set. If teachers meet these goals, they are rewarded with an increase in pay. If they do not, there is no merit bonus given. These performance-based compensation systems are often based solely on the output measure of student standardized test scores. No provisions are made to address the inequities in school conditions or social conditions that may be inherent in any given school community. Rather, the transaction of higher pay for higher student performance on standardized tests is void of any attention to disparities that may exist.

Do our educational systems ignore the need to create places of democracy within our schools and classrooms, or are we simply creating schools and classrooms that focus on successful testing outcomes? Are we creating systems that are serving the needs of legislators over the needs of families and children? Are the needs of diverse populations being addressed within our educational systems? Are the leaders we trust with creating systems for our youngest citizens truly equipped to understand the impact of inequitable social conditions on classrooms?

If the systems created are not educating our students for democracy and justice—to be participating citizens—how can leaders work in those systems for the good of all? The need for leaders to focus on transforming these systems is dire. Transformative leadership is necessary to assure that inequities in educational and social systems are overcome. But the transformative leader cannot simply begin a new school system based on transformative ideals and methodologies. Historically, education policy has necessitated the creation of educational bureaucracies. The transformative leader must work within—and astutely against—those bureaucracies to make substantive and lasting change.

How can we best prepare leaders to be transformative as they work in traditionally transactional systems? In an attempt to answer these questions, the following story of two teachers is presented. The teachers entered the profession to make a difference in the lives of children and families. Both eventually became frustrated by a school system that reduces teaching and learning to mere transactions focused on standardized test scores and rewards or punishments. They challenged each other to pursue administrative certification in an attempt to change the system by taking on formal leadership roles. Each chose their certificate program based on specific criteria. Their experiences in their preparation programs led these teachers to develop unique leadership competencies that shaped their philosophies and the ways they work on behalf of children.

The Story

This is a story of two teachers, Justine and Perry (pseudonyms), who became interested in taking leadership roles in their school systems.

Idealism: Teaching as Social Justice

These young teachers came to the profession because of their passion for teaching and their quest to make the world a more socially just place. They both attended the same teacher preparation program and landed teaching positions in a high-need urban center. Justine and Perry care deeply about the students and their families. They often spent hours after school providing academic assistance to their students. They spent their own money to provide school supplies, warm clothing, and even food for those students whose families could not afford these basic necessities of school life.

Justine and Perry planned lessons that were based on individual needs of students. Many of their students were working at levels far below the grade level they were in. Justine and Perry worked hard to give the students the skills they would need to be successful in life.

Under the union contract, teachers were required to be in school from 7:30 a.m. to 2:55 p.m. While some teachers were paid to coach sports or advise clubs, extra hours put in after 2:55 p.m. were traditionally not compensated. Both Justine and Perry stayed to help their students and families and did not receive extra pay for their efforts. But they were dedicated to the learning of their students and would go to great lengths to make sure that their students were given every opportunity for success.

Sometimes, these two teachers would eat dinner together after long days and evenings at the school. During these dinners, they typically focused on the good work they were doing, but sometimes they bemoaned the system in which they worked. There were many positive aspects of their work. Their coworkers were amazing people. Teachers worked hard to meet the needs of students. Teaching assistants and support staff provided assistance in classroom instruction and worked to bridge the gap between schools and families. Principals were dedicated, trying to support teachers in their instruction.

Reality: Compliance, Testing, and Incentives

But the system put obstacles in place that Justine and Perry considered strange. Education was supposed to be a career choice that focused on helping students to attain the levels of success necessary to be members of a caring and committed society. The focus of this system was not that. Much of the teachers' time was spent on issues of compliance. District mandates had teachers spending increasing percentages of their instructional time completing reports. This only left before and after school hours to focus on working with students and families on an individual basis. Most troubling to Justine and Perry was the obsessive focus on student attainment as measured by standardized tests.

According to mandates by the district, these annual assessments were a key focus of the work of teachers and students. Hours were spent aligning curriculum to the standards that were measured on the test. Most of the teachers felt that holding children to learning standards was important to the academic success of children. They felt that learning standards helped them to plan lessons that were meaningful and challenging to students. The professional teaching staff looked at standards in a favorable light. However some teachers suspected that these standards were not focused on student learning as much as they were on standardized test performance.

Every school-wide faculty meeting started with reports on how various grade levels performed on practice standardized tests. If your grade level performed well on the test, teachers were congratulated. If your grade level struggled with the concepts, teachers were derisively questioned about the results. A bar graph outside the principal's office indicated which classes were making appropriate gains in performance on these practice tests and which classes were not.

Additionally, there were some incentives that were being offered that seemed to be based on misplaced educational values. Teacher merit raises were being given to teachers whose children scored highest on standardized tests. A pool of money was given to each school to be divided amongst the teachers as end-of-year bonuses. The money was to be based solely on children's test scores. Those teachers who had the highest standardized test scores at each grade level were given the highest bonuses. Another bonus was given to the teacher in the school with the highest percentage of students meeting or exceeding the passing rate on the standardized test. According to the merit-pay distribution schedule, this teacher was supposed to be honored, and subsequently emulated, for his or her work. The award amount was so great that it would likely encourage others to attain such stature.

Teachers liked the idea of this merit pay. While most found the work that they did with children and the growth that they saw in the classroom to be rewarding, it was no secret that the annual salary of teachers was not on par with other professions. Teachers often saw their university classmates with advanced degrees in areas other than education out-earn them. So the "carrot" of earning a substantial bonus at the end of the year was enticing.

Alarming things happened to the collegial community of workers in the school under this merit system. Teachers who once willingly shared ideas for lessons and activities stayed in their classrooms and worked in isolation. Teachers began to make their own copies, for fear that someone would see the work that their students were doing and steal ideas that would lead to increased student learning. Classes didn't take field trips together. And teaching seemed to be focused only on the instructional areas that were on schedule to be tested via standardized tests in the spring.

Justine and Perry got caught up in this frenzy of standardized test achievement as well. Who wouldn't like the idea of some extra cash to make life a little easier? But eventually they realized that their behavior was cheating their students out of important aspects of a well-rounded education. They agreed that there needed to be a change in these practices; however, they weren't sure how they could change the system from their place in the bureaucratic chain of command. They were merely teachers who refused to jeopardize the work they loved by challenging the authority of the system. Then Perry had an idea. If they could move up that chain of command, they would be able to make some of the changes necessary to value teaching and learning over test scores. As principals, Perry and Justine would be able to help teachers focus on children and families. They could change the model of education in their schools to truly manage a school that could focus on the good work of teachers and the needs of students. Perry and Justine decided that they would go back to school and get their administrative certificates. Perhaps as school leaders they could make the changes to the educational system that would truly benefit their students.

Pathways to Educational Change: Leadership and Leadership Preparation

Remember, money is tight on these teacher salaries, so our teachers needed to make their decisions about leadership training programs carefully. The programs must be affordable and offer classes outside of the teaching day. Most teachers don't have the luxury of studying about leadership full-time, and Perry and Justine were no exceptions.

Perry had worked with student teachers from a local university and received tuition vouchers as a token of the university's appreciation. The university was well regarded. Class size was relatively small. Professors had a good reputation for being attentive to student needs. Adjunct professors who currently worked in the field of educational leadership taught many of the classes. Perry realized that this would be a good opportunity to learn about the field of educational leadership from those that were practicing educational leadership. The university had national accreditation for its educational leadership program. One of the attributes that the program met through this accreditation was a focus on leading diverse populations. That was exactly what Perry was looking for. An in-school internship was required, but the majority of that internship could be completed either during the summer and school breaks at the teacher's own school. This would relieve much of the financial burden of taking a leave of absence from teaching while pursuing this certification. An additional benefit of this program was that the placement rate of program graduates in educational leadership positions was high, with many students receiving job offers from schools where the program adjuncts worked.

Justine didn't have any student teacher vouchers from this university, so while Perry's program of choice was not out of the question, Justine looked at other programs as well. One program that really stood out for Justine was a program that had a substantial field component to it. The field component required students to not only complete an internship in a school but also to work in that school's community to see first-hand the challenges and opportunities that existed for students and families in the school. University classes were offered on weekends and evenings, so that part of the program was very convenient. However, the field components required three semesters of full-time internship practice. Justine would need to take a leave of absence from her teaching job to complete the program. Luckily, the university had a grant to compensate its students for their work in this innovative field model. While the compensation was not as much as her teacher salary, student loans could make up the difference. The hiring rate of graduates of this program was not as clear. The program graduates did become school leaders, but they also seemed to work in policy development, open charter schools, or leave education all together to become community activists.

Experts in the development of transformative leaders support programs that challenge candidates to think in new ways about inequities in our society. Brown (2004) notes that "by exposing candidates to information and ideas that they may resist and by assisting them to stretch beyond their comfort zones, a critique and transformation of hegemonic structures and ideologies can occur" (p. 78).

And so both Justine and Perry began their study of educational leadership, in order to make schools a place that provided a better educational opportunity for students, that truly delivered an education that would benefit all students and prepare them for college and careers, and that supported and trusted teachers as true professionals who do what is right for children.

Many of the classes that Justine and Perry took were similarly titled: Theory and School Administration, School Law, Methods of Supervising Instruction, and so forth. Both programs led to state certification, and the formulaic nature of those certification requirements was evident in the course offerings.

Influence of Fieldwork on Leadership Development

However, while discussing their coursework, our two teachers noted significant differences in the manner in which the courses were delivered, the expectations of the course instructors, and the content. Perry's program seemed to be more traditional in delivery. He attended lectures, read textbook assignments, and participated in hands-on group work in those classes. Discussions were interesting. Professors, especially the adjunct professors or professors who had experience in the field of education, provided insight into the various aspects of the course topic. Every class had a midterm and final exam, and assignments that were specifically aligned with the accrediting body's standards. Perry felt fortunate that he was able to complete his required internship hours in his school. He utilized his lunch breaks and planning periods to work on fulfillment of his certification requirements under the direction of the school principal. He would spend the summer supervising all aspects of the academic summer school program that took place in July and August. This was a complicated task that required strong leadership in student record keeping and assessment of skills attained in the summer program. This would need to be reported to the board of education in a formal report in September, and Perry would be given the opportunity to develop that report and to actually present it to the board. Perry was informed that this was important work and the trust that was placed in him by his principal was evidence of the good work he was doing during his internship.

Justine's work seemed to be a little different. During this field-based program she took the courses that had the same titles as Perry's, but the delivery and content were a bit different. Textbooks were used, but the majority of the reading came from current research and practitioner journals. Readings even came from some journals outside the field of educational leadership, including sociology and philosophy readings. The field of urban planning was sometimes referenced in various readings. This broad perspective was unusual but interesting to Justine. Classes certainly included some lecture and directed group work, but most courses had invited speakers from community and educational organizations. These speakers connected theory to practice for the educational leadership students. Multimedia presentations were included in class presentations. The influence of the Internet and social networking on education and society was connected to class activities. In addition to attendance requirements for traditional courses, our teacher was required to attend seminars in abstract but pertinent topics, such as poverty, power, gender issues, and gang protocol. All of this work was done in connection with the fieldwork that Justine was required to complete.

Justine's fieldwork was multidimensional and exhaustive (and exhausting!). Her internship experiences were focused on a specific urban school and its surrounding community organizations. The school leadership internship was a stand-alone internship. In this internship, our teacher learned all aspects of school leadership—curriculum, motivation, family involvement, supervision of instruction, and school compliance protocol, including fire drills, safety plans, and federal grant budgeting. As promised, the fieldwork also included community-specific projects. Justine worked in a community center, an HIV counseling organization, and a faith-based organization. These experiences provided insight into the power structure in the neighborhood of the school. They also helped Justine understand the true faces of the community in which the students lived. Justine learned much from these experiences. She learned about the students in the school and the challenges they faced daily. She learned of the supports that the community had developed to serve these children. She learned to "speak the language" of the community, making references to organizations and activities that students and families participated in. She learned there was no supermarket in the community, and that transportation to a supermarket for weekly grocery shopping was a costly challenge for most of her students and their families. She learned that gang membership was a fact of life in the community and sought ways to engage students who faced these daily challenges.In light of these amazing real-life community experiences in her program, and the focus on social justice issues that were inherent in her coursework and field seminars, Justine found it odd that eight weeks of her field experience was dedicated solely to working in a bureaucratic central office. This experience was far different from the spirited work she did in the school community. On her first day of the internship, she was assigned a cubicle. She was introduced to her internship supervisor. The supervisor explained that a federal grant was due and sent her back to her cubicle to work in isolation on completing her assigned parts of the grant. She observed that this was the protocol for much of the central office work—people working in isolation and meeting to bring the project together.

This internship experience exposed Justine to many important issues in educational-system work, including federal compliance issues in grant writing and budget development, contract negotiations, and policy regulations. The thing that stunned her the most was the paperwork that was involved in all of these issues. Paperwork was required by federal agencies, state agencies, lawyers, and union officials. Many times the only way to complete the paperwork was to ask school leaders and teachers to fill out such paperwork at the school level and aggregate it at the district level. In these eight short weeks she found herself obsessed by things that previously had no meaning in her life. Only when she reflected on this during her walks home, past the school and community where her other field work took place, did she realize that there was very little connection between what happens in neighborhoods and classrooms and what happens in bureaucracies. This dichotomy was something that Justine brought up in her seminar that weekend. Others felt it, too. How could education have become this complicated, and what could be done to have both sides of this system understand each other?

A few years passed, and both of our teachers found themselves busy with their separate lives, as often happens when coworker friends leave their place of employment. However, they eventually got together for dinner to discuss their lives, their jobs, and their accomplishments.

Working with a Bureaucracy for Standards-Based Success

Perry, the teacher who pursued the leadership certification with his student-teacher vouchers, was hired as a principal in a diverse school in a first-ring suburb. He was recommended for the position by an adjunct in his program who worked in the district. His resume, portfolio, and interview aligned nicely with the philosophy of the district. Many of the projects that he had done as part of the educational leadership program were based on the demographics and concerns of this district. Having initially pursued an educational leadership certificate because of his disgust with the transactional assessment system of his previous district, Perry prided himself on the progress he made in helping teachers deal with the mandate of standardized testing.

In completing his internship in his school's summer program, Perry realized that when a teacher has a concentrated amount of time in which to work, he or she must focus the work to get the greatest results—the "how do you get the most bang for your buck?" mentality. So rather than working from the traditional standards-curriculum alignment that teachers worked from during the school year, Perry spent time aligning the curriculum to standards that were repeatedly tested on previous standardized tests. He worked with teachers to identify the types of questions that were asked on the tests and on which standards the test questions focused. Then only those learning standards that had a record of being emphasized on standardized tests would be aligned with learning materials at every grade level.

This process resulted in a great efficiency of instruction. By teaching only those standards that would likely be tested, there was time to assure that all students understood those specific standards. Students needing remedial assistance would receive extra instruction to be sure that they understood the material at the level at which it would be tested. Those students who showed proficiency at these "power standards" would assist their classmates until the entire class could show a basic level of understanding of the material.

In their weekly lesson plans, Perry asked teachers to identify the standard that they were addressing. Only those standards that were most likely to be tested were to be addressed in instruction. Classroom assessments were to mimic the question types that the students would most likely find on the standardized test in the spring. This recording of the standard-lesson-assessment format link was carefully monitored. Weekly meetings to discuss student performance on mock standardized tests were held, with administrators carefully recording progress and helping to provide additional resources to help students who were struggling.

This concerted effort at test preparation resulted in better standardized test scores than the school had seen in quite some time. The school board praised Perry's efficient work in preparing students to take these tests. The teachers rallied around this common goal of student achievement as measured by the mandated tests. And Perry's commitment to effectiveness and school improvement was noted across the state.

Working Within a Bureaucracy for Justice and Social Change

Justine was also a principal. Her school was also very diverse. Many of her students were reading four to five levels below grade level. Her experiences through her fieldwork built her resume in very non-traditional ways. This diverse experience was one of the keys that got her the offer of working in a school that had strong neighborhood connections.

Remember that Justine was schooled in issues of social justice and advocacy. She had a thorough understanding of the community in which most of her students lived. This understanding led to her ability to communicate with parents about the needs of their children. Additionally, her experience in working within the bureaucracy of a local school system provided her with a keen awareness of the pressures that people in that bureaucracy were under and their natural inclinations to push the onus of their bureaucratic requirements on to those running schools. With these experiences under her belt, Justine devised a plan.

Justine knew that successful student performance on standardized tests was important. It was important to those at the district, state, and federal levels. The mandates were connected to school funding, and obviously school funding was essential to keeping schools open. Meeting annual yearly progress goals was essential to keeping schools open. Justine knew that keeping this school open was important to the children and families in this community. And Justine also wanted her students to meet the standards that were set by the state. The standards were good. One couldn't argue that they were concepts that every child should master. Justine had a plan that would address short-term and long-term issues associated with the standardized testing protocol of the district and its effects on her school.

Justine and her teachers knew that concentrated effort at test preparation might result in better test scores, but they weren't convinced that such preparation would result in meaningful learning. There was concern that much of the teaching was purposefully aimed at standardized test performance that limited the teaching of higher levels of thinking.

The teachers further studied the skills that were being taught through various efficiency-of-instruction initiatives in other districts. It turned out that while students passed the standardized tests, which resulted in positive public relations for the school and students meeting high-school graduation requirements, a problem was evident: Following the graduates of the school system through their entrance into college, or their career paths, the successful test takers were not considered successful in their next phase of learning. More than 50% of those students who passed the standardized test in their K-12 career were placed in remedial classes in college. How could this be? The standardized tests had shown these students to be successful. They had achieved a level of attainment on the test that indicated they had mastered the learning standard.

The problem was that students were never taught to think at the levels required for college work. They could not read college-level material critically. They could not respond to abstract ideas cohesively in writing. And their mathematical logic did not meet the most basic requirements of freshman-level, basic math in college.

Those moving into careers immediately following their high school experience did not fare much better. The lack of jobs for unskilled workers made finding employment difficult. Those jobs that were available to young adults with only a high school education were typically low-wage jobs. The successful standardized test takers are not successful in the work place. They didn't have the ability to think clearly and process information in ways that are applicable to job performance. Justine's experience was in direct alignment with Cooper (2009), who reports that "national initiatives emphasize accountability for academic achievement measured by standardized tests, but the increasing diversity of schools presents educators with significant social and cultural challenges that lie far beyond the scope of standardized assessment" (p. 695).

Beyond Compliance

For the short term, Justine and her teachers knew that standardized test performance was key to keeping their school open. So the entire of staff of the school concentrated on teaching in meaningful ways that focused on standards but also on helping students think deeply and critically about subjects being taught. Teachers met with local employers and set up internship opportunities for students. They also learned the skills that were required of their students in the workplace and aligned those skills with standard-based lessons. They met with local colleges and aligned their curriculum to ensure that students would not only meet state standards but also be trained to think critically and comprehensively in order to meet the college-level requirements of entering freshmen. And they engaged the community in these activities. Community agencies became centers for learning. Community church members, learning of these plans, invited students to intern in their workplaces. Community members mentored and tutored students.

These real-life experiences and connections to systems outside of K-12 made students excited about learning. Teachers were energized to truly prepare students for democratic thinking and productive citizenship. And, interestingly enough, they helped the school make adequate yearly progress as measured by the required standardized tests.

Justine had succeeded in keeping the school open and creating opportunities for students that led to their success in standardized testing and, more importantly, in life. She did this because she understood the bureaucracy of the school district and kept her school viable from a compliance perspective. She and her staff followed the rules but created experiences that were meaningful in the lives of children. And she also understood the bureaucracy enough to know that once you could prove yourself within the system, your reward would be respect amongst those in power.

Leveraging that respect, Justine knew that she had to go out on a limb to make changes to a system that was either not aware of or not respectful of the social conditions that exist in society. While it is reasonable to hold educators and students to standard attainment, the belief that the only way to measure attainment of "acceptable" levels of standard performance was through the administration of standardized tests at specific grade levels was unrealistic. Some students attain standard-level competency at different rates. Some students need additional supports to achieve standard-level competency. And some students need alternative ways to express their attainment of standards other than through a high-stakes standardized assessment. Additionally, the sanctioning of schools that don't meet standards on the required schedule seems to fly in the face of providing support to struggling schools and districts.

Justine knew that simply refusing to administer the standardized tests would result in the closing of her school. That was not what her students needed. But having had the experience of working in the bureaucratic central office during her administrative preparation program, Justine understood the mandates with which the district was required to comply. She creatively came up with a strategy. She would continue to advocate against the focus of learning being preparation for standardized testing. But she had another idea. It was a risky proposal, but Justine knew that she had to take a chance in order to implement a system that would better meet the needs of her students.

Cooper (2009) describes the work of transformative leaders as work that "maintains political clarity, demonstrates courage, and takes risks to advance social justice. Accomplishing these objectives is essential when leading culturally diverse and demographically changing schools" (p. 718). Additionally, Weiner (2003) notes that transformative leadership "demands people who are prepared to take risks, to form strategic alliances, to learn and unlearn their power and reach beyond a 'fear of authority' toward a concrete vision of the world in which oppression, violence and brutality are transformed by a commitment to equality, liberty and democratic struggle" (p. 102).

Using Bureaucratic Requirements to Leverage Change

Having earned the respect of her central office bureaucracy through her ability to get her school to meet adequate yearly progress goals, she proposed an alternate model of assessment for her students. The model was carefully crafted to authentically meet the learning needs of her student population but also to provide the data necessary to ensure that the central office could fulfill its state mandates. The model maintained that all students would meet standards, but rather than grade-level standards, the standards were benchmarked to be assessed throughout a three-year period. The assessment was not reliant on standardized assessments but rather on authentic assessments and portfolio reviews that were conducted by internal teaching staff as well as community members, college professors, and future employers. The authentic portfolios were proven valid and reliable by an external statistician.

As one might imagine, such an effort was met with skepticism. It was not the model approved and mandated. But it was difficult to argue that it did not meet the same ends. A pilot program was approved, with periodic standardized tests administered at the school to assure the central office that the alternate program remained true to its initial goals.

Conclusion

Justine and Perry both approached assessment mandates in unique ways. Perry conformed to the mandate but worked to make the process more efficient and standardized under a common goal of school success on the assessments.

This goal of efficiency in school processes, with little regard for meeting the broader needs of student learning, was articulated by Gause (2008), who noted that "challenges of today's educational leaders are indeed numerous and aspiring educational administrators believe to meet those challenges they must operate out of a technical/rational model of leadership without regard to issues of equity and social justice" (Academic Leadership in Education section, para. 1).

Justine saw the required mandate as something that needed to be changed but only after she proved that she could meet the same ends, and provide the same data to the central office, through a unique method of measuring student progress.

Weiner (2003) notes that "leadership, authority and power become transformative when they are directed towards the service of emancipating systemically entrenched attitudes, behaviors and ideas, as well as instigating structural transformations at a material level" (p. 93).

This narrative of two leaders' paths of assessment reform exemplifies different philosophies of what constitutes success in an assessment program. Perry's school scores were among the highest in his district. His careful focus on efficient planning and delivery of instruction led to this "success." The definition of *success* for Justine was different. She focused all resources on providing authentic learning experiences for her students. Justine's school's standardized test scores were not among the highest in the district, but the scores were high enough to show adequate yearly progress and give her the opportunity to parlay that success into a more appropriate assessment strategy for her school—a strategy that focused on addressing the issues of social inequities inherent in the current oppressive assessment system.

One could argue that the preparation of these school leaders led to these differences in assessment philosophies and practices. Perry was prepared in a traditional program—taking classes and completing internship requirements in the environment in which he already worked. He did not experience a central-office internship but was focused on the mandates handed down from the central office. Acceptance of this top-down management process focused his work on the best way to change his school inputs to meet the perceived requirements of his boss, the central office.

Justine, on the other hand, had experiences in a school, a community, and a central office. These experiences led to self-directed learning and seminar discussions about issues of concern. She was aware of the culture of the community and the resources that were available. She was aware of her responsibility to educate children in a standards-based world. And she was aware of the frustrations the central office felt around the mandates they were required to implement. Such experiences led to her ability to develop unique solutions to benefit her students and teachers, and to satisfy the necessary reporting requirements of those who were her superior in the transactional world of the educational bureaucracy.

In an ideal world, recognition of the need for a change in social conditions in order to move toward a more equitable society—and action toward that societal transformation—would be the norm. However, we live in a hegemonic world where oppressive practices are dominant. Transformative educational leaders are poised to move the fulcrum toward a more just educational system, which feeds into working toward a more just society. But to do that, they must be trained in leadership practices that recognize the transactional nature of the existing educational bureaucracies. An understanding of traditional bureaucracies is the basis for the development of skills that can challenge the status quo. By challenging the status quo through "speaking the language" and understanding their constraints, transformative leaders can move systems toward a more responsive and less oppressive bureaucracy. Transformative leaders must acknowledge the existing power structures and their place in the larger system before the challenging of those power structures can begin. Then, the challenges that transformative leaders propose can be based in true understanding of existing power structures and with the goal of moving that power to a place of increased balance for a more equitable society.

Educational leadership preparation programs play a key role in helping transformative educational leaders find the balance between necessary compliance and radical reform. Programs that are focused on strict compliance only create leaders who are valued in the hegemony. Programs that help candidates recognize the disparities in our society through fieldwork, current research, and a focus on cultural knowledge create transformative leaders who radically advocate for change. Programs that meld these two foci present a program that meets three overarching criteria: (1) giving candidates experiences to help them understand the current bureaucratic power system—including its efficiencies and deficits—and what drives it; (2) giving candidates experiences to help them understand the inequities that exist in our society and the conditions that led to those inequities; and (3) helping candidates develop skills that respect the power of the bureaucracy enough to leverage it for social change. The change cannot occur in a vacuum. It must be inclusive, informed, and skillful. Educational administration programs that are not afraid to challenge the existing power of school bureaucracies can prepare leaders who are equipped with the skills and courage to make the changes that are necessary to transform our educational system and our world into one that is more focused on equity and justice.

References

Brown, K. M. (2004). Leadership for social justice and equity: Weaving a transformative framework and pedagogy. *Educational Administration Quarterly, 40*(1), 77–108.

Cooper, C. W. (2009). Performing cultural work in demographically changing schools: Implications for expanding transformative leadership frameworks. *Educational Administration Quarterly, 45*(5), 694–724.

Gause, C. P. (2008). From social justice to collaborative activism: Changing the landscape of academic leadership. *Academic Leadership Live, The Online Journal, 6*(3). Retrieved December 3, 2010 from http://www.academicleadership.org/article/From_Social_Justice_to_Collaborative_Activism_Changing_the_Landscape_of_Academic_Leadership

Weiner, E. J. (2003). Secretary Paulo Freire and the democratization of power: Toward a theory of transformative leadership. *Educational Philosophy and Theory, 35*(1), 89–106.

Critical Thought/Creative Action

Developing a Curriculum and Pedagogy of Transformative Leadership

Eric J. Weiner

Prologue

It's a poor sort of memory that only works backwards.[1]

The Institute of Critical and Creative Thought is housed within a community center on the outskirts of Philadelphia. Taking up the top four floors of a 1970s-era brick building, originally designed as an industrial design plant specializing in the development and manufacture of durable fabrics, the Institute was the brainchild of Burton Waldorf Gartenkraut.[2] Deeply disturbed by the standardization of knowledge, the scripted pedagogies, the technocratic hegemony of school administrators, and the abject disregard for creativity and critical thought in the local public and charter schools, Gartenkraut "accidentally" developed an educational institute committed to free thinking, creative action, critical thought, and a rigorous learning regime grounded in purposeful projects born out of the needs of the surrounding communities.

He was a self-educated man, dropping out of formal school at the age of 16 and unlearning the lessons learned prior to dropping out in only a short five years. He was fond of telling anyone who might listen that, thankfully, circumstances of a decidedly dire nature led him to meet and be mentored by a motley group of dissidents and dreamers, artists and con-men, and strong women who rejected the comfort of paternalism and fought hard and sometimes violently against misogy-

---

1   Attributed to Lewis Carroll.

2   *I was named after my great-great grandfather, a Russian man of quiet insignificance and fanciful ideas. He apparently spoke nine languages, all of which, remarkably, sounded like Yiddish. I reclaimed the name many years and two generations after immigration officials unceremoniously threw the "kraut" into the New York harbor, along with all of those languages, memories, and fanciful ideas about government, art, economics, and family. Suturing the "kraut" back onto "Garten" connected memory to language, leading to a future I had yet to imagine.*

ny.[3] His education was born in the street and in the workplace, in the bar and library; it was an experiential kind of learning that privileged neither the body nor the mind, but rather, he saw in each forms of knowledge that could create a dynamic bond to a renewed sense of place and spirit. And he had the scars to prove it.[4]

At the front lines of labor disputes, he received blows to the back of the head from overzealous police and underpaid security guards. As a result of debates in the local pub about capitalism's predatory culture, his right eye still blurred in bright light from the shock of a fist that found its way into its socket. His knuckles were raw from wrenches slipping off locked nuts and his back popped from the strain of standing endlessly on the sandwich line, taking orders and making the best damn cheesesteak in Philly.[5] His eyes lost their flexibility long ago and he was constantly fumbling for glasses so he could read his cherished books, while his wrists and fingers stiffened from the hours banging away on the computer.[6] His happiness was written in scar tissue and blurry vision and it was unmoved by the scholastic cynicism being produced by the academic-industrial complex.

The Institute was originally started in the back of the local laundromat, and quite by accident, as these things usually are. It was 2020, and the local public schools in the neighborhood had essentially been gutted by regional and national policies that were designed to help raise teaching and learning standards. Since 1983, but gaining steady momentum and real power in 2010, raising standards had come to mean a few things. First, it meant eradicating bad teachers. Bad teachers were those teachers whose students failed to meet the requirements on the state's standardized tests. Good teachers' students did well on the standardized tests. Bad teachers were fired. The unions had long ago given up the fight to protect teachers from this kind of action. Second, charter schools had siphoned off the best students from public schools, taking huge chunks of money with them. These schools, although often more creatively run than their public counterparts, nevertheless were highly regulated and technocratically administered. Their goal was also to teach students to do well on the state's standardized tests, which were administered and created by shadowy corporate-government entities. The money and resources that went into developing and designing charter schools hollowed out what was left of public schools and essentially created two problems: Now we had two parallel systems of mass education—charter and public—that failed to educate children and young adults to think freely, critically, and creatively.

Adding to the burden of education was the spectacular speed in which online educational initiatives were developing as part of the epistemological infrastructure of both charter and public schools. One teacher could essentially teach an unlimited number of students the information they would need to pass the state's mandated assessments. The fetish with technology bordered on hegemonic, although there were still some who wanted to teach in actual buildings with actual students. The division between these arguing factions led some who took issue with the whole

---

3   *Of course, at the time my "dire" circumstances seemed anything but dire. The normal mix of drugs, sex, and mischief of the quasi-illegal kind was not dire to me at all, but rather a simple fact of my young life. There was nothing profound or even provocative about my choices. Frankly, I never thought twice about the consequences of my actions, let alone that they might lead somewhere other than the prison or a coffin (probably in that order).*

4   *This seems quite dramatic to me and not at all an accurate representation of my learning. I did, indeed, get scars, but how much I learned from them is still a grossly exaggerated myth. Let's just say that I was hard headed and knowledge needed a tire iron to seep into my thick skull.*

5   *This is absolutely true. The recipe, if anyone's still interested in this sort of thing, is secret. But suffice it to say that it is the bread that matters most. A bad roll ruins everything inside. The meat, strangely enough, is least important. Spices, herbs, and the cheese are next in importance after the bread. And too clean a grill will mess it all up in a second. But that's all I'm telling you.*

6   *Ha! What an image! Banging away on the computer! I rarely banged away on anything for that long, except for maybe my motorcycles. As for writing, it was vital but hardly the most important thing I was able to do as a teacher. It satisfied my own need for intellectual development, but only after I had gotten the Institute together and it started to really help people, did anyone start asking to see my writings. It is not what you write that makes who you are; it's what you do that matters. Ideas are great, but as I have always argued, the imagination must be made operational for it to become more than a means of escape.*

schooling enterprise to think that there might be an opportunity to exploit their in-fighting, while others had long ago given up on any notion of transformative action. Regardless of whether children were schooled in charter, public, or online "academies", math and reading scores still failed to match the dominance of socialist-minded countries around the globe. Complicating matters, students in the United States began to show signs of a deepening crisis of the social, political, and aesthetic imagination. On assessments by leading social-psychologists across the globe, children and young adults in the United States increasingly suffered from the intellectually debilitating conditions of narcissism and egomania. This made them, more often than not, the dumbest people in the international room, yet obnoxiously confident that they were the smartest. Challenged only by the French in their arrogance, they had neither the grace nor cultural capital to rationalize their embarrassing ignorance. They always spoke in domineering and shrill tones and constantly typed away on their phones. But what they said and wrote was so utterly ignorant of basic sociological, historical, political, geographical, and cultural referents and devoid of any holistic understanding of meaning, knowledge, and experience that they had become global punch lines for jokes about flabby intellects, tiny genitalia, and sexual repression.

By 2015, three years into Sarah Palin's first presidential term, U.S. hegemony was withering, and the kind of education that students were receiving en mass provided some reason for this. Gartenkraut had a profound distaste for schools of all sorts and a growing and solidifying disgust for the kind of people that they helped to shape.[7] He would grumble into his book as the subway lurched toward his destination, as young adults and children tapped incessantly on cell phones, reducing all communication and thought to 140 characters or less. All people born in the United States after 2015 were automatically taxed for a Web page, a Facebook account, an email account, and a future cell phone number, along with a Social Security number and Eye Recognition Identification Card (ERIC). Although reading would never die, per se, long literary forms, as well as shorter forms like poetry, were diminishing in popularity because attention spans were diminishing as well. A person might spend 12 hours a day on the computer, but he rarely spent more than a few seconds on each task. One study observed people of varying ages, born after 2005, viewing different forms of visual art in a museum. The study revealed that viewers spent, on average, no more than three seconds looking at each artifact, often not even stopping as they would stroll by the paintings and sculptures, as though they were window shopping in front of stores that held little interest for them. Like clicking through links on a web page, viewers moved quickly from one painting and sculpture to the next, barely registering any of the aesthetic moments conveyed by the convergence of form, texture, color pattern, and context.[8] Some of the visitors actually chose to sit at the "virtual art" booths, located in the lobby, to view the collection. They said the pixilated colors were more vibrant on the screen than on the canvass. With no pedagogical mechanism in place, the purpose of art had been lost in the shadow of capitalism's fetish for consumption.[9] Curiously, after the museum experience, the overwhelming response from the participants was that the art was "awesome," yet few could recall exactly what was so awesome about it. When pressed, they generally became defensive and sometimes hostile and reiterated, more loudly, "It was just awesome!"[10]

7   *No one wants to get schooled. It's embarrassing. Humiliating. I've been schooled and have done my fair share of schooling. But to take this idea out of the bar, field, locker room, or lodge and make it into a model of learning is ass-backwards! You don't school people as a principle of learning. That's the opposite of learning. When you school someone you break 'em down, demoralize them, make them feel stupid and think stupid. You train them by beating them down, taking away their ability to think for themselves. Schooled people or idiots, in the Greek sense of the word, or de-skilled in the Marxist sense.*

8   *My favorite artists help me to see and feel what reality hides from me and, in some instances, protects me from. Without them I would be lost.*

9   "Only just now awakening after years of materialism, our soul is still infected with the despair born of unbelief, of lack of purpose and aim" (attributed to Wassily Kandinsky).

10   http://i.telegraph.co.uk/telegraph/multimedia/archive/01185/arts-graphics-2008_1185335a.jpg

The reduction of experience to a series of clicks and short responses, some had begun to theorize, had initiated an evolutionary rewiring of the brain, in which concentrated study and sustained meditative practices would become not just difficult but impossible. If true, these evolutionary changes would not be realized for thousands of years, maybe more, but when Gartenkraut looked up from his book, the future looked no farther away than a few subway stops.

As was his custom, he dragged his laundry bag around the corner to the local laundromat on Friday night. It was April 13, 2020. He had been laid off from his latest job repairing motorcycles. He had some savings and lived frugally and was usually able to find work in some area in quick enough fashion to prevent eviction and starvation. He'd had many, many jobs over the years, and at age 50 was starting to wonder when he might discover his true vocation.[11] Up to this point, his life had provided him with a sense of contentment yet little happiness. In addition to a motorcycle mechanic, he had been a muralist, tattoo artist, union organizer, lobbyist for local ballot initiatives, bouncer, limo driver, dishwasher, short-order cook, ski instructor, and adult literacy tutor. He was well traveled in the United States and Canada, having crossed the continent more than a few times on motorcycles, and dabbled about in Europe, Central America, and South America.[12] He still hoped to get to Asia, but the economic war between China and the United States, raging in chilly confrontations for the last decade, made travel to the East very difficult and, in some instances, quite dangerous.[13]

As his laundry spun lazily about, he read a biography of Paulo Freire, literacy educator, freedom fighter, and what they used to call a "publicly global intellectual." He already knew quite a bit about Freire's legacy of hope and freedom through critical education, but he was finding this new biography interesting in that it was trying to understand his legacy in the context of more recent times. Technology, geoglobal economies of disproportionate scale, diminishing supplies of water, increased religious conflict, environmental degradation on massive scales never seen before, diminishing oceanic resources, and the increase in global humanitarian strife in Africa and the Middle East forced many to rethink the philosophical legacies of the past, not just in terms of what they promised but also in terms of the utopian nature of their premises. Social and political utopian discourses became suspect, as the creation of dystopian spaces increased throughout the globe. Ironically, the more dystopian the world became, the more easily people were seduced by quick-fix, individualized fantasies of (inner) harmony, (inner) peace, and individual prosperity. Social and political utopianism was out, while private, individualized utopian thinking was in. As the world seemed to become more unhinged politically, the only philosophy that registered was the philosophy of the individual. "Save yourself," one popular bumper sticker directed, because you have no control over anyone or anything else. Fantasy was the new hope, just as politics was increasingly replaced by religion as the most powerful engine of utopian promise. Secularists and scientists had slipped into the shadows of the great debates that were blasting from computers and

---

11   *This isn't exactly true. I was bored, yes. But a vocation? This was a bit beyond me, although it creates a nice literary moment in the narrative. It makes me seem like a much more introspective person than I really am. I can tell you that I did want a job that took all the knowledge and insight that lived in my bones and in my skin, what P. McLaren used to call "enfleshed," and direct it to a purpose bigger than myself. This was somewhat driven by the selfish and somewhat crazy feeling that I was soon going to die tragically. The life was starting to catch up to me, and I could feel it in the sleepless gray of morning, licking at the curtains in my rented room.*

12   *The first trip across North America took six months and changed my life. Living thin and meeting people from across the experiential continuum, I learned about myself in my dealings with others and the vagaries of the natural world. Ice storms ripped apart my tent, just as a bartender, opening his establishment, rushed to get me an onion to put on a bee sting that I had just received directly under my right eye. The lessons learned on such a trip often operate at the level of my unconscious, but become apparent years later when I find myself confronted by a problem whose solution can only be found by mining my past. This excavation often ends up somewhere along my circuitous route to the west coast. The second trip was just as notable, but made even more interesting because my bike was literally taped together with duct tape. Interesting thing, riding across an empty desert at 2:00 a.m. with tape holding together the bladder of your 20-year-old Bing carbs. Experience, theory, art, travel, literature, timing-space—interlocking circuits of knowledge and affectivity, consciousness and community.*

13   http://www.newsoffuture.com/china_and_us_largest_economy_in_the_world_future_economy.html

the recently installed sound boards lining the highways and downtown shopping malls. The people who were still relevant always had to bend their secular and/or scientific views into the new religiosity, its python grip squeezing the curiosity and creativity from the sociological imagination, just as religious freedom fighters continued to promise an escape through fantasy from the dystopian reality of everyday life.[14]

Consumed by his book, Gartenkraut failed to notice that his machine had completed its drying cycle. Dorian, a small, punkish little man, maybe 16 in age, and 5'4" in height, stared at the dead dryers, marked with yellow crime-scene tape. Half were broken, 10 were spinning, and three were stopped, the dried garments sitting flat against the bottom of the cooling cylinders. Rage. It was a simple feeling, but powerful, and it consumed Dorian as he fought the urge to kick in the glass of the broken machines with his steel-toe boots. Instead, he quickly moved toward one of the idle machines, opened the door, and started throwing the clean, warm clothes on the floor. *Fuck this*, he thought, *why should I sit here all night while some piece of shit lets his clothes take up valuable space?* In clumps, he pulled them from the dryer. He hated the thought of touching someone else's shit, but he hated waiting for a working machine to become available even more.

Gartenkraut looked up, thinking about Freire and the peasants so long ago, and saw Dorian throwing his clothes on the floor. "Up and at 'em," his mother used to say.[15] And he was. Quickly. Grabbing Dorian's arms, he threw him like a worn shirt against the dryer. Dorian, stunned for a second, tried to kick out Gartenkraut's knee with the toe of his boot. Too slow from years of inactivity, Dorian missed and then felt the most violently brutal pain rise from his chest to his throat. Gartenkraut had grabbed under his scrawny ribs and simply pulled out an inch or two, like pulling a desk drawer open, or flipping open a car door handle. Ripped a rib from the muscle tissue around it and Dorian squeaked, like a puppy's chew toy.

"Don't ever touch my shit again."

Breathing hard and trying to hold back tears, Dorian pushed down the nausea that burned the back of his throat. He was scared.

"What the fuck? You shouldn't leave your shit in a dryer when there aren't any left." He tried to suck in air, glancing down to the floor, focusing on a single, dirty sock lost beneath a washing machine. "You broke my fucking rib," was all he could manage.

---

14   From *On Imagination*

Imagination! who can sing thy force?
Or who describe the swiftness of thy course?
Soaring through the air to find the bright abode,
Th' empty real palace of the thund'ring God,
We on thy pinions can surpass the wind,
And leave the rolling universe behind:
From star to star the mental optics rove,
Measure the skies, and range the realms above.
There in one view we grasp the mighty whole,
Or with new worlds amaze th' unbounded soul.
    —Phillis Wheatley

15   *My mother was a superb cook and relatively grounded person until her mind was cooked by a combination of radiation and chemotherapy. This is what they used to do to eradicate cancer. Before Ben Hirshman discovered the cure for cancer in a combination strategy involving stem cells and "genetic erasure," cancer patients were burned and chemically saturated in an effort to kill the minority cells. When it worked it more often than not turned the infected areas into a shadow of themselves. Brain or head tumors left the surviving member a cool memory of herself. Nevertheless, her lessons of reason, humor, and pragmatism shaped my worldview in deeply spiritual ways. But it was also her influence that made me also jump out of my seat and almost kill Dorian. I am very glad I did not, as he was as much a founder of the Institute as I was.*

Gartenkraut knew this kid, or so he believed. Same piece-of-shit, texting-monkey, no-brain-matter, no-common-sense idiot that seemed to pollute the air he had to choke down every god-damn day. He was sick of it.

"I didn't break your rib, it's just the muscle that is torn. Painful as hell though," Gartenkraut smiled. "Did you not think to ask around to see if the owner of these clothes was in here? Did you not think to wait a minute to see if the owner of these clothes might show up? And why on earth would you disrespect someone else's clothes like this?"

The litany of rhetorical questions made Garkenkraut start to laugh. He really had to get a handle on his anger, he thought, as he stared hard at Dorian, trying not to reveal the grin breaking through his rough cheeks.

At this point it is necessary to take a bit of a shortcut by saying that Dorian and Burton found, after more choice words, some common ground in the decrepit condition of the laundromat. After learning about Dorian's passion for motorcycles and complete disregard for school, Burton started to feel a strange kinship to the boy. As they sat at the laundromat waiting and watching for their clothes to get clean, they learned a great deal about one another. It turned out that Dorian was building an old 1983 R80 BMW in his mother's garage. They also learned that they lived quite close to each other and that Burton had gone to elementary school with Dorian's mother, although that information would come later. The short of it is that the Institute, unbeknownst to either Burton or Dorian, had just begun.

Regular weekly meetings at the laundromat between Dorian and Burton soon involved other kids and a few adults from the neighborhood, all who seemed to be pissed off at something but had little knowledge and even fewer skills to do anything about it. On word from Dorian about a strange but badass man who seemed to know some things and who always had his head in a book about everything from history and art to motorcycles and tattoos, the hard-hit rejects from the neighborhood slid in on Friday nights to watch their laundry spin and dialogue with Gartenkraut about the troubles in their lives and neighborhood, in their schools, workplaces, and homes. Long after the clothes had dried, a hard-core group of about 12 people, ages ranging from 11 to 35, were gathered around a folding table at the back of the laundromat discussing how to best analyze the problems in the neighborhood and how to design concrete plans about how to eradicate or transform them.[16]

Together they suggested strategies to build local businesses, keep the sidewalks and streets clean and safe, establish healthcare centers that catered to the specific needs of the community, and initiate after-school sports and arts programs. Gartenkraut suggested books that could help them understand the problems in unique and complex ways. They might read poetry[17] to help them understand how white supremacy normalizes itself in the cultural expectations of all people, or read about architecture to understand the politics of space and community organizing. They read Karl Marx and Milton Friedman, Stanley Aronowitz, Chester Finn, and bell hooks. For those who couldn't read well enough to understand these texts, he helped them with their literacy. Indeed,

---

16   *It should be emphasized, if it is not obvious already, that I was not a Zen-like figure in these meetings. I had very particular ideas about how to get things done and what kinds of things needed to get done. I was nonnegotiable on taking an antiracist and antisexist stance on everything. Some who showed up initially thought that maybe I could help them try to get gay people out of the neighborhood. They quickly learned that my humanism was of a radical sort. Discrimination based on these "identities" was off the table for me. Some complained loudly, if I recall, how my ideas about free thinking were bullshit, as a consequence of my taking these positions. But from where I sat, free thinking could only be considered free if it was ethically grounded in humanistic practices of freedom and accountability. Otherwise, it was not free at all.*

17   Hughes, L. (1951), from *Montage of a Dream Deferred*. New York: Holt.
     What happens to a dream deferred?
     Does it dry up
     Like a raisin in the sun?

reading lessons became one of the most important practices in the Institute's success in helping to create transformative changes in the community.[18] Gartenkraut understood that the power of knowledge and experience existed not in their ability to directly inform people about a particular topic—although this can be an important dimension of becoming a learned person—but rather in their capacity to help people think about a variety of subjects in unique ways. Insights into human nature and social systems, he had come to understand, came not just from reading a book or hearing a lecture about human nature and social systems alone but came just as powerfully, or more so, from contemplating a poem's line breaks or a painter's choice of shape and texture.[19] Gartenkraut's influential article, published in 2048, on the science of metaphorical thinking arose primarily out of these exchanges.

Forty years after their initial meeting in the laundromat, the Institute is a model of purposeful, relevant, and creative educational practice.[20] At last count, there were 52 other unique Institutes of Critical Thought and Creative Action scattered throughout the globe. Although unique in their cultural design and orientation, their primary purpose is to serve people in their immediate community, helping them learn the knowledge and skills one needs to deal with personal issues in social and political ways. The heart of the Institute, regardless of location, is animated by a broadly defined yet principled understanding of the imagination. From the imagination arises the power to transform community and hence transform oneself.

Currently, the Institute in the United States is subsidized by private and public monies, committed graduates and other concerned community agents, as well as by a self-sustaining farm on the roof, renewable energy technologies that help it produce more energy than it uses, revenue from a growing portfolio of investments, and two small food trucks that sell latkes and matzo ball soup to workers and children in the neighborhood. When it started, the small group of founding members survived on donations and by a large matching private-public grant from Apple, Inc. and the now-defunct Bill and Melinda Gates Foundation.

The Institute in the United States has a rotating roster of teachers, with 10 core full-time transformative leaders. Each of the transformative leaders was educated at the Institute. Gartenkraut still visits, but his health prevents him from participating too rigorously in everyday activities. Because of his transformative leadership, the Institute's core principles remain intact yet avoid becoming dogmatic.

---

18 *I was horrified by the reading abilities of these kids and young adults. Basic shit, really. And if we wanted to have power to organize and change the conditions in our neighborhood, I had to teach the folks at the laundromat not just how to read, but how to teach others how to read. Soon, even the little ones who showed up with their moms would get some lessons on reading from those that I was still teaching myself. Learning how to read so that you can then teach others how to read—and read independently—is not rocket science. But it does take time and patience . . . for both people. It's some of the hardest work I have ever done. Of course, having a reason to read makes the struggle to learn how worth it. The same is true for teaching others to read. It's too hard to do without a clear purpose as to why you are doing it. Otherwise, forget. Get a shot.*

19 *I'm not sure how I came to learn these things about learning, knowledge, and experience. Somewhere in between the library, bar, gallery, subway, and home, and over many years of talking with people, I did come to understand that learning was amoebic in its shape, a cyclical metaphor that circled upon itself but avoided repetition. I have an aesthetic orientation to learning and a political orientation to knowledge. I tried to integrate these orientations into the Institute's DNA. In combination they help to highlight a truism about the social-psychologies of our experiential realities; that is, we might come away from an experience with an object of knowledge, a bit smarter than we were before, but if we come to understand that object of knowledge by first playing in its shadows, we will burn brighter as a consequence. Curiosity and imagination ripen our minds and bodies, making it difficult to erase the knowledge that comes from interpreting experience and analyzing ideas.*

20 *There are also times when there is an almost unbearable amount of conflict among all the stakeholders, a frozen analytical mind-set, a great depression of hope and possibility . . . it's not as neat and tidy as the author might want you to believe. Many times the Institute's "transformative leaders" struggled mightily to transform anything. But it is true enough that eventually we would manage to struggle through our differences and find common ground in our common concerns. If the concern was not common amongst a prevailing number of people, it would be put aside until more resources could be acquired to deal with the issue. Transformative leaders were oftentimes only as transformative as their resources permitted. Resources were so important that we spent much of our time and education investigating new and creative ways to acquire resources that would still leave us relatively independent. The acquisition of resources could not generate dependencies. Even though it is not a zero-sum game, dependencies of the ideological sort would signal the ending of a resource source.*

The core components of the Institute, arising out of Gartenkraut's experience with Dorian and the other laundromat thinkers, in general are committed to authentic practice that is theoretically informed; practice and theory that is critical, creative, and personally and socially transformative. Against the rigid, regulated, technocratic, and indoctrinating ethos of public and charter schooling, Gartenkraut set out to design his Institute based upon the following core directives: free thinking, creative action, intellectual vibrancy, curiosity and discovery, social imagination, transformative leadership, language-literacy-mind connectivity, and soul craft.[21] He understood that these conceptual referents, as he called them, needed to be taken up authentically, otherwise the Institute risked becoming just another "progressive" schooling center. He abhorred the idea of schooling so much that he would rather keep working from the laundromat than develop another school, regardless of how progressive it might appear. He knew that if these conceptual referents were not continuously used as guiding principles of action and reflection, then the devolution of the Institute was inevitable. Free thinking would be replaced by ideologically reductive discourses. Creative actions would be confined to those activities that were most likely to succeed. And leadership would begin to work in the service of its own interests. He had seen it all before. In order to resist these outcomes, Gartenkraut worked, like Freire in Brazil, with teachers, students, parents, community members, administrators, political leaders, businesses, students, and other school-based employees to develop grass-roots programs of renewal and reform that considered the whole body of the educational project. In this way, his work and the work of the Institute are holistic and reproductive; they help create sustainable systems of learning, teaching, renewal, and transformation.

The Institute's core conceptual referents, as developed by Gartenkraut, Dorian, and many others over the course of several months, were made operational, at least initially, by focusing on the

---

21 Free thinking *is nonideological, yet avoids being simply pragmatic. It signals a stance or standpoint, one that has a historical sense about itself. It is a deeply reflective kind of thinking, but reflexive as well. It is only as free as its acknowledged restraints. Free thinking is both rooted and routed. It is an ideal of thought that can never actually be reached, yet must be struggled toward if we are to be free. Free thinking can be conservative, in that it might entail conserving knowledge and resources that have been squandered or exploited; it might be transactional, in that it integrates new and old knowledge and experience in an effort to construct new knowledge; it might be radical in terms that point to a complete rewriting of the social contract, wherein it becomes revolutionary. In any case, it should always avoid becoming reactionary and recognize its purpose and unfinished nature.*
    Creative action *refers to the activities that our free thinking provokes. These creative actions are guided by a commitment to renewal, reform, conservation, and sometimes radical revision. They are community-based, while also globally articulated. They are provoked by free thinking, just as they try to build social, political, and cultural structures that will support and encourage free thought and more creative action.*
    Intellectual vibrancy *refers to the practice of reading and studying across ideologies and languages, across cultures and geopolitical spaces. It refers to the need to manage epistemological complexity in a world order intent on reducing understanding to its simplest set of political variables.*
    Curiosity and discovery *are the foundation of free thought and creative action. These things animate our humanity and find measure in our dreams. As these deaden from either ideological pressure or apathy (a function and/or effect of ideology), then our dreams for a future markedly better than the past wither on the vine of our sociological imaginations.*
    The social imagination, *following directly from Mills, is our ability to think about our private troubles as public concerns. This is fundamental in creating alternative social formations that are responsive to the personal struggles of minority peoples. If we forget that our struggles with poverty, hunger, education, male violence, rape, homicide, disease, and psychic health, among other facets of everyday life, are social-political issues, then we can't start taking social-political action to deal with these problems. One thing follows the other.*
    Transformative leadership *is a necessary dimension of social change. Without it, we lose the mechanism by which everyday people unite, organize, and act as a cohesive unit against social and political injustice.*
    Language-literacy-mind connectivity *refers to the theory and practice of literacy development pioneered by people like Paulo Freire and James Gee. Both of these thinkers understood the intimate relationship between language-literacy-mind. Words are conceptualized as markers of history, memory, thought, and action. Syntax connects bodies to actions and minds to the imagination. Reading demands a concrete set of skills, yet only becomes a meaningful practice if understood within a larger context of meaning, knowledge, power, and experience.*
    Soul craft *is a less-known dimension of the Institute, but just as important to its success and the success of its members. Soul craft refers to the process by which we take a complex accounting of the effects the social, political, and cultural environment has on our psychic and affective development. By recognizing that the external world crawls beneath the skin and conscience in a way that conditions our deepest connections to all forms of life, it is imperative that we are diligent in trying to grasp this deeper state of existence. If the other referents deal primarily with the epistemological aspects of social transformation and human understanding, soul craft is oriented to the ontological side of that same coin. It is the most controversial aspect of the Institute, but one that I feel is vitally important to the continued struggle for freedom of mind, body, and soul.*

following areas of need. They called these areas of need "impact zones" because they represented a space of power and influence; they were conceptualized as areas that had a big pay-off in terms of transformative effects once subjected to a radical reimagining. The impact zones were identified as important because they represented reproductive zones: social, political, and cultural areas of activity that helped to reproduce the hegemony of inequity and fatalism that, like a cancer, had slowly and powerfully dimmed the light of imagination in so many people. Once subjected to revision, it was thought that these zones could be the engines of social transformation and the revitalization of the social imagination. Although there have been changes and extensions to these ideas over the past 40 years, these are the ideas in their initial phase of what Gartenkraut would come to call the moment of the "operational imagination." Some of what is written is taken directly from the Institute's own archives. Some of it comes from conversations with Dorian.

Reeducating Teachers

It is not enough to replace poor and underperforming teachers with new and, we hope, better-performing teachers. Teaching, like any other profession, needs to be continually developed in concert with the changing demands of an evolving society. How effective do we think a great teacher from the 18th century would be today? It is a vocation that must be cognizant of the changing nature of the economy, youth culture, knowledge, technology, and civic responsibility. To be successful, it must be diligent in its pursuit of professional renewal and reinvention. Those who were once productive teachers often become ineffective, not because they are lazy or no longer care about their students, but rather because they have failed to keep up with the new demands and evolving expectations of a changed and changing world. This failure is then transferred to our students.

Through Critical Thought/Creative Action's teacher-reeducation program, experienced teachers are essentially retrained in the art and science of teaching: In-class encounters, professional workshops, small group discussions, online support, technological pedagogies, research-oriented learning opportunities, critical-thinking seminars, creative-action workshops, cultural study, and community-involvement projects all are designed to reorient seasoned teachers to the new, global demands of education in the 21st century. We build on teachers' deep knowledge and experience, while helping them unlearn strategies and ideas that are no longer relevant or productive in our current time. Experience cuts both ways, providing us, on one hand, with a foundation of knowledge to build upon and learn from, yet, on the other hand, keeping us rooted in the poisonous soil of outdated research and knowledge.

Redesigning Curriculum

The knowledge we need to be successful citizens, entrepreneurs, political leaders, CEOs, scientists, teachers, technicians, engineers, and so forth, is not compartmentalized as it is in school, nor does it float above the experience of life itself. Yet curriculum is too often designed whereby knowledge is disciplined—bracketed off from its relationship to everyday life—effectively severing it from experience. In failing schools, curriculum is developed as scaffolding for passing the mandated test. This practice of curriculum design only exacerbates student-teacher failure. Curriculum geared toward standardized assessments disconnects knowledge from experience—learning from purpose—making the failure of our students and teachers a foregone conclusion. This occurs because traditional curriculum design categorizes knowledge production in terms of academic disciplines and the requisite skills demanded by them. Typically, we then assess students on their lack of proficiency in these subjects using standardized tests that were designed in concert with the standardized curriculum. At no other time in our lives are we subjected to such an utterly confused program of study and evaluation. It is arguably the least-effective means of learning anything, yet the trend continues, in large part because both product and process can be easily measured by relatively inexpensive tests. Inauthentic, disconnected, decontextualized, and without a clearly defined purpose, traditional examples of curriculum need to be rewritten if we plan on raising the standard of public education.

At the Institute, we redesign curriculum so that it captures the synergistic nature of knowledge and experience, while giving students the freedom and opportunity to participate in purpose-driven activities. Born out of the real needs of real people, purposeful curriculum scaffolds the learning-teaching process by providing students and teachers with a framework for multi-disciplinary approaches to problem solving. Classes are project (problem/solution) driven instead of subject driven. The identification and satisfaction of needs—social, cultural, economic, political, educational, and environmental—define the educational project, while the redesigned curriculum provides structure and shape to the pedagogy. Creativity, critical thinking, trans-disciplinary knowledge construction, inquiry, and interdisciplinary approaches to problem solving shape the teaching and learning process. Our redesigned curriculum gives the learning process purpose and, therefore, meaning. Absent purpose and meaning, education remains anemic, while learning and teaching are allowed to atrophy.

Rethinking Schools

Our commonsense understanding of what constitutes a school is shaped by decades of misinformation and mythology. The single-room schoolhouse casts a long and dark shadow over our educational imaginations, preventing us from imagining school as anything more than a structure that houses teachers and students, divides our children by age or skill level, hurries them from subject to subject, and provides them with a predetermined set of standards to meet.

At Critical Thought/Creative Action, we shine a bright light onto the mythologies and misinformation that still condition our commonsense understandings and expectations of schools. In the glare of this light, the shadow recedes and we can begin to rethink what it means to be a school, go to school, and work in school. We break down the walls of learning, both physically and metaphorically.

Physically, going to school might come to mean going to where you need to go to experience, first hand, the thing that you want to learn about. It might mean working outside in the community with community members who share common concerns. It might mean working with artists on a mural and thereby learning about history, color, business, leadership, and so on. School might take place on a subway or in a home or in a parking lot. The possibility of creating and finding learning spaces and places are endless, just as the learning that goes on in these spaces and places is complicated by the fact that experiential knowledge is not easily compartmentalized in terms of academic subjects. In order to understand experience in all of its complexity—to transform experience into knowledge—students must employ interpretive tools from many disciplines simultaneously.

Within the actual school building, we break down the walls of learning by supporting the movement of knowledge from outside to inside to outside. Our perspective sees the actual building as beneficial, in that it can provide us with the material accouterments of learning (computers, desks, paper, chairs, a place to eat, safety, quiet, a space to organize and share our ideas, and time to think), but other than that, the walls of schools are imagined as porous, where knowledge, information, culture, power, and experience freely circulate, providing all stakeholders in the educational project an opportunity to learn from each other within the school structure. With our guidance, schooling structures become educational, promoting conviviality and thereby helping to build inquiry communities that are engaged in purposeful learning and teaching.

Redefining Community

In the recent past, geography, social class, identity, or cultural interests defined communities. At Critical Thought/Creative Action, we define communities by first identifying what the common concerns are that connect people who have an interest in the school. They might be in different locations, from different social classes, occupying different identities, and have varied cultural interests. But by first acknowledging our differences, we can then begin to identify our common concerns and needs. A collection of people who have identified a common concern or a shared unmet need, and are committed to finding solutions to that concern, is a community. It becomes a learning community when each member commits to collectively learning the knowledge and skills that must be mastered to fix the problem.

Additionally, globalization combined with new technologies demands that we redefine communities, particularly in terms of geosocial spaces. Now, more than at any other time in human history, people with common concerns can be connected with like-minded people across vast swatches of space and time. This offers us an enormous opportunity to link up people who, in the past, would never have had the opportunity to meet. Global concerns, like the environment, come to have local meaning. Local struggles over identity and rights can be a catalyst to form global learning communities. When we redefine community, we open up the possibility of restructuring the educational environment so that it is based on addressing the common concerns of the community.

Reconsidering Leadership

In an attempt to democratize authoritarian traditions of leadership, the new Left tripped over its own feet trying to distance itself from all forms of authority. Ironically, its power diminished in direct correlation to the development of an "authority complex" or, as we came to call it, "authority envy." As a critique of authoritarianism morphed into a more general critique of authority, the power to take a position and lead others wilted. To lead was to oppress, just as to use or have authority was to automatically marginalize and exploit. Teachers became facilitators, and leaders quietly abdicated their responsibility to lead in the name of equality. This process effectively lowered the bar intellectually and practically; because everyone now had a voice, many felt like they should be heard, regardless of the idiocy of their ideas. Soon everyone's ideas were no better or worse than anybody else's. There seemed to be no way to measure legitimacy without the existence of power, and no way to use power without reproducing inequitable relations of power. With this, a kind of post-structural paralysis overtook the imagination and froze the concept of leadership in overly reductive, authoritarian terms.

We reject this position by reiterating Freire's distinction between authority and authoritarianism. We also find Antonio Gramsci's insight into the role of leadership in social movements important to resurrect because he understood the connection between hegemony and leadership; that is, there is a quantifiable relationship between strong leadership and the success or failure of transformative movements. Transformative leadership is a precondition of transformative action, just as cultural pedagogy is a precondition of hegemony. This kind of action is social, political, and cultural, and is focused upon restructuring the social architecture that supports and reproduces oppressive inequities and violence. Leadership of this nature remains committed to a nonhierarchical, radically democratic procedural practice yet understands that the need for transformative action might, on occasion, overwhelm the requirement for democratic consensus on all issues concerning the constituency. Indeed, because transformative leadership more often than not leads against a majority, it becomes a necessity of power and survival to protect the constituency from the democratic tyranny of those that it fights against. In this context, democracy does not protect against injustice and violence but rather rationalizes them in procedural terms. Transformative leadership uses its authority to challenge this type of democracy on ethical and humanitarian grounds, while transformational leadership, by contrast, uses its authority to defend this type of procedural democracy.

As should be obvious, the Institute is a manifestation of my imagination, as are Gartenkraut and Dorian. Yet the idea of the Institute, and Gartenkraut's role as transformative leader, provides a backdrop against which I will talk about pedagogies that can help shape transformative leaders. Gartenkraut, although a fictional character, embodies the values, knowledge, and experiences that move people off the couch and back into their communities. His experience in the laundromat also shows how the opportunity for transformative leadership is not necessarily planned. Unmet needs, serendipity, space, time, and passion, all difficult to quantify in terms of importance, are part of the social dynamic of leadership; its deep psychology. Interlocking circuits of private and public pedagogies, in turn, condition this deep psychology. These pedagogies correlate with a finite set of social-cultural-political curricula. Together, these dynamics play upon the imagination in limited and limiting ways. The footnotes provide counter-narratives and other conceptual markers in an effort to illustrate the circuitous learning routes that form our consciousness and disposition towards each other, history, memory, and social change. Traditional schooling tends to reinforce a linear view of knowledge production as well as a hierarchical view of leadership and its responsibilities. I tried to create a transactional experience in the text between reader and author that animated the complexity of learning the lessons of transformative leadership.

In the shadow of this fictional utopia and in the context of developing transformative leaders, I will discuss what I call the "hegemonic imagination" (Weiner, 2009). I will then conclude by outlining different pedagogical exercises that can help break down the hegemonic imagination, thereby helping to foster a disposition of transformative leadership.

Fostering a Disposition of Transformative Leadership

Against the grain of common myth, there are no natural-born leaders, nor are there natural-born transformative leaders. Transformative leadership is the result of a series of planned and unplanned events and experiences. Not everyone who reads critical theory or suffers injustice or is thrown headlong into chaos and violence emerges as a transformative leader. It is equally true that neither intelligence nor education guarantees the emergence of a transformative leader. Indeed, identifying who is a transformative leader and formulating a typography of transformative leadership is a far simpler challenge than trying to untangle the social, psychological, pedagogical, and political forces that coalesce to shape an individual into a transformative leader.

What is at stake in such a challenge is the development of curriculum and pedagogies that can be employed in the service of developing transformative leaders. Complicating this project is the understanding that there are intangible dimensions of transformative leadership that cannot be known, such as genetic disposition or spiritual calling. Additionally, the specificity of transformative projects, in conjunction with the particularity of the leadership, makes any general claim about transformative leadership problematic.

Nevertheless, coming to an understanding of the coalescing forces that shape transformative leaders will provide a foundation for the development of a curriculum and associated pedagogies that can be adapted by educators in a variety of educational contexts. It is a curriculum that is project driven and responsive to shifting political and social conditions. It is conceptual as much as it is practical, with the understanding that the tools of transformative leadership are malleable and must be taught in a way that allows them to travel across contexts of leadership. The tension between generalizable skills and dispositions, on the one hand, and specific practices of leadership, on the other, is irresolvable.

Of specific concern regarding the development of a curriculum and pedagogies of transformative leadership is the role of imagination. Transformative leadership must be developed against the grain of what I have called the hegemonic imagination. Breaking into the hegemonic imagination demands a pedagogical engagement with both creative and critical trajectories of teaching and learning. For transformative leaders, creative thinking and critical thinking must converge into a fluid practice, helping those that they lead feel and act powerfully in the face of strong and potentially hostile opposition. In this way, a pedagogy of transformative leadership refers to both the means by which people are taught to be transformative leaders as well as how transformative leaders teach those that they lead.

Transformative Leadership and the Imagination

The imagination is a highly evolved social organ, dynamic in its capacity for creating new ways of seeing the world and acting in it. It can transform space and commute time; it can shift shapes and merge histories; it can literally and metaphorically transport our minds and bodies into places yet unknown; it can leave impressions upon the body, like a tattoo or fossil. But it is also quite susceptible to the dictates of social norms and the directives of power; it can operate outside of dominant institutional and ideological arrangements but too often does not. This does not mean that our social imaginations march in lock-step to an invisible "centralized scrutinator," as in Frank Zappa's "Joe's Garage," but rather that it has a delimited number of variations in its general ability to perceive what is and imagine what could be. For example, when we listen to a piece of music, view a painting, or consider another person's experiences as though they are our own, there are multiple interpretations that we could make about the music, painting, or experience, but there are just as many that most of us will never make because our imaginations are shaped and conditioned by current institutional and ideological arrangements. I explain this condition in my discussion of habitus and the hegemonic imagination. Please note that I sometimes use technical language that might be unfamiliar to many, but I make a concerted effort to define my terms. Given that language is a major tool of the imagination, it is important to recognize at the outset that our languages and literacies are two of the most powerful conditioning forces in our lives. As such, developing new languages and new corresponding literacies is a way to open new routes to the possibility of free thinking and acting.

In my consideration of the imagination, I draw on work in a number of different fields, but two that are central to my analysis are creative thinking and critical pedagogy. Both of these fields of research offer us dynamic tools by which to both understand the imagination as well as free it from its various constraints. My own take on critical thinking and pedagogy sees it as a highly social process, one that is always located in history and culture and whose primary purpose is to help people reflect, following Stephen Brookfield, upon their habituated modes of thinking and acting within specific institutional and ideological arrangements, especially those modes of thinking and acting that can work against one's class, race, and sexual interests. Additionally, I understand the concept of criticality to be a process by which we all can become more conscious of how inequities of power circulate in our lives, shaping our thoughts, feelings, and dreams. Power relations not only should be analyzed historically and contemporarily but also in terms of how they work to shape our sense of what is possible, as well as how we think about making the possible real. In this sense, my ideas are oriented towards a future not yet known, a future that is real in terms of our ability to imagine it.

The imagination is the metaphorical bridge between what is or was and what could or should be; in its operational moment it provides a guide for creative action. The light of our social imaginations, in other words, casts the shadow of human agency. One important qualification must be made at this point. That is, the imagination's capacity to distort social reality as it is attempting to see beyond it can present a danger to rational thought. We see this in the paranoid, untethered articulations of those who imagine conspiracies and the shadowy hands of government and industry. These dystopian articulations of imagination are indeed released, not in the interests of freedom and harmony but, rather, in the service of suspicion and social division. In this formulation, there are few, if any, common concerns. There is only "us" and "them." This dichotomy is a rewriting of the hegemonic imagination, even though it appears, at first, to be a breaking away from it. Absent an ethical referent, this articulation of the social imagination fails to find signification in a larger public philosophy, one that is sustainable *because* it is grounded in an ethically defensible position of social freedom.

However vital the critical process might be, it alone cannot release the imagination from dominant institutional and ideological normative constraints. A creative process has to be introduced into the theoretical and pedagogical mix in order to break down inhibiting discourses as they circulate at the level of our affective and psychic development. The creative process involves breaking down normalizing structures and the habits of emotion and cognition, which help perpetuate such structures through the creation of art, poetry, theater, film, new media, mixed media, literature, narrative, dance, spoken word, performance art, and so forth. It is animated by the need to produce, to actually create some kind of aesthetic event that rewrites or reimagines the familiar, just as it places emphasis on reorienting the unimaginable within the field of possibility. It is a process that refracts social reality as well as reflects a speculative future. The creative process that I envision should try to effectively and affectively rewrite "reality," in an effort to animate the analytical force of the critical process. This creative process, like the critical process, should always avoid didacticism in its effort to break down dominant social norms. The creative process, in particular, is most effective in its ability to rewrite reality by finding subtle ways to nudge both our conscious and unconscious toward new modes of seeing and feeling. Criticality minus creativity takes away the opportunity to rewrite our own ontological relationship to social reality. Creativity minus criticality becomes an exercise in pure aesthetics. The subversive force of imagination is felt most directly, not in its ability to acquiesce but in its drive to discover and create, to resist, to question, to empathize.

We can animate the power of critical thought and creative action by formulating pedagogical activities that tap into a person's desire for power, freedom, and justice. Developing transformative leaders, like Gartenkraut, demands learning-teaching opportunities that can help future leaders learn how to straddle the divide between dominant social structures and the development of new social formations that serve to transform those dominant structures. Leaders must be educated to think and act like transformative leaders. By engaging in the theory and practice of critical and creative studies, our future leaders can learn how to negotiate power, mediate identity, trouble common sense, and incite the imagination to dream and create beyond what is and what was. But, before we can do this, we must first come to an understanding of the social imagination and hegemony, a synthesis that makes transformative action often seem absurd or naive.

Breaking Through the Hegemonic Imagination

The Habitus of the Hegemonic Imaginary

The hegemonic imagination's power to condition our waking dreams, while making a claim to limitless freedom, lays in the celebration of its perceived ability to produce an infinite variety of thoughts, ideas, dreams, and visions. Just as neo-liberal discourses position "choice" and "opportunity" as correlates to freedom, without examining the social, cultural, and political conditions that a priori regulate (i.e., normalize) the choices that can be made or the opportunities that can be had, imagination is too often conceptualized as the key to possibility, opening an infinite number of doors, all of which promise either—and most often—an escape from reality or a different perspective on it. Because the regulatory process does not determine imagination and its output but rather suggests a field of infinitely structured and structuring structures, Bourdieu's (1990) conception of habitus is a vital, if insufficient concept, in understanding how the process of social imagining takes shape. Habitus, as he explains, is a:

> system of durable, transposable dispositions, structured structures predisposed to function as . . . principles which generate and organize practices and representations that can be objectively adapted to their outcomes without presupposing a conscious aiming at ends or an express mastery of the operation necessary in order to obtain them. Objectively "regulated" and regular without being in any way the product of obedience to rules, they can be collectively orchestrated without being the product of the organizing action of a conductor. (1990, p. 53)

Importantly, he goes on to say:

> . . . the habitus, like every "art of inventing" is what makes it possible to produce an infinite number of practices that are relatively unpredictable but also limited in their diversity. In short, being the product of a particular class of objective regularities, the habitus tends to generate all the "reasonable," "commonsense," behaviors (and only these) which are possible within the limits of these regularities, and which are likely to be positively sanctioned because they are objectively adjusted to the logic characteristic of a particular field, whose objective future they anticipate. (p. 54)

Bourdieu's (1990) theory of habitus is helpful in thinking about the hegemonic imagination because it provides a way to understand how we can imagine a seemingly infinite variety of possibilities, while at the same time be limited in the variety of possibilities that can be imagined. It is in the fact of some variation, some choice, that parameters of choice become difficult to locate and even more difficult to change. This is where the theory of habitus is less helpful. Bourdieu's theory of habitus is first and foremost synchronic in orientation and, as such, dismisses temporality as a force for changing the habitus of the hegemonic imaginary (Aronowitz, 2003). It is important to recognize that, regardless of how varied the products of the hegemonic imagination appear to be, they inevitably serve current institutional arrangements and dominant ideological interests. When disruptions arise, words like *utopian, silly, impossible, crazy,* and *dream(er)* are used to describe the ideas imagined or the imaginer him or herself to remind the imaginer that his or her thinking is outside of acceptable parameters. This is true when we speak of imagining on a social scale as well.

Social movements driven by the desire for racial equity, for example, are often belittled in the press as utopian or naïve. Radical environmental movements, likewise, have to spend enormous amounts of their limited resources defending the legitimacy of their hopes against the charge that their hopes for a "green" and equitable economic order are so far out of touch with current institutional arrangements as to be fantasy. The energy that could be used fighting for radical social change is redirected to defending the idea and possibility of radical social change itself. Schooling, of course, is a major social institution that helps to construct the hegemonic imaginary, as is the "culture industry," dominant political ideologies, religious formations, nation-state allegiances, Enlightenment ideals, bureaucratic apparatuses, and so on. The seemingly banal cultural practices of everyday life also shape the hegemonic imaginary, such as taking out the garbage for collection, getting cash at ATM machines, surfing the Internet for news, and going to the gym. It is in the everyday that histories are rewritten or forgotten, economies are reproduced or resisted, and the social imagination finds its voice and materiality.

Currently, and specifically, the hegemonic imaginary's habitus is animated by a deep skepticism of social hope and institutional transformation; a penchant for erasing or whitewashing the historical record; a turn to reactive thinking combined with a hostility to reflexive thinking; a synchronic literacy, which refers to a way of reading the world as a predetermined spatial reality; a commitment to schooling as a necessary force for social, economic, cultural, and political reproduction; a determination to conceptualize freedom in opposition to regulation; and a belief that fantasizing is the primary goal of imagination. To elaborate on each of these components is somewhat beyond the scope of this discussion. Suffice it to say that these components are interrelated, and it is the sum of the parts that determine the habitus of the hegemonic imagination. Operating within the logic of the hegemonic imagination are different trajectories of the social imagination: educational, political, and aesthetic. Each creates a challenge to transformative leadership, because each reinforces a notion of common sense that is detrimental to transformative change in their requisite field of knowledge. Each of these fields of knowledge will be discussed before moving onto various learning-teaching activities that can help teach leaders how to break through the common sense of hegemonic knowledge, thereby opening up the possibility of transforming themselves and the communities they serve.

EDUCATIONAL IMAGINATION

In the United States, the educational imagination is currently dominated by the dream and promise of positivistic knowledge. This dream is driven by an investment in measurement, standardization, and privatization. Imagining what is possible is limited by a type of thinking that makes objectivity a necessary condition of educational legitimacy. Educational theory and practice are dismissed as purely ideological if they don't meet the standards of verificationism, a methodological articulation of positivism (Cunningham, 2002). Cunningham explains, "Verificationism is always concerned with the meaning of statements rather than the nature of reality" (2002, p. 54). A struggle over meaning, however, always signifies a struggle over relations of power (Foucault, 1977, p. 114). Standardization of procedures and outcomes, coupled with muscular technologies of surveillance and oversight, defines its educational vision, just as the privatization of public education is the most respected vehicle for its realization. In recent years, No Child Left Behind is arguably the strongest national articulation of this perspective in policy form.

These parameters encourage, not simply the creation of new standardized tests, but a considerable social investment in their outcomes. The outcomes of these tests are believed to correlate with a kind of learning that is necessary for nation-state competitiveness and ideological hegemony on a global scale. This belief is rationalized by a deep commitment to the idea that positivistic orientations to scientific research can and will lead society—locally and globally—to a more ordered state. Putting aside the question of whether we can demarcate science from non-science (Cunningham, 2002), the rationalization is troubling for other reasons as well.

First, as theorists like Theodor Adorno, Max Horkheimer, and Foucault have made clear, science and technology, in the name of progress and modernization, are as much tools for domination as they are for liberation. If the recent past is any indication, they continue to be employed primarily in the service of domination, atomization, and political powerlessness. Even in cases where science and technology are utilized for cures to disease—social, physiological, and psychological—it is often to cure what they have caused to be diseased in the first place. The environment, of course, is a case in point. The irony should be lost on no one that Western science is looked to—from official sources as varied as Nobel-Prize winner Al Gore and the Bush administration—as the primary source for information and inspiration for healing environmental degradation, ignoring the fact that the degradation was caused, in large part, by an ideological investment in Western science and technology, specifically, and a belief in the benefits of "progress," generally (St. Clair, 2003). We look to science to cure cancer, just as we acknowledge that science has helped to support industrial, agriculture, and nuclear apparatuses, whose waste correlates with increases in cancer and other sicknesses and diseases. These arguments are not new, but they point to the "imaginative inertia" (Weiner, 2005) within the educational sphere, which is characterized by an uncritical investment in "scientifically proven" practices and a social investment in standardizing outcomes, while simultaneously ignoring social and economic inequities.

In a world where economic and cultural power is distributed differentially, to demand standards of outcome while ignoring standards of opportunity is to stack the deck of opportunity against those who possess limited and limiting power. In light of these arguments, it can be said with some confidence that many of the problems we see in schools today—from the spread and rationalization of culturally irrelevant teaching-learning (i.e., teaching to the test) to stagnating literacy levels in our high schools —are due directly to the institutionalization of positivistic orientations to science and technology, on the one hand, and an intense ideological commitment to roll back advances in learning and teaching made during the height of the child-centered, Dewey-influenced educational movements, on the other.

These forces limit what is possible to imagine in the educational sphere, thereby limiting what can be done educationally to transform societal structures—like capitalism, patriarchy, and white supremacy— that support, for example, racism, poverty, and sexism. What bell hooks calls "interlocking systems of domination," these social structures create the spaces in which we live, learn, work, love, and play. They are contradictory spaces, complicated by time and memory, and offer a complex set of interrelated lenses by which we can take an account of our shared social realities. But by ignoring these structures, as the educational positivists would have us do, we decontextualize the imagination, making hope no more than an expression of fantasy and escape.

POLITICAL IMAGINATION

The political imagination in the United States is currently dominated by neo-liberal and neo-conservative ideologues of various hues and temperaments, whose considerations of, and engagements with, political reality are mediated by fantasy. Their ideas about the political converge in a shared ideology of fantastic thinking; this is thinking that is materially and psychically disconnected from the imperatives of a democratic and socially substantive life, while it's the only kind of thinking valued in the official sphere of political discourse. And this is the point of fantasy: It makes no claims to knowing or caring about the needs born out of social reality, needs whose satiation can only be conceived in imagination. It only promises an escape from misery or oppression, allowing both to continue unmolested by political solutions. The connection here to fascist ideology is provocative. Walter Benjamin (1968) writes, "Fascism sees its salvation in giving these masses not their right, but instead a chance to express themselves" (p. 243). This breeds a deep level of political cynicism, solidifying a powerful form of social hopelessness. Social hopelessness is normalized under the hegemony of political cynicism, making fantasy the only viable means of escaping the political violence done by the radical indifference to individual and social rights.

Fantasy mediates fascism in the political imagination by disconnecting its metaphors of freedom and hope from the sphere of political struggle, negotiation, and cooperation. The political sphere is paradoxically represented as useless and as impenetrably powerful. Its deep bureaucratic structure breeds cynicism, even as it tries to represent itself as the primary place and space of hope; fantasizing releases us from the paradox while soothing the anomic effects of living within a political contradiction. But the anomic effects so soothed do nothing to eradicate the anomic condition. The anomic condition, in fact, depends upon, for its strength and reproduction, a softening of its effects by fantasy.

The slow development of fascism and its current significance are belied by its historical representations. Time and space get condensed in our media-dominated culture, where we absorb images of jack-booted soldiers marching lock-step in black, white, and gray tones across hi-definition fields of dirt and smoking stacks. Corporeal emaciation emerges as the dominant visual representation of fascism's effects, hollowed skulls and fragile wrists dangling at the barbed-edges of concentration camps. Concentration is hard to maintain, yet it is never easy to look away. But of course we do and, in so doing, we rewrite the narrative of fascism, effectively removing our bodies and minds from the long slog toward its imminent realization.

The psychic removal of our bodies and minds from the development and normalization of fascist imagery leaves the underlying grammar of fascism, namely, the political powerlessness of individuals, undisturbed and reinforced. On the surface of experience, contemporary articulations of fascism are animated by material comfort, individual cultural expression, and technologically mediated freedom. Without real political power, individuals experience their power primarily in the service of narcissistic interests. Personal consumption is elevated to a form of political freedom; intimate relations replace social movements as a means of protection against political violence; virtual space is completely severed from terrestrial notions of time; and techno–time-space relations constitute what appears to be a new ontology and geography.

This warping of the time-space relation seeds fantasy by generating a system of representations that fuel a kind of forgetting that is vital for fantasies of fascism; it's a forgetting that is made invisible by highly refined techniques of remembering. The nightly news, for example, conveniently reminds people what they should remember about the day's events. The *New York Times* publishes, according to its own maxim, "All the News That's Fit to Print." Consequently, these media formations remind us, not only what we need to know, but, maybe more significantly, what we can and should forget as well. Schools, religious institutions, and publishing companies also contribute to this remembering-forgetting in a similar way.

We do not miss what we forget, because we normalize what we don't know. We conceptualize our ignorance as knowledge. When ignorance becomes knowledge, the pornographic gaze at the center of the fascist fantasy goes unnoticed. Indeed, it stares back at us from our "social" and individual mirrors, showing faces shadowed by the glare of apathy and hypocrisy.

The French diplomat in Henry David Hwang's play *M. Butterfly* offers an example of someone who is in the midst, after 25 years, of remembering what the shadows hide. Sitting at his ex-lover's vanity after learning of a tragic sexual-transgender-political deception in which he is both victim and victimizer, he remakes his image by putting on his lover's kimono and applying make-up in grotesque proportions over his face, eyes, neck, and lips, not in exaggeration of what stares back from the mirror, but in an attempt to represent what he now can see. Beauty becomes ugliness and ugliness becomes truth. Before this remembering, his form appeared beautiful, but in light of his participation in the fantasy he could no longer deny his complicity in the deception, his own and his lover's. Like all tragedies, once he could see, he could not bear to remain a witness to the horror that confronted him. Because fantasy had so thoroughly mediated his reality for 25 years, he no longer possessed the knowledge and psychic dispositions to live in social reality. Without fantasy to mediate reality, death was his only escape and his only salvation. "When we experience our own destruction as an aesthetic pleasure of the first order" (Benjamin, 1968, p. 243), as the French diplomat does, fantasy no longer can be said to mediate fascism. Rather, fascism becomes the new fantasy.

In my estimation, we have not yet made this move, although it doesn't take a great leap in thought or experience to see that we are in midst of this kind of social shift in the political imaginary, evidenced, in large part, by how powerful the role of aesthetics is in political life (Benjamin, 1968, p. 243). From John Edwards's tour of impoverished towns in middle America and Rudolph Giuliani standing amidst the burning towers in downtown New York City on September 11, 2001, to Sarah Palin and Barack Obama rhetorically jousting for the right to claim ownership over the meaning and power of hope, it is hard not to see the relevancy of Benjamin's thought to our times. The anemic condition of the political imagination is disguised by its aesthetic synthesis of the technological medium and the political message. The aesthetic synthesis makes resisting the "fascism in all of us to love power, to desire the very thing that dominates and exploits us" (Foucault, 1972, p. xiii) seem an irrational response to an aesthetic representation of hope and possibility. These notions of hope and possibility have little substance beyond the aesthetics of their representation. In this way, beauty replaces rationality as a means for measuring the truth-value of information, just as it guarantees the perpetuation and celebration of an anemic political imaginary.

Aesthetic Imagination

The aesthetic imagination is concerned primarily with the aesthetic dimension, which is different in kind from the concept of aesthetics used in the previous section. The aesthetic dimension refers to the artistic form of art itself (Marcuse, 1978). Art, rather than representation, is the object of critique, as well as the impetus for sublimation. It is true that all art embodies a notion or moment of representation, but the inverse is not true; that is, all aesthetic representations are not art. In his critique of Marxist aesthetics, Marcuse (1978) explains:

> The radical qualities of art, that is to say, its indictment of the established reality and its invocation of the beautiful image of liberation, are grounded precisely in the dimensions where art transcends its social determination and emancipates itself from the given universe of discourse and behavior while preserving its overwhelming presence. Thereby art creates the realm in which the subversion of experience proper to art becomes possible: the world formed by art is recognized as a reality which is suppressed and distorted in the given reality. This experience culminates in extreme situations (of love and death, guilt and failure, but also joy, happiness, and fulfillment) which explode the given reality in the name of a truth normally denied or even unheard. The inner logic of the work of art terminates in the emergence of another reason, another sensibility, which defy the rationality and sensibility incorporated in the dominant social institutions. (pp. 6–7)

The sublimation of another reason or sensibility vis-à-vis an engagement with the radical qualities of art suggests that the introduction of aesthetics (i.e., at the surface level of representation) into political life, the kind that Benjamin (1968) argues sets the stage for the development of fascist ideologies, desublimates our reason and sensibilities further into the grammar of dominant social institutions and the logic of social relations that they support and help to reproduce. Desublimation of this nature, interpreted through the logic, grammar, and vocabularies of dominant social formations, is perceived as its opposite. When desublimation is thus perceived as sublimation, we have turned freedom on its head; to be free means simply to be aware of one's place in the established order of things—to know where not to go, what questions not to ask, and what and how not to think. Freedom is containment and containment guarantees freedom.

Sublimation, the kind that Marcuse (1978) argues art motivates, moves individuals "beyond the vital order to a 'human order,' which involves the 'capacity of going beyond created structures in order to create others'" (Merleau-Ponty, quoted in Greene, 1995, p. 55). The aesthetic imagination is therefore significant for our discussion of the hegemonic imagination, because it is the locus of sublimation and desublimation. Within the habitus of the hegemonic imagination, the aesthetic imaginary is desublimated, reducing the aesthetic dimension to a matter of individual taste and style.

This reduction is the result of the radical reification of the individual, or in ideological terms, radical individualism. Radical individualism positions the individual as *the* source of knowledge and creativity, as well as the subject of history in need of the most protection and the *only* subject of history deserving of "rights." This conception of the individual finds its philosophical roots in John Locke's discussions of property, which C. B. MacPherson—as outlined by Sehr—argues established a justification for "possessive individualism," the dominant ideological thread of thought that guided the principal designers of the American Constitution and Bill of Rights (Sehr, 1997, pp. 32–33). Today, this idea of possessive individualism finds its most powerful support from those who believe an economic marketplace unhampered by the demands of democracy will, in the end, support the social needs of the public. From libertarians to neo-liberals, the case for possessive individualism still rests on Locke's arguments that the individual's right to property is his or her best defense against social and political insecurities.

In the context of art and the imagination, the possessive individualism that MacPherson identifies in Locke's work gives the individual the sole power to decide what art is. The notion of property in Locke's work, which constituted individuals' "lives, liberties and estates" (Sehr, 1997, p. 32), must come to include, in our current times, their constructions of reality as well. By including an individual's construction of reality as an extension of Locke's possessive individualism and, hence, his notion of property, we have bridged the modern–post-modern gap, but with dangerous results. In other words, constructivist orientations to knowledge production rest on the belief that we are, first, social beings, and the meanings that we create are, at their core, social. This position challenges the fundamental premise and rationality of Locke's consideration of the individual. However, this post-modern idea, within the dominant modern ideology of possessive individualism, gets turned on its head; that is, it creates a philosophical defense of narcissism. By embracing both the constructivist belief in the social construction of knowledge and reality, and the belief that the individual is the sole recipient of rights, and therefore the most vulnerable historical agent, individuals have come to view themselves as the final arbiters of the aesthetic dimension. It's a neat trick. The individual, a social invention itself, conceptualizes itself outside of the social context in which it gets the authority to think of itself at all. Having imagined itself the sole author of its own authority, the individual conceives for itself rights that are above and beyond any consideration of the social or public, outside of their potential for violence against the individual. Under the authority of radical individualism, the individual carries his or her rights like a cowboy carries his guns, always at the ready to shoot down any and all moral appeals to the social sphere if there is any whiff of an attempt to challenge the primacy of the individual as the most forceful and fragile subject of history.

Under these conditions, the aesthetic dimension is hollowed out; no longer can the aesthetic form (poems, paintings, sculpture, plays, etc.) "break the monopoly of established reality (i.e., of those who established it) to *define* what is *real*" (Marcuse, 1978, p. 9). This is so because, under the defining gaze of the individual, art's unique language, the language of fiction—"which is more real than reality itself" (Marcuse, 1978, p. 22)—is conceived not as a language (a productive structured system of signs intertwined in relations of power), but as a blank page open to private communicative interpretations. The dissenting narratives of art are reduced to self-affirming monologues in which the individual can decide what realities art reflects and what realities art refracts. In either case, however, art no longer creates realities "more real than reality itself" (Marcuse, 1978, p. 22). It has become an "empty" vessel for individuals to fill with their ideas and attitudes about reality and, of course, art itself. As such, the reality that is created through the private communicative interpretations of individuals is *less* real than reality itself. This relation between art and the individual sustains an individualistic aesthetic at the expense of, and in spite of, the artistic form.

The individualist aesthetic is defined by the following propositions:

1. As individuals, we are the subjects of the imaginative process. Imagining begins and ends with the individual. The social and aesthetic relations of individuals are recognized as necessary, yet inconvenient, dimensions of the human and aesthetic order. Through evolutionary processes our dependence upon one another will weaken and free the individual to pursue its own ends, unrestrained by the ethic and aesthetic of social responsibility.

2. There is a connection between art and the individual, which is manifested through the individual's conception of him or herself in relation to the aesthetic dimension. Art is no more and no less than the product of the individual's perception of what art is and what it is not.

3. Although there is a definite connection between art and the individual, no one person can determine the "truth" of art. Art, therefore, is relative.

4. The artist's intentions are of little to no consequence, except in academic criticism, just as a consideration of the social effects of art is considered an ideological intrusion on the relation between the art and the individual. Purity of experience is understood as the primary goal of the interpretive process.

5. Museums and galleries (paintings, sculptures), theaters (plays), concert halls (music), and other formal showcases for art are considered unnecessary (from a hermeneutical perspective) but helpful in terms of their ability to mediate the relationship between art and the individual.

6. Art can affect the individual deeply but only in direct correlation to the individual's imaginative investment in the artistic form itself. As such, the artistic form is not the source of affectivity, but, rather, the source is the individual's investment in it.

Radical individualism creates the conditions for a radical relativism, from which the artistic form's dissenting character is replaced with a legitimating force. Delegitimization of reality via the artistic form's capacity to represent reality against the dominant categories of the real, by consequence, is negated.

The aesthetic imagination and its potential for liberating the individual from dominant categories of the real, under the regime of radical individualism, now services those same categories. This makes the aesthetic imagination complicit in the hegemony of reality, as opposed to being its foil. The aesthetic dimension is consumed within the deep psychic structures of the social mind, encouraging us to forget that it is an influential force in shaping our views of what is possible.

Techniques for Developing Transformative Leadership

The creative practices that I will outline involve breaking down normalizing structures and the habits of emotion and cognition that help perpetuate such structures. I have developed these exercises to help our future leaders break down the hegemonic imagination and become more critical and creative in their everyday lives. Social and self-transformation arise from leaders learning how to harness their passion for justice, respect for individuals, dedication to freedom, and empathy and solidarity with oppressed and marginalized peoples. Some of the exercises I present might seem beyond the pale of typical creative or critical activities. They are developed against the backdrop of the theoretical discussions that preceded them and, as such, build upon the general understanding of the imagination presented. In short, this means that the development of imagination and our creative and critical capacities might arise from unexpected places. Rather than think about the process of developing the imagination's critical and creative capacities in a linear manner, it is important to consider the fact that, through involvement with a variety of reflective, cognitively disruptive, and affectively warping exercises, we can become more critical and creative, more empathetic, and better prepared to provide transformative leadership in contexts that demand both our involvement and a deeply felt sensitivity to the possibility that our leadership is best formed in the languages, histories, memories, and experiences of the communities that we wish to help. Even though it might be difficult for some to understand the relationship between the process and its intended outcome, these practices can help generate the kinds of emotion and knowledge, insight and reflection that transformative leaders must, in part, possess. Nevertheless, for some readers, a necessary suspension of disbelief might be required in order to begin, not to mention complete, some of the exercises. It is important to remember that the process is as important, if not more so, than the final product. Critics and cynics will reduce some or all of these exercises to no more than New Age, self-help, and potentially narcissistic gibberish. If done outside of the social theory of the imagination and the conceptual referents of the Institute of Critical Thought and Creative Action, then they might have a point. But grounded in theory, made purposeful by more than simply an increased level of self-awareness, these critical and creative exercises can help individuals see themselves, not simply in the world, but also through the world's needs and their satiation. We are, indeed, intimately linked to each other, just as we are ontologically linked to the ecological foundations of the planet and surrounding systems. Please note, the more skilled one becomes in the process of critical thought and creative action, the more powerful the transformation will be. But in the end—which of course, is just a sign of new beginnings—the creative and critical process is never-ending; it is about learning, becoming, transforming, arising, imagining.

Critical/Creative Exercises for Transformative Leaders

1. FACE-TO-FACE

Part I: Stand face-to-face with a partner, about arms-length apart. Each person's job is to simply look at the other. Register body-type, dress, hair color, eye shape, height, skin color, gender, and so forth. No detail should go unnoticed. Remember, the most "normal" traits are often those that get overlooked. Don't get bamboozled by familiarity and don't be seduced by strangeness.

Part II: Write down your observations. Use descriptive language to capture what you observed in your partner. Be as detailed as possible. This is for you and you alone. Be honest. Your partner will not—should not—be allowed to see what you have written.

Part III: Think about your description in terms of "meaning." That is, think about how the descriptors you used to describe your partner come to mean something beyond the denotative definition of the words themselves. For example, if you described your partner as having "fair, milky-white skin" or "brownish-black skin," think about the difference in feelings these descriptions generate. Think about how these skin-types are represented in the larger media. Think about how the language you have used to describe your partner actually constructs a certain mental image, and think about the feelings that this mental image generates in you. Now, ask yourself why the mental image you constructed from certain uses of language makes you feel a certain way.

Part IV: Some questions to get you started:

- Are certain skin-types really more beautiful than others?

- Do certain eye shapes really make people look smarter?

- Or, is it more likely that we have learned that these things are true and have internalized these truths at the level of common sense and common experience?

- What do the descriptors that you used to describe your partner say about how you see yourself?

- Do you see yourself as fat, too thin, beautiful, ugly, smart, cool, and so on?

- How are these feelings, and the language that you use, connected to the words and language that you used to describe your partner?

- Are they part of the same discourse on beauty?

- Do they divert from dominant messages on what "cool" looks like or what "smart people" look like or dress like?

2. COLLAGE OF REPRESENTATION

Materials Needed: Magazines, newspapers, or any other kind of publication that has visual images and can be cut up; large poster board; paste; scissors

This exercise has you cutting out various representations of race, class, gender, and sexuality from the magazines you have chosen. You can do this alone, but I generally think it is more interesting and more fun if done in groups of three or four.

Part I: The main task is to create a visually compelling collage of images that tries to tell a story about the various representations you have chosen. Using magazines from different time periods is a good way to see how these representations have changed over the years. But even if you can't find older publications, you can still find noticeable differences in representation depending upon the audiences that the magazines intend to attract. Of course, you might just as well find that the representations you find are strikingly consistent from publication to publication. Pay particular attention to bodies, as well as the language that is used in conjunction with the visual representation. Try to juxtapose representations of class, for example, by placing representations of wealthy people next to representations of poor people.

Some questions that can guide your work are:

- How are women represented differently from men?

- What role does gender play in the representations you have chosen?

- Is there a relationship between gender and power implied in these representations?

- If so, how does power, or the lack thereof, get represented?

- Who benefits from these representations?

- Do you see yourself represented?

- Are you represented positively or negatively?

- What are some of the implications of these representations on how we feel about ourselves and each other?

- How do these representations shape our perception of real people?

- To what degree do you think your perceptions of real people are shaped by how they have been represented to you in magazines, television, film, and the Internet?

Your poster should attempt to play with these questions and provocations. It should not only tell a narrative about representations, but should, itself, be an alternative voice that helps people who view your poster see the representations you chose in a new light, a light that shines on the potentially destructive relationship we have to visual representations of sex orientation, class, race, gender, religion, nationality, intelligence, and health.

Part II: Share your work and your thought and affective processes with others.

3. Dialogue Across Difference

Part I: Difference is an important concept because it begs us to make an evaluation of one thing against another. Although the concept draws on our natural ability to make distinctions between two things, it also has a political and cultural orientation, making a discussion across difference easier said than done. What kind of differences should we be talking across, exactly? Well, typically, notions of difference in the context of critical thinking are oriented around questions of identity and power. So, for this exercise you should gather together no fewer than two people whose primary identities differ from one another. You can group a white woman, black man, and Asian man. Or a heterosexual man, a homosexual man, and a heterosexual woman. The possibilities for creating a diverse group are endless, but given that we all occupy multiple identities simultaneously, we need to be clear as to which identification we want to primarily speak from during the dialogue.

Granted, it is quite impossible to ignore the intersections of our multiple identities, but as an exercise in dialoguing across our cultural and political differences, it does work. First and foremost, you must also be a trusting and respectful group, or honest dialogue will never occur.

Part II: The group should pick a topic that is relevant to all that are present. It might be the state of public education, taxes, the presidential elections, a film, or travel to a specific place. The narrower the topic the better, in order to keep the dialogue focused.

Part III: It is not necessary, but if the group can have a shared artifact, like a newspaper article or a photograph, to contemplate together, it can be helpful in generating dialogue.

Part IV: Set aside a time and place that is comfortable for all parties and try to meet at least five times over the course of a few weeks to discuss the topic at hand. The dialogue itself should be honest, respectful, drawn from personal experience, open, heated, passionate, and potentially contentious. Its primary objective is to create a deeper understanding about how cultural difference shapes personal experience. Our cultural differences make the experiences we have in the same situations very different.

Part V: Explain less and listen more. Dialogue is not debate. The point is not to prove you are right, but rather to understand how another human being might have grossly different experiences in the same setting as yourself. It is less important to know, at least at this point, why the experiences they are having are so different than your own but to be able to simply acknowledge, with a deepening level of empathy, that indeed they are. Again, easier said than done. Dialogue across difference is a powerful exercise in becoming more critically and creatively minded.

Some questions and suggestions that can help guide your dialogue:

- Who gets to decide what is normal and what is different?

- Which differences matter and why?

- How does power work to marginalize some differences, while elevating others to normal status?

- How do stereotypes dampen our perceptions of people?

- Name as many stereotypes as you can, as a group, about the primary identifications from which you are speaking for the dialogue.

- Discuss how these stereotypes play out in the context of your chosen topic.

4. COMMUNITY AS CLASSROOM

This activity works on the premise that a person's sense of possibility must be made concrete through actual practice. Beyond the abstractions of hope and possibility, working within our communities toward some explicit goal can help make these ideas more concrete.

The task asks you to either find an existing community project, one that you feel passionate about and is directly connected to your immediate needs, or to identify a need in your community that is not being addressed adequately or not at all. The need could be a lack of food for those that are hungry; a lack of books for the local library; poor public transportation options for workers or students; a lack of appropriate clothes for new workers; the need for shoes; the lack of organized sports or green spaces in which to play and socialize; the need for better-trained teachers; the lack of social activities for the elderly; the need for financial literacy; the need for reading programs; the lack of after-school activities; the lack of public spaces for debate and dialogue; or some other need that you identify in your local jurisdiction. The major point is to take an accounting of a need in your community that is not being met and that you think needs to be met and join forces with an existing organization that is working to meet the need, or begin an organization yourself.

Hooking up with an existing organization is obviously easier, but you have to ask yourself whether the existing organization is working in a way that makes sense to you. If the need the organization is working to meet is, for whatever the reason, not being met to your satisfaction, then it is quite possible that a new organization is called for to attack the issue in a different way.

Time is always a consideration in these kinds of activities. So, the first thing you should do to prepare for this activity is to take a look at a typical week in your busy life and see if you realistically can devote a few hours a week to your project. Some people will find that they have no extra hours in the week to devote to a new project. These people might have to think more long-term about participating in outside projects, preparing to be more available in six months or a year. For others, cutting back on television or idle computer time might leave them significant time to devote to a project that they feel passionate about addressing.

Once you have identified potential times you would be available, and after you have identified a need that has gone unsatisfied, it is time to do some reading and research about the issue in your community. Although this sounds like a matter of common sense, too often people go headlong into a project without knowing exactly what they are doing. Just because you can recognize an unfulfilled need in your community—lack of multicultural children's reading books in your local library, for instance—does not mean you have knowledge about why the library lacks such books; whether there is resistance in the community to offer such books and, if so, from whom; and whether there are current attempts to address the absence of books. Is it simply an issue of money, or are there other reasons for the absence of multicultural children's books?

By doing your homework about these and other issues surrounding your project, you will avoid repeating mistakes of the past, offending or alienating potential allies and partners in alleviating the need, and be more informed as you outline steps to take in satisfying the need itself. Every need and its subsequent satiation are deeply caught up in a web of history and ideology, and it is vital that you educate yourself about these things lest you fulfill the cynic's circular prophecy; that is, I tried and nothing changed, therefore change is impossible and, therefore, I will never try again.

After you have educated yourself on the complexities of the issue, it is time to rally allies to your cause. You might do this by going door-to-door in your neighborhood and speaking to people about the issue. You can use your local meeting places—such as coffee shops, libraries, playgrounds, or shopping malls—to find people to speak with. You might send an email out to people in your address book who are in your area. You could design a Web page outlining the issue and why you are concerned and then send the link to people after you speak with them.

After you attract a core group of people who share your concern, it is time to strategize with the group about different ways to meet the identified need. The group should work towards focusing the issue into easily understood points and clearly stating an objective. The group should then meet to identify the means by which the objective might be met as well as the various obstacles that will necessarily make meeting the objectives challenging. These ideas should be written down and disseminated to everyone who participates.

The next step should be to get as much local support for the project as possible. Developing a widening network of local people who might have a vested interest in the issue but had not thought it possible to have the issue addressed prior to your group approaching with a clearly defined project would be a good place to start. Sometimes there is a lot of support for local projects that remains untapped simply because those who would support the issue were not the same people who would begin an organization initiating the project itself. It is best to organize people from various walks of life. This means you have to have multiple points for a variety of people to connect with your issue. The banker might see the need for more multicultural children's books in school because she recognizes the importance of a diverse workforce. People of color in your neighborhood might think the books would be important in terms of attracting their children to reading. White people might think it is important because they want their children to be exposed to cultures that are different from their own. Each issue has multiple points of connection. It is your group's responsibility to identify potential constituencies by anticipating reasonable rationales for their participation.

Once you have built up a sizable constituency of supporters, it is important to go after those in positions of power who might initially have been less than enthusiastic about your project. These are the people who would not take your calls before—even though you had identified them as being potentially vested in the project—but might be more available to you now that you have a larger group of support. These folks often represent some vital structure in the community, like a major business or governmental organization. Simultaneously, you want to contact your local media and communicate with them about your project. They will want to know why your issue is newsworthy, and it is your job to represent the issue in a way that clearly states what is at stake in *not* fulfilling the need, as well as the benefits of meeting it.

Along similar lines, your group now has to be actively involved in different kinds of actions. For example, if the library simply needs funds to purchase books, the group could hold some kind of sale in the community. Bake sales are one of the oldest forms of social action. Or a block party fundraiser where all proceeds go to buying multicultural books for the local library. Your action might be more radical, in that you might need to hold a rally outside the library to bring attention to its refusal to buy multicultural books even though it has the funds, just because it doesn't believe that they represent the culture or values of the town. This type of action should be coordinated with a call to the media informing them of the rally and, again, why it's so important.

This is the basic outline of the Community as Classroom project. The time and energy you decide to put into the project will generally reflect the level of impact your efforts have on getting the needs you identified met. But whether you win or lose your fight, the lesson remains the same: Hope and possibility are less about winning and more about fighting. For hope to remain a radical concept in the discussion of the imagination of transformative leadership, we can lose the fight or even choose not to fight, but not fighting because we don't know how cannot be an option.

5. People's Theater Project

The name of this exercise respectfully steals from Howard Zinn's evolving collection of historical essays, *The People's History of the United States* (1980). Zinn provides readers with a trenchant account of important historical events from the view of those outside of formal positions of power. His view, and one that I share, is that history is the product of social struggle—cultural, economic, and political—and, as such, needs to be retold from the perspective of those who have lost those struggles. We know that the winners of struggles have first dibs over the narrative that shapes attitudes about the struggle itself, and more often than not these accounts are less than complimentary to the losers. Official histories are as notable for what they leave out as they are for their misrepresentation of actual events.

This exercise gives you the opportunity to see an event in history from the perspective of those too often left out of the official narrative. This activity can be done alone or in groups, but as always, it is probably more fun in groups than alone. To begin this exercise you are to read one chapter from Zinn's book (I hope you read the whole thing, but for this exercise one chapter will suffice). After reading the chapter, your job will to be to write a short, one-act play, using as many of the major players from the chapter as possible. Obviously you should use your best judgment here regarding what is realistic to do in one act. Less is more in theater, and fewer characters can allow you to write deeper, more complex dialogue in such a brief theatrical account.

Describe the setting of your play and the situation your characters are in. You might choose to explain why your characters are in the situation. This information might be conveyed by a character or narrator. The possibilities for writing the play are numerous. It can be realistic or surreal. It might be done in poetry or rap, or it could be written in standard prose. Your scenery might be complex, with many objects imagined on stage, or your stage might be sparse, bathed in dark shadows. Your play might be a dialogue between characters or filled with intense action. The objective is to be as creative as you can, while using the facts of history to guide your imagination. You can end the exercise here if you want, or go on to the next step.

The next step is to create a diorama of your one-act play. A diorama is a three-dimensional representation of the play itself. The costumes, players, and set should be designed so that you have a clear visual sense of what you had imagined. Using found objects or normal art materials, arrange your characters and set in a large box (the stage) in a way that gives concrete expression to your imagination.

The final step in this exercise is to actually put on your play or do a reading of your play for an audience. You can act in your play or recruit friends to participate. Theater works on our imaginations by asking the viewer to suspend an expectation of "reality," thereby creating an alternative reality, one that is purely imaginative in nature. Yet, the reality of theater is felt in the affective traces it leaves in the performers and audiences. The theatrical imagination is a redundant conceit because theater is imagination, and as such, it demands audience participation in the very process of imagining what is being played.

Here are a few discussion questions that can help guide either a dialogue about the play by audience members or can help shape choices you make in developing your play:

- How do the characters avoid becoming stereotypes?

- What role does language play in building point of view?

- How do the sets and costumes add or take away from the story?

- What are some of the primary feelings that the play is trying to induce in the audience?

- Does the play have any surprises in it? If so, how do these surprises function to upset expectations?

- Do you feel differently about the topic addressed in the play after you saw or read it?

6. Painting of Power: Power of Painting

Materials needed: You will need a set of paints (acrylics, oils, or watercolors), brushes, a workspace, and an appropriate surface on which to paint (canvas, paper, wood, cardboard, etc.).

The point of this exercise is to engage the imagination around the issue of power. Some see power as force, control, and manipulation, while others see it as strength, confidence, and determination. Some recognize power as personal and arising from within, while others see it as social, shaping us personally from the outside. Power is one of the most important issues surrounding critical and creative thinking. It can be a hindrance to freedom or its key; its complexity lies in its totality. That is, it is always circulating in and through us, shaping, destroying, building, rewriting, and conceiving. Power is the goal of critical and creative thinking, while it is also its major challenge.

For this exercise you will paint as many renditions of power as you can. The images can be simple strokes of color, realistic renderings of events, impressions, or feelings represented by shapes and colors, abstractions, or any other thing you can imagine when thinking about the concept of power. Try to capture the complexity of power in your paintings. If you get stuck, take a look at some photographs in magazines, read some newspaper articles, or watch some television, looking for examples of power. Then go back to your canvas and paint what power feels like, sounds like, tastes like, and smells like. I know it sounds a bit weird, but getting beyond the idea of power as something we should just think about is vital in bridging the critical and creative divide. Power operates along our whole body, and by engaging the imagination in visually representing power, we bring to the fore the "how" of power.

Here are a few reflective questions to think about after you complete the exercise:

- Why did you choose the colors you did to represent power? How do these colors correspond to emotional and psychic social norms regarding the meaning and "nature" of color?

- Was power represented primarily as a positive or negative force? If so, why?

- How does your personal experience with power shape your representations of it?

- Do the shapes, images, and/or colors you chose reflect power or challenge normative structures of power?

Conclusion

Critical transformative leadership is distinguished by its commitment to eradicating marginalization and oppression and advocating for a more socially just and humane system of educational, economic, cultural, and political organization. It recognizes the decentralization of power as an eventual step in the transformative social and political process but is unwilling to abdicate its power and authority simply in the name of democratization. Beyond the scope of this chapter, further questions for consideration in the context of transformative leadership and criticality are the normative concepts of anti-schooling, de-schooling, and post-schooling. Each of these ideas suggests a complex set of interlocking epistemological and ontological assumptions about the role of transformative leadership, the function of schools, the idea of education, and the roles of the student and teacher. Moreover, the relevance of these theoretical movements must always be measured against the possibility of a far-reaching, mass-based system of education that avoids the hazards of schooling. It is still unclear as to whether an anti-schooling model of education can function on a large scale or whether we must be satisfied by a post-schooling agenda for public education. De-schooling, it seems to me, must be the signifying mechanism by which both make operational the new role of public education. It is also unclear whether democracy is an appropriate goal of critical transformative leadership or whether democratization better captures the anarchistic spirit of transformative action. If it does, then the political question must grapple with the economic question in ways that can "think" of equity in both juridical and cultural terms, neither space providing easy points of reconciliation. As I have argued, the revitalizations of the social, political, educational, and aesthetic imagination are radically important moments in the educational development of transformative leaders. It is in our ability to see beyond what we know, connect deeply to experiences outside of our own, rewrite the future against the grain of the oppressive past, and build upon and within the knowledge, languages, and cultures of history in a way that will provide us with the tools to help shape a future that we can barely imagine.

References

Aronowitz, S. (2003). *How class works*. New Haven: Yale University Press.

Benjamin, W. (1968). *Illuminations* (H. Arendt, Ed.; H. Zohn, Trans.). New York: Harcourt Brace and Co.

Bourdieu, P. (1990). *The logic of practice* (R. Nice, Trans.). Stanford: Stanford University Press.

Cunningham, J. W. (2002). The national reading panel report [Review]. In R. Allington (Ed.), *Big brother and the national reading curriculum: How ideology trumped evidence* (pp. 49–74). Portsmouth, NH: Heinemann Press.

Foucault, M. (1972). Preface. In G. Deleuze & F. Guattari (Eds.), *Anti-Oedipus* (R. Hurley, M. Seem, & H. R. Lane, Trans.; pp. xi–xiv). New York: Viking Press.

Foucault, M. (1977). *Power/knowledge* (C. Gordon, Trans.). New York: Pantheon Books.

Greene, M. (1995). *Releasing imagination*. San Francisco, CA: Jossey-Bass.

Marcuse, H. (1978). *The aesthetic dimension*. Boston: Beacon Press.

Sehr, D. (1997). *Education for public democracy*. New York: SUNY Press.

St. Clair, R. (2003). Environmental literacy. In G. A. Hull, L. Mikulecky, R. St. Clair, & S. Kerka (Eds.), *Multiple Literacies* (pp. 14–18). Columbus, OH: Center on Education and Training for Employment.

Weiner, E. J. (2005). *Private learning, public needs*. New York: Peter Lang.

Weiner, E. J. (2009). Time is on our side: Rewriting the space of imagination. *Situations: Project of the Radical Imaginary, 3*(1), 125–150.

Wheatley, p. (1767-1773), On Imagination, retrieved July 17, 2011 from http://www.vcu.edu/engweb/webtexts/Wheatley/imagination.html

Zinn, H. (1980). *The people's history of the United States, 1492–present*. New York: Harper and Row.

III

Transformative Leadership in Practice

14

Transformative Leadership in the Land of Milk and Honey

The Tension Between Public and Private Goods in Affluent School Communities

Andrew J. Barrett

My office window (a large bay window of course . . . could there be any other kind in the principal's office in an affluent suburban community?) looks out onto the parking lot of our elementary school, and this view regularly provides me with a preliminary glimpse, shall we say, of what is about to come. On a relatively recent morning, what was about to come was nothing new, in fact it was pretty par for the course (no pun intended, considering that just past the parking lot lies one of the fairways of the golf course that surrounds the school). A parent, Mrs. O'Keefe, pulled up that day in her black luxury sedan exactly one minute before our meeting was scheduled to begin. She exited her car with gusto, a Bluetooth earpiece clinging to her head and her Blackberry in hand, clearly finishing up a call before a meeting with me, the principal, regarding her fifth-grade daughter Katie's current academic placement. Mrs. O'Keefe and I had scheduled this meeting the previous day when she called and asked how to get her daughter into our gifted program. Never mind that our school does not actually offer a gifted program, but rather an acceleration and enrichment program, and never mind that we have a very specific guidebook that is shared annually with parents regarding the placement process; Mrs. O'Keefe needed to speak personally with me on this day about Katie and why she ought to be placed in the program.

Our chat began that day as these little talks often do (I am no stranger to this particular conversation). We discussed the placement process, the perceptions of Katie's parents and teachers, the structure and design of our district's curricular programming, and some of Katie's test scores, before naturally shifting into an erudite discussion about the purpose of public education. Mrs. O'Keefe, clearly an intellectual and articulate woman, wanted her daughter to have access to every opportunity available to her, and she believed that this program provided students with better opportunities for future academic success—a better ACT score, more choice and opportunity for college, and, ultimately, a more successful adulthood. In short, if this school offered it, her daughter needed to get it. As our discussion progressed, we talked about several of the divergent goals of public education that exist within the current political and educational milieu, and, while respectful and collegial, I was explicit about my belief that our first goal as a public school must be to educate students to become citizens of democracy. I suggested that, while I can certainly hope for the social mobility and eventual private sector success of our students, I cannot consider that our ultimate end.

"While I understand your perspective, my responsibility as the principal of a public school is to ensure broader educational goals for our students than simple individual achievement," I said at one point.

"Are you suggesting I look into private schools?" she asked.

"Not at all," I said. "I'm simply suggesting that a public school cannot and should not be solely concerned with the social mobility of its individual students."

She retorted quickly, "I pay nearly twenty-five-thousand dollars a year in property taxes for my child to come here. This *is* my private school."

The retelling of this actual experience encapsulates the challenges faced by democratically minded public school leaders in affluent school communities. In her book, *Dividing Classes,* Brantlinger (2003) suggests that many "educated middle class parents . . . do not think beyond their own children when they interact with schools" (p. x), and she suggests that, "the actual American educational system slants the field to give the best chances to those who are already advantaged" (p. 191). Today, in affluent school communities across the United States, homogeneous populations of upper-middle-class whites both enjoy and appreciate the comfort of the status quo, often without recognition of their own societal hegemony, and by presuming the public school's responsibility for the provision of private-sector success, these families are (often unknowingly) working to undermine the foundation of the American school system.

Transformative leadership, defined by Shields (2009) as "leadership that is firmly grounded in and cognizant of the social, political, economic, and cultural structures of society" (p. xx), represents a philosophy rife with this understanding, and one that presents both the means and the opportunity for redressing this inequity. With its focus on righting wrongs and deconstructing injustice, transformative leadership aims to break down existing societal barriers that perpetuate inequity and, as such, it represents an inherently political responsibility of a democratically minded school leader. Interestingly though, much of the discussion regarding transformative leadership focuses on schools with large proportions of minority and low-socioeconomic students; schools where injustice and inequity are already blatantly conspicuous and where society's power imbalance is already all too obvious. Thus here I focus on the tension that exists between public and private goods for transformative leaders in affluent school communities. More specifically, I seek to explore how a school leader works to become a transformative leader by navigating these tensions. In an effort to help define some of the important factors that must be considered, this chapter will explore three distinct themes. The first section will examine the dichotomy of the individual versus the collective, as it relates to transformative leadership within the typical affluent school community. The second section will highlight the existing milieu of American affluence as it relates to Labaree's (1997) framework of public versus private goods, and the third section will focus on contextualization of the public-private good conflict in the administration of the normative processes of transformative school leadership.

Our Kids or My Kid?

Should a transformative school leader in a democratic society work for the good of the collective or the good of the individual? While it is important to explicitly note upfront that true transformative leadership, "not only works for the good of every individual in the school system; at its heart it works for the common good of society as well" (Shields, 2008), we must also seek to explore the conceptual basis for this perspective, as a school leader in an affluent community will likely face this question on a regular and recurring basis. At its core, the answer to this question must begin with a shared understanding of the term *democracy* as it relates to our current cultural ethos and our system of public education; for our purposes here I believe it is important to begin with the foundation of democracy, as its underlying assumptions relate directly to our current beliefs and practices. As any elementary school student could likely share, American democracy was founded by British expatriates in the American Colonies, at least in part, as a reaction to the tyranny and oppression of the British government, and this resistance to domination, combined with a general distrust of authority, represents a basic principle of our democratic founding. As West (2004) notes, "the consolidation of elite power was the primary object of democratic revolt [and] this will to transform corrupted forms of elite rule into more democratic ways of life is an extraordinary force" (p. 204). It seems clear that, in some respects, democracy portends to wrest power from the few and place it into the hands of the many, and, in this regard, there are clear implications for school leaders who are constantly confronted with the needs and desires of affluent, power-holding members of society.

This section is titled "Our Kids or My Kid?" in an effort to highlight the dichotomous American understanding of democracy that juxtaposes the rights of the individual against the public good of civic virtue, and it is at this fault line where a transformative leader in an affluent community must precariously balance conflicting beliefs and actions. Once we consider the foundation of democracy noted above, we are all the more likely to find our public schools at a crossroads, balancing responsibility for the "American Dream" between an individualized philosophy of meritocracy and an egalitarian foundation of equality. Gutmann (2001) beautifully highlights this: "tension . . . between individual freedom and civic virtue [that] poses a challenge for educating Americans . . . [who] seem willing to settle for freedom for themselves and civic virtue for others" (p. 217). Affluent school communities epitomize Gutmann's proposition: running food drives and raising record amounts for international disaster victims while simultaneously rallying for more individualized instruction for their children. Affluent school communities somehow manage to singularly represent two divergent viewpoints, and while in some respects it would be easy to write off this divergence as unmanageable and impractical, it is both important and necessary to recognize that differing views represent the basis for democratic thinking. Green (1999) suggests that diversity of perspectives represents the basis for democracy that can, and must, lead to shared understandings and mutually constructed frameworks for democratic relations. In an affluent school community, the challenge for a transformative leader actually becomes the creation and presentation of these diverse perspectives of democracy in the face of rigid homogeneity and adherence to tradition and individual achievement. However, armed with this understanding of democratic ideals, a school leader must next consider the purpose of public education.

When a democratically oriented school leader is confronted with a situation like the one described in the introduction, it is important for that leader to have an authentic and legitimate understanding of the purpose of public schooling, for this understanding represents the basis of our systemic assumptions about educating children and the actions we take in doing so. A transformative school leader can feel so deeply encumbered by the dichotomy of the individual versus the collective, because that leader is compelled forward day in and day out by the latter, while the majority of the affluent community members with whom he or she deals strictly adhere to the former. As such, a school leader must both know and be able to articulate the democratic underpinnings of public schooling, in order to effectively navigate the assumptions and systemic beliefs of affluent parents. According to Dewey (2001), the humanist view of democracy suggests that education can "find out how all the constituents of our existing culture are operating and then see to it that whenever and wherever needed they be modified in order that their workings may release and fulfill the possibilities of human nature" (p. 173). In other words, education in a democracy must not only consider the perspectives of others and infuse that understanding into the educational program, but it must also recognize that the core of democratic education is ensuring the good of the collective through education of the individual. This is exactly what Bode (2001) suggests when he says that "the primary obligation of a democratic community to its members is to provide for each the opportunity to share in the common life" (p. 94). By recognizing and focusing on the collective and civic virtue, a transformative leader can prepare herself or himself for the challenges presented by the expectation that she or he will focus on the opposite.

Knowing and recognizing the tension between *our kids* and *my kid* will only get a school leader part of the way however. In the end, a school leader must consider the desired and appropriate outcomes of democratic education if he or she is to successfully navigate the tension between the public and private good. When Mrs. O'Keefe argued for the private good of individual achievement for her daughter, she was, in fact, arguing that the system in its current form was depriving her of a requisite opportunity—a private good to which she ought to be entitled and which she was currently denied. As Glickman (1998) notes, this is simply not the case. To the contrary, American public education is not failing because it is withholding opportunities from individuals, but rather from particular, marginalized individuals as affluent students (those like Katie from affluent families and communities) continue to do well and succeed. Instead, Glickman suggests, it is the system's failure to provide an education to *all* students—that is to say, our failure to provide education for the collective—that has resulted in our systemic failure. Shields (2009) takes Glickman's point a step further, turning to Freire to highlight the notion that we must do more than simply educate the collective, by working more deeply to empower students. We must help them to become critically aware of systemic inequities so that they may take "critical action against injustices of which one has become aware" (2009, p. xiii). Educating to or for the individual simply cannot lead to the societal and systemic critical action that is vital to the lifeblood of democracy.

With this foundation of democratic understanding and a clearer recognition of the dichotomous relationship between education for the individual and education for the collective in mind, we can now transition into another perspective of the tension between public goods and private goods in public education. The next section will focus on Labaree's (1997) framework for contextualizing the varied goals of public education based upon their relationship to public and private goods.

Continuous, Contradictory, and Competing, or Compatible?

In *"Public Goods, Private Goods: The American Struggle over Educational Goals"* (1997), David Labaree sheds light on a fundamental dichotomy of purpose that exemplifies the disparity in our political and social policies between public and private goods. Labaree focuses his sociological lens on the history of public education, as he explores our society's ever-transforming expectations for public education. How can a system designed as a public good exist in a society that increasingly expects individual results? Labaree notes that the historical goals of public education—democratic equality, social efficiency, and social mobility—represent the inner turmoil of the educational system, while also respectively symbolizing the transition of America's philosophical understanding of education from a public good to a private one. A democratically minded school leader must consider these diverse perspectives in working to develop an understanding of the purpose of public education, but also in order to contextualize the criticisms our current system receives from both ends of the spectrum. These criticisms regularly appear through the public good–private good tension, and an understanding of society's expectations can only serve to help us as we communicate about this tension with stakeholders. Before analyzing these perspectives more thoroughly, the following paragraph will provide a very brief description of the framework.

In brief, Labaree's first goal, democratic equality, represents a purely public good in that its egalitarian ethos strives to produce an educated citizenry with equitable opportunity. From the perspective of democratic equality, education is focused on citizenship training, equal treatment, and equal access, whereby students are educated in the Jeffersonian tradition. The social efficiency goal, while still technically focused on the public good, shifts to vocationalism and educational stratification in an effort to adapt schools to the goals of the marketplace. From this more neo-liberal standpoint, the educational system becomes increasingly stratified in an effort to help fill the many and varied roles necessary for the production of a healthy market. Here Labaree argues that while this stratification is clearly a marked departure from the democratic equality goal, it still represents a public good in that students are trained for positions that will ultimately serve the market and, thus, benefit society as a whole. Finally, at the opposite end of the spectrum from democratic equality lies the social mobility goal. From this perspective, public education becomes a means for providing individual status attainment; a commodity that one presumes "should provide students with the educational credentials they need in order to get ahead in the structure" (p. 50). Ultimately, Labaree suggests that the tenuous relationship between public and private goods in American education lies in the fact that "schools occupy an awkward position at the intersection between what we hope society will become and what we think it really is" (p. 41). This is the crux of the matter—the heart of the tension between public and private goods in our system of public education.

As a transformative leader considers Labaree's framework specifically in relation to school leadership in an affluent community, it is important to reflect upon these three distinct goals and discern how to best contextualize the framework in the existing milieu of American affluence. Specifically, the following section will consider the framework from three distinct perspectives: should we consider these three distinct goals as continuous—flowing progressively from one to the next; contradictory and competing—mutually exclusive from and in competition with one another; or compatible—representative of an all-inclusive understanding of the relationship between public and private goods in public schooling? A transformative leader in an affluent community with a clear understanding of these three models will certainly be better prepared to make productive and appropriate decisions for students.

In one respect, Labaree's framework represents a continuum of American perspectives of democratic education as society transitions through these goals; from democratic equality through social efficiency to social mobility. A report by the Phi Delta Kappa Educational Foundation (2000) indicates that the 19th century saw one of the greatest achievements of education reformers in the creation of universal, tax-supported public schools. Following the movement spearheaded by prominent thinkers like Horace Mann and Catherine Beecher, public education was "part and parcel of a democratic movement" (Phi Delta Kappa Educational Foundation, 2000, p. 12). Soon, capitalistic forces began to play a larger role in the educational system, and this market-based perspective led our thinking into the social efficiency model where, as Goodlad (2004) notes, "the guiding mission of schooling has increasingly become an economic one" (p. 1). This economic imperative can certainly be seen in the industrial model of education that still provides the foundation for many of our educational structures, and which often works to reinforce systemic inequities.

Today, as Labaree argues, social mobility represents the most recent incarnation of America's educational preference, and this represents the basis for our understanding of the educational milieu in the typical affluent American community. These parents look past democratic equality (they believe that their community is "beyond that") and they have converted social efficiency into social mobility, based upon the belief that their children represent the top of society's vertical distribution. In the end, their belief that the public educational system ought to provide their children with social mobility (an oxymoron considering that their children are already on top) ties directly to the earlier notion of the individual versus the collective.

Unfortunately, the continuum perspective of the public-private good tension is clearly regressive, and, as Labaree contends, this notion has, in some very real ways, undermined the educational goal of democratic equality and irreparably damaged our public schools. The increasing significance of the social mobility goal as dominant in the American democratic ethos leaves me concerned with the direction we may yet be headed; the current rhetoric about competition and charter schools may well represent further movement in this direction. For an educational leader in an affluent community, it is important to understand the continuum perspective, because it provides us with both an understanding of the historical implications of society's goals and a hopefulness that we can continue to progress; if we've regressed in one direction there is hope for us to progress in another. Buber (2001), who highlights the importance of relationships in education, notes that "faith in unity . . . is not a 'return' to individualism but a step beyond all of the dividedness of individualism and collectivism" (p. 112). In other words, build relationships and make progress for all. A democratic educational leader in an affluent community must do the former if that leader is to help foment the latter.

While it certainly seems that in some respects the tension between public and private goods has developed across a continuum, a school leader must also recognize that at times, the goals are simultaneously present and contradictory and competing. In one sense this is obvious; no tension would likely exist if only one of these goals permeated our understanding of education. Yet it will certainly come as no surprise that the contemporary affluent community is dominated by the private good ethos of social mobility. In many ways, the dominance of the notion of social mobility has become hegemonic in our conversations about public schooling, and this dominance often makes it difficult for the democratically minded school leader to make headway. Giroux (2005), a fierce critic of the neo-liberal attack on democracy and public goods, suggests that this neo-liberal hegemony is destructive to both democracy on the whole and to education, more specifically. "Democracy," he suggests, "has become synonymous with free markets" (p. 9); a notion with which Spring (1996) agrees, going so far as to say that our schools are actually reinforcing this notion through our teaching about democracy. Leading in an affluent community where stakeholders owe their own affluence to that hegemony, the conversation can become complicated very quickly. Simply put, the notion of social mobility supports a system that creates winners and losers, and the affluent generally represent the winners; this can make convincing them to step away from the status quo exceedingly difficult.

Armed with this contradictory understanding, a transformative school leader must work to transfer the discussion in an effort to help an affluent community work through the public–private good tension. Ultimately, the notion of social mobility has become so hegemonic that many parents, especially those in affluent communities, actually view the neo-liberal ethos as a personal value, and the values basis for these arguments certainly contributes to the public-private tension. In this regard, we can turn to Hodgkinson's Values Hierarchy as at least one tool for working through this tension. Evers (1985) describes Hodgkinson's model "as a first step in setting up the machinery for resolving value conflicts" (p. 38), and this model, which can most easily be understood as a three-tiered classification system for framing challenging discussions, can support a democratic leader in working toward consensus. Hodgkinson's model begins with the most relative form of values preferences and leads to the exclusively principled third tier, where he suggests consensus is impossible. The model suggests that by working to direct the conversation down a tier to Type II values, one can effectively and efficiently move the discussion to areas of consensus and consequence, which may ultimately lead to finding some common ground. This transition then guides the conversation into a place where, as Spring (1996) notes, democracy becomes a social system rather than a political one, and it is within this social system that educators can then seek opportunities to further advance meaningful equity in outputs and outcomes (Farrell, 1999). A democratic school leader must understand the contradictory components of the public–private good tension and work within that tension towards democratic practices if that leader is to be truly transformative.

In the end, while a transformative leader must certainly consider the public–private good tension from the two perspectives noted above, he or she ought to strive to consider Labaree's three goals from a compatibly holistic perspective. While the tension between public and private goods certainly exists within affluent communities—and society at large for that matter—a democratically minded school leader must seek to find a balance among the notions of democratic equality, social efficiency, and social mobility if he or she is to move forward with transformative practices for students with the support of colleagues and community members. From my perspective, it would seem that this balance can only be achieved if we begin with democratic equality, for this is the only notion of the three that can lead to the other two. Social efficiency and social mobility focus on our differences, while the notion of democratic equality finds its basis in our oneness and, ultimately, "failure to recognize what is held in common . . . means that we can emphasize only that which divides us" (Green, 2001, p. 186). Goodlad (2004) advances this notion further, noting that "serving the public good in a democracy means serving the common weal, that of both the individual and the collective" (p. 1). Thus, by beginning with democratic equality, we can also support social efficiency and social mobility.

Clearly, a holistic and contextualized understanding of Labaree's framework provides a school leader with a basis for advancing democratic practices in an affluent community. As Shields (2009) suggests, it is impossible to ignore the affluent preoccupation with social mobility and private goods, just as we cannot allow ourselves to ignore the requisite responsibilities of a democratically minded transformative leader. And so the fact remains that, as Bode (2001) suggests, "progress lies not in the substitution of new names for old habits but in the transformation of old habits into a new quality of mind and heart" (p. 97). By acknowledging the school's role in fostering both social efficiency and social mobility, a transformative leader in an affluent community can truly provide for "the free play of intelligence in the reconstruction of patterns" (p. 99) so that students can develop a more thorough and nuanced perspective of the continuum and move forward as global citizens by embracing the differing perspectives of the public–private good debate.

What Wins in the Policymaker's Office?

Our prosperity in the 20th century was fueled by an education system that helped grow the middle class and unleash the talents of our people more fully and widely than at any time in our history . . . over the last few decades, we've lost ground [and] . . . now fallen behind most wealthy countries.

Not only does that risk our leadership as a nation, it consigns millions of Americans to a lesser future.
—President Obama, 2010

This section is intended to contextualize the normative functions of modern educational leaders in affluent communities who must regularly make nuanced decisions regarding the tension between public and private goods. I quote the president here, not because he is in a position to make these types of day-to-day decisions, but rather as an example of the proposition that I have already highlighted regarding the hegemony of the social mobility goal of educational attainment, a notion so ingrained that our liberal president rhetorically supports the notion of social mobility, even while introducing a plan that is intended to encourage more equitable outcomes in our staggeringly inequitable educational system. On a local level, the rhetoric may be less soaring and eloquent, but it is often no less sympathetic to the private good function of schooling. The language of private goods permeates educational rhetoric at the local level (especially in affluent communities) in such a way as to constantly reinforce itself. Attend any school board meeting, community breakfast, Parent Teacher Association meeting, or, of late, a school district budget hearing, and one would most assuredly find conversation unswervingly infused with private good rhetoric. *This school increased its average ACT score by two points. That school is sending several kids to Ivy League colleges. This school has championship athletic teams, and National Merit finalists, and an unprecedented number of AP course offerings.* The mention of each of these areas highlights the affluent preoccupation with private goods. Even in today's political environment of unfettered spending and financial crises, the only notion that seems to chafe many affluent parents more than their local school district spending too much money is the proposition of their local school district cutting private good–focused programming to save money. Ultimately, an aspiring transformative leader must strive to contextualize and manage this preoccupation so that he or she can be equipped to carry out the important and regular functions of school leadership. The remainder of this section will address the importance of this contextualization while carrying out the normative processes of school leadership.

The contemporary school leader works within a system that, as Houston (2003) notes, is currently built upon the access paradigm of the industrial model, and this foundation is of critical importance to normative functioning and decision making of the transformative leader. With its regimented daily schedule, tracked curricular programming, and traditionally focused curriculum, our current model of schooling is all too often predisposed to lean towards the notion of social efficiency and the market, and a democratically minded school leader must be conscious of the fact that families in affluent communities represent the top of the economic structure. Freire's (1970) banking model defines this traditional approach to education so venerated by affluent parents, as one in which students become receptacles that simply absorb information from teachers, and where students are discouraged from questioning the system, challenging authority, or railing against the status quo. Why question the status quo when it has put you in a position of power? A transformative leader must turn to Giroux (1995), who reinforces Freire's abhorrence of the banking model and notes the school's responsibility to combat it by providing "teachers and students with the capacities and opportunities to be noisy, irreverent, and vibrant" (p. 299). In an affluent community, this proposition can often be seen as an anathema to traditionally focused parents. From Kaye's (1995) perspective, this is precisely because, as the current system's power holders, these parents have the most to gain by supporting the status quo. Transformative school leaders must have a clear understanding of this perspective, not only so that they can contextualize their experiences with stakeholders but also so that they do not lose sight of the important educational goals noted by Giroux. Our schools must be places of vibrancy and questioning if meaningful and equitable societal change is to occur.

Armed with an understanding of both the reasons that affluent parents reinforce the status quo and the importance of systemically challenging those beliefs, a democratic school leader in an affluent community must consider a fundamental question: How does one go about managing this shift in perspectives so that democratic practices can begin to take hold as normative school functions? Freire, whom I have already discussed, was unquestionably one of the preeminent educational theorists in history, and yet, when thrust into the bureaucratic position that provided him the power to enact his influential ideas, he faced the same challenge that a school leader in any affluent community might face: an externalized perspective that inhibited his ability to "move" stakeholders into more democratic practices. As Weiner (2003) notes, a transformative leader must be, at least in part, an active member of the dominant power structure so that he or she can not only garner a truer understanding of the deeply held systemic issues but also use his or her communication skills, capacity for relationship building, and political capital to bring about change in the status quo. Obviously, this can be a much more complicated and paradoxical prospect than meets the eye. As Freire (1970) himself suggests, one cannot be too connected to the dominant structure or one may never actually stimulate fundamental change. Democratically minded school leaders in affluent communities may:

> truly desire to transform the unjust order; but because of their background they believe that they must be the executors of the transformation. They talk about the people, but they do not trust them; and trusting the people is the indispensable precondition for revolutionary change. (1970, p. 60)

Ultimately, a school leader must find and balance upon the fulcrum between transformative ideals and the dominant systemic structure; it is only by simultaneously working within the system and shifting the perspective outward that a transformative leader can ensure that the normative functioning of affluent schools will become more just and democratic.

Moving Forward

So the question remains: How can a school leader in an affluent community lead with a democratic vision, while making the necessary and regular decisions that maintain that leader's establishment in the normative structure? I believe it is most appropriate and effective for transformative leaders to understand the public–private good tension in affluent schools in terms of a contextual transformative continuum that provides opportunities to, first, understand and interpret the inherent systemic challenges, so that the leader may then partner with stakeholders through a two-tiered understanding of shared beliefs, before finally fostering the development of new ideals and mental frameworks in the minds of stakeholders. As I have already noted, Orr (2001) suggests that Americans truly believe that social mobility and personal success represent the fundamental purpose of public education. A transformative leader in an affluent community should not begin by making this notion a subject for debate but rather recognize the belief and use it as a starting point for collaboration with stakeholders through normative practices—such as student placement or curricular programming—that foster and encourage organic dialogue with community members. In other words, simply standing up one day and suggesting the dissolution of an undemocratic program will certainly not enhance a school leader's political capital, nor will it help others to develop more democratic practices. An overt and aggressive activist stance will only work to inhibit a transformative leader in an affluent community and "limit the possibilities for the creation of structures that lead to real empowerment" (Lewis & Macedo, 1995, p. 52) by blatantly ignoring the importance of dialogue that Freire himself would have encouraged. A school leader in an affluent community must initially work from a base that recognizes the inherent private-good motivations of private good–focused constituents before making an effort to move forward with more justice-oriented practices.

Armed with this recognition, a transformative leader must then take a two-tiered approach to the work of democratizing schooling by both:

- nurturing the relationships that are a necessary prerequisite for acceptance of more just and equitable practices; and

- shifting the understanding of the curriculum in her or his school community.

Ultimately, transformative leadership ought to lead to critical action, and, as Putnam suggests, "the key to collective action is not physical capital, but social capital" (2001, p. 31). I would argue that the dominance of the private-good expectation for schooling in our country is directly related to our overarching concern with physical capital—money, status, and *stuff* that we believe will provide us with that which we most long for. Frankly though, I believe it is much simpler than that, and a transformative leader can and should make an effort to shift the perspective in our affluent school communities to social capital and civil society. The most appropriate and most natural place to do this, of course, is within the curriculum. It is important to note here what I mean by curriculum, for I do not mean to suggest that a transformative leader must go out and purchase new textbooks, worksheets, and posters that will be used by teachers. Instead I turn to Grumet (1995), who suggests that "what is basic . . . [to education] . . . is the conversation that makes sense of things" (p. 19). The curriculum is the connection, the collaboration, and the shared understanding that students, parents, and educators build together, and by developing social capital and connecting to develop shared understandings of justice and equity, a transformative leader in an affluent community can focus the conversation on the importance of our global interdependence and truly support both critical awareness and reflection that can lead to a more nuanced and just understanding of our interconnectedness.

Obviously a leader cannot be truly transformative if attitudes and beliefs are changed only so far as they occur within the structure of the existing system, and so, ultimately, a democratically minded school leader must work through the two-tiered approach noted above, and work well enough inside the existing system, to foster the development of democratic ideals that can be transferred to society at large. In this regard, a transformative leader in an affluent community must take a broadminded stance that helps to shift thinking in regard to justice in society at large. Affluent communities constructed of homogeneous white stakeholders can often lack the nuanced understanding of societal injustice that must be addressed in democratic society, and it is for precisely this reason that a transformative leader must work to develop that more nuanced awareness. This can certainly be a challenge. As Gutmann (2001) notes, "there is no defensible political understanding of education that is not tied to some conception of a good society, and there is no conception that is not controversial" (p. 225). While this is clearly the case in an affluent community, there is no doubt that it can be done. As Shields (2008) notes, "it [is] careful and consistent deconstruction of old knowledge frameworks that perpetuate deficit thinking and inequity, and their replacement with new frameworks of inclusion and equity" (p. 13) that represents truly transformative development. The process may well be slow, but results can be significant: opening minds regarding the democratic functioning within the school in an effort to help foster democratic practices outside of the school, because, as Furman and Shields (2005) note, "the experience of democracy in schools may help youth to eventually construct the democratic societies in which they wish to live" (p. 122). In the end, transformative must become the new normative.

Conclusion

The tension between public and private goods represents one of the most significant challenges facing the contemporary school leader, and this tension requires a nearly constant balancing act for school leaders in affluent American school communities. In some respects, this chapter, while certainly highlighting some of the myriad challenges inherent in this struggle, may well have produced as many questions as answers. Still, the importance of recognizing and understanding these questions cannot be underestimated. The contextualization of the inherent belief structures and systemic inclination towards private goods must occur if a democratically minded school leader in an affluent community hopes to become a truly transformative figure within that community—it is the methodical and careful deconstruction of these old knowledge frameworks that represents the first step to building new ones. Here we must end where we began: What must be developed and nurtured in the mindset of educational leaders in affluent communities is the belief that "transformative educational leadership not only works for the good of every individual in the school system; at its heart it works for the common good of society as well" (Shields, 2008, p. 18).

References

Bode, B. H. (2001). Reorientation in education. In Goodlad, S. J. (Ed.), *The last best hope: A democracy reader* (pp. 92–100). San Francisco, CA: Jossey-Bass.

Brantlinger, E. (2003). *Dividing classes: How the middle class negotiates and rationalizes school advantage.* New York: Routledge.

Buber, M. (2001). The education of character. In Goodlad, S. J. (Ed.), *The last best hope: A democracy reader* (pp. 101–114). San Francisco, CA: Jossey-Bass.

Dewey, J. (2001). Democracy and human nature. In Goodlad, S. J. (Ed.), *The last best hope: A democracy reader* (pp. 159–175). San Francisco, CA: Jossey-Bass.

Evers, C. (1985). Hodgkinson on ethics and the philosophy of administration. *Educational Administration Quarterly, 21*(4), 27–50.

Farrell, J. P. (2007). Equality of education: A half-century of comparative evidence seen from a new millennium. In R. S. Arnove & C. A. Torres (Ed.), *Comparative education: The dialectic of the global and the local* (3d ed, pp.149–177). Lanham, MD: Rowman and Littlefield.

Freire, P. (1970) *Pedagogy of the Oppressed.* New York: Continuum International.

Furman, G. C., & Shields, C. M. (2005). How can educational leaders promote and support social justice and democratic community in schools? In W. A. Firestone & C. Riehl (Eds.), *A new agenda for research in educational leadership* (pp. 119–137). New York: Teachers College Press..

Giroux, H. A. (1995). Educational visions: What are schools for and what should we be doing in the name of education? In J. L. Kincheloe & S. R. Steinberg (Eds.), *Thirteen questions* (pp. 295–302). New York: Peter Lang.

Giroux, H. A. (2005). The terror of neoliberalism: Rethinking the significance of cultural politics. *College Literature, 32*(1), 10–19.

Glickman, C. D. (1998). Revolution, education, and the practice of democracy. *The Educational Forum, 63*(1), 16–22.

Goodlad, J. I. (2004). Fulfilling the public purpose of schooling: Educating the young in support of democracy may be leadership's highest calling. *The School Administrator, 61*(5), 14–17.

Green, J. M. (1999). *Deep democracy: Community, diversity, and transformation.* Lanham, MD: Rowman & Littlefield Publishers, Inc.

Green, P. (2001). Egalitarian solidarity. In Goodlad, S. J. (Ed.), *The last best hope: A democracy reader* (pp. 176–195). San Francisco, CA: Jossey-Bass.

Grumet, M. R. (1995). The curriculum: What are the basics and are we teaching them? In J. L. Kincheloe & S. R. Steinberg (Eds)., *Thirteen questions* (pp. 15–21). New York: Peter Lang.

Gutmann, A. (2001). Democratic education in difficult times. In Goodlad, S. J. (Ed.), *The last best hope: A democracy reader* (pp. 216–230). San Francisco, CA: Jossey-Bass.

Houston, P. D. (2003). Time to re-public the republic. *School Administrator, 60*(8), 10–12.

Kaye, H. J. (1995). Education and democracy, In J. L. Kincheloe & S. R. Steinberg (Eds.), *Thirteen questions* (pp. 123–130). New York: Peter Lang.

Labaree, D. F. (1997). Public good, private goods: The American struggle over educational goals. *American Educational Research Journal, 34*(1), 39–81.

Lewis, M., & Macedo, D. (1995). Power and education: Who decides the forms schools have taken, and who should decide? In J. L. Kincheloe & S. R. Steinberg (Eds.), *Thirteen questions* (pp. 33–57). New York: Peter Lang.

Obama, B. (2010). *Weekly address: President Obama to send updated elementary and secondary education act blueprint to Congress on Monday.* March 13, 2010, retrieved January 20, 2011, from http://www.white-house.gov/the-press-office/weekly-address-president-obama-send-updated-elementary-and-secondary-education-act-

Orr, D. W. (2001). What is education for? In Goodlad, S. J. (Ed.), *The last best hope: A democracy reader* (pp. 231–239). San Francisco, CA: Jossey-Bass.

Phi Delta Kappa Educational Foundation. (2000). *Public school reform in America.* Bloomington, IN: W. J. Reese.

Putnam, R.D. (2001). What makes democracy work? In Goodlad, S. J. (Ed.), *The last best hope: A democracy reader* (pp. 25–32). San Francisco, CA: Jossey-Bass.

Shields, C. M. (2008). *Engaged and transformative leadership: Working equitably in diverse contexts.* Symposium conducted at the International Conference on Educational Leadership in Cultural Diversity and Globalization, Phuket, Thailand.

Shields, C. M. (2009). *Courageous leadership for transforming schools: Democratizing practice.* Norwood, MA: Christopher-Gordon.

Spring, J. (1996). Democracy and public schooling. *International Journal of Social Education, 11*, 48–58.

Weiner, E. J. (2003). Secretary Paulo Freire and the democratization of power: Toward a theory of transformative leadership. *Educational Philosophy and Theory, 35*(1), 89–106.

West, C. (2004). *Democracy matters: Winning the fight against imperialism.* New York: Penguin.

15

Transformative Leadership

The Exercise of Agency in Educational Leadership

Paula D. Bieneman

On its surface, educational leadership seems to be a rather practical and predictable enterprise, especially at the building level. Ask anyone. Literally, ask someone what they believe a building principal does and you will probably hear a common refrain—student discipline. Because people ground their understanding of the school principal in their own educational experiences as students, their vantage point is limited. School administration is too often defined and limited to managerial responsibilities; it is not surprising that even school principals find themselves uncertain of their roles in the current educational context. Perhaps many school principals do spend most of their time on managerial matters, but the reality is that there is so much more we could and should be doing. Time spent on noninstructional tasks, such as bus duty, attendance at school events, and managing budgets, serves as a distraction from our potential roles as transformative leaders. There is, however, much real work to be done so that all students receive an excellent and equitable education.

I have been a school administrator for nearly 20 years now, having spent the past ten years as an elementary school principal. During the past two decades, I have come to realize that educational leadership is anything but practical and predictable. Instead, it is a complex interplay of political and social realities resulting in a relatively stagnant institution that allows some children to be significantly advantaged while others simply go without. In fact, as an institution, education defies even the most zealous change agent to attempt meaningful change. Despite our contemporary society, we hold fast to our agrarian calendar and our industrial practices. We hold fast to our graded level instruction, our Crayola curriculum, and our seat time. We hold fast to our internalized beliefs and biases, and, in doing so, we hold on to the status quo and to institutionalized school failure, specifically the academic achievement gap.

Public education does not need any more managerial leaders. It does not need another round of technocrats or placeholders. Public education needs transformative leaders, leaders who are willing to ask and answer difficult questions. Children need educational leaders who are willing to acknowledge and accept their own sense of agency and who are willing to create deep and meaningful change that will benefit all students. In considering these needs, I remind myself that we, as educators, choose to participate in the current system. We decide to walk through the front doors of our schools each day. We must remember, however, that our children do not make those same choices. We compel them to attend school. Their choices are directly limited by their zip codes. Indirectly, those choices are a result of their socioeconomic status.

A Changing Educational Context

I currently work in a large elementary district in Lake County, Illinois, where I have served as a building principal for the past ten years. In our county, there is a wide range of socioeconomic contexts, with a predominantly white school district serving less than 1 percent low-income students approximately ten miles down the road from a predominantly minority district serving 71 percent low-income students. These stark contrasts are a reality throughout the county. Affluence and poverty exist in close proximity. This disparity is further emphasized and institutionalized in the educational opportunities available to the children whose lived experiences are so dramatically different.

What has been interesting during the period I have served as a principal is the changing and marginalizing dynamic in the county. While the gap between the wealthiest and poorest schools prevails, predominantly white, middle-class communities are changing. My district, for example, has experienced significant demographic shifts, reflecting a shift from a relatively middle-class, white community to a minority-majority community with an increasing number of families identified as low socioeconomic status. In 1999, more than 75 percent of the 1,982 enrolled students in my district were Caucasian. By 2010, district enrollment had risen to 2,522 and the number of Caucasian students had declined to 33.6 percent. Our district quickly realized an increasingly diverse student population. During that time, the percentage of low-income students also increased, from 8 percent in 1999 to 43.3 percent in 2010. Interestingly, at the same time the district was experiencing shifts in racial and economic demographics; the mobility rate decreased, from 17.7 to 13.7 percent, while student attendance rates increased, from 93.9 to 94.9 percent.

For an elementary principal serving in a racially and economically diverse school, closing the achievement gap is a daily reality. In so many schools serving poor and minority students, there are minimal resources to address their school needs. Staffing is limited and needs are high. My school is no exception, but rapidly changing demographics in our school community have shifted the paradigm, creating cultural and academic gaps that seem to widen with each passing year.

Overview of the Chapter

In seeking ways to understand and address these identified disparities, I look regularly to several theoretical constructs that offer promise for providing a socially just education and closing the achievement gap. Those theoretical constructs are transformative leadership, collective efficacy, and deficit thinking. In an effort to become more informed and efficacious as an educational leader, I have been working to examine the underlying beliefs and tacit assumptions of, not only those constructs, but of the practices in my own school and district. I have been critically interrogating my own belief systems and the resulting actions. In this redefined context, material realities and disparities that impinge on the success of individuals and organizations as a whole cannot be ignored (Shields, 2010). Transformative leadership theory, with its emphasis on deep and lasting change, holds promise for principals seeking to meet such challenges. To foster deep and sustainable change, transformative leaders must deconstruct and rebuild existing social and cultural knowledge frameworks about power and privilege, equity and access, and achievement. We cannot do such work without acknowledging and understanding the deficit-thinking model that has been advanced to explain school failure. Finally, as organization leaders, we must become acquainted with and expert in organizational agency. Bandura's seminal work on efficacy, specifically collective efficacy, requires our attention, because it provides evidence that teacher beliefs about their capabilities as an organization are systematically related to student achievement. Additionally, findings revealed that, even after accounting for student socioeconomic status, minority status, and prior achievement, collective efficacy was positively and significantly associated with student achievement differences among schools (Bandura, 1995, 1997b; Goddard, 2000, 2001; Goddard, R., Hoy, W. & Woolfolk Hoy, A. 2004).

Embracing transformative leadership theory as my conceptual lens (Foster, 1986; Quantz, Rogers, & Dantley, 1991; Shields, 2006, 2009), I have come to realize that every decision, even the simplest decision, has its unintended consequences. For example, a seemingly straightforward decision to offer an afterschool tutoring program for students who are not performing at grade level in reading and mathematics is more than a decision to offer academic remediation. In a resource-poor school, that decision means that, even in an ideal situation, some students will be advantaged, while others will be disadvantaged. In choosing to develop and implement the tutoring program, funds will need to be reallocated from other social or recreational programming. Those children who will now be required to attend afterschool tutoring will no longer be able to participate in concurrently scheduled events, such as chess club or basketball. To fund the tutoring, I may even have to cancel chess club or basketball, denying other child enrichment opportunities. Perhaps what is even more important is that, while I wrestle with the surface issues surrounding the tutorial program, I have yet to really drill down to confront the larger issue of disparate educational programming during the school day. Unless our daily instructional programming is consistently and effectively delivered, I am requiring some children to spend their free time remedying a problem that we as educators created. At present, I am faced with this seemingly simple dilemma. Do I provide the tutoring program to remediate the gap created by my school's lack of articulate curriculum and inconsistent grade-level expectations, or do I allow the students to fail to meet state standards and be labeled deficient? All the while, I will continue to ask the question: Who is advantaged and disadvantaged by my decision? Before demonstrating how the above theories ground and inform my leadership practice, I argue that closing the "achievement gap" is an imperative goal of moral and transformative leadership.

Closing the Achievement Gap: An Imperative for Transformative Leaders

As I learned during my first year as a principal, the starting point for discussion must be the achievement gap between white and non-white students, low-income and non-low-income children. The path of least resistance is, and has always been, the provision of services to remediate the child's perceived deficits, rather than to question the effectiveness and efficacy of the institutionalized practices. A recent study of the achievement gap charted a course for closing the gap on a state-by-state basis. The prediction was based on current trends in closing the gaps. In one state, the projected timeline for closing the achievement gap between white and black students was 105 years. The study released by the Center on Education Policy found that, in 2009, test scores for Latinos were often 15 to 20 percentage points lower than for whites. For African Americans, the gap in test scores was typically 20 to 30 points lower than for whites. The size of the test-score gap between Native Americans and whites was similar to that between African Americans and whites

(Zehr, 2010). For the most part, educational leaders stand silent, often not realizing that what we fail to say is perhaps more powerful than the words we choose to articulate.

As schools in Illinois begin to collect, analyze, and examine achievement data, that process cannot be simply a cursory glance at Illinois Standards Achievement Test data. It is, however, risky to be transparent as an educational leader. On a daily basis, I wrestle with the presentation of student achievement data. For example, in a recent board report I chose to provide an accurate summary of our current math performance data, a summary that clearly indicated that we needed to significantly improve the effectiveness of our math instruction. In doing so, I understand that data offer us one means of raising questions. For example, rather than simply offer the statement that 80 percent of our fifth-grade students met or exceeded state standards in reading in 2010, we need to look more closely. In this case, 88 percent of white fifth-grade students met or exceeded, while 75 percent of black fifth graders met or exceeded. Even more critical is an examination of who is exceeding and at what rate. Looking more closely at the same fifth-grade data, 44 percent of white fifth graders exceeded on ISAT reading, while only 5 percent of black fifth graders did. This information must be shared among all school staff and questions must be asked. Sharing this information publicly is risky, especially in an era of high-stakes accountability, because presenting the information publicly is not enough. Dialogue in response to data is critical and, all too often, lacking.

For example, in Illinois both aggregated and disaggregated data on state assessments for all public schools are available to the public via the Illinois Interactive Report Card, at www. iirc.niu. edu. One of the features on the Web site allows the viewer to examine achievement gaps between racial and income groups. At first glance, my school district's composite percentage of students meeting and exceeding on the Illinois Standards Achievement Test appears average, with 75 to 78 percent of our students either meeting or exceeding on the ISAT over the past four years. To say that three out of four students meet or exceed on that assessment is not that alarming on the surface. What is more alarming is the academic achievement gap that persists beneath that data. To be engaged in transformative leadership is to look more closely and foster dialogue about that reality.

Despite the highly politicized efforts to close the achievement gap, academic disparity continues, largely unabated. In fact, while states proudly report increases in state test scores, the achievement gap remains prominent. It is this failure to effectively address the achievement gap that requires further scrutiny. It is this failure to deliver on the promises of No Child Left Behind that inspired me to seek out more substantive ways of considering our collective failure. Certainly, if "scientifically-based interventions" and the arena of high-stakes testing had met with such failure, a more considered approach was needed. As William Congero of the Connecticut Department of Education put it at the 2007 Council of Chief State School Officers Large-Scale Assessment Conference:

> The term "achievement gap" refers to the observed disparity on a number of measures between the performance of groups of students, especially groups defined by gender, race/ethnicity, and socio-economic status. It most often describes the issue of low income/minority education in the United States; that is, blacks and Latinos and students from poor families perform worse in school than their well-off white and Asian peers. (Congero, 2007)

In response to the achievement gap in Illinois, a number of task forces, coalitions, and oversight groups have been created. Researchers from one such group, A+ Illinois, paint a bleak picture of the achievement gap. According to Sandel and Batchu (2005), "The nation's report card results show that Illinois has the largest achievement gap in the nation." In October 2004, the U.S. Department of Education released the results of the National Assessment of Educational Progress (NAEP). NAEP is a nationally representative assessment that is administered regularly over time, testing a sample of fourth- and eighth-grade students in math and reading. This assessment allows for a comparison of student achievement across states and now provides opportunities for states and districts to monitor the progress of their school-improvement efforts.

Despite a gain at the national level, Illinois did not witness such progress, failing to demonstrate a significant gain from the 2003 NAEP. Sandel and Batchu argue that the 2005 NAEP results show that Illinois continues to have some of the worst achievement gaps in the country and has been ineffective in closing those gaps. In fourth-grade math, the achievement gap between poor and non-poor students in Illinois ranked first in the nation (Education Trust and National Assessment of Progress, 2005). The state fared no better in its efforts to close the achievement gap between black and white students. That academic disparity remains significantly high, despite two years of attempted reform: In fourth-grade math, Illinois has the third-highest achievement gap between black and white students. Even more alarming, Illinois has the second-highest achievement gap in fourth-grade reading. On a more encouraging note, the achievement gap between Hispanic and white students narrowed in eighth grade. Despite that narrowed gap, Illinois remains steadily among the worst in the nation when it comes to educating Hispanic fourth-grade students (Sandel & Batchu, 2005).

On September 4, 2001, the Illinois State Board of Education issued this press release: *Year-3 ISAT scores up; achievement gap continues*. The state superintendent, Max McGee, identified an increase in student performance on the Illinois Standards Achievement Test (ISAT), but conceded that the "achievement gap" between white and non-white students remains unacceptably wide (Illinois State Board of Education, 2003). The 2003 ISAT results reveal that while 64 percent of white eighth graders met or exceeded state standards in math, only 19 percent of their black peers and 29 percent of their Hispanic peers scored comparably. When the five-year ISAT data was released by the Illinois State Board of Education, the assessment data for Illinois elementary school students showed an upward trend in mathematics at all grade levels tested and a narrowing of the achievement gap in a number of subjects at a number of grades. The results, however, revealed little gain in elementary reading scores. It is important to examine the narrowing of the achievement gap and understand that the gap between white and non-white students, poor and non-poor students is unacceptable. In third-grade math, for example, the gap narrowed from 43.8 percentage points to 39.6 percentage points (Illinois State Board of Education, 2003). ISAT reading scores at the elementary level remained static, maintaining the achievement gap for non-white and poor students.

The achievement gap at the elementary level has significant implications for the lives of the non-white students. Those students who underperform at the elementary level are also underrepresented in Advanced Placement (AP) Courses at the high school level. According to the Education Trust, African American students made up 21 percent of the public K-12 enrollment in 2004, but only accounted for 4 percent of the enrollment in AP Calculus, 5 percent of the enrollment in AP Biology, and 9 percent of the AP English enrollment. Latino students fared only slightly better. While non-white students are underrepresented, white students are overrepresented in AP enrollment (Education Trust, *Edwatch Online*, 2004).

The passage of the No Child Left Behind Act (NCLB) led to the implementation of adequate yearly progress, which has become the centerpiece of many school districts' instructional programming and school-improvement efforts. Buzz words such as *accountability, testing, academic improvement*, and *research-based* are heard resoundingly in schools and districts across the country. NCLB's first principle of accountability focused on the development of standards and high-stakes testing.

For elementary schools across the state of Illinois, high scores on the Illinois Standards Achievement Test have become the Holy Grail.

As a result, schools around the country spend considerable time and resources preparing their students for annual testing, often at the expense of higher-level thinking, fine arts, and academic enrichment. Students performing below standards frequently are required to spend more time in direct instruction of basic skills and studying with other test preparation curriculum materials. In many school districts, students identified as underperforming on standardized measures are relegated to more of the same in afterschool academic tutoring programs. Additionally, schools with limited resources must rely on a narrowing of the curriculum to emphasize test-specific content.

Useful Theoretical Frameworks

Given our limited success in addressing the achievement gap, we must begin to allow for deeper, more considered approaches that are based in research and theory. Theories abound in educational research. Underlying educational practice and school reform initiatives, whether explicit or implicit, are individual and collective belief systems that cannot go unexamined. These underlying beliefs and implicit assumptions can either contribute to the success of reform efforts or weaken the very practices designed to address students' academic and social needs. Assumptions and beliefs about culturally diverse and low-income students encountered in underperforming schools require closer examination.

Transformative Leadership

Because the decision to offer a tutoring program is just one of the many decisions I must make on a daily basis, I understand that it is exhausting to truly address institutionally created inequities that contribute to the achievement gap. To engage in transformative leadership is exhausting. It is complex. As a school principal, I understand that I am a product of the very system I seek to change. I also realize that, as a building principal, one of my most basic responsibilities is to maintain a calm and orderly environment. That expectation works in opposition to any and all actions that create conflict and disrupt the daily routine:

> Beyond these apparent, obvious explanations, a more fundamental, latent reason goes far to explain how decent, committed and hard working education professionals can fall prey to complacency and inaction. We are influenced or, in behavioural terms, conditioned by societal/organizational norms that work to thwart resistance to practices that do not conform to standard operational, mainstream procedures. Iconoclastic or subversive thinking and behaviours are punished in subtle, sometimes overt ways. (Glanz, 2007, p. 117)

For that reason, transformative leaders need to be resilient and spiritually grounded. They must be able to thrive despite adversity and they need to be willing to explore the creative tension of opposites, while working to minimize conflict. It is a delicate balancing act at best, because "susceptibility to vulnerability stifles our interest or ability to transform schools. Remaining vulnerable lowers expectations for ourselves, and more importantly, for teachers and students" (Glanz, 2007, 118). School principals are increasingly vulnerable to political and social scrutiny. We have to remain mindful of our political and social capital, spending it carefully, so that we can remain in positions to exercise our agency. We are, after all, a remarkably expendable lot who are positioned precariously in the middle, reconciling the whims of district-level administration, school board members, teachers, and parents, all while feeling overwhelmed by an onerous workload. While recognizing the need to adopt a transformative leadership approach, I also question my capacity to challenge and critique the institution and authority I represent. Certainly, school principals operating as transformative leaders will need to learn to live with cognitive dissonance if they are to be successful:

> Transformative leadership begins with questions of justice and democracy; it critiques inequitable practices and offers the promise not only of greater individual achievement but of a better life lived in common with others. Transformative leadership, therefore, inextricably links education and educational leadership with the wider social context within which it is embedded. (Shields, 2010, p. x)

For building principals, opportunities to critique inequitable practices are abundant. Unfortunately, the authority and support to challenge existing inequalities are limited, at best. There is seldom even time and space to open dialogue on such matters. For example, within a typical school day, students are present for 6 hours and 25 minutes. By contract, teachers work seven hours and five minutes, arriving 20 minutes before school and staying 20 minutes after the students are dismissed. Our contract does not allow for afterschool staff meetings, and we do not have the resources to pay staff to remain beyond the contractual day. Even with creative and resourceful scheduling, opportunities for dialogue are restricted to monthly two-hour school-improvement meetings. There is minimal time to have conversations with fellow educators. Time is a commodity that I can seldom broker, and it is one of the resources I most need to begin deconstructing deficit thinking and to begin building collective efficacy.

In many ways, transformative leadership seems antithetical to administrative survival. To question the status quo seems like political suicide. Engaging in critical dialogue exposes political and social belief systems, often positioning oneself as oppositional to those with authority and power. For example, in shifting resources or denying privilege to those who express entitlement, I risk a call to the superintendent or a threat of a visit to the school board. Building-level administrators are often informally, and sometimes formally, charged with ensuring that conflict is mitigated, that power remains where it matters, and that discord is kept to a minimum. It is especially risky to suggest redistribution of resources, to make choices that may shift advantage from the advantaged to the children of families who will not complain. Any administrator knows the risk of reducing gifted programming or reassigning benefits to "those kids."

The Lottery: A Case for Transformative Leadership

In my first year as a principal of two separate elementary buildings, I found myself in a role that is all-too-familiar for school principals—that of one caught in the middle. Prior to assuming my role as principal, the district transitioned from part-time kindergarten to a combination of full-time and part-time kindergarten. During the spring before I was hired, a "lottery" was held for incoming kindergarten students. Parents with "winning numbers" could choose between a full-day instruction program and a partial-day classroom. Parents who did not "win" the lottery had their children assigned to a partial-day classroom. Remarkably, as the early kindergarten registration closed, the district was able to award parents their program preference with only 12 students assigned to partial-day kindergarten. As summer registration came to a close, another, more significant, issue emerged. Parents who did not register in early spring did not have a choice in their children's educational programming. Those children were relegated to a partial-day program, regardless of their parents' request. For the most part, those families were new to the district. A majority of the children whose parents missed the early registration were from low-income families and were minority. As the year began, enrollment continued to increase, with all the new students assigned to partial-day kindergarten. The children were further disadvantaged by a classroom environment that was constantly changing. By the time enrollment stabilized in October, there were six full-day kindergarten classes totaling 155 students and three partial-day kindergarten classes totaling 78 students. Instead of a dozen families selecting partial-day kindergarten, approximately 70 families had their children placed in partial-day kindergarten despite their requests. Without intending to do so, the district had created disparate educational opportunities for kindergarten students, specifically for minority and low-income students.

As a result of discussions regarding the matter, a number of political tensions emerged, and I quickly realized that the issue of providing equitable educational services to students was not the issue. I came to recognize that there was limited capacity for or willingness to change. It was proposed that any children whose parents wanted them in full-day kindergarten, regardless of whether they had registered on time, should be allowed access to the full-time program. As a first-year principal assigned temporarily in a part-time capacity to that building, I was reluctant to move forward with this change to the program. I found myself debating the merits of postponing the transition to full-day kindergarten programming for all children whose families wanted the option, as a result of several vocal parents who wanted the school to stick with the original program transition plan. As a new principal, I knew that it would be safer to wait until the next year, when I would be comfortably assigned to a single building after a district-wide reconfiguration. I remember trying to invent ways to accommodate my own fear of conflict.

After several long nights spent debating the moral implications of my planned inaction, I weighed the moral imperative of providing all students with quality education and the likely potential for political turmoil. By realizing that political contexts are complex moral mazes, educational leaders can better assess the risks and rewards of serving as transformative leaders. I moved forward with the transition—offering more full-time classes—and, as tensions mounted, I became the target of a group of white parents who were openly hostile to the changes, even though their children were still provided the option of half-day kindergarten. That parent group and a small group of teachers who preferred the status quo of using the lottery system, despite the clearly disparate educational realities for the children, made my professional life difficult, to say the least. I endured more than one angry conversation about how I was changing the program for people who were not responsible enough to register early. I was advocating affirmative action, socially engineering the classrooms. The parent group even began rallying support to demand that the district not move forward with the latest restructuring. Even though the small group of parents was not being denied anything, they did not want change to occur because of "those kids."

Ten years later, I still remember the animosity and tension of that time. I still remember the difficulty of going to work every day and trying to balance my responsibilities between two buildings, while a group of parents and teachers impugned my reputation and attacked my integrity. I still remember the anxiety-ridden nights and that feeling of standing alone. What I remember more poignantly, though, are the voices of the families whose children were moved to full-day kindergarten over the winter break. I remember the grandmother who thanked Jesus that her grandchildren wouldn't be so far behind "those other children," because they had been through enough already. I remember the mother who kept saying, "Muchas gracias," again and again. I remember the 58 families who thanked me for helping their children. Those families would never come to a board meeting; they would never write a petition, and they would likely never hold the district accountable if their children fell victim to a manufactured achievement gap. I would like to believe that I would have risen to the challenge, had I known what would happen when I expanded the program, but I am not certain I would have. I was quite a bit more naïve then.

Shields (2010) asserts that "transformative leadership begins with questions of justice and democracy; it critiques inequitable practices . . ." (p. 559). Working within this framework, a principal could not simply choose to avoid the complications or contradictions of addressing this situation. In this situation, as the building principal, I not only understood that institutional power was being used to unintentionally oppress some children; I understood that it had to be used to intentionally liberate those same children. Within a few short months of becoming principal, I had to choose whether I would maintain the status quo or whether I would position myself in opposition to it. In retrospect, I knew nothing of transformative leadership at that time, but I believe that it would have been a powerful framework from which to operate. I believe it would have better prepared me to more effectively assume an activist agenda. In the end, I did come to another key realization. I came to understand that individual agency is not enough to counter the effects of institutionalized and manufactured academic disparity. To be successful, school principals need to encourage and develop others to become transformative leaders as well. I realized that I needed to promote organizational agency as well as individual agency.

Collective Efficacy

With a newly realized sense of urgency in identifying and addressing other educational disparities, I embraced the idea that "transformative leadership, therefore, recognizes the need to begin with critical reflection and analysis and to move through enlightened understanding to action" (Shields, 2010, p. 572) and I began to seek out other theoretical constructs that could inform my daily practice. Social cognitive theory eventually brought me to investigate the extant literature on collective efficacy.

Social cognitive theory asserts that individuals and collectives exercise agency through choice. Key to the exercise of agency, however, is the belief in one's efficacy or capability "to organize and execute the courses of action required to manage prospective situations" (Bandura, 1995, p. 2). Bandura (1997b) argued that efficacy beliefs, or perceptions of task-specific capabilities, are a key mechanism of behavioral change for individuals, organizations, and even nations. Perceptions of efficacy serve to influence the behavior of individuals and the normative environment of collectives by providing expectations about the likelihood of success for various pursuits.

In 1977, Bandura introduced efficacy theory, which began with the concept of self-efficacy, or "beliefs in one's capacity to organize and execute the courses of action to produce given attainments" (Bandura, 1977, p. 3). In the past 30 years, Bandura's work has expanded to include three areas of interest to educators: self-efficacy of students, self-efficacy of teachers, and perceived collective efficacy. Perceived collective efficacy is the most recent theoretical construct and may have significant implications for effective organizational agency and school-improvement efforts. Bandura (1986) identified four sources for building collective efficacy: mastery experience, vicarious experience, social persuasion, and affective states.

When studied, schools with higher proportions of students from lower socioeconomic levels and of minority status had lower collective beliefs in their efficacy to achieve academic success, and their academic achievement followed accordingly (Bandura, 1995). Bandura also found that schools heavily populated with minority and poor students achieved high levels of success on standardized measures when their educators firmly believed that they could motivate and teach the students (Bandura, 1995, p. 21). "More research is needed to know whether this finding holds in more ethnically diverse schools, and if it does, to understand why teacher perceptions differ by race" (Goddard & Skrla, 2006, p. 228). Moore and Esselman (1994) expand upon this:

> Results suggest that schools with historically poor student achievement tend to have teachers who, as a group, report a poorer image of school atmosphere which contributes to poorer perceptions of teacher effectiveness. Furthermore, path analysis suggests that this weak sense of efficacy is in part a function of the poor performance of the school's students. What is of concern is the circular nature of this relationship. (p. 14)

According to social cognitive theory, behavior, personal factors (e.g., cognitive, affective, or biological events), and the external environment are interdependent. The control individuals and collectives exert over their lives is influenced by their perceptions of efficacy. Analogous to self-efficacy, collective efficacy is associated with the tasks, level of effort, persistence, thoughts, stress levels, and achievement of groups (Bandura, 1993, 1997b). According to Bandura (1997a), "collective efficacy is concerned with the performance capability of a social system as a whole" (p. 469). For schools, collective efficacy refers to the perceptions of teachers in a school that the faculty as a whole can execute the courses of action necessary to have positive effects on students.

Collective efficacy, as measured by aggregating teacher perceptions of the staff's collective ability to teach effectively, strongly correlated with student achievement. In fact, collective efficacy was more strongly related to student achievement than was student socioeconomic status. Bandura also found that staff perceptions of collective efficacy predicted student performance as strongly as did prior student achievement (Bandura, 1997b). The significance of this research is that it poses a direct challenge to previous research that argued that schools cannot overcome the biases attributed to socioeconomic status (SES). Bandura made an effective argument that collective efficacy could be a promising construct for understanding and realizing systemic school improvement. Goddard successfully replicated Bandura's research, although he used different statistical means for measuring collective efficacy (2000).

In Goddard, Hoy & Woolfolk Hoy (2000), collective teacher efficacy is defined as "an emergent group-level attribute, the product of the interactive dynamics of the group members" (p. 482). The emergent nature of the attribute is more than a sum of individual group members. Bandura identifies "the group's shared belief in its conjoint capabilities to organize and execute courses of action required to produce given levels of attainment" (Bandura, 1997a).

The reality of continuous and sustainable school improvement is that, in spite of external pressure and increased political scrutiny, educators—not politicians—remain solely responsible for creating learning environments that are conducive to academic achievement. Teachers operate collectively within an interactive social system, rather than as isolates. Understanding that belief systems are a precursor to action is critical. It appears that collective-efficacy beliefs influence group performance by shaping the behavioral and normative environment of schools. As Bandura (1997a) observed, "people working independently within a group do not function as social isolates totally immune to the influence of those around them" (p. 469). It is this work on collective efficacy that holds promise that organizational agency exists that will lead to continuous school improvement, particularly in schools with risk factors.

Bandura's research on collective efficacy provides educators with a new construct for examining the achievement gap. Rather than continue to focus on student demographics, such as SES and ethnicity, Bandura's work shifted the focus to organizational factors. When Bandura (1993) controlled for student demographics, previous school achievement data, and teacher experience, the relationship between schools with high levels of collective efficacy and high academic performance was established. This realization is particularly timely, as current literature continues to emerge on high-poverty, high-performing schools, specifically the 90/90/90 schools. In 90/90/90 schools, academic success, defined as 90 percent of the students meeting identified standards, is attained despite student populations made of up 90 percent low-SES and 90 percent minorities.

As a staff, we continue to explore our own belief systems and tacit assumptions, using the research on collective efficacy. To establish a baseline measurement of our own collective efficacy, staff members have completed the Collective Efficacy Scale and reviewed the data. Additionally, we have shared articles about efficacy and worked to build efficacy in our school community. Bandura's four sources of collective efficacy—mastery experience, vicarious experience, social persuasion, and affective states—are integrated into staff development, as we work to build our collective efficacy. Moving forward, I realize that building collective efficacy is an iterative process that is critical to school improvement. Not only does collective efficacy offer a useful paradigm for school reform, but it also strengthens the argument that we, as educators, are producers of experiences. Bandura (2000) argues that "unless people believe that they can produce desired effects and forestall undesired ones by their actions, they have little incentive to act" (p. 75). To successfully enact organizational change, transformative leaders need to create hope by deconstructing existing social and educational realities. By finding and sharing evidence of efficacious organizations with similar demographic challenges and highlighting their successes, we allow for possibilities previously denied.

Deconstructing Deficit Thinking

As an educator, I also understand the complex interplay between belief and practice. In particular, I understand the power of perception and long-held "truths" about school failure, known as deficit thinking. As transformative leaders we must be the catalyst for continued examination of deficit thinking. To create more a more just and equitable educational system, the deficit-thinking paradigm must be deconstructed, and we need to critically examine the root cause of educational disparities and underachievement (Shields, 2010). Cooper (2009) argues that "in the midst of demographic change, students need leaders and advocates who are prepared to be cultural change agents . . ." (p. x). To effectively lead for social justice, school principals must reject "ideologies and practices steeped in blatantly biased or color-blind traditions" (Cooper, 2009, p. 695). To begin this work, educational leaders will need to not only become more aware of the deficit-thinking model but also to gain the skills necessary to counter dynamics that marginalize students and limit their opportunities for success.

In American public schools, Valencia (1997) argued that the dominant paradigm shaping educators' expectations and subsequent practice is that of deficit thinking. "The deficit thinking paradigm, as a whole, posits that students who fail in school do so because of alleged internal deficiencies (such as cognitive and/or motivational limitations) or shortcomings socially linked to the youngster—such as familial defects and dysfunctions" (p. xi). Deficit thinking as a phenomenon has been researched extensively in education (Delpit, 1995; Garcia & Guerra, 2004; Shields, Bishop, & Mazawi, 2005; Valencia, 1997; Valencia, R. & Guadarrama, I. 2001). Contemporary deficit thinking is built on a long and storied history, with roots as far back as the 17th century.

Hawkins (Valencia, R. & Guadarrama, I. 2001) asserted that "some scholars would have us believe that educability is largely dependent on individual intellectual ability and that social, political and economic conditions within the schools and society are largely unrelated to 'why some of our children are so much more educable than others'" (p. 375). Instructional practices and educational assumptions that emerge from the deficit-thinking paradigm mask organizational and social issues, often overshadowing the abilities of students and teachers.

As recently as 1994, Herrnstein and Murray attempted to influence contemporary society with *The Bell Curve: Intelligence and Class Structure in American Life,* making the case that the deficit paradigm could be supported by their interpretation of their data. Herrnstein, a Harvard professor, and Murray, a public-policy analyst, sought to legitimize the deficit paradigm by arguing that IQ varies among racial and ethnic groups. Perhaps more unsettling, their claim that these variations might be genetic further fueled the pervasive beliefs about the deficits inherent in minority groups. Although this publication is 17 years old, Herrnstein and Murray's argument is still echoing in public schools throughout the nation.

Recently, while attending a multidistrict teacher institute day, I heard a group of white educators from a predominantly African American community argue that "these kids aren't able to think critically . . . they just do not come to school with the necessary background." Further discussion revealed a widely accepted belief that critical-thinking skills were not on the curricular agenda for many of the classrooms represented in that training session. That this belief system was so readily offered and supported in a staff development day focused on critical thinking was appalling.

A deficit-thinking model asserts that students who underperform or underachieve in schools or on school-based assessments do so because of internal deficits (Valencia, 1997). Theories regarding the sources of these perceived deficits include intellectual limitations, cultural or economic disadvantage, a lack of motivation, and poor home environment. Deficit thinking argues that poor school performance is "rooted in students' alleged cognitive and motivational deficits, while institutional structures and inequitable schooling arrangements . . . are held exculpatory" (Valencia, 1997, p. 9).

To ensure test preparedness and address these "deficits," school district curriculum and instructional materials are "teacher-proofed" and rely heavily on prescriptive approaches to learning. These approaches focus on the alleged limitations of the student, requiring no change on behalf of the institution. Although these attempts at intervention may contribute to higher test scores, they do little to provide students with the quality of instruction necessary in a democratic society (Shields, 2009). Studies of comprehensive school reform argue that these initiatives frequently fail due to an unwillingness to interrogate the causes of underachievement and school failure, particularly among low-income and minority students. As a result of the nation's attempt to close the achievement gap and adequately respond to NCLB mandates, "compensatory education" programs remain current practice. Despite William Ryan's impassioned critique of deficit thinking in *Blaming the Victim* (1971), the current high-stakes testing accountability continues a tradition of deficit thinking. As data are disaggregated and schools scrutinized for subgroup academic performance, the possibility of sanctions for low performance holds serious consequences for students and educators (Urrieta, 2004).

Several common refrains in education that exemplify deficit thinking include "These kids do not come to school ready to learn," or "These parents just do not value education." It is the litany of phrases that begin with "these children" that serve as an indicator of deficit thinking. Educators too often elaborate on "these children" by pointing to the lack of prerequisite knowledge and skills, and uncaring parents who are unable or unwilling to value education and who do not support their child's schooling. Given these external and overwhelming challenges, many educators argue that their school is doing a satisfactory job given the challenges of "these children," or they accept, with resignation, that they can do no more for "these children" (Finnan & Swanson, 2000). Many educators are, after all, able to point to the children with whom they are successful, further emphasizing deficit beliefs and returning the onus to the student and his subgroup.

In societies where inequity and inequality exists, Freire argued that assistencialism was the social response to that disparity. According to the oppressor, or dominant culture, certain groups of people lack the knowledge and skills to know what is necessary for their own success and those belonging to the more "able" culture had the rationality to identify what was needed (Urrieta, 2004). Assistencialism is one of those forms of domination that assume that some groups of people need the assistance of education and other social programs to live successfully.

> Although the deficit thinking model has been rebuked by a number of scholars for many decades and is held in disrepute by many current behavioral and social scientists, it nevertheless manifests, in varying degrees, in contemporary educational thought and practice. Furthermore, not only does deficit thinking demonstrate an adherence to current social thought and educational practice, but by all indicators it continues to gain ground as we approach the twenty-first century. (Valencia, 1997, p. x)

Working toward systemic change in low-performing schools, Berman et al. (1999) found that efforts to raise achievement were hindered by school districts' and educators' tendencies to place the problem within the student (and family) or within the school, without examining the links between school practices and student outcomes. These researchers suggested that there is insufficient "exploration of the institutional and individual practices, assumptions, and processes that contribute to and/or fail to weaken these patterns" (Garcia & Guerra, 2004, p. 10).

At present, few educators are even aware of this construct and its unintended, yet destructive, effects. Recently, I served as adjunct faculty at a private university. I taught in two separate master's programs—one for reading specialists and one for administrators. During the course of that year, I introduced students to the research on deficit thinking. None of the nearly 80 educators were even familiar with the notion of deficit thinking, and none had examined pathologizing practices in their own classrooms and schools. Becoming aware is a critical first step for transformative leaders. It is necessary to identify, contextualize, and challenge tacit assumptions about our students and our communities. Without such examination, the deficit paradigm governs our daily lives, and we allow it to position both children and educators as victims, fostering discouragement and hopelessness.

When we position ourselves as victims, we essentially argue that the 6.5 hours a day, 174 days a year (or 1131 hours) children spend with us are insignificant. We argue that we are insignificant. There is evidence to the contrary. As I have suggested, there are other realities that we have yet to accept, realities that involve changing our sense of collective efficacy and fostering sustainable, transformative leadership, while working to deconstruct deficit thinking.

Reconstructing Social and Cultural Knowledge Frameworks

It is not enough, however, to promote dialogue; educational leaders must look for and maximize opportunities to improve instruction by challenging deficit-thinking paradigms, understanding human agency, and building collective efficacy. To do this, principals must be willing to accept their roles as transformative leaders. Understanding that changes to practice cannot occur only at the periphery is critical. The very act of teaching is an act of human agency, with unlimited potential for transformative leadership. For me, acknowledging my own human agency and advocating for educational equity is a moral and spiritual imperative. It consumes me and compels me to examine and reexamine the daily reality of my school context.

That sense of moral purpose is the one driving factor that pushes me to consider moving to the next level of educational leadership—the superintendency. At one point, I believed that I could effect needed change as an elementary principal. I thought that attempts to create dialogue, to engage other voices, and perhaps to even engage in subtle activism, would be enough. They simply are not. That level of leadership must come from and be fostered by the superintendent, with building principals being empowered and supported to advance an agenda that has, as its goal, organizational transformation. This is especially true in school districts like mine—districts that have greater potential than we admit.

Somehow, we need to create a sense of urgency—to better inform our community of the benefits of a well-educated populace and the risks and costs of an undereducated citizenry. Challenging the status quo requires a commitment by educators to demonstrate that change is the responsibility of the system and the educators within it. It also requires us to demonstrate the possibilities for success. To be transformative, I believe, is to provide examples of those possibilities at multiple levels within the organization—the classroom, the building, and the district.

For example, during the first year of our performance grouping in reading, I deliberately assigned the most efficacious and capable teachers to the lowest performing students. There were three sections of first grade. That year, the performance grouping fell neatly into three categories, with one section exceeding grade-level expectations, one at grade level, and one significantly below grade level. By the middle of the year, the lowest section was performing at the level of the middle group. Eventually, that lowest performing group surpassed the average performing group. By reviewing and sharing student-reading data with the first-grade team, as well as the other grade-level teams, a question was raised regarding teacher efficacy. That example, and others that followed, generated a more thorough interrogation of our beliefs about our own agency and the perceived deficits of the children.

The examination of student data over the years fuels many of our discussions. To date, there are teachers in our building who get results—significant results—with children other teachers identify as deficient. Over the years, our achievement gaps have closed significantly, suggesting that we have the capacity to succeed. In response to staff concerns that our changing demographics are the reason our achievement gap has reopened in the past two years, I share data. For example, in 2002, our population was 70.6 percent white, yet our scores were 65 percent met or exceeded expectations; in 2003, 62.3 percent white and scores were the lowest, at 60 percent meeting or exceeding expectations. Additionally, our school size was small, 333 students in 2002 and 326 in 2003. Yet, in 2007, when our school enrollment increased to 490 and we were a minority-majority school, 82 percent of our students met or exceeded. If changing demographics were the issue, our achievement should not have increased so significantly, surpassing that of a predominantly white student population. Discussions informed by data have allowed us to examine and reexamine our assumptions about who we serve and with whom we succeed.

Final Thoughts

What I have learned during the past ten years as a building principal is that this type of work is unending and exhausting. I almost feel as though I am beginning the dialogue again, starting over. What I have also realized is that I am going to have to rethink a few of my non-negotiables at this one moment in time. I am going to have to be willing to stretch existing relationships, create tension in an otherwise calm environment, and find spiritual strength if I am going to challenge the status quo that I helped create. But, there are those moments that remind me that our school is on track.

At the beginning of the year, I had shared research with the staff regarding vocabulary disparities in children entering school, with students from lower SES groups knowing substantially fewer words than children from professional families. In an effort to address that disparity, grade levels were asked to explicitly teach academic vocabulary. Despite some initial resistance, teachers began teaching an articulated vocabulary. At differing points in the school year, I can honestly say that I wished I had not taken on that issue; yet at other times, I was glad that I had. At the end of a rather long and exhausting day, one of my fifth grade teachers came by to share the results of her recent reading assessment. The online assessment provides an overall reading indicator as well as subindicators for vocabulary, fiction, non-fiction, and long passages. In just a few short months, the teacher shared her students' vocabulary scores had increased dramatically. Her excitement was inspirational and I found myself reviewing the data for all of our students, considering the many ways I could share that data with others. I realize now that I have multiple frameworks from which to operate. I can present that vocabulary data to build collective efficacy, by encouraging dialogue about how and why that success was realized. I can review that vocabulary data to challenge deficit thinking, by identifying students in the different subgroups and sharing their achievement data. I can ask others to share their success stories with vocabulary. Looking back, and forward, I realize that my own sense of agency has been strengthened as I have grounded myself in transformative leadership. The question is no longer "Should I serve as a transformative leader?" but rather, "How can I better serve as transformative leader?" To answer that question, I continue to rely on theoretical constructs, such as collective efficacy and deficit thinking, to inform and guide my efforts.

Throughout the years, the questions I have asked and been asked have changed based on my research, my experiences, and our collective experiences as a school. The questions no longer revolve around who is meeting state standards; they have evolved into a critique over who is and who is not exceeding state standards. There are, of course, times when I am not even certain what questions will be raised next. I would like to believe that I capitalize on every opportunity to lead transformatively, but I am not that noble.

I realize that "what is essential is how we ground our approaches, position ourselves, conceptualize the roles, and live our lives in institutional settings" (Shields, 2006, p. 64). In my daily life as an elementary school principal, I am grounded in theories that reject deficit thinking and promote collective efficacy, or organizational agency. As an elementary school principal, I have adopted an agentic perspective and positioned myself as a transformative leader who is willing to live with tension and challenge in order to create schools that are equitable, inclusive, and socially just.

There are times I find myself shrinking from that responsibility, ready to stand aside and stop tilting at windmills. It usually happens on a Monday, with the long week ahead of me, but then I hear the announcement that Community Meeting is beginning and I go to join my community. Every time I walk into the gym and witness 600 students and teachers moving together, dancing and singing, I accept the reality that I still have so much real work to do, because there is so much promise to realize.

References

Bandura, A. (1977). Self-efficacy: Toward a unifying theory of behavioral change. *Psychological Review, 84*(2), 191–215.

Bandura, A. (1986). *Social foundations of thought and action: A social cognitive theory.* Englewood Cliffs, NJ: Prentice-Hall.

Bandura, A. (1993). Perceived self-efficacy in cognitive development and functioning. *Educational Psychologist, 28,* 117–148.

Bandura, A. (1995). On rectifying conceptual ecumenism. In J. E. Maddux (Ed.), *Self-efficacy, adaptation, and adjustment* (pp. 347–376). New York: Springer.

Bandura, A. (1997a). *Self-efficacy: The exercise of control.* New York: W.H. Freeman & Co.

Bandura, A. (1997b). Exercise of personal and collective efficacy in changing societies. In A. Bandura (Ed.), *Self-efficacy in changing societies* (pp. 1–45). Cambridge: Cambridge University Press.

Bandura, A. (2000). Exercise of human agency through collective efficacy. *Current Directions in Psychological Science, 9*(3), 75–78.

Berman, P. Chambliss, D. & Geiser, K.D. (1999). *Making the case for a focus on equity in school reform.* Emeryville, CA: RPP International.

Congero, W. (2007, June). *Examining achievement gaps.* Paper presented at the CCSSO Large-Scale Assessment Conference, Connecticut Department of Education, Nashville, TN.

Cooper, C. (2009). Performing cultural work in demographically changing schools: Implications for expanding transformative leadership frameworks. *Educational Administration Quarterly, 45*(5), 594–724.

Delpit, L. (1995). *Other people's children: Cultural conflict in the classroom.* New York: The New Press.

Education Trust and National Assessment of Progress (2003). Education Watch: Illinois. *Key Education Facts and Figures*: Achievement, Attainment and Opportunity, From Elementary School to College. Edwatch Online Summary Reports. Retrieved 2004, from www.edtrust.org

Education Trust, *EdWatch Online*, 2004 State Summary Reports, www.edtrust.org.

Finnan, C., & Swanson, J. D. (2000). *Accelerating the learning of all students: Cultivating culture change in schools, classrooms, and individuals.* Boulder, CO: Westview Press.

Foster, W. (1986). *Paradigms and promises.* Buffalo, NY: Prometheus.

Freire, P. (1970). *Pedagogy of the oppressed.* Boston: Bergin and Garvey.

Freire, P. (1978). *Education for critical consciousness.* New York: Seabury Press.

Garcia, S., & Guerra, P. (2004). Deconstructing deficit thinking: Working with educators to create more equitable learning environments. *Education and Urban Society, 36*(2), 150–168.

Glanz, J. (2007). On vulnerability and transformative leadership: An imperative for leaders of supervision. *International Journal of Leadership in Education, 10*(2), 115–135.

Goddard, R. D. (2000). *Collective efficacy and student achievement.* Paper presented at the annual meeting of the American Educational Research Association, New Orleans, LA.

Goddard, R. D. (2001). Collective efficacy: A neglected construct in the study of schools and student learning. *Journal of Educational Psychology, 93*(3), 467–476.

Goddard, R. D., Hoy, W. K., & Woolfolk Hoy, A. (2000). Collective efficacy: Its meaning, measure, and impact on student achievement. *American Educational Research Journal, 37*, 479-507.

Goddard, R., Hoy, W., & Woolfolk Hoy, A. (2004). Collective efficacy beliefs: Theoretical developments, empirical evidence and future directions. *Educational Researcher, 33* (3), 3–13.

Goddard R. D., & Skrla, L. (2006). The influence of school social composition on teachers' collective efficacy beliefs. *Educational Administration Quarterly, 42*(2), 216–235.

Hawkins, T. (1984). 'Vote of confidence', Commentary in 'Back Talk'. In R. R. Valencia (Ed.), *Conceptualizing the notion of deficit thinking. The evolution of deficit thinking: Educational thought and practice* (pp. 1–12). London: RoutledgeFalmer.

Herrnstein, R., & Murray, C. (1994). *The bell curve: Intelligence and class structure in American life.* Washington, DC: Free Press.

Illinois State Board of Education (2003). 5-year ISAT test data show mixed results. http://www.isbe.state.il.us/news/2003/jul23–03.htm.

Moore, W., & Esselman, M. (1994, April). *Exploring the context of teacher efficacy: The role of achievement and climate.* Paper presented at the annual meeting of the American Educational Research Association, New Orleans, LA.

Quantz, R. A., Rogers, J., & Dantley, M. (1991). Rethinking transformative leadership: Toward democratic reform of schools. *Journal of Education, 173*(3), 96–118.

Ryan, W. (1971). *Blaming the victim.* New York: Random House, Inc.

Sandel, K., & Batchu, B. (2005). *The gap persists: Closing Illinois' achievement divide.* A+ Illinois. Retrieved 2008 from http://www.aplusillinois.org

Shields, C. M. (2006). Creating spaces for value-based conversations: The role of school leaders in the 21st century. *ISEA, 34*(2), 62–81.

Shields, C. M. (2009). *Courageous leadership for transforming schools: Democratizing practice.* Norwood, MA: Christopher-Gordon.

Shields, C. M. (2010). Transformative leadership: Working for equity in diverse contexts. *Educational Administration Quarterly, 46*(4), 558–589.

Shields, C. M., Bishop, R., & Mazawi, A. E. (2005). *Pathologizing practices: The impact of deficit thinking on education.* New York: Peter Lang.

Urrieta, L. (2004). Assistencialism and the politics of high-stakes testing. *The Urban Review, 36*(3), 211–226.

Valencia, R. (1997). *The evolution of deficit thinking: Educational thought and practice.* Washington D.C.: Falmer Press.

Valencia, R. R., & Guadarrama, I. N. (2001). 'High-stakes testing and its impact on social and ethnic minority students. In L.A. Suzuki, L.A., et al (Eds.), *Multicultural assessment: Clinical, psychological, and educational applications* (pp. 561–610). San Francisco, CA: Jossey-Bass.

Valencia, R. & Suzuki, L. (2001). *Intelligence testing and minority students: Foundations, performance factors, and assessment issues.* Thousand Oaks, CA: Sage Publications.

Zehr, M. (2010). Study: States must move faster to close achievement gaps. *Education Week, 30*(15). Retrieved 2010, from www.edweek.org.

16

Transformative Leadership in a Diverse Setting

Iris H. Jun

Historically, educational leadership has largely been associated with structural frames of clasical organizational theory, with a hierarchy of leadership positions and traditional methods of management (Karpinski & Lugg, 2006). According to Weber (2005), bureaucratic structures regulate and govern the activities of a formal organization, such as schools and school districts. Duties of the members of a bureaucracy are clearly delineated, and the assignment of roles is given based on technical qualifications (Weber, 2005)—for instance, district superintendents and school principals. In the case of bureaucratic educational organizations, the traditional idea of an educational leader may encompass acts of decision making, policy forming, curriculum setting, planning structural organizations, and developing teacher management systems (Karpinski & Lugg, 2006). Leadership theories, such as distributive or transactional leadership, therefore, can be applied directly to structures of educational organizations.

Transformative leadership, however, goes beyond traditional notions of educational and organizational leadership theory and introduces a moral, ethical, and democratic component (Sergiovanni, 2006; Shields, 2004). I would say that transformative leadership transcends a simple application of a leadership theory and becomes a philosophy of leadership that can be filtered through and with other forms of leadership theory. The underlying ethical and moral component of transformative leadership requires educational leaders to think about areas of their organization at a different level, beyond just the management—and even simple transformational changes—of structures. The actions and movements engaged by transformative leaders are often, therefore, motivated by social justice and equity (Dantley & Tillman, 2010; Karpinski & Lugg, 2006; Sergiovanni, 2006; Shields, 2004). Transformative leaders identify societal inequities, such as marginalization based on race, culture, religion, and gender, and work to eliminate them from the programs and policies in their schools (Dantley & Tillman, 2010; Karpinski & Lugg, 2006; Shields, 2004). The purpose of the chapter is to provide an example of an application of transformative leadership theory in a diverse high school setting. The chapter will include anecdotes from a case at a suburban high school in the Midwest and argue the need for transformative leadership to address them.

Key Characteristics of Transformative Leadership

Transformative leadership has many characteristics. All of them are deeply rooted in moral and ethical values (Shields, 2004). While researchers (Cambron-McCabe, 2010; Dantley & Tillman, 2010; McKenzie et al., 2008) warn against essentializing transformative leadership, for the purpose of this chapter, I will delineate some characteristics that transformative leaders exhibit in order to illustrate transformative leadership through the anecdotal cases at Northwest High School.

First Characteristic: The Notion of Critique

One characteristic of transformative leadership is the idea of critique. Transformative leadership requires an element of outward critique of educational organizations and systems as well as an introspective look at personal beliefs and areas of deficit thinking (Dantley & Tillman, 2010; McKenzie et al., 2008). Therefore, an outward critical perspective should entail a deep examination of current practices in school settings that perpetuate the marginalization of students (Dantley & Tillman, 2010). Transformative leaders need to spend some time taking an honest look at policies, programs, curriculum, and everyday practices in their schools in order to determine whether they are equitable and promote social justice. In addition, leaders need to look introspectively, to examine underlying beliefs that may not promote equity and social justice. Furman and Gruenewald (2004) stress the importance of transformative leaders to have the ". . . willingness and ability to engage in the political act of analyzing and critiquing the taken-for-granted assumptions of Western society" (p. 65). When leaders take the time to look for situations in their schools that promote the "taken-for-granted assumptions" and acknowledge the areas of their schools that need reforming and redirection, they are practicing one element of transformative leadership.

Starratt (1991) also calls for educational leaders to consider the ethic of critique, the ethic of justice, and the ethic of caring as a tripartite framework for making ethical judgments. While Starratt is careful to warn his readers that the three ethics are not meant to stand alone, I will make the claim that the ethic of critique has direct implications for transformative leadership. Drawing from social theories that came out of the Frankfurt School, Starratt (1991) explains that the ethic of critique uncovers the shortcomings of a bureaucratic system, mainly its failure to carry out values such as equality, the common good, human civil rights, and democratic participation. The ethic of critique requires educational leaders to recognize competing interests and needs of groups and individuals that may be in opposition to each other. In order to do this, especially in a hierarchical system such as schools, leaders must take into consideration the realities of the social arrangements of its constituencies (Starratt, 1991). The challenge for educational leaders is to make social and political arrangements more conducive to having all stakeholders critique and evaluate certain situations. Rethinking the way things have always been and exercising critique will allow all members of the school community to make better, more democratic decisions.

Second Characteristic: Empathy

Related to the notion of critique and having a critical perspective is the idea of empathy. Going back to Starratt's (1991) three-part notion of the ethics in leadership, administrators can draw from the ethic of caring to set a foundation for community building in a school system. First, an ethic of caring can set the cultural tone of the school by creating a sense of community or family (Starratt,

1991). Secondly, an ethic of caring can create solidarity. Solidarity based on trust—mutual trust between administrators, teachers, students, parents, and community members—is the strongest. All parties need to feel sincerity from each other and gain a strong trust in each other. According to Weiner, Freire states that solidarity based on trust will diminish the gap between members of the school's community—including certified (teachers, administrators) and noncertified staff (cooks and maintenance workers), students, parents, and community members—and by doing so will narrow the space of ". . . what is said and what is done" (Weiner, 2003, p. 92). Lastly, I believe an ethic of caring promotes an acceptance of difference. Difference, not for the sake of competition, but for cultural democracy, requires an increase in moral vision—a vision for unity and the acceptance of differences (Giroux & Green, 1995; Shields, 2009).

Moral imagination is tied to the ability to empathize with others whose voices may not have been heard in the past or heard in the present (Johnson, 2001). Moral imagination and moral empathy should be a part of administrators' practice, especially as it relates to students who are marginalized. According to Johnson (2001), moral imagination provides general guidelines of morality that come from an enhanced moral understanding and self-knowledge. Therefore, having a better understanding of morality enables educational leaders to form, not only personal convictions, but convictions that can affect others around them, particularly marginalized groups. Moral imagination happens by refining how notions of right and wrong develop, envisioning new possibilities, and changing the way others are perceived. So rather than focusing on rules of moral law, leaders can use their moral imagination to learn empathy. In other words, moral imagination helps form moral empathy (Johnson, 2001).

Third Characteristic: Schools as Places of Democracy

Another characteristic of transformative leadership I would like to highlight is the notion that schools are places of democracy. A primary goal of public school is honing the intellect of individuals, but this goal must be infused with a notion of democracy, along with ideals of equity and justice (Shields, 2009). If a primary goal is to promote democracy and social justice, administrators need to begin thinking and acting transformatively. Of course, the practical application of transformative leadership will be different depending on the situation, because the idea of democratic schools is a complex one and may not look the same in every public school (Postman, 2001). However, I believe that some of the key elements of democracy and transformative leadership in schools are: education for civic duty and social improvement, opportunities for students to expand and grow personally and collectively, opportunities for participation in society or a community, and inclusion and consideration of the individual and the collective (Shields, 2009). Transformative leadership in a truly democratic school should, therefore, look very different from a technical and mechanistic form of traditional organizational leadership.

In addition to places of academic excellence, leaders who practice transformative leadership view schools as places of democracy (Dantley & Tillman, 2010; Shields, 2004). Quantz, Rogers, and Dantley (1991) state that transformative leadership theory recognizes that schools are arenas of cultural politics and that transformation of schools must come from authority that is based on democracy. Shields (2004) also recognizes the importance of the placement of democratic thinking in leadership. Decision making in schools with transformative leaders involves democratic participation that cannot be established by having a directionless meeting with an open invitation (Shields, 2004, 2009). Rather, democratic participation involves teaching administration, teachers, and even students how to participate, making everyone feel comfortable and safe enough to participate in informed and intelligent gatherings that enable more democratic decision making (Shields, 2004).

Democracy in education involves a citizenship in which members take seriously the responsibility to participate in informed decision making. Decision making requires an inclusive dialogue between all stakeholders. Stakeholders include school community members, other administrators, school leaders, teachers, students, parents, and community members. Pedagogy cannot be omitted from the effects of democracy, as democratic pedagogy is necessary for stakeholders to be educated and taught *how* to participate democratically—a skill that cannot be assumed to be human nature or innate (Dewey, 2001). Many stakeholders in a school system need to learn how to engage more deeply, some need to be empowered through democratic pedagogy, and all need to practice "radical" or "thick" democracy (Barber, 2001; Furman & Shields, 1995; Torres, 1998).

Fourth Characteristic: Dialogue

The final characteristic of transformative leadership I will highlight for the purpose of this chapter is dialogue. Dialogue in an educational democracy should occur at every level, wherever possible. It is an opportunity to open up to the thinking of others (Freire & Macedo, 2000; Sidorkin, 1999). Opening up to the thinking of others does not necessarily mean that it puts all agents at the same level as one another (Freire & Macedo, 2000). It does, however, mean that administrators open lines of communication to all and do not decide on which voices are given priority over others (Sidorkin, 1999). More importantly, all agents of meaningful dialogue ". . . retain their identity . . . actively defend it, and thus grow together" (Freire & Macedo, 2000, p. 248). This type of relationship between agents of meaningful dialogue, as noted before, requires time and patience (Burbules, 1993). Educators themselves cannot be the agents of political change, per se, given the limitations of the social space of a school that assume specific roles and expectations for different members of school community. Instead, the education of students promotes skills for democratic purposes that can result in political change. Essentially the education becomes the agent that encourages students to make political change. The skills involved include critical thinking, informed decision making, and the courage to have open dialogue and speak out against injustices (Shields, 2009). The idea of crossing borders, according to Torres (1998), comes from Paulo Freire's acknowledgment that all students, not just students of color, come from culturally diverse backgrounds. In order for educators to educate for empowerment and not oppression, the act of crossing borders by administrators, teachers, and students is necessary. Essentially, crossing borders means that all three parties take on the roles of teacher and learner and step into the role of other people's experiences, cultural or otherwise. Giroux and Greene (1995) think of border crossing as more than just an experience, but as an opportunity to rethink relations between the dominant and subordinate groups and to think of ways to change negative aspects of that relationship.

Freire critiques much of education that essentially dehumanizes students as a banking system in which teachers can deposit knowledge and information. Torres states that Freire's pedagogy of liberation invites dialogue toward the struggle for liberation. Once again, the practice of true dialogue is seen as a critical component in democratic education, but this time in pedagogy. Dialogic education will lead to citizenship training—teaching students their responsibility and right to practice democracy and promote their common good and well-being (Torres, 1998). Therefore it is crucial to teach students to voice their opinions and to identify the experiences that shape them as people. It is equally crucial for educators and leaders to take into consideration students' opinions and experiences, as they create curriculum and policies on their behalf (Shields, 2004). In doing so, curriculum becomes a way to make sense of student experiences and backgrounds (Shields, 2009). In addition, an educational leader who has an ethic of justice in mind will encourage instructors to incorporate specific ethical learning activities, not only within classroom curriculum but within extracurricular programs as well (Starratt, 1991).

Dialogue "as a way of being" (Shields, 2004, p. 115) means educational leaders and teachers must always be in relation to and with one another and have opportunities to deeply understand and know each other (Shields, 2004). In an educational setting where ontological dialogue exists, leaders should provide settings, or "positive spaces" (Shields, 2004, p. 116), where participants seek agreement or understanding of different perspectives (Shields, 2004, 2009). Shields (2004) claims that when administrators and teachers cannot have meaningful dialogue in safe, positive spaces to discuss differences and develop strong relationships, schools fall into pathologies of silence. "Pathologies are misguided attempts to act justly, to display empathy, and to create democratic and optimistic educational communities" (Shields, 2004, p. 117). Pathologies occur when administrators, leaders, teachers, students, and parents cannot have conversations that lead to trust and, in turn, lead to genuine understanding of each other (Shields, 2004, 2009). If school leaders want to transform their schools to be places of academic and educational excellence, administrators need to help teachers overcome these pathologies of silence and provide safe spaces for students to come with their lived experiences, without fear of marginalization (Shields, 2004, 2009). Therefore, dialogue—among educational leaders and teachers, between teachers and teachers, and teachers and students—is critical to transformative leadership.

The remainder of the chapter will first present an overview of Northwest High School and then analyze some situations where the key elements of transformative leadership summarized in this section could have been helpfully applied. The name of the school and all subsequent names of administrators and teachers are pseudonyms.

Northwest High School and Suburban Township High School District AAA

Located in a large suburb in the Midwest, Northwest High School (NWHS) is one of five high schools in Suburban Township High School District AAA. The district serves about 13,000 students in four major suburban towns, and portions of seven neighboring communities. All five high schools are nationally recognized Blue Ribbon Schools of Excellence by the United States Department of Education. At the same time, paradoxically, not all five schools have made adequate yearly progress, and some are in the process of restructuring. The demographics of NWHS rapidly changed in the 1980s and 90s, and the minority subgroups have steadily increased in the last 15 years. For the purpose of the No Child Left Behind legislation, NWHS has students in the following subgroups: White, Black, Hispanic, Asian/Pacific Islander, Multiracial/Ethnic, Limited English Proficient (LEP), Students with Disabilities, and Economically Disadvantaged. The achievement gap between minority groups (Black and Hispanic) and the White and Asian populations can stretch over 50% in reading and writing on the state standardized test. The gap between students with disabilities and whites and Asians is higher, although not by much, compared to the Hispanic populations, and the gap between LEP students and whites and Asians is the greatest, with a 75% difference in reading and over 60% in mathematics.

The disparities in achievement led administrators and teachers to develop an overwhelming number of new initiatives and programs to target the subgroups and help those students achieve higher. Initiatives and programs included summer academies for incoming freshmen, sophomores, and all English Language Learners (ELLs), double period math and English classes for "bubble students" who, through initial tests were projected to score right below standard, math and English tutoring centers, all-academic tutoring centers, and behavioral management programs. The initiatives and programs were all well intended and came from a motive to help students achieve higher, but all of them, unknowingly by staff and administrators, operated from deficit thinking.

Organizationally, the five-school district is highly bureaucratic and hierarchical, purely because of its size and volume. The centrally located MacFarland Administration Center houses the superintendent, Dr. Rona Newberry, and her cabinet. Each high school building has a principal, four assistant principals, and two directors, the athletic director, and the director of student services. In addition to this administrative team, each principal has a leadership team of department chairs, which acts as an advisory board to the principal regarding building issues and management, but mostly on curricular and instructional matters. Department chairs must hold an administrative certificate, but are not considered full-time administrators because they also teach a minimum of two classes. Often the line of communication comes from Dr. Newberry, in conjunction with the district's board of education, to the principals, to the administrative teams, to the department chairs, and then to the teachers. Meetings occur weekly, district-wide and by building, to disseminate information, and things run smoothly for the most part. Directives usually come from the superintendent and her cabinet, with much deliberation and council from building principals, assistant principals, directors, and district department chairs. While the many directives may come from the district level, buildings have the autonomy to apply them as they see fit for their population and culture. The organization of the district is important to note, as it follows the technical notions of educational leadership and organization described above. In addition, leadership and organizational theory can be applied by a variety of members of the district and school, from principals to administrators and department chairs.

The Need for Transformative Leadership at Northwest High School

For the remainder of the chapter, I will focus on a variety of anecdotal cases at Northwest High School specifically, and how different levels of administrators and leaders can enact transformative leadership. I believe transformative leadership can be practiced at all levels because the notion transcends the other types of leadership theory. The examples given here will examine the behaviors of the building leaders, from the principal, Dr. Scott Green, assistant principals, and directors to department chairs and other teacher-leaders.

Three out of the four assistant principals in the building, along with the dean, primarily deal with the discipline matters of the school. They manage referrals, which range from small infractions, such as repeated insubordination or disruptions in classrooms, to more serious offenses, such as fighting and gang representation or recruiting in the building. The assistant principals work closely with counselors to develop plans of service for and with students who repeatedly get referred to the office. Sometimes they work with the resident police consultant, especially with regards to truancy tickets and gang-related issues. The assistant principals at NWHS are Ms. Jackson, Mr. Kim, and Mr. Mizetti; the dean for the school year is Mr. Chartwell; and the police consultant is Officer Ortiz. The director of student services, Dr. Richard Feldman, oversees the guidance department, and other student service-related staff, such as the school nurses, psychologists, and social workers. As described earlier, department chairs head their subject-related departments and serve on the leadership team with the principal and the administrative team. Department chairs are regarded by the administrators and teachers as experts in their fields, and manage the teachers in areas of curriculum and instruction. In addition, chairs of the larger departments often enlist the help of teacher-leaders to carry out a variety of initiatives and programs.

Because transformative leadership theory carries undertones of a philosophy and a way of thinking, leaders at any level, from teacher-leaders to principals, can portray the four elements outlined earlier. The examples given here will discuss how transformative approaches might make a difference for equitable treatment and more socially just outcomes for marginalized students and families in the community.

Metal Detectors at the Cinco de Mayo Celebration

Due to an increasing number of Spanish-speaking students, the district hired Manuel Sanchez as its Spanish-speaking social worker 15 years ago. Since then, Mr. Sanchez has worked tirelessly as an advocate for students and their families. He also cosponsors the Cultural Awareness Club with Eric Carpenter, a guidance counselor. Among other things, the club organizes the annual Cinco de Mayo celebration, a combination of food, entertainment, and dancing. The event has brought members of the Hispanic community into the school building and has created a sense of belonging for families. Over the years, unfortunately, there have been incidents that make it difficult for the administration to fully support the event. Vandalism, gang representation, people from other communities causing disruptions, and the outbreak of fights caused the administration to work with Mr. Sanchez and Mr. Carpenter and the club to make some changes to the evening, including having ticket sales, closing doors after 8:00 pm, changing the venue, increasing police security, and restricting from the event students with a discipline record related to gang activity.

One year, during the week of the event, Manny Gonzalez, a student known to be affiliated with the Latin Kings, but who did not have gang representation on his discipline record, came in to see Mr. Kim in the discipline office. Manny was visibly upset about something, but Mr. Kim was not in his office, so his secretary gave Manny some paper to write him a note. The note indicated Manny's concern about a rumor that a rival gang from another town was planning on bringing guns to the Cinco de Mayo party at NWHS. Manny was seriously considering not attending this event and asked the administration to think about canceling it. The note prompted Mr. Kim to call Manny down to the office from class, where he took the time to get more of the story. Manny admitted that he felt less certain about his claims now, but that he still felt the administration should consider doing something about the threat. Mr. Kim called an emergency meeting with the rest of the assistant principals, the principal, the police consultant, and the director of student services to decide on what to do about the Cinco de Mayo celebration that year. They also brought in Mr. Sanchez and Mr. Carpenter to make them aware of the situation and get their input. Dr. Green's first response was to suggest canceling the event altogether. The others hesitated supporting this idea, and considered other options, including shortening the event, bringing in heavier police presence, restricting the event to students only, and lastly, getting the advice of the district office. Dr. Newberry, the superintendent, suggested using the portable metal detector that the district had recently purchased. In the end, the group decided to use the portable metal detector and to bring in more police, including plain-clothed and uniformed officers.

Later that week, Dr. Green started the leadership meeting with highlights of the week. He continued with other announcements from the Administrative Council meetings that occur weekly at the district office with other school principals and the superintendent. In between two relatively insignificant announcements, Dr. Green announced that the district would utilize its portable metal detectors at the Cinco de Mayo celebration at NWHS that year. The quick announcement caused a couple of chairs to turn heads and talk amongst each other. Mr. Kirkland, the art department chair, finally interrupted Dr. Green and questioned why the administration had decided to use metal detectors at the Cinco de Mayo event. Dr. Green responded by stating that there was a viable threat and that the metal detectors and stronger police presence would ensure safety at the event. He had originally considered canceling the event, so the use of the metal detectors was, in his opinion, the better option. Many of the other chairs seemed to agree. Ms. Harris tried to explain that the metal detector, since it had never been used before, along with a strong, visible police presence at the event, could cause families to be worried or nervous. One of the other chairs responded, "Wouldn't they feel safer knowing that the police were there to protect them from this threat?" to which Ms. Harris replied, "No, not if they don't understand why the police are there in such force. And considering the climate these days, our Hispanic families don't trust the police and are afraid of local authorities." Dr. Green ended the discussion by stating that the decision had been made final by the superintendent and that there was nothing they could do about it.

Ms. Harris scheduled a meeting with Dr. Green the next day. She expressed her concerns again, and asked him to make an announcement explaining the presence of the police at the start of the event. Dr. Green handed her a prepared letter with an explanation he had written in English. While Ms. Harris appreciated the fact that he thought to write a letter, she had to remind Dr. Green that many of the members of the community could not read or understand a letter in English. She offered to have the letter translated by one of her department members, and then suggested again that he make an announcement with a microphone, with Mr. Sanchez translating at the beginning of the evening. He hesitated but eventually agreed.

Enhancing Communication

This anecdote sheds light on the lived experiences of so many of our minority students—primarily, the gross marginalization that occurs in many schools across the country. In this section, I hope to illustrate the social phenomenon that occurred that evening, and its implications as they relate to transformative leadership. The notion of transformative leadership addresses the marginalization of students, and in this case, community members, and how leaders in schools can redraw the lines of equity and social justice.

In the above case, I believe that Dr. Green and the administrative team could have done more to include others in the decision to use metal detectors. The result may have been the same, but when more stakeholders are involved, it can be a more informed and generally agreed upon decision in the end. Dr. Green could have used the leadership meeting to provide details about Manny's letter, the circumstances surrounding it, and the events leading to consulting the district office. Dr. Newberry, the superintendent of the district, could have also explained her thought process in bringing the portable metal detector. The decision to use it was Dr. Green's decision, and no one on the administrative team could feel they could argue. The relationships in this hierarchy are primarily positional, leaving subordinates forced to accept decisions made by their superiors. This type of relationship is in direct opposition to the notion of democratic decision making that Starratt (1991) promotes in the ethic of critique and is directly opposed to the principles of transformative leadership outlined earlier.

The Need for Dialogue

Dialogue is important for democratic leadership and education (Shields, 2009). It is a concept that is often misunderstood by administrators in a busy climate of accountability. Discussions in a nondemocratic environment often center on an agenda and have a clear and immediate purpose. During leadership meetings, Dr. Green merely makes announcements about items on an agenda. Typically, chairs and other administrators speak if they feel the need to provide the group with more details about an item on the agenda or to highlight positive news about their particular department. Some weeks, an item on the agenda may spark more dialogue or interest from the group, but usually the meetings progress in the same manner week after week. While Dr. Green rarely cuts a discussion short or shows disrespect to his colleagues on the leadership team, the conversation often flows in one direction. The content remains superficial and does not promote democracy. According to Burbules (1993), dialogue is not just the mere act of talking to one another or even *at* one another. He considers dialogue a relation to one another that involves true bonds of respect, trust, and concern and requires patience, commitment, understanding, and a willingness to work through disagreements (Burbules, 1993). Therefore, in order to practice a more democratic form of leadership at NWHS, Dr. Green can conduct his leadership meetings so that it becomes a safe place for discussing deeper issues. The topics on the agenda are not necessarily irrelevant or unnecessary, but the announcements that are simple can be written into the agenda document so that more time can be spent discussing issues or other items on the agenda at a deeper level.

In an educational system arranged hierarchically, such as NWHS, administrators and teachers may feel uncomfortable with the idea of opening lines of communication in such a way that might cause them to lose power. Freire and Macedo (2000) recognize that parents and students do not have the professional expertise to participate in all of the decisions of a school. They do, however, have the right to a genuine line of communication with the school where their voices can be heard and understood. In so many instances, the voices of the Hispanic community at NWHS are muted. In the case of the Cinco de Mayo event, Dr. Green reluctantly agreed to make an announcement about the police presence at the beginning of the night, but this never happened. In addition, parents and students were never invited to ask questions or have an open forum about the particular threat prior to the Cinco de Mayo event.

NWHS has a reputation for its positive climate among staff and students, but it falls very short of the ethic of caring Starratt (1991) describes. It is evident in this case on many occasions. Because the warning about the threat came from a student and was obviously viable, it was understandable for the administration to proceed as they did. However, incidents at past Cinco de Mayo celebrations increased the level of suspicion for police and administration. Suspicion widened the gap between the dominant and the Hispanic communities. In addition, Mr. Sanchez and Ms. Harris and her department had made positive connections with the Hispanic community in the town, but for many parents in that community, their contact with assistant principals had primarily been for discipline and behavioral issues regarding their children.

Using Moral Imagination

The notion of moral imagination—or empathy—is also missing from this example. The administrators and the leadership team at NWHS could have gained more insight into the decision if they had engaged in moral empathy. The entire student body knew about the Cinco de Mayo celebration because of the numerous announcements made throughout the week. The celebration began at 7:00 p.m., as student athletes returned from their games and parents picked their children up from practices. Upon arriving on school grounds, they saw a number of police cars, and the officers in bulletproof vests standing by the entrance of the school. Many students and parents might have wondered why there was such a heavy police presence at the school that evening, until they remembered that the Mexicans were having their Cinco de Mayo dance, further perpetuating the assumptions made by many in the community regarding the local Hispanic community. Moral empathy on the part of the leadership team might have given them some insight into the effects of the negative association of police presence at a Cinco de Mayo dance. Some Latino parents were grateful for the protection, but others might have been confused or intimidated by such a heavy presence at the event. Receiving the translated letter from the principal eased some of their concerns, but many of them did not even know who Dr. Green was or that he was even there at the dance.

Mr. Sanchez and Mr. Carpenter missed the opportunity to use what happened as a teachable moment for the students in the Cultural Awareness Club. Mr. Sanchez and Mr. Carpenter could have taught their students how to practice their critical-thinking skills, and given them the platform to have open dialogue and speak out against the injustices of the decision to use metal detectors with members of their own community. In addition, the skills of how to engage in a democratic society should be embedded within objectives and standards of curriculum across disciplines. Had that been the case at NWHS, students in the Cultural Awareness Club may have already been able to engage in dialogue with their teachers and administrators and fight for their right to voice their concerns.

Transformative leadership in this situation could have resulted in a more equitable, respectful, and less marginalized environment for students, staff, and the community. As seen throughout the example, the principles of empathy, democracy, dialogue, and the ethic of critique were missing. Had leaders taken the time to empathize with the families and community members who had to walk through the metal detectors, they might have stopped the exercise altogether and understood the humiliation and embarrassment. If leaders believed and applied the notion that school should be places of democracy and safe dialogue, a better solution than metal detectors may have been implemented—a solution that would not have further marginalized this particular group of students and members of the community. As one can see from this example, transformative leadership also takes courage—courage to speak out against decisions and actions that discriminate, ever so slightly, and make the changes needed to create a more socially just and equitable environment for all. The same is true in the following situation, generally referred to as the "brown line."

The "Brown Line"

Historically, the suburb in which NWHS is located was homogenous, until the early 1980s. The demographics of the suburb, and subsequently the high school, changed rapidly in the 1990s. In addition to higher numbers of minorities moving into the community and affecting enrollment, there was a higher number of economically disadvantaged students. The school began to see a gang presence and worked forcefully to remove members of gangs from its building. The diversity of the student population became more of a challenge after the No Child Left Behind legislation revealed that there was an achievement gap between the white and Asian subgroups and black, Hispanic, and economically disadvantaged subgroups. Administrators and teachers worked tirelessly to create programs and initiatives to help increase the achievement for all students but in particular the subgroups who were not meeting or exceeding standards. The efforts were made with the best of intentions, but subsequently the school began operating through deficit thinking. The discussion became more about what the students in the black, Hispanic, and economically disadvantaged subgroups could *not* do, what they did *not* come into the building knowing, how they did *not* know how to behave, or did *not* know how to follow the rules and expectations of the school. While the conversations also led to how the school and programs could help the students' achievement, the underlying mentality that the students in the subgroups were also subpar was also prevalent.

The division seemed clear to the students as well. The Advanced Placement (AP) classes followed the trend of the rest of the country, with very few minority students enrolled. Also following the trend, the special education program serviced many minority families and their children. The majority of the students placed in the lower tracked classes were minority students. The discipline office received many referrals for minority students. It became very evident to the student population that the students belonging to the subgroups were "those kids." Never was this more apparent than in the student cafeteria, where groups of students sat in their obvious cliques and the formation of the "brown line" began. Ms. Harris, the English as a Second Language (ESL) department chair, first heard about the "brown line" from Mr. Cervantes, a teacher assistant in the department. Many of the students who are scheduled for half a period in a resource class and the other half in lunch complained to Mr. Cervantes that the lines for lunch were so long that by the time the students got down to the student cafeteria, stood in line to get their lunch, and finally sat at their seats, they only had five minutes left to eat. They also complained that they hated waiting in the "stupid brown line" for the free and reduced priced lunch options and wished they could get their food somewhere else in the cafeteria. Mr. Cervantes decided to bring the situation up with Ms. Harris, since she could make the decision to allow students during lunch periods to leave early. Ms. Harris could not believe that a "brown line" existed and made Mr. Cervantes go to the cafeteria a few times to investigate if what the students said was, in fact, true. Each time, Mr. Cervantes reported back with the same story until, finally, Ms. Harris investigated herself. Sure enough, the "brown line" existed; both students and teachers confirmed its existence—the line where the students who participated in the free or reduced-priced lunch program stood to get their lunch and where the majority of the students who participated in the free or reduced-priced lunch program were brown-skinned.

Upon learning of the "brown line," Ms. Harris approached Dr. Green. Dr. Green spoke with the woman in charge of food service for the school, Ms. Margaret Dillon. She explained that the line existed because it was an option where students could get the entire hot meal for free or at a reduced price. She also explained that students could receive parts of their free and reduced priced meals elsewhere, in fact, in every other line except for one—the only line where hot lunch items were not available. The students on free and reduced-price lunch chose to stay in the "brown line" because it was where they were told to get the hot lunches. Students thought it was the only line option for them and did not think it segregated them. In fact, the design of the cafeteria allowed for a "brown line" to form and exist without any questioning. While not completely satisfied with the explanation of the "brown line," Ms. Harris did not inquire further, and accepted the situation for what it was.

As mentioned earlier in the chapter, an transformative leadership includes the ethic of critique (Starratt, 1991). Examining the taken-for-granted assumptions that take place in schools often takes courage. Ms. Harris's unwillingness to take the matter further until a few years later illustrates where the ethic of critique falls short of its intent. Whether Ms. Harris did not feel there was a safe space to bring her concerns or whether she thought she was told to accept it, this is an example of a pathology of silence (Shields, 2004). Pathologies of silence occur in schools when stakeholders, such as administrators, leaders, teachers, students, and parents, cannot have conversations about areas of inequity and injustice in safe, positive spaces (Shields, 2004). In the case of the "brown line," the investigation only occurred from person to person. In other words, Dr. Green, Ms. Harris, and Mr. Cervantes all did individual investigations on the matter, and had answers, but no real solutions. In fact, no one seemed willing to acknowledge the existence of the "brown line" or do anything to abolish it.

Overcoming Marginalization

The "brown line" at NWHS quintessentially exemplifies, almost literally, the marginalization of minority groups, such as those who are economically disadvantaged. A transformative leader, whether it was the department chair, Ms. Harris, Dr. Green, or even Mr. Cervantes, would have first seen the situation and have had the courage to speak out against it, which I believe Mr. Cervantes did. In terms of dialogue, and the notion of schools being a place of democracy, again the elements are missing. There was no doubt that Dr. Green wanted to rectify the situation, but he wanted to do it with little fanfare, which is understandable. Therefore, he did not mention the situation to the rest of the leadership team, since it was not an item on the agenda of a leadership team meeting, nor did he address or make it known to his administrative team. Instead, he spoke to the cafeteria staff and quickly got the answers to help Ms. Harris and Mr. Cervantes. Discussion was not held to help students make choices that would protect their identity as students who were economically disadvantaged. In terms of dialogue and places of democracy, the other leaders in the building were not even aware of the situation and did not have the opportunity to share ideas to remedy the situation or to even help communicate and educate the students on how to receive their free or reduced-priced lunches without stigma.

Reflections on the Brown Line

The "brown line" shows clearly, as did the incident at the Cinco de Mayo celebration, the need for leaders who will take time to listen to others, to communicate about marginalizing and oppressive situations, and who will courageously challenge them. Once again, dialogue with the (dis)affected students and their situation is called for. Once again, moral imagination—administrators putting themselves in the place of these students, understanding the messages they are sending, the message that these students are second-class citizens and do not require positive attention—cannot be over-estimated. Transformative leaders who recognize the importance of relationships and inclusive learning environments would challenge inequitable practices, work to deconstruct excuses, and to implement new ways of thinking about the lunch line. Instead, in this case, the "brown line" was permitted to persist, while leaders failed to take the requisite action in a more thorough fashion. The deficit thinking that continues to marginalize "brown" students is shown once again in the incident below.

Committing to the Mustangs, Committing to Social Justice

"Commit to the Mustangs" (CTTM) is a building-wide program that uses positive behavior incentives to reconnect with school policies and to communicate the expectations of behavior across the school—students and staff and faculty alike, including hall supervisors and paraprofessionals. Rather than focusing on the negative behavior, the adults affirm positive behavior and highlight positive behavior. The type of deficit thinking slowly disappears when the entire student body is addressed and everyone is on the same page in terms of behavioral expectations.

In addition, students and teachers created "The Mustang Promise" in response to the bullying and negative behavior often associated with extremely violent incidents, such as what occurred at Columbine High School in Columbine, Colorado in 1999. Students and teachers modeled the program after "Rachel's Challenge," which is a national program named after Rachel Scott, the first victim shot and killed in the incident. While the programs in and of themselves do not directly affect the marginalized, or use the language of social justice or transformative leadership, they do, however, provide the platform for discussion on issues related to social justice. For example, one of the lessons of the Mustang Promise used the documentary, *Invisible Children*. In the past, the school may have responded to crisis situations around the world by merely sponsoring a food drive or raising money through class competitions but never had discussions about the lives of people all over the world, which may be very different than that in the suburbs. This time, however, the school had discussions in all classrooms that sparked an awareness of students in other countries, such as the "invisible children" of Uganda. Students saw the trailer for the documentary during the period, and the committee for the Mustang Promise showed the documentary during lunch hours.

A few years ago, students came up with the idea of "Mix It Up" to shuffle students around in the student cafeteria and encourage students to take the opportunity to talk to those with whom they did not normally talk or eat. "Lunchapalooza" evolved from the Mix It Up lunch concept, with the goal that by the end of the three-day event, students would feel more comfortable with each other, not only in the cafeteria, but also throughout the building. It evolved to be a celebration of students and the year's promises and lessons. The year the Mustang Promise introduced *Invisible Children*, the first day of Lunchapalooza was a huge success. The school collected thousands of books during the drive and continued to raise awareness on the atrocities young Ugandans face every day. The other days of the event, students celebrated through several different musical acts.

The committee for the Mustang Promise consisted of department chairs, teachers, and students, and since the inception of the idea to have a program to address bullying and violence, it has been student led and driven. What began as a response to bullying and negative behavior in the high school became a platform for the school to also address other issues of social justice. The long-term effects of what students might have engaged in or learned during the presentation of the documentary, or the discussions that occurred in the classrooms as a result of that, will never be known. What can be known is that students were educated on the circumstances in Uganda, and they were taught about the wretched conditions, which drove them to implement a book drive. The students learned enough, to be able to make educated decisions about how to respond civically as as members of the world community but did not reach their home community. The discussion allows for democratic pedagogy and democratic leadership for social justice. Other topics related to the Mustang Promise and CTTM opened the lines of communication regarding the conditions of potentially marginalized groups of students, such as bisexual, gay, lesbian, transgender, and questioning students, who often tend to be bullied.

Potential Contributions of Transformative Leadership

Transformative leaders have two components of student learning in mind. The first issue principals need to consider is whether or not current practices for student learning cover strong academic content, critical and higher order thinking, and diversity (Kose, 2009). Transformative leaders provide teachers and administrators the professional development needed to train and help those teachers evolve their lessons and instruction so as to increase rigor in classes. The second concerns the alignment of ". . . academics and multicultural, justice-oriented content in preparing all students for an increasingly diverse, complex, and globally interconnected society" (Johnson & Uline, 2005; Kose, 2009). Kose thus shifts the previous notion of socially just teaching to socially just *learning* for teachers and students. Therefore, transformative leaders can decrease marginalization through professional development programs that include topics about cultural and social diversity (Kose, 2007, 2009). As a result, transformative leadership can open the lines of dialogue about issues that may otherwise be divisive or cause tension.

The literature on transformative leaders indicates that, as a result of their efforts, student and staff learning increases and cultural capacity grows (Kose, 2007, 2009; Shields, 2004; Theoharis, 2007). Cultural capital helps in bringing about moral empathy and an element of the ethic of critique, which can bring about social justice and equity in the school. Principals who help enhance student learning through the enhancement of staff learning help to create good teaching, successful instructional experiences, and a positive climate for all students—in particular, previously marginalized students. Enhancement of staff learning comes through staff development efforts in areas of diversity, such as culturally responsive teaching, building relationships with the community and parents, understanding students from culturally and linguistically diverse backgrounds, and lesbian, gay, bisexual, transgender, and questioning (LGBTQ) students (Scheurich & Skrla, 2003; Shields, 2004).

In addition to increasing teacher awareness of issues related to diversity in schools, administrators and teachers need to increase their self-awareness of attitudes and assumptive beliefs they hold about students from diverse backgrounds and interests (Kose, 2007; Scheurich & Skrla, 2003; Shields, 2004). This addressing of attitudes by transformative leaders creates about the ability to confront "taken-for-granted" assumptions in order to look at areas in schools that can be changed (Shields, 2004). Staff and professional development are the correct avenues of increasing awareness at both levels. Human resources departments have the responsibility of searching for and creating time for administrators and teachers to address these issues, as ongoing professional development programs emphasize the need for teachers to have the space to collaborate, team teach, interact, and educate each other (Shields, 2004). Coordinated efforts in transformative leadership and professional development, therefore, must exist for teachers and administrators to gain more self-awareness and outer awareness of diversity in culture, beliefs, and practices, which, in turn, leads to a more positive environment for students of a diverse background. This self-awareness and outer awareness of diversity can occur through dialogue. Dialogue, as Shields (2004) stated, requires time, patience, trust, and effort.

Conclusion

Educational leaders practicing transformative leadership have a commitment to go beyond traditional notions of democracy and, instead, promote a radical application of democracy in their schools. Democratic schools practice deep, meaningful dialogue with all members of the school community. Educational leaders cannot distance themselves from others in a democratic environment. It is a commitment to a ". . . truth that depends on a multiplicity of different voices" (Sidorkin, 1999, p. 63). Closely tied to dialogue is the practice of democratic decision making. Using moral empathy and trying to understand others, in addition to open dialogue, significantly changes the way educational leaders make decisions for their schools. Developing trust among all stakeholders, promoting "democratic faith . . . grounded on a lucid understanding of the weaknesses . . . people are capable of . . ." (Lummis, 2001, p. 43), and fostering solidarity are all ways to incorporate community in a democratic school.

Democratic education changes the way schools create curriculum for their students. Democratizing pedagogy will prepare students to addresses social issues and injustices and engage in social justice work (Shields, 2009; Westheimer & Kahne, 2004). Curriculum will teach children how to think critically, form opinions, make decisions based on those opinions, and voice them to raise the critical consciousness of those around them (Shields, 2009). Through these four important areas of practice, educational transformative leaders can promote democratic education within their schools aimed ". . . at the empowerment of free and equal citizens, people who are willing and able to share together in shaping their own society" (Gutman, 2001, p. 229).

References

Barber, B. R. (2001). An aristocracy of everyone. In S. J. Goodlad (Ed.), *The last best hope: A democracy reader* (pp. 11–23). San Francisco, CA: Jossey-Bass/A Wiley Company.

Burbules, N. C. (1993). *Dialogue in teaching*. New York: Teachers College Press.

Cambron-McCabe, N. (2010). Preparation and development of school leaders: Implications for social justice policies. In C. Marshall & M. Oliva (Eds.), *Leadership for social justice: Making revolutions in education* (pp. 35–52). Boston, MA: Allyn & Bacon.

Dantley, M. E., & Tillman, L. C. (2010). Social justice and moral transformative leadership. In C. Marshall & M. Oliva (Eds.), *Leadership for social justice: Making revolutions in education* (pp. 19–34). Boston, MA: Allyn & Bacon.

Dewey, J. (2001). Democracy and human nature. In S. J. Goodlad (Ed.), *The last best hope: A democracy reader* (pp. 159–175). San Francisco, CA: Jossey-Bass/A Wiley Company.

Freire, A. M. A., & Macedo, D. (Eds.). (2000). *The Paulo Freire reader*. New York: Continuum.

Furman, G. C., & Gruenewald, D. A. (2004). Expanding the landscape of social justice: A critical ecological analysis. *Educational Administration Quarterly, 40*(1), 47–76.

Furman, G. C., & Shields, C. M. (1995). How can educational leaders promote and support social justice and democratic community in schools? In J. L. Kincheloe & S. R. Steinberg (Eds.), *Thirteen questions* (pp. 119–137). New York: Peter Lang.

Giroux, H. A., & Greene, M. (1995). Educational visions: What are schools for and what should we be doing in the name of education? In J. L. Kincheloe & S. R. Steinberg (Eds.), *Thirteen questions* (pp. 295–302). New York: Peter Lang.

Gutman, A. (2001). Democratic education in difficult times. In S. J. Goodlad (Ed.), *The last best hope: A democracy reader* (pp. 216–230). San Francisco, CA: Jossey-Bass/A Wiley Company.

Johnson, J. F., & Uline, C. L. (2005). Preparing educational leaders to close achievement gaps. *Theory into Practice, 44*(1), 45–52.

Johnson, M. (2001). Moral imagination. In S. J. Goodlad (Ed.), *The last best hope: A democracy reader* (pp. 194–203). San Francisco, CA: Jossey-Bass/A Wiley Company.

Karpinski, C. F. & Lugg, C. A. (2006). Social justice and educational administration: Mutually exclusive? *Journal of Educational Administration. 44*(3), 278–292.

Kose, B. W. (2007). Principal leadership for social justice: Uncovering the content of teacher professional development. *Journal of School Leadership, 17*(3), 276–312.

Kose, B. W. (2009). The principal's role in professional development for social justice: An empirically-based transformative framework. *Urban Education, 44*(6), 628–663.

Lummis, C. D. (2001). The democratic virtues. In S. J. Goodlad (Ed.), *The last best hope: A democracy reader* (pp. 33–48). San Francisco, CA: Jossey-Bass/A Wiley Company.

McKenzie, K. B., Christman, D. E., Hernandez, F., Fierro, E., Capper, C. A., Dantley, M., Gonzalez, M. L., Cambron-McCabe, N., & Scheurich, J. J. (2008). From the field: A proposal for educating leaders for social justice. *Educational Administration Quarterly 44*(1), 111–138.

Postman, N. (2001). Democracy. In S. J. Goodlad (Ed.), *The last best hope: A democracy reader* (pp. 3–10). San Francisco, CA: Jossey-Bass/A Wiley Company.

Quantz, R. A., Rogers, J., & Dantley, M. (1991). Rethinking transformative leadership: Toward democratic reform of schools. *Journal of Education, 173*(3), 96–118.

Scheurich, J. J. & Skrla, L. (2003). *Leadership for equity and excellence: Creating high-achievement classrooms, schools, and districts*. Thousand Oaks, CA: Corwin Press.

Sergiovanni, T. J. (2006). Adding value to leadership gets extraordinary results. In T. J. Sergiovanni, *Rethinking leadership: A collection of articles* (2d. ed., pp. 65–71. Thousand Oaks, CA: Sage Publications.

Shields, C. M. (2004). Dialogic leadership for social justice: Overcoming pathologies of silence. *Educational Administrative Quarterly, 40*(1), 109–132.

Shields, C. M. (2009). Introduction. In C. M. Shields, *Courageous leadership for transforming schools: democratizing practice* (pp. 1–14). Norwood, MA: Christopher-Gordon.

Sidorkin, A. M. (1999). *Beyond discourse*. Buffalo, NY: SUNY Press.

Starratt, R. J. (1991). Building an ethical school: A theory for practice in educational leadership. *Educational Administration Quarterly, 27*(2), 185–202.

Theoharis, G. (2007). Social justice educational leaders and resistance: Toward a theory of social justice leadership. *Educational Administration Quarterly, 43*(2), 221–258.

Torres, C. A. (1998). *Democracy, education, multiculturalism*. Lanham, MD: Rowman & Littlefield.

Weber, M. (2005/1922). Bureaucracy. In J. M. Shafritz, J. S. Ott, & Y. S. Jang (Eds.), *Classics of organizational theory* (6th ed., pp. 73–78). Florence, KY: Wadsworth Publishing.

Weiner, E. J. (2003). Secretary Paulo Freire and the democratization of power: Toward a theory of transformative leadership. *Educational Philosophy and Theory, 35*(1), 89–102.

Westheimer, J., & Kahne, J. (2004). What kind of citizen? The politics of educating for democracy. *American Education Research Journal, 41*(2), 237–269.

17

Northern Lights and Shooting Stars

Observing Educational Leaders in the North

Claire Lapointe[1]

In August 1999, *National Geographic* published a special issue on the vanishing cultures of the world and the precarious and rather alarming situation of the global linguistic heritage. In the issue, Canadian anthropologist Wade Davies explained how, every year, dozens of native languages disappear and compared this phenomenon to the extinction of animal or vegetal species. According to Davies, the impoverishment of the world's diverse linguistic heritage is as menacing to humankind as the disappearance of natural biodiversity.

The reason why anthropologists are so preoccupied with this issue is because language is the fundamental support of a people's culture. When a language disappears, it is the particular *weltanschauung*, or vision of the world, of a people that vanishes, little by little. Another disturbing effect of language loss is the diminished cultural diversity present around us, and our subsequent narrowed capacity for comprehensive and rich analysis and interpretation of social and natural life. This shrinkage of world visions results in the emergence of an ever more homogenous and limiting cultural system, which, in turn, can generate intolerance, even totalitarianism. According to Davies (1999, 2009), cultural diversity prevents humankind from wearing blinkers and widens its view on the world, thus protecting it from socially menacing prejudice.

From this perspective, it becomes obvious that, by protecting world minority languages and cultures, we are in fact protecting humanity itself, and that majority linguistic groups should not consider the loss of a language as a problem for the people whose language it is but, rather, as an issue which directly affects all of us. Such an understanding of this problem calls for solutions that will ensure the protection of endangered languages and cultures. In this chapter, I will discuss the important role schools—and school leaders—play in the protection of endangered languages and cultures and share some of the results of a recently completed research project. This project deals with the very meaning of educational leadership in a culture in which the language is endangered:

the Inuit culture. But, before describing the context of the research project, I want to first explain why I used a transformative leadership framework for the analysis.

Recent studies have led to the identification of a form of leadership that is rooted in a vision of social justice, equity, and action for emancipation (Quantz, Rogers & Dantley, 1991; Shields, 2010; Weiner, 2003). Such a vision is required of principals who want to encourage school practices and structures that can effectively protect and help maintain endangered languages and cultures. According to Shields (2010):

> Transformative leadership begins with questions of justice and democracy; it critiques inequitable practices and offers the promise not only of greater individual achievement but of a better life lived in common with others. (p. 559)

Transformative leaders are profoundly aware of and take into account issues of power and privilege, inequity, and patterns of discrimination in greater society. They engage in emancipatory leadership practices in order to transform both the culture and the structure of their schools. In order to do so, transformative leaders first engage in a critical analysis of their school context and uncover formal and informal ways things are being done that are detrimental to the promotion of educational and social equity. Subsequently, transformative leaders must take action and strategically endeavour to transform school practices, striving to bring about greater justice and tangible results for the disadvantaged groups, both in their schools and in society in general. Furthermore, transformative leadership is firmly rooted in the ethic of critique and can, therefore, be closely associated with ethical leadership (Starratt, 1991; Langlois, 1997, 2004; Langlois & Starratt, 2001). Studies I have conducted since 2000 on the role school leaders play in linguistic minority settings have led me to conclude that school principals who possess this vision can initiate authentic, long-lasting, and effective transformations, which, in turn, help protect and maintain endangered languages and cultures.

Schools as Agents of Socialization and Protectors of Languages

Before discussing the role schools play in helping to protect endangered languages and cultures, and in promoting not only their survival, but their prosperity, it is important—given today's complex and very diverse demographic reality—to first clarify the concept of linguistic minority, as understood in my field of research (Bishop & Glynn, 1998; Burnaby & MacKenzie, 2001; De Klerk, 2000; Hoffmann, 2000; Lapointe, 2003; Lasagabaster, 2001; Tacelosky, 2001).

By linguistic minority, I refer to ethnolinguistic groups that are among the original or first inhabitants of a country, region, or state, and are usually identified as official or regional linguistic and cultural minorities. Examples of such groups in Europe are Corsicans, Alsatians, and Bretons (France); and Catalonians, Basques, and Galicians (Spain). In New Zealand, there are the Maoris and, in Australia, the Aborigines. Inuit, First Nations, and French-Canadians are recognized minority groups in Canada who have specific rights and privileges enshrined in the constitution. This sets them apart from other groups of linguistic minorities who have more recently migrated from their home countries to a new one, and about whom a distinct and sometimes complementary field of research exists.

According to Allardt (1984), a linguistic minority group, as defined here, can be identified using four criteria: it possesses a language different from that of the majority group or groups, and it has a common ancestry, distinct cultural features, and a strong social organisation. A number of factors are closely linked to the survival of minority languages (Davies, 1999; Landry & Allard,

1998), including fluency level and the degree to which the language is regularly spoken at home, in the minority community and in the larger social environment as well as the level of social organisation of the minority group and the political and legal power wielded by its institutions. According to Landry and Allard who have studied a number of linguistic minority groups in different parts of the world (see among others Allard & Landry, 1994, 1998; Allard, Landry & Bourhis, 1997; Landry, 1994; Landry & Allard, 1994a, 1994b ; Landry, Allard & Henry, 1996; Landry & Bourhis, 1997; Magord, Landry & Allard, 1994), the socialization process of children and the degree of ethnolinguistic vitality of their community are at the core of the dynamics which link these survival factors.

Given the decreasing influence of traditional sources of socialisation, such as the family and religious institutions, schools have become the principal agents in the socialisation process of children. That is why governments, in different parts of the world, have enlarged their mandate in order to include the protection and revitalisation of endangered minority languages (Lapointe, Godin, & Langlois, 2005). It is important to keep in mind the fact that languages don't have rights, people do (Foucher, 2002). This is why the mandate given to schools in official or regional linguistic minority settings "is to contribute to the sense of identity, security and dignity of minority-language children and youth, which constitute fundamental human rights" (Langlois & Lapointe 2007, p. 243).

What Does It Mean to Be an Educational Leader in a Linguistic Minority School?

In the context just described, it is obvious that schools and school leaders have a very unique mandate, given the fact that, besides delivering regular educational services, they must also find ways to provide the kind of environment in which a rich linguistic and cultural socialisation in the mother tongue is cultivated (Lapointe, 2002). My personal experience as a scholar and educator in an official linguistic-minority setting in Canada has led me to initiate a research program on the meaning of educational leadership in these contexts. Through my research, I wanted to find answers to the following questions: What is the particular story of these leaders? Are there new dimensions that their experiences add to current models on educational leadership? Are they challenged by the formidable task of trying to bring about more social justice and equity for their students and their community?

First, between 2002 and 2005, a study was conducted in several French-language-minority settings across Canada (Langlois & Lapointe, 2007; Lapointe & Langlois, 2004, 2005), followed by a second study, between 2005 and 2009, in an Inuit context (Lapointe, Langlois, & Montpetit, 2010). In this chapter, I will share some of the results from this second study and reflect on the presence of transformative leadership in Inuit schools.

The Challenge of Social Justice in Canada's First Nations and Inuit Education

In the early 1970s, the National Indian Brotherhood of Canada (NIBC), subsequently the Assembly of First Nations, identified education as a fundamental issue in leading to their full autonomy. In a document entitled *Indian Control of Indian Education* (1972), also known as the *Red Paper*, the NIBC described how former education policies put in place by the Canadian government had not only failed, they had been profoundly detrimental to the well-being of First Nations children and the development of their communities. According to the NIBC:

> Unless a child learns about the forces which shape him: the history of his people, their values and customs, their language, he will never really know himself or his potential as a human being. (. . .)

We want education to provide the setting in which our children can develop the fundamental attitudes and values which have an honoured place in Indian tradition and culture. (1972, p. 9)

Thirty-five years after the adoption of the first education policy written by the First Nations
themselves, Aylward (2007) and Wotherspoon (2006) highlighted some of its accomplishments,
such as the capacity to protect and maintain aboriginal values and still adapt to new socioeconomic
conditions, while Carr-Stewart (2006) observed that the aspirations of the First Nations peoples
had only been partially realized. Like in many other countries, Canada's aboriginal peoples are faced
with major social and economic issues, such as generalized unemployment, drug addiction, domes-
tic violence, high drop-out rates, adult and youth suicide, and teenage pregnancy (Mueller, 2006;
Sarrasin, 1998). Risk factors are so prevalent among youth that the graduation rate of aboriginal
students is by far the lowest in all Canadian provinces, compared to non-aboriginals (Carr-Stewart,
2006; Larose, Bourque, Terrisse, & Kurtness, 2001; Sarrasin, 1998; Wotherspoon, 2006). There
are, however, positive factors, which enhance the interest in and attraction of aboriginal children
and youth to going to school, such as trust-based relationships between students, parents—especially mothers—and school personnel, as well as culturally and linguistically relevant pedagogical
practices (Eriks-Brophy & Crago, 2003; Larose et al., 2001; Spada & Lightbown, 2002).

As research has shown, the quality of both school-family relationships and pedagogical practices depends, to a large extent, on who school principals are and what they do. But what happens
when there are no aboriginal people ready to take on the role of being school principal? Are "white"
principals sufficiently aware of the distinct role aboriginal schools play in promoting an endangered
language and culture? How deep is their understanding of the unique social-justice issues at stake?
How committed are they to equity for aboriginal people? These are some of the questions my
research team and I wanted to look at, as we conducted our study in Nunavik, an Inuit territory
north of the province of Québec.

Nunavik, the Place to Live

Nunavik, which means "the place to live," is a regionally-governed Inuit territory located north of
the 55th parallel, in the province of Québec, in North Eastern Canada. Larger than the state of California, Nunavik has a small population of less than 11,650 people living in 14 villages, accessible
only by plane or by snowmobile in the winter. Ninety percent of the population is Inuit, whose first
language is Inuktitut, and more than half are 25 years old or younger.

The Kativik school district, where the study was conducted, is the only school district in Nunavik. It is responsible for 15 schools, which share facilities with the village community centers. Inuit
directors are in charge of the community centers and non-Inuit principals manage the schools.
Inuktitut and culture courses are taught by Inuit teachers, whereas most other subjects are taught
by non-Inuit staff. The turnover rate among non-Inuit teachers is very high, most of them staying
only for two years.

With regard to language, education is provided in Inuktitut from kindergarten through second
grade, at the end of which parents choose between French or English as a second language. In the
future, as more Inuit teachers are trained, schooling in Inuktitut will be offered up to sixth grade,
which is the last year of elementary schooling in Québec. At the present time, 50% of the teaching
time in third grade is in Inuktitut and the other 50% is in the second language chosen by the parents. From fourth through eleventh grade[2], the introduction rate of the second language is decided
locally by each village Education Committee. In 2007 to 2008, when the research project took
place, 2,335 students attended school in Nunavik, 46% of whom were learning French as their

second language, and 54% English. In 2006, the graduation rate among Inuit students was 20%, compared to 75% for the province of Québec as a whole.

Conducting Our Study

Between January and May 2008, interviews were conducted with nine of the twelve non-Inuit school principals, two women and seven men. While four of the principals had between four and five years of teaching experience in Nunavik prior to becoming principal of an Inuit school, the other five had none, even though regulations stipulate that principals must have had a minimum of five years of teaching experience in Nunavik in order to become school principal. Five of the participants had been principals in Nunavik for about four years, one for two years, and three were in their first year in that position.

The interview guide consisted of a set of open-ended questions, which aimed at identifying the general perception and experience of participants about their role as principals in an Inuit school, their main tasks and responsibilities, the qualities and skills they valued as educational leaders, their relationship with the pupils, the staff, and the Inuit community, and the ethical challenges they encountered. Interviews lasted between 45 minutes and 2 hours. They were tape-recorded and then transcribed in their entirety. The data were analyzed through an iterative process, in which significant testimonies and experiences shared by the participants were highlighted, meaningful words and expressions identified, and their core meaning extracted.

For the purposes of this paper, I will present the results related to two of the questions asked which, in my view, are fundamental with regard to equity and transformative leadership in Nunavik. Firstly, how do non-Inuit school principals refer to the Inuit people, its language, and its culture? Secondly, what do they say about the role of non-Inuits in Inuit schools?

Results

Too Little, Too Late? Discourse of Non-Inuit Principals on the Role They Play in Protecting the Inuit People, Its Culture, and Language

Participant discourse on the role they and their schools play in protecting the Inuit people, its culture, and language can be positioned on a continuum, going from what appears to be a lack of understanding of the issues at stake, to critical reflection on the issues, to socially engaged actions (see Figure 17.1).

Figure 17.1 Continuum of Discourse on Role Played by Non-Inuit Principals on Their Protection of Inuit People, Culture, and Language

No real action taken in the school (P 1 and 8)	Impement culturally adapted practices at school (P 6 & 9)	Structure the school | differently (P 3 & 4)	Are challenged by the major changes they think must take place (P 2 & 7)	Is engaged in major action at school and village level (P 5)

Here are excerpts from Participants 1 (four years in Nunavik [N]) and 8 (seven years in N), whose discourse appears to indicate a lack of sensitivity for and understanding of their role as defenders of an endangered culture and language.

> I try to keep some local colour, to kind of emphasize the cultural aspect. . . . I think it is important for them to stick to their roots. But we have to meet department expectations, to be more and more rigorous, and I can see we are heading in that direction which is a very good thing. (P1)

> [About protecting the language and culture,] I can't say that I've contributed much to it. I do respect it, but I haven't really done anything very specific or directly related to those issues. (P8)

As we can see, the position expressed by these two principals reflects what I call a "folkloric understanding" of the vanishing culture and language issues. It is as though they wear blinders that prevent them from being aware of the unique context where they work and its implications with regard to their role as principals. Such a position can have a rather negative impact on Inuit children and their community because, by its indifference, it prevents the school from playing a key role as an agent of cultural and linguistic socialisation. Fortunately, only two of the nine principals we interviewed appeared to take that position. The seven other principals were all aware of the situation, and their actions varied from school-based transformations to village- or even territory-based endeavours. For instance, Participants 6 (less than one year in N) and 9 (eight years in N) felt that the solution consisted of intervening at the school level through a culturally adapted pedagogy, or in making sure that all communications were done in all three languages spoken at school.

> Any given language reflects people's thoughts. Aboriginal people don't think like Francophones, and Francophones don't think like Anglophones. . . . Above and beyond the culture and Inuktitut courses that children have each day, every year we have at least one day dedicated to the Inuit culture, and we invite elders to speak to the children. The children need to hear their elders when they say that they are losing their language. They must value their own language. It is these young people who are going to keep the language alive. . . . I have come to believe that an aboriginal who has succeeded the best is one who has two cultures, who is completely bicultural, one who is proud of his or her aboriginal culture and who can function, one who is proud that he or she has learned how to function in the white culture. (P6)

> At all our meetings, everything is translated into all three languages: Inuktitut, French, and English. Always, everything that is said. It is very important. Unfortunately, it takes a very long time, but I think it is very important and we must respect it. I hope it is respected all over Nunavik. (P9)

Contrary to the first two principals, Participants 6 and 9 demonstrated a reflective attitude rooted in an ethic of critique, which is fundamental for transformative leaders. They recognized the unique character of each culture present at the school and understood how each of them constitutes a richness, which needs to be protected for the benefit of the whole community. Even though these participants were not Inuit, they felt responsible towards the Inuit students and took action in order to nurture the children's sensitivity to the survival of the Inuit language and culture.

As we see in the following quotes, two other participants (P3, seven years in N; and P4, less than one year in N) were engaged in a deeper reflection upon the future of Inuit culture and language and the role their school had to play in this regard. Furthermore, they seemed to be engaged in a more critical analysis of the provincial school curricula that the Inuit school system must follow, acknowledging the presence of important contradictions between the white school system and the needs of the Inuit people.

> The children have the right to speak Inuktitut in class, even if the teacher doesn't speak it, as long as it is done respectfully. . . . By giving more importance to the culture and the language, I make decisions which I wouldn't have made in the South,[3] or I accept things I wouldn't have accepted. (P3)

> If I go back 50 or 60 years, they were still hunting, fishing, picking berries, and so on. Now, Inuit children have Gameboys, Nintendos . . . . there is the alcohol problem, drugs. I think it is us, white people, who have brought these things with our culture. . . . I decided to change the schedule from 45-minute classes to 75-minute ones, and the Inuit teachers told me: "At last, we'll be able to do something [in the language and culture classes] . . . . With 45 minutes, we didn't have time to do anything right." . . . At the same time, I am caught in a dilemma. If I want kids to graduate, they not only have to learn their mother tongue, but they have to improve their mastery of their second language, plus in many cases even learn a third language. If people in the South had a better understanding of the history here, the culture, why Inuit do things the way they do, and all that, the school calendar probably wouldn't be 190 days long. (P4)

Like Participants 6 and 9, Participants 3 and 4 were engaged in a critical reflection on the particular situation of Inuit schools. However, their reflection went one step further, resulting in unconventional decisions and transformative actions in the school—that is, actions that aimed at taking social justice issues into consideration in order to provide Inuit students with a more equitable and inclusive learning environment.

As we move towards the right of the continuum, we can see that Participants 2 (three years in N) and 7 (less than one year in N) expressed their concerns as well as critically reflected upon the superficial content children were offered with regard to Inuit culture, and the obligation for them to learn two—if not three—languages, when they had difficulties maintaining their own one. These participants questioned what was being done in schools and wondered about how to answer such questions.

> I have the feeling their culture has been lost in religious propaganda. They were brainwashed over the last century, always hearing that things they believed in or had were not beautiful, nothing was any good, everything was dangerous. We, the whites, we scared them. (P2)

> Every year, in grades three, four, and five, then in grades six and seven, they make those damned embroidered mittens with little stars on them and they'll make them next year, too. Is that what you should expect from school? As a people, as a nation, here in the North, what do you really expect from school? . . . What use is it to them to learn French for years on end? I don't know. Is it meeting their needs? I think French is not something they need. Not here in Nunavik. You can do very well with English and Inuktitut. Why do parents want their kids to learn French? For what purpose? Is it just some idea or do they really need it? (P7)

Again, insights shared by Participants 2 and 7 were rooted in an ethic of critique expressed in the way they acknowledged past discriminatory treatments or denounced the inadequacy of curricula with regard to cultural activities and language acquisition. Participant 7, who was French-Canadian and, therefore, himself belonged to a North American linguistic minority, took a very strong stance by asserting that people in Nunavik should not have to learn French, even though they live in the province of Québec, where the official language is French.

Finally, at the far right end of the continuum, Participant 5 (eight years in N) expressed a particularly refined understanding of the situation in which the Inuit find themselves, an understanding which is embedded in a critical reflection upon school practices. He described how, as a school principal, he was engaged in social transformation at the village level, and also at the territorial level in Nunavik.

Inuktitut is a healthy language, but it is a vanishing language. You see, you have 8,000 Inuit on the shores of the Hudson Strait, which is about to become a major sea canal, probably more important than the Panama Canal, in a region that has mines, probably diamonds and hydroelectric resources. So 8,000 Inuits living in 14 small villages. We are trying to avoid cultural genocide! Let's be clear about this! A people whose previous generation was born in igloos and whose current generation lives like young Americans. Elders don't understand the adults, who in turn don't understand the youth and the children. Because the older ones were born in igloos, the adults were deported to schools in the South, and their children are culturally uprooted, even though they live in the North. And they expect the school principal to be able to offer them solutions, to help them see how we will be able to ensure the survival of the Inuit language and culture. With the elders who are disappearing, taking with them an amazing [cultural] treasure trove, which they were not able to transfer to the next generation because they didn't talk to each other. Very often, they don't even speak the same Inuktitut; they don't have the same vocabulary; they don't go hunting or fishing together anymore so they don't share the same language. . . . The village councils are looking for solutions, but the clock is ticking; time is running out very quickly. . . . But they don't see it, they don't know it is happening. So, as school principal, I have to share what I see with them so that they, too, can see what is happening. I have to do something and prepare the children for the challenges that are imminent. (P5)

Of all the participants, this last one appeared to possess the keenest knowledge and understanding of the Inuit school context, expressed both in his description of the past and present social realities and his prospective analysis of the future ahead. Grounded in a critical perspective, he expressed deep concerns for the Inuit people and his desire to act in order to empower students, demonstrating, by so doing, a strong transformative leadership.

Inuits Must Become Principals: The Role of Non-Inuit Principals in Inuit Schools

The different understandings participants had of the role non-Inuit principals should play in Inuit schools can also be represented on a continuum (see Figure 17.2), with, on the left side, the absence of any mention of this question by one participant, and, on the right side, a critical analysis of the issue by four participants, who stressed the urgent need for transformative action, which would enable Inuit people to take complete ownership of their schools.

Figure 17.2 Continuum of Discourse of Non-Inuit Principals on Their Role in Inuit Schools

No mention (P 1)	Non-Inuit need a basic knowledge of language (P 8)	Need to transfer expertise to Inuit (P 9)	Critique imposition of 'white system' on Inuit (P 2 & 3)	Critique presence of non-Inuit principals (P 4, 5, 6 & 7)

It should be noted that the two participants who seemed to have the least critical understanding of the issue were the same two who said that, as school principals, they didn't do anything in particular in order to make sure their school would contribute to the protection of the Inuit language and culture. Participant 1 (four years in N) didn't refer at all to the question of non-Inuit principals, and Participant 8 (seven years in N) expressed a view that if future non-Inuit principals had a basic knowledge of Inuktitut, they would be able to better meet the needs of the school:

> I know it is important to understand those things (Inuit culture, history, language), but I don't understand them well enough to talk much about the issues, to explain things. Is it necessary? I don't think so. I think I do a pretty good job, but sometimes I regret not knowing the language better . . . I didn't think I would stay in the North for so long. . . . However, it is going to become necessary [to speak the language] with the plan to have teaching in Inuktituk in grades four, five, and six. It is going to take however long it takes, but it will happen, and then it won't be just an asset, it will be necessary to have at least a practical knowledge of the language to be able to function as a principal on a daily basis. (P8)

I find it intriguing that, even though these two participants have worked in Nunavik for many years, their understanding of and sensitivity to the challenges facing the Inuit people were very limited. As mentioned by Langlois (2004), in the absence of authentic awareness to ethical issues, it is very unlikely that leaders will engage in ethical action. I believe the same is true of transformative leadership: In the absence of real awareness to social injustice, leaders won't be able to initiate and sustain transformative actions in their school and their community.

Another principal (Participant 9, eight years of experience in Nunavik) described the role of non-Inuit principals as that of experts who have the responsibility to transfer their expertise and to make sure Inuit people make it their own, while learning from them as well. This participant mentioned the fact that he or she will have to leave some day and be replaced by another person, Inuit or not.

> We are here to meet their needs. You have to keep that in mind, because our work can be frustrating; but you have to always remind yourself that you are here for them. Often, the Inuit look up to us, because we have more education, like we are always right . . . like we always know the right way to do things. But when we promote and prioritize cultural and linguistic projects, well, then, they have the expertise and we follow them, we learn from them. . . . And when there is something they don't know, I try to use my experience to help them, to teach them. I try my best. And at some point, someone else will take my place and will do things differently. (P9)

Although Participant 9 appeared to understand how important it was to empower the Inuit community in order to better serve the Inuit students, the participant did not seem to be aware of the major linguistic and cultural challenges that might very well prevent this community surviving as a society of its own, unless Inuit school principals are trained and take leadership of Inuit schools. Comparatively, the next two participants demonstrated such awareness but expressed a certain feeling of powerlessness facing the situation. They criticized the fact that they must follow the rules given to them by the Québec Department of Education, while knowing full well that these rules do not respect Inuit culture and education:

> Don't forget that we are tourists here. . . . Unfortunately, and I say unfortunately with a fair degree of certitude, we are going way too fast . . . the Education Department's policies will fail. I believe there is pressure to accelerate the process of integration. The damn provincial high school exams, the damn tests are the same ones used in the South . . . We have not given ourselves enough time to accompany these people . . . we'd need another 10 to 15 years. (P2)

> It means, and I don't want to sound racist here, that we're trying to make a "white people's" system work in a culture which is not a white culture. Sometimes, you are seen as the person who upholds this system, by the kids, the parents or by the community. (P3)

Finally, at the extreme right end of the continuum are found four participants who saw themselves as consultants, volunteers, even colonisers. They questioned their presence as principals in Inuit schools, which, in their view, should be led by Inuit people who speak the language and have a profound understanding of the issues at stake. They reflected on how rules and policies emanating from "the South" dispossess the Inuit people of their autonomy and of what might be their last chance to save their language and preserve their true cultural identity.

I say that we are, like, just visiting here. You just have to listen to what Inuit people say about teachers, principals. What do they say? "You are only passing through; we are going to stay in the community." And they are right, we are only passing through. We try our best to help them. I think it is like a service contract. We have experience, we try our best to help them, to give them some tools, but we must not do things in their stead. We have to empower them. So that they can try to do things by themselves once we have left. Unfortunately, it is not the short one-hour session that we get on our arrival (where we learn Nakurmik, Ilaali, Kinauvit, meaning thank you, my pleasure, what is your name?) that will do the job. . . I think the school board has to think this over, for its staff, because what does a language do? It facilitates people's social integration. So, if people in the community see that the gallunaat, the white people, the strangers, have the rudiments of their language, it sends a completely different message. But we are seen as colonisers. (P4)

I think I shouldn't even be here in this school. Because I don't have the required experience and qualities. In my school, 80% of the teaching and learning time is in Inuktitut. I should be training someone from here to replace me as soon as possible, to ensure communications, out of respect. . . . Take advantage of my being here, of my experience, to make sure that an Inuit person can take my place very soon. The school board wants to train local people to occupy these positions in the North. I agree completely, I agree that we must develop northern leadership with people from within the community. (P5)

Were my educational values challenged? Heavens, yes! When I started asking myself questions like: "How do these people learn?", "How do they teach their children?", questions like that, I had to stop. I couldn't do anything for a while. Because all of my values about education were challenged. I met people who not only didn't use the wheel, they had chosen not to use the wheel. Like the Zulus who said to the white people: "Keep your culture, we are not interested in going in that direction." "But you don't understand!" "Yes, we understand and we just don't want to go in that direction." I think we should leave. Inuit schools should be led by Inuit people for Inuit people. That is what I think. We can be hired to give a hand, to help shoulder the work. But in order for Inuit people to take ownership of their governance in Nunavik, we must leave. That's why I try to tell my students: "Come to school, get your diploma, and take our place. You must replace us. You must take your future into your own hands." (P6)

I am like a paid volunteer.[4] There is like a dichotomy here: I am the principal but I am only here to help, I can only cooperate . . . because there are so many things which are not from my culture, things I will never fully understand. I must always widen my horizons, open up my leadership to those who are going to stay here . . . but I am not one of those who are going to stay. I could stay here one year, two, maybe four, but I don't belong, so it is very different. I see myself like a paid volunteer, a consultant. I might be able to understand a few things, but do I feel them? No. I find my school looks like a white people's school, with white people structures, white people decor. There are a few Inuit sculptures, Inuit pictures, but darn it, you find them in Montreal as well . . . For instance, the center director, she likes to work sitting on the floor with all her papers around her. If another Inuit arrives, he or she will sit next to her and work with her. Once, we had a meeting like that; she sat on the floor, then all the Inuit staff sat on the floor, and, finally, all the qallunaats (whites) all sat on the floor. The atmosphere was really different. We played, they taught us Inuit games, then, at some point, I said "OK, let's start the meeting" and that was that! Ideally, an Inuit has to be principal. It would help so much and the sooner, the better! (P7)

Thoughts shared by Participants 4, 5, 6 and 7 indicated their strong awareness of how inadequate non-Inuit principals are and all stressed the necessity for Inuit people to become school principals in Nunavik. I can also see two different levels of critical analysis and transformative leadership among these principals: the stand of Participant 4, who supported the need for white principals to learn Inuktitut, while feeling, at the same time, like a coloniser, is at a more basic level; whereas the reflection of Participants 5, 6, and 7, for whom Inuit people must become principals, are at a higher level of analysis.

Perspective

When I started this research project with my colleagues, my understanding of the phenomenon of educational leadership in a linguistic-minority setting was based on my own personal and professional experience as a Canadian Francophone living outside of Québec, someone whose rights to an education in French were enshrined in the Canadian constitution (see Langlois & Lapointe, 2007). My experience was enriched by reading about other such experiences from the rare studies published based on this line of enquiry, as well as by conversing with First Nations educators in Canada and the United States. But it was only while conducting this study that I realized the scope of the challenges facing the Inuit people, and that will continue to face them, as they strive to preserve their language and culture within the world community.

Can Nunavik schools play their role efficiently as agents of linguistic and cultural socialisation? Or will they become instruments of cultural assimilation? My analysis of the question of educational leadership in a linguistic-minority setting, starting over 15 years ago and having been strongly enriched by this study conducted in Nunavik, brings me to the conclusion that, without the presence of a transformative leadership among school principals, it will be impossible for Inuit schools to successfully carry out their mandate of protecting and transmitting the Inuit language and culture. However, as I suggested in a theoretical model of educational leadership (Lapointe, 2002), in order to progress from basic participative leadership to an emancipatory form of leadership, which I now recognize as transformative, school principals who work in official or regional linguistic-minority schools must have a profound knowledge and deep understanding of the history, culture, and language of the minority community. If they don't meet these prerequisites, they will fail to bring about the required transformation to school culture and structure that would ensure the survival of the endangered language and culture, as well as the protection of fundamental human rights of the community they are serving. Indeed, it is this acute understanding of the dynamics in action that will enable school leaders to make courageous decisions and engage in emancipatory change.

Indeed, just as true social justice at school and by schools cannot exist in an underprivileged community if there is an absence of critical reflection on the part of the school leaders, the level of protection of language and culture will be proportional to the capacity of the individuals who manage the system to understand issues of human rights, of justice, and of equity, which are fundamental to their responsibilities and which must guide their decision making. The message from these research participants is clear: The ultimate survival of the Inuit language and culture will be ensured by transformative Inuit school principals, who are responsible for monitoring the correct implementation of Inuit curricula *today*, for tomorrow will probably be too late.

Notes

1. I want to thank the Social Sciences and Humanities Research Council of Canada for its support for this research project, as well as my co-investigators, Dr. Lyse Langlois, Professor Carolyn Shields, and Mr. David Montpetit.

2. In Québec, elementary school has six grades and high school, five grades, for a total of 11 years of schooling.

3. In Nunavik, people refer to the "South" to designate the populated region along the St. Lawrence River, where most of the population of Québec lives.

4. In French, the word used here was "coopérant," which has no obvious and direct translation in English

References

Allard, R., & Landry, R. (1994). Subjective ethnolinguistic vitality: A comparison of two measures. *International Journal of the Sociology of Language, 108,* 117–144.

Allard, R., & Landry, R. (1998). French in New Brunswick. In J. Edwards (Ed.), *Languages in Canada* (pp. 202–225). Cambridge, U.K.: Cambridge University Press.

Allard, R., Landry, R., & Bourhis, R. (1997). La disposition cognitivo-affective sur le plan ethnolangagier d'élèves francophones et anglophones du Québec. In G. Budach & J. Erfurt (Eds.), *Identité franco-canadienne et société civile québécoise* (pp. 151–164). Leipzig: Leipziger Universitätsverlag.

Allardt, E. (1984). What constitutes a language minority? *Journal of Multilingual and Multicultural Development, 5*(3), 193–205.

Aylward, M. L. (2007). Discourses of cultural relevance in Nunavut schooling. *Journal of Research in Rural Education, 22*(7), 1–9.

Bishop, R., & Glynn, T. (1998). Achieving cultural integrity within education in New Zealand. In K. Cushner (Ed.), *Intercultural Perspectives on Intercultural Education* (pp. 38–70). Mahwah, NJ: Lawrence Erlbaum Associates.

Burnaby, B., & MacKenzie, M. (2001). Cree decision making concerning language. *Journal of Multilingual and Multicultural Development, 22*(3), 191–209.

Carr-Stewart, S. (2006). First Nations education: Financial accountability and educational attainment. *Canadian Journal of Education, 29*(4), 998–1018.

Davies, W. (1999). Vanishing cultures. *National Geographic, 196*(2), 62–89.

Davies, W. (2009). *The wayfinders: Why ancient wisdom matters in the modern world.* Toronto, ON: House of Anansi Press.

De Klerk, V. (2000). To be Xhosa or not to be Xhosa . . . that is the question. *Journal of Multilingual and Multicultural Development, 21*(3), 198–215.

Eriks Brophy, A., & Crago, M. (2003). Variation in instructional discourse features: Cultural or linguistic? Evidence from Inuit and non-Inuit teachers of Nunavik. *Anthropology & Education Quarterly, 34*(4), 396–419.

Foucher, P. (2002). Le droit et les langues en contact: du droit linguistique aux droits des minorités. In A. Boudreau, L. Dubois, J. Maurais, & G. McConnel (Eds.), *L'écologie des langues* (pp. 43–68). Paris: L'Harmattan.

Hoffmann, C. (2000). Balancing language planning and language rights: Catalone's uneasy juggling act. *Journal of Multilingual and Multicultural Development, 21*(5), 425–441.

Landry, R. (1994). Minority education: A theoretical model. Paper presented at the Council of Europe *Educational Research Workshop on Minority Education,* Bautzen, Germany, October 11–14.

Landry, R., & Allard, R. (1994a). Diglossia, ethnolinguistic vitality and bilingual behavior. *International Journal of the Sociology of Language, 108,* 15–42.

Landry, R., & Allard, R. (1994b). Ethnolinguistic vitality: A viable construct. *International Journal of the Sociology of Language, 108,* 5–13.

Landry, R., Allard, R., & Henry, J. (1996). French in south Louisiana: Towards language loss. *Journal of Multilingual and Multicultural Development, 17*(6), 442–468.

Landry, R., & Bourhis, R. (1997). Linguistic landscape and ethnolinguistic vitality: An empirical study. *Journal of Language and Social Psychology, 16*(1), 23–49.

Langlois, L. (1997). *Les défis de la gestion scolaire d'après un modèle de leadership éthique: Une étude de cas* (Unpublished doctoral dissertation). Université Laval, Québec, Canada.

Langlois, L. (2004). Responding ethically: Complex decision-making by school district superintendents. *International Studies Educational Administration Management, 32*(2), 78–93.

Langlois, L., & Lapointe, C. (2007). Ethical leadership in Canadian school organizations: Tensions and possibilities. *Educational Management, Administration and Leadership, 35*(2), 247–260.

Langlois, L., & Starratt, J. (2001, October). *Identification of superintendent and school commissioners' ethical perspective: A case study and overlapping ethical framework: Data talking to the model.* Paper presented at the Conference on Ethics and Leadership, Virginia University, Charlottesville, VA.

Lapointe, C. (2002). Diriger l'école en milieu linguistique minoritaire. In L. Langlois & C. Lapointe (Eds.), *Le leadership en éducation Plusieurs regards, une même passion* (pp. 37–48). Montréal, QC: Éditions Chenellière/McGraw-Hill.

Lapointe, C. (2003, April). *Educational leadership in official-language minority settings: Searching for a relevant theory.* Paper presented at the American Educational Research Association, University of Chicago, Chicago, IL.

Lapointe, C., Godin, J., & Langlois, L. (2005). The leadership of heritage: Searching for a meaningful theory in official-language minority settings. *Journal of School Leadership, 15*(2), 143–158.

Lapointe, C., & Langlois, L. (2004, October). *School principals as promoters of unity in diversity: The case of French-language minority schools in Canada.* Paper presented at the 9th Annual Values and Leadership Conference, Southern Palms Resort, Christ Church, Barbados.

Lapointe, C., & Langlois, L. (2005). Re-visiting educational leadership in a complex democratic society: The case of linguistic minority schools. Paper presented at the *Annual Meeting of the University Council of Educational Administration*, November 2005, Nashville, TN.

Lapointe, C., Langlois, L., & Montpetit, D. (2010, April). *Reconciliating the past and the future: Ethnopedagogic leadership in Inuit schools.* Paper presented at the American Educational Research Association, Denver, CO.

Larose, F., Bourque, J., Terrisse, B., & Kurtness, J. (2001). La résilience scolaire comme indice d'acculturation chez les autochtones: Bilan de recherches en milieux innus. *Revue des sciences de l'éducation, 27*(1), 151–180.

Lasagabaster, D. (2001). Bilingualism, immersion programmes and language learning in the Basque country. *Journal of Multilingual and Multicultural Development, 22*(5), 401–425.

Magord, A., Landry, R., & Allard, R. (1994). Identités acadiennes en Louisiane, en Poitou et à Belle-Ile. *Études canadiennes/Canadian Studies, 37,* 159–180.

Mueller, C. (2006). Creating a joint partnership: Including Qallunaat teacher voices within Nunavik education policy. *International Journal of Inclusive Education, 10*(4–5), 429–447.

National Indian Brotherhood of Canada/Assembly of First Nations. (1972, December). *Indian Control of Indian Education.* Policy paper presented to the Minister of Indian Affairs and Northern Development, Ottawa, Canada.

Quantz, R. A., Rogers, J., Dantley, M. (1991). Rethinking transformative leadership: Toward democratic reform of schools. *Journal of Education, 173*(3), 96–118.

Sarrasin, R. (1998). L'enseignement du français et en français en milieu amérindien au Québec: Une problématique ethnopédagogique. *Canadian Journal of Applied Linguistics, 1*(1–2), 107–125.

Shields, C. M. (2010). Transformative leadership: Working for equity in diverse contexts. *Educational Administration Quarterly, 46*(4), 558–589.

Spada, N., & Lightbown, P. M. (2002). L1 and L2 in the education of Inuit children in northern Québec: Abilities and perceptions. *Language and Education, 16*(3), 212–240.

Starratt, R. J. (1991). Building an ethical school: A theory for practice in educational leadership. *Educational Administration Quarterly, 27*(2), 185–202.

Tacelosky, K. (2001). Bilingual education and language use among the Shipibo of the Peruvian Amazon. *Journal of Multilingual and Multicultural Development, 22*(1), 39–56.

Weiner, E. J. (2003). Secretary Paulo Freire and the democratization of power: Toward a theory of transformative leadership. *Educational Philosophy and Theory, 35*(1), 89–106.

Wotherspoon, T. (2006). Teachers' work in Canadian aboriginal communities. *Comparative Education Review, 50*(4), 672–694.

18

Redefining the Notion of Youth

Contextualizing the Possible for Transformative Youth Leadership

Shirley R. Steinberg

Introduction: What's Wrong with You?

When I was hired as a high school drama teacher in 1987, it was expected that I "bring" back a dying program by producing and directing an enormous musical production. Creating a theatrical community while mounting *Grease* was part of my own personal mandate. The students, musicians, stagehands, all of us, became parts of a dynamic whole. The group was a social and artistic organism, enjoying one another. Jeremy was cast as Kenickie, the hell-raising greaser who becomes the potential father attached to Rizzo's possible pregnancy. Lanky, funny, and flexible, Jeremy had a dynamite voice, he was perfect for the part. Early one morning, following the previous evening's run-through of "Greased Lightning," my office phone rang:

Hello

I'm looking for Ms. Steinberg

You found me, can I help you?

This is Reverend Erb

I'm so glad you phoned, Jeremy is doing so well, he is amazing.

That is why I am calling. I have a problem with you.

In what way?

I don't like the play you are directing, I don't like the part Jeremy is playing, I think it sends the wrong messages to our children, and I don't like what I hear about you.

Is there anything else?

I don't like that these young adults are doing, what I think you call, improvisation. Drama games. They are not following scripts. The whole play and the drama program are not what we want them to be learning. This is a school, and your values are not appropriate.

What is it you want me to do?

My son refuses to quit the play. I think you should tell him he can't have the part.

I can't do that. Jeremy deserves the part, it is his decision.

That's precisely the problem, you are teaching a program which allows students to make the decisions.

I'm sorry you feel that way, you are welcome to discuss it with the administration; however, they approved this production.

Obviously, I can't get anywhere discussing this with you.

Thank you for calling.

Wait, just one more thing. . .this is what I really want to ask you. . ..

(pause)

What is wrong with you, Ms. Steinberg?

Wrong with me?

There has to be something wrong with you. The students stay late after school; you take them to plays; you all go out for dinner.

Yes.

No one likes teenagers. Only someone with something wrong inside wants to be around them that much.

Reverend Erb was right. Most people (grownups) don't like teenagers, they don't trust them, and certainly wanting to be around them is suspect. It was then that I decided to devote my career to facilitating young adults to become leaders, to be viewed as worthwhile, trustworthy, and brilliant. The old boy was speaking the language of the dominant North American parent: *kids are bad, kids are sneaky, kids raise hell, kids are not capable of making good decisions.*

Our son, Ian, and his best friend, Nathan, were hanging out a few years later, I was working on a book about schools and wanted to ask the boys a few questions. Nathan was up to answering my questions:

You are 16. You are in school. What do you think the purpose of school is for you?

To keep us in.

In?

Yeah, to keep us out of trouble, off the streets until we learn how not to get into trouble. They just want to keep us in.

Fear of Youth

Historically, adolescents and youth were not a distinct societal subculture. Indeed, until the twentieth century, North American 'teens' were often working at a young age, and certainly few were educated. In the 1950s, the notion of the rebel youth appeared, poster child James Dean became a grown-up's nightmare, along with rock n' roll, the hell-raising 50s led into the tune in, turn on, drop out 60s. Popular images of youth created a suspect society driven by desire and the ability to terrify adults. Psychologists and sociologists struggled to deal with youth; psychologizing, pathologizing, and institutionally marginalizing youth became the practice. What was wrong with youth? Everything.

Schools attempted to balance out youth subcultural movements by counter images of *the good girl* and *the manly, responsible boy.* Certainly, the Cleavers never had problems with Wally or the Beaver; Patty Duke complied; Father always knew best, and popular television created images of teens who did not question, did not rebel, and certainly, did not emulate Kenickie on the stage. Notions of drag racing, hoods, loose girls and back talking to parents were lower class behaviors, by the kids from across-the-tracks. Leadership by teens was reduced to two categories: *Preppies* (my word), the Paul Petersonesque kids with starched shirts and ties: and *Hoods*, those from lower or blacker/browner social classes who ran in gangs. Popular culture throughout the first thirty years of television did not portray empowered, functional youth as leaders.

Empowerment was not discussed. Schools did not address the possibility of creating a curriculum of leadership for youth. . .sort of like they don't do this now. Historically, and presently, the idea of youth leadership is not engaged. Youth are to be feared, controlled, contained, and, as Nathan noted, "kept in."

A fear of youth is part of our fabric. Woven between the threads, young men and women are unloved, often not understood, and often feared. Academic, school, and parent discourse address issues *about* youth in constant discussions about:

- eating disorders

- bullying

- teen mothers

- gangs

- youth suicide

- homelessness

- disrespect for parents

- boredom in school

- failure to succeed

- lack of initiative

- sexualities

- identities

- language (as in slang, crude, or non-standard)

Conversations about youth reveal that *they are a problem*. Yet we do not have the conversations about why *we* perceive a problem. Curricula are designed to make sure youth know that they need to change, they need to take responsibility, and yes, Nathan was right, they need to be kept in.

All this to say, that in this chapter, I will not look at the "youth problem" nor articulate any confirmation that youth are "at risk." I will engage in a conversation about youth leadership, its possibilities and challenges. Bottom line, youth are not a deficit in our culture or educational system. The deficit vision of youth is psychologized, pathologized, institutionalized, and marginalized. . . in a phrase, adults fear youth.

How Do We Discuss Youth Leadership If We Don't Want Youth to Lead?

Leadership is a clumsy term to deal with, the non-transformative kind. I'm not sure how to replace it, but want to state upfront, I don't like it much. It implies a hierarchy with the leader at the top, and then the leadees following below. Some may be given tasks or delegated responsibility, but leadership tends to expect that the leader will ultimately have the power. As a critical theorist, leadership for me becomes problematic. In a critical pedagogical world, noting how power works and replicates itself, how does one become a leader without assuming power? And, how do we work with youth to become leaders who do not intend to wield power? This is a tough one, and I want to keep it in mind in this discussion.

The notion of transformative youth leadership must be grounded in the articulation that youth are distinct beings and citizens, with specific needs, cultures, and views of the world. Instead of seeing youth as mini us, we need to redefine youth by seeing how youth define themselves—they are not a subculture; they are young men and women with cultures. Within these youth cultures, subcultures are created (usually by the youth themselves). I have observed in my work with youth, that many adults are reluctant to name youth cultures, instead discuss them with distain, pathology, or marginalization: *She's in her Goth phase. Facebook has taken them over. World of Warfare is just his way of avoiding being with the family. I was the same way, I hated all adults. She just needs to understand that her appearance is not acceptable in our home. This music is out of control. He thinks he is gay; we are ignoring it; he will grow out of it. This hip hop thing, it is violent; we don't allow it in our home.* Rarely are young women and men given credit and respect for the decisions they make on a daily basis. Issues of identity become points of ridicule, and many teachers and caregivers view choices as phases, stages, or unimportant fads.

Certainly, teacher education does not prepare secondary and middle school teachers to facilitate youth leadership and empowerment; most parents and caregivers are not wired to assist empowerment, rather to squelch it. Often citing yellowed memories from their own lives, adults forget that they somehow made it through adolescence and teen years and actually did lots of good things during that time. Memories from adults are often categorized in two ways:

1. I did it, regret it, and don't ever want my kids to know I did it or to do "it" themselves: or

2. When I was that age, I did what I was told, what was expected, did not ask for my own "space," I was part of a family.

Incanting the term, *youth leadership*, most educators and parents speak out of both sides of their mouths, giving the term, and taking the power. . .no one seems to want kids to lead, to make responsible decisions, and to eventually replace a stagnant status quo. Ironically, it will happen. Thirty years ago, no one would have ever guessed that a presidential nominee's theme song would be one by Fleetwood Mac. There is almost a 'get over it' pedagogy that we must enact in order to overcome the youth phobia shared by many adults. . .especially those who design curriculum and create pseudo leadership roles for youth.

What We Need to Know

Creating a socially just youth leadership curriculum has obstacles, and the more urban the area, the more disenfranchised, the harder the challenge becomes. However, we must use the dialectic of challenges and opportunities. We must view our youth as novel entities, who may be similar or dissimilar from other young men and women. We rid ourselves of assumptions and create a space and pedagogy of leadership for schools and students, researching and observing each group on its own. We must focus attention on:

- The socio-cultural context of a school or community organization

- The backgrounds of each young man and woman

- The positions of empowerment and disempowerment from which each youth operates

- The knowledges youth bring to the classroom or organization

- The languages spoken by the youth, both cultural and sub-cultural

- The ways these dynamics mold teaching and learning

Keeping in mind the complexity and contradictions of the category of youth leadership, we must look at the unique features in creating a transformative youth leadership program. These are features which be kept in the forefront, especially in working with urban and marginalized youth.

- What are the considerations of population density as it applies to where youth live?

- Sizes of schools, availability of community centres. Are large suburban and rural counterparts more prepared to serve higher numbers of lower socio-economic class students? Are many students likely to be ignored and overlooked in the crowds of an urban area? In this context, it is difficult for urban and marginalized students to create and feel a sense of community. This creates an alienation which often leads to low academic performance, high dropout rates, and unanticipated leadership, gang affiliation, and negative subculture associations.

- What does the examination of geographic areas marked by profound economic disparity reveal? Disproportionate percentages of minority students and their families are plagued by centralized urban poverty, which hampers their quest for academic success on a plethora of levels. In urban schools and drop-in community centers (if they exist), there are an appalling lack of resources, financial inequalities, horrendous infrastructural violations, dilapidated buildings, and no space. . .no space for youth to just be. . .to be trusted, to make decisions.

- Urban areas have a higher rate of ethnic, racial, and religious diversity. In densely populated urban locales, people come from different ethnic, racial, and religious backgrounds, not to mention economic, social, and linguistic arenas, and they live close to one another. Nearly two-thirds of these urban youth do not fit the categories of white or middle class, and within these populations high percentages of students receive a free or reduced price lunch. Achievement rates for poor minority youth consistently fall below of those of whites and higher socioeconomic classes, and often their failures are the final proof that quitting school, engaging in illegal activity, is success.

- How does our work reach gay, lesbian, bisexual, transgendered and questioning youth?

- Where do indigenous youth fit into a closed definition of youth? Immigrant and migrant youth?

- Adults who sit on school boards, city councils, and on youth task forces, experience and factionalize infighting over issues on resources and influence, and often fighting is reduced to the youthphobia notion, that they are not to be leaders. . .as the reverend told, me, *there has to be something wrong with me.* How could I tolerate and trust youth? There are no attempts to incorporate the voices of youth within these boards, councils and task forces. Youth are discussed as the societal deficit. . .the youth problem.

- Often administrators and leaders who work with teachers are undermined by ineffective business operations. The facilities rely on basic resources, especially in urban settings, and no one has the ability to change the reality. I am working with youth in East New York (Brooklyn) now and have made it a point to count the amount of play yards with functioning hoops for basketball, basketballs, and a minimum of jump ropes and hand balls. Youth drop centers are often in the cast-off basements or temporary buildings of a past era, and groups are reluctant to add financially to the structure of a soon-to-be condemned building and space.

- Work with youth does not tend to include initiatives for health and well-being. Naturally, the more socially deprived the youth, the worse the health and safety issues. School administrators will be more concerned with providing a warm building on a cold day, than fixing unsanitary and disease-producing bathrooms—poor spaces for youth, if any are provided for them to meet. The community fears youth meeting in groups; malls are closed during certain hours, or kids must be accompanied by adults. Street corners, steps of stores, these become the places for youth to meet.

- A mobility issue also haunts disenfranchised and urban schools. Students, teachers, and community leaders, and especially administrators, leave frequently. Good work may be being done but halts when an adult is replaced. Analysts have noted that the poorer the student, the more moves he or she is likely to make. High teacher turnover, one out of every two teachers in urban and poor schools leaves in five years. . .community organizers are volunteers or so poorly paid that they are unable to advocate for even a minimal raise.

- Urban and poor schools serve higher immigrant populations. Each group experience has needs particular to their own ethnic group, yet they have little governmental or educational help to get them started.

- Urban schools have characteristic linguistic challenges. In New York City, for example over 350 languages and dialects are spoken. Because the leaders and teachers are white or middle class, it is hard to have the general sense of heritage and educational backgrounds to make use of linguistic diversity. Indeed, linguistic diversity is seen as a problem, rather than a unique opportunity.

- Context is important. We know the responsibilities many young men and women carry. Once again, in lower socio-economic strata, or in specific cultures, youth take on adult roles as small children. Minding baby brothers and sisters/nieces and nephews, tending to aged grandparents, translating personal and medical knowledge between adults and doctors or social workers. . .these conditions throw youth into powerless leadership positions of translation and decision making.

- Mentors, teachers, and social workers are less likely to live in a community, which is profiled economically or culturally. Consequently, youth do not have consistent leadership models upon which to build or seek advice.

Eschewing the Modernist Constructions of Youth

Along with contextualizing the above thoughts is a short deconstruction of previous notions and definitions of youth. Keep in mind that 'teenager,' as a separate designation of *an older kid*, started to appear in literature in the late 1930s, early 40s. No historical reference launches fireworks for *the* day that the word first was used. Originally, it described literally, kids who were in the teens, 13–19. Most who work in adolescent and youth studies have different definitions. I loosely look at the ages between 11 and 21 but also can see that teenager or youth are tentative words, and along with them come expectations both cognitively and performatively. Jean Piaget addressed the notion of adolescence, observing that sometime around the age of 12, adolescents began to enter the formal operational stage, a more enlightened and sophisticated cognitive developmental stage. He saw that scientific, logical, and abstract thought was enacted by this age group and understood that many young people could stretch concrete thought to abstractions. He saw them as able to understand words and ideas in meaning-making terms, consider relationships, and have an operating knowledge of concepts like justice, morals, fairness, etc. My criticisms of Piaget have been discussed in the work done with Joe Kincheloe in postformal thinking (Kincheloe & Steinberg, 1993). Our main issue was that Piaget as the final word in youth construction was exactly that. . .and there are no final words. Piaget's developmentalist approaches are limited, essentialistic, and not capable of considering the nuances of youth. . .especially in a postmodern era. We cannot work with youth, teach youth, or facilitate youth empowerment for leadership using the tired methods of developmentalism. . .with a redefined notion of youth, adulthood, and the cultural capital of technology and cyberspace, the development of youth has changed (of course, I would argue that the Piagetian model never created the appropriate read on youth).

Youth development is not in stages: it is culturally and socially defined by the surroundings and experience of each young adult. Facilitating youth to become socially aware and ethical leaders requires a deep read of the lived world of each young man or woman. There are no Coveyesque or Tony Robbinsian ways to methodologize youth, no applicable Fullanization that can take place to acknowledge the importance of working with youth to create individualized and contextualized leadership empowerment. The discussions with youth on empowerment and leadership must be tentative and on-going, and, they must be done with those who *like* youth, who are not afraid of youth, and who are committed to a vision of engaged youth leadership.

A Transformative Critical Pedagogical Youth Leadership

We must ask, in the Freirean fashion of dialogue: *what can be done in youth leadership?* What is it we are trying to facilitate and enact? Freire (1970) reminds us that empowerment cannot be taught; rather, we can act as conduits to creating safe spaces and opportunities for empowerment/enlightenment to take place. As critical educators, we learn first, to view the world from the eyes of those who are not part of the dominant culture. In this case, we view from the perspectives and ways in which youth see the world. How do youth see power? Do they identify with their place in the world, in the web of reality? Do they recognize opportunities? Are they comfortable with becoming leaders and mentors? What is it like to be a young man or woman today? How can one organize? Can character be built? What are the ethics of leadership? How does trust fit in with leadership? What communication skills are needed in leadership? Is there an *attitude* of leadership? Leaders are not born, they develop, and it is our mandate to secure dialogue and place in which to mentor and usher development. Youth leadership in a critical sense includes character, responsibility, respect, and knowledge. Those who work with youth to create viable leadership opportunities acknowledge each of these traits. . .and in this context, I would assert that respect is paramount in youth engagement. Our work with youth should be committed to facilitating the development of a democratic citizen, one who is conscious of being part of a whole, of society.

We encourage and mentor the notions that a young leader learns to articulate vision and understands her or his place within power structures and society, in general. We encourage leadership by doing and modeling and by seeking/researching those who lead but may not be known as *leaders*. I often use the example of the Canadian athlete, Terry Fox, a young amputee with cancer, who determined to run the width of Canada in order to bring awareness to cancer research. Fox began in Newfoundland with little fanfare, just a kid with a metal leg and a vision. Momentum gathered, and he became a symbol of persistence, faith, and leadership. Fox was a leader who did not seek to lead but to do good work. Leadership can be created by good works. This is not to confuse the notion of leader with role models or heroes. Often media-driven, those who are defined as role models are part of the Hollywoodization of leadership. Many are called heroes but incorrectly. A hero is one who does not seek to do heroic deeds but is thrust into being a hero through altruistic motivation and selflessness. It is an important pedagogical act to differentiate between a leader and a role model or hero. A leader does not aspire to be 'followed,' but she or he aspires merely to do, as I said earlier, *good work.* Paulo Freire also serves as an example of a leader, a quiet intellectual with political indignation, who was imprisoned and exiled; Freire didn't seek fame; he sought to create socially just dialogue which would serve to open paths to empowerment. Engaging in a conversation about youth leadership demands that youth identify those who serve to define leadership and good work. Part of a critical pedagogy of youth leadership asks that young men and women deliberate upon what characteristics a youth leader needs and who exemplifies those characteristics.

Youth can be engaged in defining youth leadership; discussions about listening, respect, desire to learn, sharing, delegation, lifetime learning, are all part of coming to terms with leadership qualities. We ask when one should lead and when a leader supports another to lead. Leadership also means giving up the lead if necessary. Youth should be leaders, they are leaders; however, with the decades of seeing youth as hoodlums, ganstas, thugs, and reprobates, it will take time to change, not only society's view of youth, but the self-identity of young men and women themselves.

Only a Beginning

Avoiding the platitude-laden liberal tripe about youth, we name the needs, issues, and social conditions surrounding our youth. We act as mentors and treat youth as young leaders. . .younger colleagues, engaging in respect and collegiality as we create a safe and healthy leadership vision. We ask that youth contribute to the vision, that it is not imposed upon them, and that we assist them in discovering their abilities and potentials as leaders. We do not create a defined *leader* but a flexible view of one who leads; some will be tacit leaders, some will be overt, some will share leadership, and some will support it. . . .youth leaders are not the new curricular thing, the new black of pedagogical lexicons; youth leaders are necessary to nurture in order to create a healthy and optimistic environment.

A critical pedagogy of transformative youth leadership can impact youth in a global context, creating a space for youth leadership studies, research, mentorship, internships, and empowerment.

References

Freire, P. (1970). *Pedagogy of the Oppressed.* London: Continuum Books.

Kincheloe, J. L., & Steinberg, S. R. (1993). ""A Tentative Description of Post-Formal Thinking: The Critical Confrontation with Cognitive Theory." *Harvard Educational Review,* Vol., 63 No. 3, Fall.

IV

Studying
Transformative Leadership

19

Promoting Equity and Social Justice

A Task Too Heavy for Individual School Principals?

Jorunn Møller

The Scandinavian countries have exemplified a strong commitment to comprehensive education and social justice, inspired by social democratic politics for ensuring equality. This implies a conviction that a more democratic and egalitarian organization of society is both possible and desirable, and that education can have an important role to play in attaining this kind of society (see, for example, Apple, 2000; Beane & Apple, 1999; Furman & Starratt, 2002; Grace, 1995; Woods, 2005). Becoming a knowledgeable and engaged citizen who is responsive to diversity within and across nations is a process. It requires both knowledge about democracy and experiences of democracy through democratic leadership in practice. Neither is sufficient on its own. Education should facilitate the development of students' consciousness and agency.

During the last decade in Scandinavia, there have, however, been increasing concerns about the quality of schooling, and we have witnessed a development towards a stronger focus on educational quality, in terms of student achievements and more output-oriented means of governing. The focus has shifted to more or less well-defined expectations of what has to be achieved and by whom, and only those outcomes that meet the predefined criteria are considered successful (Hopmann, 2007). New strategies for reinventing government by establishing New Public Management, NPM, both at the central and the municipal level have emerged. On the one hand, it is argued that introducing New Public Management has been motivated by concerns about reducing disparities in educational outcomes across different social groups. Therefore, there is a need for strengthening of state responsibility in terms of monitoring public sector services (Røvik, 2007). On the other hand, it is often argued that the cost of public sector is too high, and NPM is an instrument for efficient service production, governed by a performance oriented culture with a focus on results and efficiency (Heinrich, 2005; Olsen, 2002).

Still, there is broad agreement on the normative basis of democratic education, and the educational policy intends to create equal and equitable life conditions for all social groups, regardless of social background, gender, ethnicity, and geographical location. There might be disagreement about how to define democratic education, but most definitions will include the following set of qualities: recognition of the basic values and rights of each individual, considering other people's perspective, deliberation in making decisions, embracing plurality and difference, and promoting equity and social justice (see Møller, 2006, pp. 54–56).

In this chapter, I start by elaborating upon transformative leadership, as this type of leadership begins with questions of democracy and links educational leadership with the social context within which it is embedded. Therefore, it offers a lens to understanding leadership that strives for equity and social justice and addresses both individual achievement and the public good. Based on findings from the project named "Revisiting Successful School Principals Five Years Later within a Norwegian Context," I will then provide examples of two principals who, over time, have demonstrated a strong commitment to working for equity and social justice in their schools and analyze their stories through this lens of transformative leadership. An important question is: How may school principals contribute to making schools more inclusive, socially just, and, at the same time, academically successful?

Transformative Leadership as an Analytical Lens

It may be difficult to distinguish between transformative and transformational leadership, and the two terms are often used interchangeably in the literature. If we translate the terms into Norwegian, both terms are translated with an identical word, *transformativ*. The two terms have many overlaps, but there are also clear distinctions if we explore their roots more closely (Shields, 2010).

Transformational leadership owes much to the work of Burns (1978), Bass and Avolio (1994), and later to Leithwood, Jantzi, and Dart (1990), who adapted the framework for analyzing and evaluating school leaders' practices. Transformational leadership focuses on the capacity to develop infrastructure, and, as Leithwood and colleagues have framed it, it is about setting direction, developing people, and redesigning the organization. Intrinsic components are moral and ethical behavior. Even though moral questions of goodness and duty are a major concern, the focus is primarily on what happens within the organization. This is an important distinction from *transformative leadership*, which focuses more on sociological and cultural elements of the organization and the wider society in which they are embedded (see Shields, 2010). Transformative leadership gives emphasis to the need to recognize that the inequities experienced in the wider society affect one's ability both to perform and to succeed within the school. Transformative leadership owes much to the work of Freire, and later to the work of Foster (1986), who emphasized the need to change the conditions in which we live.

In a review of the literature, Shields has framed the distinction between the two terms like this: "transformational leadership focuses on improving organizational qualities, dimensions, and effectiveness; and transformative educational leadership begins by challenging inappropriate uses of power and privilege by challenging inappropriate uses of power and privilege that create or perpetuate inequity and injustice" (Shields, 2010, p. 564). In her review, she has identified seven key elements of transformative leadership: a combination of both critique and promise; attempts to effect both deep and equitable changes; deconstruction and reconstruction of the knowledge frameworks that generate inequity; acknowledgement of power and privilege; emphasis on both individual achievement and the public good; a focus on liberation, democracy, equity, and justice; and evidence of moral courage and activism (2010, p. 562). The project "Revisiting Successful School Principals" did not intend to study the principals through the lens of transformative leadership, but for the purpose of this chapter the data have been reanalyzed through this lens.

Examples of Successful Schools Five Years Ago

Leadership in Norwegian schools is situated in a democratic governance structure with policies that aim to educate students for citizenship in a democratic society. This means that school leadership is a moral activity, which cannot be fully grasped without including a discussion of what we mean by an education based on democratic values. The task ahead is not just about formulating a vision for democracy and inclusiveness. It is an empirical question as to what degree these missions influence the students' experiences. To illustrate this argument, I will use data from two of the successful Norwegian schools we examined in 2003 within the framework of the International Successful School Principalship Project (ISSPP).[1] The schools, Skog and Brage, had both gained public recognition for being successful in their work for democracy in a multiethnic environment.[2] Both schools had a principal with a strong commitment to comprehensive education and social justice, inspired by social democratic politics for promoting equity. However, the analysis demonstrated disparities in creating challenging learning environments for *all* students, and these differences were closely linked to the leadership approach by the principal at the local school (Vedøy & Møller, 2007).[3]

Our findings demonstrated that, although the principals at these two schools had visions about democratic and inclusive schooling for all students, their leadership practices were quite different. At Skog primary school, which was located in a semi-rural municipality, deficit thinking seemed to masquerade as the principal and the teachers' talk about social justice. This primary school had about 350 students, of whom 20% were language-minority students. The enrolment area mainly included students from the average socioeconomic status group. The staff at Skog School was mainly a homogenous group, with predominantly female teachers in their fifties. Most of them had worked at the school for a long period of time. A specialist teacher at Skog School had sole responsibility for much of the adapted education for minority-language students. The teachers expressed their gratefulness for having a skilled person who handled students when they did not have the capacity and time to do extra work with these students. The specialist cooperated to some extent with the bilingual teachers, but few other regular teachers were involved. In this way, experts had the responsibility for minority-language students, and their knowledge and practice were, to a very little extent, shared with the rest of the teachers. When the principal at Skog portrayed his interaction with minority students and their parents, *care* was the key term. His way of caring was characterized by a focus on the students' histories and family backgrounds:

> I think it is important to invest some time to care . . . when it comes to inclusion . . . it has something to do with religion. Because, and especially for the group we discuss now, they belong to . . . most times they belong to other religions. We need to be open to the diversity of religions and not exclude anybody on that basis. . . . What kind of attitudes do these students experience in their different homes? What ways of thinking do they meet? What kind of reactions can we expect to get, if we send a message home, saying we want you to discuss this or that with your children? . . . All in all it has to do with caring, and a wish to get involved in what they really stand for.

However, explaining and understanding students with reference to their difference in home cultures gave rise to a focus on students' deficits in relation to the majority culture. Also, through an implicit discourse of pluralism, where power relations were taken for granted in favor of the majority and harmony in the staff was stressed, the principal ultimately suppressed democratic processes. The staff backed out of collective responsibility concerning the minority students (see Vedøy & Møller, 2007). Analyzed through the lens of transformative leadership Skog could not be recognized as successful. As demonstrated above the school did not promote equity for *all* students in practice.

Brage, a combined primary and lower secondary school with about 400 students—of whom 22% were language minority students—was located in a town with roughly 30,000 inhabitants. The enrolment area included students from both high- and low-socioeconomic-status groups. One area consisted of detached and terraced houses and had a high socioeconomic standard. The other area consisted of blocks of flats, inhabitants living under poor socioeconomic conditions, many single parents, recipients of social welfare, and a high number of language minorities. Minorities were described as equals at the school, and the principal hired a diverse staff. He expected all teachers to be responsible for the minority students' education, for the common good, and for the development of a diverse society. *Respect* was the key term for descriptions of meetings between majority and minority, or more specifically, between people in general. The principal's answer to success was structure, respecting the students, and giving emphasis to learning processes, learning outcomes, and hard work. He had a clear sense of purpose related to how to create a learning environment in which all children would not only feel they belong but also in which they could be successful. He argued very strongly that one should not establish a dichotomy between discourses of social justice and working for high academic achievements on the part of the students. Through an explicit discourse of critical multiculturalism based on respect, the principal opened the school up for democratic processes (see Vedøy & Møller, 2007).[4]

In many ways, these findings echo Shields's (2006) analysis of how her three schools chose different strategies to promote social justice, with very diverse result. Her principals also had a reputation for promoting social justice, but only one of these schools could serve as an example of schoolwide transformation and success. According to Shields, the knowledgeable principal was crucial for such an achievement. Moreover, the principal was able to engage her staff in extensive dialogue about how to make meaningful change, in order to make sure that the decisions were grounded in theories of social justice. Our analysis showed that the approach chosen by the principal at Brage seemed promising to fulfill a vision of democratic and inclusive schooling for all students.

Revisiting Successful Schools After Five Years

When we revisited some of our successful schools five years later, the project aimed to better understand what these principals do in today's more demanding accountability context. Developments in educational policy and reforms in the public sector in general during the last five years have raised new expectations towards schools, and principals are particularly challenged to respond to new and sometimes contradicting expectations. New evaluation procedures have been introduced to produce data about student achievement levels, and schools are increasingly perceived as the unit of measurement, clearly implying new expectations of public reporting. Along with this development, content aims in the national curriculum have been reformulated into competence aims, which are easier to evaluate, and accountability has become a central issue of educational reform. The massive attention PISA[5] has received in Norway owes much to the emerging age of performance measurement and accountability. While we previously took for granted that teachers could be trusted to do a good job, there are now other social groups wishing to define educational quality, and they ask for more external regulation of teachers' work (see Møller, Vedøy, Presthus, & Skedsmo, 2009).

As a basis for the discussion in this chapter, I will use data from two of the schools that were revisited in September 2008, and I have selected Brage combined school (grades 1 through 10) and Ospelia upper-secondary school (grades 11 to 13). In these two schools, the same principals were still in their posts. Both schools had demonstrated five years earlier that they managed to create excellent learning environments for all students, and both schools had principals who were driven by their commitment to social justice. Only Brage had a large percentage of minority students. (Skog was not among the schools which were selected for a revisit, as our analysis five years previously showed that the school was not promoting equity in practice.)

Brage had, since 2003, gradually increased the number of students to 575 students. The school had about 20% students with minority-language background, and there were all together 16 or 17 different first languages in the school. The students, as they did five years earlier, came from two different socioeconomic areas. Approximately one half of the students were still living in an area with low-socioeconomic-status groups, while the other half of the students had a rather wealthy background. An important development in the student population over the last few years was that the school received fewer minority-language students who did not have any proficiency in Norwegian when they started school in grade one. The reason for this development was that most of the new entrants now had attended kindergarten. As a consequence, there was a considerable difference between the minority students five years earlier, who knew little Norwegian, and 2008's students.

In our interview with the principal at Brage compulsory school, he emphasized that he had not changed his understanding of what counts as a good school. It was the same as five years earlier. The answer seemed to be structure, respecting all the students, and an emphasis on learning and hard work. The principal had this to say about students' learning outcomes:

> In 2006, the first year with students graduating after all their 10 years of compulsory education at Brage, we had the seventh-best exam results in Norway. We even beat the best school in Oslo and the whole bunch there. Last year we had a group of students that were . . . that I never in my life-time thought would be able to get any results at all, and then they were totally or slightly above the average. That is maybe the most impressing result we have had . . . I looked at the list of students, and, yes there is Mustafa and Ibrahim, all the way down. So, everyone understands that we couldn't have done it well this year. . . . But there is no damn way we are going to make this into an excuse. Now we have started a major work to improve the students' fluency in Norwegian. We focus on it; we will not sit back and say that this is because of many minority-language students.

He had a quite distinct approach to leading a multicultural school, with focus on the resources you have and making the best out of it, instead of complaining over lack of resources. In his opinion, the variations in student results were mainly a result of student enrolment: "We just have to accept that. That is why making school results public is totally pointless." The principal had a clear sense of purpose about how to create a learning environment in which all children may not only feel they belong but also in which they may be successful. He was proud of what he had accomplished, as the following quote illustrates:

> I have regular meetings with all the team leaders, and every second Wednesday I have meetings with the teacher responsible for special educational needs. When we have team meetings we discuss every single age group. Which students are in trouble, how teaching is developing, what kind of pedagogical arrangements are being used. In this way I have extreme control over what is going on in this school. And we put in efforts whenever needed. . . . Remember, we have 575 students, but we only have 11 students who require special needs education and who follow an individual subject program. Eleven students! Normally we would have had 50, right, given the enrolment of students at this school. But we have only 11 students!

He had an educational background in special needs education, and from that experience he knew how extremely important it was to be systematic in his work. He liked to state most things in their extreme form and portrayed himself as successful, especially with the most difficult students. In many ways the principal was positioning himself as a rebel who enjoyed provoking. He was also critical in regards to regional expectations of schools to create a local vision. Such a process was a waste of time, according to him:

> I won't be bothered about dragging the staff into meaningless processes about visions and all sorts of rubbish; we don't do that here, really. I can't imagine anything more heartbreaking than to entering a Web page, and it says something like School X is a good place to be, a good place to learn. What the hell does that mean? Right? And they have probably used Monday after Monday for years to come up with this vision with yellow Post-it notes and put them up and stuff . . . really, the teachers here should be spared from that.

Focus on student outcome is considered a good thing. Education is a way to give all students opportunities for social mobility in society, and this means that basic skills like reading, writing, and calculation ought to be focused on. These are tools students need in order to get social access. A successful school for the principal at Brage is a school that has the ability to care for every single student. One has to react early in order to use the resources in an effective way. The principal portrayed himself as very close to the students. He cared and had respect for both children and adults, and the interviews with the teachers confirmed this picture. The principal had clear expectations of staff members and students, related to responsibility, challenge, and support. He described himself as optimistic and persistent in his pursuit of high achievement for all. This school had also, throughout many years, been recognized in the local community for working successfully with special educational needs students. The principal was also aware of giving all parents a voice. Because the socioeconomic-status groups varied so much among the parents, he had chosen to focus on individual parental conferences instead of large meetings with all the parents. Furthermore, in each grade, parents were in charge of social activities within the community.

The principal at Ospelia upper-secondary school emphasized that the criteria for a good school were the same as when they had been formulated five years earlier: to see the whole student and to get the best out of each individual. The school's practices and the principal's involvement in the student council and student participation had also been enduring. In our analysis five years earlier, we had concluded that Ospelia had managed to sustain their progressive visions from the early 1970s. Furthermore, we had constructed a picture of a principal who "lived" his ethic of caring, and who argued that promoting equity and social justice was the main concern (Møller, 2006).

Since our last visit, Ospelia had had a large growth in student population, from 550 to 700 students. This was due to increased settlement and migration to the community. The county government had decided to expand the existing school instead of building a new one, and a rebuilding project had started, with the principal heavily involved in planning and following up. There had also been a change in the recruitment of students, in terms of getting more students with weak academic achievements and low school motivation. One reason may be that Ospelia had obtained a reputation and a history of dealing successfully with students with special educational needs. It may have also been due to Norwegian students' preferences of upper-secondary level. In more recent years, there was a tendency to choose schools located in more urban areas, and Ospelia is located in a rural environment.[6] Every student has the right of entry to upper-secondary schools, but their selection of school is regulated by scores at national exams, and the bright students choose first within such a system.

Ospelia had tried to adapt to the new student population. An environmental health worker was positioned at the school to meet the new needs and to prevent drop-out. This had proved to be a very successful strategy. Prevention of high drop-out rates was emphasized politically, and the principal had made an effort to influence local politicians with respect to choosing a model that works. Another step to meet the students' needs was the focus upon visible leadership and more explicit expectations of teachers and students. The principal had started to perform classroom observations to show interest and keep in touch with the students and the classroom processes. But he emphasized that this was not in order to control the teachers.

The principal stressed that the school's mission was to provide a good teaching and learning environment for all their students, regardless of socioeconomic or cultural background and abilities but in particular for those students with great problems. Therefore, an evaluation of the schools' average academic achievements had to be linked to the recruitment of students. The school had a low drop-out rate, and this was highlighted as an important criterion of success. He had not changed his criteria for what constitutes a good school:

> Success always requires that we ask the following question: Success in or for what and for whom? Who are our "consumers"? The students? The parents? The teachers? My focus is the students. A successful school has employees who value and pay great attention to every student, who continuously seek to establish a culture of care and achievement. If you have a school with leaders and staff who, first and foremost, have an eye for every student, their needs and their talents; who are sensitive to student background characteristics, then we have the necessary platform for a good school. Last, but not least, it has to do with mutual trust and good social relationships between students, teachers, school leaders. . . . Of course, we also have to pay attention to student outcomes, and on average it isn't totally bad, however—our drop-out rate is very low, and that is a very important issue nowadays.

On the one hand, both the principal and the teachers considered a low drop-out rate as an important success criterion, not in the least due to the marked change in student enrolment. On the other hand, there was a much stronger focus on learning outcomes and student achievement in society compared with five years earlier. At Ospelia, the student learning outcomes were average compared to other upper-secondary schools in the county, below average in the program for general studies, but above average in the vocational program for technical and industrial production. Given the background of the students enrolled in these programs, the principal was satisfied with the result. The principal talked about having an eye for every individual, and simultaneously showing a concern for the common good. Also, he was very alert when it came to the recruitment of teachers. He emphasized that he was preoccupied with hiring people with the right set of core values and personal traits more than academic skills:

> When we interview applicants for teacher positions, a main issue for me is the social part. I don't focus so much on their academic achievements, but more on personal characteristics, how they relate to colleagues and students. [Interviewer: But would you say they also hold high-quality competencies in subject areas?] High-quality capacity and qualification for teaching is taken as a point of departure, but I don't take any notice of marks. I don't. I may pay attention to the average scores, but first and foremost I emphasize the personal characteristics.

As a whole, our interviews with the principals at Brage and Ospelia demonstrated that they both had a broad definition of success. Improving and supporting working conditions, focusing on staff motivation, and close cooperation with parents were all vital factors for creating a successful school. They talked about equity and equality, and the moral imperative was at the forefront for those working in these schools. Both principals and teachers wanted to 'make a difference' despite relentless demands from national and local authorities, but the ways they addressed issues of educational equity and social justice were often more implicit than straightforward. They described their work as a blend of human, professional, and civic concerns, and in their work they intended to cultivate an environment for learning that was humanly fulfilling and socially responsible. A common characteristic was equity and social justice as personal commitment—an ethic of care and a concern for the common good.

Neither of the principals limited their understanding of success to excellent student outcomes, but took the students and the school context into consideration when they defined success. Support from parents was considered a criterion for success, particularly at compulsory level. The two schools were characterized by open and friendly environments, where teachers supported each other and new staff members were well taken care of. A professional ethos seemed to be guiding their work. The principals emphasized that they had not changed their understanding of what counted as a good school and that their leadership strategies were related to a concern for the welfare of others and working for the common good. A successful school was a school that had the ability to care for every single student. In the interview material as a whole, there were many accounts that spoke of a strong emotional commitment to their profession, and teachers were expected to take significant responsibilities and make important decisions in their everyday work (Møller et al., 2009).

Discussion

Should these two school principals serve as examples of sustained work for promoting equity and social justice in schools and beyond? Do these principals contribute to making schools more inclusive, socially just, and, at the same time, academically successful? The answer may be 'yes' and 'no'.

These principals see themselves as guardians of certain values, which are now at risk because of development towards a more output-oriented means of governing. There seems to be a change in society's values, and steps are taken to introduce market forces into the public sector. At the same time, outcome-based expectations are often imbued with paradoxes and ambiguity, and as such, the situation is creating leeway for practitioners to interpret the policies. Norwegian schools are both autonomous institutions and embedded in—and are accountable to—a municipal-county governance structure. At municipal level, leadership responsibility is shared between professional administrators and elected politicians. Through this link, education is connected to broader community affairs. The principals' actions are not dictated by the shifting political contexts in which they work, but they demonstrate, to some degree, responsiveness to this context. Through the lens of transformative leadership, we may identify a combination of both critique and promise in these schools, but their actions do not seem to move beyond the local context.

At the same time, we need to understand the school's role as an element of the social-democratic welfare state in Norway, where the school emerged, first and foremost, as a public institution. The welfare-state model stressed the redistributive role of the state, and social inclusion underpinned by high levels of taxation and public spending. A dominant view after the Second World War was that the state had a particular responsibility to promote the collective values and interests of society, and high value was placed on education (Telhaug, Mediås, & Aasen, 2006). This legacy of the social-democratic educational model was based on a vision of a homogeneous society. As such, it implied a rather simplistic definition of the common good. When the society became more multicultural, common goals and the common good were no longer self-evident. During the last 25 years, the Norwegian educational policy has been contested, but it has also to some extent maintained a social-democratic foundation. Equity based on social inclusion and solidarity is still emphasized, but at the same time we have moved from highlighting equal life opportunities for all citizens, to appraisal of greater individual autonomy and diversity. Today we give more attention to individual academic achievements and equity is balanced by the demands for efficiency (Aasen, 2007). Nevertheless, it is reasonable to argue that, in spite of the changes in educational policy, social-democratic progressivism is still recognizable in the schools, and there are still very few private schools in the country—2.6% of students in compulsory school.

In addition, the Norwegian school is not only seen as a place for the students but is also often the cultural core of the local community. This turns the local and the regional distribution of schooling into an always-contested issue (Møller, 2009). It is probably the many small, local communities that give Norwegian society its distinctive character. Whenever the local educational authority suggests closing down small schools, the parents mobilize against the decision. Applying a transformative leadership lens to such stories brings evidence of moral courage and activism by parents on behalf of their own children within the local community. In contrast, principals may demonstrate moral courage in their struggle for a more just society, but they are not activists in such cases. Instead, they try to balance the interests of different stakeholders, while at the same time addressing a concern for the common good.

The regional policy dimension has been particularly central in Norway, and throughout history the municipal level has played a strong role alongside a tradition of 'implementation from above'. Educational institutions have been, and still are, important for ensuring the survival of the many small communities in a country where the population is widely dispersed. Also, during the first part of the 1900s, the local teachers became agents of the civic society. They had the cultural and social capital to act on a trans-local level and to mobilize people to work for social justice. As a background for understanding the conceptualization of leadership within the Norwegian education sector, one has to know that the schools and their teachers played a crucial role in the processes of nation-building and shaping of national identities up until the 1970s. Often the teachers became involved in a variety of activities. The teacher ran the local youth club, sport activities, mission society, and other charities (see, for example, Ahonen & Rantala, 2001). Even though the role of teachers as tenets of civic society has declined during the last 40 years, this image continues to influence the expectations people have of teachers, particularly in the rural or semirural areas. In the cities, such an image has more or less disappeared.

A more recent feature—a consequence of the restructuring of the municipal governing of the schools—is the fact that many principals today coordinate various functions that earlier were taken care of at the municipal level. It increases the principal's workload, and the list of what is required by school leaders is wide-ranging, putting them under more pressure. Therefore, a timely question is 'do we expect too much of the principals?'

Conclusion

In this chapter, I have mapped out the practices of two Norwegian school principals, whom we revisited five years after their participation in the International Successful School Principals Project (ISSPP). The discussion in the chapter draws mainly on the school principals' own stories about their criteria for the good school and how these criteria inform their work for equity and social justice within the school. Although general claims cannot be presented based on the data collected in the study, the analysis has illuminated some aspects of the schools' endeavor for equity and social justice.

As demonstrated, the two principals each have a broad definition of success. A successful school is a school that succeeds in taking care of all children, regardless of social-economic or cultural background and abilities, all major elements in the Norwegian educational policy. In other words, the principals are very supportive of the current educational policy, which intends to create both equal and equitable life conditions for all social groups. One aspect of equity is equal access to the educational system, and fairness is understood as the educational system's ability to distribute financial and economic resources in such a way as to meet the needs of all the users in order to provide equal opportunities. Another aspect of equity concerns the individual level: This addresses the diversities among students and, therefore, the necessity for unequal treatment in order to meet the needs of individual learning abilities.

The principals' stories mirror, to some degree, the central debate at the national level and demonstrate how the PISA findings have had consequences for educational policy. The governing of Norwegian schools has been influenced by the discourse of New Public Management, with a focus on managerial accountability, but schools seem, so far, to have the option of paying little attention to managerial accountability. They do not run any risk with this approach. Managerial accountability has, essentially, the status of being the 'anticipated future'. Hopmann (2007) has termed the Norwegian response to new accountability expectations 'muddling-through'—for example, planning, coordinating, and reporting on a local level, with no real stakes and with inconclusive outcomes.

So, despite new expectations from schools, the main findings demonstrate a situation of continuity at the local school. The continuity is reflected in the stories of the principals' capacity to promote good relationships among the staff members, and the moral imperative of developing the whole child, which is still at the forefront of the work being done in these schools. These stories highlight that the school's main aim is to provide good learning opportunities so all children can become good citizens in the future. Improving and supporting working conditions, focusing on staff motivation, close cooperation with parents, and working for equity, are all vital factors in achieving this goal. Furthermore, there is leeway for school principals to interpret the national educational policy to match their own values. There seems to be broad agreement on the normative basis of civics education for schools, but our methodological approach does not allow for any conclusions about how and how well schooling fulfills this function.

However, the task ahead is not just about modeling and developing democratic practices within the school. It is also about challenging the wider power structures in which the school is embedded and committing oneself to work for social change, as the framework of transformative leadership implies. In the reported study, the principals do not challenge the wider power structures in society. On the contrary, power structures are taken more-or-less for granted, and it is apparent that these principals do not move beyond their local context. But is it reasonable to expect school principals to be activists? A vision of transformative leadership is very demanding and, as such, may be criticized for placing too much on the shoulders of school leaders. As a school leader one also has to work within the dominant structures of power and authority. Is it likely that they will exercise oppositional power to become voices for change and transformation?

The findings based on Revisiting Successful School Principals showed that, although the main focus was on what happened within the organization, these principals were deeply concerned about inequities in the wider society. They tried to address equity within their schools as best they could, while criticizing educational policy that would generate inequity. They were driven by their commitment to social justice and worked hard within the system to balance all the demands placed on their shoulders, in order to ensure more equitable learning environments for all students. It is also important to underline that the power of a principal to act cannot be understood if the unit of analysis is limited to the school itself, because its source is delegated by the state. Their work is embedded in wider social structures of power. They may challenge existing power structures—and they do to some extent, as shown in the stories of Brage and Ospelia—but at the same time they have to be compliant with a hierarchical structure. If not, they will lose their job.

Internationally, there are evidences of a widespread erosion of public trust in representative democracy in many countries, and 9/11 has changed the debate on multiculturalism, and also led to a review of what we understand by democracy (MacBeath, 2004). We know not only that poverty is closely linked to student achievement but also that schools can make a difference in students' lives. As a consequence, teaching about and for democracy cannot be a theoretical notion. Teacher and student learning mirror one another, and democratic leadership includes a consideration of the ways in which external social structures are reproduced through the administration of schooling. Transformative leadership in practice, with its focus on liberation, democracy, equity, social justice, and the acknowledgement of power and privilege, calls for a collective endeavor in the local community and the wider society. It is a challenge for political leadership at central level. School principals may nonetheless play a key role in including the stakeholders at the local level in the work for a more democratic schooling. Those of us who are educators at universities also have a responsibility to work with principals and teachers in order to reveal the conditions that create social inequalities in school, including a consideration of the ways in which external social structures are reproduced through the administration of schooling. It is an important start, and a promising way forward, to achieving the success of all students.

Notes

1. It should be noted that the Norwegian case schools that participated in the ISSPP study were not selected based on their academic outcomes, but on public recognition. Norway had to use a different set of criteria for selecting the cases, because there were no public test results and no public inspection reports. However, some schools had received public recognition by the Ministry of Education and Research based on the schools' efforts to improve the learning environment. Some schools received their recognition because they could demonstrate success in providing students with a voice in the school; others could demonstrate that they worked in a very systematic way with regard to personalized education in school subjects. A third group had developed excellent conditions for embracing plurality and difference and promoting equity.
2. At the national level, the immigrant population constitutes about 9%, but in the Oslo area there are, on average, 30% students from language minorities in the schools. Brage and Skog have 20% minority students.
3. The study of these two schools was part of a doctoral project, which allowed for in-depth studies over a period of nine months (Vedøy, 2008).
4. Brage was one of the schools we revisited five years later.
5. Programme for International Student Assessment
6. Prior to 2004, students had to choose a school located in their neighborhood.

References

Aasen, P. (2007). Equality in educational policy. A Norwegian perspective. In R. Teese, S. Lamb, & M. Duru-Bellat (Eds.), *International studies in educational inequality, theory and policy* (Vol. 2, pp. 127–142). New York: Springer.

Ahonen, S., & Rantala, J. (2001). Introduction: Norden's present to the world. In S. Ahonen & J. Rantala (Eds.), *Nordic lights. Education for nation and civic society in the Nordic countries, 1850–2000* (pp. 9–29). Helsinki, Finland: Studia Fennica, Historica 1.

Apple, M. (2000). Between neoliberalism and neoconservatism: Education and conservatism in a global context. In N. C. Burbules & C. A. Torres (Eds.), *Globalization and education: Critical perspectives* (pp. 57–79). New York: Routledge.

Bass, B. M., & Avolio, B. J. (1994). *Improving organizational effectiveness through transformational leadership.* Thousand Oaks, CA: Sage Publications.

Beane, J. A., & Apple, M. W. (1999). The case for democratic schools. In M. W. Apple & J. A. Beane (Eds.), *Democratic schools: Lessons from the chalk face* (pp. 1–26). Buckingham, U.K.: Open University Press.

Burns, J. M. G. (1978). *Leadership*. New York: Harper & Row.

Foster, W. (1986). *Paradigms and promises. New approaches to educational administration*. Buffalo, New York: Prometheus Books.

Furman, G., & Starratt, R. J. (2002). Leadership for democratic community in schools. In J. Murphy (Ed.), *The educational leadership challenge: Redefining leadership for the 21st century* (pp. 105–134). Chicago, IL: National Society for the Study of Education/The University of Chicago Press.

Grace, G. (1995). *School leadership: Beyond education management: An essay in policy scholarship*. London: Falmer Press.

Heinrich, C.J. (2005). Measuring public sector and effectiveness. In G. Peters & J. Pierre (Eds.), *Handbook of Public Administration* (pp. 25–37). London: Sage Publications.

Hopmann, S. (2007). No child, no school, no state left behind. Comparative research in the age of accountability. In S. T. Hopmann, G. Brinek, & M. Retzl (Eds.), *PISA according to PISA—A European perspective* (pp. 363–416). Münster, Westf.: LIT Verlag.

Leithwood, K., Jantzi, D., & Dart, B. (1990). Transformational leadership: How principals can help reform school cultures. *School Effectiveness and School Improvement, 1*(4), 249–280.

MacBeath, J. (2004). Democratic learning and school effectiveness. Are they by any chance related? In J. MacBeath & L. Moos (Eds.), *Democratic learning. The challenge to school effectiveness* (pp. 19–52). London: RoutledgeFalmer.

Møller, J. (2006). Democratic schooling in Norway: Implications for leadership in practice. *Leadership and Policy in Schools, 5*(1), 53–69. (Special issue on international perspectives on leadership for social justice.)

Møller, J. (2009). Approaches to school leadership in Scandinavia. *Journal of Educational Administration and History, 41*(2), 165–177.

Møller, J., Vedøy G., Presthus, A. M., & Skedsmo, G. (2009). Fostering learning and sustained improvement—The influence of principalship. *European Educational Research Journal, 7*(3), 359–371.

Olsen, J.P. (2002). Towards a European Administrative Space? *Arena—Centre for European Studies, University of Oslo* (26).

Røvik, K.A. (2007). *Trender og translasjoner. Ideer som former det 21. århundrets organisasjon. (Trends and Translations. Ideas which have shaped the organization of the 21st century)*. Oslo: Universitetsforlaget.

Shields, C. (2006, October). *Thinking about social justice: Bridging the gap between theory and educators conceptions*. A Paper Presented at the CCEAM Conference (Commonwealth Council of Educational Administration and Management), University of Cyprus, Lefkosia, Cyprus.

Shields, C. (2010). Transformative Leadership: Working for equity in diverse contexts. *Educational Administration Quarterly, 46*(4), 558–589. Online version available at http://eaq.sagepub.com/content/46/4/558

Telhaug, A. O., Mediås, O. A., & Aasen, P. (2006). The Nordic model in education: Education as part of the political system in the last 50 years. *Scandinavian Journal of Educational Research, 50*(3), 229–243.

Vedøy, G. (2008). "En elev er en elev," "barn er barn" og "folk er folk"— Ledelse i flerkulturelle skoler [Leadership in multicultural schools]. Doctoral thesis, University of Oslo, Faculty of Education.

Vedøy, G., & Møller, J. (2007). Successful school leadership for diversity: Examining two contrasting examples of working for democracy in Norway. *ISEA, International Studies in Educational Administration, 35*(3), 58–67.

Woods, P. (2005). *Democratic leadership in education*. London: Paul Chapman Publishing.

20

Transformative Leadership

How Do Montréal School Principals Ensure Social Justice in Their Disadvantaged School?

Jean Archambault and Roseline Garon

Education in Canada is relatively well positioned among other countries and is generally considered to be of high quality and a system that ensures social equity. In fact, many countries envy our education system (Dubet, 2010). Nevertheless, in Canada's French province of Québec, as in other provinces, there are still too many young people who quit school without a diploma. Not surprisingly, they come mainly from disadvantaged areas— another example of how the link between poverty and success in schools continues to operate (Perry & McConney, 2010; Sirin, 2005). This is why, even in a country as wealthy as Canada, and particularly in the province of Québec, it is so important to continue working at breaking this link and at increasing equity and social justice. About 15 years ago, there was such an opportunity when the government of Québec implemented a special initiative for disadvantaged schools in urban areas. We saw an opportunity for us to initiate our own research program within this initiative and in collaboration with the practitioners who worked at this initiative. Our main research objective was to describe elementary school principals' work so as to better understand their work and to offer them better professional development activities.

The aim of this chapter is to present the development of a framework for studying transformative leadership (Shields, 2003) exerted by elementary school principals in urban areas. Transformative leadership is seen here as an interesting theoretical basis for our analysis, as it expands the view of transformational leadership (Leithwood & Jantzi, 2006), where learning is a priority, to include notions of power, social justice, and equity (Shields, 2010).

Two studies of our own gave us insight into principals' work, but many questions concerning social justice and transformative leadership remained. This is why we made a second analysis of our data in order to understand how our elementary school principals ensure social justice in their disadvantaged schools. It is this second analysis that brought us to elaborate a framework for content and method to be used to further study transformative leadership in principals' daily work.

Our research program takes place in Montréal, the largest urban area of Québec. Montréal is composed of 16 municipalities and has a population of 1.85 million, about 26% of the population of the province of Québec. Fifty percent of Montréal's population is both French and English speaking, but for the other half, the French language is predominant. This urban area is situated on an island (Island of Montréal) where one out of three inhabitants was born outside Canada. In fact, the Island of Montreal receives three out of four immigrants that come to Québec (Ville de Montréal, 2010).

Montréal, a Disadvantaged Urban Area

In addition to being the largest, Montréal is also the poorest city of the province of Québec, and is even one of the poorest urban areas in Canada. Two thirds of Montrealers have an income that is under the mean income of C$34,300, and nearly 30% of its families live with low income, that is, they use 20% more than the general mean of the population does for food, lodging, and clothes (Statistics Canada, 2010).

Not surprisingly, in Québec, it is within this area—the Island of Montréal—that the majority of elementary schools with low-socioeconomic status are concentrated. In fact, 184 elementary schools on the Island of Montréal are considered low-socioeconomic-status schools (Gouvernement du Québec, 2009). These schools serve 57,000 of the 101,000 students in Montréal elementary schools, and hold characteristics very similar to those of urban areas elsewhere in Canada and the United States, and even in Europe (Berliner, 2005; Institut national de recherche pédagogique, 2007; Levin, 2004), including a marked academic delay among students from disadvantaged neighbourhoods. The schools also exhibit a concentration of factors similar to those found elsewhere but also very specific to the Island of Montréal, which combine and accumulate to make the situation worse: higher community unemployment rate; concentration of immigrant families, many of whom do not speak French—yet French school is compulsory for immigrants; numerous single-parent families; two main linguistic communities—one Francophone, the other Anglophone; and an important network of funded private schools that drain public schools of their best students. It has also been observed that a significant number of students from disadvantaged neighbourhoods are less successful overall: They experience greater learning difficulties, lag farther behind their peers academically, and are not as successful at consolidating learning. Fewer of these students obtain a diploma, and they often drop out of school earlier, meaning that they can find themselves without any qualifications and with fewer job opportunities (Gouvernement du Québec, 2009).

These elementary schools have benefited since 1997 from additional fiscal resources allocated by the Supporting Montréal Schools Program (SMSP), an action line of Québec's educational reform (Gouvernement du Québec, 1997). Indeed, it is the particular situation of Montréal and the concentration of poverty in the city that incited the government of Québec to offer assistance to Montréal's schools and to embed this support in Québec's educational reform (Gouvernement du Québec, 1997). The SMSP was created to offer this assistance. By establishing this program, the government of Québec recognized the unique challenges of low-socioeconomic-status schools, particularly the educational challenges facing teachers and school principals in the Montréal urban area.

The Supporting Montréal Schools Program

The objective of the Supporting Montréal Schools Program is, "To promote the personal and educational success of students from disadvantaged neighbourhoods, while taking into account their needs and characteristics, and contributing to the creation of a committed educational community" (Gouvernement du Québec, 2009, p. 5). SMSP presently provides support to the 184 lowest socioeconomic-status elementary schools from three French and two English school boards on the Island of Montréal. These target schools were chosen by using widely recognized indicators, such as low income, unemployment rates, and mother's own school attendance. Particularly, services and professional development activities are directed towards school principals so that they can implement strategies viewed as essential in disadvantaged neighbourhoods, in order to improve the success of students.

These schools receive financial, material, and human support from the SMSP's professional team. In addition to basic funding and specific and additional allocations given to the schools, they can also benefit from collective services, such as professional development networks, educational tools produced by the SMSP, an interregional bank of interpreters, various forms of support offered by the SMSP's professional team, as well as research and development activities in collaboration with university researchers. This support is ensured to the schools, in order for them to implement seven strategies that are considered to have a positive impact on learning, educational paths, and the motivation of students from disadvantaged neighbourhoods (Archambault, Ouellet, & Harnois, 2006). Because of their presumed positive impact, these strategies are compulsory for SMSP schools, but target schools implement them gradually and in an ongoing process, while taking into account their own situation and the specific needs of their students. School teams are responsible for the implementation of these strategies, which is coordinated by the school principal. These strategies involve (Gouvernement du Québec, 2009):

1. instructional interventions that promote learning and success for all;

2. emphasis on the development of reading competency;

3. a guidance-oriented approach;

4. continuous professional development of the school principal and the school team;

5. access to cultural resources;

6. cooperative links with students' families; and

7. cooperative links with the community.

The fourth strategy is of particular interest for the present chapter.

Strategy 4: School Principals' Professional Development

On a regular basis, SMSP's professional team initiates a reflection on one of the seven strategies in order to evaluate its relevance and its effectiveness and to improve the services offered to the schools. It is the fourth strategy, "continuous professional development of the school principal and the school team," that became the center of interest three years ago. Regarding this strategy, SMSP's professional team had set up professional development groups for school principals. But some questions arose: What would be the pedagogical content for these groups? What do school principals need to develop? In fact, what is distinctive about leading a school in a disadvantaged area?

Leading an elementary school, be it in a disadvantaged area or not, is a complex endeavor. It requires that school principals possess particular attitudes and competencies, especially when their schools are located in disadvantaged areas (Dupuis, 2004; Haberman, 1999; Lapointe & Gauthier,

2005; Leithwood, Seashore Louis, Anderson, & Wahlstrom, 2004; Muijs, Harris, Chapman, Stoll, & Russ, 2004). All the more so, it seems that certain leading practices may have more effect in disadvantaged schools than in advantaged ones (Garon & Lapointe, 2007).

It is this questioning and this reflection that led us to establish a research program with the Supporting Montreal Schools Program, examining the work of elementary school principals on the Island of Montréal, an urban area with a significant concentration of poverty (Archambault and Harnois, 2008).

A Collaborative Research Program

Our research interest in elementary school principals coincided with the practical interest of the SMSP, especially regarding school principals' professional development. This is why we worked with SMSP's professional team to define school principals' needs and research objectives. This work was done with SMSP's professional staff according to a collaborative research paradigm, as outlined by Lieberman's "Collaborative Research: Working with, Not Working on. . ." (1986). Researchers and practitioners negotiated their needs and their expectations and planned the research program together, making sure to attain what Desgagné calls *double vraisemblance,* or double likelihood, where, because rigor and relevance are both preserved, mutual benefits are obtained (Desgagné, Bednarz, Couture, Poirier, & Lebuis, 2001).

"Working with" means, of course, working with school principals. And we chose to work with typical principals who were not necessarily exemplary or outstanding but who showed interest in working with us. Working with typical principals allowed us to sound out the real baseline of their daily work in school and to be better prepared to cater to them in professional development.

The two studies presented here are part of this larger research program done with SMSP. We will describe secondary analyses of these two studies' findings, examining them from the "transformative leadership for social justice" point of view.

First Study: Principals' Discourse

In our first study, we interviewed 45 typical elementary school principals in eight focus groups. Archambault, with a member of SMSP's professional team, conducted two interviews with each group. At the first meeting, we asked principals to talk largely about their jobs: what were the tasks of a principal in a low-SES school? What were the qualities, the competences, and the attitudes required of a school principal in low-SES school? The second meeting was used to delve more deeply into the answers of the first meeting. We began by giving principals a summary of their first meeting's answers, and we also presented them with the main findings of a review of the literature on performing schools in disadvantaged areas (Archambault & Harnois, 2006) in order to confront these findings with their answers and to further stimulate responses from the principals.

All interviews were digitally recorded and an integral transcript was developed. The material, which was in Microsoft Word format, was subsequently coded and analyzed, using qualitative data analysis software, according to a simple thematic coding method.

Findings

We found that school principals saw leading a school in disadvantaged area as (1) an extra burden placed on them, (2) necessitating particular competencies and attitudes, (3) having to exert a transformative leadership that advocates social justice, and (4) being sustained by ongoing professional development.

It is the third finding that interests us here. Having recently reviewed it, we knew of the flourishing literature on leadership for social justice (Archambault & Harnois, 2009a) and on transformative leadership (Shields, 2003, 2006). Nevertheless, this subject was not discussed by school principals at the first meeting. At the second meeting, we presented leadership for social justice as being one of the main features of performing schools in disadvantaged areas (Archambault and Harnois, 2006). But at this second meeting, we were a little surprised by school principals' answers to our questions.

At first, they told us that there were no prejudices or false beliefs in their school. They emphasized the fact that their personnel had been working in the school for many years and knew the neighborhood and its characteristics. Being aware that false beliefs and prejudice are present in disadvantaged areas (Archambault & Harnois, 2009b; Gorski, 2008; Normore & Blanco, 2006) and that deficit thinking prevails (Archambault, 2010; Flessa, 2007; Portelli, Shields, & Vibert, 2007), we went on to question the principals. At this time, they began to acknowledge that there were prejudices, false beliefs, deficit thinking, and lowering of expectations in their schools:

> At the beginning of the meeting we were told that teachers think that all children can learn, but at last we realize that many of them hold prejudices. (Principal 5)

Let's take a closer look at what the principals said regarding social justice.

A Strong Belief in Children's Capacities, but Prejudices in Their School

The principals said that they believed all children could learn and had the capacity to succeed. For most of them it was a fundamental belief:

> They are as capable to succeed as any other children elsewhere. (Principal 41)

> What is major for me is the strong belief that all students are capable of learning . . . If we don't hold this belief, we stand outside of the school's mission. (Principal 1)

Nevertheless, the principals indicated that there were prejudices against people living in poverty in their schools. These prejudices took different forms: they were against the way of life of people from poverty, against what they looked like and who they were, especially when it came to considering children living in poverty as having deficiencies or deficits:

> We look very much at children's deficiencies. We say that they are understimulated. (Principal 25)

> We should begin with not taking them as retarded because they don't know or they are not interested in books . . . we should rather discover what they know. They have some knowledge. (Principal 5)

When it came to describing parents as being unable to care for their children, other prejudices or false beliefs emerged, concerning expectations for student-learning and their capacity to learn. A belief in every child's capacity to learn was clearly not held by everybody:

> . . . prejudices that parents do not take care of their children, [who] are left alone . . . that parents do not help with homework. (Principal 33)

. . . it is the belief that all of them can learn, but in our schools there are prejudices and not every-body shares this belief and not everybody has high expectations for the children. (Principal 3)

Prejudices That Principals Ought to Fight . . .

The principals we spoke with considered it an important part of their work to support teachers' professional development, which consists of bringing about changes in attitudes and beliefs, fighting against prejudices, and exerting a leadership that promotes social justice. They saw moral implications as important, and all those we interviewed wanted to make a difference for these students. Many of their efforts to bring about change were aimed at their school team:

I think that much of my work consists of raising teachers' awareness about this reality, about the young at school and about their families. (Principal 41)

There is no room for the child in the classroom. It is the program or the project that counts and it is the child who must adapt, and not the contrary . . . I have teachers who don't see the child in poverty. They only see the subject matter [they have to teach them]. (Principal 1)

There is this fire burning inside of me. I believe in what I say . . . I think there are social inequi-ties, that these kids . . . we ought to do something for them . . . what we have already done is not enough. (Principal 14)

. . . Using Educational Strategies

The principals reported using several strategies to fight against those prejudices and false beliefs: sending reminders to the school team, distributing information on the neighborhood and on poverty, promoting professional development—or sometimes interventions—aimed at changing behaviours—in order to increase equity and to avoid segregation or exclusion:

On a regular basis, I remind my personnel of what it is to be a child in disadvantaged areas. I use videos during team meetings and we discuss those issues every three months, but I have to remind them of what is working in a disadvantaged area, children's needs . . . I do that because, yes, there are prejudices. (Principal 9)

I have been able to question these kinds of after school retention they had on [this past] Friday, mainly for young boys who had pushed someone else at recess on the schoolyard . . . And I won my point and made it stop when I told my teachers: "Listen, it (after school retention) does not work, it is always the same 10 to 15 young black boys. I know them well and it is not fun." Our [For my teachers] role was to be dull and to make them do dull things. But this is not educational at all. (Principal 1)

Transformative behaviours exhibited by these school principals included fighting against preju-dices and false beliefs about children of poverty and their families, reminding the school team on a regular basis of the characteristics of the school environment, raising teachers' awareness about the importance of maintaining their expectations at high levels for children's learning, and keeping an eye on practices that segregate or discriminate against children in order to change them. These behaviours helped reduce inequities and, in the long run, helped children gain confidence in their learning capacity, an essential condition if children are to learn effectively.

Learning Not a Priority

One would think giving high priority to learning would be a preferred strategy for increasing eq-uity and decreasing prejudices. But for many principals in disadvantaged areas, learning does not always come first. Some principals confessed that for many reasons—mainly the overburdening work, the feeling of emergency, and unexpected occurrences—educational aspects of the school often fell second. . . we are told

> "your main role is to be an instructional leader." But in disadvantaged areas, look, there are so many other glaring things [going on]. Yes, we have it in our head, but in day-to-day reality, it is something else [that has our attention]. (Principal 42)

Principals Reveal Their Own Prejudices and False Beliefs

During the interviews, principals also revealed their own prejudices against children in poverty and against their families: first, towards children's characteristics—particularly towards their deficiencies, deficits, distresses, woes, exhibitions of hostility and violence, and finally towards the expectations one can sustain with regard to these children. Of particular importance here is the fact that most prejudices and false beliefs exhibited deficit thinking, which is detrimental to learning and social justice (Portelli et al., 2007; Valencia, 2010):

> . . . our kids are basically the same as every other kids. But when they come to school, some things are missing. There are deficiencies or lacks in their needs. (Principal 44)

> You already start with a slower pace that moves forward, but more slowly. (Principal 37)

> Even when you succeed in helping him or her to understand the text, he or she is blocked by his own cultural background. (Principal 9)

> What is different in disadvantaged areas? Children are suffering. (Principal 39)

> Violent environment; basic needs not answered. (Principal 44)

Second, they show prejudices towards family values. When they express those views, we see a sense of exclusion in the "us versus them" discourse, as much as in the perception of the role of the school consisting of inculcating "good" values. They also show prejudice towards families often considering them as responsible for their children's school problems—being themselves under-educated and having had bad school experiences themselves, these parents are not present in their child's school life and, therefore, cannot support their child's school experience.

> You should be open to accept[ing] children's parents that do not necessarily have the same values . . . [or] the same way of seeing things as us. (Principal 2)

> Sometimes I think they have strange moral values. But they have some.

> . . . values like "My uncle has a big car, he earns big money." But they have values. (Principal 13)

> For many reasons, parents are in [an] emergency [situation], they are not in the flow of life, as we are. They have to answer basic needs. (Principal 11)

> Parents: They are afraid of education. They haven't been successful, so how do you bring them back in? What skills can they bring, especially when a number of them are illiterate themselves? (Principal 23)

> When parents are undereducated and when the parent lacks abilities, it is difficult to give his or her child resources or means. (Principal 24)

Interpretation of the Findings

At the very beginning of the second meeting, the principals believed that their environment was free from prejudices and false beliefs. Further discussion and questioning brought them to change their point of view, and they began to talk heavily about the prejudices and false beliefs of their school team. They even described their role as being one of fighting against these prejudices and false beliefs in order to protect social justice. Yet, during the two meetings, principals also exhibited prejudices and false beliefs very similar, on the whole, to those of their school teams. One could hypothesize that it is our questioning that sensitized them to their school team's prejudices and that, nobody being against virtue, it became morally just to them to rise up against those prejudices and to claim to be fighting against them. Furthermore, given that they themselves showed these kinds of false beliefs and prejudices, one could ask if their level of awareness towards prejudices and false beliefs was really that high, and if they would have thought of fighting against false beliefs and prejudices without our questioning during the interviews. Still, they described strategies they used to protect social justice in their schools. Some principals, especially, reported being really active in promoting social justice.

These findings being a little astonishing, we wanted to know more about what principals do to address these issues. This is why we went on to further examine how school principals not only fought prejudices or false beliefs, but also, more broadly, how they exerted transformative leadership so as to pursue social justice in their school (Shields, 2010; Theoharis, 2010). Thus, we went on to reexamine transcripts of observations collected in the second study, from this new point of view.

Second Study: Transformative Leadership in School Principals' Daily Work

Findings of the first study left one big unanswered question that was relevant for both researchers and principals: Beyond their discourse, what do principals do while leading a disadvantaged school and keeping at heart the idea of social justice? That is the question we aim to answer by reanalysing data from the second study.

Methodology

In the second study, we observed (via shadowing) 12 typical elementary school principals for three days. All these principals, except for one, had participated in the first study. For each of the three days, they were followed by a research assistant who recorded in notes everything they did. We then transcribed these notes and analyzed them in accordance with the social justice issue. Compared to the first study, where we collected discourse data from principals, here we collected actual behavioural data in order to describe what school principals really do and how they actually assume their transformative role.

Findings

One of the observed principals directly encouraged teachers' social justice practices. For example, he nodded in agreement to a teacher who spoke about his or her potential to improve the students' disadvantaged context. Another principal talked about effective teaching practices during a general teacher meeting, and got teachers to think about the possibility that they may have lowered their expectations for their students. Still another principal organized an activity to collect data, in order to know better the students.

In a somewhat different way than in the interviews, observations help illustrate the principals' biases or prejudices, which we found out about though what they told us in the first study. For example, one principal said to a teacher that it was difficult to get parents to collaborate, even if the teacher had just told the principal that a student's parents participate well. In addition, it is rather interesting to find out that one principal believed in the capacity of every child to succeed and, at the same time, held prejudices against the willingness of economically "disadvantaged" parents to collaborate.

Nevertheless, we realize that several behaviours we observed cannot be categorised for analysis, because we do not know the reasons why actions have been undertaken by the principal. For example, many times, we observed situations where a principal helped a parent or a student with advice or money. Was it because the principal thought that the parent or student would never get it by themselves, or, on the contrary, was it because the principal thought that this help would empower the parent or student? In the same way, we could not infer principals' motivations or intentions in fostering relationships with the community that would be related to social justice.

Interpretation of the Findings

Overall, in the second study we found that very few observation data are related to social justice; that is a, first, interesting—though not surprising—finding. Indeed, given the fact that in the first study, principals had to be questioned directly on the subject to even talk about this, it speaks for itself. In fact there is much similarity between principals' discourse and the behaviours observed. In the same way as principals told us in the focus groups, we could find in observation data some behaviour consistent with the promotion of social justice and also some clues for the prejudices principals hold, sometimes even within the same principal. Portelli et al. (2007) also observed this fragility of the contour in the discourses of their participants:

> These discourses are neither discrete nor universal, but are contingent on the interaction between context and interpretation. Thus, the boundaries between them are fluid, such that in practice multiple discourses function not only within the same school and context, but often within the same person. (p.7)

Wouldn't this fragility mean that principals understand only superficially the issues of the dominant culture, of poverty, and, more broadly, of social justice? And last, many behaviours could not be categorised as social justice behaviours or not, because principals' intentions were rarely explicit.

These findings globally reveal the necessity, first, to elaborate a framework for studying transformative behaviours aimed at preserving social justice, and, second, to choose a method that would allow us to have access to the motivations and intentions underlying what principals do.

Elaboration of a Transformative Leadership Behaviour Framework

Reviewing literature, we soon realized that most authors on transformative leadership, following Bogotch's call (2002), claim that this competence requires that people not only believe or be in agreement with or talk about social justice, but, as important, that they do something to promote social justice (Beachum & McCray, 2010; Shields, 2003, 2010; Theoaris, 2010). As a result, we decided to take a closer look at the theoretical literature about behaviour and behaviour change. Then, integrating this literature with the literature about social justice and transformative leadership, we worked at elaborating a conceptual framework and a method that would allow us to study school principals' transformative practices.

Behaviour and Behaviour Change

Many theories have been elaborated in health education to describe behaviour and behavior change (Eccles, Grimshaw, Walker, Johnston, & Pitts, 2005; Fishbein, 2000). They may be grouped around motivational theories, action theories, or stage theories (Eccles et al., 2005). Because health education researchers often have to elaborate, implement, and evaluate intervention programs, they contribute to developing these theories (Fishbein et al., 1992; Hagger, Chatzisarantis, & Biddle, 2002). According to their studies, four elements are generally addressed that may take many forms: knowledge, attitudes-values-beliefs, reported behaviour, and actual behaviour and skills. Each of these elements has been included in our conceptual framework. It is interesting to note that self-reported behaviour and actual behaviour could be different, and that we should take both into account.

A Framework to Study Transformative Leadership Behaviours in Context?

Examining the transformative leadership and social justice literature, we found five aspects that have to be taken into account by transformative leaders in order to effect change in their school (Shields, 2010; Theoharis, 2009):

1. Elements of the dominant culture

2. Context of students from disadvantaged environments

3. Personnel's and students' knowledge, attitudes, and behaviours linked to social justice

4. Strategies to promote change and social justice

5. Barriers to the promotion of change and social justice and means to overcome them

Integrating elements of behaviour change into what we find in the transformative leadership literature results in the framework of Figure 20.1, presented on the next page. Each column represents one of the four elements of behaviour change, whereas each line represents an element to be taken into account by transformative leaders. We can see how these elements combine with aspects of behaviour change to show every part of the framework that should constitute the discourse or the behaviour of transformative leaders—or both. Let's take a closer look at the framework.

In order to study principals' transformative leadership practices for social justice, we must be able to find, in discourse data or in observation data, some awareness on the part of principals of elements of the dominant culture, such as knowledge of the fact that dominant people benefit from privileges, while oppressed people suffer from discrimination, awareness of where oppression exists in the school's community, or an understanding of power issues and where they manifest in classrooms and elsewhere (Beachum & McCray, 2010; Fraser & Shields, 2010; Shields, 2006). Principals' use of words or concepts referring to race, class, gender, handicap, sexual orientation, and so forth, can serve as indications of a certain awareness on their part. However, according to most work on transformative leadership, awareness or knowledge of the effects of power struc-

Knowledge	Attitudes, Beliefs, Values	Self-Reported Behaviours	Observed Behaviours
Personnel awareness of privileges and inequities	*Will to change so as to promote social justice*	*Strategy implementation to effect change towards social justice*	*Strategy implementation to effect change towards social justice*
Knowledge of dominant culture's characteristics	Will to increase ones own and other people's awareness of dominant culture's characteristics	Reported behaviours aimed at increasing ones own and other people's awareness of dominant culture's characteristics	Observed behaviors aimed at increasing ones own and other people's awareness of dominant culture's characteristics
Knowledge of the context of students from disadvantaged areas	Will to increase ones own and other people's knowledge of the context of students from disadvantaged areas	Reported behaviours aimed at increasing ones own and other people's knowledge of the context of students from disadvantaged areas	Observed behaviours aimed at increasing ones own and other people's knowledge of the context of students from disadvantaged areas
Knowledge of attitudes, particular knowledge and bahviours related to social justice for school personnel and students	Will to increase ones own and other people's knowledge about attitudes, particularly knowledge and behaviours related to social justice for school personnel and students	Reported behaviours aimed at increasing ones own and other people's knowledge about attitudes, particular knowledge and behaviours related to social justice for school personnel and students	Observed behaviours aimed at increasing ones own and other people's knowledge about attitudes, particular knowledge and behaviours related to social justice for school personnel and students
Knowledge of strategies to increase social justice and to induce change	Will to identify and implement strategies to increase social justice and to induce change	Reported behaviours aimed at increasing social justice and inducing change	Observed behaviours aimed at increasing social justice and inducing change
Knowledge of the barriers to social justice and change and of the means to overcome them	Will to identify and overcome the barriers to social justice and change	Reported behaviours aimed at identifying and at overcoming the barriers to social justice and change	Observed behaviours aimed at identifying and at overcoming the barriers to social justice and change

Figure 20.1 Operational Framework for the Study of Transformative Leadership

tures—or even good intentions about exerting transformative leadership—is not enough (Shields, 2003). People must report or show attitudes and behaviours that demonstrate they understand—or help others understand—that these privileges and discriminations really exist, and that they know where they take place. In our study of principals' practices, we must also define characteristics of this understanding, which would represent clues of transformative leadership in their reported behaviour or in their actual observed behaviour. Thus, our framework has to take this discourse and its translation into actual behaviour into account.

A transformative principal who leads a disadvantaged school should know the context of life of his or her students. However, according to Lyman and Villani (2002), this context is complex. For example, some relatively quiet, nonviolent, multiethnic schools in Montréal are more financially poor than culturally poor, and education for parents and children from this neighbourhood is a fundamental value. Many parents have been well educated in their country of origin. In contrast, there are some other homogeneous milieus where violence is a daily routine and education a burden. These schools show both types of poverties, financial and cultural, and may be more ethnic, or not. For a transformative leader, it would be necessary, in order to ensure social justice, to use specific approaches tailored to the school and based on precise data. Therefore, studying how principals promote social justice should imply verifying what they know and let it be known about their students and their context, or undertake to do that; principals examining preexisting data or collecting actual data, in order to avoid relying only on their own perceptions, may well prompt their own concerns about social justice.

As the principals should have a deep knowledge of their students and of their context, they should also have a good idea of the knowledge, attitudes, and behaviours of both the school personnel and the students themselves concerning social justice. Where do they stand? Are they already convinced that there is a dominant culture or dominant cultures that they have to counter or fight with active strategies? Or do principals have to start from the beginning and have the school community reflect upon and work on the issue of power and social justice? What about the students? Do some of them exert power over others? Are they aware of the exercise of power by dominant cultures? Where do they stand regarding poverty? Do they know if there are differences between poor and rich children? between different ethnic communities?

One can recognize transformative leaders by their actions that are guided by an intention. But to be efficient, knowing effective strategies to promote social justice or change may be useful. Strategies can operate at different levels, from people to school structure, and from community to district. On this matter, Shields (2010) and Theoharis (2009, 2010) talk about promising tracks that bring precision to our framework, such as strategies aimed at changing curriculum-teaching-learning issues; the inclusive organizational culture and structure; professional development; and parent and community mobilization.

Finally, even though it may be counterproductive to dwell on barriers (Garon & Leroux, 2009), knowing them and the means to overcome them, wanting to identify them, or reporting actions aimed at surmounting these barriers are all elements that can emerge from interviews or observation intended to study transformative leadership and social justice practices. For example, acknowledging personnel's resistance to change and developing strategies to mobilize and include all members of the personnel in the fight for social justice are something to look for in interviews or observation.

Resulting Method

It seems obvious that obtaining a clear and complete picture of transformative behaviours requires combining two methods of data collection: observation and interview. But, in contrast with what we did in the studies just described—that is, interviewing and observing separately—what we need is interviewing principals on what they just did. One way to do this, for example, is to present observation transcripts to principals and have a researcher question them on different aspects of the transcript, in order to stimulate reflection-in-*action*. This general method of stimulated-recall interview, or the more specific self-confrontation interview on what they have done or not (Clot, Faïta, Fernandez, & Scheller, 2000; Yvon & Garon, 2006), has often been used to study professional practice (Vesterinen, Toom, & Patrikainen, 2010). Data from observation and interviews are then analysed with the framework described earlier.

Future Research

In Québec, some researchers manifest interest in poverty's social, economic, and moral challenges. But only a few of them work directly on school principals' work. This is why it appears so important to us to carry on with our research program. This research program must not only produce knowledge on the issue but also inform school principals' compulsory preparation curricula at the university level and professional development programs at the SMSP level. For now, the preparation curricula deals quite partially with the subject of exerting transformative leadership for social justice in schools in disadvantaged areas. The conceptual framework and the matching research method described earlier will serve as a foundation for our next study. In so doing, we want to make sure that we contribute to the concomitant advancement of both research and training.

As for research, we will be able to develop and refine our conceptual framework and to pinpoint the strengths and weaknesses of both data collection methods—interview and observation. As for professional practice, we will gain a better idea of Québec school principals' needs for training. Should training be concerned with their knowledge, their attitudes, or their behaviour? Of the five elements that tell transformative leaders apart from the others, which ones are lacking and which ones should be addressed first? Answering these questions should help faculties to renew their curricula and professionals in charge to improve their services so as to better suit school principals' needs for training. Moreover, data collected as interview and observation transcripts could be adapted to become instructional material. For instance, it would be possible to develop scripts for case studies or to draw critical incidents in order to induce reflection and conversations among school principals.

Conclusion

In Québec, equity and social justice are in everyone's public discourse. Québec's government has implemented measures to reduce poverty and to foster social justice. Nevertheless, poverty and inequities persist, as if the discourse were not enough. Poverty and inequity is also an issue in Québec's schools, and our research program shows that school principals do have a discourse about inequities and social justice in their schools. It is clear for them that social injustice persists.

Given the recurring interest and the abundant literature on the subject of social justice (Archambault & Harnois, 2009a; Frattura & Capper, 2007), our findings from the studies presented here are surprising. We found that principals at first did not see problems of social justice in their schools; then, when further questioned, they were able to describe prejudices and false beliefs exhibited by their personnel and advocated their fight against these prejudices and false beliefs—yet, at the same time, they exhibited their own prejudices and false beliefs. These prejudices and false beliefs were of the same kind as the ones they were fighting against with their personnel. Furthermore, we found very few behaviours related to promoting social justice on the part of the principals that we observed.

Compared to outstanding principals who turn their schools around using transformative leadership (Shields, 2010; Theoharis, 2009), we found that typical school principals' work does not seem to be influenced by social justice. Yet, when they are shown social injustice, they acknowledge it. Talking about it is clearly not enough.

Our work as researchers is clearly to better understand school principals' work. But it is also to help them understand the importance of power imbalance in their schools and the necessity of talking about this imbalance and, mostly, to act to improve it. This is why it is also our work to improve training. Our initial preparation programs and professional development programs for school principals should take social justice into account.

The framework we presented here, to be used to study transformative leadership practices for social justice, can be useful in school principals' preparation. Indeed, not only can we be aware of better principals' practices, but we can also train them better if we take elements of the framework into account (see Figure 20.1). First, professional development should consider the many aspects of behaviour change—that is, principals' knowledge, attitudes, beliefs, and values, as well as their reported behaviour and, primarily, their actual behaviour. Knowing better where they stand for each of these aspects will allow us to focus on the right things during professional development. Second, these aspects of behaviour change should be worked upon in order for principals to increase their awareness of the aspects of social justice they will have to look after in their school: the elements of the dominant culture, its differential impacts on students, and the exercise of power; the context of students from disadvantaged environment, their ways of life, their values, knowledge, and skills; personnel's and students' knowledge, attitudes, and behaviours linked to social justice, as in prejudices and false beliefs; strategies to promote change and social justice; and barriers and resistances to the promotion of change and social justice, and the means to overcome them. By taking into account each element of this framework when training school principals, one could contribute to better preparing principals to inhabit a transformative leadership role for social justice.

References

Archambault, J. (2010). Maturité scolaire et vision éducative. *Vivre le primaire, 23*(1), 14–15.

Archambault, J., & Harnois, L. (2006). *Des caractéristiques des écoles efficaces, provenant de la documentation scientifique*. Research report, Université de Montréal et Programme de soutien à l'école montréalaise (MELS).

Archambault, J., & Harnois, L. (2008). *La direction d'une école en milieu défavorisé: ce qu'en disent des directions d'écoles primaires de l'île de Montréal*. Research report, Programme de soutien à l'école montréalaise (Ministère de l'Éducation, du Loisir et du Sport), Université de Montréal, Faculté des sciences de l'éducation, département d'Administration et fondements de l'éducation, 155 p.

Archambault, J., & Harnois, L. (2009a). *Le leadership de justice sociale en éducation. Extraits de la littérature scientifique*. Research report, Université de Montréal et Programme de soutien à l'école montréalaise (MELS).

Archambault, J., & Harnois, L. (2009b). *Le leadership de justice sociale en éducation. Fausse croyances et préjugés au sujet de la pauvreté. Extraits de la littérature scientifique et professionnelle*. Research report, Université de Montréal et Programme de soutien à l'école montréalaise (MELS).

Archambault, J., Ouellet, G., & Harnois, L. (2006). *Diriger une école en milieu défavorisé. Ce qui ressort des écrits scientifiques et professionnels*. Research report, Ministère de l'Éducation, du Loisir et du Sport, Programme de soutien à l'école montréalaise, p. 19.

Beachum, F. D., & McCray, C. R. (2010). Cracking the code: Illuminating the promises and pitfalls of social justice in educational leadership. *International Journal of Urban Educational Leadership, 4*(1), 206–211.

Berliner, D. (2005). Our impoverished view of educational reform. *Teachers College Record, 108*(6), 949–995. Retrieved July 14, 2008, from http://www.tcrecord.org/content.asp?contentid=12106

Bogotch, I. (2002). Educational leadership and social justice: Practice into theory. *Journal of School Leadership, 12*(2), 138–156.

Clot, Y., Faïta, D., Fernandez, G., & Scheller, L. (2000). Entretiens en autoconfrontation croisée: Une méthode en clinique de l'activité. *Pistes, 2*(1), 1–7. Retrieved February 18, 2009, from http://www.pistes.uqam.ca/v2n1/pdf/v2n1a3.pdf

Desgagné, S., Bednarz, N., Couture, C., Poirier, L., & Lebuis, P. (2001). L'approche collaborative de recherche en éducation: Un nouveau rapport à établir entre recherche et formation. *Revue des sciences de l'éducation, 27*(1), 33–64.

Dubet, F. (2010, November). *Les sociétés et leur école*. Paper presented at l'Université de Montréal, Canada.

Dupuis, P. (2004). L'administration de l'éducation: Quelles compétences? *Éducation et francophonie, XXXII*(2), 132–157.

Eccles, M., Grimshaw, J., Walker, A., Johnston M., & Pitts, N. (2005). Changing the behavior of healthcare professionals: The use of theory in promoting the uptake of research findings. *Journal of Clinical Epidemiology, 58*(2), 107–112.

Fishbein, M. (2000). The role of theory in HIV prevention. *AIDS Care, 12*(3), 273–278.

Fishbein, M., Bandura, A., Triandis, H. C., Kanfer, F. H., Becker, M. H., & Middlestadt, S. E. (1992). *Factors influencing behavior and behavior change: Final report—Theorist's workshop*. Rockville, MD: National Institute of Mental Health.

Flessa, J. J. (2007). *Poverty and education: Towards effective action. A review of the literature*. Research report, Elementary Teachers' Federation of Ontario.

Fraser, D. F. G., & Shields, C. M. (2010). Leaders' roles in disrupting dominant discourses and promoting inclusion. In A. L. Edmunds & R. B. Macmillan (Eds.), *Leadership for inclusion* (pp. 7–18). Rotterdam, the Netherlands: Sense Publishers.

Frattura, E. M., & Capper, C. A. (2007). *Leading for social justice. Transforming schools for all learners.* Thousand Oaks, CA: Corwin Press.

Garon, R., & Lapointe, P. (2007). *Pratiques de gestion éducatives en contexte de réforme et défavorisation.* Paper presented at the 35th Annual Conference of CSSE, Saskatoon, Saskatchewan.

Garon, R., & Leroux, M. (2009). *Étude de la résilience de directions d'école primaire en milieu défavorisé.* Research report: Montréal.

Gorski, P. C. (2008). The myth of the culture of poverty. *Educational leadership, 65*(7), 32–36.

Gouvernement du Québec. (1997). *Prendre le virage du succès. Plan d'action ministériel pour la réforme de l'éducation.* Québec: Ministère de l'Éducation du Québec.

Gouvernement du Québec. (2009). *The Supporting Montréal Schools Program.* Québec: Ministère de l'éducation, du Loisir et du Sport.

Haberman, M. (1999). *Star principals serving children in poverty.* Indianapolis, IN: Kappa Delta Pi.

Hagger, M. S., Chatzisarantis, N., & Biddle, S. J. H. (2002). A meta-analytic review of the theories of reasoned action and planned behavior in physical activity: Predictive validity and the contribution of additional variables. *Journal of Sport and Exercise Psychology, 24*(1), 3–32.

Institut national de recherche pédagogique. (2007). *Apprendre et enseigner en milieux difficiles.* Lyon, France: Centre Alain Savary (INRP).

Lapointe, C., & Gauthier, M. (2005). Le rôle des directions d'écoles dans la dynamique de la réussite scolaire. In L. DeBlois & D. Lamothe (Eds.), *La réussite scolaire. Comprendre et mieux intervenir* (pp. 455–482). Collectif du CRIRES, Ste-Foy, QC, PUL.

Leithwood, K., & Jantzi, D. (2006). Transformational school leadership for large-scale reform: Effects on students, teachers, and their classroom practices. *School Effectiveness and School Improvement, 17*(2), 201–227.

Leithwood, K., Seashore Louis, K., Anderson, S., & Wahlstrom K. (2004). *Review of research: How leadership influences student learning.* Executive summary, University of Minnesota (CAREI), University of Toronto (OISE), The Wallace Foundation.

Levin, B. (2004, December). Pauvreté et éducation au centre-ville, *Horizons, 7*(2), 45–50.

Lieberman, A. (1986). Collaborative research: Working with, not working on. . .. *Educational leadership, 43*(5), 28–32.

Lyman, L. L., & Villani, C. J. (2002). The complexity of poverty: A missing component of educational leadership programs. *The Journal of School Leadership, 12*, 246-280.

Muijs, D., Harris, A., Chapman, C., Stoll, L., & Russ, J. (2004). Improving schools in socioeconomically disadvantaged areas—A review of research evidence. *School Effectiveness and School Improvement, 15*(2), 149–175.

Normore, A. H., & Blanco, R. I. (2006). Leadership for social justice and morality: Collaborative partnerships, school-linked services and the plight of the poor. *International Electronic Journal for Leadership in Learning, 10*(27). Retrieved March 29, 2011, from http://www.ucalgary.ca/iejll/vol10/blanco

Perry, L. B., & McConney, A. (2010). Does the SES of the school matter? An examination of socioeconomic status and student achievement using PISA 2003. *Teachers College Record, 112*(4), 7–8. Retrieved September 4, 2009, from http://www.tcrecord.org, ID Number: 15662.

Portelli, J. P., Shields, C., & Vibert, A. B. (2007). *Toward an equitable education: Poverty, diversity, and students at risk.* Ontario Institute for Studies in Education, University of Toronto, National Library and Archives Canada.

Shields, C. M. (2003). *Good intentions are not enough. Transformative leadership for communities of difference.* Lanham, MD: Scarecrow Press.

Shields, C. M. (2006). Creating spaces for values-based conversations: The role of school leaders in the 21st century. *International Journal of Educational Administration, 34*(2), 62–81.

Shields, C. M. (2010). Transformative leadership: Working for equity in diverse contexts. *Educational Administration Quarterly, 46*(4), 558–589.

Sirin, S. R. (2005). Socioeconomic status and academic achievement: A meta-analytic review of research. *Review of Educational Research, 75*(3), 417–453.

Statistique Canada/Statistics Canada. (2010). Les seuils de faible revenu. Retrieved on October 30, 2010, from http://www.statcan.gc.ca/pub/75f0002m/2009002/s2–fra.htm

Theoharis, G. (2009). *The school leaders our children deserve: Seven keys to equity, social justice, and school reform.* New York: Teachers College Press.

Theoharis, G. (2010). Sustaining social justice: Strategies urban principals develop to advance justice and equity while facing resistance. *International Journal of Urban Educational Leadership, 4*(1), 92–110.

Valencia, R. R. (2010). *Dismantling contemporary deficit thinking.* New York, Routledge.

Vesterinen, O., Toom, A., & Patrikainen, S. (2010). The stimulated recall method and ICTs in research on the reasoning of teachers. *International Journal of Research & Method in Education, 33*(2), 183–197.

Ville de Montréal. (2010). *Montréal en statistiques. Profil sociodémographique, agglomération de Montréal* [Online bulletin]. Montréal : Service de la mise en valeur du territoire et du patrimoine. http://ville.montreal.qc.ca/pls/portal/docs/PAGE/MTL_STATS_FR/MEDIA/DOCUMENTS/PSD_AGGLOM%C9RATION_DE_MONTR%C9AL.PDF

Yvon, F., & Garon, R. (2006). L'analyse du travail par l'auto-confrontation croisée: Transfert d'un dispositif méthodologique de l'ergonomie à l'éducation. *Recherches qualitatives, 26*(1), 51–80.

21

The Helpless, the Bullies, the Misguided, the Advocates

School Leaders and Inclusive School Reform

George Theoharis and Marcia Ranieri

This chapter recognizes the growing body of scholarship demonstrating the key roles school leaders play in creating and maintaining equitable and excellent schools (Scheurich & Skrla, 2003; Theoharis, 2009). In complement, Villa, Thousand, Meyers, and Nevin (1996) found that school administrators' own beliefs about inclusive services for students with disabilities were the best predictor of the quality and success of inclusive school reform. In looking at leadership that creates inclusive and equitable schools for marginalized students with a particular focus on students with disabilities, Frattura and Capper (2007), McLeskey and Waldron (2006), and Theoharis (2009) have identified leaders whose work very closely aligns with what Shields (2010) and others describe as transformative leadership. These leaders' work seeks to bring deep change to the educational realities of students with disabilities, change that results in personal and professional tension and dissonance as it challenges organizational and societal norms.

This chapter is a product of a secondary analysis of four different qualitative research projects that each focused on leadership, school reform, and issues of inclusion and equity. The purpose is to highlight the ways transformative school administrators lead in contrast to other leaders tackling similar issues. In addition, this chapter makes the necessary connection between the social-justice aims of transformative leadership and inclusion of students with disabilities. The first of these studies was a study of seven school leaders who came to the field of educational administration with the commitment to create more equitable and socially just schools and made great strides in accomplishing that (Theoharis, 2007; 2009). The second of these studies involved schools and their leaders who chose to engage in an inclusive school-reform initiative between a university and a partner urban school district (Causton-Theoharis, Theoharis, Bull, Cosier, & Dempf-Aldrich, in press; Theoharis & Causton-Theoharis, 2010). The third project involved studying schools leaders and their interest in and commitments to creating more equitable and just schools, as a part of their involvement in a university and state department of special education project to identify and replicate promising practices in special education. The fourth project was similar to the first but involved studying district office leaders who had strong commitments to further an inclusive and equity-oriented agenda and made notable strides in moving their district in that direction (Theoharis & Frattura, 2009). All four studies involved ongoing work with school leaders, school visits, observations of these leaders on the job, interviews with each of the school leaders, discussions or interviews with teachers and others who work with the leaders, and a review of documents.

Inclusive School Reform, Advocacy, and Transformative Leadership

Equity-oriented, inclusive school reform provides all learners with access to the general education curriculum. A defining aspect is that all students—including students with significant disabilities, autism, emotional disabilities, learning disabilities, and so forth—are taught in heterogeneous classrooms with their peers (McLeskey & Waldron, 2006; Theoharis & Causton-Theoharis, 2010). Studies suggest that the impact of an inclusive model of service delivery affects all students, not just those labeled as having a disability (Burnstein, Sears, Wilcoxen, Cabello, & Spagna, 2004). Equity-oriented inclusive school reform is also designed to harness the integration of school resources (Frattura & Capper, 2007; Theoharis & Causton-Theoharis, 2010). Villa et al. (1996) found that school leaders are the best predictors of successful inclusion; thus, the intersection of inclusive school reform and school administration is a key starting point to examining transformative leadership.

Central to this reform is placing students with varying abilities in the same classrooms as well as facilitating meaningful interaction throughout the school day via the collaboration and integration of both general education teachers and specialists. As with any innovation or educational reform effort, the successful inclusion of students with disabilities requires fundamental change in the organizational structures of schools and in the roles and responsibilities of teachers (Burnstein et al., 2004). Structured professional development to help educators collaborate, take on new and fluid roles that blur the lines between general educator and specialist, and incorporate paraprofessionals is necessary for this transformation to occur within the schools committed to inclusive reform. McLeskey & Waldron (2006) noted that the change process is based on the belief that inclusive schools cannot be developed from a prescribed model; instead, the school must reflect its own beliefs, attitudes, culture, and skills. The result of this process is that schools are more responsive to the individual needs of all students. The framework and collaborative reform that McLeskey and Waldron proposed consider the attitudes and beliefs of school professionals, clarify the goals of a local inclusive program, recognize barriers to reorganizing special and general education instruction, and address the reasonable concerns of school personnel and parents. We see this kind of leadership as transformative, in that students with disabilities are and historically have been marginalized and forced to receive fewer educational experiences. Thus, enacting authentic inclusive reform requires transformative leadership.

Anderson (2009) defined *advocacy leadership* as laying out a postreform agenda that moves beyond the neo-liberal, competition framework to define a new accountability, a new pedagogy, and a new leadership role definition. He continued to say that drawing on personal narrative, discourse analysis, and interdisciplinary scholarship will push schools to move away from current inauthentic and inequitable approaches to school reform and towards an alternative vision of our current education system. Advocacy leadership requires that school administrators take action to create a school community, and a broader community, that is more equitable and just. As such, the intersection between advocacy and inclusion provides an important vantage point for understanding transformative leadership.

Wasonga (2009) studied 32 principals who gradually transformed their schools to be high achieving, and found advocacy to be a resounding trend in the data as a result of her study. Principals noted that their intention was to educate students to the best of their ability while they were in school with them. These leaders were advocates for their marginalized students. They were focused on creating schools where their students received the best education possible, while working tirelessly to overcome the obstacles that stood in their way. Wasonga (2009) stated that "overall, advocacy was about giving every student every chance possible to learn, grow, develop, and become a good citizen" (p. 201). Successful leaders focused on each of these areas each and every day in their schools.

Increased collaboration was the key when there were intense obstacles to creating change. Wasonga (2009) explained that turn-key principals

> use relationships and values such as respect, trust, and humility to break social barriers, enhance collaboration, develop common interest, and increase understanding of issues. They exercise social control with purpose to facilitate the use of deep democratic processes and the invitation of voices that would otherwise be silenced or left behind. (p. 204)

Similarly, the implication of effective inclusive schooling of students with disabilities requires collaboration. This includes a mutually beneficial professional environment, increased roles of teachers as advocates for students, and knowing the extent to which inclusion affects an entire school community (Colucci, Epanchin, Hocutt, & LaFramboise, 2004). The fundamental principle of inclusive education is the valuing of diversity within the human community:

> When inclusive education is fully embraced, we abandon the idea that children have to become "normal" in order to contribute to the world. . . . We begin to look beyond typical ways of becoming valued members of the community, and in doing so, begin to realize the achievable goal of providing all children with an authentic sense of belonging. (Kunc, 1992, p. 39)

In seeking to change their organizations for the better, these leaders included other stakeholders in deep and meaningful ways. Inclusive reform does so similarly, in that it necessitates that all learners feel connected and belong to the greater community of the school. Transformative leaders do more than engage children with disabilities—they advocate for change in schools and communities, spark a passion for inclusion amongst teachers, paraprofessionals, and families, but, most of all, they put the child at the center of their focus. They also give parents the practical guidance they need to make it work (Jorgensen, Schuh, & Nisbet, 2006).

Transformative ideals also owe much to the work of Freire (1970/1998), who used the terms *transform, transformation,* and *transformative* to describe the changes that may occur as a result of education. Freire called for personal, dialogic relationships to undergird education, because without such relationships, he argued, education acts to deform rather than to transform (Shields, 2010). School leaders who see the problems facing them and advocate for marginalized students (in this case, students with disabilities) while creating school structures, climate, and collaborative teams, bridge advocacy leadership and transformational leadership. Effective leaders within inclusive reform typify this. We argue that schools cannot be considered equitable for all until all students have access to general education teaching, curriculum, and peers. This means eliminating segregated campuses, schools, rooms, and programs, requiring advocacy by school leaders as they commit to inclusive reform. The social justice underpinnings of this inclusive advocacy are the focus of this chapter on transformative leadership.

Contrasting Leadership Orientations

This chapter focuses on the leadership styles or orientations of administrators across these four studies. This is done to illustrate the differences between inclusive advocacy, which we see as transformative leadership, and other contrasting orientations, which we see as both less effective and not transformative. For clarity of presentation, we describe the contrasting leadership orientations based on the way each leader approached his or her practice of advancing inclusive school reform. The four orientations that were constructed through the analysis are (1) the helpless, (2) the bullies, (3) the misguided, and (4) the advocates. It is important to be clear that none of the leaders fell solely into just one of the constructed styles. Each leader possessed aspects of multiple orientations. While each leader manifested multiple orientations at different times and in different ways, we provide general features of each orientation and examples of the kinds of behavior and beliefs for each orientation, across all of the leaders involved in this secondary analysis. We refer to the different leaders by pseudonym.

The Helpless Orientation

The *helpless* orientation was seen when leaders threw up their hands and both felt and acted like they could not change a particular situation or current reality. Principal Scott felt helpless in the face of his boss, the assistant superintendent, who set up a weekly meeting where she provided ongoing critique of his work and offered unsolicited advice. Director Judy was seen as helpless because she felt she could not influence the sheer number of initiatives the district was engaged in or mandated to do. Principal Dale felt helpless in the face of rising paperwork requirements that came from central office.

For some leaders helpless was not an occasional feeling or way or acting, it was their predominate leadership stance around inclusive reform. The leaders whose predominate orientation was helpless agreed that providing access for students with disabilities is the right thing to do, but they had no idea how to move their school in that direction, and often conveyed the message that "there is nothing I can do," or "my hands are tied" by either regulations, district policy, resistant teachers, or special education administrators. For example, Principal Mack wanted to adopt, in his words, "a fully inclusive model." Yet, he felt he could not get people together to make this work effectively. He could not find ways to provide professional development or resources to support that learning, he did not expect teachers to take on new roles, he did not feel he could ask teachers to be part of ongoing discussion and planning for a new inclusive model, and he left students in self-contained or pull-out special education rooms. He provides a clear example of someone who believed inclusive services would be better but could do nothing to get his school there. A transformative leader, by definition, acts with moral courage and so cannot operate from a predominantly helpless orientation.

The Bully Orientation

The bully orientation was seen in a variety of leaders. This makes sense, in that principals and central office administrators are in positions where they often need to implement ideas or programs that might not be popular or have widespread support. We classify bully behavior as forcing action against another's will, and sometimes this included a spiteful or vengeful attitude in dealing with other staff or families. Assistant Superintendent Connie used the bully orientation as she replaced principals without their input or much discussion because they were not supporting the inclusive reform efforts. Principal Olivia exhibited bully behaviors as she focused on micromanaging teachers' lesson plans and specialists' schedules, in that she would berate staff for failing to provide this information or not providing it in the manner she wanted.

The leaders whose predominate orientation was bully were interested and focused on school improvement and the necessity of raising test scores. While this group might be sympathetic to including students with disabilities, who have historically been taught in pullout or self-contained settings, they are interested in rapid results first and foremost. The bullies over-rely on mandates and direct supervision to implement inclusive reform but have not embraced beliefs about the philosophical underpinning of inclusion and seeing all students as competent and valuable assets. In general, since leaders who exhibited a predominate bully orientation were engaged in inclusive reform, they felt or knew that greater access to general education for students with disabilities would provide greater achievement, and so in essence they believed inclusive services were the best thing for students. The way they went about making that happen, however, exhibited their bully orientation. This channeled them into being unable to create an authentic sense of belonging and inclusion in their schools, as they fell back on excluding certain students and their families when challenges arose.

Special Education Director Ann knew inclusive services were right, yet she berated general and education teachers for their weak collaborative attempts. This was ongoing and became expected and thus impacted the culture. It did not create better collaborative teams. She demanded that their practice change but provided almost no opportunities for input of professional learning. Principal Olivia was regularly reprimanding teachers and paraprofessionals for things we felt were minutia. This created a culture where no one would take risks, which led to minimal collaboration or new ideas.

We see that the bully orientation does not mesh well with transformative leadership. If an administrator is focused on an inclusive and socially just goal, while excluding, belittling, or berating others, that is not transformative. Martin Luther King Jr. explained this as it relates to transformative leadership: "Ends are not cut off from means, because the means represent the ideal in the making, and the end in process. Ultimately, you can't reach good ends through evil means, because the means represent the seed and the end represents the tree" (King, as cited in Washington, 1991, p. 255. The bully orientation creates a community of mistrust, anger, and avoidance. This in turn breaks ties, disconnects individuals from the school community, and detracts from the goals of a transformative leadership focus.

The Misguided Orientation

School administrators who espouse inclusive philosophy, but who, when translating that to practice, create more separate programs or separate ways for students to receive service, typify the *misguided* orientation. Being misguided is not the same as making mistakes. Leaders who intentionally create communities within schools that exclude certain students from the lunch room, limit students with disabilities' access to rigorous academics or their general education peers, or schedule all students with disabilities in the same physical education class are misguided. When we refer to those who are misguided we denote those leaders who think they are doing meaningful work; however, they are just creating more exclusive programs and spaces. This involved, for example, setting up self-contained special education rooms and schools, or, in the spirit of inclusion, clustering all the students with disabilities or students learning English into one room, creating an overly dense cluster of student needs. This is in contrast to heterogeneous grouping and natural proportions. In the midst of implementing inclusive services, Principal Judy proposed that two students with emotional disabilities be moved to another school. This was in direct opposition to the philosophy behind the reform, that all students should be members of the general education classroom and that the school would redeploy resources to provide the appropriate services. So, while she was leading inclusive reform, she made misguided efforts that excluded two students from her school.

Principal Lee was a strong proponent of the inclusive services his school was implementing. He championed creating a section of high school content that would be co-taught between general education teachers and special education teachers, while keeping the high-tracked and AP classes separate from the "inclusive" ones. This resulted in running a dual system within the high school—a high track and an inclusive track, and at times up to 60% of the "inclusive" classes were made up of students with disabilities. This work missed the mark in creating authentically inclusive classrooms and school and is misguided in that it created a low-track system that separated students with disabilities into particular classrooms.

In investigating the practice of inclusive reform, the leaders whose predominate orientation is misguided are not transformative because they maintain marginalization and segregation of students with disabilities. Ultimately, these leaders did not create more inclusive schools or systems.

The Advocate Orientation

The *advocates* represent the leaders who have grown to embrace their own agency in changing their school structures, policies, and culture. They have developed a sense of responsibility to ensure an equitable education, gain necessary personal knowledge to support their work, and tirelessly advocate for students with disabilities. Special Education Director Martin saw a district that operated many separate and segregated programs for students with disabilities, along with principals who were happy to abdicate responsibility for students receiving special education. He engaged in reforming the services across the district as well as implementing professional development with principals as he felt both needed to and could change their service delivery.

Principal Tracy inherited a special education program that relied on pullout and self-contained services. Instead of creating large clusters of students with special needs and adding them to elementary classrooms in the name of inclusion, he led a redesign process where teams of teachers spent significant time and energy creating balanced classrooms. Teams of general educators and special educators were then given professional autonomy to decide upon how to collaborate and support the students with disabilities—as long as students were being served in heterogeneous groups.

While imperfect, the schools run by advocate leaders represent a fundamental and deep shift in beliefs and structures. Students who challenge the education system—in this case, students with the entire range of disabilities—are valued as essential community members who are educated in heterogeneous classrooms with groupings of peers with and without disabilities. The advocates focused on the need for all students to be included as a way of changing the entire focus of the school. We are not arguing that simply advocating will result in inclusive schools or make one a transformative leader. We are arguing that leaders in these studies whose predominate orientation was that of advocate had a particular, socially just focus to their advocacy. They were focused on ending separate programs and marginalized education for students with disabilities. Their advocacy was centered in a socially just vision of inclusive schools that placed the needs of traditionally marginalized students at the center of the work of their schools.

Examining the Styles

We have just provided examples and definitions of the four orientations of school leaders engaging in inclusive school reform. The remainder of this chapter will provide three contrasting pairs of leaders—each pair will have a leader whose primary orientation is that of an advocate, as well as a leader of one of the other orientations (helpless, bully, misguided). This is done to illustrate the differences, both glaring and subtle, between leaders who take a day-in and day-out advocacy stance and other leaders seeking similar ends but whose leadership practice strays from advocacy. Not all leaders who advocate create inclusive schools and not all leaders who advocate are transformative. However, for this chapter and the secondary analysis of these four research projects, a necessary orientation we found for both creating meaningfully inclusive schools and operating from a transformative stance was an orientation of advocacy.

The first pair includes one leader with a predominant orientation of helpless with another leader with that of an advocate. The second pair contains a predominant orientation of bully with an advocate; the third combines a predominant orientation of misguided and an advocate.

First Pair: Helpless and Advocate

This section will compare two elementary principals—one whose predominant orientation was helpless, Principal Gale, and one whose was advocate, Principal Meg. When faced with staff who were angry about the proposed inclusive service delivery, Principal Gale felt she could not change their minds and then decided that they were not going to implement a new inclusive service delivery after all. After making a decision to initially move toward more inclusive services, her action of back-peddling was done because she felt she could not change the minds or practices of a vocal minority. This helpless stance left a group of students with cognitive disabilities in a self-contained room where, according to Principal Gale, "they were receiving a joke of an education." She recognized that those students would benefit tremendously from being in a general education classroom, but did nothing about it.

Principal Meg, an advocate, felt it was her responsibility to change the services at her school—to eliminate pullout and self-contained programs for students with disabilities as well as English Language Learners. She applied for district, state, and federal waivers to policies in order to create small heterogeneous classes where the teacher was responsible for reaching all students. She became a vocal advocate across her urban district for inclusive school reform.

Principal Gale and Principal Meg demonstrated behaviors and feelings of all four orientations. Table 21.1 provides examples of the ways in which they embodied those different orientations. Their predominant orientations are evident in that their work gravitated back to that location, thus greater numbers and more substantial actions and feelings were found there. It is important to realize that Principal Gale's school never implemented inclusive reform, which meant many students with special education needs were not given full access to the general education curriculum and peers. Her leadership has led to the continuation of self-contained and pullout services. The achievement of all students and, in particular, students with disabilities has remained low. In contrast, Principal Meg's schools (she has led similar inclusive reforms at two elementary schools) have seen significant achievement gains for all students and, in particular, for students with disabilities and students learning English. She has led the elimination of self-contained and pullout programs for both special education and ESL and replaced them with inclusive services in heterogeneous classrooms.

Second Pair: Bully and Advocate

This contrasting pair includes two middle school principals—one who operated largely as a bully, Principal Judy, and one who predominately was an advocate, Principal Dale. Principal Judy made the decision to move forward with inclusive reform, which allowed many students with disabilities

Table 21.1 Comparison of Leaders with Predominant Orientations of Helpless Versus Advocate

Leader and Primary Orientation	Helpless	Bully	Misguided	Advocate
Principal Gale—*Helpless*	Cannot change culture of teaching teams Cannot tell people to change practice Cannot expect related services to be in the classroom Hands tied by union representative and vocal minority Nothing she could do, because some vocal staff did not want to change Allowed students with cognitive disabilities to continue receive "a joke of an education"	Minimal communication about planning or school improvement (e.g., "I control the information.")	Decides to adopt inclusive services but never implements in the face of staff resistance	Uses shared decision-making structures Encourages more collaboration Expects teachers to have ideas and solutions to solve their own problems
Principal Meg—*Advocate*	Feels hands tied by district initiative about gifted and talented programs	Makes service-delivery changes, even when staff does not want to	Values co-teaching but sees general education teacher as more important.	Sets up schedule and services so students receive all support in the classroom, guided by an articulated belief that classroom teaching and learning as best intervention. Keeps students in heterogeneous groups. Outspoken with district colleagues about inclusive services. Democratic and shared decision-making structures.

access to general education curriculum and peers; this certainly had an aspect of advocacy. However, she operated from a bully orientation, and staff felt this was something they were being forced to do; her personal style was intimidating and vindictive to those who were not supportive. During their first year of implementation, Judy told some of her specialists to "put away those stupid games you play in your special rooms and get teaching in the classrooms." Principal Judy created teams of

Table 22.2 Comparison of Leaders with Predominant Orientations of Bully Versus Advocate

Leader and Primary Orientation	Helpless	Bully	Misguided	Advocate
Principal Judy—*Bully*	Cannot change how the district allocates staff Cannot change the students who are shipped to the school for special education services	Vindictive about staff who challenge her Adopts "inclusive services are happening—like it or not" stance Creates teams each year based on her perspective: "I will decide who will work together."	Does not extend inclusion of students with disabilities to afterschool programs Articulates that the students whose behavior is the most challenging should go to another school and seeks ways to achieve that	Adopts inclusive service delivery for all students Expects and reinforces teachers to engage in ongoing learning Ensures that all teaching and related services to be brought to the general education classroom.
Principal Dale—*Advocate*	Overwhelmed by the amount of paperwork and district directives	Makes service delivery changes, even when staff does not want to.	Asks for a particularly complicated student with significant behavior and disability to be removed from his school	Sets up schedule and services so students with disabilities receive all support in the classroom Sets up co-teaching teams where teachers have professional autonomy to decide how to use the staff they had and how to co-teach Detracks math while including students with disabilities, so all students receive math instruction in heterogeneous groups Democratic and shared decision-making structures.

special education teachers and general education teachers based on her ideas for the best teams and with little input from staff. Her bullying stance drove the reform to take shape but created a school climate where staff felt intimidated and not invested.

Principal Dale led inclusive service delivery changes at his middle school, which also resulted in all students with disabilities being included in general education classes. Like Principal Judy, Dale moved forward without the entire staff on board. His sense of advocacy was driving the need to change a system of pullout and self-contained special education that was marginalizing students, even though some staff and parents resisted. He also led with detracking of math classes. Unlike Principal Judy, he did not micromanage his staff or intimidate them. He created teaching teams with teachers' input and granted them the autonomy to decide how best to use their time, as well as which paraprofessionals were assigned to their teams. Staff embraced the opportunity to work together, coteach, and try new things without fear that Principal Dale would reprimand them as they were getting used to new collaboration and sharing roles within the classroom. He made certain that students with disabilities were taught in heterogeneous groups in the general education classroom, but in such a way that set a tone of inclusivity and empowerment for staff.

Principal Judy and Principal Dale demonstrated behaviors and feeling across the four different orientations. Table 21.2 details examples of the ways in which they embodied the different orientations, but also illuminates their predominate orientation. Additionally, it is important to know that both schools were high-needs, high-poverty, racially diverse urban middle schools. Both implemented inclusive school reform, which eliminated pullout and self-contained programs for students with disabilities. Over the years, this gave hundreds of students with disabilities access to the general education curriculum, classroom, and peers in ways they had not had previously. Both schools saw a drop in discipline and both made similar significant gains in achievement. The climate at each school was different, however, in that staff at Principal Judy's school felt intimidated and morale appeared to be low; they implemented inclusive services and co-teaching but did not seem to embrace the changes, nor did they deeply invest themselves in changing their practice. In addition, the inclusive philosophy did not permeate the school, as every year a number of teachers would push for a couple of students to be sent to other schools. Additionally, they did not provide inclusive support for students with disabilities in their new afterschool or summer programs. At Principal Dale's school, it was palpable that staff members were invested in their newly created inclusive teams. The climate felt much happier than Principal Judy's school in terms of staff enjoying their work and putting in effort to change their teaching practices.

Third Pair: Misguided and Advocate

This final pair contrasts the leadership of Special Education Director Barry, a predominately misguided orientation, with that of Special Education Director Debra, a predominate advocate. While the four qualitative projects that provided data for this chapter included leaders spanning numerous states, for this pair it was important to note that these two leaders are special education directors in the same state. This is key, as special regulations, language, and oversight vary from state to state and it is important to see that, while compliance with special education regulations is a key part of special education administration, leadership can and is enacted differently under the same constraints, resulting in different outcomes.

Director Barry spoke articulately about the need for inclusive services and his beliefs about social justice equating to providing inclusion to students who had historically been marginalized. He supported an inclusive-reform partnership between the university and two schools in his district. Yet, he saw inclusion as one special education program among many, not a guiding philosophy for all students. This led him to maintain a busing system that sent students with disabilities to different schools around the city for different types of programs, in contrast to an inclusive approach, which brought all services to students at the school they would typically attend. Students with disabilities were sent across the city to self-contained, pullout, and inclusive programs instead of each school providing these. As the district rolled out citywide initiatives to create comprehensive afterschool and summer programming for all elementary students, Director Barry played no role, which left students with disabilities marginalized, in that many were not allowed to attend and those that were part of these programs often were separated from their peers.

In contrast, Director Debra saw inclusion of students with disabilities as a driving philosophy for her work and for the district. Inclusion was not seen as a program to implement but as a way to

Table 21.3 Comparison of Leaders with Predominant Orientations of Misguided Versus Advocate

Leader and Primary Orientation	Helpless	Bully	Misguided	Advocate
Special Education Director Barry—*Misguided*	Cannot change that some staff do not want to collaborate or include students with disabilities Cannot change how principals do not take ownership for students with disabilities	-	Maintains busing system that sends students with disabilities to schools around the district based on "space" in a particular program Purchases separate literacy curriculum for students with disabilities Plays no role in district initiative offering afterschool and summer programming: inclusion of students with disabilities not part of afterschool or summer programs Articulates self contained school for students with emotional disabilities as a lab for ideas about behavior management for the rest of the district. Allows students with significant communication needs to be isolated	Supports inclusive reform initiative at a number of schools Finds resources to support specific requests from principals at these schools
Special Education Director Debra—*Advocate*	Cannot control the amount of initiatives.	-	Maintains off-campus, self-contained community placements for a few students	Democratic in practice and sharing of information Works schedule and services to allow for students with disabilities to receive all support in the general education classroom Sets up co-teaching team: teachers have professional autonomy Infuses inclusive philosophy into other initiatives: Reading First, state grants Opens district to visitors from other districts

guide decisions. The philosophy that Director Debra used was that students with disabilities were authentic and valued members of the general school community. This led her to bring teams of elementary, middle, and high school teachers together, in order to figure out how to provide services for students with significant disabilities within the general education classrooms. When the district took on new initiatives, like Reading First, Director Debra played a major role in the implementation, in that it was done inclusively for students with disabilities, with attention to heterogeneous grouping. She also felt that creating inclusive services in her district was not enough, and so she opened her district to visitors from around the state to come and see the inclusive-based philosophies driving all of the practices across the district.

Director Barry and Director Debra demonstrated behaviors and feelings across three of the four different orientations. Table 21.3 provides examples of the ways in which they embodied the different orientations. In addition, Table 21.3 illuminates their predominant orientation. Both Director Barry and Director Debra worked in high-needs, high-poverty districts in the same state. It was clear that staff across Director Debra's district and school community were both committed to and proud of their inclusive practices. Their district student achievement has grown steadily over the past 5 to10 years and the students perform above state averages—and students with disabilities perform particularly well. They have been recognized by universities and the state for their commitment and success at delivering inclusive services. Director Barry's district has seen modest gains in student achievement across the district and minimal improvement in the achievement of students with disabilities. It is one of the lowest performing districts in the state. Their commonly held belief across this district is that some children should be included and some should not, combined with a resounding belief that students with disabilities are primarily the responsibility of special education staff.

Conclusion

We are not implying, nor can we prove, that the leaders with the advocate orientation are the reason why their schools and districts both raised achievement and created inclusive services in heterogeneous groups for all students with disabilities. Yet it is compelling to see how their advocacy leadership has created schools and districts where marginalized students—students with disabilities—are being seen and educated as valued and authentic members of the general learning community. The advocate leaders across these studies felt they had a mission to guide and lead their schools to be safe places that fostered growth and acceptance amongst all parties. In conclusion, we highlight some of the key aspects of the advocate leaders, which we argue relate directly to transformative leadership.

First, they balanced a democratic and collaborative style with a strong commitment to keep the inclusive needs of students with disabilities at the center. They maintained these two conflicting realities—collaboration and their vision of inclusion. They felt that they were responsible for changing the way students with disabilities were educated and that they, as leaders, were responsible for making it happen. They were collaborative, but did not see this as "someone else's responsibility." This advocacy of their inclusive vision through collaboration connects directly to how Shields (2010) outlines transformative leadership—these administrators started with the realistic notion of marginalized students, and they worked with and persevered through tension and conflict.

Second, they worked beyond their school community. They took a message of inclusive and socially just reform to leaders and community members outside of their local school context. In other words, they were champions and allies for students with disabilities both within and outside of their school. Again, this carries out the activism and the goal to seek broader equitable social change that Shields (2010) describes as a key to transformative leadership.

Third, they did not see inclusive reform as an add-on, distinct, or separate initiative. This is in stark contrast to seeing inclusive reform as a special education initiative. The advocates rejected that view. This is a key aspect of transformative leadership, as well, in that the advocate leaders did not see inclusive service for students with disabilities as separate from running their school effectively; they saw it as a necessary and foundational piece of creating a more socially just school. Their zeal for creating a school where students with disabilities had access to general education teaching, the same curriculum, and collective groups of peers yet were as equally valued as any other student. This was a guiding philosophy they brought to all of their work.

These aspects of successful inclusive reform are key aspects bridging transformative leadership (Shields, 2010) and advocacy (Anderson, 2009). The leaders felt it was their responsibility to create not only inclusive schools but to also take that message beyond their workplace. They worked collaboratively to change the organization and culture but did not let democratic structures move them away from creating inclusive services. They felt compelled and responsible for ensuring inclusivity for all students across their organizations. We argue that in combination, these aspects of their advocacy leadership moved these administrators to operate from a transformative and inherently political location and in doing so created more equitable and just schools.

References

Anderson, G. L. (2009). *Advocacy leadership: Towards a post-reform agenda in education.* New York: Taylor & Francis.

Burnstein, N., Sears, S., Wilcoxen, A., Cabello, B., & Spagna, M. (2004). Moving toward inclusive practices. *Remedial and Special Education, 25*(2), 104–116.

Causton-Theoharis, J., Theoharis, G., Bull, T., Cosier, M., & Dempf-Aldrich, K. (In press). Schools of promise: A school district-university partnership centered on inclusive school reform. *Remedial and Special Education.*

Colucci, K., Epanchin, B., Hocutt, A., & LaFramboise, K. (2004). Working together: Emerging roles of special education teachers in inclusive settings. *Action in Teacher Education, 26*(3), 29–43.

Frattura, E. & Capper, C. A. (2007). *Leading for social justice: Transforming schools for all learners.* Thousand Oaks, CA: Corwin Press.

Freire, P. (1998). *Pedagogy of the oppressed* (New rev. ed.). New York: Continuum Publishing Company. (Originally published in 1970.)

Jorgensen, C. M., Schuh, M., & Nisbet, J. (2006). *The inclusion facilitator's guide.* Baltimore, MD: Paul H. Brookes Publishing Co., Inc.

Kunc, N. (1992). The need to belong: Rediscovering Maslow's hierarchy of needs. In R. A. Villa. J. S. Thousand, W. Stainback. & S. Stainback (Eds.), *Restructuring for caring and effective education: An administrative guide to creating heterogeneous schools* (pp. 25–39). Baltimore, MD: Paul H. Brookes.

McLeskey, J., & Waldron, N. (2006). Comprehensive school reform and inclusive schools. *Theory into Practice, 45*(3), 269–278.

Scheurich, J. J., & Skrla, L. (2003). *Leadership for equity and excellence: Creating high-achievement classrooms, schools, and districts.* Thousand Oaks, CA: Corwin Press.

Shields, C. M. (2010). Leadership: Transformative. In P. Peterson, E. Baker, & B. McGaw (Eds.), *International Encyclopedia of Education* (Vol. 5, pp. 26–33). Oxford: Elsevier.

Theoharis, G. (2007). Social justice educational leaders and resistance: Toward a theory of social justice leadership. *Educational Administration Quarterly, 43*(2), 221–258.

Theoharis, G. (2009). *The school leaders our children deserve: Seven keys to equity, social justice, and school reform.* New York: Teachers College Press.

Theoharis, G., & Causton-Theoharis, J. (2010). Include. Belong. Learn. *Educational Leadership, 68*(2), 225–238. Retrieved October 10, 2010 from http://www.ascd.org/publications/educational-leadership/oct10/vol68/num02/Include,-Belong,-Learn.aspx

Theoharis, G., & Frattura, E. (2009, November 19). *Intersecting Policy and Professional Development: District Office Leadership for Equity, Inclusion and Social Justice.* Paper presented at the annual meeting of the

UCEA Annual Convention, Anaheim Marriott, Anaheim, California. Retrieved November 10, 3020, from http://www.allacademic.com/meta/p378306_index.html

Villa, R., Thousand, J. S., Meyers, H., & Nevin, A. (1996). Teacher and administrator perceptions of heterogeneous education. *Exceptional Children, 63*(1), 29–45.

Washington, J. M. (ed). (1991). *A testament of hope: the essential writings and speeches of Martin Luther King Jr.* New York, Harper Collins.

Wasonga, T. (2009). Leadership practices for social justice, democratic community, and learning: School principals' perspectives. *Journal of School Leadership*, 19(2), 200–24.

22

Developing a Leadership Education Framework

A Transformative Leadership Perspective

Lauren Stephenson

With a particular emphasis on emerging transformative leadership perspectives, this chapter reports on leadership perspectives specific to the Emirati context that aligned with several of Shields's (2010) transformative leadership characteristics. These characteristics include leadership development through community engagement, giving back to the community. and service learning. These elements informed the development of the conceptual framework for student leadership education at Zayed University and led the participants to a better understanding of the nature of transformative leadership and its utility in the United Arab Emirates (UAE) context.

In 2009, the provost requested that a year-long Conversation on Leadership (CoL) project explore ways to institutionalize leadership education, develop research, and create a more coherent conceptual framework for student leadership education. The university's previous leadership initiatives had proved successful but only for a relatively small cohort, and there was concern about the sustainability, range, and inclusivity of those programs. A wide range of leadership development initiatives were already in place, and it was important to tie those activities to a broader conception of leadership education and development, one that not only encompassed personal development and curricular initiatives but also integrated overt behavioural skills with deep structural and principled leadership knowledge and skills (Komives, Longerbeam, Owen, Mainella, & Osteen, 2005, 2006; Lord & Hall, 2005) that are critical for effective collective leadership in today's world. It was intended that ZU construct a distinctive philosophy of leadership and leadership education that would address the specific needs of Emiratis and the development of the UAE and would be grounded in the different leadership challenges its students faced within work, family, and societal contexts. The project's intended outcomes included a review of the status of student leadership education at the university and agreement on a draft conceptual framework, which would serve as a basis for the development of a student leadership education curriculum.

Given that the author was a key participant in the project, engaged in the longitudinal, ongoing process of learning about leadership and leadership development, a case-study approach was used. It provided an opportunity to document a unique, multi-layered process of individual and collective learning about leadership and student leadership education. The following broad questions were investigated:

1. What are we talking about when we talk about 'leadership'?

2. What leadership perspectives are most appropriate for our students?

3. How do we develop leadership?

This chapter is significant in that it provides an account of a unique, collaborative, pluralistic process of learning about leadership undertaken by a university community as it worked toward the development of an undergraduate leadership education curriculum. This chapter contributes to the knowledge base on leadership education through the development of a better understanding of the importance of transformative leadership perspectives for student leadership education in the region and in higher education contexts in general.

Background

Prior to federation in 1971, the UAE was known as the Trucial States, with each emirate having its own independent ruler. Since federation, the UAE has operated as a 'nation-state' and socio-economic development has been rapid. The UAE has had many economic and social successes in the name of progress. However, it has also faced some of the challenges that newly emerging countries can often face. These challenges include the pace and scope of economic growth and societal change. This fast pace has led to what Kazim (2000, cited in Clarke & Otaky, 2006) has described as three differing discourses within current UAE society: "conservative" (seeking to preserve social patterns from earlier times), "progressive" (welcoming global perspectives), and "moderate" (trying to balance between the first two). These discourses are apparent in the different issues arising within recent leadership discourse (e.g., the place of international consultancies, language and cultural identity—the role of English and Arabic, gender-related achievement, critical thinking, leadership perspectives, and policy making).

It is important to recognize that the country is less than 40 years old, and thus, caution is needed in drawing comparisons with older, more complex and well-established systems in the west. It is important also to bear in mind that the UAE is a wealthy, small nation, with a somewhat diverse Emirati population (Kazim, 2000, in Clarke & Otaky, 2006), and that some of the social issues affecting more diverse populations are less evident there (e.g., extremes of poverty and wealth, religious and linguistic diversity).

Zayed University was inaugurated in 1998, initially as a university for UAE women, but recently it has begun to include Emirati males and a small cohort of international students. Its academic program is a learning outcomes based model (LO), and one of the key outcomes is leadership knowledge and skills. At the time of the current project's commencement, a range of formal and informal leadership development initiatives were already in place, and it was seen as important by the university senior management to tie those activities to a broader conception of leadership education and development that not only encompassed skills but also personal development and curricular initiatives.

Student leadership development has recently become a more important aspect of the UAE's educational system, but, particularly in the booming economy of the last decade, UAE leaders have focused on the educational reform of school administration, assessment methods, and curriculum implementation as a means of enabling citizens to participate more fully in society through leadership roles. The [translated] vision statement of the UAE Ministry of Education (n.d.) is as follows:

> An educational system that harmonizes with the best universal educational standards, prepares the student for a beneficial and productive life, develops his ability for continuous learning to deal with the era's facts and to contribute to achieving enduring development for the community. (para. 1)

This statement is followed by a mission statement that identifies the importance of students, teachers, and parents working together to achieve "the highest levels in educational performance in ways that help deepen the spirit of responsibility in all levels and develop people's obligation toward serving their community" (UAE Ministry of Education, n.d., para. 2). Both statements underscore ideals of transformative leadership, such as community engagement and service, and these ideals are reflected many times in statements from our research participants.

Review of Relevant Literature

This section briefly describes authentic, shared, democratic, and transformative leadership perspectives. These perspectives were chosen because they resonate best with the Zayed University undergraduate student body. They all focus on the importance of networks and relationships. Apart from shared leadership perspectives, they all also include a moral-ethical component typically found in authentic (Avolio & Gardner, 2005; Luthans & Avolio, 2003; May, Chan, Hodges, & Avolio, 2003), democratic (Woods, 2004) and transformative (Shields, 2010) perspectives.

Leadership Theories

Authentic leadership is closely related to charismatic, transformative, ethical, spiritual, and servant leadership perspectives (Avolio & Gardner, 2005). In reviewing the literature, there are five characteristics of authentic leadership that consistently appear: self-awareness, self-regulation and development, relational transparency, positive psychological capital, and a positive moral perspective. Yet, there is still no agreement on how they are included within an authentic leadership perspective.

For Bhindi, Smith, Hansen and Riley (n. d., p.3) authentic leadership is "the transformation of oneself and others to a higher moral and ethical purpose. It is earned by the leader and bestowed by followers." Authentic leadership, then, is dependent upon the recognized integrity and credibility of the leader. It is a dynamic and collective process that recognizes the critical relationship between leader and follower. It results in both greater self-awareness and self-regulated positive behaviors on the part of leaders.

> Authenticity is knowing, and acting on, what is true and real inside yourself, your team and your organization and knowing and acting on what is true and real in the world. It is not enough to walk one's talk if one is headed off, or leading one's organization, community or nation, off a cliff! (Terry, 2003, para.3).

Authentic leadership fosters positive self-development and encompasses a positive moral perspective (Luthans & Avolio, 2003; May et al., 2003).

For Avolio and Gardner (2005), authentic leaders have a deep sense of self and a conscious commitment to core, and enduring beliefs, principles, values, and ethics that are modeled in all that they do. This earns them the trust of others. Authentic leaders' confidence, hope, and optimism stem from their strong beliefs in themselves (Luthans & Youssef, 2004). They make clear to others exactly what is expected at individual, dyad, group, and organizational levels. As such, authentic followers display behavior paralleling what characterizes authentic leaders, such as internalized regulatory processes, balanced processing of information, and relational transparency (Avolio & Gardner, 2005). Through authentic leadership, people are better able to find meaning and connection at work because of greater self-awareness. Optimism, confidence, hope, mutual trust, commitment, and resiliency are also restored by promoting positive ethical climates, transparent relationships, and inclusive structures and decision making (Avolio & Gardner, 2005).

Recent leadership literature has also distinguished between leading as being the quality of one person, the appointed leader, and leadership as a collective phenomenon, referred to as shared, distributed, or participative leadership. Shared leadership is becoming increasingly popular, as the limitations of the single "heroic" leader are recognized, along with the realization that capturing the ideas, skills, innovations, and creativity of the collective greatly enhances individual and organizational learning (Stephenson, 2008). Drawing from Engestrom's (1999, 2000) activity theory and Archer's sociological theory (1995), shared leadership is a way of thinking about leadership as a social process that emphasizes institutional, cultural, and social phenomena as emergent properties of lived experience (Woods, 2000, 2004). Shared leadership is no longer bounded by formal leadership positions but rather, is seen as the professional work of everyone (Lambert, 2003). From this perspective, individuals are empowered to take action, making their work more meaningful and effective. Rather than focusing on leadership behaviors, shared leadership is the result of social relationships that lead to responsibility, learning, mutual respect, and sharing (Gastil, 1997). Nemerowicz and Rosi (1997) identify the following characteristics of shared leadership: a common good is sought; people are interdependent, and all are active participants in the process of leadership; all work to enhance the process and to make it more fulfilling; communication is crucial, with a stress on conversation; democratic processes, honesty, and shared ethics are valued; the quality of people's interactions is the distinguishing factor, rather than their position; and leadership is evaluated by how well people are working together.

Lawler's (2001) outline of workplace democracy captures some of the key characteristics of shared leadership, where organizations replace hierarchical structures with lateral forms of organization that rely on teams, networks, technology, agile structures, distributed leadership, and employee participation. However, hierarchies do not necessarily preclude shared leadership, which can still operate within hierarchical organizations in the form of teams, committees, and informal work groups (see Graetz, 2000; Harris & Chapman, 2002). Therefore, shared-leadership approaches can vary depending upon who is included and the balance those included actually have between autonomy and control.

However, democratic and transformative leadership perspectives are richer and more challenging concepts than Lawler's workplace democracy, because they are in the service of moral and ethical purpose. According to Woods (2004), democratic leadership "entails rights to meaningful participation and respect for and expectations toward everyone as ethical beings" (p. 4). Unlike in shared leadership, moral purpose (Fullan, 2003) and ethical principles are at the very heart of democratic and transformative perspectives.

Transformative leadership stems from Burns (1978), but also draws on the theoretical work of scholars such as Brown (2004), Foster (1986), Freire (1970), Quantz, Rogers, and Dantley (1992),

Shields (2003a, 2003b, 2009, 2010), and Weiner (2003). It differs from other leadership perspectives, for example, transformational and shared leadership, in that it focuses on both democratic process and content and on critical approaches to the practice of leadership. Here, democracy and democratic leadership are instrumental and de-politicized (Woods, 2004). According to Shields (2010), transformative leadership begins by considering individual, organizational, and societal goals for education transformation and social justice. It takes into account the disparities and inequities in the wider society and attends to the ways in which these disparities affect the ability of organizations to be successful and the ability of individuals to experience both equitable access and equitable educational outcomes. Transformative leaders work, broadly, for goals related to both academic excellence and for overcoming inequitable practices, both within and outside of schools. Transformative leadership is an analytic and normative concept that recognizes the need for leaders to address beliefs, assumptions, practices, and policies that oppress or exclude some groups. It holds as its key values liberation, emancipation, democracy, equity, and justice (Shields, 2010). It links education and educational leadership with the wider social context within which it is embedded, focusing on the generation of transformative actions that permit the full inclusion and participation of all, that eliminate deficit thinking, that address issues of power, privilege, and hegemony, and that hold all to appropriate high expectations. (Shields, 2010).

Democratic and transformative leadership perspectives also conceptualize leadership as emergent and dispersed. Transformative leadership recognizes the need to begin with critical reflection and analysis and to move through greater understanding to action for social justice (Shields, 2010). A transformative perspective also includes shared leadership as well as leadership focussed upon an individual leader at certain times. Woods (2004) refers to these phenomena as democracy-creating and, the inclusivity of transformative leadership is based on human status and agency, rather than on organizational needs and priorities (Woods, 2004).

Leadership Development

Democracy-creating builds conditions for democratic processes and participation, whereas democracy-doing involves distributed acts of democratic leadership and initiative by members of the community. Just as shared leadership is inclusive, so too is transformative leadership; however in various U.S. institutions, one finds that there is a wide range of curricular and co-curricular leadership activities and programs, ranging from full majors in leadership studies to service learning projects, leadership workshops, leadership conferences, and student-led clubs and organizations. What is common is the focus on foundations of leadership, strategic leadership, personal development, organizational leadership, and ethical leadership. Some universities decentralize the process, while others centralize their leadership development programs. Regardless of the degree of centralization, most student leadership development frameworks are based on one or more leadership theories. According to McIntire (1989), there are three typical models: the student-affairs model (development of student leaders within campus activities and organisations); the academic-focused model (a combination of academic and co-curricular activities); and the training model (leadership training through applied practice, which is typical in professional settings).

Typically, leadership identities are developed as learners move through stages, focussing initially on the self and gradually moving toward a collective-leadership focus (see Komives et al., 2005, 2006; Lord & Hall, 2005). In most of these programs, what is also common is the shift from theory to practice, from roles to processes, from knowledge to learning, from individual action to collective action, and from detached analysis to reflexive understanding.

According to Allio (2005), effective leadership development programs should be learner-centred and link contemporary theories to actual experiences. An effective program should include outcomes, learner abilities, assessment, evaluation, and curriculum. According to the International Leadership Association's *Guiding Questions: Guidelines for Leadership Education Programs* (2009), essential areas for curriculum development, instructional effectiveness, and quality assessment are the context, conceptual framework, content, teaching and learning, and outcomes and assessment.

From a transformative leadership perspective, an effective leadership program should ensure that all students not only succeed in tasks associated with the formal leadership curriculum but also experience leadership opportunities in learning contexts or communities where social and cultural capital is enhanced on a level playing field, as they begin to contribute as members and leaders in the community.

The Conversation on Leadership Project

The Conversation on Leadership project was initiated by the provost, who believed that its two-fold focus on leadership curriculum development and strengthening the biennial Women as Global Leaders (WAGL) conference would be beneficial to the university's overall leadership goals. Following an initial WAGL planning committee meeting, faculty were invited to express interest and nominate project leaders, and a final decision on the project leadership team was made by the provost. A chairperson was appointed, together with two co-chairs who represented the two main campuses. Between them, the three team members had extensive experience in leadership education and student development.

Besides renewing the university's commitment to developing its students as principled leaders, the conversation aimed to stimulate thinking about the best ways to help students achieve the leadership outcome, elicit thoughts on ways to further infuse the university experience with academic and experiential opportunities for students to move toward the leadership learning outcome, and raise the ethical consciousness of the campus.

The Conversation on Leadership project, reported on in this chapter, aimed to collect data that would enable Zayed University's leadership educators to make important choices about the development, organization, and evaluation of ZU's student leadership education program. Specifically, the project aimed to achieve the following outcomes: review the current status of student leadership education at Zayed University; draft a conceptual framework to serve as a basis for the 2010 to 2011 development of ZU's student leadership education curriculum; and identify new directions and ideas for the WAGL conference.

The project was characterized by two broad strategies. First, it was inclusive of all faculty, staff, and students in the university as active participants and actors, who reflected and provided feedback on their perspectives of leadership through a rich variety of university-wide interactive discussions and presentations. This aimed to provide students, in particular, with a 'voice' to express themselves on issues of leadership and make the process participatory and "bottom-up." The second strategy was to give voice to 'local' or "indigenous" leadership perspectives, which do not necessarily emanate from Western academic literature.

The project team comprised three levels of involvement in a 'flat' distributed structure. A leadership team of three (chair and two co-chairs) had overall responsibility for project implementation. They were assisted by a Steering Committee of senior university personnel, who provided feedback and guidance on aspects of the project. The project events and activities were coordinated by a team of 25 representatives of colleges and academic units across three campuses, whose task was to involve other faculty, staff, and students at the unit level. Leadership-related activities and events were planned, both at a cross-campus and within-unit level. A framework of key questions was developed to allow consistent feedback to the project team from members of the university community, so that there was a coherent means of interpreting data as they emerged.

In the beginning phase of the project, the leadership team met weekly to discuss a possible model for the project. From the outset, a process of negotiation was evident. The initial thinking of one team member was to have a series of three international experts make presentations and workshops on leadership approaches for students, which would be followed by feedback, leading to a final decision about which approach seemed to best fit ZU student curriculum requirements. The proposed model was presented to the Steering Committee for approval, together with an initial budget proposal. At this point questions arose about the budget feasibility. In addition, the semester teaching program was underway, and it was unclear to the leadership team whether international experts could be located and encouraged to visit ZU in the time available. The model was reconsidered by the leadership team, who decided to run with a new focus, wherein leadership practitioners from the UAE and the region would be selected by academic-unit representatives to make presentations to ZU students, faculty, and staff. The modified model and a revised budget were presented to the Steering Committee and were accepted.

Other project developments were developing simultaneously. The unit representatives (reps) were a key component of the project model. They were faculty or staff who were selected by the dean or director of each unit to actively guide the unit's project activities and events. Unit reps were charged with the following: work with one student class to serve as a cohort for the Conversation on Leadership project; identify and liaise with other unit faculty, staff, and students who could assist in the project; develop with the dean or director a plan of activities for the unit; identify 'experts' in leadership education who could contribute to the project (e.g., as guest speakers); document and publish "conversations" after CoL events; report back in monthly progress to the leadership team; communicate unit-level tasks to the leadership team for advertising purposes; and facilitate the implementation and evaluation of unit-level tasks and conversations.

An inaugural meeting was held to brief the unit reps, and regular meetings were held with them during the year to plan for specific activities and events and to monitor the project. In addition, the leadership team met with student council and clubs representatives to gather feedback and advice about project activities. Regular updates on the CoL project were provided at faculty and staff meetings and to deans and directors.

During the project, the leadership team, unit reps, staff, faculty, and students collaborated to develop a program of events and activities that would contribute to the Conversation on Leadership. The program comprised three strands. One strand was public events, including displays, interactive events, and the guest speaker series. The second strand was specific to academic units and comprised a range of coursework- and academic-related activities. The third strand was the inauguration of a service-learning program. Events that occurred in the three strands included guest talks, videos, films, displays, debates, Web-page development, surveys, interviews, book fairs, student club activities, student council activities, competitions, TedX, round-tables, and lunch discussions. Prominent in the conversation were members of the scholarly and wider community that study leadership development or practice leadership in their daily lives. Throughout the year, they visited the university for several days of discussion. The conversation prepared the way for the university, in spring 2010, to make deliberate adjustments in the curriculum for the 2010 to 2011 academic year, and to take other actions that would quickly imbue the Zayed University experience with new inspiration for emerging leaders, thus creating a more coherent student leadership education framework and institutionalizing leadership education, development, and research to include ethical dimensions and leadership for the betterment of others.

Throughout the year, data were collected and analyzed regularly in order to compare and contrast students' views with those of faculty and staff. These data, along with the literature review and the various feedback reports from the unit representatives and students, fed into the final conceptual framework.

A specific framework of questions was developed to provide a consistent flow of data from feedback about events and to avoid the project becoming simply a collection of unrelated events. Invited speakers were sent a list of guiding questions to consider as they prepared their presentation. Where possible, each unit rep took a specific class of students to the presentations and other events. These participants were asked to provide feedback according to another set of guiding questions. This process resulted in a useful dataset of leadership perspectives.

A draft leadership education conceptual framework was created towards the end of the spring semester and circulated among faculty, staff, and students. Unit reps were asked to gather feedback on the draft framework, and it was also put online for electronic feedback. In June 2010, the leadership team made a final analysis of the data and feedback and produced a framework for the development of a leadership education curriculum. Further recommendations were made about programmatic requirements that would support the next phase implementation. This section has provided a broad overview of the project development. I now turn to the methodology used in the study.

Methodology

A case-study approach was used in this study. Data collection was ongoing and used the following methods:

Baseline data collection: A mingling activity to collect multiple opinions, online surveys, and document analysis were used to establish baseline understanding of current leadership perspectives.

Discussion: Individual and group discussions were held about leadership perspectives and about the draft leadership conceptual framework and its effectiveness.

Journals: The researchers each kept an ongoing reflective journal to capture their own learning as the project was implemented.

Interviews and conversations: Semi-structured interviews and conversations with participants occurred to build upon data collected earlier.

Baseline data were collected at the beginning of the project to establish respective student, staff, and faculty perspectives. During the year, a series of student leadership events and keynote speaker presentations were organized and contributed to by each academic unit. Data were collected by means of a standardized set of leadership-related questions asked following the events, activities and exhibitions. Additional data were collected through focus-group interviews, individual interviews, document analysis, and reflective journals. This set of key questions was developed to allow consistent feedback to the project team from members of the university community, so that there was a coherent means of interpreting data as they emerged.

Data analysis was based on the identification of significant themes. In order to do this, data were constantly analyzed using an inductive process. A cyclical process was used, allowing for analysis and interpretation based on questions of meaning and local significance, as well as for thematic categories constructed directly from the data. In keeping with a qualitative approach, the data-analysis technique involved impressionistic, informal pattern and thematic recognition.

The next section reports on some of the leadership perspectives emerging from the data, specific to the Emirati context, that resonated with several of Shields's (2010) transformative leadership characteristics, such as community engagement, giving back to the community, and service learning. These perspectives influenced the structure and development of the leadership education conceptual framework.

Findings

An analysis of the data from student feedback identified several recurring themes. These included learning leadership, communication, gender, lived experience and public service, and service learning, all of which are important elements of transformative leadership.

The majority of undergraduate students said that their perception of leadership had changed as a result of their participation in the Conversation on Leadership project. For most it had changed from a position of trait theory to leadership learning. The following quotes capture this recurring theme.

> What [was] said about leadership wasn't the same as my original idea. I thought that leaders are born with leadership skills. But, now I know that if you want to be a leader you have to develop your skills and knowledge. Therefore, leadership isn't inherited [and] we can learn it if we want. (Aida)

Other students also went beyond individual, "heroic" notions of leadership and identified aspects of sharing leadership and empowering others:

> I learned that leadership is not limited to certain people, but everyone can be a successful leader. I learned that I should learn leadership from everyone and teach everyone. (Ebtisam)

The preceding comments indicate that students had modified their views to encompass the possibility of learning leadership. If leadership education is to help them develop an understanding of transformative perspectives, this has implications for the nature and content of the leadership curriculum.

The importance of effective communication was identified as a second critical aspect of leadership development:

> To be a leader you should share, communicate, and accept other opinions and ideas. (Aida)

Several students commented specifically on how important listening was as a skill in order to begin to understand the diverse opinions, values, beliefs, and practices of others:

> Listening is the best skill to make a person a good leader . . . because when you listen you show respect to others and sometimes other peoples' ideas are very useful. (Asma).

> I learned that if someone wants to lead a group of people, a company, or even a country, he/she must first listen carefully to others by discussing, sharing information, and, most importantly, learning from them. Everyone is your teacher and everyone is your student. (Farah)

Many students commented on issues of cultural identity and the advantages of moving beyond the boundaries of specific nationality groups and communicating with a wider range of people, as evident in Aida's comments:

> The speaker said something that caught my attention and I found it very interesting. She suggested that we meet new people and share our ideas with them . . . such as our culture and knowledge. They can possibly teach us more than people we already know. She said that our lives are "like circles" and when we meet new people the circles become bigger and bigger. I agree that we should accept others in order for them to accept us because as she said everybody is different. (Aida)

However, other students were quite vocal about "Emiratization" and expressed concern over foreigners taking leadership roles that UAE women should take on:

> It is better to have a female leader who is local rather than a foreigner. (Elham)

Another significant finding was the role of negotiation and persuasion when young Emirati women communicated with their families on issues that were sometimes at odds with cultural norms:

> You have to respect your family's idea[s] . . . but to achieve your ambition you need to do your best to change our family's minds if we want to achieve [some] of your life goals. (Ayesha).

> Nothing is too difficult to reach. We should have the enthusiasm and eagerness to persuade others, and especially the family, about the courses we wish to take. (Dana)

Aida's comments use a common battle metaphor to highlight the challenges involved as well as the courage and determination sometimes required in better communicating one's goals and in persuading others to support one's attempts to achieve them:

> We have to fight for our ideas and ambitions, because if we don't do this we will regret this for the rest of our lives. What she said makes me think of my real ambition, which was to study abroad. Her words give me the hope that I can convince my parents to do what I really want to do. (Aida)

The ability to communicate effectively is a critical part of transformative leadership practice. The preceding comments show that students were developing a critical awareness of inclusivity, equity, and acceptance in relation to diverse groups and gender issues. The comments also identify aspects of contestation and a need for greater understanding of equity in diverse contexts.

On many occasions, the students raised issues around the topic of gender in relation to their leadership development. Some students who had never interacted with any men apart from their immediate family members and who were initially anxious became better able to contemplate the idea of being and working with men:

> My thoughts about leadership have changed a lot, because before I thought I couldn't be in a place with males or even express my ideas to them, because as a female I feel too shy working, or even being in, a place full of men. (Roudha)

The perceived roles of women in society are clearly changing, and our students were clearly challenging the stereotypical discourse about the "oppressed Arab woman," as they identified aspects of authentic female leadership:

> Previously, I had thought that leadership education was very difficult and the people who had power and were tough were the only ones who could perform better in leadership. I thought that men were better leaders than women. However, I have changed my mind. People who are good leaders are people who are helpful, respectful, listeners, kind, strong, and imaginative. Most women are capable of being as good a leader as a man as long as they have self-confidence. (Maitha).

> She has shown me that being a leader does not mean that a female goes out of her character and is "tough" so her opinion gets the respect it deserves, no . . . she needs to be herself and confident about who she is, and she needs to treat each person how they want to be treated, so we need to learn about the people we deal with. (Ohood).

> Leadership is not just among men. Women have a big role in changing the society and leading the country as well. (Elham)

Several students commented on the importance of role models and the increasing number of visible female Emirati role models in UAE society. Maitha's quote, given after viewing an exhibition of prominent female Emirati leaders, exemplifies this point:

> Compared to the past, Emirati women faced many challenges to get their chances in education and work placement. However, as time passed and as our country united with the greatness of our late father and leader Sheikh Zayed, Emirati women got better opportunities to study and work side by side with men to develop our country. (Maitha).

These comments indicate that students were aware of different ways of thinking about gender roles and were beginning to demonstrate moral courage and activism in challenging stereotypes. In addition, they were beginning to identify some of the kinds of values that underpin transformative leadership. The very foundation of transformative leadership is the notion of critique and promise, which is also emerging in the above quotes.

The fourth theme, lived leadership experience and the importance of public service was recognized by the majority of students in the Conversation on Leadership project:

> I believe [learning] leadership is not all about reading books. . . it's 50 percent education and 50 percent doing and communicating. (Maitha).

Many talked specifically about community engagement and gaining experience in the wider community and work places:

> To learn leadership we must apply what we have learned to the real world, and what a person learns from working in the community is actually the "real" deal. (Farah)

> Encourage students to do some activities together outside ZU to give them the chance to participate in some activities and share their ideas with others and in teams. (Fayza)

The importance of public service and giving back was emphasized by students over and over again. Some focused on individual interpersonal aspects:

> We have to graduate from ZU and have good leadership, because this will help us in our careers in the future. (Fatma)

Others emphasized societal and collective needs and identified specific leadership qualities and skills that resonate with a transformative perspective:

> Leadership is having the qualities of honesty, patience, and justice. (Sarra).

> Having "a big heart" is the quality necessary for good leadership for this country. (Moaza).

> I learned that four things can help us to be successful leaders, which are: to be determined, by setting goals for a better future; ambitious, by going to places where others failed; receptive, by being willing to listen to others and learn; and enthusiastic, by caring to make a difference. (Ebtisam).

> Leadership means caring enough to make a difference. (Fayza).

Others identified elements such as principled leadership:

> I think that good leadership basically means "to do something that everybody can get the benefit from." (Kamla).

A third group commented on improving family life:

> Leadership skills will really help us to raise our children, to raise them in an appropriate way that we want and to prepare them for the future as well. (Aisha)

A fourth group identified another transformative leadership perspective that focused on making positive change in UAE society:

> The UAE is pushing us towards success and these [Emirati female leaders] added one more achievement to their lists, which is encouraging the rest of us to make our dreams come true and gain confidence to work hard for our country and to make our county proud of us . . . the future of our country is in our hands. (Moaza)

Another important reason for giving back was that of preserving national pride and identity, which is of particular concern to UAE citizens, as over 80 percent of the UAE population are foreigners:

> Great stories of achievements [of previous national leaders] should never be forgotten or wasted, and should be told to the next generations to give them hope, encouragement, and passion to keep on developing their country. (Kaltham).

> We should contribute [to] the development process, each in [our] own way, because, after all, we should first return the favor to this country which gave us and is still giving us more than any other county. (Nada)

The preceding group of quotes encapsulates several transformative leadership processes, including the emergence of changing societal knowledge frameworks that acknowledge power and privilege as well as the dialectic between individual and social contexts (Shields, 2010). Transformative leadership's basic foundations of critique and promise, and its emphasis on deep and equitable change, are also evident in the participants' quotes above.

The final theme identified in the data was the importance of service learning in student leadership development. Specific service-learning examples included the service-learning day, when six different groups of students,—along with faculty and student-life coordinators—left the three university campuses in Dubai, Abu Dhabi South, and Abu Dhabi North, to invest in a day of service learning within each respective community. Some examples from the day follow.

Abu Dhabi business students and others developed a computer database to be used for communication with all orphan sponsors and orphans in the UAE, in celebration of World Orphan Day. This project, completed for the Middle East's Red Crescent, aimed to facilitate easier access to sponsor and orphan records, in order to streamline future communication. The student responses to the day indicate their growing awareness of how transformative leadership can impact the marginalized and disadvantaged:

> Community service makes me feel better, and I know that having fun and watching movies is not everything . . . there is more to think about. (Nada)

> Creating a database can make a difference in the lives of the orphans and shows me how business tasks can impact people's lives. (Suhaila)

Another student, who visited the Gulf Autism Center, commented on how the experience had impacted her personally as plans were finalized in a follow-up session for a continued partnership of fundraising, visits, and training to work further with the students:

> The leader of the Gulf Autism Center is so passionate about her vision for the students . . . and the trip motivated me to find something I am passionate about. (Fatma)

A group of male students from the north campus took part in the first stage of a project that aimed to have university males serve as mentors for Emirati youths. The connections made between university students and local youths led to a greater understanding of the meaning and purpose of doing service.

Education students spent the day with Special Needs Family Center participants, working together on arts and crafts and academic work, followed by games during recreation time. "When you help others in a project, you learn that working with others and for others is the role of the leader," remarked a student volunteer. Another captured several of the volunteers' thoughts in this statement:

> I now ask myself how I can learn and study to build a future, and how I can change myself, make a difference in my own life, family, society, and the whole world around me, without force, but [through an exchange], understanding, flexibility, knowledge, and hard work. (Maryam)

Again, plans were made for future collaboration, and there were goodbye hugs all around as ZU students departed.

The service-learning day allowed students, many for the first time, to experience what it was like to serve others in different community agencies and settings. Not only did this experience raise their awareness of groups with differing needs in wider society, but it also provided a strong motivational impetus to continue leadership development at the university and in the society.

The Leadership Education Framework

The CoL project did not start from a blank slate. The leadership team was cognizant of the students' leadership perspectives from previous programs that had been undertaken, including campus-wide institutes and activities targeting specific groups of students. In addition, there was evidence of a range of current programs and activities occurring independently within Student Life and academic units. These programs, courses, and activities had added a rich strand of leadership development to the ZU curriculum. A key issue that emerged, however, was that almost 30% of faculty and 20% of students who participated in the baseline data collection were unclear or not aware of what leadership development opportunities currently existed. This finding supported the thrust behind the CoL project, which was to investigate ways of institutionalizing leadership education. Particular elements seen as successful by significant numbers of faculty, staff, and students included class and coursework activities, leadership-skills development, student council, clubs, carnivals, and field trips. These data suggest that such elements should be retained and built upon.

Over a 12-month time frame, Zayed University faculty, staff, and students were involved in conversation, events, and activities centered around the theme of leadership. One of the outcomes of this was the creation of an initial framework to guide the development of a campus-wide student leadership-education curriculum that would span a student's entire program at ZU through curricular, cocurricular, and extracurricular learning (Figure 22.1).

Figure 22.1 Draft conceptual framework for student leadership education at Zayed University

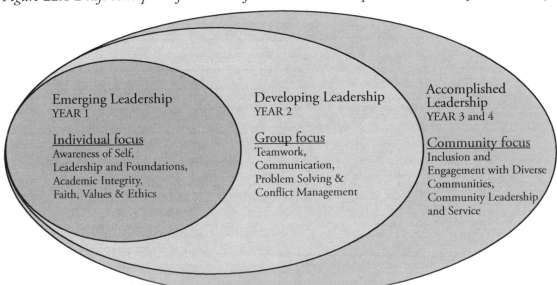

The framework was developed from three major sources: data collected during the current leadership project, a review of research and literature in the field, and the analysis of some existing approaches and models (e.g., at Marquette University). The framework aimed to define what effective leadership looks like in practice at different stages of development and growth. The basis of the framework drew on leadership perspectives from Shields (2010), Avolio and Gardner (2005), Gastil (1997), Nemerowicz and Rosi (1997), and Woods (2004). It also drew on social-constructivist perspectives and social-identity theories (see Holland, Lachicotte, Skinner, & Cain, 1998) that focus on both individual and collective perspectives (see Brown & Duguid, 1991).

The framework is underpinned by five key beliefs:

1. Leadership competencies can be learned and developed.

2. Leadership is contextual and is influenced by culture.

3. Leadership development is a lifelong process.

4. Leadership is learned best through leadership in action and through reflection on that action.

5. Leadership is based on a foundation of ethics and manifests itself in service to others.

Although the framework appears fairly straightforward in design, its implementation will be more fluid, organic, and evolving, and thus necessarily more complex. It may be better conceptualized as three dimensional, interwoven, and layered to reflect the complexity of the definitions of leadership and processes of leadership development that are currently challenging the leadership field. The boundaries in the design are artificial, since movement between individual, group, and collective processes is neither necessarily linear nor one way, nor will it certainly be accomplished by all students within a specific time frame.

The framework is both a process- and product-oriented model that allows for both individual and collective expression of leadership. It is flexible enough to provide basic leadership education for those students who are interested in a more distributed or subtle style of leadership, and also for a more exclusive group of student-leaders who aspire to a more visible and individualistic leadership style. The framework comprises three levels, with a focus on specific elements of transformative leadership at each one.

The micro-level of emerging leadership equates with Lord and Hall's (2005) surface-level leadership knowledge and skills and with Komives et al.'s (2005) key categories—changing view of leadership and developing self—and operates during the student's first-year experiences at university. During this time, the emphasis is largely on the individual. Just as transformative leadership recognizes the need to begin with critical reflection and analysis (Shields, 2010), so too does this micro-level. At a personal level, it is a time when the students develop a greater awareness of themselves and transformative leadership processes, such as the dialectic between individual and social and the acknowledgment of power and privilege (for example, identifying and articulating gifts, talents, values, and skills; building self-confidence; demonstrating openness to change; seeking feedback; appreciating multiple leadership styles; and identifying opportunities for growth). Second, they explore the foundations of leadership (for example, understanding theories about leadership; articulating a personal leadership style; understanding cultural and gender influences on leadership; developing personal management skills, such as time management, stress reduction, and effective communication; and developing relationships). The third element of the micro-level of leadership education is related to faith, values, ethics, and academic integrity. This means learning about the relationship of faith to leadership, making value-based decisions, identifying and applying academic integrity and ethical principles, and demonstrating a commitment to social justice.

The students' second year comprises the meso-level, or developing leadership practice. This level is similar to the stage in transformative leadership where students move through enlightened understanding to action. This level is also similar to Lord and Hall's (2005) intermediate leadership knowledge and skills and Komives et al.'s (2005) key category—group influences. Here the key focus is on leadership in group or team situations. Students learn, for example, how to understand group dynamics and development, how to work with others towards goals, how to share leadership and empower others, and how to develop trust and collaboration. Communication is a second important element at this stage and involves experiences in motivating and empowering others through writing, speaking, and artistic expression; articulating abstract ideas; listening effectively; and identifying common purposes and shared goals. The third aspect of leadership learning at the meso-level is concerned with problem solving and conflict management. This means that students need to learn about and experience dynamics of group decision making, how to gather information from diverse sources, how to think critically, and how to manage and resolve conflict while showing empathy and respect for others' perspectives.

The final macro-level, or accomplished leadership learning is similar to principled, deeply structured leadership knowledge and skills (Lord & Hall, 2005). It also relates to Komives et al.'s (2005) key category of developing influences. It occurs during students' third and fourth years, when they are in their major programs. At this level, the focus is on leadership in the wider community. From a transformative leadership perspective, this level is where students are able to take action that addresses Shields's (2010) goals of individual, organizational, and societal transformation. Students learn about and experience inclusion and engagement with diverse communities (for example, interacting effectively with people from diverse backgrounds and becoming involved in community activities and decisions, integrating perspectives and experiences of others in group and community decisions, and demonstrating empathy and respect for others). A second important component of leadership learning at the macro-level is making connections to the wider community through service learning and transformative leadership practices. Such practices involve using one's talents to benefit others, demonstrating commitment to community through quality and quantity of interactions, demonstrating moral courage, emphasizing deep and equitable change in social conditions by giving of oneself in service to those in need, reflecting and reacting to the needs of the community, and demonstrating advocacy in community issues.

I now turn to discussion of the particular transformative leadership perspectives that resonated with ZU students during the project.

Discussion

What becomes immediately clear from the findings is that leadership in this region or in any other cannot be understood apart from culture and gender. By its very nature, leadership is about relationships of power in a particular context. The UAE context is much more complex than the preconceived notions of oppressed Arab women and stereotypes around women's roles. Both men and women support women in their aim of self-improvement. The nuances of culture, community, religion, national identity, and language are an integral part of Zayed University's concept of leadership and leadership development.

The majority of students demonstrated an emerging awareness of transformative leadership aspects, such as critique and promise; deep and equitable change in social conditions; deconstruction and reconstruction of social-cultural knowledge frameworks that generate inequity for women; acknowledgment of power and privilege; dialectic between individual and social, liberation and emancipation, equity and justice for women; individual transformation; and, to some extent, emergent societal transformation (Shields, 2010). The data from the students indicate the tensions and challenges with which they live in modern Emirati society. Their comments indicate a developing awareness of the importance of moral courage for transformative action, but they are still at the surface-level leadership skills described by Lord and Hall (2005) and the early stages of self-development noted by Komives et al. (2005). As such, service-learning and community-based initiatives were identified as critical activities to engage our students in civil society and to provide leadership opportunities relevant to their particular leadership realities and needs. As students participate in civil society, they will develop greater social responsibility, which, through incremental change, can gradually meet the needs of the nation.

The prominent role of faith in understandings of leadership was evident in the values, principles, and beliefs students held about leadership. These stemmed from the teachings of Islam, where leadership and faith are closely aligned. What also emerged from the data was evidence that student views about leadership were related to more than one theoretical perspective, including authentic, shared, and transformative leadership. Authentic leadership was evident in comments about principles, values, ethics, and enduring beliefs (Avolio & Gardner, 2005). The students demonstrated optimism, hope, and increasing belief in themselves and their emerging ability to lead (Luthans & Youssef, 2004). It was clear that principled, ethical leadership practice with moral purpose is important for the students. Ethical principles are at the very heart of authentic and transformative leadership perspectives. For example, the value placed by ZU students on practical experiences of public engagement and community service challenges the public discourse about youth in the region as being disengaged and demotivated (Assaad, 2010). While they now use the rhetoric of engagement for public well being, what is critical is turning that rhetoric into the reality of action and into reflection in and on action (Komives et al., 2005; Lord & Hall, 2005). This implies that a concept like transformative leadership is perhaps more relevant and useful than are more technical, objective approaches.

Student comments also indicated that they were clearly moving away from the trait theory or heroic-leader model toward a recognition that shared leadership is appropriate and meaningful as students take on leadership roles in the community. Another aspect that emerged from the student data was the importance of listening to others. Communication was seen as a critical aspect of leadership, with a specific focus on conversation with others (Nemerowicz & Rosi, 1997). This resonates with Gastil's (1997) view that social relationships lead to responsibility, learning, mutual respect, and sharing of leadership.

Leadership education in the Gulf can be perceived as challenging (Al Dabbagh, 2010; Neal, 2010) because "materials are largely based on leadership concepts and theories emanating from the U.S." (Neal, 2010, p. 13), and it is also challenging to teach leadership without being critical of established structures, the status quo, and the nuanced subtexts that exist (Neal, 2010). Al Dabbagh (2010, p. 17) also critiques the "import" model, where expertise and material are brought to the UAE with little genuine engagement with region-specific realities and needs. To counter these issues, Zayed University's student leadership–education conceptual framework considers the Emirati voice and builds on Emirati values and traditions. It also encourages students to think beyond themselves and their institutional boundaries, thus addressing Al Dabbagh's (2010) concern that in the UAE individuals rarely transcend their institutions, "which hampers the public orientation of [leadership development] programs" (p. 17). ZU's framework not only focuses on leader development at the intrapersonal level (Komives et al., 2005; Lord & Hall, 2005) but also addresses interpersonal collective and transformative leadership development levels in order to ensure the inclusion of the qualities that enable teamwork and joint effort. These qualities are those which research suggests "Emirati youth may be predisposed to given the communal structure of their society" (Assaad, 2010, p. 11).

The students' leadership perspectives clearly link to the leadership education framework stages of emerging, developing, and accomplished leadership, moving from critical reflection and analysis, through to enlightened understanding and action for deep and equitable change and transformation (Shields, 2010). It is important to remember that there will, however, be overlap of leadership skills and an interplay between surface- and deeper-level leadership skills (Lord & Hall, 2005) and the key categories (Komives et al., 2005). The micro-level of leadership concerns itself more with intrapersonal skills (Komives et al., 2005; Lord & Hall, 2005) and aspects of authentic leadership in the form of self-awareness, faith, values, principles, beliefs, and ethics (Avolio & Gardner, 2005; Gastil, 1997). The meso-level is concerned with interpersonal skills and shared leadership perspectives. The macro-level is community-focused and resonates with aspects of Shields's (2010) transformative leadership perspective, as discussed previously.

It is also expected that the implementation of the framework will provide greater opportunities for students to reframe their thinking about leadership in civil society; to alter dominant conceptions and mental models that perpetuate deficit thinking; and advance new leadership perspectives and frames of thinking, such as those characteristics found in transformative leadership (see Shields, 2010). It also encourages the development of social relationships and networking to bring diverse groups together, with the aim of creating greater individual and collective leadership, social responsibility, justice, and deep and equitable change in social conditions.

The next section provides recommendations for institutionalizing leadership education, development, and research through curricular and cocurricular activities and programs.

Next Steps and Recommendations

The discussion thus far has highlighted key elements that must be considered in any discussion of leadership education in the Gulf tertiary context. The Zayed University experience may well have something to offer other undergraduate leadership programs within the broader regional and Gulf perspective. It is clear that there are certain fundamental principles that must be adhered to in the development of any such program: the definition of leadership, ownership, and institutionalization, and a cross-disciplinary approach.

It is important that this breadth of understanding of what constitutes leadership is an integral part of any new program and that those aspects of authentic, shared, democratic, and transformative leadership that resonate with students are emphasized. University graduates are expected to be able to contribute in meaningful ways to society for the betterment of all. In order to do this, the kind of experience and curriculum provided at universities must allow for the emergence of transformative perspectives and understandings, to ensure a greater focus on equity and social-justice issues.

The curriculum should include formal leadership development as an academic component of all students' education. This academic component should be supplemented with practical leadership activities that focus on building leadership skills and dispositions, and opportunities to reflect on those activities. The development of extracurricular events, such as the guest speaker series, leadership book club, leadership luncheons, debates, movies, and fairs, to promote and maintain the visibility of leadership on campus is critical. When planning extracurricular events and inviting key leadership practitioners to address the student body, consideration should be given to those practicing leaders who exemplify elements of transformative leadership in their societies. Exposing students to role models of this sort throughout their university program will increase their depth of understanding of transformative leadership perspectives and serve as a catalyst for their own practice.

Program developers should also involve role models from the community as mentors and coaches whenever possible in such curricular activities as internships and capstone projects. One way that this can be done is to continue to link leadership development to community needs by developing the scope and structure of the service-learning program; establishing a leadership scholarship program; expanding opportunities for alumnae-student dialogue as a way to determine leadership knowledge, skills, and dispositions that are in demand in the UAE workforce; and establishing mentoring programs with other students from around the globe and with local and regional education and business leaders. Assessment of leadership development is also critical, and specific programmatic leadership assessment points and practices should be identified.

Any new program must be collectively owned and valued by all members of the university community. Deans and senior administrators have a key role to play here, and they, themselves, must be actively and collaboratively involved in the development and implementation of the program. The leadership education program must be incorporated within the formal operating structure of the university, and its ongoing development and implementation must be an integral part of the everyday life of the university.

One of the key successes of the Zayed University Conversation on Leadership project was the opportunity for faculty, staff, and students to work in ways that crossed disciplinary boundaries and allowed a community of learning to emerge. This is a significant factor that must be addressed in the next stages of program development, in order to avoid an individualistic perspective on leadership education. We must continue to bring students into the design of leadership education programs to bring to the fore their assumptions and frameworks for thinking about principled transformative leadership.

Conclusion

Zayed University's Conversation on Leadership project reported on in this chapter showed that there were clear opportunities for the development of transformative leadership knowledge and practice among undergraduate students. There is a developmental level of leadership practice and learning that is very important to consider. Students new to a university have an emergent level of understanding of leadership practice. If we are to encourage the growth of understanding and practice of transformative leadership perspectives, then the program of leadership education has to be very carefully planned. Countries in the Gulf region are currently facing a range of economic and social challenges arising from rapid and continuous change alongside other global factors, such as the recent international financial and political crises. As a result, it would seem that transformative leadership practice has much to offer in the region. However, this is a challenging task because leadership practice is nuanced within the complexities and contestations of culture, community, religion, national identity, language, and gender. There are currently many opportunities for transformative leadership within civil society, and already community agencies and businesses engaging in social entrepreneurship are emerging to address such issues as human trafficking, human rights, substance abuse, child abuse, environmental concerns, and equitable access to educational resources. The region will need the kind of emerging leaders who have graduated from comprehensive and multifaceted programs of leadership development and who bring with them the understanding and skills necessary to contribute to the continued growth of a socially just, inclusive, and equitable society.

References

Al Dabbagh, M. (2010, February). *Leadership development.* Workshop proceedings, Appreciating and Advancing Leadership for Public Wellbeing, February 14–16, 2010, NYU Abu Dhabi, UAE.

Allio, R. J. (2005). Leadership development: Teaching versus learning. *Management Decision, 43*(7–8), 1071–1077.

Archer, M. (1995). *Realist social theory: The morphogenetic approach.* Cambridge: Cambridge University Press.

Assaad, C. (2010, February). *Youth and bicultural identity—Privilege or dissonance?* Workshop proceedings, Appreciating and Advancing Leadership for Public Wellbeing, February 14–16, 2010, NYU Abu Dhabi, UAE.

Avolio, B. J., & Gardner, W. L. (2005). Authentic leadership development: Getting to the root of positive forms of leadership. *The Leadership Quarterly, 16*(3), 315–338.

Bhindi, N., Smith, R., Hansen, J., & Riley, D. (n.d.). Authentic leadership in education: A cross-country phenomenon—or, leaders in their own mind? Accessed on 10 November 2010 from http://www.woodhillpark.com/attachments/1/NZEALS%20%20Authentic%20Leadership%20Summary.pdf

Brown, K. M. (2004). Leadership for social justice and equity: Weaving a transformative framework and pedagogy. *Educational Administration Quarterly, 40*(1), pp. 77–108.

Brown, J. S., & Duguid, P. (1991). Organizational learning and communities of practice: Toward a unified view of working, learning and innovation. *Organization Science, 2*(1), 40–57.

Burns, J. M. (1978). *Leadership.* New York: Harper & Row.

Clarke, M., & Otaky, D. (2006). Reflection 'on' and 'in' teacher education in the United Arab Emirates. *International Journal of Educational Development, 26*(1), 111–122.

Engestrom, Y. (1999). Activity theory and individual and social transformation. In Y. Engestrom, R. Miettinene, and R.-L. Punamaki (Eds.), *Perspectives on activity theory* (pp. 19-38). Cambridge: Cambridge University Press.

Engestrom, Y. (2000). Comment on Blackler et al. Activity theory and the social construction of knowledge: A story of four umpires. *Organization, 7*(2), 301–310.

Foster, W. (1986). *Paradigms and promises.* Buffalo, NY: Prometheus.

Freire, P. (1970). *Pedagogy of the oppressed.* New York: Herder & Herder.

Fullan, M. (2003). *The moral imperative of school leadership.* Thousand Oaks. CA: Corwin Press.

Gastil, J. (1997). A definition and illustration of democratic leadership. In K. Grint (Ed.), *Leadership*) (pp. 155–178). Oxford: Oxford University Press.

Graetz, F. (2000). Strategic change leadership. *Management Decision, 38*(8), 550–562

Harris, A., & Chapman, C. (2002). *Democratic leadership for school improvement in challenging contexts.* Paper presented at International Congress on School Effectiveness and Improvement, Copenhagen, Denmark.

Holland, D., Lachicotte Jr., W., Skinner, D., & Cain, C. (1998). *Identity and agency in cultural worlds.* Cambridge, MA: Harvard University Press.

International Leadership Association. (2009). *Guiding Questions: Guidelines for Leadership Education Programs* [living document]. Retrieved on May 17, 2010 from http://www.ila-net.org/Communities/LC/GuidingQuestionsFinal.pdf

Komives, S. R., Longerbeam, S., Owen, J. E., Mainella, F. C., & Osteen, L. (2005). Developing a leadership identity: A grounded theory. *Journal of College Student Development, 46*(6), 593–611.

Komives, S. R., Longerbeam, S., Owen, J. E., Mainella, F. C., & Osteen, L. (2006). A leadership identity development model: Applications from a grounded theory. *Journal of College Student Development. 47*(4), 401–420.

Lambert, L. (2003). *Leadership capacity for lasting school improvement.* Alexandria, VA: Association for Supervision and Curriculum Development.

Lawler, E. E. (2001). The era of human capital has finally arrived. In W. Bennis, G. M. Spreitzer, & T. G. Cummings (Eds.), *The future of leadership* (pp. 14–25). San Francisco, CA: Jossey-Bass.

Lord, R. G., & Hall, R. J. (2005). Identity, deep structure and the development of leadership skill. *The Leadership Quarterly, 16*(5), 591–615.

Luthans, F., & Avolio, B. (2003). Authentic leadership development. In K. S. Cameron, J. E. Dutton, & R. E. Quinn (Eds.), *Positive organizational scholarship. Foundations of a new discipline* (pp. 241–259). San Francisco, CA: Berrett-Koehler.

Luthans, F., & Youssef, C. M. (2004). Human, social, and now positive psychological capital management: Investing in people for competitive advantage. *Organizational Dynamics, 33*(2), 143–160.

May, D. R., Chan, A. Y. I., Hodges, T. D., & Avolio, B. J. (2003). Developing the moral component of authentic leadership. *Organizational Dynamics, 33*(3), 247–260.

McIntire, D. D. (1989). Student leadership development: A student affairs mandate. *NASPA Journal, 27*(1), 75–79.

Neal, M. (2010, February). *Leadership, religion, and culture—Drawing on and adapting tradition.* Workshop Proceedings from Appreciating and Advancing Leadership for Public Wellbeing, February 14–16, 2010, NYU Abu Dhabi, UAE.

Nemerowicz, G., & Rosi, E. (1997). *Education for leadership and social responsibility.* London: Falmer.

Quantz, R. A., Rogers, J., & Dantley, M. (1992). Rethinking transformative leadership: Toward democratic reform of schools. *Journal of Education, 173*(3), 96–118.

Shields, C. M. (2003a). *Good intentions are not enough: Transformative leadership for communities of difference.* Lanham, MD: Scarecrow/Technomics.

Shields, C. M. (2003b). Dialogic leadership for social justice: Overcoming pathologies of silence. *Educational Administrative Quarterly, 11*(1), 111–134.

Shields, C. M., (2009). *Democratizing practice: Courageous leadership for transforming schools.* Norwood, MA: Christopher-Gordon Publishers.

Shields, C. M. (2010). Transformative leadership: Working for equity in diverse contexts. *Educational Administration Quarterly, 46*(4), 558–589.

Stephenson, L. (2008). Leadership theories, educational change and developing a learning organization. In C. Coombe, M. MClouskey, L. Stephenson, & N. Anderson (Eds.), *Leadership in English language teaching and learning* (pp. 7-16). Ann Arbor, MI: University of Michigan Press.

Terry, R. (2003). *Authentic leadership: Courage in action.* San Francisco, CA: Jossey-Bass. Retrieved on November 10, 2010, from http://www.action-wheel.com/authentic-leadership.html (online extract).

UAE Ministry of Education. (n.d.). Retrieved on October 17, 2010, from http://www.moc.gov.ae/English/Pages/VisionMission.aspx

Weiner, E. J. (2003). Secretary Paulo Freire and the democratization of power: Toward a theory of transformative leadership. *Educational Philosophy and Theory, 35*(1), 89–106.

Woods, P. A. (2000). Varieties and themes in producer engagement: Structure and agency in the schools public market. *British Journal of Sociology of Education, 21*(2), 219–242.

Woods, P. A (2004). Democratic leadership: Drawing distinctions with distributed leadership. *The International Journal of Leadership in Education, 7*(1), 3–26.

23

Arab Women

Emerging Leadership Patterns and Identities

Barbara Harold

The role of women in Arab society has generated a range of reports and literature, much of which has painted a somewhat negative picture of women's lives. This perspective has tended to bias Western perspectives towards Arab women; it is time for other perspectives to be shown that can provide a balance for the often pessimistic views expounded. Women's leadership experiences are an area that offer possibilities for a fresh look at their role in civil society. In recent years, there has been an increase in studies of women's leadership in the Arab world (see Dubai Women Establishment [DWE], 2009). Research has been done from both an 'insider' and an external standpoint. The Arab world is a diverse one and women's levels of participation range from very restricted to full participation at the highest ranks of governance. It was noted in the recent *Arab Women: Leadership Outlook 2009–2011* (AWLO) report that:

> It is clear that women leaders in the Arab world are becoming more visible and their influence is felt across many sectors of business, despite the fact that they continue to represent a small minority in Arab society. Yet this minority increasingly punches above its weight and these women leaders act as role models and agents for change in Arab society. (DWE, 2009, p. 17)

At the same time that other countries in the Middle East are developing opportunities for women's leadership, the United Arab Emirates (UAE), in particular, has undergone rapid social, human, and economic development over the past four decades since its federation. The issue of leading and sustaining social progress has been at the forefront of recent local and national meetings of key organizations, including the Federal National Council and the Dubai Women's Establishment. Of significance also is the creation of various foundations with goals to research and develop social, human, and economic agendas; women and youth issues; leadership; and administration. In addition, the Emirates's leaders and key educational authorities have been focused on administrative and curricular reform in the nation's schools to ensure the sustainability of educational development. While there has been considerable research into educational leadership internationally, much more remains to be known about women leaders in the Gulf region and their culture, leadership, and learning.

In addition to the inclusion of data from the wider Arab region, this chapter uses data from three studies related to educational leadership, conducted by the author and a colleague, to discuss the way UAE women's leadership identities and roles are developing within the framework of contested meanings, shifting with time and context. The developing identities of participants in the three projects were the result of the interaction between their internal values, beliefs, and assumptions and the contexts in which they lived their experiences. This development parallels, and is a vital factor in, the sustainability of the broader social, economic, and educational development that is shaping UAE society. This chapter will also explore the elements of leadership-identity development in general, and the concept of transformative leadership in particular, to investigate what dimensions of transformative practice may be emerging from the former.

Literature Review

Given that the topic of this chapter is concerned with emerging patterns of leadership-identity development and how they might link to the concept of transformative leadership, it is helpful to initially explore perspectives in the literature about identity development. Drawing on the previous work of Harold and Stephenson (2008) and Stephenson (2004), the next section addresses current theories of identity.

Theories of Identity

According to Holland, Lachicotte, Skinner, and Cain (1998, p. 3) "identity is a person's self-understanding about who they are, who they say they are and trying to act as though they are who they say they are." In their view, the development of identities is a historically contingent, socially enacted, culturally constructed frame of social practices where individual and collective behaviours are mediated by a sense of self, or, in other words, an identity (Holland et al., 1998).

A 'communities of practice' concept is forwarded by Brown and Duguid (1991) and Wenger (1998) to highlight the connections between identity and learning and the role played by practice in the construction and maintenance of individual and collective identities. This chapter draws on social-identity theories from the perspective that identity is an ongoing process of interaction of person and context and, thus, interpretation and reinterpretation of experiences so that individuals understand who they are and who they wish to become (Beijaard, Meijer, & Verloop, 2004).

Britzman (1991, p. 3) explains that identities are dialogic relationships, "produced because of social interaction, subject to negotiation, consent, and circumstance, inscribed with power and desire, and always in the process of becoming." Holland et al. (1998, p. vii) theorize that if identities are being lived then they are unfinished and in process, and meanings that attach to certain identities shift with time and vary from place to place. Identities are shaped through the tensions between knowing and being, thought and action, theory and practice, and the objective and the subjective.

Wenger's (1998) model also emphasizes the dialogic nature of identity construction. In his model, the development of leadership identities is an ongoing process that changes as an individual learns through lived experiences, shaping and reshaping meanings that result from the social nature of identity development in specific contexts. Wenger (1998) identifies seven ways that identities are constructed and emphasizes the complexity of identity construction as a result of life's experiences. In his view, identities are configured by life, experience, and negotiation; across ongoing lifespan experiences; through social experiences; by the incorporation of past and future into the present; at the nexus of current practices; and through the interplay of global and local contexts where those practices are located; and finally, through the individual's participation in varying communities and practices at different stages of life. Similarly, for Lemke (1997) it is in the larger system of interdependent networks of activities and communities of practice that meaning making and learning occur.

> We embody our past, as our environment embodies its (and so our collective) past, and in our interaction not only memory but culture and historical and sociological processes are renewed and continued, diverted and changed. (Lemke, 1997, p. 10)

For Salling Olesen (2001, p. 296), identity is a process of ongoing concern for the professional in a field. She identifies two main objective elements: work practices, with their more or less contradictory and coercive conditions, and the social interactions, missions, and changes to which the professional has to and wants to relate; and the cultural institution, consisting of the profession as an institution and a professional discourse:

> Learning and experience building is a process of subjective flexibility, in which a learning subject, meeting new and changing phenomena and social practices, redefines itself cognitively and emotionally (Salling Olesen, 2001, p. 95).

The foregoing views on identity development have clear implications for how we think about leadership identity, implying that leadership beliefs and practices are similarly built up over time from individual and collective social experiences within a cultural framework and that they are dialogic, fluid, and enacted within specific social contexts. Inherent in these theories is a view that leadership identity develops and matures over time. This is an important point in relation to transformative leadership practice, which requires in the leader a maturity and wisdom to understand and critique broader issues within the social milieu in which the leader operates. The following section explores the issue of leadership-identity development as discussed in recent literature.

Leadership-Identity Development

Identity development has also been the focus of attention in recent leadership literature. A useful theoretical model has been proposed by Lord and Hall (2005), for example, who suggest that a leader's self-identity is a central focus, as it provides a means for the leader to organize knowledge and a source for self-motivation—and potentially a source for personal material, such as narratives and values, that may motivate others (Lord & Hall, 2005, p. 592). In their terms, leadership skills develop progressively from novice through intermediate to expert. Throughout this progression, factors of identity, emotional regulation, and meta-cognition play a critical role in the development of deep cognitive structures associated with leadership expertise (2005, p. 591).

Komives, Longerbeam, Owen, Mainella, and Osteen (2006) have also proposed a progressive model of leadership-identity development. They claim that individuals move through six stages: awareness, exploration-engagement, leader identified, leadership differentiated, generativity, and integration-synthesis. This growth in leadership identity is impacted at each stage by changing views of leadership, self-development, group influences, developmental influences, and changing views of self with others. For Komives et al. (2006), the critical transition period is between the third and fourth stages, where the leader moves from an individual positional perspective to a recognition that leadership involves meaningful engagement with others. Transformative leadership also recognizes the progressive nature of leadership development, with an initial focus on critical self-reflection, moving through to enlightened understanding, and finally to action "to redress wrongs and to ensure that all . . . are provided with as level a playing field as possible" (Shields, 2010, p. 573).

According to van Knippenberg, van Knippenberg, De Cremer, and Hogg (2005), leadership development is a relatively understudied element in leadership research. In their introduction to a special edition of *Leadership Quarterly* dealing with theories of leadership identity, they identify several emerging topics worthy of further research; for example, the role of follower self-conception as both a mediator and moderator of the relationship between leadership and follower behavior (Lord, Brown, & Freiberg, 1999; van Knippenberg, van Knippenberg, De Cremer, & Hogg, 2004); the integration of social-identity theories with those of leader fairness (Lipponen, Koivisto, & Olkkonen, 2005; Tyler & De Cremer, 2005); and leadership effectiveness from the perspective of the leader's self-conception (Lord & Hall, 2005). Van Knippenberg et al. (2005) raise questions that could potentially inform understanding of collective transformative leadership practice, such as, "What leads leaders to engage in behaviors that affect follower self-construal (e.g., group-oriented behavior)?" and "What leads leaders to act in ways that build follower self-efficacy?" (van Knippenberg et al., 2005, p. 497).

An overview of recent research into Arab women's leadership indicates that the dominant perspective has been transformational leadership (e.g., Al-Lamky, 2007; DWE, 2009; Yaseen, 2010). This is most likely because the concept of transformative leadership (see Shields, 2003; Stephenson, Shields, & Harold, 2010) is a relatively new one in leadership theory, growing with the recognition that transformational perspectives alone are inadequate to meet the complex social, academic, and equity needs of many school contexts. In educational leadership situations, transformation leadership tends to operate within the organizational setting, focusing on organizational change and improvement, increased administrative and curricular effectiveness, and the professional learning of others in the organization. Transformative leadership practice looks beyond the organization to the deconstruction and reconstruction of social-cultural knowledge frameworks that generate inequity (Shields, 2010). This implies a leadership identity that is well developed, mature, and confident, because the leader may well be in a position where he or she has to meet challenges and situations that require wisdom and courage.

Methodology

The data for this chapter are drawn from studies that fall predominantly within a qualitative paradigm. The methods used include review of recent leadership studies and conference presentations in the wider Middle Eastern context, together with an analysis of material emerging from studies done in the United Arab Emirates in particular (see Harold, 2008; Harold & Stephenson, 2008; Stephenson, 2011). The latter studies used interview, reflective journals, self-reports, and document analysis to investigate leadership perspectives of undergraduate and graduate students and local educational and business leaders. Using a qualitative and interpretive paradigm, where research is considered a social act that is itself shaped by social and cultural conventions, the project methodologies drew on oral history and grounded-theory methods and narrative inquiry, respectively. The first project was carried out by a group of preservice teachers using an oral history methodology wherein they interviewed senior family members who had attended school in the 1960s and 1970s in the United Arab Emirates in order to get an inside perspective into what education was like at that time. The second project focused on experienced female educational leaders' narratives of self, their learning, and the development of their leadership skills.

These two projects used forms of narrative inquiry. Narrativists believe that human beings live out stories, are told stories, and are storytelling beings (Stephenson, 2004). Narrative inquiry is a form of narrative experience that allows the complexities, challenges, and ambiguities of our individual and social life experiences to be linked to experiential inquiry.

The third UAE project used a qualitative framework, where in-depth analysis of the process of ongoing individual leadership learning was carried out by a retrospective analysis of data gathered within the last four years from a graduate educational leadership program at Zayed University. Graduates were asked to draw on personal and theoretical points of view to reflect on their current leadership perspectives and philosophies, in the context of their culture and religion. A grounded-theory approach (Glaser & Strauss, 1967; Strauss & Corbin, 1990) was used to analyze data.

Additional perspectives were drawn from the proceedings of a workshop organized by the New York University Wagner Graduate School of Public Service (NYU Abu Dhabi Institute, 2010). This was held in the UAE in February 2010 and the participants were scholars and practitioners invited from a range of academic and civil society contexts throughout the Middle East. Their leadership-related work and research was varied, but all were concerned in some way with transformational and transformative perspectives, including women's leadership, civic engagement, migrant worker issues, youth empowerment, education reform, and civic engagement.

Findings

An analysis of data from the three UAE projects indicated that there were two overarching themes emerging from the material. The first key theme was that of change—perspectives of women's roles and women's opportunities in society, balancing roles, the nature of education, patterns of support, and impact of new theories. Second, there was a clear continuity of ongoing influences—parental support, the importance of family, impact of friendship, role models, influence of Islam, and learning from previous experience.

Change

The following section expands on these influences and, following a sequential historical perspective, highlights the way that these women's leadership identities have developed through the interplay between continuity and change over time and are grounded in the local context. It also comments on the links between the UAE research and other leadership studies done in the wider region. Following exemplars of each element of leadership identity is a brief discussion of its link to transformative leadership perspectives. These are expanded upon later in the discussion section of the chapter.

Perspectives of Women's Roles

The oral history data clearly showed the impact of traditional roles and expectations on the education of the participants when they attended school in the 1960s and 1970s:

> Because of the traditions of the society and families toward girls' education, I was not able to continue my education immediately after grade five. . . . Many people did not allow their daughters to go to school because of their beliefs toward girl's education. (Alya)

When I was five and it was the time to register me in a school my father refused and said that he didn't want his daughter to go to schools. (Nahla)

Within the school system there were also restrictions on girls' dress and behaviour:

The administration of our school was very strict with us. They were restricting everything that girls could ever do. For example, kohl and long nails weren't allowed. (Hamda)

Nahla indicated in her story that opportunities for women were still relatively limited at that time:

Education and work were not very common for women at that time, so there were not much working opportunities for women and even when they existed the social restrictions were very hard. (Nahla)

The five experienced female Emirati leaders attended school at a similar time to participants of the oral history project. However, by the time they became adults they had contested the traditional role of women in the community by taking on specific leadership positions. Raja, for example, was chosen as headmistress when she was 23 years old, over 30 years ago. This was groundbreaking in the cultural context. She continued to challenge stereotypes of Emirati women as she became a more prominent leader and role model for young Emirati women. Her perspective is clearly shown in the following quote:

I have a vision. [I want people to know that] the UAE has businesswomen, but to also change the misconception in the West about Middle Eastern women, [that they are] neglected, on the shelf, in tents, on camels . . . make it very clear that woman plays her role. (Raja)

Not only did another local woman leader, Aysha, challenge the expected role of women at that time, she took on leadership roles and actively sought to shift the perceptions of other young women as she encouraged their development as educational leaders:

These [teachers] that I focused on, I realized they are flexible, ready to learn and [have] a strong personality [so] I gave them many things to do especially preparing . . . workshops with me. I [wanted] to give them responsibility [and set high expectations for leadership success]. The two [teachers] joined me and are now very successful in their jobs. (Aysha)

Anood was older than the other key leaders and in her earlier life had tended to follow the more traditional cultural expectations for women. However, education had always been important for her and even in retirement she still continued to develop her knowledge and skills:

[Because my role with the kids was over] I decided to learn to recite the Quran by heart. I am also learning Arabic language grammar. I plan to continue at night school. (Anood)

The graduate data indicated that, for those participants, women's roles in the current context were not seen as fixed. Majida, for example, commented on how the graduate program had impacted her views of herself as a female leader:

[The course] created a shift in my ways of thinking about leadership, and encouraged me to be eager to explore more issues of leadership. Actually, it changed my concept and ideas of women as leaders. (Majida)

Alia was aware that opportunities for women were changing in the local context and she wanted to take advantage of that herself:

> One of the things that I am concerned about is the role of women in the UAE. In these day women have taken their chance to hold different positions. In fact, we can see a woman as a [government] minister, where before this position was only for men. These changes in our society make me want to develop myself in order to help my country in some way. (Alia)

Majida's experiences in the leadership course had focused her thinking in more specific ways and changed some of her views about opportunities for women leaders:

> A new idea I am interested in is the idea of empowering women in leadership in the UAE. (Majida)

Like Alia, she was aware of changes in society, but was also aware that more work needed to be done:

> Women face unique challenges. The Quran stress that men and women are equal [but] I feel that [until recently] there weren't training programs or study programs to engage and prepare women for leadership. (Majida)

These women clearly reflect transformative leadership elements in their statements, which indicate their awareness for new roles and possibilities for women leaders in their society. Raja, for example, was aware of realities and perspectives outside her own country that led to erroneous beliefs about modern Arab women and she wanted to change those. Others, such as Alia and Majida, were developing understandings about gender issues within their own society that they believed needed attention. From a transformative perspective, they were engaging with critique and possibility and deconstructing and reconstructing knowledge frameworks.

Balancing Roles

In all of the UAE projects the theme of balancing roles came through clearly. The first of these dimensions related to balancing between work and family responsibilities. Many of the participants mentioned how this impacted them. Although they valued education and work they felt their responsibilities as mothers very strongly and strove to balance between the two. Alya in the oral history project reflects the importance of parenting:

> I was not able to complete my grade 12 final year because of the family responsibilities as a mother for my children, who needed me to be there with them. . . . I considered this experience was a great achievement from my point of view with all the hard responsibilities that I had and the different roles that I played. (Alya)

Mona, one of the experienced women leaders, had to weigh her dual responsibilities before choosing to develop a leadership opportunity to write a curriculum text for the Ministry of Education:

> I already had three children and I was thinking about how I was going to leave [them] but the book writing was an opportunity to be taken. This started another chapter in my life. (Mona)

Similarly, Anood understood the weight of responsibility in being a mother and a teacher but still managed to balance the two successfully:

The nicest part of my [leadership] journey was seeing my children complete their education. Teaching and mothering were critical. I was a leader at home and in teaching the Quran. Life was so different before. What was important for me was to take things easy . . . teach the students [the Quran] and bring up my own children. I had double the work but I did it. I did not think it was too difficult for me. (Anood)

Research done by Al-Lamky (2007) and the AWLO project (DWE, 2009) raises another dimension and dilemma that Arab women leaders face in balancing roles. This is finding a balance between societal expectations of women—especially those held by Arab men—and the opportunities for leadership that emerge from education, experience, and personal drive. Al-Lamky (2007, p. 59) comments that the emphasis on women's "sentimental and emotional" role as mother-wife is seen as contradictory to the "rational and economic" role of men and, thus, they face challenges when taking on leadership roles in male-dominated fields. Ironically, it is the emphasis on broader subjective values of care and support shown by the women in Al-Lamky's study that is a critical element in transformative practice.

The Nature of Education

Within the UAE studies the theme of the nature and importance of education was also common. All of the participants had been successful in their schooling. As they reflected on past and present, some of the oral history participants could see significant differences:

Education before differs from education now because the whole system changed as a result of the development that the UAE went through. After comparing between education before and now, I noticed a huge change in the curriculum and its contents the school system, the teaching methods, the timing, teaching materials used, and teachers' status and position in the society now. (Shaikha)

The women in the experienced leaders' project were critically aware of problems in the education system and strove to initiate change for the better. Aysha, for example, took a lead in professional development for teachers:

I was giving this feeling to teachers to encourage them, but the feeling was not enough. There was a need to do more, so I started workshops and seminars and was involved in organizing the first English conference in the UAE at Zayed University in 1998. (Aysha)

Not only was she supporting the teachers in her own subject area, but she was also actively involved in distributing leadership across other curriculum areas as well. Her leadership style showed elements of transformative practice in the sense that she actively used her position, knowledge, and power to strengthen other teachers in new kinds of pedagogical practice that would offer a better curriculum for children. In addition, as the following quote shows, she was constantly seeking ways to share her power by mentoring and encouraging others to take up leadership in their school programs:

When we were training English teachers we were training them to give lessons to teachers from other subjects. I was building their characters without telling them feel that. Here my focus was on individuals. These teachers were leaders in the schools. You will find these teachers were everywhere, like butterflies. They deserve somebody to support and back them. (Aysha)

Women leaders in Al-Lamky's (2007) study also noted the importance of education. One of her participants commented, for example: "My mother was herself an educationalist and a leader who emphasized the returns and importance of education in our lives" (Al-Lamky, 2007, p. 56).

In the AWLO study too, education was noted as a key element in the expression of responsibility in leadership. One participant stated:

> Educated women should share the knowledge they gained with others, as they are holding social responsibilities. When women gain power, authorities, and knowledge they are responsible for helping others reach that stage as well. (DWE, 2007, p. 22)

This view connects with the requirement that a transformative leader acknowledge their own power and privilege and to use it for the betterment of others.

Patterns of Support

As the stories emerged from the women's experiences it was obvious that a significant element in their development was the support of key people in the school, family, and workplace. While there is evidence of continuity of support over time, it has been included under the theme of change to highlight some new patterns of support that emerged as a result of change over time. Here, we look at other patterns of support.

Alya, for example, reflected on how the support of teachers in her early years had impacted on her own support for her children's learning:

> I believe that what I had got in these years helped me to have a background on how to teach my children and develop their love and encourage them to love learning and education. (Alya)

The experienced educational women leaders drew support from each other and from colleagues in the field:

> My colleagues were always ready to help, for example, at conferences. We were called the 'gang'—people called us to organize conferences. (Aysha)

The support of husbands was mentioned by several of the participants. This was something new in the culture, as is reflected in the quote to follow. Mona noted this as she spoke about an opportunity for leadership that had arisen when her children were still young:

> [My supervisor] said he would talk to the principal and my husband. That was my first step towards leadership. The principal was very supportive. My husband and parents were very cooperative and very supportive. (Mona)

The graduate students also identified this new pattern. Tahani, for example, mentioned both her parents as having initial positive leadership influences but then went on to also identify her husband as someone who had provided the impetus to continue to develop those earlier effects:

> My husband . . . encouraged me to step out of my comfort zone to seek further knowledge and continue my education. (Tahani)

In the AWLO report, also (DWE, 2009), 55% of participants cited husbands as being strongly supportive:

The future does not depend on the woman or her qualities alone. It depends on factors around her that help—most of all on the husband's support and the husband's culture. (DWE, 2009, p.23)

The AWLO report (DWE, 2009) also identified the strong influence of family networks for their participant leaders, with 67% and 66% of participants citing mothers and fathers, respectively, as being of central importance to their ongoing leadership development.

Unlimited support from families coupled with the surrounding environment gives Arab women a better chance to become distinguished leaders compared with non-Arab women. (DWE, 2009, p. 27)

Other studies in the region support the importance of family influences in the development of women leaders. Al-Lamky's (2007) study of elite female leaders in Oman, for example, noted:

All the women interviewed for this study acknowledged their parents or at least one of them, typically the father, to have facilitated an early sense of independence, self confidence and assertiveness. The role of the mother was also prominent; typically a strong character leaving clear marks on their development. (Al-Lamky, 2007, p. 56)

The foregoing quotes underscore the critical way in which the lived experiences of these women have contributed to their sense of identity by allowing them to develop, within a supportive and nurturing environment, the confidence, determination, courage, and core values that are more likely to lead to transformative action.

Impact of New Theories

The graduate leadership program at Zayed University exposed the cohorts to a wide range of theoretical perspectives and models. The program's initial focus on systems thinking, shared leadership, and servant leadership undoubtedly influenced the way our graduates thought about leadership concepts. For example, the second cohort was introduced to more content about organizational theory and leadership, and this was reflected in their comments about these topics. Several noted the importance for the leader to be able to have a broad understanding and knowledge of the organization in order to make changes and improvements:

I think that the leader should understand the culture and the structure of the organization, should be aware of the contemporary imperatives, should formulate a vision, should create the proper atmosphere to enable change, and should enhance coherence between all the parts of the organization. (Sabah)

A leader in an organization should clarify the organization's role and responsibility in the society, as well as modify the roles and positions of their team members. The leaders should be able to share their mission and vision to achieve their aim as team. (Afra)

While these two quotes tend to reflect *transformational* perspectives, Sabah's mention of "contemporary imperatives" allows for the possibility of a *transformative* view.

Certain leadership approaches appealed to the graduate cohort as they developed their own identity. Distributed leadership was one of these, as it aligned closely with the concept of Al Shura leadership (see Al Hinai & Rutherford, 2002):

I found myself [using] distributed leadership. Actually, I believe that [distributed] leadership is the best way of leading. (Alia)

However, new ideas were not accepted uncritically, as Ayesha showed in her comment:

I don't think that distributed leadership works in the school. It may possibly work in the industrial sector [but] in my school there are actually three powers (principal–vice principal–supervisor): how can they have an equal strength of power in the school if they oppose each others' ideas and decisions? (Ayesha)

Ayesha's comment, in particular, showed the emerging recognition of the complexities of the role and exercise of power, a key element of transformative leadership.

Continuity

This chapter has thus far discussed keys themes relating to change in the participants' lived experiences as they develop their own leadership identities of self. The next section focuses on themes of continuity as they emerged from the data.

The Importance of Family and Parental Support

Across the three projects, comments about the importance of family and parental support appeared consistently. Mothers were identified by several women as being a key influence on their leadership growth. Participants in the oral history project noted:

My mother insisted that I get educated, as she believed then that education will make us as girls stronger and more confident. (Nahla)

I had the motivation to continue my study because I was the only daughter at home and my mother wanted me to continue studying instead of sitting at home without any purpose. (Shaikha)

The place of mothers was also reflected in comments from the experienced leaders. Anood's statement indicated continuity and family values grounded in the local context of Islam:

The first step was with my mother, who insisted on my education. She took me to a lady who was teaching the Quran. I finished learning the Quran at 15 years old. I then had to teach my own sister. (Anood)

For the graduates, the impact of mothers' support in developing their leadership identities was also clear, as evidenced in the following comments:

Through [my mother's] hard work and support we succeeded in finishing our graduate studies and each daughter became a leader in her own way. (Tahani)

My mother's personality was characterized by her strong perspective in leading and managing and solving problems in my life had a positive effect in the way she raised me. (Mona)

Mona, too, commented on how her parents supported her early education and development as a lifelong learner:

We were taught international values, honesty, respect, love. Taught at school and at home. Parents showed a lot of love and affection but did not live in a materialistic world. Parents wanted us to value and be grateful for what we had. (Mona)

Raja's key influence was from her father, and her comment also highlights the continuity of family values and learning from past experience:

My father taught me to be a woman who works and cares for her family. A woman who cares for her family is the most important thing. The most important thing is success within the family. Therefore, I concentrated on my children—I have given them my life. Whatever I lacked I wanted my children to have. (Raja)

Impact of Friendship

The role friendship plays in Arabic culture is significant, particularly for women. Hamda's comments (from the oral history) about her own schooling capture this well:

There was a strong relationship between students in the classroom and even outside the classroom. There were no barriers between us. We played, ate, and studied together. We had a very simple life, not like nowadays. We were like a family. After the third classes, we had a break. In this break, I sat with my friends, talked with them, or sometimes if we had homework for the next day, we sat together and did it. I loved my friends a lot and we still contact each other even now. (Hamda)

The experienced female Emirati leaders also valued friendship, and the following comments show its importance in their lives from when they were children up to their current work:

I have always kept my relationship with everybody that wherever we reach we never forget the old good days. [Since] I was 10 years old I [still] have the same friends as then. I don't get into new relationships very easily. I am stable. (Raja)

I chose [to study] art because of my friends . . . I just wanted to enjoy my school days— to be with my friends. 'Til now we are still friends from grade five—always together—even in university most of us chose English—to share. This is something that told me to work in groups—teamwork— helping other as friends and colleagues. This was one of the good things in my life. (Abla)

Role Models

Role models significantly impacted participants' identity formation over time and location. These role models ranged from family mentors and friends to colleagues, teachers, and national and religious leaders. The strong value placed on education by their role models was noted by several participants. For example, the oral history participants were attending school at the time of the federation of the Emirates and some mentioned this point in relation to the new leader of the nation, who valued education very highly:

At that time, some families didn't send their children to school because they didn't know how valuable education was. After 1972, Shaikh Zayed Bin Sultan, may God bless his soul, motivated people to complete their study and let their children enter school. (Shaikha)

Some women spoke of their own teachers as key role models for them as students:

Teachers were the models of education and they had a special status in the society. In addition to that, people noticed that there is nothing better than being educated. (Shaikha)

Teachers had a great reputation in the society, and the teaching career was and still [is] considered the best profession for women. (Nahla)

A number of participants identified their father as a key role model. Raja, one of the experienced leaders, was influenced strongly by her parent's character:

My role model is my father, who is over 80 and still working. [He says] "I don't want to retire." I feel I have his genes. . . . I learnt from my father to be stable and to think on the matter. (Raja)

Among the graduates, others also cited their father as an early role model. Tahani and Kaltham identified specific traits that they admired:

My father, who practiced medicine, was my first role model. He was charismatic, honourable, straightforward, and honest. A man with a vision who had a lot to offer. (Tahani)

I grew up to see my father as a leading figure. He used to work in the military, and he always told me, "If you want to grow up and be a leader you should gain others' confidence through your good manners and never ever force your opinion on others . . . use negotiation and compromise to reach your goal . . ." (Kaltham)

Like Raja, Anood took much from a parent as a role model. For her, her mother's influence was strong:

My father was a pearl diver—gone for three to four months a year—so my mother took on [both] the mother and father role[s]. [As a result] I learned how to be strong from her. . . . I learned many things from my mother . . . generosity, patience . . . her doors were open all the time. She tried to be with all her relatives. In Islam if relatives are in need, first give to them, then give to strangers. (Anood)

Raja herself had been a role model for Abla when the latter first started her teaching career:

My principal was Raja in the then only secondary [girls'] school. I was so lucky to be with that lady . . . . She taught me what leadership is . . . my first lesson was how to encourage, how to choose the right person in the right place, how to build something in her character. I still remember—she used to send me to represent the school—others too. She gave me the first lesson in leadership. (Abla)

Other principals were also mentioned by some in the graduate study as having had an impact on their views of leadership:

I remember a principal who encouraged teachers to do what she wanted and they really did it with happiness by her persuading and convincing them. She was very personable. What most I appreci- ated about her is how she delegated the workload. If there was a problem, she would sit down to speak to the person in private. She was always teaching me new things. (Majida)

For both cohorts, the leadership examples set by local leaders were frequently cited as having had an influence on their own views. Here, they mentioned particular leaders and designated them as transformational and charismatic leaders:

> One of the great transformational leadership examples is what we are experiencing by living here in Dubai. This style is represented through HH Shaikh Mohamed Bin Rashed Al Maktoum's vision to transform Dubai to rank as one of the first cities in the world. (Tahani)

Influence of Islam

An ongoing and pervasive influence for all of the participants was their strong belief in and lived experiences of Islam as they negotiated their identity development. This was evident from their earliest days of schooling, as mentioned by Alya:

> I entered school for the first time in 1963 when I was six years old. The first stage of my days of school was from grade one to grade five. In the afternoon time we went to study and recite the holy Quran with a teacher who was named Al Mutawa. (Alya)

The experienced leaders also commented on the place of Islam in their lives from childhood:

> I'd recite the Quran before school . . . . I did very well in reading and reciting the Quran and was helping my friends. (Abla)

> I stopped teaching [the classes then] so that I could teach my own kids Islamic studies. This was very important for me to do. (Anood)

They went on to endorse its impact on their current leadership practices and values:

> [Leadership] is a gift from God firstly . . . (Raja)

> God dominates everything— it happened for me to have to do something in this life. (Abla)

The influence of Islam was a similar theme within the graduate data on leadership. For some it was simply a given:

> My own conception of leadership is based on a combination of my beliefs and Islamic values. (Asia)

> Throughout history people have been trying to define leadership at it has evolved. Therefore, I will choose the holiest definition by our Prophet Mohammad (peace be upon him) when he said: "Each of you is a guardian, and each of you will be asked about his subjects." (Majida)

Several reiterated the importance of moral and ethical values and behaviour that were inherent within Islam and that formed an implicit element of leaders' work:

> In the Holy Quran and the Hadith, a great emphasis is given to moral and ethical values in Islam. These ethics and values are not just a set of rules to be followed, they are a whole lifestyle and this comprises the foundation of my personal beliefs and values. (Tahani)

In Islam, leaders are encouraged to implement their Islamic principles and values by creating an ethical institution, practicing authority in ethical ways, and applying it in daily practices and challenges. (Asia)

Some participants referred to the leadership of Prophet Mohamed (PBUH) as an exemplar to guide them in their own approach to leadership. Often they referred to specific messages from the Holy Quran to reinforce this:

Prophet Mohamed founded one of the world's great religions, and became an immensely effective political leader. Today, thirteen centuries after his death, his influence is still powerful. He is surely right and we love the prophet Mohamed (peace and blessings be upon him) as he lives with us and we always find him a great leader who has all the necessary qualities for success in every aspect of life. (Suhaila)

A further aspect of leadership practice that was connected with Islam by some participants was that of personal change:

Change from inside must come first. In the Holy Quran, in Al Ra'ad, part 13, page 250, it says, "Verily never will God change the condition of a people until they change it themselves (with their own souls)." (Shaima)

The views expressed by participants in our study align with the ideas expressed by Shah (2006) in her seminal article about the Islamic perspectives on leadership in educational contexts. She notes that in Islam:

Education is for the holistic development, and religion is not a mere set of moral principles, but a complete system encompassing and integrating the political, social and economic, as well as personal, moral and spiritual aspects of life. (Shah, 2006, p. 368)

There are clear links between this perspective and the characteristics of transformative leaders in the sense that both points of view are concerned with the betterment of the individual and society. Inherent in an Islamic perspective on educational leadership is a holistic view of the learner. Shah (2006) states:

From an Islamic perspective institutional leadership continues to involve more than organizational management involving responsibilities for the holistic development of the learners and the wider society. The teacher is perceived as a leader within and beyond the classroom context, expected to fulfill the leadership role as a guide to knowledge and conduct and to be a role model. (Shah, 2006, p. 371)

Learning from Previous Experience

One theme of continuity that came through, predominantly from the experienced leaders, was that of learning from previous experience. In reflecting on her career change from school principal to company CEO, Raja made the following comments:

Yes, I did make mistakes. A human should make mistakes and from these mistakes they learn. In my personality, before I sleep I always reflect [and] question myself and evaluate [or] judge my daily performance in life. When I start my next day I try to overcome those mistakes through constant analysis. Yes, I am very focused and organized. (Raja)

As their parents had done before, what these women had learned as they developed their own leadership identities was something that they were passing on to their own children, thus continuing the cycle of parental support and leadership:

> When raised that way and you "feel leadership" you feel you always want to be on top. I try to do it with my daughter. I believe—when you put a child [there] at the beginning—he will always be leading in his life. (Abla)

Other Current Leadership Patterns

The NYU workshop identified other patterns of leadership development found across the region. One of these was the fluid leadership identities of participants themselves as "practitioner-academics, as business and social entrepreneurs, and as local actors and global citizens" (NYU Abu Dhabi Institute, 2010, p. 5). One participant reported on research on women's negotiation and leadership in the region, which showed that gender is a relational concept that must include understanding of the role of men and the relationships of power that bind women and men together. The study also found that context and culture are impacted by the hegemonic effect of globalization and that "culture" as a lens to understand leadership can be potentially disempowering, establishing simplistic conceptions of oppressed Arab women (Al Dabbagh, 2010, cited in NYU Institute, 2010, p. 12). Another participant (Bouraoui, 2010, cited in NYU Abu Dhabi Institute, 2010, p. 12) shared findings from her life-history research with Arab women, which showed that women "exercise leadership strategically, drawing on a wide repertoire of leadership practices and deploying them based on the situation" (p. 12).

Discussion

The preceding sections provide an overview of the varied dimensions to the development of leadership identity among some groups of Arab women and make some initial links between those aspects and transformative leadership. I now turn to a discussion of the significance of these dimensions in relation to theories of identity development and transformative leadership theory and practice.

There is a clear resonance between the aspects of Wenger's (1998) model of identity development, which highlights the interplay between "the remembered past and the anticipated future [which] are constantly integrated into and renegotiated in the ever-changing negotiated, dynamic present" (Clarke, 2005, p. 35). Lave and Wenger's (1991) concept of situated cognition, which is concerned with how learning occurs in practice and context and explores the situated character of human understanding and communication, also provides a window to examine the ways in which the graduate students operated in the program. It views action as being situated in the individual roles of members within communities.

Many references were made by participants across all the studies to early role models, including those from home and family, the workplace, and in societal leadership roles. These references reflect the high cultural value placed on family roles and obligations, which, in Arab society, often come first before other societal duties.

The findings across the studies identified several similarities to Komives et al.'s (2005) grounded-theory study on the development of a leadership identity, including the role of adult influence, reflective learning, meaningful involvement, deepening self-awareness, applying new skills, changing views of self, group influence, and broadening views of leadership. However, Komives et al.'s (2005) study does not explicitly address belief systems, such as religious influence and cultural assumptions. They state that "other aspects of self-awareness were the development of personal values and a sense of personal integrity that became more important over time" (2005, p. 600). However, the majority of participants referred to Islam as a significant influence on their concepts of leadership, including the importance of value-centered leadership where ethics and moral purpose are central tenets. Such tenets also underpin a transformative approach to leadership.

The interwovenness and content of dimensions of leadership identity shared by participants relate strongly to Wenger's (1998) theories of identity construction. For example, the social aspect of identity construction was evident in the strong links between the participants' Islamic cultural experiences and the values that they saw as critical for effective leadership. The multifaceted nature of identities was shown through their comments about the development of their views in relation to home, school, workplace, and academic contexts. The interplay between global and local contexts was indicated by the way in which they made links between their current views, constructed from a Middle Eastern perspective, to new material from wider international practices. The incorporation of past and future into the present was evident—for example, where graduate participants drew on positive or negative earlier experiences and then, looking forward to how they intended to practice leadership, linked those ideas to their present context. The findings across the three UAE projects aligned with Lord and Hall's (2005) theoretical model, in the sense that leadership skills develop progressively from novice through intermediate to expert. Lord and Hall's (2005) theoretical factors of identity, emotional regulation, and meta-cognition were also evident in the comments of the participants. In terms of leadership skills, the graduate students could perhaps be seen as being at a novice or intermediate level, whereas the experienced leaders in the studies by Al-Lamky (2007), DWE (2009), Harold and Stephenson (2008), and Stephenson (2011) were clearly at the expert level. Furthermore, what was shown in Harold and Stephenson's (2008) study was the nature of the progression from novice to expert. This dimension has particular relevance to the development of understandings about transformative approaches to leadership. By its very definition transformative leadership practice requires that leaders have a depth of knowledge built on lived experience, which allows them to engage in challenge and critique and to recognize those aspects of society that are inequitable and that impinge on their work as leaders. This kind of maturity was evident in the comments of the experienced leaders in our study and was emerging from the graduates' thinking as they interacted with new theories and ideas in the coursework.

An examination of comments about how leadership identity was changing or had changed as a result of the leadership program also highlights the links between those explanations and several of Wenger's (1998) elements of identity formation. There are links in the findings, also, to Beijaard, Meijer and Verloop's (2004) concept of identity as growing from interpretation and reinterpretation of experiences so that individuals understand who they are and who they wish to become. For the graduates, through interacting as a community of practice in the class setting, sharing and receiving feedback about personal experiences, and critically analyzing leadership experiences from wider contexts, the interpretation-reinterpretation process became an integral part of the participants' learning about and constructing themselves as leaders now and in the future.

What is implied from the findings is the multidimensional, fluid nature of leadership identity and practice. Data from the three UAE projects indicated a continuum of leadership identity growth that was constantly evolving through engagement with interdependent networks of people, communities of practice, and ideas. Perceptions of Arab women's leadership practice need to be cognizant of the nuances within which it operates (NYU Abu Dhabi Institute, 2010). Related to this dimension is the way that women's lived experience in an Islamic culture is deeply intertwined with their leadership practice and impacts their ability to take transformative action.

The relational concept of gender is particularly important in any analysis of Arab women's leadership identity and practice. Al-Lamky's (2007) work has highlighted the complexity of women's leadership in societies where gender roles and power relations are still clearly defined and yet are also impacted by cultural change and globalization. What emerged clearly from all the studies cited was the importance of male support and encouragement being received by the female participants, which allowed them to continue to build their leadership practice. These findings indicate that much more needs to be known about the nature of gender and power relations within family contexts in order to avoid stereotyped views. A transformative approach would require female leaders to challenge and critique gender relations to identify ways to reconstruct gender relations in a more equitable way.

What is evident in the data is that Arab women leaders who are seen as successful do not necessarily face gender barriers within the family level as evidenced by support from fathers and husbands. The data show that, in fact, men are being advocates for women in these situations, a factor that also challenges stereotypes about men in the region. However, the women may still require moral courage to deal with challenges to their position in wider society and deep and equitable change in social conditions. This dimension is intimately concerned with dialectic processes between the individual and social (Shields, 2010). Data from the studies show that while many of the participants were aware of important goals for societal transformation, that emphasis needs to now translate into how to take action for social justice. This is particularly important for the graduates who are at a point of moving into leadership positions in their organizations.

Another important factor is that most of the research into women's leadership identities in the Arab world has focused on how they get ahead as individuals. Much more needs to be known about what is happening from a collective perspective. The data from the experienced leaders' study gave some indication that those women gained strength, support, and satisfaction from working collectively. From a transformative leadership perspective, more research is needed about how to harness the skills of both emerging and experienced female leaders and also their capacity to improve not only themselves but also the communities in which they work.

What is interesting in the analysis of leadership exemplars and research from the Middle East is how elements of transformative leadership emerge from the data and are intertwined with transformational elements. For example, there was an understanding of the processes of transformational leadership, such as an understanding of organizational culture and helping members grow and develop within it. But some leaders were able to extend that understanding into the ability to critique and challenge wider societal issues of equity. Some of the research focuses attention on how women call on a repertoire of leadership skills to react to specific situations. This view of leadership suggests that their leadership practice may be characterized across a range of theoretical constructs that are utilized as required within particular contexts and to respond to particular needs. What is clear from the data is that experienced leaders are integrating transformative goals at the personal and organizational levels and are incorporating principled and ethical approaches into their work in education, and some have moved to the societal level of transformative action, balancing critique and promise and overcoming deficit thinking, particularly in relation to gender.

Conclusion

The studies described in this chapter have focused attention on women in the Gulf region and their patterns of leadership-identity development and emerging transformative leadership practice. The examples given highlight the way women's identities and roles are developing within the framework of contested meanings, shifting with time, and being grounded in the region's communities, culture, and religion. The identities of participants in the projects discussed were developed through an interplay between continuity and change and were the result of the interactions between their internal values, beliefs, and assumptions and the contexts in which they lived their experiences. This reconstruction of cultural and knowledge frameworks parallels and is a critical factor in the sustainability of the broader social, economic, and educational development that is shaping societies in the UAE, Gulf countries, and the wider region. These broad societal developments challenge the stereotypes and preconceived notions held by outsiders about women in the region. It is clear that elements of transformative leadership practice are emerging and in use within the individual and collective contexts occupied by these women and that they are acting courageously to advance greater social justice and opportunities for other women to take up leadership roles.

> The path to achieve transformative change may be tough and seemingly unattainable; however, chances for success in realizing meaningful inclusiveness can be increased by cultivating a vision for the future, and a clear direction aimed at altering women's realities and tackling socio-economic and cultural structures that sustain inequities. (Al-Lamky, 2007, p. 64)

References

Al Hinai, H., & Rutherford, D. (2002, September). *Exploring the Alshura school leadership model in Oman.* Paper presented at the Annual Conference of the British Educational Leadership, Management and Administration Society (BELMAS), Birmingham, England.

Al-Lamky, A. (2007). Feminizing leadership in Arab societies: The perspectives of Omani female leaders. *Women in Management Review, 22*(1), 49– 67. Retrieved on 11 November 2010 from http://search. proquest.com/docview/213184855/fulltextPDF?accountid=15192

Beijaard, D., Meijer, P. C., & Verloop, N. (2004). Reconsidering research on teachers' professional identity. *Teaching and Teacher Education, 20*(2), 107–128.

Britzman, D. B. (1991). *Practice makes practice: A critical study of learning to teach.* Albany, NY: State University of New York Press.

Brown, J. S., & Duguid, P. (1991). Organizational learning and communities of practice: Toward a unified view of working, learning and innovation. *Organization Science, 2*(1), 40–57.

Clarke, M. (2005). Teaching Identity: The discursive construction of an evolving community of practice. Unpublished doctoral thesis: University of Melbourne.

Dubai Women Establishment (DWE). (2009). *Arab women: Leadership outlook, 2009–2011.* Dubai: Dubai Women Establishment.

Glaser, B. G., & Strauss, A. L. (1967). *The Discovery of grounded theory: Strategies for qualitative research.* Chicago: Aldine Publishing Company.

Harold, B. (2008, July). *Connecting past, present and future for pre-service teachers: An account of an oral history project.* Paper presented at Teacher Education Federation of Aotearoa/New Zealand (TEFANZ) conference, Waikato University.

Harold, B., & Stephenson, L. (2008, September). *Learning to be leaders: The construction of professional identity by Emirati teachers and leaders.* Paper presented at British Educational Research Association (BERA) Annual Meeting, Herriot-Watt University, Edinburgh, Scotland.

Holland, D., Skinner, D., Lachicotte, W., & Cain, C. (1998). *Identity and agency in cultural worlds.* Cambridge, MA: Harvard University Press.

Komives, S. R., Owen, J. E., Longerbeam, S. D., Mainella, F. C., & Osteen, L. (2005). Developing a leadership identity: A grounded theory. *Journal of College Student Development, 46(6),* 593–611.

Komives, S. R., Longerbeam, S. D., Owen, J. E., Mainella, F. C., Osteen, L. (2006). A Leadership Identity Development Model: Applications from a Grounded Theory. *Journal of College Student Development, 47(*4), 401-418.

Lave, J., & Wenger, E. (1991). *Situated learning: Legitimate peripheral participation.* Cambridge, UK: Cambridge University Press.

Lemke, J. (1997). Cognition, context, and learning: A social semiotic perspective. In D. Kirshner & J. A. Whiston (Eds.), *Situated cognition: Social, semiotic, and psychological perspectives.* (pp. 37–54). Mahwah, NJ: Lawrence Erlbaum Associates.

Lipponen, J., Koivisto, S., & Olkkonen, M. (2005). Procedural justice and status judgements: The moderating role of leader ingroup prototypicality. *The Leadership Quarterly, 16*(4), 517–528.

Lord, R. G., Brown, D. J., & Freiberg, S. J. (1999). Understanding the dynamics of leadership: The role of follower self concepts in the leader/follower relationship. *Organizational Behavior and Human Decision Processes, 78*(3), 1–37.

Lord, R. G., & Hall, R. J. (2005). Identity, deep structure and the development of leadership skill. *The Leadership Quarterly, 16*(4), 591–615.

New York University (NYU) Abu Dhabi Institute. (2010). *Appreciating and advancing leadership for public wellbeing.* Workshop proceedings, February 14–16, Abu Dhabi.

Salling Olesen, H. (2001). Professional identity as learning processes in life histories. *Journal for Workplace Learning, 13*(7/8), 290–298.

Shah, S. (2006). Educational leadership: An Islamic perspective. *British Educational Research Journal, 32*(3), 363–385.

Shields, C. M. (2003). *Good intentions are not enough: Transformative leadership for communities of difference.* Lanham, MD: Scarecrow/Technomics.

Shields, C. M. (2010). Transformative leadership: Working for equity in diverse contexts. *Educational Administration Quarterly, 46*(4), 558–589.

Stephenson, L. T. (2004). *Individual learning within an organisation: An autoethnographic learning journey* (Unpublished doctoral thesis). University of Sydney, Australia.

Stephenson. L. (2011). Developing a leadership education framework: A transformative leadership perspective. In C. M. Shields (Ed.), *Transformative Leadership: A Reader* (pp. 313–333). New York: Peter Lang Publishing.

Stephenson, L., Shields, C. M., & Harold, B. (2010). *Transformative leadership: Crossing boundaries in the UAE.* Paper presented at the Commonwealth Council for Educational Administration and Management, Sydney, Australia (September 29–October 1, 2010).

Strauss, A., & Corbin, J. (1990). *Basics of qualitative research.* Newbury Park, CA: Sage Publications.

Tyler, T., & De Cremer, D. (2005). Process-based leadership: Fair procedures and reactions to organizational change. *The Leadership Quarterly, 16*(4), 529–545.

van Knippenberg, D., van Knippenberg, B., De Cremer, D., & Hogg, M. A. (2004). Leadership, self, and identity: A review and research agenda. *The Leadership Quarterly, 15*(6), 825–856.

van Knippenberg, B., van Knippenberg, D., De Cremer, D., & Hogg, M. A. (2005). Research in leadership, self, and identity: A sample of the present and a glimpse of the future. *The Leadership Quarterly, 16*(4), 495–499.

Wenger, E. (1998). Communities of practice, learning meaning and identity. Cambridge: Cambridge University Press.

Yaseen, Z. (2010). Leadership styles of men and women in the Arab world. *Education, Business and Society: Contemporary Middle Eastern Issues, 3*(1), 63–70.

24

Educating Leaders for Social Justice

Christa Boske

This study examines how participants understand their relation to self and others in addressing issues of social justice in U.S. public schools. The University Council for Educational Administration (UCEA), an international consortium of research universities committed to promoting educational leadership practices to the benefit of children, their families, schools, and society, stresses that there is an urgency to prepare school leaders to be able to interrupt oppression and develop meaningful school leadership practices (Donmoyer, Imber, & Scheurich, 1995). UCEA encourages faculty to embark on pedagogy that is centered on preparing school leaders to address contemporary issues facing U.S. schools. This urgency promotes the need for those who prepare school leaders to consider the implications of transformative leadership. Although some may refer to the terms *transformational* and *transformative* as synonyms, there are subtle but significant differences between them. Transformational leadership centers on collective interests of groups (Leithwood & Jantzi, 1990) and places the leader at the heart of shared decision making, fostering consensus, and building a productive school culture that encourages participation in school decisions. Words such as *liberation, emancipation,* and *equality* are central to transformative leadership, which focuses on exhibiting value-based leadership (Astin & Astin, 2000), working with others towards higher levels of engagement, and advocating morality, in order to foster social justice work in schools (Shields, 2003). The promotion of such practices often raises issues for faculty to consider, including programmatic climate, ability and willingness to address oppressive practices associated with underserved populations, and commitment to engaging students in transformative work in schools (Boske & Tooms, 2010; Brown, 2004, 2006; Marshall & Oliva, 2010; Tooms & Boske, 2010).

Although there has been an increase in the number of educational leadership preparation programs that claim to incorporate social justice–oriented approaches, the number of programs that have brought such practices to fruition, however, is quite limited (Cambron-McCabe & McCarthy, 2005; Lopez, 2003; Marshall, Young, & Moll, 2010). Conversations centered on social justice in schools range from the dangers of promoting assimilation models with the increasing numbers of children of color in public schools (Ladson-Billings, 1994), school policies that fail to serve marginalized student populations due to gender, race, class, sexuality, and ability (Marshall, 1993, 2005), which students are served in schools (Delpit, 1995), and the longstanding achievement gap between mainstream and marginalized children in public schools (Apple, 1993; Darling-Hammond, 1997; Delpit, 1995; Larson & Ovando, 2001; Marshall & Oliva, 2010; Valenzuela, 1999).

For the purpose of this chapter, the researcher asserts social justice is context-specific (Furman & Shields, 2005) and connects social justice-oriented work with action (Bogotch, 2002). Those who lead for social justice and equity commit themselves to empowering marginalized populations (for example, due to race, class, gender, language, sexual identity, ability [mental and physical], as well as other historically disenfranchised groups) and interrupt oppressive practices in schools (Blackmore, 2002; Dantley, 2002; Dantley & Tillman, 2005; Riester, Pursch, & Skrla, 2002). Transformative leadership essentially opens up new possibilities for meaningful change to enhance equity, social justice, and civic responsibility so as to empower underserved populations. It requires an increased consciousness, passion, courage, and risk taking (Dantley & Tillman, 2005; Marshall & Oliva, 2010 Shields, 2003; Shoho, 2006; Tooms & Boske, 2010). Transformative leaders take seriously the need to listen to the voices of those who have been silenced and to move to the margins to protect disenfranchised populations. Such leadership is activist-oriented, morally transformative, and pursued with the intent of eliminating unjust practices (Dantley & Tillman, 2005). In many ways, school leaders who promote transformative leadership often extend the boundaries of what is deemed appropriate by challenging the status quo in quiet, strategic ways.

Educational leadership programs that emphasize the need for transformative educational school leaders require critical thought and reflection with regard to personal beliefs, lived experiences, and cultural identity. Attempts by preparation programs to promote transformative leadership include affording school leaders with spaces to build the capacity and will to transform schools through school policies and practices that address the lived realities of disenfranchised populations (Theoharis, 2007; Tooms & Boske, 2010). Sometimes discussions center on disparities facing children of color (Ladson-Billings, 1994), school policies that fail to serve marginalized populations (Marshall, 1993; Marshall & Gerstl-Pepin, 2005), or longstanding achievement gaps between mainstream and marginalized children in U.S. public schools (Apple, 1993; Darling-Hammond, 1997; Marshall & Oliva, 2010). The leader-in-training must be aware of leadership as a powerful intervening variable in determining whether children from diverse backgrounds are successful or not (Reyes, Scribner, & Paredes Scribner, 1999; Skrla & Scheurich, 2003).

Those who prepare school leaders must reconsider how programmatic decisions influence curricular activities, content, and pedagogy in order to foster transformational experiences for aspiring school leaders (Boske & Tooms, 2010; McKenzie et al., 2008; Quantz, Rogers, & Dantley, 1992; Shields, 2004; Young & Brooks, 2008). Future educational leaders for social justice must have the ability and willingness to raise the academic achievement of all students in schools, prepare students to live as critical citizens, and provide those faculty interested in this work with inclusive, heterogeneous spaces that enrich their experiences and engage them in the curriculum (Boske & Tooms, 2010; McKenzie et al., 2008).

The way in which people think and learn through multi-layered lived experiences impacts the way they understand, make meaning, and make sense of the world. Because people are storytelling organisms who, individually and collectively, lead storied lives, their ways of knowing and responding to the world are essential to understanding the ways people think and learn (e.g.,

Cahnmann-Taylor & Siegesmund, 2008; Dewey, 1934; Eisner, 2008). Ultimately, they engage in sense-making, which is the process by which people draw meaning from their lived inquiries while engaging in complex reflective processes. One means of promoting this type of work is to afford school leaders with spaces to deepen their understanding regarding the courage and skill set necessary to sustain social justice and equity work in schools. Promoting reflective spaces such as this has the potential to provide school leaders with safe emotional spaces to reflect on the impact of their sense making on their school leadership identities (Boske, in press; Terrell & Lindsey, 2009).

The chapter begins with a brief literature review regarding transformative leadership, which centers on social justice and equity-oriented work. Next, the researcher describes the methodology, provides an overview of the participants, and analyzes the data. In the discussion section, a conceptual framework for being a catalyst for social justice and equity-oriented work is presented. The researcher concludes the chapter with implications for those who prepare educational leaders.

Literature Review

Leading for social justice is a highly emotional endeavor requiring courage, integrity, imaginative possibilities, and self-awareness. This type of work urges school leaders to engage in transformative processes to address issues such as power, gender, ethnicity, and culture (Shields, 2003). As school leaders address issues of marginalization within U.S. public schools, they discover the emergence of fundamental structural inequities (Darling-Hammond, 2005; Ladson-Billings & Tate, 2006), insufficient school funding (Kozol, 1991), and lack of highly qualified school personnel within urban and rural communities (Darling-Hammond, 2002, 2005). Within U.S. public schools, children are exposed to the effects of these inequities through the perpetuation of school practices that reproduce and reinforce cultural and educational traditions of white, middle-class, English-speaking, Christian, heterosexual communities (e.g., Tooms & Boske, 2010; González, Moll, & Amanti, 2005; Marshall & Oliva, 2010).The impact of social justice and equity issues on the lives of underserved populations is so profound that those who prepare school leaders are reconsidering their curriculum and pedagogy to provide spaces for candidates to recognize, analyze, and respond to systemic inequities (e.g., Boske, in press; Boske & Tooms, 2010; Brown, 2004, 2006; Ladson-Billings & Tate, 2006; Marshall & Oliva, 2010; McKenzie et al., 2008).

With the nation's schools serving increasingly culturally diverse populations, children and families are in need of school leaders who are prepared and committed to empowering underserved populations. School leaders need the knowledge, skill set, and courage to engage in culturally responsive practices that reject color-blind and oppressive ideologies (Cooper, 2009). Exemplary school leadership is essential to bringing about systemic changes (Blackmore, 2002; Bogotch, 2002; Grogan, 2002). School leaders who understand how critical it is to deepen their understanding about the lived realities of others are needed to answer the call to lead for social justice (Marshall & Oliva, 2010); however, school leaders who answer the call must commit to deepening their understanding and empathic responses in order to address unjust conditions in U.S. public schools (Boske & McEnery, 2010; Theoharis, 2007).

Envisioning socially just practices requires school leaders to ensure *all* students have access to high-quality educational experiences in which children are held to high standards and expectations. Democratic schools are inclusive, acknowledging the worth of each individual within the school community and appealing for a renewed understanding of democracy as a way of life. Empathic schools recognize the need for interaction and interconnectedness that occurs with a caring, supportive environment in which people feel safe, valued, and respected (Noddings, 2003; Shields, 2003). Social justice work in public schools requires school leaders to identify a vision of a desired end. School leaders need to consider multiple contexts in order to recognize whether their beliefs and practices fit the defined sociocultural experiences of the school community (Tooms, Lugg, & Bogotch, 2010). This work urges school leaders to be aware of what they stand for, emphasizing the need to specify for whom, by what means, and at what cost they are willing and able to create schools that are socially just, democratic, and empathic.

Drawing from various analyses of social justice work in schools, Furman and Shields (2005) argue that leading and learning require school leaders to create socially just and deeply democratic communities. They contend social justice is "not based on a single attribute, but a broad and holistic conception of learning" (p. 124). Both call for school leaders to understand multiple aspects of addressing equity and social justice in public schools including: (1) robust and dynamic understanding of social justice; (2) acknowledgment of injustices related to power and privilege; (3) recognition of individual prejudice as well as collective inequities; and (4) a concern for pedagogical implications of social justice.

Context of the Study

This inquiry begins when faculty at a northeastern United States university revisit their educational leadership program's vision and mission during the 2008 to 2009 school year and determine the need to revise their program in order to provide preservice school leaders with spaces in which to critically examine issues of social justice and equity (also see Marshall & Oliva, 2010; Theoharis, 2007; Tooms & Boske, 2010; Young & Brooks, 2008). After one year of reconsidering the impact of social injustices within U.S. public schools, faculty deem issues of social justice and equity as pertinent issues in preparing school leaders and interrupting oppressive school practices (Valencia, 1997).

Participants in this study enroll in the educational leadership program's first Leading for Social Justice course in the spring of 2010, which is a required course for all school leadership candidates within the university. To inform the structure of this course, the researcher borrows from scholars in the field of educational leadership who focus on preparing candidates for social justice and equity-oriented work in U.S. public schools. The course centers on the following: (1) creating safe spaces for aspiring school leaders to increase their awareness of social justice and equity issues (Capper, Theoharis, & Sebastian, 2006; Furman & Shields, 2005); (2) engaging students in critical inquiry that promotes social justice–oriented practices through transformative pedagogy and transformational learning (Brown, 2004, 2006; Henderson & Gornik, 2007); (3) emphasizing the need for reflection to further develop school leadership identity by looking within (Boske, in press; Terrell & Lindsey, 2009); and (4) immersing students in transformative field-based projects with the goal of improving the educational experiences of all children by creating spaces for preservice leaders to build bridges between themselves and those they serve, especially those who live on the margins (Boske, 2009; Greene, 1995; Langer, 1953; Skrla, McKenzie, & Scheurich, 2009).

Methodology

Based in the tradition of grounded theory, this study examines how participants understand their relation to self and others in addressing issues of social justice in U.S. public schools (Strauss & Corbin, 1998). This approach provides the researcher with spaces to translate analyzed categories into theory (Glaser, 1978). The researcher chose to employ a grounded-theory approach to develop a new theory that explains the dominant process of the social area being investigated, (Creswell, 2007; Dey, 1999; Glaser & Strauss, 1967). The phenomena under investigation in understanding how candidates understood themselves in answering the call to lead for social justice are quite limited to examining transformative pedagogy in preparation programs (Brown, 2004, 2006), understanding how practicing school leaders resist oppressive practices once they enter the field (Theoharis, 2007), promoting supportive curriculum and pedagogy for graduate students of color (Young & Brooks, 2008), and formulating ideas about what type of pedagogy is necessary to make transformative changes in aspiring school leaders (McKenzie et al., 2008); therefore, grounded theory is not overly influenced by literature in the field of educational leadership. Secondly, the paucity of the literature also implies that exploratory, descriptive research requiring an inductive approach would be appropriate for this investigation. Thirdly, the research problem of interest is the process of understanding the lived experiences of participants enrolled in a course on leading for social justice, and again, grounded theory is particularly suited to the investigating these processes (Glaser, 1978).

Grounded theory addresses individual experiences (Glaser, 1978) and affords the researcher with systematic yet flexible guidelines to collect rich, multidimensional data with which to construct data-grounded theories (Lincoln & Guba, 1985). Charmaz (2006) describes grounded theory as an "approach that places priority on the phenomena of study, and sees both data and analysis as created from shared experience and relationships with participants and other sources of data" (p. 130), which includes the researcher. The goal of curricular activities (i.e., weekly audio-video reflections, written responses, art making) is to generate substantive categories, which is necessary in order to solicit the maximum variations from the participants (Glaser, 1978; Glaser & Strauss, 1967). The reflective questions provide opportunities to explore the participants' experiences (Charmaz, 2006; Holstein & Gubrium, 2003). Utilizing a constructivist approach emphasizes eliciting participants' situations and experiences in an attempt to "tap into his or her assumptions, implicit meanings, and tacit rules" (Charmaz, 2006, p. 32). This approach provides the researcher with a specific focus within one context, centered on how participants understand and respond to issues of social justice and equity in schools.

Participants

Participants in this study include 15 students from a northeastern university who enroll in the Leading for Social Justice course for preservice school leaders. One black student (male), one Asian (Chinese female), and 13 white students (seven males and four females) participate. All of the participants identify as heterosexual. One student identifies as an English-language learner and spoke her native language at home. All of the participants identify as Christian. Three students hold school leadership positions (one high school assistant principal, one high school principal, and one central office administrator). Of the remaining ten students, three students do not work in schools and seven students hold teaching positions in rural, inner-city, or suburban school districts. Participants grant consent to the study after completing the course and receiving their final grades.

Situating Self

Decisions about research methods depend on the specific context and issues studied, as well as on other components of research design (Creswell, 2002). The researcher, as the instructor, functions as a research instrument and makes observations to deepen her understanding of how the participants understand issues of social justice in U.S. public schools (Maxwell, 2005). This study and her lived experiences as a white, formerly closeted school leader, out lesbian scholar, with a partner of 14 years and a Latina child, drive her beliefs and school practices. The researcher contends that her line of inquiry centers on the belief that her work should benefit underserved populations and interrupt unjust school practices (Bogdan & Biklen, 1998).

Data Sources

Participants engage in a wide range of course activities and projects including: (a) a written analysis of Jonothan Kozol's *The Shame of the Nation* (2005); (b) a written reflection and examination of the implications of the documentary *With All Deliberate Speed*; (c) conducting equity audits in public schools, which are based on Skrla et al.'s (2009) work; (d) responding to weekly audio-video reflections (10 to 25 questions each week) centered on developing a school leadership identity (Delpit, 1995; Leary & Tangney, 2003; Tooms et al., 2010), defining social justice work in schools (Furman & Shields, 2005; Marshall & Oliva, 2010) and contemplating the implications of cultural proficiency (Terrell & Lindsey, 2009); (e) preparing a manuscript for possible publication on a social justice issue facing U.S. public schools; (f) translating ways of knowing to metaphor to artmaking (Eisner, 2008; Langer, 1953); and (e) working with community artist mentors to create an artmaking research gallery exhibit based on the students' social justice stance. All audio-video reflections are coded and transcribed.

Participants respond to open-ended questions based on Terrell and Lindsey's (2009) culturally proficient leadership framework. They complete 15 weekly audio or video reflections (15 students x 15 reflective responses = 225 total reflections). What emerges from the reflections are questions that guide the research: (1) What are participants' ways of knowing?; (2) How are participants responding to issues of social justice and equity-oriented practices?; and (3) How do participants understand themselves as school leaders? In order to establish trustworthiness, the researcher invites participants to engage in the research study after they receive their final course grades. Both participant-member checks and triangulation of data from multiple sources are noted in the data collection section (Creswell, 2007). Analysis within the multiple data source groups are shared with participants to check for accuracy and gain perspective on descriptive and interpretive work throughout the research process.

Limitations

One limitation of this study is that it centers on the findings from just one northeastern U.S. school leadership preparation program. The findings are specific to this program and location. Although participants are all from one university location, the findings could be transferable to other settings of comparable demographics or profiles. The other limitation is the use of open-ended reflective questions. Open-ended questions center on the researcher's limited perceptions and the participants' comfort levels and abilities to respond to the questions (Scheurich, 1997). Despite the noted limitations, this study is significant for preparing educational leaders because it contributes to deepening understanding of how candidates understand their relation to self and others in an effort to address issues of social justice.

Analytic Process

The data consist of participants' weekly audio or video standardized open-ended reflective responses. This format allows for freedom in response. Data also consist of students' equity audits, written narratives to open-ended questions, social justice research stances, metaphors, and art making. All reflections are transcribed and coded. Charmaz (2006) reminds us, "Coding is the pivotal link between collecting data and developing an emergent theory to explain these data" (p. 46). Open coding is used to break down, analyze, compare, and categorize data (Strauss & Corbin, 1998). Incidents and events are labeled and grouped via constant comparisons, which leads to the emergence of themes, properties, and patterns within the texts of the reflections (Glaser & Strauss, 1967). Analytic memos are created throughout the research process to track data and establish patterns (Charmaz, 2003; Maxwell, 2005). Open codes are combined with other, conceptually similar open codes to form axial codes. The axial codes are collected, placed into categories, and developed into the themes presented in this paper. The methods support the study's internal validity by triangulating the data with field notes, audio-video reflections, and written narratives (Fielding & Fielding, 1986; Maxwell, 1992). Emergent themes are used as a framework to present the findings based on, first, how participants understand issues of social justice and equity as school leaders and, second, how participants utilize their new ways of knowing and responding to interrupt oppressive school practices.

The actual analysis of the data involves three readings of the reflections, written assignments, and artmaking. The first phase consists of naming the data with the content of the reflections and artmaking (Charmaz, 2006). This is followed by a process of constant comparison, which provides a more selective focus regarding the most frequently recurring codes (Charmaz, 2006). The researcher identifies conceptual categories, which reflects commonalities and theoretical saturation is achieved when new data about the categories no longer emerge from the data being analyzed (Strauss & Corbin, 1998).

Findings

Findings from the data analysis indicate that all of the participants perceive changes in their awareness, attitudes, beliefs, and school practices regarding issues of social justice and equity, changes that center on developing a deeper understanding of the need to assess the dominant values and goals of schools in an effort to protect those who live on the margins. Transformative leadership is at the heart of sharing power. These school leaders recognize their ability and willingness to realign structures and relationships to achieve authentic, meaningful, and sustainable change. Such changes afford those who live on the margins opportunities to be visible and heard. Emerging themes reveal the following: (1) a deepened sense of self in relation to others; (2) new ways of knowing; (3) new ways of responding; and (4) being a catalyst for change. The conceptual framework for being a catalyst for social justice and equity-oriented work is described in the Discussion section.

Deepened a Sense of Self in Relation to Others

Students of color are initially aware of social justice and equity issues, but note the need to deepen their commitment to social justice and equity-oriented work in schools by creating bridges between themselves and their communities of color. They share personal experiences of being discriminated against throughout their childhood and academic careers due to their race, native language, or immigration status. Their lived experiences as members of marginalized populations inspire them to internalize issues of social justice and equity within both their personal and professional lives.

For white participants, they become aware of their power and privilege and tendency to perpetuate oppressive practices in schools. They also share feelings of anxiety and fear regarding their unfamiliarity with social justice issues, as well as their responsibility as school leaders to interrupt oppressive practices within U.S. public schools. The ways in which they initially understand themselves as school leaders center on descriptors, rather than centering on the impact of beliefs, assumptions, and socially constructed ways of knowing. For example, Alyssa, a white female high school teacher, describes herself as a school leader during the first week of class.

> Organized, confident, welcoming, genuine, trustworthy, hopefully passionable, structured, consistent, good role model, busy, prepared, anticipates setback, faith, and making changes are some of the more important ones. I would like to be a middle school principal one day. Currently I work in a high school and this includes some of the things that I have seen in the middle school level in a principal aspect. (Alyssa)

Initially, participants do not associate themselves with practices aligned with social justice and equity work in schools. Rather, they center on "positions" and "duties" associated with their job titles, versus their final reflections, which ultimately focus on "answering the call" to lead for social justice.

As participants engage in course assignments, they deepen their awareness of social and political movements and identify the implications of such reform in 21st-century schools. White students also note that transformative learning experiences encourage them to examine their role in perpetuating oppressive school practices—which are later deemed unacceptable by all participants. White males often express frustration, anger, and sometimes rage when asked to examine the impact of their power, privilege, and entitlement in perpetuating oppressive school practices. These specific issues raise concerns for white males as they grapple with connections between personal understandings of oppression, their relation of self to others, and the promotion of social justice–oriented work in schools.

New Ways of Knowing

Lived experiences throughout the course afford participants with opportunities to broaden their perspectives and deepen their understanding of the lived experiences of marginalized populations. They stress how critical conscious-centered and activist-oriented opportunities create spaces in which they can examine what is meant by creating more just and empathic school experiences for underserved populations. Patricia, a white female school leader in a rural community, shares how the course experiences influence her ability to recognize the impact of "otherness" on her understanding of what it means to lead for social justice.

> Who I am reflects my lived experiences. I realize I am more than an over-achiever and perfectionist . . . organized . . . I am what I have lived. I came to know this world and developed my beliefs and attitudes because of my experiences and thinking about the implications of these experiences. I see the world differently than the teachers who work in special education. I realize my passion for making sure we do right by these children was influenced by how I see the world and what I know about this world through what I have lived and witnessed in my career. This not only impacts how I live my life . . . it's how I lead. (Patricia)

Other participants critically assess how they understand the implications of formal curriculum in relation to promoting culturally responsive practices. Many of them note conversations centered on improving the achievement scores of "subgroups" by stressing "their deficits" versus "their strengths." They pose questions regarding the impact of cultural misconceptions and assumptions made about specific cultural student groups on their campuses.

> On my campus, the students who don't speak very good English aren't looked upon as equal. They are put into our classrooms and not much consideration is given to them. I hear teachers say those

students aren't very smart. I think teachers believe these students are a burden and all of this is just extra work. (Justin, a white male high school teacher)

Participants share how, often, teachers are placed in positions in which they are not encouraged to deepen their understanding of underserved populations (i.e., due to race, class, religion, sexual identity, or ability). For example, Margaret, a white female elementary teacher, notes her frustration with shifting from "this common practice of pushing test-taking" to "proactively engaging in understanding how to critically think about meaning making."

> Principals keep making demands on us and don't seem to make social justice a priority, let alone a topic up for discussion. It seems as though there just isn't enough time or enough people to do all the work that needs to be done. It would make more sense if school leaders understood how important it was for [us] to talk about this. I mean, let's be proactive, talk about what we think and why we think that way. It makes me sad to see so much time spent on disciplining students rather than looking at ourselves and what we do to perpetuate this. (Margaret)

Many participants describe their efforts to engage in critical conversations centered on oppressive practices as "uncomfortable"; however, such spaces "deepen" their ways of knowing. They emphasize the need for ongoing support throughout their coursework if they are to be successful, transformative leaders in schools. The pressure of thinking critically about the implications of their personal beliefs and understandings of their world are often "painful" and "uncomfortable" experiences, especially for those with power and privilege as members of the dominant culture.

> When I think about this stuff, I just want to crawl into a deep, dark hole. It's hard to think about what it means for me to be a white male and a member of the dominant culture. I never stopped and thought about this before. Now that I know what this means and how dominance has really played a role in who gets what in education, I have the responsibility to do something. I can't just sit in my dark hole and remain there. I need to get up, crawl out, and make some changes in my life. (James, a white male high school leader)

The inherent challenges for participants center on allowing themselves spaces to increase their critical consciousness and deepen their empathic responses towards children and communities, especially for those who live on the margins. Through the process, participants recognize the need to look within, redefine what it means to be a transformative school leader, and "push the boundaries" within their schools to increase the critical consciousness of children, families, teachers, and community members.

New Ways of Responding

Explicit remarks are made by participants regarding links between evolving social justice–oriented work and their own lived experiences of being marginalized (i.e., due to their race, language, class, gender, or perceived immigration status), especially students of color. For example, Huang, an Asian female teacher who works in a suburban school district, and Jackson, a black male high school leader, emphasize how their racial identity often informed their ways of knowing and responding to their school communities.

> I didn't realize how often the children who did not have were placed to wayside. We just focus on the students who can and forget about the situations that put these students in positions where they

take a backseat to learning. My people do not consider the hardships these children face and we need to remember what it is like to be other. (Huang)

Many participants also redress fundamental inequities witnessed throughout their childhood experiences, school leadership preparation, and professional careers (i.e., regarding materials, resources, and facilities). They also examine the impact of people's values and their attitudes towards children from marginalized populations (i.e., the belief that certain cultural groups were more intrinsically capable of succeeding than others). However, for students of color, the significance of providing their communities of color with positive role models is significant to becoming transformative school leaders.

I am probably the only black male school leader they ever saw, let alone a teacher. And being a principal makes it even more important. How I work with the kids is critical. I realized I have the responsibility to do what's right for our kids and keep pushing the issues. [Other teachers] watch how I respond [to] the kids and wonder why I have a different impact on them. I don't think they ever stopped to realize I respect the kids and listen to their concerns. I try to be a support in their life and show them someone cares about them. (Jackson)

Participants who are members of the dominant culture describe different ways of responding to otherness. As they reflect on the lived experiences of those excluded from mainstream society, these participants emphasize the need to look within and recognize how power and privilege influence how they respond to those who live on the margins.

I never stopped to think about whether or not we were meeting the needs of kids who were gay. I didn't even know if they were here or not. After the equity audit, I got to know how many kids identified as being LGBTQ and the need to open up opportunities to talk about their experiences and what we need to do to help them be successful here. (James)

Over the course of the semester, participants in this study develop a deepened sensitivity towards students who identify as outliers (i.e., children in special education, English-language learners, lesbian/gay/bisexual/transgender/queer/intersex/ally (LGBTQIA). As they increase their awareness, they realize their ways of responding to underserved populations are also in need of change. Participants stress how the process urges them to examine how newly lived experiences are internalized and how they impact their intellectual capacity and ability to interrupt oppressive practices in schools. Anna, a white female elementary teacher who works in a suburb, shares how identifying and examining newly lived experiences influences her ability to recognize the impact of otherness and respond differently to underserved populations.

I realize I have been fooled. I never knew how embedded my school practices were and how often I did what I did just because that was the way I was told to do it. We tend not to stop and think about what it is to be other. We get caught up in all this test taking and objectify the students into test scores and subcategories. I started challenging how we address our students and the language we use to remind ourselves these are someone's children. I have tried to put myself in the shoes of our families, especially the ones who are often blamed for everything that goes wrong. I think more often before I speak and really think about what we are saying about our children. (Anna)

Addressing issues of social justice and equity encourages participants to take a critical stance regarding the construction of meaning, the role of power and privilege, and how power perpetuates the marginalization of underserved populations through curriculum, pedagogy, and school policies. They describe efforts to "raise the bar" and interrupt daily oppressive practices in schools.

> The more I know, the more I realize I need to stand up and say something, because no one else is obviously going to. Every time I hear negative things about our kids, I come back with a positive. I tell them I don't want to hear anything negative—nothing. I remind them we are here to support our kids and this is the way I teach. I ask them if they would like someone talking about their child like that. That conversation usually ends in silence. (Mark, a white male elementary teacher)

Recognizing the need to think systemically about the impact of their responses towards underserved populations is commonly voiced by participants. They stress the need to examine the distribution of power, as well as influence, of institutional school practices on meeting the needs of all children, and the need to promote culturally responsive practices throughout the district. For instance, Janice, a white female elementary teacher, emphasizes the need to "move beyond testing" and urged teachers to think critically about "what" they were teaching and "why" they were promoting specific practices. Other participants, like Brad, a white male high school teacher, emphasize the need to reconsider the realities facing children and their families and the need to bring issues of social justice "to the table" through conversations within his department.

They share challenges they have faced in creating spaces in which colleagues and school leaders could reconsider the interconnectedness between people's live histories and beliefs and the ways in which they respond to all students and their families. Participants stress the significance of transformational learning, activist-oriented activities, such as the equity audit, as a means of creating open safe spaces to investigate the implications of the data.

> The equity audit was the first time I could remember anyone talking about what we do on our campus and why we do it and who is it really serving. Presenting the data in this way and creating places for us to talk about what equity is, how we interact with students, and what we need to improve their experiences at this school were issues always put off because of time. Now that we completed the equity audit and discussed what this means to us, we are ready to move forward and start thinking about what works and what needs to change. (Amanda, a white female rural school leader)

Some participants recognize their ability to build the capacity to address unjust practices in schools and stress the need for faculty support to guide them through challenging current school practices. They describe these opportunities to discuss a myriad of models as essential to their growth as school leaders. For instance, in order to interrupt oppressive practices, Marcus stresses the need to "put the issues on the table" in objective ways. Some participants also note how they involve students on their campuses in attempts to deepen their own critical consciousness and efforts to address social justice issues.

> I started surveying and interviewing students on my campus and discovered we weren't doing everything we thought we were doing. Many of us thought we were creating a safe and positive climate, but I learned that for many of the students who tend to be quiet, [they] choose to remain silent because they don't believe anyone is really looking out for them. (Barbara, a white female teacher)

Participants emphasize the need not only to increase their critical consciousness or that of their peers but also to reconsider the curriculum in order to create social change through civic engagement. Empowering students to interrupt oppressive practices on campus is expressed as a priority for most participants; however, the means to implement such changes often depends on their current positions of power and how they perceive their power within a specific school or district.

Participants realize the need to initiate "grassroots" movements in which they directly connect with colleagues, students, families, and school leaders interested in promoting social justice work. Their new ways of responding to underserved populations in schools center on creating "ripples in the pond." Participants often describe these ripples as significant to transforming the way in which school communities respond to the needs of all children.

Being a Catalyst for Change

At the conclusion of the participants' coursework,[1] they share common experiences in which they identify themselves as *bridge builders* (i.e., eradicating social injustices and inequities by engaging in meaningful dialogue and actions centered on community needs), *catalysts* (i.e., interrupting hegemonic practices and inspiring others to engage in such work), and/or *movers and shakers* (i.e., creating alliances to promote socially just practices). The weaving of social justice concepts, transformational learning, transformative leadership, and reflective practices create spaces for them to explore their beliefs, attitudes, and current school practices in an effort to deepen their ways of knowing and responses toward marginalized populations. Participants stress the significance of experience in meaning making and in developing an ability and willingness to interrupt oppressive school practices by facilitating spaces for vigorous dialogue about the lived experiences of disenfranchised populations. Some participants note the significance of gathering, analyzing, and proposing solutions for overcoming challenges through equity audit data collection (i.e., student achievement, teacher quality, programmatic quality, and disciplinary practices). And some include the need to acknowledge school policies centering on the elimination of social injustices and inequities in U.S. public schools.

Participants emphasize the need to develop meaningful relationships with children and their families through the implementation of culturally responsive pedagogy. Such practices are opportunities for school leaders to build bridges between district professional development seminars, culturally proficient practices, and school policies that perpetuate the marginalization of faculty, children, and school community families who continue to live on the margins (e.g., due to sexual identity, race, class, language, ability [mental and physical], immigration status, and gender). They emphasize the need to look within and reflect on the impact of their school leadership identity on decision-making practices. By looking within and deepening their understanding of self, participants describe a deeper understanding of how oppressive practices create barriers to addressing social justice and equity issues embedded within the fabric of American public schools. For example, Martha, a white female teacher, notes that the integration of theory and practice with form and feeling through artmaking "moved her in unexpected ways" and provided a process for her to engage in reflective work she deems "significant to making her the leader she aspired to be." The course experiences provide participants with a foundation from which newly lived experiences will function as catalysts, which will reconstruct who they are as school leaders, as well as create new ways of knowing and promoting social justice–oriented work in schools.

Discussion

Learning to make connections between significantly improving students' academic achievement, increasing critical consciousness, and responding to underserved populations by engaging in inclusive school practices is at the center of what it means for these participants to identify themselves as transformative leaders. However, findings also suggest there is a need for faculty to provide spaces to deepen their understanding regarding the impact of personal histories, beliefs, and ways of knowing, which influence to what extent, if any, they address issues of social justice, power, and inequity in schools (Cherryholmes, 1988). They recognize issues of social justice are not only perpetuated within their school districts but are widespread throughout the United States, which impinges on the success of all children (Kozol, 2005). As students increase their awareness regarding the lived experiences of underserved populations, they describe a deeper sense of empathy, ethic of care, and willingness to take seriously the need to safeguard democratic practices. They contend such efforts not only protect those who live on the margins, but they are essential to engaging and sustaining social justice and equity work in schools (Kouzes & Posner, 1999).

Participants realize that deepening their empathic responses is the first step to interrupting oppressive school practices; however, as a result of their course field experiences, they acknowledge the level of apprehension of school leaders to "share their power" by collaborating with marginalized populations or providing these populations with opportunities for their voices and lived experiences to play a role in curriculum and school policy. In order to eliminate oppressive school practices, students stress the need for all school community members to be afforded spaces in which they increase their critical consciousness. Participants suggest their ability to engage in transformative work in schools is embedded within their reflective practices, and focus on the moral courage necessary to combat injustice (Shields, 2003). Within these spaces, students actively engage in the struggle for social justice, and recognize a continuum of transformations. This continuum ranges from understanding the relation of self to others, to critically examining the implications of school policy on underserved populations, to "making change at any cost," because "it is the right thing to do." As candidates move along the continuum towards activist-oriented work, they identify themselves as pivotal players in sustaining equitable change in public schools (Bass & Avolio, 1994; Boske, 2009; Shields, 2003).

Their efforts extend beyond their classrooms and campuses. Students identify as transformative school leaders who support and respond to the needs of all students, especially for those who have been silenced (Delpit, 1995). The interconnectedness of their activist-oriented efforts, promotion of school-community members as agents of change, and need for societal transformation are all critical to identifying themselves as leaders for social justice (Brown, 2004, 2006; Marshall & Oliva, 2010). Embedded throughout these realizations is a shift in their ways of knowing and responding to their work in schools. Participants recognize how they initially utilized power and privilege to perpetuate oppressive practices, which often deem one group as superior to another, and shifted their understanding and responses towards utilizing privileged positions as bridge building, in order to empower children and families who lived on the margins (Tooms & Boske, 2010).

This work requires courage, integrity, and willingness to aspire to bring a heightened awareness of the knowledge of self into practice. The transformations encourage school leaders to make a personal and professional commitment to advocate for the empowerment of those who have been silenced. The process affords school leader with spaces to promote a vision of the complexities to make schools better places for all children by examining, understanding, and responding to the whole education. This work encourages school leaders become reflectively conscious who are more aware of their social-emotional strengths as well as shortcomings. These spaces offer them opportunities to engage in holistic growth-oriented work in schools, such as becoming grassroots activists. Students not only deepen their understanding of what is meant by social justice and equity work in schools, they also deepen their sense of self as a leader. These spaces are nested throughout their transformative learning opportunities along the way. The learning plays a pivotal role in affording school leaders with opportunities to examine the impact of their newly lived experiences, ways of knowing, and implications for their new ways of responding to those they serve (see Figure 24.1).

Figure 24.1 Transformative Leadership: A Catalytic Framework for Social Justice and Equity-Oriented School Leadership

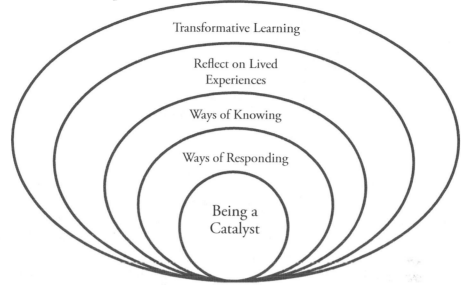

Throughout this holistic growth-oriented process, participants express their tendency to feel overwhelmed with the responsibilities and lifelong commitment necessary for this work to significantly change the lived experiences of underserved populations. They recognize the need to come to terms with their anxiety in an effort to deepen their perspectives and increase the knowledge and skills that leaders for social justice need. They interrogate their personal behaviors as well as those within the schools and community at large that perpetuate unjust practices (Dantley, 2005). The transformative process provides spaces to raise critical consciousness, embrace personal issues on race and other markers of distinction and identity, and prepare them to lead in meaningful ways (Giroux, 1997; West, 1999). As they release prior ways of knowing and internalize new understandings, they respond differently to the world around them. Their transformative actions support them in identifying themselves as catalysts. Participants take seriously the creation and promotion of safe places for all children, make connections between their leadership roles and activism, and embody the process.

Students realize this journey of self and relation to others constantly evolves. They also recognize this journey is somewhat dependent on their school leadership preparation program's initiatives. Participants note how faculty afford them with spaces to develop their school leadership identities, and sense of self as a social justice school leader (Boske, in press; Marshall & Oliva, 2010; Terrell & Lindsey, 2009). The nested growth-oriented experiences assist participants in coming to terms with their beliefs, understandings, and ways of responding to issues of race, class, sexual identity, and ability (Boske, in press; Dantley, 2005; Terrell & Lindsey, 2009). They develop a commitment to social justice and equity-oriented work in schools and feel compelled to address unjust practices in their schools, especially those centered on race, class, and ability.

Throughout their coursework, they stress the need to continue cultivating this same level of consciousness with students, families, teachers, and the community at large. Their goals not only center on transforming self, they also focus on becoming catalysts whose goals are making radical transformations in their schools as well as society. The act of becoming a catalyst is a political one. Participants contend their courageous conversations engage a myriad of school community members in raising their critical consciousness (Singleton & Linton, 2006). Together, they work with school members to encourage new ways of knowing centered on inequities in schools. These new understandings are reinforced through critical dialogic conversations with other school community members including, but not limited to teachers, families, students, and school leaders. These conversations legitimate multiple voices within the learning community. Within these spaces, participants work collectively to share data regarding ways in which schools produce and interrupt inequities embedded throughout their school practices (i.e., children receiving free or reduced lunch being enrolled in lower-level courses, children identified as needing special education services, overrepresentation of children of color being disciplined). For example, the creation of equity audit teams is the first time any of the participants recall conducting conversations centered on increasing critical consciousness as a collaborative (see Skrla et al., 2009).

Making authentic, meaningful connections between participants' work, improving the educational experiences of children, and relation of self to others is essential to building bridges between themselves and those they serve in schools (e.g., equity audits, critical conversations, and artmaking) is at the heart of what it means to become a catalyst for transformative change. As they identify as catalysts, they deepen their understanding of how their newly lived experiences influence their decision-making practices as well as their willingness and ability to interrupt oppressive school practices (Langer, 1953; Terrell & Lindsey, 2009). Their developing school leadership identity is understood as a process as opposed to deferring their roles as simply following mandates and school policy. This process of understanding oneself as a catalyst also encourages participants to realize the need to "navigate rough waters," because they will face "countervailing pressures" to maintain the status quo (Theoharis, 2007, p. 4). For instance, participants stress how often tensions rose when speaking about the need for culturally responsive practices (Gay, 2010; Ladson-Billings, 1994, 1995, 1997) on their campuses as well as providing data questioning whose knowledge bases matter most when developing curriculum in schools (González et al., 2005).

Students describe their school leadership identity as both self- and co-constructed (with peers, family members, instructors, and community at large). They emphasize a renewed sense of responsibility, purpose, and call to action, all of which are primarily discovered throughout their ongoing reflective process. The role of transformative learning, which seems to foster newly lived experiences, impacts how participants understand themselves as being catalysts. This growth-oriented process "creates a fire in the belly." The fire seems to encourage them to continue on their journey towards leading for social justice and equity-oriented work in schools. They recognize their worth in the role of promoting collective action and reconsider their capacity and willingness to build bridges between themselves and others.

Implications

There are inherent challenges in preparing school leaders to take a more critically conscious stance towards deepening empathic responses towards marginalized children and communities (Boske, in press; Brown, 2004, 2006; Lopez, 2003). Those who prepare school leaders will continue to face the challenge of creating spaces in which candidates critically inquire about the structures, systems, and norms that result in inequitable schooling. Students living on the margins need advocates to build bridges, influence educational policies, and address social justice issues (also see Cambron-McCabe & McCarthy, 2005; Tooms & Boske, 2010). The conceptual framework presented in this chapter provides tremendous possibilities for teaching and learning. However, those who prepare school leaders must consider the significance of context in promoting what it means to be a transformative leader. These findings could be transferable to other settings of comparable demographics or profiles, and cultural contexts (i.e., if school is a place where young people and adults explore deep understandings of culture and power, and where they recognize and celebrate diversity within the community of difference); however, those who prepare school leaders will need to continuously negotiate and renegotiate, as well as construct and reconstruct, ways of knowing about community, political ideals, history, leadership, and what is meant by "social justice work" as well as "transformative leadership" within specific contexts. For those who serve within the United States, social justice, most would agree, attempts to build bridges between individuals, groups, and communities (e.g., Merchant & Shoho, 2010; Tooms & Boske, 2010); however, it is a messy and complex process with overarching principles striving for visibility. In an effort to build bridges with these principles in mind, specific stances will take precedence over others and play a pivotal role in where, with whom, and for whom these bridges are built. Therefore, conceptualizing universality with transformative leadership may be difficult, because individuals or groups advocate for and from their particular viewpoints, which are often embedded within cultural, political, and societal norms.

Placing the learning self at the center of educational leadership programmatic practices emphasizes the need for school leaders to reconsider context and the impact of knowledge and experience in throughout their process of meaning making (Boske, 2009, in press; Ellsworth, 2005). School leaders' meaning making evolves as they engage in a myriad of pedagogical media, which afford them safe spaces to examine their ways of knowing and responding to issues of social justice and equity in schools. Their reflections and social justice stances emerge as new ways of understanding themselves in relation to others (Boske, in press; Terrell & Lindsey, 2009). The process is a constant exchange of personal and situational experiences, which necessitates participation and involvement. School leaders are placed in positions in which they boldly confront their inquiries and their willingness and ability to engage in undertaking imaginative possibilities. The interweaving of social justice concepts, transformative learning, and examining of the impact of catalysts on understanding themselves as leaders for social justice are all essential to living their inquiries within this meaning-making process. They are encouraged to engage in new ways of understanding through perception, selection, and responsiveness. The relationship between how they understand themselves within specific contexts is reorganized throughout the ongoing process of knowing, reflecting, and responding.

The experience expands values of personal knowing, interpretations, and expressions that evolve into a newly constructed way of understanding oneself as a school leader, which is most significant to this process. Examining the impact of lived experiences, however, relies heavily on the school leader's ability and willingness to engage in meaningful dialogue and active participation in sense making. Faculty who engage in these curriculum media must afford school leaders with spaces to deepen the interconnectedness between their lived experiences, ways of knowing, and responses towards those who live on the margins. Such opportunities encourage both faculty and school leaders to be absorbed by the complexities of relations and identify themselves as media for learning and change.

Placing such efforts at the center of programmatic considerations is essential to promoting transformative school leadership. Such efforts promote (a) the creation of safe spaces for candidates to explore their emotion-laden experiences with social justice work in schools (Boske, in press; Capper et al., 2006); (b) offer opportunities to reconceptualize the meaning of leading for social justice (Brown, 2004, 2006; Furman & Shields, 2005), and (c) afford candidates with spaces to strategize efforts that encourage them to function as bridge builders between schools and communities at large (Merchant & Shoho, 2010; Tooms & Boske, 2010). These transformative school leaders offer opportunities to work as a collective to improve the lived experiences of all children and families. Their efforts encourage new and innovative ways to challenge the status quo, interrupt unjust practices, and advocate for the visibility of those deemed invisible.

If educational leadership preparation programs center on engaging candidates in transformative school leadership through catalytic learning experiences, they afford them with opportunities to immerse themselves in their own learning processes. The impact of individual histories and lived experiences—which influence attitudes, beliefs, thinking processes, and conceptualizations of what it means to lead in socially just ways within specific contexts—all play a pivotal role in programmatic decisions regarding the need for critical reflection and activist-oriented practices (Boske, in press; Brown, 2004, 2006). Candidates will recognize the need for school leaders to deepen their critical consciousness by looking within and by promoting critical reflective practices among school community members (Mezirow, 1991). They will also develop the intellectual capacity to understand how to achieve high student achievement for all students, especially for those who live on the margins. Furthermore, these school leaders will know how to create purposeful and inclusive learning communities centered on interrupting oppressive practices due to a student's race, class, sexual identity, immigration status, religion, gender, native language, or ability. Such practices place significance on to what extent the school leader learns to reevaluate lived experiences and develop new meaning making. When school leaders immerse themselves in spaces such as these, new ways of knowing and responding to the world will take precedence over prior understandings and responses (e.g., Boske, in press; Mezirow, 1990).

School leaders are not the only ones who might reconsider ways to raise critical consciousness and implement activism-oriented school practices centered on social justice in their schools. Those who prepare school leaders might also rethink how this catalytic conceptual model might provide spaces for faculty to discuss ways they might promote critical consciousness in their teaching and learning as well. The connective process precedes meaningful learning for all of those interested in promoting social justice and equity-oriented work in schools. Because the process centers on change of self and, ultimately, on change regarding ways of knowing and responding, faculty who prepare teachers might inquire about the implications for educators who aspire to similar calls to action in schools. The creative open-learning process affords faculty a worthwhile direction centered on establishing spaces for ongoing conversations as well as on teaching and learning for social justice and equity in U.S. public schools.

Conclusion

This study represents the culmination of a two-year process among a small group of faculty members at one northeastern university attempting to create a spaces for candidates to critically think about connections between research, relation of self to others, social justice, and leadership education. Although there is a need to improve the welfare of children and families from disenfranchised populations, it is clear that educational leadership programs must strive to provide spaces for school leaders to develop dispositions toward activism (Sleeter, 1996), understand the emotion-laden inner journey of social justice work (Langer, 1953; Terrell & Lindsey, 2009) and commit him or herself as a leader for social justice (Brown, 2004, 2006; Marshall & Oliva, 2010; Theoharis, 2007). What is needed are spaces in which to further develop school leaders' capacity and willingness to look within and accept responsibility for being the catalysts for addressing issues of social justice and equity in schools. The implications for transformative learning opportunities, such as the conceptual framework presented in this chapter, are essential to collectively developing leaders for social justice. The dialogue among school leaders who grapple with the intersections of power, culture, empowerment, and community are central to this movement. The synergy created by developing a deeper sense of self, new understandings and ways of responding, and sense of community is an ongoing process that continuously negotiates and reconstructs ways of knowing, all in an effort to become more transformative.

Note

1. Coursework included weekly reflections (see Terrell & Lindsey, 2009), dialogue regarding the development of self-identities and school leadership identity (see Delpit, 1995; Leary & Tangney, 2003), equity audits (see Skrla et al., 2009), social-justice research (see Furman & Shields, 2005; Marshall & Oliva, 2010) and artmaking (see Eisner, 2002; Greene, 1995; Langer, 1953; Shapiro, 2010).

References

Apple, M. W. (1993). *Official knowledge: Democratic education in a conservative age.* New York: Routledge.

Astin, A. W., & Astin, H. S. (2000). *Leadership reconsidered: Engaging higher education in social change.* Battle Creek, MI: W. K. Kellogg Foundation.

Bass, B. M., & Avolio, B. J. (1994). *Improving organizational effectiveness through transformational leadership.* Thousand Oaks, CA: Sage Publications.

Blackmore, J. (2002). Leadership for socially just schooling: More substance and less style in high risk, low trust times? *Journal of School Leadership, 12*(2), 198–222.

Bogdan, R. C., & Biklen, S. K. (1998). *Qualitative research for education: An introduction to theory and methods.* Boston, MA: Allyn & Bacon.

Bogotch, I. (2002). Educational leadership and social justice: Practice into theory. *Journal of School Leadership, 12,* 138–156.

Boske, C. (In press). Audio and video reflections to promote social justice. *Multicultural Education and Technology Journal.* Special Issue.

Boske, C. (2009). Imaginative thinking: Addressing social justice issues through MovieMaker. *Multicultural Education and Technology Journal, 3*(3), 213–226.

Boske, C., & McEnery, L. (2010). Taking it to the streets: A new line of inquiry for school communities. *Journal of School Leadership, 20*(3), 369–398.

Boske, C., & Tooms, A. K. (2010). Clashing epistemologies: Reflections on change, culture and the politics of the professoriate. In G. Jean Marie & T. Normore (Eds.), *Educational leadership preparation: Innovation and interdisciplinary approaches to the Ed.D. and graduate education* (pp. 33–52). New York, NY: Palgrave Macmillan.

Brown, K. (2004). Leadership for social justice and equity: Weaving a transformative framework and pedagogy. *Educational Administration Quarterly, 40(1),* 79–110.

Brown, K. (2006, December). Leadership for social justice and equity: Evaluating a transformative framework and pedagogy. *Educational Administration Quarterly, 42(5),* 700–745.

Cahnmann-Taylor, M., & Siegesmund, R. (2008). *Arts-based research in education: Foundations for practice.* New York, NY: Routledge.

Cambron-McCabe, N., & McCarthy, M. M. (2005). Educating school leaders for social justice. *Educational Policy, 19*(1), 201–222.

Capper, C. A., Theoharis, G., & Sebastian, J. (2006). Toward a framework for preparing leaders for social justice. *Journal of Education Administration, 44*(3), 209–224.

Charmaz, K. (2006) *Constructing grounded theory: A practical guide through qualitative analysis.* London: Sage Publications.

Charmaz, K. (2003). Grounded theory: objectivist and constructivist methods. In N. K. Denzin & Y. S. Lincoln (Eds.), *Strategies of qualitative inquiry* (2d ed.) (pp. 249–291). Thousand Oaks, CA: Sage Publications.

Cherryholmes, C. (1988). *Power and criticism: Poststructural investigations in education.* New York: Columbia University Press.

Cooper, C. W. (2009). Performing cultural work in demographically changing schools: Implications for expanding transformative leadership frameworks. *Educational Administration Quarterly, 45*(5), 694–724.

Creswell, J. W. (2002). *Educational research: Planning, conducting, and evaluating quantitative and qualitative approaches to research.* Upper Saddle River, NJ: Merrill/Pearson Education.

Creswell, J. W. (2007). *Qualitative inquiry and research design: Choosing among five traditions* (2d ed). Thousand Oaks, CA: Sage Publications.

Dantley, M. (2002). Uprooting and replacing positivism, the melting pot, multiculturalism, and other impotent notions in education leadership through an African American perspective. *Education and Urban Society, 34*(3), 334–352.

Dantley, M. (2005). The power of critical spirituality to act and to reform. *Journal of School Leadership, 15*(5), 500–518.

Dantley, M., & Tillman, L. C. (2005). Social justice and moral transformative leadership. In C. Marshal & M. Oliva (Eds.), *Leadership for social justice: Making revolutions in education* (pp. 16–30). Boston, MA: Allyn & Bacon.

Darling-Hammond, L. (1997). *The right to learn: A blueprint for creating schools that work*. San Francisco, CA: Jossey-Bass.

Darling-Hammond, L. (2002) Learning to teach for social justice. In L. Darling-Hammond, J. French, & S. Garcia-Lopez (Eds.), *Learning to teach for social justice* (pp. 1–7). New York: Teachers College Press.

Darling-Hammond, L. (2005). New standards and old inequalities: School reform and the education of African American students. In J. E. King (Ed.), *Black education: A transformative research and action agenda for the new century* (pp. 197–224). Mahwah, NJ: Erlbaum.

Delpit, L. (1995). *Other people's children: Cultural conflict in the classroom*. New York: The New Press.

Dewey, J. (1934). *Art as experience*. Toms River, NJ: Capricorn Books.

Dey, I. (1999). *Grounding grounded theory*. San Diego, CA: Academic Press.

Donmoyer, R., Imber, M., & Scheurich, J. J. (1995). *The knowledge base of educational administration: Multiple perspectives*. Albany, NY: State University of New York Press.

Eisner, E. W. (2002). *The arts and creation of mind*. New Haven, CT: Yale University Press.

Eisner, E. (2008). Art and knowledge. In A. Cole, & J. Knowles (Eds.), *Handbook of the arts in qualitative research: Perspectives, methodologies, examples, and issues.* (pp. 3–12). London: Sage Publications.

Ellsworth, E. (2005). *Places of learning: Media, architecture, pedagogy*. New York, NY: Routledge.

Fielding, N. G., & Fielding, J. L. (1986). *Linking data*. Beverly Hills, CA: Sage Publications.

Furman, G. C., & Shields, C. M. (2005). Leadership for social justice and democratic community. In W. A. Firestone & C. Riehl (Eds.), *A new agenda: Directions for research on educational leadership.* (pp. 119–137). New York: Teachers College Press.

Gay, G. (2010). *Culturally responsive teaching: Theory, research, and practice* (2d. ed.). New York: Teachers College Press.

Giroux, H. A. (1997) *Pedagogy and the politics of hope*. Boulder, CO: Westview Press.

Glaser, B. G. (1978). *Theoretical sensitivity: Advances in the methodology of grounded theory*. Mill Valley, CA: Sociology Press.

Glaser, B. G. , & Strauss, A. L. (1967). *The discovery of grounded theory: Strategies for qualitative research*. Hawthorne, NY: Aldine.

González, N., Moll, L., & Amanti, C. (2005). *Funds of knowledge: Theorizing practices in households, communities, and classrooms*. Mahwah, NJ: Lawrence Erlbaum Associates.

Greene, M. (1995). *Releasing the imagination: Essays on education, the arts, and social change*. San Francisco, CA: Jossey-Bass.

Grogan, M. (Ed.). (2002). Leadership for social justice (Part I, Special issue). *Journal of School Leadership, 12*(2), 112–115.

Henderson, J. G., Gornik, R. (2007). *Transformative curriculum leadership* (3d ed.). Upper Saddle River, NJ: Pearson.

Holstein, J. A., & Gubrium, J. F. (2003). *Inside interviewing: New lenses, new concerns*. Thousand Oaks, CA: Sage Publications.

Kouzes, J., & Posner, B. (1999). *Encouraging the heart*. San Francisco, CA: Jossey-Bass.

Kozol, J. (1991). *Savage inequalities*. New York: Crown Publishers.

Kozol, J. (2005). *The shame of the nation: The restoration of apartheid schooling in America*. New York: Three Rivers Press.

Ladson-Billings, G. (1994). *The dreamkeepers*. San Francisco, CA: Jossey-Bass.

Ladson-Billings, G. (1995). But that's just good teaching! The case for culturally relevant pedagogy. *Theory into Practice, 34*(3), 159–165.

Ladson-Billings, G. (1997). Toward a theory of culturally relevant pedagogy. *American Education Research Journal, 32*(3), 465–491.

Ladson-Billings, G.J. & Tate, W. (2006). *Education research in the public interest: Social justice, action, and policy.* New York: Teachers College Press.

Langer, S. K. (1953). *Feeling and form: A theory of art.* New York: Scribner.

Larson, C. L., & Ovando, C. J. (2001). *The color of bureaucracy: The politics of equity in multicultural school communities.* Belmont, CA: Thomson Learning, Inc.

Leary, M. R., & Tangney, J. P. (2003). *Handbook of self and identity.* New York: Guilford Press.

Leithwood, K., & Jantzi, D. (1990). Transformational leadership: How principals can help to reform school cultures. *School Effectiveness and School Improvement, 1*(4), 249–280.

Lincoln, Y. S., & Guba, E. G. (1985). *Naturalistic inquiry.* Beverly Hills, CA: Sage Publications.

Lopez, G. R. (2003). The (racially-neutral) politics of education: A critical race theory perspective. *Educational Administration Quarterly, 39*(1), 68–94.

Marshall, C. (1993). *The unsung role of the career assistant principal.* Washington, DC: National Association of Secondary School Principals.

Marshall, C., & Gerstl-Pepin, C. (2005). *Re-framing educational politics for social justice.* Boston, MA: Allyn & Bacon.

Marshall, C., & Olivia, M. (2010). *Leadership for social justice: Making revolutions in education* (2nd ed.). Boston, MA: Allyn & Bacon.

Marshall, C., & Ward, M. (2004). "Yes, but . . .": Education leaders discuss social justice. *Journal of School Leadership, 14,* 530-563.

Marshall, C., Young, M. D., & Moll, L. (2010). The wider societal challenge: An afterword. In C. Marshall & M. Oliva (Eds.), *Leading for social justice: Making revolutions in education* (2nd ed., pp. 315 325). Boston, MA: Allyn & Bacon.

Maxwell, J. A. (1992). Understanding and validity in qualitative research. *Harvard Educational Review, 62*(3), 279–300.

Maxwell, J. A. (2005). *Qualitative research design: An interactive approach* (2d ed.). Thousand Oaks, CA: Sage Publications.

McKenzie, K. B., Christman, D. E., Hernandez, F., Fierro, E., Capper, C. A., Dantley, M. E., Gonzalez, M. L., Cambron-McCabe, N., & Scheurich, J. J. (2008). From the field: A proposal for educating leaders for social justice. *Educational Administration Quarterly. 44*(1), 111–138.

Merchant, B. M., & Shoho, A. R. (2010). Bridge people: Civic and educational leaders for social justice. In C. Marshall & M. Oliva (Eds.), *Leading for social justice: Making revolutions in education* (2nd ed., pp. 120–138). Boston, MA: Allyn & Bacon.

Mezirow, J. (1990). *Fostering critical reflection in adulthood.* San Francisco, CA: Jossey-Bass

Mezirow, J. (1991). *Transformative dimensions of adult learning.* San Francisco, CA: Jossey-Bass.

Mezirow, J. (2000). Learning to think like an adult: Core concepts of transformation theory. In J. Mezirow & Associates (Eds.), *Learning as transformation: Critical perspectives on a theory in progress* (pp. 3–34). San Francisco, CA: Jossey-Bass.

Noddings, N. (2003). *Caring: A feminine approach to ethics and moral education,* 2d. Berkeley, CA: University of California Press.

Quantz, R., Rogers, J., & Dantley, M. (1992). Rethinking transformative leadership toward democratic reform of schools. *Journal of Education, 173*(3), 96–118.

Reyes, P., Scribner, J. D., & Paredes Scribner, A. (Eds.). (1999). *Lessons from high performing Hispanic schools: Creating learning communities.* New York: Teachers College Press.

Riester, A. F., Pursch, V., & Skrla, L. (2002). Principals for social justice: Leaders of school success for children from low-income homes. *Journal of School Leadership, 12*(3), 281–304.

Scheurich, J. J. (1997). *Research method in the postmodern.* London: Falmer Press.

Scheurich, J. J., &Skrla, L. (2003). *Leadership for equity and excellence: Creating high-achievement classrooms, schools, and districts.* Thousand Oaks, CA: Corwin.

Shapiro, L. (2010). Releasing emotion: Artmaking and leading for social justice. In C. Marshall & M. Oliva (Eds.), *Leading for social justice: Making revolutions in education* (2nd ed., pp. 242–258). Boston, MA: Allyn & Bacon.

Shields, C. M. (2003). *Good intentions are not enough: Transformative leadership for communities of difference.* Lanham, MD: Scarecrow Press.

Shields, C. M. (2004). Dialogic leadership for social justice: Overcoming pathologies of silence. *Educational Administration Quarterly, 40*(1), 111–134.

Shoho, A. (Ed.). (2006). Preparing leaders for social justice [Special issue]. *Journal of Educational Administration, 44*(3), 196-208.

Singleton, G. E., & Linton, C. (2006). *Courageous conversations about race*. Thousand Oaks, CA: Corwin.

Skrla, L., & Scheurich, J.J. (2003). *Educational equity and accountability: Paradigms, policies, and politics*. London: Routledge.

Skrla, L., McKenzie, K., Scheurich, J. (2009). *Using equity audits to create equitable and excellent schools*. Thousand Oaks, CA: Corwin Press.

Sleeter, C. E. (1996). *Multicultural education as social activism*. Albany, NY: SUNY Press.

Strauss, A. (1987). *Qualitative analysis for social scientists*. Cambridge, MA: Cambridge University Press.

Strauss, A., & Corbin, J. M. (1998). *Basics of qualitative research: Techniques and theories for developing grounded theory* (2d ed.) Thousand Oaks, CA: Sage Publications.

Terrell, R. D., & Lindsey, R. B. (2009). *Culturally proficient leadership: The personal journey begins within*. Thousand Oaks, CA: Corwin Press.

Theoharis, G. (2007). Social justice educational leaders and resistance: Toward a theory of social justice leadership. *Educational Administration Quarterly, 43*(2), 221–258.

Tooms, A. K. & Boske, C. (2010). *Bridge leadership: Connecting educational leadership and social justice to improve schools*. Charlotte, NC: Information Age Publishing.

Tooms, A. K., Lugg, C. A., & Bogotch, I. (2010). Rethinking the politics of fit and educational leadership. *Educational Administration Quarterly, 46*(1), 96–131.

Valencia, R. R. (1997). *The evolution of deficit thinking: Educational thought and practice*. London: Falmer.

Valenzuela, A. (1999). *Subtractive schooling: U.S.-Mexican youth and the politics of caring*. New York: State University of New York Press.

West, C., (1999). *Cornel West reader*. New York: Basic Civitas Books.

Young , M. D., & Brooks, J. S. (2008). Supporting graduate students of color in educational administration preparation programs: Faculty perspectives on best practices, possibilities, and problems. *Educational Administration Quarterly, 44*(3), 391–423.

Afterword

Towards an Appreciation of Critical Transformative Leadership

Carolyn M. Shields

There you have it—a set of reflections and studies that offer critical new perspectives on leadership. The authors included in this volume have provided evidence of the robustness of the concept of transformative leadership, as they have written about the ways in which it both extends and is enriched by theories of democracy, identity, advocacy, and social justice. We have also read studies conducted in Australia, Canada, Scandinavia, the United States, and the United Arab Emirates, all demonstrating the relevance of the tenets of transformative leadership for various contexts—developing and developed worlds, as well as Arab, Caucasian, and multicultural settings.

Here, we have identified a constellation of elements that comprise transformative leadership, although no single article includes all of them. These authors have argued that conversations about race, identity, curriculum, and pedagogy are all part of transformative leadership, as are the core components of dialogue, equity, privilege, and moral courage that I identified in the Introduction. Similarly we have seen how transformative leadership is ideological. Burns's (1978) call for "ideological leaders [to] dedicate themselves to explicit goals that require substantial social change and to organizing and leading political movements that pursue these goals" (p. 248) echoed through the chapters by Starratt, Blackmore, and others. His concept of intellectual leadership that identifies and focuses on these purposes, on the value-laden nature of leadership, and on the need for engagement with our wider society resounds throughout the pages of this reader.

Further, the need for moral courage is abundantly evident. We constantly hear that these are difficult times in which to exercise educational leadership. President Obama, on January 25, 2011, in his State of the Union address, painted a bleak picture of the current state of education in America, saying:

> As many as a quarter of our students aren't even finishing high school. The quality of our math and science education lags behind many other nations. America has fallen to ninth in the proportion of young people with a college degree. And so the question is whether all of us— as citizens, and

as parents— are willing to do what's necessary to give every child a chance to succeed . . . (Obama, 2011, para. 3)

Obama went on to suggest that the early responsibility of parents and families was shared by schools. And, he asserted, although many schools don't meet the test, that "when a child walks into a classroom, it should be a place of high expectations and high performance" (para. 36). Interestingly, as he continued, he advocated increased respect for educators, saying that "in South Korea, teachers are known as 'nation builders'" (para. 39.

In this volume, you have read ways in which educators can—and should—become known as nation builders. We must acknowledge the central importance of education to the development of both civil society and the prosperity of a nation. This begs for the rejection of technical solutions to complex problems. It eschews more of the same—increased testing, new programs, additional teacher assessment, or more modern schools. Instead, it requires educators to attend to the issues, problems, and solutions advocated in the preceding chapters. I repeat the tenets here. Transformative educators will:

- acknowledge power and privilege;

- articulate both individual and collective purposes (public and private good);

- deconstruct social-cultural knowledge frameworks that generate inequity and reconstruct them in more equitable ways;

- balance critique and promise;

- effect deep and equitable change;

- work towards transformation—liberation, emancipation, democracy, equity, and excellence; and

- demonstrate moral courage and activism.

This kind of leadership does not occur in a vacuum, but requires leaders to be aware of other theories and research. We have also heard how attending to concepts of deep democracy (Carr; Moller), identity (Requa; Sayani; Stephenson), linguistic minorities (Lapointe), race (Mohan), power (Reyes & Bogotch; Weiner), and others will inform and guide transformative leaders. The key is the purpose or goal of deep and equitable transformation of our schools and of the societies in which they are embedded.

Before you set this reader aside, let us reflect one more time on the elements that these authors found compelling and on the potential of transformative leadership to move our field and our society forward. Transformative leadership is not just a way to improve test scores or to ensure that students from minority or disadvantaged groups are provided with the resources needed to meet the requisite state expectations (although this is generally an outcome of transformative approaches). It is not simply a way to engage in effective or efficient managerial practices. It is not simply about school performance or making adequate yearly progress (AYP). It is not about producing better school-improvement plans, developing better parent advisory committees, or adopting the latest improvement fad—regardless of the impact and popularity of Professional Learning Communities, Response to Intervention, or Positive Behavior Intervention Systems. It is not even a leadership theory primarily designed to create schools that are more inclusive and socially just. It does not jump on purported panaceas such as vouchers or charter schools without stopping to reflect on the answers to some key questions: Who will this advantage? Who will be disadvantaged even further? Who will be included and who excluded? Who benefits and who will lose? Whose voices have been heard and whose silenced?

Transformative leadership is a robust way of thinking about leadership that requires multiple styles and strategies. At one point, a transformative leader will be collaborative, sharing leadership tasks and collaborating with multiple partners. Another time, a transformative leader will operate in a hierarchical, top-down way; and on still another occasion, that same leader may well engage in bargaining and securing agreement related to a mutually beneficial transaction. In other words, the style will vary with the circumstances. But what remains constant is the purpose: to work for, and to advocate, goals that are equitable, inclusive, socially just, and deeply democratic (a term I understand as a way of living together in respect and mutual benefit and not as a form of governance). Being transformative necessitates taking a critical approach to leadership that recognizes that, in whichever organization one works, it is essential to have a broad and comprehensive vision of the goals that will promote the kind of global society we wish to help build. It is not just another new theory in a new package, but, rather, a robust set of concepts that must undergird leadership practice—whatever one decides to call it—if the outcomes are to be an improvement in the education and subsequent opportunities for everyone.

When William Shakespeare wrote, "A rose by any other name would smell as sweet," he may have succinctly expressed a common feeling among educational leaders that there is too much emphasis on leadership styles, theories, strategies, or approaches. Indeed, here we have found authors not only discussing tenets of transformative leadership, but also using other related and complimentary terms. It matters less what it is called than what it involves. If our focus is on equality, efficiency, and effectiveness, as generally propounded and understood in neo-liberal terms, we will never attain the goals of a more equitable and mutually beneficial society. If, on the other hand, the ways in which we understand, study, and practice leadership include the concepts advocated here, there is the potential for our leadership to be transformative. For that reason, I believe that transformative leadership is not simply just another leadership fad, and that the focus on equity, inclusion, justice, and transformation suggests that it isn't just about semantics.

It is about starting where we are. It requires all of us, as leaders, to know ourselves—what guides and grounds us, what our non-negotiables are, what we believe, what we are willing to fight for, and what we are trying to accomplish. It requires that leadership be firmly grounded in moral purpose. It calls for a clear understanding that, as leaders, we must use the power we inevitably wield wisely and justly. And, as many of the chapter authors have argued, it requires that we work to translate our vision into transformative action—always engaged in, and often as advocates for, the communal life of our neighborhood, school, community, nation, and world.

We have articulated a daunting task—one that calls for a clear sense of purpose, moral courage, and engagement (even advocacy and activism). We sincerely hope that as you reflect on the challenging ideas presented here, you will not find them overwhelming, but instead will be convinced of their merit and possibilities. We even dare to hope you will be inspired—even stimulated and galvanized—to ensure that the education we offer our children will, as George Washington Carver (n.d) urged, "unlock the golden door of freedom." It is to that end we are called to act courageously and to advocate unceasingly.

References

Burns, J. M. (1978). *Leadership*. New York: HarperCollins.

Carver, G. W. (n.d.) retrieved April 30, 2011, from http://www.great-quotes.com/Educational_Quotes.htm.

Obama, B. H. (2011). State of the union 2011: Winning the future, address to Congress. Retrieved January 26, 2011, from http://www.whitehouse.gov/state-of-the-union-2011

About the Contributors

Jean Archambault is associate professor of educational administration, Faculté des sciences de l'éducation, Université de Montréal. He is in charge of the 2nd cycle professional programs and of the educational management sector. He was formerly a pedagogy counselor for the Montreal School board and for the Supporting Montreal Schools Program for low socioeconomic status schools of the Québec Ministry of Education. He was at the forefront of Québec's educational reform, working in a target school where implementation was experimented. He earned an M.A. degree in clinical psychology from the Université du Québec à Montréal and a Ph.D. in psychopedagogy from the Université de Montréal. On the educational scene for more than 30 years, he taught in many universities and published numerous papers intended for school principals, teachers, and educational professionals. His research interests focus on educational change and transformative leadership, particularly concerning school principals in disadvantaged areas. He has published two books in French: with Chantale Richer, *Une école pour apprendre* (2007), and with Roch Chouinard, *Vers une gestion éducative de la classe*.

Deneca Winfrey Avant received her bachelor's degree in social work in 1996 from Jackson State University, her master of social work degree, specializing in school social work, from the University of Illinois at Urbana-Champaign in 1998, and a master of education in leadership and administration from the University of Illinois at Chicago in 2003. In 2005, Dr. Avant began her doctoral program at the University of Illinois at Urbana-Champaign in the Department of Educational Organization and Leadership. During her program, she was an instructor in the Educational Psychology Department and research team leader for the Summer Research Opportunity Program. Dr. Avant earned her doctor of philosophy in May 2009 and joined Illinois State University as an assistant professor of social work in June 2009. Dr. Avant's research interests include social work roles in Response to Intervention and transformative leadership for social justice. Dr. Avant is affiliated with several organizations, including the School Social Work Association of America and the American Educational Research Association. In her free time, she enjoys traveling, watching movies, spending time with her husband, Andre, their bichon frise, and her sorority sisters.

Andrew J. Barrett currently serves as curriculum director for Geneva SD 304 in Illinois. He is also a doctoral candidate in the Educational Policy, Organization, and Leadership Department at the University of Illinois at Urbana-Champaign. Andy received his master's degree in educational administration and leadership from Aurora University and his bachelor of arts degree in elementary education from Monmouth College, both in Illinois. His research interests include democratic practices in education, transformative leadership theory, and social justice. His doctoral research focuses on the relationship between democratic education and the social construction of American affluence. More specifically, he seeks to understand how school principals in affluent communities experience and contextualize the tension between private good expectations and public good responsibilities for schooling. In addition to his professional and academic pursuits, Andy enjoys reading, playing the guitar, and spending time with friends and family. His most valued supporters are his wife Sarah, an elementary school teacher, and the light of their lives, their four-year-old son, Theo.

Paula D. Bieneman is a doctoral candidate in the Educational Policy, Organization and Leadership Department at the University of Illinois at Urbana-Champaign. Paula began her 23–year career as a teacher with VisionQuest, a wilderness program for incarcerated youth. Today she serves as an elementary school principal in Illinois, having worked as a high school English teacher, an alternative-school division leader, a high school dean of students, and a central office administrator. She earned both her B.S. in secondary education and her M.Ed. in administration at the University of Illinois at Urbana-Champaign. Her professional interests include examining theoretical constructs, such as collective efficacy, transformative leadership, and social justice, to encourage dialogue and inform the school-improvement process. Paula's doctoral research examines the nature of collective efficacy in racially diverse elementary schools. The study examines the impact of organizational agency and conducts a deeper interrogation of the underlying belief systems and tacit assumptions that are steeped in deficit thinking.

Jill Blackmore is professor of education in the Faculty of Education at Deakin University and director of the Centre for Research in Educational Futures and Innovation. Her research focuses on globalization and internationalization, educational restructuring and redesign, and changes in educational work and organisations from a feminist and social justice perspective. Her publications include Blackmore, J., Brennan, M., and Zipin, L. (2010) (eds.) *Repositioning University Governance and Academic Work*,; and Blackmore, J. and Sachs, J. (2007) *Performing and Reforming Leaders: Gender, Educational Restructuring and Organisational Change.*

Ira Bogotch is professor of education leadership at Florida Atlantic University. He currently serves as associate editor for the *International Journal of Leadership in Education* and on the editorial boards of *Urban Education*, the *Scholar-Practitioner Quarterly*, and *Professional Education*. His scholarly research and essays have appeared in many peer-review journals, both nationally and internationally. He was the U.S. regional editor for the *International Handbook on Leadership for Learning*, to be published in 2011, and will be coediting, with Carolyn Shields, the *International Handbook on Social [In]Justice and Educational Leadership*, scheduled for publication in 2013.

Christa Boske is assistant professor in educational administration at Kent State University. She encourages school leaders to promote humanity in schools, especially for disenfranchised children and families. Christa's recent work has been published in the *Journal of School Leadership*, the *Journal of Research on Leadership Education*, *Multicultural Education and Technology Journal*, and the *Journal of Curriculum Theorizing* (in press). Her scholarship is informed by her work as a school leader and social worker in residential treatment and inner-city schools. She coedited a book with Autumn K. Tooms titled *Bridge Leadership: Connecting Educational Leadership and Social Justice to Improve Schools*, published in 2010 by Information Age Publishing. Christa has another edited book scheduled for publication in the fall of 2011 titled *Educational Leadership: Building Bridges Between Ideas, Schools, and Nations*, also by Information Age Publishing.

Paul R. Carr is associate professor in the Departments of Sociology and Interdisciplinary Studies at Lakehead University, Orillia. His research focuses on democracy, critical pedagogy, media literacy, and peace studies, and he has some 50 articles and book chapters published in these areas. His most recent book is *Does Your Vote Count? Critical Pedagogy and Democracy*, published by Peter Lang in 2010. He is coeditor of another book currently in press, entitled *The Phenomenon of Obama and the Agenda for Education: Can Hope Audaciously Trump Neoliberalism?*, to be published by Information Age Publishing, and has also coedited four other books, including *The Great White North? Exploring Whiteness, Privilege, and Identity in Education* (Sense Publishers, 2007), which won awards from the Canadian Race Relations Foundation and the Canadian Association for Foundations in Education. His website is www.paulrcarr.net.

Michael E. Dantley is associate provost and associate vice president for academic affairs and professor of educational leadership at Miami University, Oxford, Ohio. Prior to his current position, Dr. Dantley served as associate dean for academic affairs in the School of Education, Health, and Society at Miami. Dr. Dantley teaches courses in organizational and leadership theory, ethics and leadership, the principalship, educational leadership theory, and philosophy and change in the Department of Educational Leadership. His research focuses on leadership, spirituality, and social justice. He is currently, however, pursuing research that explores new ways to conduct qualitative research on spirituality and leadership as well as research that explores the link between principals' moral development and the ways these principals define and demonstrate their commitment to social justice. Dr. Dantley's scholarship has been published in numerous venues, including *Educational Administration Quarterly*, the *Journal of School Leadership Urban Education*, and the *Journal of Negro Education*. He has written chapters in edited texts including the new *Sage Handbook of Educational Leadership*, *Leadership for Social Justice: Making It Happen*, *Inspiring Practice: Spirituality and Educational Leadership*, and *Keeping the Promise: Educational Leadership and the Promise of Democracy in Our Time*. Dr. Dantley lectures at universities throughout the United States and Canada on current issues in urban school leadership.

Roseline Garon is associate professor of educational administration, Faculté des sciences de l'éducation, Université de Montréal. She is responsible mostly for research courses, and concurrently she holds the function of secretary of the Faculté des sciences de l'éducation. She has also been in charge of the 2nd cycle professional programs. She earned an M.A. in psychology from the Université du Québec à Montréal and a Ph.D. in educational psychology from the Université de Montréal. Her research interests are the resilience of school principals in disadvantaged areas and the study of their leadership practices. She has published one book in French with Manon Théorêt, *L'effort à l'école, un goût à développer. Intervention pédagogique transversale destinée aux élèves du primaire* (2000).

Barbara Harold is an experienced educator with a background in elementary teaching, followed by more than 25 years in the tertiary sector as a teacher educator. Her doctoral thesis investigated issues of power, change, and leadership in the implementation of government policy in rural schools in New Zealand. Since joining Zayed University in 2001 she has continued teaching, research, and publication in the areas of leadership, educational reform, and professional learning, and she is experienced in qualitative methodology, ethnographic research, and grounded theory development. Dr. Harold recently chaired Zayed University's year-long Conversation on Leadership project, which successfully completed a conceptual framework for the development of a campus-wide undergraduate leadership-education curriculum. She has also been director of the College of Education Centre for Professional Development and has led workshops and seminars in the United Arab Emirates and wider Gulf region. In addition, she has disseminated her research at national, regional, and international conferences in the United States, United Kingdom, United Arab Emirates, Saudi Arabia, New Zealand, and Australia. Her current research interests are in leadership identity development and school reform.

Iris Jun began teaching English as Second Language (ESL) in 1996 at a high school in the suburbs of Chicago and has been a coach, sponsor, curricular leader, and department chair. As department chair of ESL, she has participated in major programmatic and curricular changes, started initiatives for parent and community outreach programs, and created staff development for content area teachers on instruction for English language learners, culturally relevant pedagogy, and the ESL program in general. She received her master's degree in linguistics at Northeastern Illinois University in Chicago, Illinois and a second master's degree in educational leadership and organizational change at Roosevelt University in Chicago. She is currently pursuing her Ph.D. in educational organization and leadership at the University of Illinois at Urbana-Champaign, where she is cultivating her interest in transformative leadership and leadership for equity and social justice.

Lyse Langlois holds a doctorate in school policy and educational administration. She is professor in the Department of Labour Relations at Université Laval, Québec, Canada, specializing in the field of human resources and applied ethics. Professor Langlois has developed a model of ethical decision making and conduct in educational organizations, thus making a unique contribution to ethics as a management issue. In the area of educational administration, she has followed up her conceptual work with empirical research, which has contributed to knowledge in the following areas: (a) individual ethical conduct in organizations; (b) ethical dilemmas in educational administration; (c) ethical leadership; and (d) institutionalization of ethics in the workplace. Dr. Langlois is a full member of the Interuniversity Research Center on Globalization and Work (CRIMT) and member of the director board of the Institute of Applied Ethics. She was elected to the Board of Governors of the Center for the Study of Leadership, Values, and Ethics at Pennsylvania State University. She has published several articles on the ethical leadership and ethical decision-making process. Her latest book, *Anatomy of Ethical Leadership: To Lead Our Organizations in a Conscientious and Authentic Manner,* was published in French by the Presses de l'Université Laval (2008) and in English by AU Press (2011).

Claire Lapointe received her Ph. D. in educational administration and policy studies from Université Laval in 1995. She is full professor and head of the Department of Educational Administration and Foundations at Université Laval, Québec City, Canada. Prior to teaching at the university level, Professor Lapointe worked in the field of education in various Canadian provinces, as well as in several countries, including Germany, French Polynesia, New Zealand, and Gabon. Her research interest in the cultural aspects of educational leadership stems, therefore, from her wide-ranging experience as an educator and educational administrator in different parts of the world since 1976. Professor Lapointe has published extensively on the subjects of gender equity in education, organizational culture, school leadership in linguistic minority settings, and, with Professor Lyse Langlois, on ethical leadership in education. In January 2010, she became a member of the Québec Conseil Supérieur de l'Éducation, an independent body appointed by the provincial government, with the role of advising the Minister of education.

Erica Mohan completed her Ph.D. in the Department of Educational Studies at the University of British Columbia. Her doctoral research examined the influence of the K–12 schooling experience on the racial and ethnic identity development of multiethnic students. Her broader research interests include antiracist education and education for social justice—interests that stem, in part, from her experiences of teaching and learning in a variety of settings, including Central and South America and across North America. Erica has been involved in several large-scale research projects in both Canada and the United States, and her publications, which also include several book chapters, have appeared in the *International Journal of Qualitative Studies in Education* (QSE), *Teacher Development*, and the *Journal of Cases in Educational Leadership*. In addition to her academic work, for the past two years Erica has been working with homeless youth in California.

Jorunn Moller is professor in the Department of Teacher Education and School Research, and vice dean for research in the Faculty of Educational Sciences at the University of Oslo. Her professional interests are in the areas of educational leadership and governance, reform policies, and school accountability. She has been involved in a range of research projects on educational leadership and policy change, and also is participating in international research networks in the field of school leadership. At present she is engaged in a five-year project that aims to analyze the role of administration and institutions in the implementation of the current educational reform in Norway. She also is involved in the International Successful School Principal Project (ISSPP). Address for correspondence: University of Oslo, Department of Teacher Education and School Research, P.O. Box 1099, Blindern, 0317 Oslo, Norway. Email: jorunn.moller@ils.uio.no; website: *http://www.uv.uio.no/ils/english/people/aca/jorunnm/index.html*

Marcia A. Ranieri is a full-time doctoral student at Syracuse University in the teaching and leadership program. Prior to coming to Syracuse, Ranieri was a high school Spanish teacher and school-building leader in a suburban New York district for eight years. She received her undergraduate degree in Spanish education from Geneseo, her master's in bilingual education from the University of Buffalo, and her C.A.S. in educational leadership from Syracuse University. Her research interests include social justice leadership, gender, and inclusion. Ranieri is a member of the Reduction of Stigma in Schools Program, a partnership between Syracuse University and the School of Education that works with district leaders and classroom teachers to facilitate discussion and create awareness around the issues that LGBT (lesbian, gay, bisexual, and transgender) students face each day in our schools. In addition, Ranieri is the bilingual parent outreach coordinator for the

Syracuse University Parent Advocacy Center, where she assists bilingual parents in gaining more equitable access for their students with disabilities. Ranieri has received recognition in the field for her work with diversity efforts as well as for excellence in teaching. Marcia can be reached at mranieri@syr.edu.

Steve Rayner is professor of education at Oxford Brookes University in the United Kingdom. He is an internationally recognized scholar in the field of individual differences in learning, teaching, and leadership, and in the field of management of inclusive education. Recent research includes the study of international knowledge production in cognitive style research, examining the construction and use of personalizing pedagogies associated with web-based learning, evaluating pedagogies and impact in educationists' learning leadership at doctoral level, and investigating academic leadership in the role of the professoriate in the "U.K. University." Steve previously worked as professor of leadership and diversity in education at the University of Gloucestershire, U.K. He was formerly headteacher of Penwithen School (Dorset LEA) and taught in secondary and special education, before moving to the School of Education at the University of Birmingham, where he worked more recently as the director for doctoral studies. A forthcoming publication is: Rayner, S., & Cools, E, (Eds) (2011) *Style Differences in Cognition, Learning, and Management: Theory, Research, and Practice*. See Routledge Studies in Management, Organizations and Society at http://www.routledge.com/books/series/routledge_studies_in_management_organizations_and_society_SE0536/.   To contact by email: srayner@brookes.ac.uk.

David Requa is a graduate student in the Ph.D. program in educational administration and leadership in the College of Education at the University of Illinois. He also serves as a graduate research associate in the college's Bureau of Educational Research and the Office of School University Research Relations. Prior to that, he served as an administrator and superintendent in Rantoul and Braidwood, Illinois after teaching in Springfield and Danville, Illinois. He practiced law in Illinois from 1979 until 1999, when he returned to teaching. He earned his B.S. from the University of Illinois in music education in 1974, his J.D. from the University of Illinois in 1979, his M.Ed also from the University of Illinois in 1996, and completed a Certificate of Advanced Study in Educational Administration at Eastern Illinois University in 2005.

Daniel Reyes-Guerra is assistant professor of educational leadership at Florida Atlantic University. He teaches several courses, including School Improvement on the doctoral level and Educational Governance and the Principal Internship on the master's level. His research, writing, and service agenda include educational leadership program development, innovative district-university partnerships and internships, strategic leadership actions and thinking, and the promotion of social justice and democracy in public schools. He has served on the American Educational Research Association (AERA) Leadership and Teaching in Educational Leadership Special Interest Group (LTEL-SIG) and has published articles in the *Community Education Journal*, *Leadership Review*, and *International Journal of Leadership Development*. Correspondence concerning his book chapter should be addressed to dreyes@fau.edu.

Anish Sayani spent 14 years teaching high school English, social studies, leadership, and special education in both British Columbia and Texas, before receiving his Ph.D. in educational leadership at the University of British Columbia, Canada. He has been a staff developer for three years in Monument Valley, Utah, where he mentors teachers and administrators. He has also spent over 10 years teaching and leading religious education for the Shia Ismaili Muslim community in Canada. Currently, he teaches in the Faculty of Education at the University of British Columbia. Anish's research interests include leadership for social justice and the role of identity and dialogue as foundations for leadership. He lives in Vancouver, B.C. and is fortunate to be a father of two inspirational boys, Noah and Misha.

Carolyn M. Shields, who has a Ph.D. from the University of Saskatchewan, took up her role as dean of the College of Education at Wayne State University in July 2011. For the past 20 years, she has been a professor of leadership at the University of Illinois at Urbana-Champaign, the University of British Columbia, and the University of Utah. She is past president of the Canadian Association for Studies in Educational Administration and former Canadian representative to the Board of the Commonwealth Council for Educational Administration and Management. Her teaching is in the area of transformative leadership, deep democracy, equitable policy, social justice, and research methodology. Her research focuses on how educational leaders can create learning environments that are deeply democratic, socially just, and inclusive of all students' lived experiences, and that prepare students for excellence and citizenship in our global society. These interests are reflected in her presentations and publications: over 100 articles, hundreds of conference and keynote presentations, and seven books, the most recent of which is *Courageous Leadership for Transforming Schools: Democratizing Practice*. She has received recognition for both her teaching and her career contributions to the field of educational leadership.

Robert J. Starratt, known to his friends as Jerry, is professor of educational administration at Boston College. His work with schools has taken him to various states in the United States, as well as to Australia, Canada, Ireland, Sweden, India, and several countries on the Pacific Rim. Starratt is author of numerous books and articles, including *The Drama of Schooling/The Schooling of Drama, Centering Educational Administration,* and *Leaders with Vision*. His recent publications have focused on moral and ethical issues in education. He received the Don Willower Award for Lifetime Achievement in the field of Educational Leadership and Ethics, and the Roald Campbell Award for lifetime service and achievement in the field of Educational Administration, from the University Council for Educational Administration.

Shirley R. Steinberg is the Director and Chair of The Werklund Foundation Centre for Youth Leadership in Education, and Professor of Youth Studies at the University of Calgary. She is the author and editor of over 35 books in critical literacy, critical pedagogy, urban and youth culture, and cultural studies. Her most recent books include: *Kinderculture: The Corporate Construction of Childhood* (2011); *Teaching Against Islamophobia* (2011); *19 Urban Questions: Teaching in the City* (2010); *Christotainment: Selling Jesus Through Popular Culture* (2009); *Diversity and Multiculturalism: A Reader* (2009); *Media Literacy: A Reader* (2007); the award winning *Contemporary Youth Culture: An International Encyclopedia*; and *The Miseducation of the West: How Schools and Media Distort Our Understanding of the Islam World* (with Joe L. Kincheloe) (2004). She is currently finishing two books: *Writing and Publishing* (Fall 2011) and *The Bricolage and Qualitative Research* (Fall 2011) and *The Critical Qualitative Research Reader* (with Gaile Canella) (Spring 2012). A regular contributor to CBC Radio One, CTV, *The Toronto Globe and Mail, The Montreal Gazette,* and *Canadian Press*, she is an internationally known speaker and teacher. She is also the founding editor of *Taboo: The Journal of Culture and Education*, and the Managing Editor of *The International Journal of Critical Pedagogy*. The organizer of The Critical Pedagogical Congress, she is committed to a global community of transformative educators and community workers engaged in radical love, social justice, and the situating of power within social and cultural contexts.

Lauren Stephenson is an experienced educator with a background in English-language teaching and educational leadership. She has over 15 years experience in the tertiary sector as a teacher educator. She holds a Ph.D. in educational leadership and organizational learning from the University of Sydney in Australia. She recently cochaired Zayed University's Conversation on Leadership project, which aimed to develop a campus-wide undergraduate leadership education curriculum. She has also held leadership positions in Zayed University's College of Education Graduate Programs Division, in its Center for Professional Development of United Arab Emirates (U.A.E.) Educators, and has led workshops and seminars in the U.A.E. and wider Gulf region. In addition, she has disseminated her research at national, regional, and international conferences in the United States, United Kingdom, Europe, U.A.E., and Australia. Her teaching, research, and publications are in the areas of educational leadership, teacher professional learning, organizational learning, teacher education, collaborative research, and language education. She is experienced in qualitative methodology, ethnographic research action research, and mixed methods.

George Theoharis is associate professor in educational leadership and inclusive elementary education and the director of field relations at Syracuse University. He has extensive field experience in public education as a principal and as a teacher. George teaches classes in educational leadership and elementary–early childhood teacher education. His interests and research focus on issues of equity, justice, diversity, inclusion, leadership, and school reform. George's published works appear in such journals as *Teachers College Record*, *The School Administrator*, *Educational Administration Quarterly*, *The School Administrator*, *Educational Leadership*, the *Journal of School Leadership*, *The International Journal of Inclusive Education*, and *Equity & Excellence in Education*. He has a recent book titled *The School Leaders Our Children Deserve (2009)* about school leadership, social justice, and school reform. He runs a summer leadership institute for school administrators focusing on issues of equity and inclusion, as well as a school reform project called Schools of Promise. His Ph.D. in educational leadership and policy analysis is from the University of Wisconsin–Madison. He lives in Fayetteville, New York and has two adorable children, Ella and Sam.

Anne Marie Tryjankowski, Ed.D. is assistant professor of graduate education and leadership at Canisius College in Buffalo, New York. She has extensive experience as a classroom teacher and central office administrator in high-need, urban public schools. She has also worked in education policy, specifically in school choice and charter school policy, as the managing director of the Education Innovation Consortium. She is currently the coordinator of the Institute for Transformational Leadership in Education at Canisius. The Institute works to teach leaders at the teacher, administrator, and community levels to think and act collaboratively in order to affect policy and practice within local, regional, and national education communities. Dr. Tryjankowski's teaching and research activities are focused on urban education and social justice, including the role of faith-based initiatives in community revitalization, leadership preparation, teacher leadership, school choice models, and appropriate uses of assessment.

Eric J. Weiner is associate professor of education in the College of Education at Montclair State University in New Jersey. He is widely published in the areas of critical pedagogy, social theory, literacy, and democratic education. His book *Private Learning, Public Needs: The Neoliberal Assault on Democratic Education* (2005) examines the threat posed by neoliberal ideology upon democratic education and democratic agency. His work can be found in journals such as *Educational Philosophy and Theory, Educational Foundations, Journal of Advanced Composition, Journal of Adult and Adolescent Literacy,* and, most recently, *Situations: Project of the Radical Imaginary.* Dr. Weiner's work bridges the gap between academic discourses and vernacular discourses, between critical and creative realms of thought and action, and across and through traditional academic disciplines.

Studies in the Postmodern Theory of Education

General Editor
Shirley R. Steinberg

Counterpoints publishes the most compelling and imaginative books being written in education today. Grounded on the theoretical advances in criticalism, feminism, and postmodernism in the last two decades of the twentieth century, Counterpoints engages the meaning of these innovations in various forms of educational expression. Committed to the proposition that theoretical literature should be accessible to a variety of audiences, the series insists that its authors avoid esoteric and jargonistic languages that transform educational scholarship into an elite discourse for the initiated. Scholarly work matters only to the degree it affects consciousness and practice at multiple sites. Counterpoints' editorial policy is based on these principles and the ability of scholars to break new ground, to open new conversations, to go where educators have never gone before.

For additional information about this series or for the submission of manuscripts, please contact:

Shirley R. Steinberg
c/o Peter Lang Publishing, Inc.
29 Broadway, 18th floor
New York, New York 10006

To order other books in this series, please contact our Customer Service Department:

(800) 770-LANG (within the U.S.)
(212) 647-7706 (outside the U.S.)
(212) 647-7707 FAX

Or browse online by series:
www.peterlang.com